Alamein

Alamein

JON LATIMER

JOHN MURRAY
Albemarle Street, London

First published in 2002
by John Murray (Publishers) Ltd,
50 Albemarle Street, London W1S 4BD

A catalogue record for this book is available from the British Library

ISBN 0-7195-6203 1

Typeset in Monotype Garamond
by Servis Filmsetting Ltd, Manchester

Printed and bound in Great Britain by
Butler and Tanner Ltd., Frome and London

To my Mam

Contents

Illustrations

(between pages 224 and 225)

The author and publishers would like to thank the following for permission to repro-
duce illustrations: Plates 1 and 20, Tank Museum Collection, Bovington; 2, 3, 4, 5, 6,
7, 8, 9, 11, 13, 14, 17, 18, 21, 22, 24, 25, 26, 28, 30, 31, and 32, Trustees of the Imperial
War Museum, London (2, HU57040; 3, E12633; 4, E15219; 5, E15750; 6, E15788; 7,
E15644; 8, E15078; 9, MH27544; 11, E19019; 13, E17426; 14, E17425; 17, E15782;
18, E14658; 21, E15022; 22, CM3812; 24, E18472; 25, E18800; 26, E18807; 28,
CM3446; 30, E16494; 31, E19130; 32, E18884); 10, 12, 19, 23 and 29, Australian War
Memorial, Canberra (10, 025177; 12, 128995; 19, PO1614.017; 23, PO2127.019; 29,
PO2743.001); 15 and 16, Public Record Office, London; 27, © Hulton Archive.

Acknowledgments

The Desert Campaign has been described as the most overwritten campaign in history. That is a testament to its enduring interest, and there is certainly a phenomenal body of information to be waded through in attempting to produce a new account. In the course of my research I have encountered and found of great value a number of superb individual accounts of life in the front line at Alamein. These range from those published soon after the war and sadly now largely forgotten, such as Captain H. P. Samwell's *An Infantry Officer with the Eighth Army*, to those written perhaps 40 years later, such as Norman Craig's *The Broken Plume*. Also invaluable have been those books based on personal accounts held by the Imperial War Museum, in particular James Lucas's *War in the Desert: The Eighth Army at El Alamein*, Alexander McKee's *El Alamein: Ultra and the Three Battles* and Adrian Gilbert's *The Imperial War Museum Book of the Desert War 1940–1942*. Also of enormous value was Philip Warner's *Alamein*, a collection of first-hand accounts submitted following an appeal in the *Daily Telegraph* in 1978. I am also extremely grateful for the use of many accounts and letters held by various museums, some unpublished, and I wish to thank all those who have responded so generously to my enquiries.

Once again thanks to John Hall of University of Wales, Swansea, for being so helpful, to Jim Whetton, for loan of his father's book *Z Location or Survey in War*, and to Alison Jones and the library staff at UW Swansea, Swansea Central Library, the National Army Museum reading room, and all the staff at the departments of Documents, Printed Books and Sound Recordings and in the Photographic Archive of the Imperial War Museum and at John Rylands Library, University of Manchester, and

King's College Library and the Liddell Hart Centre for Military Archives, London; also to my old friend John McHugh for patiently accommodating me when in London, and to Stan Greaves, Lucy Jones and Laurie Hannigan for the same service in Sydney and Canberra. Special thanks to Willi Prochnow-Slettin for help in contacting the Afrika Korps Veterans Association. Also thanks to Rex Trye and Dal McGuirk in New Zealand and to Windsor Jones of Queen Elizabeth II Army Museum, Waiouru, Jock Phillips, chief historian at the New Zealand Ministry of Culture and Heritage, Kevin L. Stuart of the Alexander Turnbull Library, Wellington. Thanks too to Jillian Brankin and the staff of the Australian War Memorial; Helen Wakely of the Wellcome Library; Major K. Gray, The Royal Green Jackets Museum; Major P. J. C. Beresford, The Royal Hussars Museum; Major (Retd) J. O. M. Hackett, The Worcestershire and Sherwood Foresters Museum; Lieutenant-Colonel Roger Binks, The Royal Scots Dragoon Guards Museum; Ian Hook, The Essex Regiment Museum; Penny James, The Queen's Royal Surrey Regiment Museum; Alan Readman and Richard Childs of West Sussex County Record Office; Bob Burns, The Royal Sussex Regiment Museum; Richard Callaghan, Redoubt Fortress Museum, Eastbourne; George Fraser, Durham Light Infantry Museum, and William Meredith at Durham County Record Office; Bryan Johnson BEM, The Warwickshire Yeomanry Museum; David German, The Staffordshire Yeomanry Museum; James Orme and Lieutenant-Colonel Richard Jenkins, The Royal Wiltshire Yeomanry Museum; Lieutenant-Colonel Neil McIntosh MBE, The Green Howards Museum; Lieutenant-Colonel T. C. E. Vines, The Prince of Wales's Own Regiment of Yorkshire Museum; W. W. Smith, The Gordon Highlanders Museum; Colonel H. B. Waring, The Queen's Own Royal West Kent Regiment Museum; Marion Harding and Michael Ball, The National Army Museum; Major J. S. Knight, The Queen's Own Hussars Museum; Dr John Rhodes TD, Royal Engineers Museum; Dr Anthony Morton, Royal Logistics Corps Museum; Cliff Walters, Stella McIntyre, Adam Forty and Tim Stankus, Royal Signals Museum; Rod McKenzie, The Argyll and Sutherland Highlanders Museum; Lieutenant-Colonel Stephen Lindsay and Thomas B. Smyth, The Black Watch Museum; Lieutenant-Colonel Angus Fairrie, The Queen's Own Highlanders Museum; Angela Tarnowski, Derby Museum and Art Gallery; Major John Ellis, The Cheshire Military Museum; Clive Morris, The Queen's Dragoon Guards Museum; Dr Peter Liddle and Tracy Craggs, The Second World War Experience Centre in Leeds; and, once again, David Fletcher, historian at The Tank Museum. Thanks also to Grant McIntyre, Stephanie Allen, John Murray, Caroline Westmore, Gail

Pirkis and Jane Blackstock at John Murray. Special thanks to Bob Davenport, and last, but by no means least, to my agent, Andrew Lownie.

An extract from 'Lili Marleen' (original words by Hans Leip, English words by Mack David, music by Norbert Schultze, © 1944 Chappell & Co. Inc., USA, Warner/Chappell Music Ltd, London W6 8BS) is reproduced by permission of International Music Publications Ltd. All Rights Reserved. An extract from 'To-morrow' by John Masefield is reproduced by permission of The Society of Authors as the literary representative of the estate of John Masefield.

Swansea, February 2002

Maps

KEY TO SYMBOLS

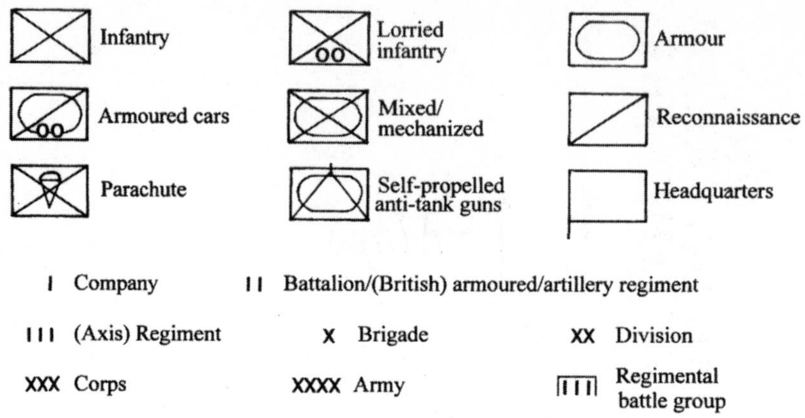

Infantry

Lorried infantry

Armour

Armoured cars

Mixed/ mechanized

Reconnaissance

Parachute

Self-propelled anti-tank guns

Headquarters

I Company   I I Battalion/(British) armoured/artillery regiment

I I I (Axis) Regiment   X Brigade   XX Division

XXX Corps   XXXX Army   Regimental battle group

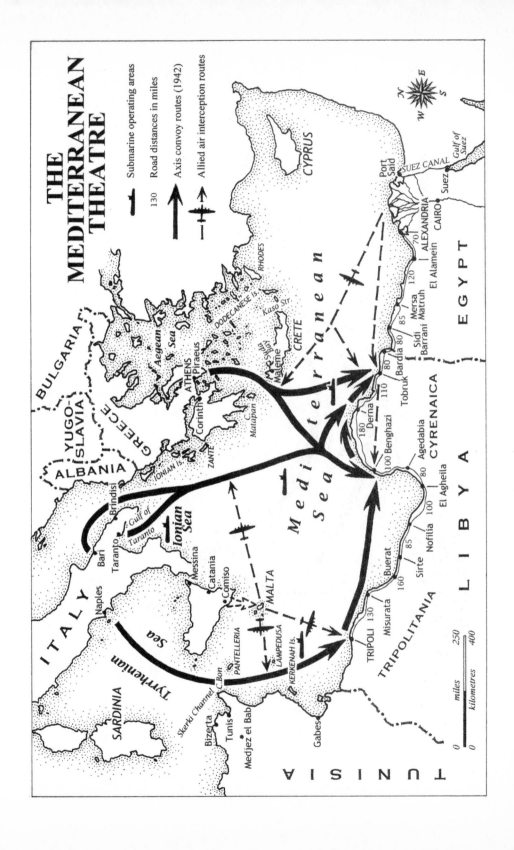

THE
MEDITERRANEAN
THEATRE

Submarine operating areas

130   Road distances in miles

Axis convoy routes (1942)

Allied air interception routes

N
W E
S

ITALY
Naples
Bari
Brindisi
Taranto
Gulf of Taranto
Ionian Sea
Messina
Catania
Comiso
MALTA
PANTELLERIA
LAMPEDUSA Is.
KERKENAH Is.
Tyrrhenian Sea
SARDINIA
Bizerta
Tunis
Medjez el Bab
C. Bon
Skerki Channel
Gabes

TUNISIA

SICILY

BULGARIA
YUGO-SLAVIA
ALBANIA
GREECE
ATHENS
Corinth
Piraeus
C. Matapan
ZANTE
IONIAN IS.
Gulf of
Aegean Sea
DODECANESE IS.
RHODES
Kaso Str.
Suda Bay
Maleme
CRETE
CYPRUS

Mediterranean Sea

LIBYA
TRIPOLITANIA
Tripoli 130
Misurata
Buerat
160
Sirte
85
Nofilia
100
El Agheila
80
Agedabia
100
Benghazi
180
Derna
110
Tobruk
80
Bardia
80
Sidi Barrani
85
Mersa Matruh
120
El Alamein
70
ALEXANDRIA
CAIRO
EGYPT
CYRENAICA

Port Said
SUEZ CANAL
Suez
Gulf of Suez

miles 0   250
kilometres 0   400

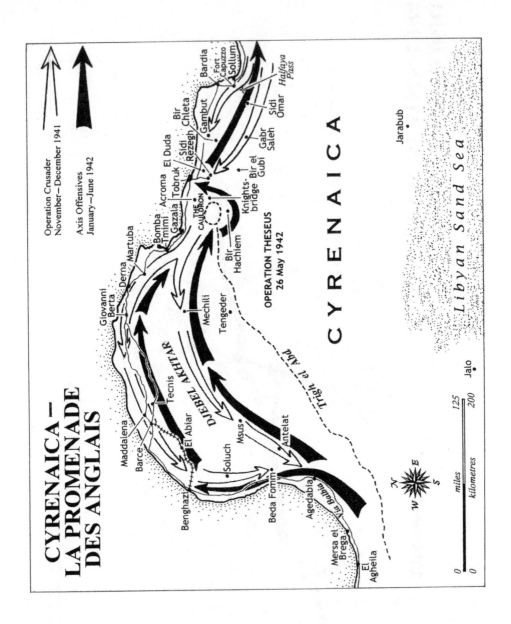

CYRENAICA –
LA PROMENADE
DES ANGLAIS

Operation Crusader
November – December 1941

Axis Offensives
January – June 1942

OPERATION THESEUS
26 May 1942

CYRENAICA

Libyan Sand Sea

Jarabub

Jalo

miles
0   125
0   200
kilometres

N
W E
S

Bardia
Fort Capuzzo
Sollum
Halfaya Pass
Gambut
Sidi Omar
Bir Chleta
Sidi Rezegh
Gabr Saleh
Acroma
El Duda
Bir el Gubi
Knights-bridge
Tobruk
Gazala
THE CAULDRON
Bir Hachiem
Bomba
Tmimi
Martuba
Derna
Giovanni Berta
Tecnis
DJEBEL AKHTAR
Mechili
Tengeder
El Abiar
Maddalena
Barce
Benghazi
Soluch
Msus
Antelat
Beda Fomm
Agedabia
Via Balbia
Mersa el Brega
El Agheila
Trigh el Abd

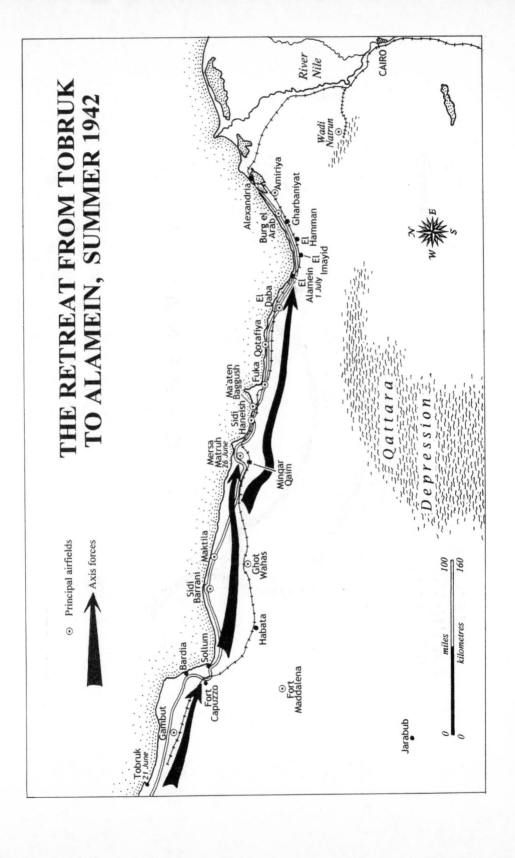

THE RETREAT FROM TOBRUK TO ALAMEIN, SUMMER 1942

⊙   Principal airfields

▲   Axis forces

Tobruk
21 June
Gambut
Bardia
Sollum
Fort Capuzzo
Sidi Barrani
Maktila
Ghot Wahas
Habata
Fort Maddalena
Jarabub
Mersa Matruh
26 June
Sidi Haneish
Ma'aten Baggush
Minqar Qaim
Fuka Qotafiya
El Daba
El Alamein
1 July
El Imayid
El Hamman
Gharbaniyat
Burg el Arab
Amiriya
Alexandria
Qattara Depression
River Nile
Wadi Natrun
CAIRO

N
E
S
W

miles   0   100
kilometres   0   160

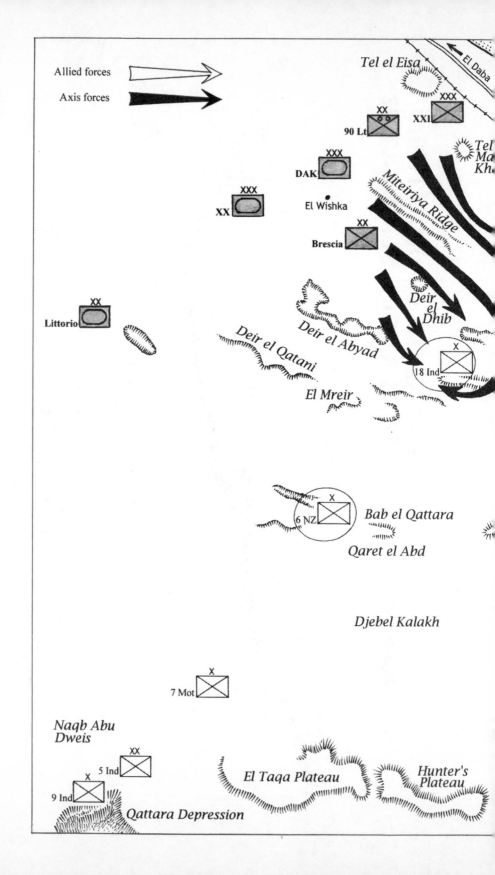

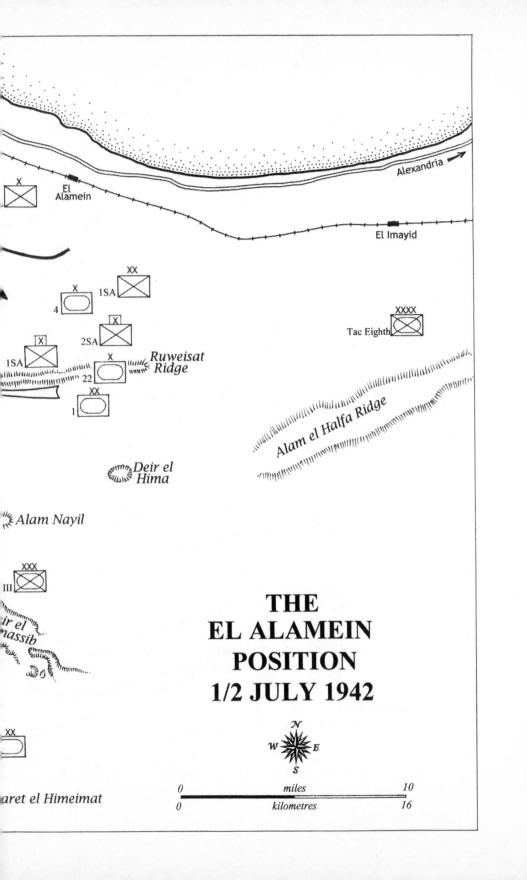

X
El
Alamein

Alexandria →

El Imayid

XX
1SA

X
4

XXXX
Tac Eighth

X
2SA

X
22   Ruweisat
Ridge

X
1SA

Alam el Halfa Ridge

XX
1

Deir el
Hima

Alam Nayil

XXX
III

ir el
assib

**THE
EL ALAMEIN
POSITION
1/2 JULY 1942**

XX

N
W · E
S

0   miles   10
0   kilometres   16

aret el Himeimat

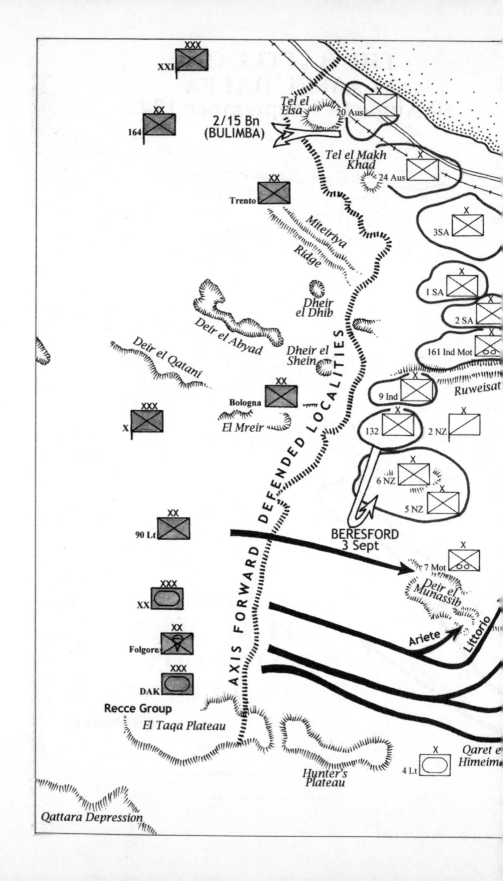

THE BATTLE OF
ALAM EL HALFA
30 August–3 September 1942

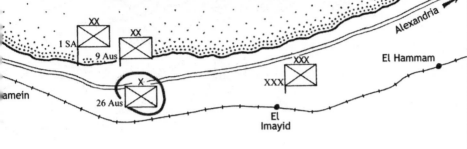

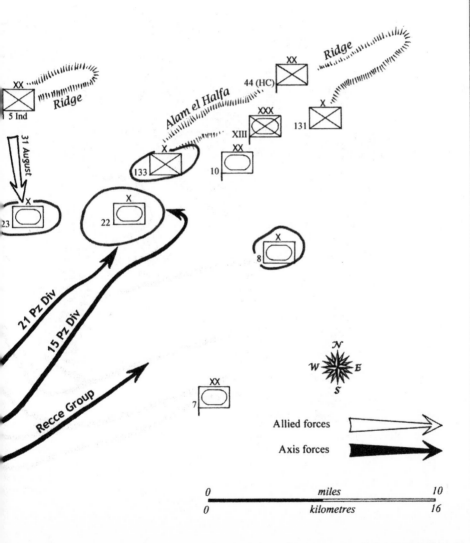

Alexandria

El Hammam

1 SA

9 Aus

26 Aus

El Imayid

amein

Ridge

5 Ind

31 August

Alam el Halfa

44 (HC)

Ridge

131

XIII

133

10

23

22

8

21 Pz Div

15 Pz Div

Recce Group

7

N
W E
S

Allied forces

Axis forces

| 0 | miles | 10 |
| 0 | kilometres | 16 |

Cairo

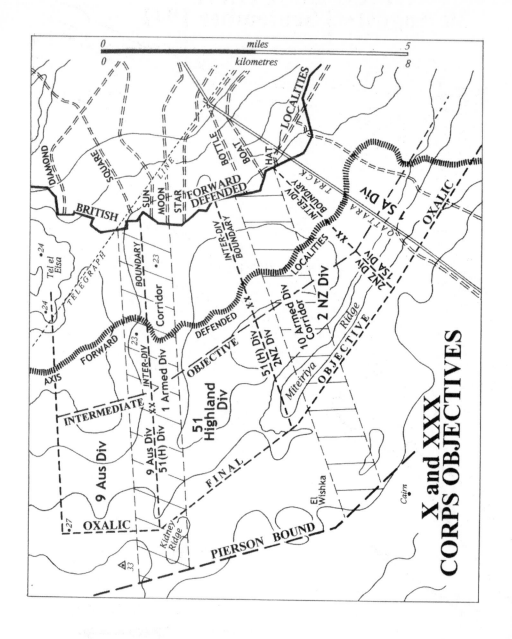

X and XXX CORPS OBJECTIVES

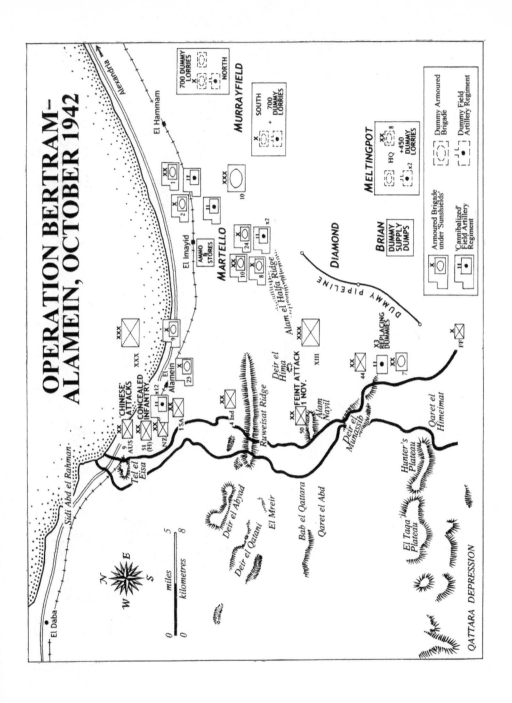

OPERATION BERTRAM –
ALAMEIN, OCTOBER 1942

MURRAYFIELD

700 DUMMY LORRIES
NORTH

SOUTH
700 DUMMY LORRIES

MELTINGPOT

HQ
450 DUMMY LORRIES

BRIAN
DUMMY SUPPLY DUMPS

10

MARTELLO

AMMO STORES

24

x2

10   8

Alam el Halfa Ridge

DIAMOND

DUMMY PIPELINE

9

xxx

El Alamein   23

Deir el Hima

X3 REPLACING DUMMIES

44   7

FF

Alam Nayil

'CHINESE' ATTACKS
CONCEALED INFANTRY

x12

1 SA

XIII

FEINT ATTACK 1 NOV.

50

Deir el Munassib

9 AUS   51 (H)   NZ

4 Ind

Ruweisat Ridge

Hunter's Plateau

Qaret el Himeimat

Tel el Eisa

Sidi Abd el Rahman

Deir el Abyad

Deir el Qatani

El Mreir

Bab el Qattara

Qaret el Abd

El Taqa Plateau

QATTARA DEPRESSION

El Daba

Alexandria

El Hammam

El Imayid

N E S W

miles
0   5
kilometres
0   8

Armoured Brigade under 'Sunshields'

'Cannibalized' Field Artillery Regiment

Dummy Armoured Brigade

Dummy Field Artillery Regiment

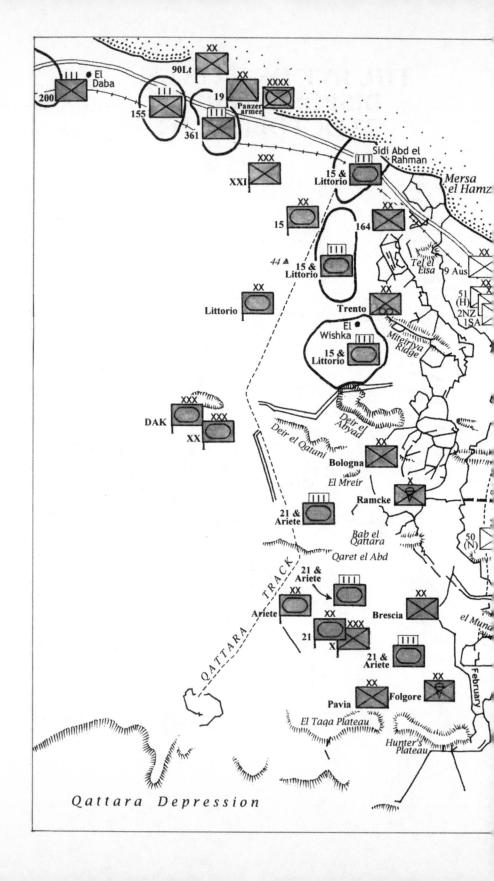

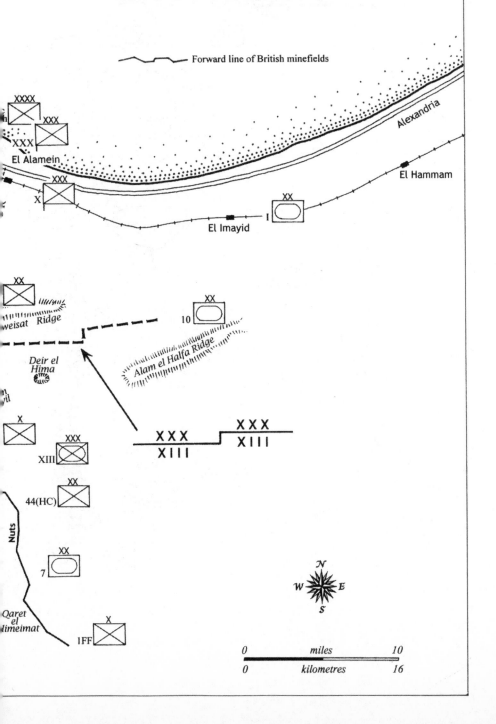

THE EVE OF BATTLE –
DISPOSITIONS ON
23 OCTOBER 1942

〰〰〰 Forward line of British minefields

XXXX

XXX

XXX

El Alamein

XXX

X

Alexandria

El Hammam

XX
I

El Imayid

XX
weisat Ridge

10
XX

Alam el Halfa Ridge

Deir el
Hima

X

XXX
XIII

XXX
XIII

XXX
XIII

44(HC)
XX

Nuts

7
XX

Qaret
el
Imeimat

1FF
X

N
W   E
S

| 0 | miles | 10 |
| 0 | kilometres | 16 |

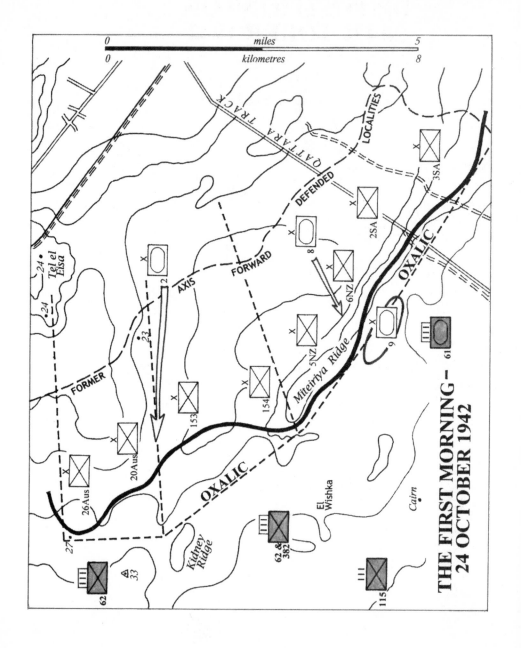

THE FIRST MORNING—
24 OCTOBER 1942

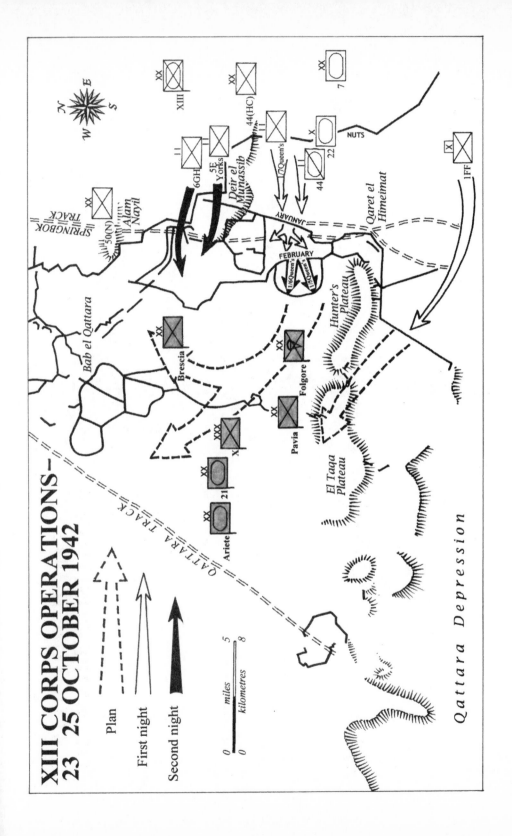

XIII CORPS OPERATIONS—
23–25 OCTOBER 1942

Plan

First night

Second night

miles
0   5

kilometres
0   8

XIII

7

44(HC)

NUTS

22

1FF

17Queen's

44

6GH

5E Yorks

Deir el Munassib

JANUARY

Qaret el Himeimat

SPRINGBOK TRACK

50(N)

Alam Nayil

Bab el Qattara

FEBRUARY

1/6Queen's

1/5Queen's

Hunter's Plateau

Brescia

Folgore

Pavia

El Taqa Plateau

21

Ariete

QATTARA TRACK

Qattara Depression

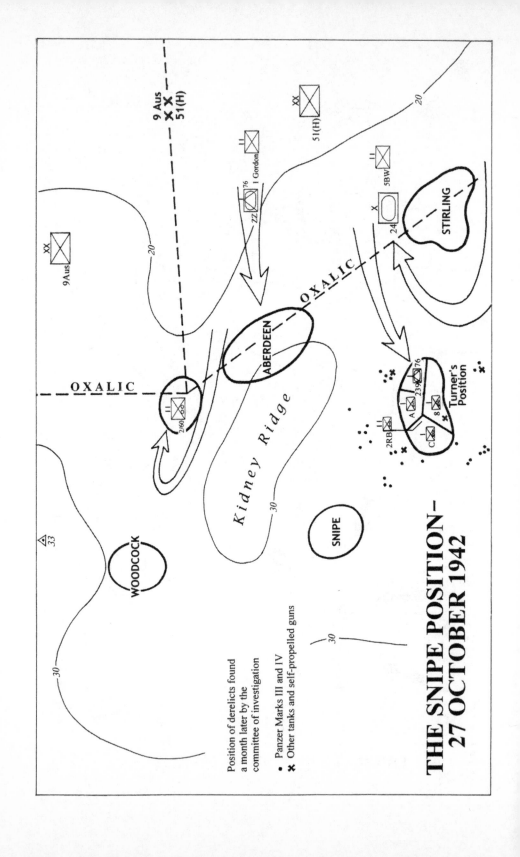

THE SNIPE POSITION—
27 OCTOBER 1942

9 Aus
XX
51(H)

51(H)

I Gordon

5BW

24

STIRLING

XX
9Aus

OXALIC

OXALIC

ABERDEEN

Kidney Ridge

2/60

Turner's
Position

23

A

8

C

2RB

20

30

30

SNIPE

WOODCOCK

33

30

Position of derelicts found
a month later by the
committee of investigation

• Panzer Marks III and IV
✗ Other tanks and self-propelled guns

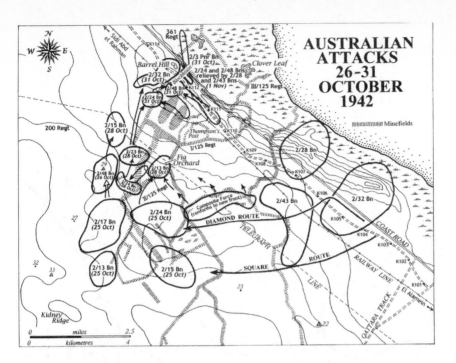

AUSTRALIAN ATTACKS 26–31 OCTOBER 1942

361 Regt
Sidi Abd el Rahman
SK114
Barrel Hill
2/32 Bn (31 Oct)
2/3 Pnr Bn (31 Oct)
Clover Leaf
2/24 and 2/48 Bns relieved by 2/28 and 2/43 Bns (1 Nov)
2/48 Bn (31 Oct)
III/125 Regt
K113
2/24 Bn (31 Oct)
K112
K111
200 Regt
2/15 Bn (28 Oct)
Thompson's Post
SK110
29
2/23 Bn (28 Oct)
Fig Orchard
2/13 Bn (28 Oct)
2/48 Bn (26 Oct)
I/125 Regt
K109
K108
2/28 Bn
K107
2/32 Bn
2/15 Bn (31 Oct)
II/125 Regt
2/24 Bn (25 Oct)
Composite Force (conforms to new front)
2/43 Bn
K106
K105
27
2/17 Bn (25 Oct)
DIAMOND ROUTE
TELEGRAPH
K104
COAST ROAD
K103
32
33
2/13 Bn (25 Oct)
2/15 Bn (25 Oct)
SQUARE
ROUTE
LINE
RAILWAY LINE
K102
K101
El Alamein
23
QATTARA TRACK
Kidney Ridge
22

Minefields

miles 0 — 2.5
kilometres 0 — 4

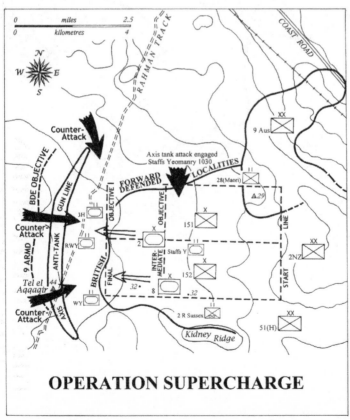

OPERATION SUPERCHARGE

miles 0 — 2.5
kilometres 0 — 4

COAST ROAD
RAHMAN TRACK
Counter-Attack
XX 9 Aus
Axis tank attack engaged Staffs Yeomanry 1030
BDE OBJECTIVE
GUN LINE
FORWARD DEFENDED LOCALITIES
OBJECTIVE
28 (Maori)
Counter-Attack
ANTI-TANK
3H
Δ29
151
X
START LINE
OBJECTIVE
9 ARMD
RWY
2
Staffs Y
INTERMEDIATE
XX 2NZ
Tel el Aqqaqir
44
152
X
AXIS
BRITISH FINAL
32
8
32
Counter-Attack
WY
2 R Sussex
Kidney Ridge
XX 51(H)

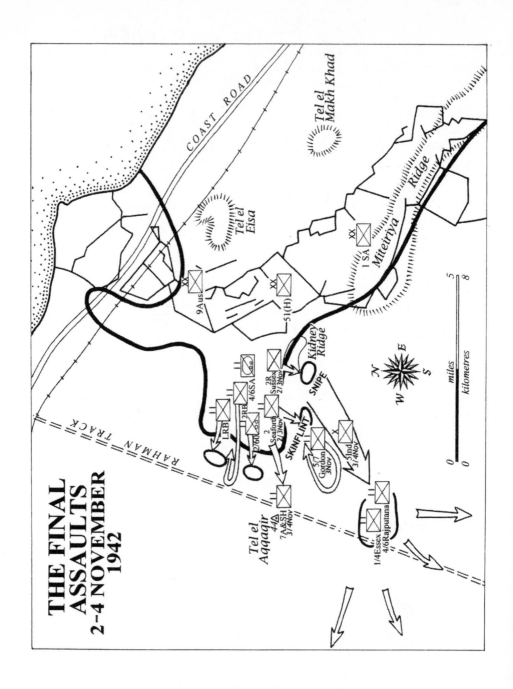

THE FINAL ASSAULTS 2–4 NOVEMBER 1942

COAST ROAD

Tel el Makh Khad

Tel el Eisa

Miteiriya Ridge

XX 1 SA

XX 9 Aus

XX 51 (H)

Kidney Ridge

Tel el Aqqaqir

RAHMAN TRACK

4/6 SA

LRB

2 RB

2/60

2 Seaforth 2/3 Nov

2 R Sussex 2/3 Nov

SNIPE

SKINFLINT

5/7 Gordon 3 Nov

5 Ind 3/4 Nov

44 7 A&SH 3/4 Nov

1/4 Essex 4/6 Rajputana

N E S W

miles 5

kilometres 8

0

Introduction

Alamein is possibly the one battle of the Second World War whose name is familiar to most Britons today, and it is of particular significance to the history of that war in that it was the last battle in which British forces achieved success under exclusively British command. It was also the first time in the war that the Allies achieved a major victory over the Germans. Although they had seen limited success in previous operations, Alamein was the decisive action in the two-year struggle between Eighth Army and the Deutsches Afrikakorps (which had been transformed by this stage into the German–Italian Panzer Army) led by Generalfeldmarschall Erwin Rommel – 'the Desert Fox'. That the victory was decisive is unquestionable: it drove the Axis forces from Egypt and clean across Libya into Tunisia, where, in conjunction with General Dwight D. Eisenhower's Anglo-American Army, Eighth Army destroyed them, removing them from Africa for ever. However, there remains controversy, largely over the merits of the British commander, Lieutenant-General Bernard Law Montgomery. Montgomery went on to greater things, and made many enemies in the process, but his name will be for ever associated with Alamein. Whatever one's view of him, however, Alamein was not simply a victory for Montgomery, or even for Eighth Army: it was a victory for modern armaments, for the Royal Navy in preventing supplies (particularly petrol) arriving from Italy, and for the Middle East Air Forces in destroying supplies and supporting the ground forces.[1]

While it signalled the beginning of the counter-offensive of the western Allies which carried them ultimately to central Germany, Alamein was not on the same scale as the titanic struggles of the

1

Eastern Front, in comparison to which Rommel's campaign was only ever a sideshow for the Germans, whereas Montgomery was backed by the full weight of British strategy. At Alamein a Commonwealth force of 195,000 men in 11 divisions (four armoured) defeated four weak German and eight Italian divisions (some 50,000 Germans and 54,000 Italians); Axis forces on the Eastern Front at the time amounted to 232 divisions (171 of them German, including 24 armoured divisions) – manpower totalling millions.[2] Nevertheless, for the Commonwealth countries and for Great Britain in particular, suffering as she was from the strain of three years of war during which ultimate and disastrous defeat seemed perilously close on many occasions, the victory was of colossal significance. Initial success against the Italians in Libya and Ethiopia had been swiftly overshadowed by events in Greece and Crete and subsequently the Western Desert. The stock of the British Army – not high following the carnage of the First World War – was particularly low by the summer of 1942. With political pressure mounting on the Prime Minister, Winston Churchill, a victory was not merely desirable, it was absolutely essential. When news of the outcome at Alamein arrived, church bells which had been silent since the beginning of the war (being reserved for warning of invasion) were rung with glee at the news of the first tangible victory – a sure sign that the tide of the war had finally turned.

Thucydides remarked that those who take part in a campaign know least about it. The personal reminiscences of even senior officers bear this out, stressing the confusion that surrounds them at all times, whereas most ordinary soldiers, sailors and airmen are too close to death to consider anything but their immediate situations, and usually too dog-tired to remember events clearly afterwards. But what really happened does matter, because wartime propaganda – about Italian cowardice, for example – lives on in peace as myth, warping our under-standing of the past, and the past is an essential part of ourselves.[3] Throughout my research of this battle I have been confronted by the ongoing debate about the relative merits of the various generals involved. Indeed, few generals have ever inspired such controversy as Montgomery, the matter of competence being complicated by a par-ticularly prickly and egotistical personality.[4] Hindsight about the conduct of military operations is a game much overplayed by authors, especially those who have no personal experience of the confusion such operations entail.[5] I have therefore attempted not to take sides in the controversy over personalities, but as far as possible to describe what happened and, as far as I am able, to explain why.

Certainly memories of Sir Harold Alexander – Montgomery's

Commander-in-Chief – have benefited from his gentlemanly nature, whatever his military limitations. Also, the halting of the Axis drive towards the Nile Delta was for many years ignored, and Sir Claude Auchinleck – Alexander's predecessor – was denied the credit he deserved for this. Montgomery's personal antipathy to Auchinleck, who nevertheless inspired immense confidence and admiration among everyone else who served with and under him, rebounded and contributed to the backlash which from the 1960s onwards led many to question Montgomery's ability. It is a shame that Montgomery's sometimes unedifying personality has diminished his achievement at Alamein, for, while Eighth Army undoubtedly enjoyed many advantages over its Axis opponents, it would be quite wrong to believe that the outcome of the battle was a foregone conclusion. Indeed, ironically, if Auchinleck had succeeded in driving Rommel back at the end of July 1942 – which he came very close to doing – the conditions for victory in October might not have obtained; Rommel's lines of communication might have been much shorter and Montgomery's correspondingly longer, thus reducing the significant superiority in *matériel* that the latter enjoyed. Similarly, at any point other than the Alamein position, an open desert flank would surely have led to fluid and mobile operations which would have suited the Germans far better than the 'rough house' that the battle became. As it was, Montgomery was in a position to launch a battle with the stage management that he believed was necessary in a fashion that best suited the qualities of British arms.

When the fourth volume of Churchill's account of the war, *The Hinge of Fate*, came out in 1952, Auchinleck's former Deputy Chief of Staff, Eric 'Chink' Dorman-Smith, issued a writ for libel. When Montgomery's own *Memoirs* came out in 1958, the reaction to his humourless egotism was even stronger, and Auchinleck was livid at the imputations that the situation in the Middle East was hopeless when Montgomery took over. Montgomery was forced to climb down, and future editions of his *Memoirs* were printed with a correction. The renowned military writer Basil Liddell Hart noted that 'Montgomery's tendency to paint everything black prior to his arrival on the scene has long been a running joke among his fellow soldiers. Also his tendency to sweeping and unfounded assertions. I have known him for thirty years and long wondered how a man so careful and thorough in his own work could indulge in sweeping assertions so easy to disprove.'[6] Then, with the help of Correlli Barnett and John Connell, the reaction against Montgomery intensified with the publication first of Connell's *Auchinleck* in 1959, followed by Barnett's *The Desert Generals* in 1960. Montgomery's biographer of the 1980s, Nigel Hamilton, then somewhat overcorrected this when he demanded that 'the historian pay tribute to the salutory manner in which [Montgomery] transformed the tide of history'.[7] But even during the 1990s it was possible to read books that attacked Montgomery – such as Bob Leach's *Massacre at Alamein?*, which, however dubious its conclusions, demonstrates the depth of passion still felt by those involved – and there remain those who categorically refuse to acknowledge his achievement.

I feel that the camps which favour particular British generals associate so closely with their heroes (as do many of Rommel's biographers) that each is incapable of viewing the others dispassionately. Perhaps if Montgomery had possessed a more generous personality and had not been so dismissive of the contribution of others – especially Auchinleck – he might now be acknowledged as the greatest British soldier of the twentieth century and even have earned plaudits from those overseas, notably in America, who now revile him. It was not a case of 'Behold, the conquering hero comes': Montgomery did not transform a beaten army, but rather took a blunt but fundamentally sound blade and sharpened it before wielding it with maximum force. Liddell Hart claimed that the performance of Eighth Army before Montgomery took over was impaired by its Commonwealth composition – a charge that, not surprisingly, is strongly refuted by Commonwealth historians.[8] Leach complains bitterly that Montgomery took 13,500 casualties during his offensive, but fails to notice that Auchinleck took a similar number during his series of July attacks without achieving a decisive breakthrough. Indeed, the July battles did generate considerable criticism within Eighth Army – and not only among the Commonwealth formations. Where Auchinleck is open to criticism is over the mounting casualty lists of the July battles, in which, as Army Commander, he failed to recognize early enough the limitations of the armour, the drawbacks of a purely British command, and the lack of training in co-operation throughout his army.[9] And the fact that those who served in Eighth Army before Alamein are not allowed to wear an '8' on their Africa Star is a disgrace.

Above all these personalities, however, was one of yet more brooding greatness. In the 1960s, when his previously implacable bitterness had mellowed, Dorman-Smith wrote, 'One cannot understand the vagaries of our warfare unless one returns to the study of Churchill himself. Wasn't he a bit like a headmaster of a public school? . . . War cabinet as housemasters; chiefs of staff and field commanders as prefects – bad boys could be sacked . . . And Monty as head boy!' (Montgomery, however, was a plain middle-class Briton with his roots in Victorian convention and insecure for most of his life. He had a monkish quality,

Chink decided: 'The Army was his monastery and by 1946 he had become the infallible father superior.')[10]

Churchill dominated Britain's conduct of the war from May 1940 onwards. The myth of the lovable bulldog was a product of his forcefully expressed defiance of Hitler at the time of Britain's darkest peril, and also of his own account of events and of later political considerations. Churchill seemed to believe he had inherited the military qualities of his great forebear John Churchill, first Duke of Marlborough. He enjoyed the privileges of his class, which gave him an education at Harrow and a commission in the 4th Hussars. He progressed effortlessly into politics, and commanded a battalion of Royal Scots Fusiliers during the First World War. As a result of his many positions of responsibility, including stints as First Lord of the Admiralty, he believed he understood far more about military matters than he did. When he became Prime Minister he also took over as Minister of Defence, and he discharged these immense responsibilities during the period of Britain's greatest trial – when, it should not be forgotten, he was already approaching his seventies. Consequently, he found it difficult to trust the much younger men who had to conduct the detailed business of war.

Churchill has been accused of being a romantic lover of war, but it is probably fairer to say that he was a lover of romantic war – of cavalry charges such as that of the 21st Lancers at Omdurman in 1898, in which he took part. The Army's decision to go for total mechanization during the 1930s had created both benefits and drawbacks. The latter included a need to devote a large proportion of the best manpower to maintenance – a source of constant irritation to Churchill, who complained there was too much 'fluff and flummery behind the fighting troops'.[11] By January 1941 the General Staff calculated that each division in the Middle East (some 18,000 men) required a 'divisional slice' of 41,000 men to maintain it in the field. This was in part because units had to be maintained in undeveloped countries at the end of lengthy sea lanes, but it was also an inevitable result of mechanization.[12] Churchill's references to war in the desert being like war at sea suggest a simplistic attitude. He never understood the problems of providing adequate communications: the difficulties in building and maintaining roads and tracks in the desert; the need to maintain and extend railways, improve harbour facilities, provide camps, water installations, workshops and assembly plants, and the importance of scores of other undertakings all demanding skilled labour and technical expertise. Churchill would overshadow events in the Middle East until the end of the campaign, but his influence was not always constructive.

Many commentators have favourably compared the supposed tactical excellence of the German Army during the Second World War with that of the British, considering in particular the difficulty experienced by the British in practising combined-arms tactics – integrating armour, infantry, artillery and engineers. Some conclude that the British won only by the application of overwhelming superiority of *matériel*. This analysis has, however, been shown to be erroneous.[13] Montgomery has been criticized for ensuring his logistic arrangements were in order before starting operations, while Rommel has often been praised for the opposite – attitudes that defy all logic. While operating across the short continental distances in Poland and France, against opponents lacking air superiority and handicapped by doctrinal weakness and operational error, German means were sufficient. But in Russia and North Africa, and later in Normandy, failure was largely due to logistical overreach; in the face of which all Rommel's tactical brilliance could not be transformed into operational victory. Indeed, the 'brute force' theory of Montgomery's generalship ignores the simple fact that logistics matter, even if in this case the tempo of operations suffered in the short term from the prominence that British commanders gave to supplies. But, during 200 years of fighting overseas far from home bases, the British Army had learned the hard way the price of neglecting preparations.[14] In this respect, the importance of seapower in intercepting Rommel's supplies cannot be overstated, but nor should we ignore other developments such as the Takoradi air-reinforcement route. During the twentieth century more than at any time previously, victory followed superiority in industry and logistics, and the work of all those involved in these aspects of the war has too often been ignored.[15]

The Western Desert battlefield of Egypt and the eastern Libyan province of Cyrenaica, on which the campaign that culminated at Alamein was fought, was mostly scorching wilderness, a fiercely hot pitch extending from the Mediterranean to the Sahara, with Alexandria and Tripoli as the goals. These goals were close to 1,000 miles apart, and naturally the nearer one side was to its opponent's goal, the further it was from its base, with all that this entailed for its ability to maintain itself, still less build up the necessary stores to mount offensive operations. To use another metaphor, it was as if each side was tied by a bungee rope to its base. The further it advanced from that base, the greater was the restraining effect of that distance, and more easily could the defender swat away the increasingly feeble stretch for the final objective.

The terrain itself was far from the shifting sand dunes of romantic vision, but varied from dun to grit grey, which its limestone base turned an almost incandescent white in the midday heat. Apart from camel thorn, there was little vegetation, and the only fauna were scorpions, a few reptiles, including little horned vipers, and small mammals, including the occasional gazelle and the jerboa – the famous 'desert rat'. Only fleas and flies – the two great scourges of desert soldiers – were abundant, for these know no boundaries. Apart from in some small settlements on the coast, particularly around the Djebel Akhtar, the fertile strip of mountains in Cyrenaicia, there were no humans to get caught up in the maelstrom, save the few passing Bedouin occasionally glimpsed going apparently from nowhere to nowhere. Near the sea was an insignificant railway station called El Alamein, which took its name from the ridge between the railway and the sea: Tel el Alamein, the hill of twin cairns. It was well known to British and Commonwealth soldiers as one of the few places where it was easy to get down to the beach to wash off the all-pervading dust.[16]

That such a battle should have been fought by three great powers in such a seemingly worthless place is due to earlier history. 'Great Britain,' wrote Lord Esher, a member of the Imperial Defence Committee early in the twentieth century, 'either is or is not one of the great powers of the world. Her position in this respect depends solely upon sea command – and upon sea command in the Mediterranean.'[17] At Alexandria was the Royal Navy's base in Egypt, and from there the Navy directed its Mediterranean operations. In 1921 Winston Churchill described the Middle East as the centre of the Empire, to be defended at all costs; later he referred to it as the 'hinge of fate on which our ultimate victory turned'.[18] Egypt was therefore of vital importance to British strategy.

Malta was the keystone of Churchill's strategy in the Mediterranean, and he knew that its occupation by the enemy would stymie all the schemes he had been working to realise, including the proposed invasion of North Africa and assaults on the 'soft underbelly of Europe'. Malta was essential to success at Alamein, and victory at Alamein would be essential to relieving Malta. Thus once more maritime strategy would underpin all Britain's efforts, on land and in the air as well as at sea.

PART I

An Obscure Railway Halt

1

Colonial Rivals

A thousand years have passed away,
    Cast back your glances on the scene,
Compare this England of to-day
    With England as she once has been.

Fast beat the pulse of living then:
    The hum of movement, throb of war
The rushing mighty sound of men
    Reverberated loud and far.

Charles Hamilton Sorley

'If we have decided to face the risks and sacrifices of war, it is because the interests of Italy requires it of us,' Benito Mussolini announced from the balcony of the Palazzo Venzia at 1900 hours on 10 June 1940. Unfortunately, he forgot to inform his men in Italy's Libyan colony that they were now at war with the neighbouring British in Egypt. As evening approached, a line of armoured cars from 11th Hussars (Prince Albert's Own) – famed as the 'Cherry-Pickers' for their red trousers, worn since an incident during the Peninsular War – drove towards the double strand tangle of rusty barbed wire that stretched some 400 miles along the barren Egyptian–Libyan frontier. As quietly as possible, the drivers pressed the armoured Rolls-Royce bonnets against the wire, steadily and slowly, backwards and forwards, in an obviously practised manner. Soon the wire strained and broke, and the crews – wearing rubber-soled shoes, lest the wire prove electrified – dragged it away and pulled out the fence posts to create permanent gaps. Then they drove deep into Libya to cut telephone wires and cause havoc with the border garrisons. Gingerly approaching Fort Maddalena, Troop Sergeant-Major 'Nobby' Clarke saw a solitary lorry driving towards the fort, headlights blazing, and opened fire – the first shots of the Desert War. By dawn on 12 June all the Cherry-Picker patrols had returned unharmed, having shot up numerous camps and lorries and captured 70 bewildered Italian prisoners.[1]

In 1875, Prime Minister Benjamin Disraeli had made a secret deal with Tewfik Pasha, the Khedive of Egypt, to buy shares in the recently opened Suez Canal. The Canal would draw Great Britain deeper and deeper into Middle East affairs. Although the Khedive was a constitutional monarch nominally the viceroy of the Sultan of Turkey, Egypt was run by a system of 'Dual Control' in which Britain and France, together with other European powers holding bonds in the Canal, controlled all financial and political levers. On 9 September 1881 there was a nationalist coup in Egypt. Although the Khedive was said to be delighted with this event, the British perceived a threat to their interests and the result was an invasion of Egypt.[2] On 13 September 1882, with their pipers to the fore, the Black Watch and the Cameron Highlanders led the assault at the Battle of Tel el Kebir. Thirty-five minutes later that very model of a modern major-general, Sir Garnet Wolseley, had won a small, neat and thoroughly professional victory.

Wolseley sent a signal: 'The war in Egypt is over; send no more men from England.' However, many more men came: a consul-general, a sirdar (commander-in-chief) to run a new Egyptian Army, and a 14,000-man British Army of Occupation to ensure the Suez Canal was secure for British trade.[3]

During the First World War, Egypt was turned into a fortified camp when threatened by the Ottoman Turks, and later Palestine and Arabia came under British control. Although the British Protectorate of Egypt ended on 28 February 1922 and the country was declared an independent sovereign state, Britain reserved the right to control security of communications with the Empire, the protection of foreign interests and minorities in Egypt, the defence of Egypt itself, and control of Sudan. In 1936 Britain and Egypt signed a new treaty which formed the legal basis of Britain's position in Egypt throughout the Second World War, providing for a twenty-year military alliance with a peacetime British garrison of 10,000 men, British control of the Canal area, and essential facilities in time of war.[4] Egypt was the western shield of an area vitally important to Britain, particularly since this was bounded by the Italian colony of Libya. In September 1911 Italy had gone to war with Ottoman Turkey in order to snatch this last African possession of the Ottomans, which she achieved after a difficult campaign that also led to the Italians landing on Rhodes and gaining control of the Dodecanese Islands.[5]

For much of the early period of Mussolini's rule from 1922, relations between Britain and Italy had remained cordial. Before the Abyssinian

Crisis of 1935 Mussolini generally aligned his foreign policy with that of Great Britain. Initially he disliked Adolf Hitler and despised his anti-Semitism. As Nazi Germany's aggressive intentions became apparent, Britain, France and Italy organized a conference at Stresa in April 1935 in an attempt to prevent German rearmament. There, following discussions with Ramsay MacDonald, the British Prime Minister, and Sir John Simon, the Foreign Secretary, Mussolini decided that were he to invade Abyssinia there would be no British attempts to mobilize the League of Nations against him – just as the League had made no move over his bombardment of Corfu in 1923, the Japanese invasion of Manchuria, or Nazi Germany's violation of the Treaty of Versailles. Beginning in October 1935, the Italian invasion of Abyssinia was brutal in the extreme. Now Britain's relations with Italy were becoming strained.

However, a 'Peace Ballot' organized by the League of Nations Union on 27 June had shown that over 10 million out of 11.5 million people canvassed were in favour of League actions to prevent member states attacking one another; the British Cabinet therefore felt obliged to take action after all. Economic sanctions surprised and antagonized Mussolini, and he stopped trying to prevent Germany's rearmament. He nevertheless remained mistrustful of Hitler. But the succession of Stanley Baldwin as Prime Minister in June had produced a policy of opposition to Mussolini and appeasement of Hitler – because, according to Anthony Eden, Baldwin's Foreign Secretary, an agreement with Hitler 'might have a chance of a reasonable life whereas Mussolini . . . is a complete gangster'. Any chance to bring Italy on to the Allied side had been missed.[6] British handling of the dictators bore out George Orwell's description of England as a 'rather stuffy Victorian family . . . in which the young are generally thwarted and most of the power is in the hands of irresponsible uncles and bedridden aunts'. What was to be expected of its ruling class 'was not treachery, or physical cowardice, but stupidity, unconscious sabotage, an infallible instinct for doing the wrong thing'.[7] Britain would in due course have to fight Italy for three years, when, with France on the verge of falling to Nazi Germany, and sensing the chance of rich pickings from the British Empire, Mussolini declared war.

Although at that time Britain also appeared to be on the verge of total defeat, Mussolini could not persuade his commander in Libya, Maresciallo Rodolfo Graziani, to begin the invasion of Egypt until 13 September, by which time the British had already seized the initiative by harassing frontier posts and columns, inflicting some 3,500 casualties for the loss of only 150. The British then fell back to their defence line at Mersa Matruh, but Graziani refused to move beyond Sidi Barrani, some 60 miles inside Egypt.

For too long there has been a fatuous contempt for Italian arms in Anglophone countries, largely as a result of wartime propaganda. The truth is that Italian soldiers were tough and hardy, and on innumerable occasions they fought as bravely as any soldiers in the world. But the Italian record in adapting operational concepts to technology was almost uniformly disastrous. In both the Army and Navy, doctrine inhibited the adoption of new technology; but in the Air Force the absence of doctrine had the same effect. All three services suffered from intellectual rigidity and lack of interest in developments elsewhere, and combat came as a profound shock. Pre-war foreign commentators noted that army commanders were oblivious to the importance of training, and what training there was remained unrelated to any effective tactical system. This particularly affected junior leaders, and the deliberate stunting of the NCO cadre produced an army in which competent junior leaders were the exception. An officer corps that lacked energy and self-confidence ensured that these problems persisted throughout the war. The Italian High Command wilfully refused to make improvements, through fear of exposing shortcomings to their Germans allies and to their own public. The result was an army that rejected armour; a navy staff that already considered itself inferior to the Royal Navy before the outbreak of war and that neglected radar and coastal warfare; and an air force that favoured biplane fighters.[8]

The Regio Esercito (Royal Italian Army) was clearly not ready to fight a modern war. A German staff officer noted, 'The command apparatus is . . . pedantic and slow. The absence of sufficient communications equipment renders the link to subordinate units precarious.'[9] But it takes more courage, not less, to enter battle with obsolescent second-rate equipment and an inept doctrine.[10] It was the Italian soldier's misfortune to serve under a system that left him wholly unprepared. The Italians were not really interested in war, many of them having an affinity with Britain that had been strengthened in 1914–18 and that now leached away their enthusiasm, while others remembered that fighting Austria-Hungary and then Germany had led to 600,000 Italian dead during the First World War. Their militaristic image was no more than a Fascist illusion. Thanks to Fascism – which perpetuated privilege – a strong caste system dominated the rank structure of the army, preserving elitist distinctions that had largely died out elsewhere. Both the British and the Germans were aghast at the way in which Italian officers looked to their own comfort first and were out of touch with the men they were supposed to lead.[11] Rommel would subsequently offer a plea in mitigation for the Italian soldier, who was, he said, poorly equipped and poorly led by an officer class that did not always consider it necessary to put in an appearance in battle, and that continued to enjoy meals of several courses while the troops did not even have field kitchens. He might have added that the officers' lifestyles included many other amenities, including travelling brothels.[12]

Although full mobilization had been declared in Italy on 10 May and Italian forces overseas were reinforced, there was a severe shortage of technical skills and experienced leaders. For all Mussolini's talk of '8 million bayonets', never more than 3 million men were mobilized, and most formations were heavily under strength both at home and overseas. Equipment was universally poor – from small arms with a wide variety of calibres, and grenades which posed little threat beyond a few feet, to First World War artillery. Nevertheless, Italian gunners often operated their pieces to the bitter end. More serious in a desert war was the chronic shortage of motor transport; what there was was of poor quality and largely unequal to the terrain. Apart from the useless L3 tankette – known as the 'Sardine Tin Scout' – the Italians lacked an effective medium tank. The M13/40 was only a marginal improvement on the M11/39, but Italian industry placidly continued to produce it.[13] While German and British tanks would be uprated with better armour and armament, the Italians produced the M14/41: it took a year to develop, had some 5 millimetres more armour than the M13/40, a few more miles per hour road speed, and a fuelling range stepped up by about 12 miles. It was little wonder that the British and Germans nicknamed the Italian tanks 'steel coffins'.[14] Also, the Italians had nothing like enough anti-tank and anti-aircraft guns. So, although the Italians' 208,000 men in Libya – organized in two armies: Fifth and Tenth – vastly outnumbered the British in Egypt, and despite the 2,000 or so aircraft of the land-based Regia Aeronautica and the powerful and modern ships of the Regia Marina, Italy could enter the war with little confidence.

In August 1939, General Sir Archibald Wavell was appointed to the newly created military post of Commander-in-Chief Middle East. The outbreak of war in September saw a substantial increase in the responsibilities of the Middle East commanders, particularly Wavell and his Royal Air Force counterpart, Air Vice-Marshal Sir Arthur Longmore, Air Officer Commanding-in-Chief (AOC-in-C) Middle East.[15] Together with Admiral Sir Andrew Cunningham, Commander-in-Chief Mediterranean Station, they were now responsible for an area measuring some 2,000 by

1,800 miles, encompassing nine countries in three continents, and their commitments would grow further during the next year. Longmore's Middle East Air Forces had just 32 squadrons in the entire theatre, and in Egypt and Palestine there were 50,000 British troops in total, already tasked since Easter 1936 with suppressing an Arab rebellion in Palestine, where Britain ran a protectorate under a League of Nations mandate. Thus there were not 'two kings in Israel' at the time but three – an arrangement of which American observers were highly critical. However, as the later AOC-in-C Middle East Air Marshal Sir Arthur Tedder subsequently said, 'the respective commanders are normally reasonable men who have the same purpose at heart'. Besides, the Axis command would also rely on a large measure of co-operation, which was usually much less forthcoming.[16]

Some of the blame for British military defeats in the period 1940–42 must be laid at the doors of politicians between the wars, who approved spending programmes that favoured the Royal Navy and Royal Air Force to the exclusion of the Army.[17] Other aspects of the Army's failure were systemic military ones. It is wrong, however, to assume that the Army had learned nothing from the First World War: in fact it made strenuous efforts to develop a doctrine appropriate to a modern mechanized battle fought against a major continental opponent. This entailed generating firepower in order to neutralize enemy defences and bring about battlefield mobility, seeking to avoid the stalemate and high casualties of the trenches. Unfortunately, the development of such a doctrine was at cross-purposes with the continuing requirement to garrison an empire, for much of the British Army's equipment at the start of the war was designed for ease of transport rather than firepower. Critics of the regimental system have overstated the extent to which it led to an insularity and parochialism that inhibited all-arms co-operation. What inhibited this most of all was a lack of a uniform doctrine and the opportunity to practise it: when the opportunity was available, co-operation was generally good.[18]

Unfortunately, class prejudice did persist among British troops: members of rifle regiments tended to talk only to other 'Greenjackets', and Guardsmen and cavalry maintained their traditional aloofness. Lieutenant-Colonel E. O. Burne expressed violent opposition to plans to reform the practice of the cavalry seeking out and recruiting the smartest young officers, which he justified by arguing that the Englishman was the inventor of the club 'and naturally he likes to belong to the best club. A good regiment is regarded as a good club by both officers and men, and round it are built up innumerable welfare associations and social societies. The argument that popular regiments get a monopoly of the best class of officer is but a point in favour of the old system.' He continued, 'Under the new system [which aimed for a more balanced allocation of officers] the R[oyal] A[rmoured] C[orps] will not get good officers at all. The powerful trade unions [*sic*] of the Guards Brigade and Rifle Regiments will see to that.'[19] As for the infantry of the line, clearly they would have to take their chances.

Within the cavalry and infantry, the public-school 'amateur' ethos still held sway and sporting prowess was seen as more important than technical ability.[20] British regular soldiers during the 1930s signed on for a minimum of seven years, but many stayed longer. The life was spartan, with a marked dedication to sport – due as much to a lack of equipment for meaningful training as to anything else. At least one regular battalion was still using flags to represent anti-tank guns on exercise in 1939. But the toughness of life in places such as the North-West Frontier of India served the Army well in due course. The lack of professionalism is illustrated by the discouragement of 'shop' talk in the officers' mess; where topics considered more appropriate were 'fuss and feathers', Royal Birthday Parades and other ceremonial. Nevertheless, one lesson all officers learned was that Britain did not possess an unlimited supply of soldiers: the health and well-being of the men was committed to them as a solemn responsibility. This was in marked contrast to Italian practice.[21]

Its personnel and training policy significantly degraded the Army's combat capability, although not for the reasons often cited. The command and control of British troops relied on subordinates doing as they were told and not exercising their initiative – a product of First World War experience which seemed to suggest that on a chaotic battlefield the only way to ensure co-operation was through unity of control. The continued emphasis on training in close-order drill was designed to teach 'instant, exact and unhesitating obedience of orders'.[22] Furthermore, the training of officers was often haphazard and unsatisfactory, and the high ratio of officers to men hampered the promotion of initiative among both junior officers and NCOs alike. Until the introduction of the War Office Selection Board system in April 1942, the officer corps remained the preserve of the upper and middle classes. Now, owing to the demands of wartime, the overwhelming majority of those commissioned, like the men they commanded, had been civilians before the war. Ironically, although the General Staff wanted to equip and organize for mobile mechanized operations, an autocratic system together with an officer corps with heavily diluted professionalism threatened to negate many of the potential advantages of such a blitzkrieg approach.

British officers either went to a service school to learn the intricacies of their arm or, if they were from the cavalry or infantry, they went to the regimental depot, where they spent nine months learning more drill and the routine and discipline of the unit, as well as being improved in minor details of dress and deportment. Even the three months spent by infantry officers at the School of Musketry in Hythe served to create musketry instructors rather than tactical leaders.[23] The difficulty that British infantry experienced in applying fire and movement in their minor tactics was due to faulty pre-war doctrine and organization and the lack of effective infantry firepower. Many riflemen were reduced to little more than ammunition carriers for the Bren light machine-guns, but the Bren could generate only a fraction of the firepower of the German MG-34 and later MG-42. Throughout the war, the infantry found itself intimidated by German light machine-guns and mortars and so relied on tanks and artillery to generate the firepower necessary to enable it to manoeuvre across the battlefield. But these heavier arms were organized at a higher level, and the time-consuming process of requesting support through divisional channels significantly retarded the tempo of operations.

The Army failed to imbue its junior leaders of different arms with a common sense of its doctrine. Throughout the war, the difficulty experienced by units in co-operating resulted from the General Staff's laissez-faire attitude to the promulgation of doctrine and the conduct of training. Organizational changes were easier to implement, but they masked the inherent weakness of the rigid hierarchical command system that prevented commanders from grasping fleeting battlefield opportunities. The oft-noted unwillingness of British troops to push beyond their objectives was due to a doctrine that set specific and limited goals and taught rapid consolidation ahead of ruthless exploitation which might leave the attacker exposed to the sort of well-organized counter-attacks for which the Germans had a reputation from 1916 to 1918. Instead, technological and doctrinal solutions were sought to increase the tempo of operations, although these were hampered by the decision in the late 1920s that effectively ended attempts to create permanent all-arms formations – balancing infantry, armour and supporting arms – and by the acceptance in the 1935 edition of *Field Service Regulations* of the bifurcation of armour into 'infantry' and 'cruiser' tanks – an enduring source of trouble throughout the war.[24] The former were slow and heavily armoured, being intended to provide close support to infantry assaults; the latter were fast and lightly armoured, to act in cavalry fashion.

Certainly, neither type of tank was properly armed. The standard tank gun – the 2-pounder – was adequate against the Italians, but far from effective against German armour and significantly had no satisfactory high-explosive round to deal with anti-tank guns. When British armour came up against the German 88 mm anti-aircraft gun used so effectively as an anti-tank gun at ranges of 1,500 yards and more, the British tanks had to close to within 600 yards before they could reply at all, while all the time they were horribly exposed. The Matilda infantry tanks had a limited range of operation and were mechanically unreliable, so that the only way to conserve them was not to drive them, which seriously restricted the scope for training. The cruisers – also notoriously unreliable – were seriously underpowered, so they could not be up-armoured. Neither type of tank could be up-gunned because of the size of the turret ring, itself limited by a tank's width after the War Office insisted that tanks must be transportable by rail (on the British gauge, narrower than the Continental).[25] Even by late 1942 there was a widespread dissatisfaction with every British-designed tank in service, and many British armoured units at Alamein were still equipped with the hopelessly inadequate Valentine infantry tank and even the Matilda. American Grants, and still more Shermans, therefore proved something of a revelation when they were issued to British forces in 1942.

In such an atmosphere it was hardly surprising that, despite inventing the tank and producing in Liddell Hart, J. F. C. Fuller and Percy Hobart some of the foremost proponents of armoured warfare during the inter-war years, Britain entered the war with a hopelessly muddled armour policy. The Royal Armoured Corps was formed by combining much of the cavalry with the battalions of the Royal Tank Corps (the Royal Tank Regiment after 1938). Thus, regiments of hussars, lancers and dragoons, together with their county brethren from the yeomanry (largely officered by the fox-hunting classes – whether one hunted was literally a stricter requirement for a commission than any military criterion), had to turn their centuries' old cavalry tradition and genuine affection for horses into something quite different. That they continued to refer to 'chargers', 'lead horses' and 'stables' was indicative of an unfortunate hippomania. The propensity of British armour to charge enemy anti-tank gun screens owed much to frustration with flawed equipment but also to deficiencies of training that reinforced the idea that armour could operate without intimate support from infantry and artillery.[26] That the tank regiments were amateurs in the ways of armoured warfare should not, however, detract from the fact that when their members rode to their canned deaths by roasting they did so with panache and even gaiety, victims perhaps of the peace-loving society that bred them – one that fumbled its defences and neglected its peacetime armed forces precisely because it was civilized enough to regard war as a tragedy, and quite unlike the ruthless totalitarian powers it opposed. But British amateurishness was also a reflection of a public opinion 'lulled by the appeasement policy of its leaders and by the emotional blandishments of a facile pacifism'.[27]

One great advantage that the British enjoyed was the experience they derived from active peacetime garrisoning in the desert and the opportunity, at least for the Mobile Division, which became 7th Armoured Division on 16 February 1940, to train under desert conditions, especially in navigation and use of the sun compass (a sort of sundial).[28] Most people's immediate impression is that the desert is quite flat and featureless apart from a few low ridges and conspicuous high points of rock; but this is deceptive.

To the experienced soldier the ground reveals innumerable folds and undulations capable of hiding a vehicle or a group of men. Concealment is further assisted by the prevalence of dust and by the shimmering haze created by heat during the middle of the day – though at night the desert could be bitterly cold. Along the coast of Libya runs an escarpment up to 300 feet high which turns south-east once it crosses the border with Egypt. Away to the south, depressions fall away to similar depths below sea level – the most famous being the Qattara Depression, effectively impassable to armies, which was to mark the southern edge of the Alamein battlefield. Most of the desert to the north was firm enough to take wheeled as well as tracked vehicles, having a base of rock below a shallow carpet of fine sand. But, in places, expanses of soft sand could trap and bog the unwary. Neither the rock nor the sand was well suited to the infantryman trying to burrow down into the earth to find protection, but the former – needing drills or explosives to break it up – was the worse.

Desert life entailed hardship, with monotonous food and little water. The British soldier's staples remained unchanged from the First World War: corned beef (bully), canned meat and vegetables (known as 'M and V' or 'Maconochie', after the manufacturer), hard-tack biscuits, and jam – as well as the inevitable tea. Corporal N. D. Hatfield recalled that quick brew-ups at short halts 'were usually made by the well-tried method of filling with sand a perforated petrol-can with the top cut off, pouring petrol on the sand, putting a "dixie" on top and igniting and, hey presto, we had boiling water within a few minutes! The water was of course chlorinated and contained plenty of sediment.'[29] The water was invariably foul, noted Gunner L. E. Tutt. 'It often curdled the tinned milk that we used in our tea so that the mugs became filled with soft orange-coloured curds.' Nevertheless, 'we could never get enough tea, sugar and tinned milk. Our mugs of scalding sweet tea became a drug and to be deprived of them was sheer hell. Morale and good fellowship were in direct proportion to our supply of brews.' John Longstaff agreed: 'In my view a cup of char won the war. Give a Tommy a cup of char and whatever morale he had beforehand it was right high up after his cuppa char.' This was the authorities' opinion too: in 1942 the British Government bought that year's world tea crop, and distributed the surplus to other Allied nations. Tinned fruit (usually from Commonwealth sources) and potatoes, as well as bacon and soya links masquerading as sausages, together with bread baked in Royal Army Service Corps (RASC) field bakeries, helped to vary the diet and keep the soldiers generally healthy, although attempts to provide dehydrated cabbage proved something of a failure, as Gunner Tutt described. 'No matter how the cook prepared it, it always ended up looking and tasting like stewed gas cape.'[30]

While Axis forces usually relied on centralized cooking, the British often devolved the responsibility down to vehicle crews, allowing more scope for inventiveness. Crews soon perfected the technique of 'brewing up' and moving on in 20 minutes, and 20 ways of cooking bully. Whenever the British were close to Alexandria an enterprising unit would arrange for delicacies to be brought up by anyone with an excuse to make a visit there, however brief.[31] 'Up the blue' – in the open desert – very occasionally there would be gazelles to hunt for fresh meat, and sometimes a Bedouin would appear seemingly from nowhere, enabling a trade – the British swapped tea or cigarettes for eggs. According to Harold Fitzjohn, these exchanges were not always straightforward, as the nomad would always ask for a written chit or pass to prove his loyalty to the Allied cause. 'He'd ask the Germans for the same. I suppose he had a pocket full of them. We used to make one out and it used to say "Whatever happens, do not trust the bastard." After much thanking and "salaaming" he would go on his way clutching his pass.'[32]

Accurate maps were essential not only for navigation but for fixing the positions of the innumerable minefields that came to dot Egypt and Libya. Maps could be highly deceptive: for example, with practically no rainfall except along the narrow coastal strip, many places shown as 'Bir', meaning 'Well', were not inhabited, but merely the sites of ancient boreholes. The emptiness of the desert and its essentially flat nature made navigation and location-fixing all the more difficult, so that, while the desert conveyed freedom of movement tactically, it imposed extra and enormous strain on those tasked with administration. Every bullet and shell, every single morsel of food, and every single drop of precious fuel or water had to be brought to the right place at the right time, with the constant nagging fear of getting lost. When Major-General Douglas Wimberley first went into the desert with 51st (Highland) Division, he found out the hard way how difficult navigation was when it took him two hours to reach the officers' mess tent from his dugout some 400 yards away.[33] Colin Hayes, an established artist in civilian life, was a Royal Engineers surveyor. Much of his work involved placing beacons (usually made from oil drums with a number painted in large figures) and accurately positioning them on the map usually by astronomical observation:

> The information was then rushed back to the printing section and over-printed on every batch of fresh maps. So a map would consist of a grid and lots of numbers and dots. Occasionally it would have something like 'many tracks' written on it as well, just to make it look as if there was something else there. But mostly it was more like a naval chart than a map.[34]

The points thus established supplemented the surveyors' existing 'trig' points.

Sand got into everything, recalled Lieutenant-Colonel R G. Green – 'one's hair, eyes, ears, tea (the blessed drink) and our food. If your tank was hit the first thing you would know would be the clouds of sand blown up from the floor of the fighting compartment.'[35] Sand – like the mud in Flanders where the fathers of so many combatants had fought twenty-five years previously – was often ground into dust 'as fine as snuff or flour which can seep through closed lips and eyelids, through any clothing, which gets into food and gun-barrels and aeroplane engines; which, when it blows, makes men pray for deliverance'.[36] Dust clogged the filters of engines and drastically reduced the distances that vehicles could cover before needing overhaul – already reduced by the wear imposed by constantly driving over rugged terrain which, apart from a single metalled coast road, was completely devoid of routes which did not impose fearsome strain on tyres, shock absorbers and suspensions.

From the interior blew a hot wind, the *khamseen*, often accompanied by sandstorms which were one of the few things capable of stopping operations. 'If a sandstorm came, and they would come without warning, you would hope that it would clear off before the enemy,' said Colonel Green.[37] Bob Sykes, an Eighth Army soldier, described how

> one sandstorm sounded like a train coming, and way out a big black bank of cloud was rushing towards us . . . The sandstorm came at us like an express

train at about 40 m.p.h. with increasing gusts of wind. All oxygen seemed to go out of the air, and the flies were maddening and swarming. The heat was terrific and I sweated so the sand caked onto me – in my eyes, nose and ears. I sat down in my dugout and waited, thinking it would be over in a few minutes, but suddenly I nearly panicked – the sand was coming through every crack. I thought I would be buried. I fought my way out . . . the sand was whipping the skin off my face and hands. It was almost pitch black and I felt entirely alone. Then a light appeared and the sun began to look a dirty orange. The noise slowly abated and the wind died down: I had ridden out my first sandstorm.[38]

Meanwhile, the Italians faced a storm they could not hope to ride out. The Regia Marina suffered a crippling defeat at the hands of the Fleet Air Arm at Taranto in November 1940, and then Operation Compass, beginning on 9 December, proved a complete success with the defeat of the Italians in Egypt and the capture of over 38,000 prisoners. When Graziani's invading army stopped, he set up a series of fortified camps south of Sidi Barrani. These were hopelessly ill-organized, lacking mutual support and unable to dominate the ground between them, so that, when Wavell directed Western Desert Force under Lieutenant-General Richard O'Connor to launch what was initially to be a five-day raid, O'Connor was able to get behind them and defeat them in detail.

The war correspondent Alan Moorehead was astonished by what the British found in the camps: 'wines from Frascati and Falerno and Chianti . . . Parmesan cheeses as big as small cart-wheels . . . delicate tinned tongue and tunny fish and small round tins of beef. The vegetables were of every kind . . .' He also found a letter in which the writer noted, 'We are trying to fight this war as though it was a colonial war in Africa. But it is a European war in Africa fought with European weapons against a European enemy. We take too little account of this in building our stone forts and equipping ourselves with such luxury. We are not fighting Abyssinians now.'[39] Indeed, the Ethiopians were never equipped with Matilda tanks, which, however inadequate, had armour that was impenetrable to Italian guns.

Following up his success, O'Connor was given permission to invade Cyrenaica. With his force renamed XIII Corps, he took Bardia (5 January 1941) and Tobruk (26 January) before completing the destruction of the Italian Tenth Army at Beda Fomm on 7 February with a total haul of 110,000 prisoners (including 22 generals and an admiral), 180 medium and 200 light tanks, innumerable soft-skin vehicles and 845 guns captured, at a cost of 500 British dead, 1,373 wounded and 55 missing.

It was an astonishing feat, but already the focus of events had moved across the Mediterranean. Italy had attacked Greece the previous October, and Greece, which had put up a stout resistance, was now threatened by Germany through the Balkans. Wavell, under pressure from Churchill (prompted by Eden, his Foreign Secretary), began transferring forces to Greece now that it seemed the western flank was secure. When O'Connor wished to press on to Tripoli, he was therefore restrained.[40] However, his achievements did not go unrewarded: he was granted a knighthood, and appointed to command British Troops Egypt.

One unfortunate result of O'Connor's success was that some lessons learned were not necessarily the correct ones. His forces operated widely dispersed, to minimize the effects of air attack – essential until the Desert Air Force achieved air superiority – but this made tactical concentration and concentration of firepower difficult.[41] The success of 'Jock' columns – small ad-hoc groups of infantry and artillery – in harassing the Italians also led to a tendency towards dispersal that persisted long into 1942.

With O'Connor sent back to Egypt, in February 1941 Lieutenant-General Philip Neame VC took command of the remaining troops in Cyrenaica. The newly formed Cyrenaica Command was not expected to face a renewed threat from Tripolitania for several months, and Neame foresaw a largely administrative task, relying on the local telephone system for communications. With Wavell's eyes focused on Greece, Neame had only two weak and inexperienced formations as a garrison: 2nd Armoured Division (which possessed only one armoured brigade, partially equipped with captured Italian M13/40 tanks, and a threadbare support group) and 9th Australian Division (two of whose brigades had been replaced by raw, partially trained formations).[42]

Meanwhile, Hitler had decided it was necessary to prop up his ally. In October 1940 Generalmajor Wilhelm Ritter von Thoma had been sent to Libya to assess the prospects for German intervention. He reported that 'the supply problem was the decisive factor – not only because of the difficulties of the desert, but because of the British Navy's command of the Mediterranean'. He went on to stress that only motorized forces could operate, and that four panzer (armoured) divisions were needed to be decisive, which must replace Italian troops.[43] Not only was this politically unacceptable, it also would mean committing too many forces required for plans to invade the Soviet Union, so Hitler lost interest. But, with Italian defeat looming, on 11 January 1941 he issued Directive No. 22, stating that 'Germany should assist for reasons of strategy, politics, and psychology.'[44] He had already agreed to dispatch the aircraft of Fliegerkorps X to Sicily in order to attack British shipping – a development Churchill noted with foreboding.[45] Now he authorized creating the nucleus of a *Sperrverband* (blocking force) which would become 5th Light (Motorized) Division. Hitler had little difficulty in choosing a commander, whom he summoned on the morning of 6 February 1941 to the Reich Chancellery to receive his new appointment as Befehlshaber (Commander-in-Chief) German Troops in Libya. Promotion to Generalleutnant followed the next day, and Erwin Johannes Eugen Rommel set off immediately to take up his new command.

2

Enter Rommel

Heiss über Afrikas Boden die Sonne glüht,
Unsere panzermotoren singen ihr Lied,
Deutsche Panzer im Sonnenbrand
Stehen im Kampf gegen Engeland.
Es rasseln die Ketten, es dröhnt der Motor,
Panzer rollen in Afrika vor.

Afrikakorps song*

Rommel had, according to the Italian officer Alessandro Predieri, 'two very rare and precious gifts':

> The first is luck, which you will remember, Napoleon prescribed to his generals . . . The second gift is that of being able to keep his bearings in the midst of all the confusion of modern desert warfare. His instinct tells him immediately where a difficult situation is going to develop, and off he goes with his Kampfstaffel [Headquarters Group], which he treats like a Praetorian Guard, and puts things right, charging around like a junior officer.[1]

The son of a schoolmaster from Heidenheim in Württemberg, Rommel revealed his impetuous military character within days of first seeing action as a lieutenant in August 1914.[2] Following an astonishing exploit in November 1917 in which he led a small detachment of mountain troops around the flanks of a large Italian position at Monte Mataiur, north of Trieste, capturing both the position and some 6,000 prisoners, he performed another at Longarone, in the Piave valley north of Treviso, by capturing no fewer than 8,000 prisoners in one day, for which he was awarded the *Pour le Mérite*, the highest German decoration for bravery at the time. This was a defining moment in his life. Rommel

---

* The sun glows hot over Africa's soil,/Our panzer motors sing their song,/German tanks under the burning sun/Stand in battle against England./The tracks rattle, the motor roars,/Panzers are advancing in Africa.

was utterly single-minded in his devotion to soldiering, and he was greedy for success and the acclaim it brings. Despite his decoration, he never forgot that someone else was rewarded for Monte Mataiur. As a fellow instructor at the Infantry School in Dresden later commented, 'You can understand Rommel only by taking his storming of Monte Mataiur into account. Basically he always stayed that lieutenant, making snap decisions and acting on the spur of the moment.'[3]

Yet, immediately after Longarone, Rommel was posted to staff duties – which he detested. Worse, he never qualified for the General Staff, though his promotions led to resentment between himself and its officers. When his book *Infanterie Grieft An* (*Infantry Attacks*) was published in 1937, he came to Hitler's notice and embraced the Nazis while his fellow officers were still in two minds. In August 1939 he was appointed to command Hitler's headquarters for the invasion of Poland, and in the following year he commanded 7th Panzer Division for the invasion of France. In spectacular fashion he captured most of 51st (Highland) Division at Saint-Valéry-en-Caux, and earned the name 'Ghost' Division for his formation in the process. It was a brilliant performance, based on the premiss that the enemy would be too disordered to attack his vulnerable flanks.

During the summer of 1940 Rommel's reputation grew as the Nazi press exploited his success assiduously. Hitler's regard for him was already arousing jealously and mistrust in others. Of all the factors that contributed to the Rommel legend, none is more important than the special position Rommel held in Hitler's estimation.[4] Hitler deliberately chose to foster two heroes: one in the snow – Edouard Dietl – and one in the sun – Rommel. Both performed in the wings, away from the main stage, and both appeared loyal instruments of Hitler, not possessing the type of intellect that might threaten his position. Over the next 18 months Rommel's fame would grow to such proportions that many Eighth Army soldiers thought more highly of him than of their own commanders and his unexpected 'jack-in-the-box' appearances so tickled their sense of humour that this admiration bordered on the affectionate.[5]

Rommel arrived in Tripoli – the main landing place for Axis supplies – on 12 February 1941, and immediately set off for the front at Sirte in a light aircraft. Significantly, this was almost 300 miles away (half as far again as the distance normally considered the limit for supplying a force by road), and Oberkommando des Heeres (OKH – Army High Command) estimated a requirement of 39 transport columns (each of 30 two-ton trucks) to supply Rommel's force. With 15th Panzer Division from Germany, reserves and troop-carrying vehicles added to

5th Light (Motorized) Division, his force would need proportionately 20 times as much motor transport as was allocated to the armies preparing to invade the USSR. This would stretch the Wehrmacht's capacity to the limit, and more troops or longer distances would necessarily mean shortages at the front.[6]

One of Rommel's first acts after visiting the front was to order 100 dummy tanks to be made up from canvas and wood mounted on cars, while a parade in Tripoli on 14 February involved panzers rejoining the column behind the reviewing stand to increase their apparent numbers. Rommel addressed some of his new arrivals. 'The desert is waiting for us. We are about to embark on a great safari!' '*Heia Safari!*' replied an enthusiastic subaltern, and was echoed by others in the audience. It would become their battle cry.[7] On 19 February his command was officially designated Deutsches Afrikakorps (DAK), but he retained his own original title, since Befehlshaber was one rung higher in military jargon than Kommandierender General (corps commander).

For the moment, he was content to get his small force deployed with characteristic drive and energy, but Rommel's ambitions were limitless. Despite specific and clear instructions to the contrary – for Berlin was concentrating on invading the Soviet Union – he never concealed his intention of capturing Cairo and the Suez Canal. Visiting Berlin in March, he explained that he would soon conquer Egypt and began talking about restoring and expanding a German East Africa. The Chief of the General Staff, Generaloberst Franz Halder, asked what he would need for the purpose. When Rommel said another two panzer corps, Halder was contemptuous, asking, 'Even if we had them, how are you going to supply them and feed them?' 'That,' relied Rommel equally contemptuously, 'is quite immaterial to me. That's your pigeon.'[8] These personal frictions would have ramifications later on. Hitler must have known that Rommel would, if necessary, appeal directly to him, and this proved the case more and more as the tide of war gradually turned against the Germans. Rommel had a special channel for such communication in Leutnant Dr Alfred Ingemar Berndt, a member of Dr Josef Goebbels's Propaganda Ministry, who was appointed to Rommel's staff as overseer of propaganda but often acted as an envoy.[9]

In a lightning strike beginning on 31 March 1941, Rommel scattered 2nd Armoured Division, captured Neame and O'Connor, and drove the British from all of Cyrenaica with the exception of Tobruk, into which 9th Australian Division retired. 'My superiors in Tripoli, Rome and perhaps Berlin too must be clutching their heads in dismay,' declared Rommel. 'I took the risk, against all instructions, because the opportunity was there for the taking. Probably it will all be pronounced all right later.'[10] An assessment by Wavell on 2 March had discounted the threat to Cyrenaica on the basis that the Germans would not be ready to attack before the summer. This accorded with all indications of their capabilities, but even the German High Command could not account for Rommel's intentions.[11] The German press lapped up his success, measuring it in kilometres – even though they were kilometres of nothing. But the problem that would bedevil all Rommel's actions in Africa – supply – was now far more pressing than glamorous tactical manoeuvring, and he was quick to blame others when it led to failure.

Contrary to the widespread belief among Commonwealth forces at the time, the Germans were hopelessly ill-prepared for desert warfare. Unable to get useful information from the Italians, the Germans initially overestimated water requirements. They also soon discovered that the double-tyred back wheels of their lorries sank into the sand. The climate was unlike anything most of them had ever experienced, and not until their second year in Africa did German soldiers become accustomed to this.[12] That they adapted was thanks to their ability to improvise – a characteristic that the American military historian Trevor Dupuy attributed not to any innate propensity for war, but to the long-standing effectiveness of the German General Staff.[13] It is difficult not to feel, however, that their strong sense of national identity, of being *Germans*, strengthened by the exhortations of the Nazis, also played a part. But the German soldier shared the irreverence of all soldiers for the army in general and for his superiors in particular. One diarist recorded his opinion of General Staff officers as 'old bald-headed bureaucrats and conceited young whippersnappers'.[14] The pith helmets, shorts and knee-length stockings issued caused much hilarity. 'We look like a lot of bloody Tyroleans,' said one. The pith helmets were soon discarded and replaced by a sloppy peaked cap – the *Einheitsfeldmütze* – which became a DAK symbol.[15]

The British also completely misunderstood German doctrine – a failure made worse by stereotypical views of both the Germans and themselves. David Hunt, a British intelligence officer, recalled that during his officer training he was told that 'the Germans were fiendishly clever and worked out schemes of the utmost ingenuity . . . But, my instructors would insist, the moment their plans began to run into difficulties they were at a sad loss. The British, I was told, were always at their best in these circumstances; but the Germans were quite unable to improvise.'[16] Hunt's subsequent experience in North Africa and Italy convinced him that the opposite was true. With its system of 'mission command', the German approach rejected the concept of war as a 'scientific' discipline. Commanders issued directives, but subordinates were allowed wide freedom of action to secure their commander's *intention*. Thus, whenever a fluid situation emerged, they had a greater scope for thought and action.[17] Junior leaders were taught that 'inaction was criminal: it is better to do something which might turn out to be wrong than to make no decision and remain inactive'.[18] Furthermore, German officer cadets received superior tactical training which enabled them to step up into positions of higher responsibility. They were already fully trained soldiers before starting officer training and, while the British cadet was taught the bare essentials of platoon tactics, the German cadet was taught everything an infantry battalion commander needed to know and could theoretically command at that level. This had two benefits: junior officers were able to accept command responsibilities with a minimum of further training and there was a common understanding of the army's tactical doctrine.[19]

Their panzers were generally superior to British tanks. While British tanks were designed to fight different types of battle, panzers were designed to fulfill different roles in the same battle: the Mark III had an effective 50 mm high-velocity gun (which was improved to a long version), and the Mark IV was armed with a 75 mm capable of firing an effective high-explosive round to nearly 2 miles.[20] Panzer divisions moved in compact all-arms groups organized so that panzers, infantry, artillery and anti-tank guns could each quickly give the others support.[21] The panzers would withdraw, enticing the British armour on to the anti-tank-gun screens, and then be ready to counter-attack from the flanks. It was a common British misconception that most tank casualties were caused by panzers, in fact the majority were caused by anti-tank guns.[22] Furthermore, panzer commanders could lead from the front, because they were equipped with mobile command posts fitted with adequate communications. They could monitor their panzers' progress by radio without having constantly to wait for consolidated situation reports, and their battle drills allowed them to deploy on the simplest of oral instructions – something the British eschewed for a long time. Consequently, when both sides' command and communications systems failed under the strain of combat, the Germans were better able to adapt quickly; and, while both sides made mistakes, the Germans could often enough regain the situation while the British could not.[23]

On 10 April, Rommel declared (in complete contravention of his orders) that 'Our objective is to be made known to every man; it is the

Suez Canal. To prevent a breakout from Tobruk the offensive is to be pushed ahead by every means possible.'[24] In racing for the Canal, he was setting a precedent that he would follow to the end. However, he did not realize that he had already reached his logistical limit and that the troops who faced him would not simply collapse. Ninth Australian Division would prove his nemesis. Its commander, Leslie Morshead, was like most of his men not a professional soldier, although he had been soldiering all his life. He had begun with the Citizen Military Force while a schoolmaster, before distinguished service with the Australian Imperial Force during the First World War. He was a fighting leader in whom 'the traditions of the British Army had been bottled from his childhood like tight-corked champagne'.[25] Between the wars he combined a successful business career with the Orient Line with command of a militia brigade for seven years, and in 1941 his men rapidly bestowed on him the nickname of 'Ming the Merciless', after the evil megalomaniac in the *Flash Gordon* films. If battles are a contest of wills there was no chance of Morshead being found wanting. 'Battles and campaigns are won by leadership . . .' he said later, 'by discipline . . . by hard work. And above all that, by courage, which we call "guts", gallantry, and devotion to duty.'[26] Now Morshead and his men set about showing these qualities in abundance.

Rommel attacked within days of sealing in the mostly Australian Tobruk garrison, on 13/14 April, but was bloodily repulsed. Another assault was launched at the end of the month and secured an important piece of high ground but no further progress. Rommel had no option but to settle down for a siege. The truth was that his brilliant advance had failed to bring decisive victory but had extended his supply lines by 700 miles – a problem only partially offset by the capture of Benghazi. More seriously, he was soon on extremely bad terms with his Fliegerführer Afrika (air-force commander), Generalmajor Stefan Frölich, who disliked Rommel's bullying manner so much that he actively avoided him.[27] Rommel's personal file in Berlin soon bulged with complaints from subordinates and others, and it is hardly surprising that his abrasive style did not lend itself to smooth relations with the Italians, though he was nominally under Italian command – at first under the Governor-General of Libya, Generale Italo Gariboldi.

Rommel's supply problems have since been defined in terms of Malta, from where strong and aggressive British air and naval forces acted very effectively against Axis shipping carrying supplies from Italy to Libya. Important though Malta was, the Italians were still able to land sufficient supplies on the African shore to sustain the Axis forces. Temporary crises of shipping occurred, but generally the Regia Marina performed its convoy duties well. Over 90 per cent of personnel, 80 per cent of stores and supplies, and 85 per cent of vehicles arrived safely. The problem lay in internal communications. As the only port of any size was Tripoli, supplies had to be brought up by road, and between 35 and 50 per cent of the fuel landed was needed to move everything else eastward.[28] Seapower enabled the British to supply Morshead in Tobruk while Rommel spent the summer living from hand to mouth, unable to concentrate sufficient strength for an effective tilt at the fortress.

Seapower had also allowed the British to evacuate their expeditionary force from Greece and subsequently from Crete when that was invaded in May by German parachutists and mountain troops (although at terrible cost). It also enabled reinforcements to be rushed to Egypt in the form of the fast convoy Tiger carrying some 150 tanks. But it could not overcome the army's deficiencies in doctrine and training, which Rommel cruelly exposed during two attempts to relieve Tobruk in May and June – Operations Brevity and Battleaxe.

One factor in such British defeats as Crete had been Churchill's impulsive reading of Ultra, the signals intelligence resulting from Allied cracking of Axis codes, particularly from the German Enigma machine. Churchill used Ultra to browbeat generals, when it was merely one source of information. Other sources in North Africa were the twice-daily reports of the Long Range Desert Group (LRDG), which lay up in the enemy's back areas watching the roads and counting what passed.[29] There was also aerial photography, tactical radio intercept ('Y') and interrogation of prisoners and captured documents. Although of enormous significance, the importance of Ultra relative to these other sources is sometimes overstated. But, even though full warning by Ultra had not brought victory in Crete, Churchill had used Ultra to bully Wavell into premature action over Battleaxe.[30] He believed he had full access to Axis plans, and was ignorant of the dangers inherent in basing strategy on single pieces of uncorroborated evidence, however unimpeachable their source.

In fact Churchill had long doubted Wavell's ability, and was determined to replace him with General Sir Claude Auchinleck, Commander-in-Chief India. They swapped places on 5 July. Unfortunately, however, Auchinleck and Churchill could not work well together. Auchinleck was a superb leader – much admired and respected both by close associates and by his soldiers – but Churchill's impatient telegrams annoyed him considerably, and he made this clear. Like Wavell before him, he therefore failed to gain the confidence of his political master.

*

Shortly after replacing Wavell, Auchinleck announced his intention of driving the enemy out of North Africa and told Churchill that the offensive would begin on or around 1 November. Auchinleck had served in Mesopotamia during the First World War, and the disaster that surrounded the siege of Kut al Amara had convinced him that troops should never be asked to fight until properly trained and that they must have proper logistic support. Churchill persisted in the belief that a unit was ready to fight the instant it disembarked and that equipment was ready the moment it was unloaded, and he demanded that Auchinleck take the offensive immediately. Auchinleck refused. General Sir Alan Brooke, appointed Chief of the Imperial General Staff (CIGS) on 25 December, found himself constantly having to filter Churchill's growling urge to hit the enemy whenever and wherever possible through a calico of practical reality.

Auchinleck waited patiently as the steady flow of men and equipment arrived. During the summer and early autumn, over 600 new tanks and 800 guns were unloaded. Headquarters Western Army was formed in Cairo on 10 September, with Lieutenant-General Sir Alan Cunningham appointed in command, and from midnight on the 26th, as Headquarters Eighth Army, it assumed command of all troops in the Western Desert.[31] Western Desert Force, reconstituted in the spring, once again became XIII Corps at the end of October, under Major-General Alfred Godwin-Austen, while reinforcements permitted the formation of a second corps – known initially as the Armoured Corps, but soon designated XXX Corps, with Major-General Willoughby Norrie appointed commander.

Although all the fast cruiser tanks would be concentrated in XXX Corps, the slow infantry tanks would remain with XIII Corps. Thus the two-speed nature of British armour which Rommel had already noted as a weakness persisted to dog Wavell's successor. Nevertheless, the British possessed a material superiority. Eighth Army comprised 118,000 men, with 126 light, 529 cruiser and 205 infantry tanks supported by 849 medium, field and anti-tank guns. Apart from this field force, another infantry division was in reserve, while in Tobruk there was a reinforced infantry division and about 100 tanks in an army tank brigade.[32] In the air, the British deployed 512 aircraft, and these were faced by about 350 German and Italian machines, although the latter would have the advantage of operating much closer to their forward airfields. At the outset of Rommel's first dash across Cyrenaica he enjoyed almost total air superiority and the British were forced to confine their movements to the hours of darkness. From now on this situation would be steadily reversed. In July, Tedder – newly appointed AOC-in-C – had organized the first tactical air force and took steps to improve its ground mobility by reorganizing 204 Group into Air Headquarters Western Desert, which would control what became the Desert Air Force (DAF).[33]

'British' was a misleading term for Eighth Army – many of its members were as close to Britain in the Western Desert as they would ever get. As well as 1st South African Division (all volunteers and mostly Afrikaners) in XXX Corps, XIII Corps included 4th Indian and the New Zealand Divisions. On his appointment to command the latter, Major-General Bernard Freyberg had pointed out that 'the New Zealand forces are not an integral part of the British Army – they are a distinct New Zealand force, proud of their own identity'.[34] The officer–men relationship was much more relaxed than in British units. Most New Zealanders had a great respect for their officers and regarded them as equals – senior rather than superior – and there was a reciprocal respect of officers for men – hence Christian-name terms.[35] Freyberg – known affectionately as 'Tiny', because he was over six feet tall – was born in Surrey but grew up in New Zealand. He started adult life as a dentist; then, as a member of the Hood Battalion, Royal Naval Division, he swam ashore at Gallipoli and won the first of three DSOs. He later gained a VC in France, and after the war he stayed on in the British Army, retiring on medical grounds in 1937 as a major-general. When war broke out again he offered his services to the New Zealand government and became commander of the New Zealand Expeditionary Force. Rommel came to regard the Kiwis as the elite of Eighth Army. They were certainly different, rather like a large tribe and stronger than a normal British division, with a cavalry regiment and an extra infantry battalion – the superb 28th (Maori) Battalion. Assessing the relative merits of fighting troops is, however, fraught with danger and necessarily subjective. Some myths have since been demolished.[36] Major-General Francis 'Gertie' Tuker, the commander of 4th Indian Division, thought the New Zealand Division 'a very ponderous affair . . . like dear old Freyberg'.[37]

Soldiers from the Commonwealth – particularly Australia – held themselves in high regard, which they generally justified.[38] After fighting around Sollum and Tobruk, the commander of the German II Battalion 104th Rifle Regiment remarked that 'The English and Australians are tough and hard opponents as individual fighters, highly skilled in defence, unimaginative and inflexible in attack, cold-blooded and skilled in in-fighting, experienced in assault and capable of standing hardships of all kinds.'[39] Major Charles Finlay described the qualities of the Australian soldier: 'Discipline has different connotations for different people. The Australian "Digger" had the discipline which allowed him to think and not do things automatically . . . What I mean by that is the Australian private soldier understood what was required of him and what his duties were, and didn't have to wait for the section or platoon commander to issue him with orders.' Peter Jeffrey of 3 Squadron Royal Australian Air Force agreed: 'I don't think the "Pommie" was a softie in any shape or form; I think he was a very brave man and I think he put up with all sorts of conditions. I think the main difference was he just didn't have the initiative, he waited to be told, instead of getting on himself.' Most British observers tended to agree, although Harold Harper of Eighth Army dissented: 'A lot of [the Australians'] casualties were quite unnecessary in my opinion, because of their indiscipline. They would go into a situation fearlessly – let's be fair, they were fearless soldiers – but without adopting the correct tactical methods of approach shown by British infantrymen.'[40]

By mid-November the garrison of Tobruk was mostly British and Polish: fears that the 'Rats of Tobruk' were enjoying themselves too much had prompted wives and sweethearts to press the Australian government for their relief, and the Royal Navy had replaced them with the British 70th Division in another brilliant operation. Opposing the garrison was the recently created Panzergruppe Afrika, deploying 102,000 men with 380 tanks and 1,140 guns, including those of DAK. In August, DAK's original 5th Light (Motorized) Division (now redesignated 21st Panzer Division) and 15th Panzer Division had been joined by a third DAK division, originally created as Afrika Division zur besonderen Verwendung – for special purposes – but in November redesignated 90th Light Division. It was created from various units already in or en route to Africa, including 361st Africa Regiment raised from Germans in the French Foreign Legion given a 'second chance'. Attached to DAK was an Italian infantry division. Also formed was Sonderverband 288 – 288th Special Unit – which was originally intended to operate deep behind Allied lines to exploit Arab nationalism and anti-British factions such as those of Raschid Ali in Iraq or the Vichy regime in Syria. However, by the time it was operational, in August 1941, events had overtaken it and both Iraq and Syria were firmly occupied by the British. It was then attached to 90th Light Division, and was eventually designated Panzergrenadier Regiment Afrika on 31 October 1942. There were two Italian armoured divisions and a motorized infantry division (XX Corps), as well as four Italian infantry divisions (XXI Corps) supported by a siege train of artillery. Most of the Italian infantry – 'stiffened' by German units – invested the fortress of Tobruk, while the mobile formations were deployed between Tobruk and the frontier with Egypt.

Auchinleck's offensive was code-named Crusader,which also inspired the choice of a sword for Eighth Army's badge and the name of its weekly newspaper.[41] The plan involved what was rapidly becoming the classic desert manoeuvre: a wide sweep south around the exposed southern flank of the enemy's defences. The Axis positions at Sollum, Halfaya and Capuzzo would be outflanked, while the Tobruk garrison would break out 'to catch Rommel's infantry divisions between hammer and anvil'.[42] Although Auchinleck's original start date was 1 November, he came to regard the middle of the month as more realistic, and Churchill chafed at the further delay while intensive preparations continued – including the extension of the Western Desert Railway some 75 miles west from Matruh and the laying of a water pipeline close by. Further delays were caused by late delivery of 150 tanks from the United Kingdom, and transport shortages hindered some of the training programme, so that Auchinleck was forced to postpone the start of the operation until 18 November.[43]

Rommel was meanwhile trying to put together a plan to overcome the troublesome fortress once and for all, and when Crusader was launched on 18 November he ignored it at first. Near the coast, Halfaya was invested by XIII Corps, while XXX Corps reached its objectives in the area of Gabr Saleh. The lack of opposition caused uncertainty at Eighth Army Headquarters, prompting Cunningham to change his plan. The armour would now destroy the Italians at Bir el Gubi before driving for Sidi Rezegh, immediately south of Tobruk. This resulted in 'some of the most extraordinary and complex movements in the history of the war'.[44] Much of the fighting now revolved around the airfield at Sidi Rezegh. Rommel, unconcerned by the attack, ordered DAK to concentrate between the incursion and Egypt, but its commander, Generalleutnant Ludwig Crüwell, who was beginning to appreciate British intentions, directed his panzers into the British flank. Cunningham, seeing the possibility of trapping and destroying most of the Panzergruppe, ordered the Tobruk garrison to begin its breakout on the morning of the 21st, but Rommel finally acknowledged that this was a serious offensive and ordered the concentration of DAK at Sidi Rezegh. Thus, when the breakout battle began, Tobforce, striking out from Tobruk, faced much more serious opposition than anticipated. A gunner from 3rd Royal Horse Artillery recalled:

> We all met Mr Death that day at Sidi Rezegh . . . We were being blown to pieces a bit at a time by the enemy and we could not do a thing about it. We had our faithful anti-tank guns, 2-pounders, against the German 88s. Our shells tried so hard to penetrate his armour. We had only peashooters, but we fought on. Men died by their guns.[45]

In XIII Corps's area on 22 November, Bardia, Capuzzo and Sidi Omar were attacked in the belief that DAK was withdrawing westward. When 6th New Zealand Brigade heard of the crisis at Sidi Rezegh it marched throughout the afternoon and night. Following a navigational error, it arrived at Bir Chleta, where it captured DAK Headquarters, narrowly missing capturing Crüwell, who had left only minutes before. At Sidi Rezegh, 21st Panzer Division resumed the assault and forced 7th Armoured Division to abandon its positions, with 7th Armoured Brigade having effectively ceased to exist. Now Rommel planned from 23 November to crush the remains of XXX Corps in a pincer before moving to relieve his frontier garrisons.

Both sides were under false impressions about the situation. Cunningham still thought XXX Corps was writing down the Axis armour and that the New Zealanders were in position to link up with Tobforce. Rommel thought he had also destroyed 4th Armoured Brigade, when it was in fact only scattered. But Eighth Army would suffer disaster on the following day: Crüwell's panzer regiments smashed into 5th South African Brigade about 8 miles south of Sidi Rezegh, practically destroying it. Nevertheless, 23 November – *Totensonntag** – was once more a day of the dead for the Germans: they lost another 72 tanks and many infantry to the British armour, which, although badly mauled, was still operating. Elsewhere, Tobforce continued to extend its salient and 6th New Zealand Brigade was stopped some 6 miles short of Sidi Rezegh.[46]

Cunningham's losses became apparent to him only that evening, and in the chaos he was unable to discern much hope. He asked Auchinleck to fly up from Cairo to decide Crusader's fate. Auchinleck arrived as it was getting dark on the 23rd and received a bleak prognosis from Cunningham. Auchinleck realized it might be correct, but insisted that 'the strategical initiative remained with us: we were attacking, he was defending'.[47]

Rommel was also under misapprehensions, but these led him to over-optimism. He decided that the crisis had passed and that an invasion of Egypt would finish the British off. On the morning of 24 November he personally led DAK in 'the dash to the wire'. This surprised everyone, and reports verging on panic flooded into Eighth Army Headquarters. But Auchinleck remained unperturbed and issued a detailed instruction 'to attack the enemy relentlessly', reminding Cunningham that his immediate objective was the destruction of Axis

---

* *Totensonntag* was declared a solemn day of remembrance in 1816 for those who fell in the Napoleonic wars.

armour and that Tobruk would be relieved.[48] Auchinleck's coolness was soon vindicated, for Rommel's drive rapidly came unstuck. The panzers ran out of fuel, ammunition and water, and British artillery caused them no end of grief, though they managed to get into Bardia. Meanwhile the New Zealand Division was heading for Tobruk and Tobforce continued to fight its way southward; by the day's end, a narrow link had been established between them. At midday on 26 November, Auchinleck assumed command of Eighth Army. The decision to dismiss Cunningham was not taken lightly, and he was persuaded to go into hospital in Alexandria under an assumed name for treatment for nervous exhaustion. That evening, Rommel realized that his foray into Egypt had been futile and he ordered a return to the area around Tobruk. Two days later a combined assault was made by DAK against the New Zealand and Tobforce positions around Ed Duda and succeeded in cutting Freyberg's division in two. Following this, the New Zealanders were withdrawn eastward on 1 December. Once more Tobruk was surrounded, but with XIII Corps Headquarters now inside the perimeter. Although the situation appeared to be the same as before the offensive began, both sides were close to exhaustion, and in this the Axis was at a disadvantage. The British received personnel and *matériel* reinforcements, while Rommel had few reserves. Fighting continued for several more days, but on 6 December Rommel was forced to withdraw, abandoning his troops – who had held out valiantly throughout – at the frontier.[49]

In this battle perhaps more than any other, Malta had a direct and massive influence in destroying the supplies so vital to sustaining the Axis. This point was not lost in Berlin, and as a result on 2 December Hitler issued Directive No. 38, dispatching Luftflotte II (Air Fleet II) from the Eastern Front 'to secure mastery of the air and sea in the area between Southern Italy and North Africa in order to secure communications with Libya and Cyrenaica and, in particular, to keep Malta in subjection'.[50] In October he went further, ordering two dozen U-boats to enter the Mediterranean, despite navy protests. Thus Rommel's strategy, pursued independently since April, was now affecting other theatres.

On 28 November, Generalfeldmarschall Albrecht Kesselring was appointed Oberbefehlshaber Sud (Commander-in-Chief South) and commander of the Luftwaffe in the Mediterranean. Kesselring was one of the best staff officers and administrators produced by any service, and his courage as a Luftwaffe commander was legendary. An optimist with a permanent toothy grin and the nickname 'smiling Albert', he had orders to see that Rommel got his supplies – although Rommel accused him of adopting the airs of a supreme Wehrmacht commander in the south. However, he was not to be Rommel's superior. The curious set-up gave him a sort of watching brief over German land forces and absolute control of air forces. He was officially subordinate to Generale Ettore Bastico, the governor-general of Tripolitania, and through him to Comando Supremo, the Italian High Command, headed by Generale Ugo Cavallero (with German representation by Generalleutnant Enno von Rintelen), but he also received orders direct from OKW (Oberkommando der Wehrmacht – the German Armed Forces High Command). The result was a web of negotiation and intrigue rather than a firm system of control, and, although he often complained about this complicated structure, Rommel was able to exploit this for his own purposes. He riled senior Italian officers, but got away with it because by now it was apparent to everyone that he had Hitler's backing.[51]

Eighth Army also had a new commander. After sacking Cunningham, Auchinleck sent for Major-General Neil Ritchie, his Chief of Staff at GHQ, to take temporary command. Ritchie was a strange choice, having commanded nothing larger in the field than a battalion. It seems that Auchinleck intended to keep close personal control of Eighth Army, and certainly for the first ten days Ritchie acted as no more than a deputy to him. Possibly Auchinleck intended the appointment to be no more than a stopgap, and Ritchie himself suggested that someone should be sent out from Britain. Unfortunately, Auchinleck's temporary appointment became permanent when Churchill announced it in the House of Commons without indicating its temporary nature.[52]

In the meantime, the pursuit did not go well for the exhausted British forces; and Rommel inflicted a check on them in the Gazala area. By Christmas he was back at Agedabia, and then withdrew to El Agheila, where he had begun his offensive operations some nine months before. He was not dismayed, however, and while Auchinleck planned to resume the offensive around 10–15 February – once stocks had been built up through Benghazi – he took the opportunity presented by weak screening forces to his front to knock the British off balance once more. On 21 January 1942 he launched his attack near Agedabia and routed 2nd Armoured Brigade, newly arrived from Egypt.*

---

* The following day he was promoted to Generaloberst and his command was renamed Panzerarmee Afrika to encompass all Axis forces operating in Cyrenaica. In the Commons, Churchill called him 'a great general' – much to Hitler's delight and the displeasure of Auchinleck, who issued the extraordinary request that 'I am therefore begging you to dispel the idea in every way that you can that Rommel is anything but an ordinary German general . . . I am not jealous of Rommel' (Irving, *The Trail of the Fox*, p. 5).

Within Eighth Army, relations among the senior officers were poor. The corps commanders were senior to Ritchie, and felt their experience more valuable than his. There now followed a worrying set of arguments between Godwin-Austen and Tuker on the one hand, who argued in favour of abandoning Benghazi, and Ritchie on the other, who felt Benghazi could be held and took 4th Indian Division directly under army command. Auchinleck became so concerned about the situation that he flew up to Eighth Army Headquarters, although he neither took command nor interfered with Ritchie's running of operations. Tuker later wrote that 'Godwin-Austen had asked for bread and been given a stone. The one thing he did not get out of Army was a positive, definite plan.'[53] When Rommel launched a new attack on 27 January he exploited the lack of firm control emanating from Eighth Army, while Tuker felt he had no option but to retreat from Benghazi – having first demolished vital installations.

Thereafter, events overtook Ritchie, who retreated as far as Gazala – abandoning the bulge of Cyrenaica, including its precious airfields. Rommel, who throughout was perilously short of supplies, decided against further pursuit. He was fully aware that a resumption of the advance would renew his supply problems, and demanded another 8,000 trucks from OKH (nonsense given that the entire German armoured force at this time mustered 14,000 in total). Before he could resume his advance to Tobruk and Egypt, Comando Supremo then asked how he intended to supply his force. Rommel confessed he did not know: the logistic services would somehow have to 'adapt themselves' to the tactical situation.[54]

By now Paris radio was referring to Cyrenaica as *La Promenade des Anglais* – the pendulum had swung across it no fewer than five times since 1940. But nobody actually wanted it. The whole point of the campaign was to capture the ports at either end, and Rommel's eyes remained firmly fixed on Alexandria.[55] Eighth Army, now in a defensive line running from Gazala to Bir Hacheim in the south, would have to prepare where it stood to face any future Axis offensive and to launch its own. And with the entry of Japan into the war in December 1941 the British strategic situation had taken a dramatic turn for the worse. All of a sudden, with Malaya overrun and Singapore surrendering on 15 February 1942, land and air forces were being diverted to the Far East, while the Australian government was calling for the return of its troops from the Middle East. Godwin-Austen felt that his position in command of XIII Corps had been undermined by Ritchie's actions and asked to be relieved.[56] Auchinleck accepted his resignation and replaced him with Lieutenant-General W. H. E. 'Strafer' Gott. Godwin-Austen had impressed his subordinates as a robust, shrewd and energetic leader,[57] and his departure 'was the latest of many misjudgements which had started to shake the confidence in the leadership'.[58] But when Auchinleck's Deputy Chief of Staff, Major-General Eric 'Chink' Dorman-Smith, suggested replacing Ritchie, Auchinleck demurred on the grounds that he could not keep sacking Eighth Army commanders. Besides, he felt that, if he did, the replacement for Ritchie sent out from Britain would be Lieutenant-General Bernard Law Montgomery, and there had been considerable antipathy between them since Montgomery had been one of his subordinates in 1940.[59]

3

The Fall of Tobruk

Vor der Kaserne,
Vor dem grosser Tor,
Stand eine Laterne,
Und steht sie noch davor,
So woll'n wir uns da wieder seh'n
Bei der Laterne wollen wir stehn
Wie einst Lili Marleen
Wie einst Lili Marleen.

'Lili Marleen'*

Just before ten o'clock, someone called out, 'What about our bedtime song?' Denis Johnston, a BBC war correspondent, was deeply moved to hear a German woman sing both armies to sleep in a deep and lovely contralto. He lay down in his bedroll and, looking up at the desert stars, found his emotions gripped and wrung like a damp rag.[1] Written by Norbert Schultze and Hans Leip, and originally recorded by Lale Andersen in 1939, 'Lili Marleen' became a huge hit with both armies after its first broadcast on Radio Belgrade on 18 August 1941, probably because it was *not* a war song but a song of farewell – always popular with servicemen, men thinking not of dying bravely for their countries but of returning, safe, to their families, sweethearts and friends. For three years it was played every night without fail (except three times after the fall of Stalingrad, when Goebbels forbade all entertainment),[2] and it became personal to the men of Eighth Army. Few had an opportunity to hear it, however, since this required access to a radio, but the wartime grapevine was highly efficient. In addition men brought songs

---

* Underneath the lantern,/By the barrack gate,/Darling I remember/The way you used to wait./T'was there that you whispered tenderly/That you loved me,/You'd always be/My Lili of the Lamplight,/My own Lili Marlene. [Loose translation for singing.]

from home with them – mostly slushy moon–June love songs[3] – and those that passed through Durban on troopships remembered an unknown 'Lady in White' (she was Perla Siedle Gibson) who sang for them no matter what the time of day or night.[4]

The shared ordeal of desert warfare produced a bond between those who served 'up the blue' on both sides. Although not on terms of affection, they shared 'Lili Marleen' (which neither the Italians nor the British could improve on), and there was a mutual respect born of common hardship, with few breaches of the accepted rules of war, almost as if the desert war were a private affair. The British went one step further, and came to regard the desert as a kind of club with its own language – a soldierized bastard-Arabic employed in the accents of London, Liverpool, Glasgow, Johannesburg, Sydney and Auckland. 'Griff' meant 'rumour'; 'jankers' was 'punishment'; *'mahleesh'* meant 'couldn't matter less', and 'take a *shufti*' was 'have a look'. Membership was open only to those who fought there, and members were contemptuous of outsiders, who were 'white knees'. Many a general – not least Montgomery – had to persuade these independent 'British' that he was 'one of them'. The club also had its own dress code. Except in combat, this amounted to no more than shorts and boots. Officers were no more formal, and often wore the soft suede footwear known to this day as 'desert boots'. They also took to wearing vividly coloured neck scarves – functional for dust and sweat, and pretty for the hell of it. This fashion crossed no man's land, and Rommel even took to wearing his *Pour le Mérite* over one. The cavalry regiments, ever mindful of their role as leaders of military *haute couture*, took things yet further, wearing made-to-measure khaki drill-type shirts, corduroy trousers, and even sheepskin jackets to keep out the chill of the desert nights.

Although Ultra gave the British a strategic advantage, it could not improve their tactical performance. One tenet of German doctrine was speed, to which end the Germans were prepared to sacrifice caution and sometimes reconnaissance. But in certain aspects of intelligence they were also well served. The Horchaufklarung (Y Service) was extremely effective. The desert campaign created new difficulties for signallers due to distance, dust, and adverse radio conditions. Delicate electrical equipment needed careful handling and constant mainten-ance.[5] At the start of the war, few British infantry officers had much experience of radio as a means of control, especially radio telephony. Although the quality and quantity of radio sets improved between 1940 and 1942, speech over large distances was usually difficult, sometimes impossible, and always insecure. This meant, according to one officer, 'having to shout at the top of one's voice coded stuff such as: "Monument nuts playbox peddler" etc. through a wild mixture of what sounded like an Egyptian funeral, dance music and the foreign tongues of announcers'.[6] Encipherment and wireless telegraphy imposed further delays, and communications difficulties played a very significant part in the two 'Benghazi handicaps' of April 1941 and February 1942.[7]

The virtual collapse of its signals system because of such difficulties was one reason why Eighth Army's armoured formations became so widely scattered during Crusader. But, even when working properly, situation reports were usually 12 or more hours old by the time they reached Army Headquarters, and often the lag was 24 or even 36 hours.[8] Indeed, the more skilled and efficient German intercept service was often quicker at reading and forwarding British messages than were the British themselves.[9] Under the command of Leutnant Alfred Seebohm, 3rd Company 56th Signals Battalion (later 621st Radio Company) soon identified British operators personally – a task made easier by the lack of security consciousness among them – and could draw conclusions from, for example, their relocation. According to Lieutenant Keith Douglas, the idiom of British radio traffic was like the conversation of the two Englishmen in Hitchcock's *The Lady Vanishes*. He felt that the yeomanry certainly found correct radio voice procedure and code unenterprising, and supplemented it with 'veiled talk'. This had two main sources of allusion – horses and cricket – so that losing a tank track became 'I shall need the farrier, I've lost a shoe', and 'Now that chap has retired to the pavilion, how many short of a team are you?' Armoured cars were 'our friends on ponies', and the technical adjutant of Douglas's regiment was known as 'our bald-headed friend'.[10] Such peculiarities were easily picked up by the Germans, and, once a headquarters had been identified, direction-finding could locate and follow it. This proved especially valuable when the British sought to attack.[11]

Beyond this, however, Rommel benefited from what was known as the 'Good Source'. This began during the winter of 1941/2, after the Italian Servizio Informazione Militare (SIM) persuaded a clerk at the American Embassy in August 1941 to photocopy the 'Black Code' used for US diplomatic signals. From autumn onwards, both SIM and its German counterparts, the Abwehr, could read all messages sent in this code – including those of the American military attaché in Cairo, Colonel Bonner Fellers. With considerable frankness, the British briefed Fellers on matters of strategic and tactical importance, and he duly passed this information on to Washington and, unwittingly, within a few hours of transmission, to Rommel.[12]

Luftflotte II's aerial assault on Malta intensified throughout January and February, and on 12 February Grossadmiral Erich Raeder, Commander-in-Chief of the German navy, the Kriegsmarine, had an audience with Hitler in which he explained to an unusually receptive Führer that Britain's position in the Middle East depended on her oil supplies. If these could be captured, not only would Britain be knocked out of the war, but a link-up could be effected with the Japanese on the shores of the Indian Ocean.[13] Hitler ordered Raeder to examine what became known briefly as 'The Great Plan' – the British nightmare scenario of a pincer through Egypt and south from the Caucasus. But responsibility for Mediterranean operations would remain the province of Comando Supremo in Rome. Cavallero became embroiled in the discussions, and a circular argument soon developed: no drive could be launched on the Nile until sufficient supplies had been built up; no build-up could take place while Malta's aircraft and submarines remained active; no attack could be launched on Malta until the British air bases in Cyrenaica behind the Gazala line had been driven back.

The Italians proposed so grandiose an invasion of Malta that it could not take place before the end of July, which would have delayed Rommel's offensive until the autumn. Kesselring tried to persuade them to be more realistic, but the negotiations dragged on.[14] Eventually the plan was referred to the Axis leaders' summit of 29–30 April (at a conference attended by many senior generals but no admirals from either side), where compromise plans to take Tobruk (Operation Theseus) and to deal with Malta (Operation Herkules or Operazione C3) were agreed: Panzerarmee Afrika – as Panzergruppe had become – would attack first, capture Tobruk and advance to the Egyptian frontier, whereupon all available aircraft and shipping would be diverted to a decisive attack on Malta.[15] Generalmajor Bernard Hermann Ramcke, a paratroop veteran of Crete, was employed to train the tough Italian Folgore Parachute Division for a combined operation with his own German brigade.[16] Kesselring intensified air attacks on Malta, and by April these averaged six per day. The fierce bombardment had immediate effects: in the first five months of 1942 Malta's aircraft and submarines sank only a fifth of the Axis shipping tonnage they had accounted for in the last five months of 1941, and on 10 May Kesselring declared that Malta had been effectively neutralized. Rommel was better supplied than ever before, though Churchill leaned still more heavily on Eighth Army for an early offensive. Yet, even as Malta's fortunes reached their lowest ebb, Hitler, with that improvidence characteristic of the master plotters of war, found himself short of aircraft. With the island's neutralization only 'partial and temporary', according to an Italian appreciation, he was forced to choose between Malta and his overarching dream of defeating Russia.[17]

On 27 February Auchinleck had signalled Churchill that he did not expect to have sufficient strength for offensive operations before June and that any such attempt made sooner would risk failure and expose Egypt to invasion. After renewed pressure from London he brought forward his earliest possible date for an offensive to 15 May. He stressed that this was not definite, but since Brooke had guaranteed that no more forces would be withdrawn from the Middle East, and that the number of medium tanks would have increased to 450 by mid-May, he felt that he might be ready about then. Ritchie meanwhile was to give maximum attention to offensive preparations, and as a result the defences of the Gazala line were far from impressive.[18] They consisted of a loose system of 'boxes' stretching southward to Bir Hacheim. Each box formed a defensive perimeter surrounded by mines and wire and contained infantry, artillery, anti-tank and anti-aircraft detachments, but between them were large gaps that could not be covered through which Eighth Army's own armour was due to advance in the forthcoming offensive. The line was held in the north by XIII Corps, while XXX Corps covered the south with 1st Fighting French Brigade under command of XXX Corps holding Bir Hacheim.[19] Significantly, Tobruk was not to be defended again in the manner of the previous year. It was now a huge store dump and administration area, its wire serving to keep out light-fingered looters rather than the enemy.[20] The Royal Navy insisted that it could not supply it, and Auchinleck therefore ordered Ritchie to prevent its investment.

The armoured formations in XXX Corps included Crusader and Honey tanks – both still outclassed by the Mark III and IV panzers – but there were also 175 of the new American Grant tanks, mounting a 75 mm gun. Unfortunately, this was a low-velocity weapon mounted on the side of the tank in a way that prevented the tank from taking hull-down positions (in which a tank could hide behind a fold in the ground with only its turret showing). Ken Giles, a friend of Keith Douglas, later described what it was like to fight in a Grant:

> The '75' is firing. The '37' [the Grant's secondary gun] is firing, but it's traversed around the wrong way. The Browning is jammed. I am saying 'Driver advance' on the A [intercom] set, and the driver, who can't hear me, is reversing. And as I look over the top of the turret and see twelve enemy tanks fifty yards away, someone hands me a cheese sandwich.[21]

*

Rommel began his offensive in the early afternoon of 26 May. The plan was for DAK to attack Bir Hacheim, but Rommel then handed this task to the Italians and some confusion ensued. This was exacerbated when DAK, which was now to outflank the defensive line to the south, ran into the new Grant tanks and 6-pounder anti-tank guns, which German intelligence knew nothing about. The following day the confusion became greater as the British got behind the lead elements of DAK to attack its supply columns. However, the DAK forward elements were faced with only piecemeal counter-attacks, owing to a misreading of the situation. Auchinleck had suggested to Ritchie that the Germans might attack through the centre of the line. Although this never happened, Ritchie and his staff knew that Auchinleck was privy to very secret and sensitive sources of information (Ultra), and his suggestion was therefore given very high credence at Army Headquarters. By the time it was appreciated that the Axis *Schwerpunkt* was really around the southern end of the line it was too late to concentrate forces. But Rommel did not have things all his own way, and by nightfall, he as well as Ritchie was in danger of losing control.[22]

Rommel had pushed his German troops into an area that became known as 'The Cauldron', a depression in the desert measuring 4 miles by 2, some 5 miles south-west of the 'Knightsbridge' box. He had suffered severe losses as a result of British resistance, but now planned to break through the British line from behind and thus shorten his communications. As Ritchie believed the Germans were beaten, Rommel succeeded with little interference.[23] Ritchie himself had been planning to attack with XIII Corps, but by 31 May he decided that the Axis armour must first be destroyed. Meanwhile, as he was planning this, Rommel attacked 150th Brigade's box, which menaced one of his supply routes. He finished it off on 1 June after, Panzerarmee reported, it 'resisted stubbornly'.[24] Ritchie's counter-stroke – Operation Aberdeen – did not start for another four days, by which time Axis defences were well prepared. Despite initial success, it was a resounding defeat for the British, who lost 200 tanks, 4 field artillery regiments and an infantry brigade.

Thus ended the second phase of the Gazala battles, leaving Rommel in a much stronger position than previously and Eighth Army's morale severely shaken. A young hussar officer wrote later that 'no soldier who fought in that battle can ever excuse those high ranking officers who at the time were damned but have since been resurrected'.[25] Meanwhile the infantry began to look askance at the armour, and there are many stories of armoured formations questioning orders – a result of inadequate tactical doctrine and training.[26]

Rommel now concentrated on the Fighting French at Bir Hacheim, who had already been under ferocious attack for ten days. Despite the critical importance of this position to the British for holding the bottom of the Gazala line, and its truly heroic defence, no attempt was made to relieve it; yet if it fell the Gazala battle would be surely lost. The French commander, Brigadier-General Pierre Koenig, wanted his men evacuated, believing their resistance had been futile. He pleaded with Ritchie that he had no water or ammunition, and he was given permission to break out on the night of 10/11 June.

The next morning XIII Corps (less 150th Brigade) was still intact and Eighth Army still had superiority but did not attack – largely because of poor leadership – leaving Rommel to do so. The battle raged throughout 12 June around Knightsbridge and east at El Adem, resulting in the sharpest defeat yet of the British armour, involving the loss of some 120 tanks.[27]

Auchinleck spent 12 June with Ritchie but did not interfere, and flew back to Cairo the following day. Thereafter the situation rapidly deteriorated. But even now Ritchie continued to view the situation favourably – at least in his signals to Auchinleck, who replied that he regarded the news with 'some misgiving', adding, 'I am sure, however, there are factors known to you which I do not know.' In that remark lies the tragedy of the summer: Auchinleck did not know all the facts, being dependent on the signals sent him by his field commanders – who were not above taking an optimistic view in order to please their master.[28] Although the responsibilities on Auchinleck as Commander-in-Chief had been reduced in scope and scale compared to those in Wavell's day, they remained vast, and, while he has been criticized for not taking closer control of the battle sooner, it was not strictly his role to do so. With the growing German threat to the Caucasus and the Middle East from the north, he has been accused of 'looking over his shoulder' at Syria and Palestine. Churchill and the Chiefs of Staff had urged that he take personal command as early as 20 May, but did not arrange to relieve him of his other responsibilities.[29]

In the meantime, British operational blundering continued to provide Rommel with a window of opportunity. On 14 June the remainder of 50th (Northumbrian) Division and 1st South African Division – in danger of being surrounded and cut off – broke out from the Gazala position to dash headlong towards Egypt. Losses, especially of transport and equipment, proved disastrous. Ritchie signalled Auchinleck, concluding, 'Do you agree to me accepting the risk of investment in Tobruk?' This must have perplexed Auchinleck, who did not know that the Northumbrians and South Africans had been ordered back to the frontier. He replied that same afternoon that 'Tobruk must be held and the enemy must not be allowed to invest it. This means that Eighth Army must hold the line Acroma–El Adem and southwards and resist all enemy attempts to by-pass it . . . I order you to do it.'[30] Yet, despite the clarity of these instructions, Ritchie felt it necessary to confer with Gott, whose fearlessness and imperturbability in the face of crisis were almost legendary throughout Eighth Army. Somehow, between them, they decided that the investment of Tobruk was inevitable and that the fortress could hold out without difficulty for two months, despite entirely different circumstances from those of the previous year. The defences had deteriorated considerably over the winter. Many of the mines had been lifted for use in the Gazala defences, the anti-tank ditch had largely silted up, and there were insufficient anti-tank guns to prevent a determined armoured assault.

Even before Auchinleck sent further explicit and categorical instructions at 1950 hours that Tobruk was *not* to be invested, Ritchie replied to his earlier orders by explaining that reorganization would take a few days and concluding that 'I will be faced with a decision to allow Tobruk to be invested or to order the garrison to fight its way out.'[31] But the garrison implied in the signal did not as yet exist, and when it was cobbled together it was wholly inadequate. Richard Casey, Minister of State in Cairo, signalled Churchill, who was preparing to leave for Washington, that the Acroma–El Adem line would be held. Late that same evening Auchinleck held a conference attended by Brigadier Francis de Guingand, Director of Military Intelligence, who gave his opinion that Rommel 'would welcome such a development [as a second siege of Tobruk and] would consider the task of capturing [Tobruk] a reasonably easy one'.[32] During the conference a signal arrived from Churchill, who, given his colossal responsibilities, must have forgotten the decision expressed in Middle East Operation Instruction No. 110 of 19 January, in which Auchinleck clearly stated that in the event of withdrawal 'it is not my intention to try to hold permanently Tobruk or any other locality west of the frontier'.[33] This decision had been confirmed at a meeting of the Middle East Defence Committee on 4 February 1942 and acknowledged by Ritchie.[34] But Churchill believed that 'as long as Tobruk is held no serious enemy advance into Egypt is possible. We went through all this in April 1941.' De Guingand saw Auchinleck 'studying the signal with great concentration, and then in his own hand drafting the orders to Ritchie'.[35] Tobruk was to be held.

On 15 June the contingency demolition orders were cancelled and XIII Corps was ordered to hold the port. Gott then instructed Major-General H. B. Klopper of 2nd South African Division to do this.

Churchill sent another telegram to Auchinleck on 16 June, stating he was 'glad to have your assurance that you have no intention of giving up Tobruk'.[36] Thus, tragically, Auchinleck had no alternative but to accept Churchill's policy, misguided though it was through lack of the true facts. Meanwhile, as both Ritchie and Gott gave Klopper assurances that they would not permit the enemy to invest Tobruk, Rommel had other ideas: seeing that the greater part of the British infantry had escaped from the Gazala line, he decided at once to swing towards El Adem and knock away what he called the 'cornerstone of Tobruk'. Concentrating overwhelming force in the El Adem area, he completely forestalled Ritchie so that the events of 15–17 June decided the fate of the port.[37] During the night of 15/16 June, Knightsbridge was evacuated with permission from Gott. Eighth Army was being pushed northward, and Ritchie realized he could not stop the Axis forces cutting off and trapping XIII Corps. In the early hours he ordered Gott to move east to the frontier. Three days later Klopper informed Ritchie of his confidence, while Churchill assumed that Tobruk would once more defy the Axis. But this confidence was misplaced. If Tobruk had had any chance of surviving, the charge of 4th Armoured Brigade on 17 June against the German concentration between Belhamed and El Adem had ended it. Another 30 tanks were lost, and Eighth Army's armour effectively ceased to exist.

The second siege of the fortress could never be a repeat of the first, however brave the defenders. Furthermore, 2nd South African Division had never been issued with desert-worthy transport by Eighth Army, so the South Africans were unable to manoeuvre even within their own brigade sectors except on foot.[38] Rommel swiftly applied the plan for the reduction of the fortress forestalled by Crusader the previous year, only this time with even greater force, and on 20 June the assault was launched against the south-eastern corner. Under cover of heavy air and artillery fire, this was soon penetrated. The result was inevitable and swift. As dawn broke, the battle was all over bar the mopping up; some small groups broke out and escaped, but by 0945 hours Panzerarmee was already issuing orders to reassemble for the next advance. The Axis took 33,000 prisoners, and Axis soldiers hurried to grab a share of the loot while they could. One of them, puffing and wheezing under the weight of a crate, called out, 'Beer, lads! Lots of it.' The labels read 'Münchner Löwenbräu', while other stickers showed it had reached the British via Portugal.[39]

The reaction on the Allied side was one of disbelief. '[Tobruk] was impregnable,' wrote Captain B. L. Bernstein, intelligence officer of 3rd South African Brigade, credulously echoing the propaganda. 'The whole thing was a ghastly mistake!'[40] Churchill in faraway Washington had been reminded by Admiral Sir Andrew Cunningham of the unanimous decision of the Commanders-in-Chief not to hold the port, which decision he regarded with scorn.[41] He was conferring with President Franklin D. Roosevelt when the latter was handed a telegram which he passed to his guest without comment – it was one of the heaviest blows of the war to Churchill. 'Defeat is one thing,' Churchill growled to Roosevelt, '*disgrace* is another.'[42] But the ill wind of the fall of Tobruk blew some good: Roosevelt responded by offering to send 300 of the new Sherman tanks and 100 self-propelled 105 mm howitzers – equipment which would play a significant role in the final battle in the desert.[43]

Kesselring's declaration that Malta was neutralized had proved premature: between 9 and 18 May the island received significant reinforcements of Spitfires – Luftwaffe intelligence was proving no better than it had been two years previously in the west.[44] The Axis air forces were not sufficient both to neutralize Malta and to support a headlong dash to the Nile, but, believing Eighth Army's plight worse than his own, Rommel urged immediate pursuit. Besides, his timetable was already badly out of joint: in particular, the heroic French defence of Bir Hacheim 'meant nine days of losses in material, personnel, armour and petrol', which, according to the Luftwaffe Historical Section, 'were irrecoverable'.[45] Rommel's scheme would take him 300 miles beyond Tobruk and 700 beyond Benghazi, and both Kesselring and the Italians opposed it, knowing that if Malta were not dealt with the task of supplying Panzerarmee would be immensely difficult. But when Kesselring arrived at Tobruk at midday on 21 June to offer congratulations, to confer, and to begin preparations for Herkules he found Rommel choking on the leash.

A summit meeting was held in a roadman's hut, and was also attended by Bastico. There was strong disagreement on what to do next. Rommel's promotion to Generalfeldmarschall that same day removed any chance of pulling rank – which was not Kesselring's style in any case – and Major Friedrich von Mellenthin, who witnessed it as Rommel's intelligence officer, described the discussion as 'exceedingly lively'.[46] When Kesselring announced he would withdraw his air units for Herkules anyway, Rommel said he had already sent Berndt to argue his case personally with Hitler.

Faced with a great opportunity, his gambler's instinct overcame all other considerations. 'With all the equipment and supplies we've picked up we can knock off Malta and knock out Egypt simultaneously,' he declared.[47] He would reach the Delta before the British organized effective defences and would force the Royal Navy and the RAF to abandon the eastern Mediterranean, thus ending his supply problems at a stroke. Rommel appeared to believe he need only demand the impossible from the logistics staffs to get it – just as with fighting troops.[48] However, in recent days the Italian freighters *Allegri* and *Giuliani* had been sunk, and on the day of the meeting the German steamer *Reichenfels* was sunk by torpedo-carrying aircraft. Rommel peremptorily broke off the council and told DAK commander Walter Nehring, 'You with your corps through the desert down under; the 90th Light down the Via Balbia. Go!'[49]

When Berndt presented the case to a Führer already nervous about Herkules, Hitler readily backed Rommel against the advice of Kesselring, von Rintelen, the Supermarina (the Italian Naval Staff) and Comando Supremo. He cabled Mussolini on 22 June that 'it is only once in a lifetime that the Goddess of Victory smiles'.[50] And, having intercepted one of the last signals sent by Colonel Fellers, saying the British had been decisively beaten and the time was ripe for Rommel to take Cairo and the Nile Delta, the Italians agreed that Rommel had a good chance of success.[51] Rommel promised to be in Cairo in ten days. The attack on Malta was postponed – in effect indefinitely. When the head of airborne troops, Kurt Student, went to see Hitler for a final conference in July, 'he simply turned [Herkules] down flat'.[52] By allowing this change of plan 'the Italian Supreme Command and I made a mistake', wrote Kesselring after the war. 'I should have known that a tactical victory can be exploited only if the supply system functions smoothly. I should furthermore have known that Rommel cannot be bridled once he smells victory.'[53] Perhaps no other decision on the Axis side since the formation of DAK was to have such far-reaching consequences for the Middle East theatre, but it would take only take a fortnight to show that the eager Desert Fox had led his masters into 'a major strategic blunder'.[54]

Ritchie now planned to hold Egypt on a line pivoted on Mersa Matruh. This, however, was still exposed to outflanking from the south. Rommel duly ploughed on, and Eighth Army retreated in a final state of rout and dissolution.[55] Losses totalled 80,000, and by nightfall on 25 June Rommel was in front of the Matruh defences, having covered 100 miles in a day. Thus Ritchie had no time to prepare the position, and on 26 June Auchinleck arrived and finally relieved him of command.[56] Auchinleck left his Chief of Staff, Lieutenant-General T. W. Corbett, behind in Cairo as his deputy and took Dorman-Smith with him as his personal staff officer. Corbett was described by de Guingand as a 'complete fathead'; Auchinleck later acknowledged that his deputy had not 'been a success'.[57] Also, Dorman-Smith was a man 'bubbling with ideas' according to Auchinleck's biographer John Connell, but according to the CIGS, Brooke, only some of these '(not many) were good, and the rest useless. Archie Wavell had made use of him, but was wise enough to discard all the bad and retain only the good. Auchinleck was incapable of doing so and allowed himself to fall too deeply under Chink's influence.'[58]

Auchinleck and Dorman-Smith agreed that all troops were to be kept mobile and that only men for whom there was first-line transport (that is, transport integral to their units) would remain; the rest would move back immediately to the Alamein position. This meant splitting formations into battle groups determined by the amount of artillery available – disguising, ironically, that both Auchinleck and Dorman-Smith were firm believers in massed artillery and of fighting battles using divisions as divisions, albeit mobile ones.[59]

Rommel continued to press with whatever came to hand, and confused fighting went on throughout 26 and 27 June, with Gott trying to conduct the mobile defence that Auchinleck had ordered. Whatever the scheme's merits, its adoption on the very eve of battle was 'perhaps inopportune'.[60] By scraping troops and tanks together from every possible source, Auchinleck had 159 tanks (including 60 Grants) in 1st Armoured Division in the desert south and east of Matruh, while at Matruh itself were 50th (Northumbrian) and 10th Indian Divisions, brought over from Syria under command of X Corps, with Freyberg's New Zealand Division at Minqar Qaim. These units all comprised ad-hoc groupings of infantry and artillery. Two battle groups – Gleecol and Leathercol – held the centre; but there would be no last stand at Matruh, especially after these battle groups were destroyed.[61] The only effective resistance to the Axis advance now came from the Desert Air Force, which by strenuous efforts raised its numbers of serviceable aircraft from two-thirds during the first week of the Gazala battles to three-quarters of its total strength.

If anything made the difference to Eighth Army in its hour of defeat, it was the DAF. The Luftwaffe was initially based only 40 miles away from the battlefield, but it could manage only 50 per cent serviceability (the Regia Aeronautica achieved around 60 per cent). More important now was its lack of mobility: the acute shortage of motor transport and petrol played a vital part in thinning out the Axis air effort. (For the Cyrenaica operations the Luftwaffe had accumulated only 20 days' worth of fuel.)[62] Only on 26 June did Rommel decide to bring forward his air units at the expense of his Italian infantry, who had to walk. But during this period the DAF acted so vigorously against his airstrips that he was able to get little offensive air support. The intensity of British air operations at this time was largely due to superb organization permitting mobility and flexibility (only five unserviceable aircraft were abandoned during the entire retreat) and to Tedder's boldness in throwing forward every available aircraft. The work rate was phenomenal: aircraft were flying up to seven sorties a day, and fighter pilots as many as five.[63]

Between X Corps and XIII Corps on the ground, Rommel could have been surrounded, but neither side fully understood the situation. Freyberg was hit in the neck by a splinter that could have killed him, and then 21st Panzer Division managed to scatter the New Zealand Division's main transport park. Gott, falsely believing that the panzers had come through, not around, the Kiwis, and that this magnificent division was finished, ordered his XIII Corps to withdraw during the night. This was accomplished in a wild mêlée that left X Corps isolated in Matruh with no option but to sit tight during the next day and to break out the following night – leaving behind 6,000 prisoners and 40 tanks. On 29 June streams of vehicles charged eastward across the desert, all trying to avoid each other. Most of the Axis now travelled in British lorries running on British petrol. That morning elements of 21st Panzer Division caught a British column near Fuka and took another 1,600 prisoners.[64] Rommel joined the vanguard commander, Hauptman Georg Briel, and said, 'Well Briel, you will advance with your men to Alexandria and stop when you come to the suburbs. The Tommies have gone.' Briel was stunned. Rommel smiled. 'When I arrive tomorrow we'll drive into Cairo together for a coffee.'[65]

Auchinleck had ordered withdrawal to the Alamein line at 0415 hours on 26 June, and signalled Brooke that the plan would involve deploying the maximum amount of artillery – kept fully mobile by employing only the minimum amount of infantry necessary for local protection. The following day 1st South African Division moved into the position. The intention was to keep the army in being at all costs by aiming for maximum mobility 'unimpaired by the necessity for defending fortified positions'.[66] Auchinleck also wanted the New Zealanders to form battle groups, but Brigadier L. M. Inglis, commanding the division in Freyberg's absence, and aware of a previous refusal by Freyberg at Minqar Qaim, informed Auchinleck that he could not obey. 'The expected explosion did not follow,' he said after the war. 'I was merely asked why I objected and what I proposed to do. The reason was that if I broke up the division and dispersed it over a wide front I had as much chance of stopping Rommel as a piece of tissue paper would have had.'

He then received a briefing from Dorman-Smith, who said he was 'considering whether to advise [Auchinleck] to withdraw on Alexandria or on Cairo or partly on one and partly on the other'. An incredulous Inglis replied that all that was needed was for Eighth Army to face west and fight. The Alamein position must, he said, be the limit of withdrawal. Dorman-Smith said that these comments were disrespectful to the Commander-in-Chief, and the two did not part harmoniously.[67]

Auchinleck had shown poor judgement in choosing subordinates. De Guingand felt that the Commander-in-Chief was a lonely figure who needed people he trusted around him, and that this may have accounted for some of his choices. Ritchie had been out of his depth as Army Commander. Corbett, a fellow Indian Army man, was, according to Churchill, 'a very small agreeable man, of no personality and little experience'.[68] And Auchinleck's reliance on Dorman-Smith – a man whose intellectual arrogance had made him deeply unpopular throughout the Army – caused considerable friction. Initially Dorman-Smith was responsible for supporting Auchinleck's work as Commander-in-Chief, with Brigadier John Whiteley as principal staff officer of Eighth Army, but he quickly antagonized other members of the army staff. Lieutenant-Colonel Charles Richardson, general staff officer (GSO) 1 (Plans), resented that discussions that should have been led by Auchinleck were led by Dorman-Smith, and found his optimism irritating, his energy wearing and that he had become too arbitrary and academic to bother with diplomacy. The custodian of Ultra, Major Edgar 'Bill' Williams, was equally distrustful.[69]

In Alexandria the residents went indoors, and as early as 27 June Major David Parry arriving from the desert found the city seemingly deserted. Then 'suddenly a little Greek popped out of a shop like a rabbit out of its hole. Rushing across the road, he seized my arm, and, quite terrified, asked if it was true that Rommel was about to enter the city.' Having seen the New Zealand Division moving up, fresh and fully equipped, Parry replied that Rommel 'was not entering the city today and would never enter it'.[70]

Developments continued apace. On 28 June the US Army Middle East Air Force was established, with Major-General Lewis H. Brereton in command.[71] On 29 June Mussolini flew to Derna, piloting his own aircraft and followed by another carrying the white charger on which he planned to make his triumphal entry into Alexandria. The plane crash-landed at Derna and, although Mussolini escaped injury, his barber and chef were killed. But at least his horse, bands and flags got through.[72]

On the same day, however, Fellers – the 'Good Source' – ceased broadcasting. He had been identified largely thanks to Ultra, but had already made a significant contribution to Axis intelligence during the offensive.[73] Meanwhile, when 7th Motor Brigade overran Italian XX Corps Headquarters and part of a division, Rommel responded to calls for help by demanding that the Italians destroy the enemy and reach their objective, following up an hour later with '[I] trust your corps will now find itself able to cope with so contemptible an enemy'.[74] It seemed that the British were beaten. Axis propaganda made the most of it and broadcast to the women of Alexandria, 'Get out your party frocks, we're on our way!' Cairo was rife with rumour and intrigue, and the Egyptian populace was by no means worried by the prospect of an Axis takeover. Cairene taxi drivers made jokes like 'Today I drive you to Groppi's – tomorrow you drive me!'[75]

The worst day of the 'flap' – the dash to leave for Palestine or Syria – the day the British position in the Middle East was in gravest danger, was Wednesday 1 July. The Royal Navy evacuated Alexandria and dispersed to Haifa, Beirut and Port Said; even HMS *Queen Elizabeth* was floated off the harbour bed where she had lain since a daring Italian attack and made her way first to Port Sudan, then to the USA for a complete refit. The atmosphere of panic was compounded by a pall of smoke over central Cairo as staff at Greyfriars, as General Headquarters Middle East Forces was known, tried to burn documents – a remarkably difficult task without an incinerator, earning the day the epithet 'Ash Wednesday'. 'The bulk were simply burnt in the open,' observed Julian Amery, a captain with the Special Operations Executive. 'But then the wind got up and a mass of secret documents were blown away little more than scorched, rising like so many phoenixes from their ashes and pursued all over the city by irate and frenzied officers.'[76] Ordinary Tommies were far more sanguine about the situation. A graduate member of the ruling Wafd Party went to see the columns of fleeing British for himself, but was disappointed to see no panic, only boredom. When one truck stopped there was a mad scramble to get off, but the academic was dismayed to see that this desperate rush was not to escape but to make tea; some of the Tommies were even kicking a football, and he returned home sad and disillusioned.[77]

What panic there was died almost as quickly as it arose. By the evening of 3 July the crowds of refugees had returned and the meretricious Delta life had resumed. Why the mood changed back so suddenly is not clear. It was certainly not yet apparent that the tide of war had changed, although it had – having reached its furthest point around an obscure railway halt some 60 miles west of Alexandria: El Alamein.[78]

4

The Alamein Line

Visiting the South Africans in the Alamein box in July 1942, Denis Johnston heard one of them singing an old Boer War ditty, while wearing the khaki about which the song was so sarcastic.[1] One of Auchinleck's first steps as Commander-in-Chief Middle East had been to order construction of a defensive position at Alamein, and work had begun in August 1941 with engineers, civilian labour when available, and varying degrees of enthusiasm in its progress.[2] When it first arrived in Egypt, 2nd South African Division was set to work with the South African Engineer Corps (SAEC) as contractors 'and the Division the hired labour'.[3] But, when hardly a man in the ranks and certainly none in 3rd South African Brigade discerned the slightest possibility that these positions would ever be occupied in battle, the gruelling work of excavation with inadequate tools on rock-like desert had been slow.[4]

---

*The Khakis [British soldiers – from the colour of their uniforms] are just like crocodiles,/They always drag you to the water;/They throw you in a ship for a long long trip,/Heaven only knows where to.//O take me back to the old Transvaal,/There where my Sarie lives./Down there among the mealies [maize]/By the green thorn-tree,/There lives my Sarie Marais.

Now, with Rommel bearing down, they were busy digging, wiring and mining themselves in to those very same positions.

Yet it was no accident that the war came to Alamein. If at first sight the stretch of desert between the sea and the salt marsh and quicksands of the Qattara Depression was no different from any other, then those very edges made it different. To outflank the natural barrier to the south would require a massive detour and crossing the shifting sands of the Sahara. Here was the one place with secure flanks which precluded the tactics that had brought Rommel to the verge of Cairo. The British had known this as a result of the pre-war garrisoning of Egypt, when its role in a potentially secure defence line against invasion from the west had been recognized.[5] The most thoroughly developed of the boxes was around Alamein's railway station, where to the north ran the coast road and which was protected by the sea. Another position was some 15 miles inland, including the peak at Qaret el Abd. To the south were two ridges which would assume great significance in due course – Miteiriya and Ruweisat – and further south still the desert became more ragged, broken by sharp-edged escarpments and flat-topped hills, the most significant of which was Qaret el Himeimat. The southernmost position was sited to cover the pass down to the Qattara Depression at Naqb Abu Dweis, and provided excellent observation in all directions. An enemy approaching the Alamein line would thus find himself channelled into three avenues of 'good going' formed in the north between the coast and Ruweisat Ridge; in the centre between Qaret el Abd and south of Ruweisat Ridge; and in the south between Djebel Kalakh and Himeimat.

However, from these boxes it would be possible to do little more than hammer an enemy with whatever artillery could be squeezed within them, and any expansion would require considerable extra troops – especially anti-tank guns – in order to defend the boxes from all sides. The minimum requirement for the whole line was calculated as two infantry and two armoured divisions plus reserves.[6] Only the first of the positions was anywhere near complete, and losses had been so great that on 1 July Eighth Army could field only one complete infantry division (the New Zealand Division), the incomplete 1st South African Division, and 9th and 18th Indian Brigade Groups, together with the almost complete 1st Armoured Division. But the Axis forces were strained by what Clausewitz called the 'diminishing power of the offensive'.[7] By the evening of 1 July their chances of snatching victory were rapidly dwindling, although Eighth Army had at this time ceased to function as an army and even corps control was uncertain. It was rather as individual units and formations acting with little concert that it finally stopped an enemy 'exhausted by victory'.[8] Throughout Auchinleck remained calm, despite confusion through loss of contact between Eighth Army and X Corps, and 1st Armoured Division was able to regroup and beat off the exhausted DAK attack.[9]

It has been suggested that 'First' Alamein was not in fact an Alamein battle at all, but only the end of the Battle of Gazala.[10] To dismiss a battle which took place at Alamein as part of one that took place two weeks before and many miles away would be as confusing as it would be illogical.[11] Nevertheless, Charles Richardson, a senior Eighth Army staff officer, lamented that 'the only Battle of Alamein that can be recognised by those of us who were there is accorded second place. I can state from my continuous presence as GSO 1 (Plans) throughout those weeks that no battle entitled to the name "First Alamein" ever took place.'[12] The New Zealand historian Peter Bates – himself a former Eighth Army soldier – is perhaps right in giving it the name that Auchinleck himself gave it in his order of the day of 30 June: 'We are fighting the Battle of Egypt,' he said.[13] And, despite the haphazard and disconnected nature of operations over the following four weeks, Rommel was stopped and Egypt was saved.

To Eighth Army could now be added a complete and fresh formation already battle-proven – Morshead's 9th Australian Division. During the three months before Rommel's assault on the Gazala line, the Australian government had discussed this division's future employment with the British. Churchill, quoting American promises of support in defence of Australia and the need to economize on shipping, persuaded the Australian government not to press for its early recall, and orders for a move to Egypt were received by the division on 25 June. It began to move towards Egypt the following day, glad to have an end of garrison duties in Syria.[14] The division was over strength in men but very short of transport and equipment – especially anti-tank guns. On its way forward it discovered a large ordnance base at Amiriya, near Alexandria, where it made good its deficiencies without bothering to go through the proper channels and earned itself a new nickname from the pro-German propagandist William Joyce, 'Lord Haw Haw', in which it took some delight – 'Ali Baba Morshead and the Twenty-Thousand Thieves'.[15] As the Australians moved forward, they struggled past streaming columns heading in the opposite direction. 'Sometimes the retreating columns were not only nose-to-tail, but two and three abreast. All their personnel except the drivers – and often the drivers too – slept where they sat. There were bits and pieces of broken units – here and there an anti-tank gun, here and there a Bofors, here and there a 25-pounder.'[16]

For a long time after Auchinleck took over, Eighth Army intelligence overestimated the strength of Panzerarmee, so that it seemed at the beginning of July that Auchinleck's dishevelled army could be outmanoeuvred and trapped as it had been at Tobruk or Matruh. With the opening on 28 June of the German offensive into southern Russia, towards the Caucasus and its oilfields and threatening the north of Middle East Command, Auchinleck was fully aware of the implications for his position being outflanked from the north.[17] Although determined to stop the enemy at Alamein, he was also determined to keep the army 'in being', going back to the Suez Canal if necessary. Plans were made for these contingencies, and, however unlikely further retreat may have been, they undoubtedly affected morale. While Norrie later declared that 'Alamein was the last ditch and it was a real case of "Do or Die", with every chance of stopping the enemy', Gott appeared to be have been thinking more of the alternative.[18] He showed Brigadier Howard Kippenburger (in temporary command of the New Zealand Division while Inglis visited Cairo) a letter from Corbett outlining these plans. Kippenburger was appalled by the unnecessarily doom-laden meeting – a sign of the enormous strain if a man of Gott's integrity and courage could be so affected.[19]

Although Kippenburger determined to keep quiet over the matter, others shared Gott's pessimism, including Major-General Dan Pienaar of 1st South African Division, who told Norrie that he thought 'it was wrong to stand at El Alamein, and that the best place was to go behind the Suez Canal'.[20] This view was not shared by his men, however: 'We were determined to avenge Gazala and Tobruk,' wrote Captain Bernstein, 'and we knew it would be a "last man, last round" action, for with Alamein lost, the Nile valley and Egypt were as good as gone.'[21] In fairness to Pienaar, who was a student of the Bible and a fatalist, his approach to the enemy demonstrated a Gilbertian sense of humour. He sowed German mines in front of Italian troops and Italian mines in front of the Germans, and instituted an artillery programme to coincide with the nightly playing of 'Lili Marleen'. He also told Denis Johnston that the retreat would go no further – 'Not so far as I'm concerned. I've retreated far enough and here I stop whether we hold the damn thing or not.'[22] And he told an American war correspondent, 'You can quote me on this. Rommel will not get the Alexandria naval base; he will not get the Suez Canal; he will never dine in Cairo unless as a tourist after the war.'[23]

Auchinleck himself was also determined to fight, and sensed that Rommel must be overreaching himself. On 1 July he addressed an order of the day to Eighth Army in which he stated, 'The enemy is stretched to the limit and thinks we are a broken army . . . Show him where he gets off.'[24] Indeed, as the Italian historian Antonio Tedde noted, 'The clarity, precision and firmness of Auchinleck showed that Eighth Army had found a commander. Rommel, with Ritchie's replacement, ceased to be the master.'[25] The South Africans formed mobile columns consisting of a battalion each and two batteries of artillery, leaving 3rd South African Brigade to hold the Alamein box reinforced with three extra infantry companies and some artillery. The box was some 7 miles across, and the Springboks were able to hold only the western face, leaving the east unoccupied. When the German attack came in, much of its artillery fire was from captured 25-pounders: Captain Bernstein sardonically noted that a dud shell which landed near Brigade Headquarters was stamped, 'Made Iscor, Pretoria.'[26]

The South Africans' neighbour to the south was 18th Indian Brigade at Deir el Shein. German intelligence was faulty, and the German attempt to push between the Alamein and Bab el Qattara boxes instead drove into 18th Indian Brigade, supported by nine Matilda tanks but not by 1st Armoured Division as the British plan called for. After eight hours of bitter fighting the brigade was overrun and all but destroyed.[27] Nevertheless, DAK had been held up and had lost another 18 of its remaining 55 tanks.[28] Auchinleck was not disheartened by this tragedy, but decided that his line was too extended and that the Bab el Qattara and Naqb Abu Dweis boxes would have to be abandoned. The New Zealand Division was to leave a column at Bab el Qattara and prepare for a mobile role, while 5th Indian Division would act similarly at Qaret el Himeimat.[29]

On 2 July the infantry battle continued around El Alamein while the British and Axis armour clashed inconclusively further south as both tried to outflank the other. Major David Parry spotted Auchinleck driving around in his car, apparently giving pep talks, except it

> was no pep talk. Auchinleck explained that Rommel was now fully extended and that his advanced troops were now dangerously exposed. So it was essential that the Eighth Army, seriously disorganized, was given a few days to reorganize and establish defence positions at Alamein. The answer – all the fighting troops which could be rallied would be formed into a striking force to bloody the enemy's nose within the next twenty-four hours . . . So the CinC assumed the duties of corps, division, brigade and even battalion commander, collected together a miscellaneous force from the remnants of Eighth Army, and gave orders direct to those involved.

Within hours the attack was launched, Rommel's advanced troops were stopped, and 3,000 Axis prisoners were taken.[30]

*

Churchill needed a victory. On 1 July he was facing a motion, put before the House of Commons on 27 June, that 'while paying tribute to the heroism and endurance of the Armed Forces . . . [the House] has no confidence in the central direction of the war'. With his mind focused by the unfavourable result of a by-election in Maldon, he had also been given a report by Sir Stafford Cripps, the Leader of the House of Commons and a member of the War Cabinet, that fed receptivity to armchair criticisms. Cripps expressed doubts as to whether senior commanders had 'a real appreciation of the tactics and strategy of modern mechanical warfare, and to whether it is not necessary to have a complete change in command'. These observations, coming from a politician sitting comfortably thousands of miles away and with no meaningful military experience of his own, nor any means of sounding the opinions of those on the spot, ignored the fact that the Commons motion criticized the central direction of the war in London – meaning the politicians – and, as the opening words of Sir John Warlow-Milne in the debate stated, was 'not an attack upon officers in the field'. Churchill received a substantial vote of confidence by 475 votes to 25, but the very tabling of the motion was indicative of the pressure he was now under.[31]

And the Opposition had a point. Though it had been plain since the fall of France that the 2-pounder gun was hopelessly inadequate as an anti-tank gun or tank armament, British war production had continued to produce it, and by July 1942 thousands had been stockpiled. When the newly appointed Minister of Production, Oliver Lyttelton, tried to explain to the Commons that to switch production to a more effective gun would have temporarily reduced output, he was howled down.[32] However, the losses in France in 1940 and the desperate need to re-equip in the face of threatened invasion, coupled with production realities, meant that until 1942 the field forces often had to make do with obsolescent equipment. To put the 6-pounder into immediate mass production in early 1941, with the threat of invasion still extant, would have meant sacrificing the output of 600 2-pounders for only 100 of the new weapon, and the Ministry of Supply and the War Office reluctantly agreed that it was more important to get any weapon into the hands of the troops rather than the best one. Thus it was not until early 1942 that the 6-pounder had begun to reach the troops.[33]

In fact, while Churchill told the Commons that the British were 'in the presence of a recession of their hopes and prospects in the Middle East and the Mediterranean unequalled since the Fall of France', the war diary of the German 90th Light Division noted Desert Air Force bombers flying overhead every 20 or 30 minutes. While these bombers were unable to inflict much damage on the dispersed German units, 'the morale effect is so much more important'. Wistfully the diary observed that Panzerarmee did 'not seem able to take this last fortress of the English in front of the Nile Delta with the available forces'.[34] A captured Italian diary described how troops were ordered to stay underground during the day to avoid observation from the air. 'We came out of our holes at night to take the air, otherwise we are buried all day, and with a slit trench as deep and narrow as mine is it's no fun. There are two of us in mine and when we want to turn around it's agony, as we are as tightly packed as anchovies in a tin.'[35] Success in air warfare depends on having efficient aircraft in sufficient numbers. While Tedder concentrated his whole available force to meet the immediate threat, Kesselring, with a potential force of up to 3,000 aircraft, managed to support only 20 per cent of it in Africa.[36] The RAF and the Royal Navy's maritime onslaught had not only starved the enemy's existing forces but had severely limited their reinforcement. Rommel's swift change of plan after the fall of Tobruk had seriously unbalanced the Axis air forces, and he became increasingly worried that the steady drain on transport vehicles – itself almost entirely due to Allied air action – prevented his air forces from moving forward to support Panzerarmee.[37]

Despite all Rommel's exhortations to attack 'with the utmost energy', it was at Ruweisat Ridge at dusk on 3 July that one could say the tide of war turned against the Axis in North Africa.[38] Rommel demanded yet another effort from his faltering troops, but DAK was down to around a tenth of its strength and could deploy only 26 tanks against over 100 in 1st Armoured Division.[39] Rommel called a halt, justifying this by the low fighting strength and exhaustion of his troops, and Auchinleck was aware of this through Ultra shortly after midnight.[40]

Panzerarmee was now desperately short of fuel – a situation made worse by the sinking of the tanker *Avionia*, which had been closely tracked by Ultra. Eighth Army outnumbered Panzerarmee and was being reinforced more quickly. Auchinleck and Dorman-Smith planned to 'pursue and destroy' the enemy in a plan codenamed Exalted, but instead, according to Friedrich von Mellenthin, 'there followed a week of missed opportunities for the British and thereafter, more weeks of costly and mismanaged operations'.[41]

The army was still fighting in improvised columns. Robcol, under Brigadier Rob Waller, comprised an infantry battalion and a field artillery regiment, plus a battery and a detachment from two others, an anti-tank battery, anti-aircraft and machine-gun detachments, and later additional infantry detachments.[42] Squeakcol comprised one battalion, a battery of field artillery, and anti-tank and anti-aircraft detachments. Ackcol, which was under the command of Squeakcol, comprised an anti-tank regimental headquarters and three companies of infantry, plus detachments.[43] Auchinleck later commented, 'It worked all right. But it was against all rules and regulations. It was pretty desperate really.'[44] When at 0300 hours on 3 July orders were sent to 9th Australian Division to form battle groups and for a brigade to be sent forward immediately, Morshead flew up to see Auchinleck and a heated conversation took place in which the little Australian refused to allow his command to be broken up piecemeal. 'They are going to fight as a formation with the rest of the division,' he said. Morshead was spoken to very brusquely, he later recalled. But Auchinleck could not afford to allow the diplomatic niceties that governed his command of Commonwealth troops to delay their deployment, so he agreed that the whole division should move forward.[45]

Command difficulties permeated Eighth Army. On 5 July, Major-General Herbert Lumsden, commanding 1st Armoured Division, arrived at XXX Corps Headquarters and 'immediately and brusquely' demanded that his division be relieved.[46] Nothing Norrie said would calm him, and 'the over-excited and emphatically undisciplined' Lumsden carried on complaining while Dorman-Smith watched in 'fascinated horror' and wondered why Norrie did not put Lumsden under arrest. While Lumsden's comments had some justification, Norrie's calm may well have been attributable to the knowledge that he himself was due to be relieved in two days' time: Auchinleck was sending him back to Britain, to be replaced by Major-General W. H. Ramsden, then commanding 50th (Northumbrian) Division.[47] Following the Gazala battle, Pienaar of 1st South African Division had no faith in Ramsden or his staff, and in his diary Morshead recorded his unease at being subordinated to a commander whose immediately previous responsibilities had been less than his own, particularly as Morshead was now the senior officer of the Australian Imperial Force in theatre and held the rank of lieutenant-general, which had not yet been conferred on Ramsden. The constant elevation of British regular officers above more experienced Commonwealth ones rankled, especially where there was little faith in the former. Ramsden failed to win Morshead's confidence and found him an intractable subordinate, as he twice complained to Auchinleck.[48] But there was little anyone could teach Leslie John Morshead about soldiering, as he had long since proved, and there was nothing Auchinleck could do about his attitude.

Meanwhile, the DAF was demonstrating the limitations of light bombers in the close air-support role by persistently dropping their bombs on the South Africans in the Alamein box. The difficulties of precision bombing at the best of times were aggravated by the haze and dust when bombing from 7–8,000 feet, but the problem was overcome to a certain extent by a decision taken by Air Headquarters on 6 July that it would itself define the bomb line (beyond which it was deemed safe to attack from the air) rather than have the army do it. On 7 July there was a remarkable moment of unintended co-operation when bombers hit a group of enemy vehicles just as a field battery was preparing to fire against the same target.[49]

Auchinleck now realized that he did not have the strength to sweep around the south-west flank of the Axis forces, and on 6 and 7 July he decided on a modified and less ambitious offensive. This required pulling the New Zealanders back from the Bab el Qattara box on the night of the 8th, which led Rommel to think that all Eighth Army was again retreating and to direct the Italian Littorio Division to fill the gap. Rommel was thus spreading his already weak forces very thinly, while Auchinleck was concentrating in the north.[50] Having decided to attack there, Auchinleck now instructed Ramsden to take the ridges of Tel el Eisa* with the Australians and Tel el Makh Khad just south of the coast road with the South Africans in Operation Reefknot. Once these were taken, he proposed to advance with battle groups on Deir el Shein.

On 10 July, two companies of 1st Natal Mounted Rifles attacked Tel el Makh Khad and then withdrew in an operation that 'appears to have achieved little but the bewilderment of the participants'.[51] The attack on Tel el Eisa, however, was provided with formidable artillery and air support and 32 Valentines from 44th Royal Tank Regiment. Nevertheless, in order to achieve surprise, the lead assault by 2/48th Battalion was made silently on a narrow frontage and captured Point 26 before dawn. Then the artillery opened fire and the Australians quickly followed up on to Point 23. At 0715 hours two companies swung south and, now under heavy shell fire, moved on to Tel el Eisa station some one and a half miles to the south-west of Point 23, attacking with great élan and capturing 106 prisoners (mostly German) and 4 guns. On their right, 2/24th Battalion met stiffer resistance, but by the day's end it had taken over 800 (mostly Italian) prisoners for the loss of 6 dead and 22 wounded.[52] Most significantly, however, it had overrun 621st Radio

---

* Tel el Eisa means 'Hill of the Lord' but is often referred to as 'Hill of Jesus' due to faulty reporting by war correspondents, who also got its location wrong (Oakes, *Muzzle Blast*, p. 107).

Company, killing or capturing most of its members, including the immensely valuable Seebohm. This was an irreparable loss for the Germans,[53] who, with the uncovering of Colonel Fellers, had lost two rounds in the information battle in two weeks. In contrast, Eighth Army was well provided with operational intelligence regarding both the combat state and the order of battle of the Axis forces. Ultra was a prime source, but army Y was scarcely less important.[54] Meanwhile, Tedder reported to Air Chief Marshal Sir Charles Portal, Chief of Air Staff, that his priority was enemy supplies, which he was 'taking every possible step to interrupt both at sea and in port'. On 10 and 11 July, Wellingtons flew 58 and 76 sorties from Egypt against Tobruk, and for many weeks their scale of operations far exceeded those of UK-based units.[55]

A short distance to the south, two sorties were made from the Alamein box on 11 July. One, by a combined British and Australian force of infantry, armour and artillery called Daycol, was embarrassed by hundreds of surrendering Italians. The Allies took 1,023 prisoners and destroyed 8 guns. The other sortie was made by a South African battle group called Matie Column, comprising infantry from 2nd Regiment Botha, tanks from 44th Royal Tank Regiment, and a squadron from 6th South African Armoured Car Regiment. This group cleared the enemy from Tel el Makh Khad, but was then withdrawn, which served only to further sour relations – already strained to say the least – between Pienaar and Ramsden.

Two days after these operations, Rommel launched an attack against the Alamein box using 21st Panzer Division supported by every gun and aeroplane he could muster, but got nowhere under massive concentrations of artillery fire. It seemed that neither side could concentrate decisive force, and Inglis wrote bitterly to Freyberg that the army needed 'a commander who will make a firm plan and leave his staff to implement it, crash through with it; and once the conception is under way, move about the battlefield himself and galvanise the troops who are looking over their shoulder'. To Inglis it seemed that both sides' concept of attack 'seems to be shoot with artillery and stop when suitably shot up'.[56]

In this sour atmosphere, 2nd New Zealand Division* approached its first major operation – codenamed Bacon – around the Alamein pos-

---

* The New Zealand Division became 2nd New Zealand Division on 8 July: 1st, 4th and 5th New Zealand Divisions formed the home army; 3rd New Zealand Division was in Fiji, and Middle East base units became 6th New Zealand Division as a deception measure.

ition. The plan was for two New Zealand and one Indian brigades to attack in a north-westerly direction on to Ruweisat Ridge, which would then become the forming-up point for an advance by 1st Armoured Division into the enemy's rear. Beginning on the evening of 14 July, by first light 4th and 5th New Zealand Brigades had occupied the western end of the ridge and taken some 2,000 Italian prisoners; but 5th Indian Brigade was still struggling to take the eastern end when 15th Panzer Division counter-attacked and the infantry found themselves cruelly exposed. While this was going on, Kippenburger had driven about 'almost frantic with helplessness' looking for the British armour that was supposed to be up with his infantry by now. By the time he located 2nd Armoured Brigade, his infantry were in direst peril and the apparent lack of urgency on the part of the British armour would have tried the patience of a saint. Eventually, the armour came up, having met resistance and not before much heavy fighting on the ridge throughout the day.[57] Steadily, 4th New Zealand Brigade was whittled down from the west: 'they did all the infantry could possibly do and then got overrun – the bloody armour again' noted Major Denver Fontaine bitterly.[58] They were all but destroyed, while 5th New Zealand Brigade was forced to withdraw. In total, 2nd New Zealand Division lost 1,115 killed or missing and 290 wounded.

However, the armour had not been idle: it had fought its own battle according to its training, but this was a different battle from that of the infantry. It was as though they spoke different languages. While Kippenburger noted that 'the fundamental fault was the failure to co-ordinate infantry and armour', he acknowledged that 'I do not think that we of the infantry did nearly so much as we could or should have done to ensure that we fought the battle together.'[59] It was an infantry-man's illusion that tank fighting was relatively comfortable – though understandable, given how hard the infantry's own conditions were. However, a detailed and dispassionate report from the Medical Research Section at GHQ described the strain on tank crews. They usually got up sometime before daylight to drive to their appointed position, with little time to wash and breakfast. Fighting usually took place during the early morning or late afternoon, to put the blinding sun into the eyes of one side or the other – fighting during the midday heat haze was difficult if not impossible. Although fighting seldom lasted for more than three hours of daylight, the rest of the day was spent on watch, patrolling, or preparing to receive an attack. These long periods of expectation were found more nerve-racking than actual fighting, especially in the cramped sardine-tin interior of a tank.

Occasionally it would be possible for one or two of the crew to dismount to stretch their legs or make a brew, but it was common to spend the entire period of daylight in the tank. The discomfort from engine fumes and noise was compounded by wearing headphones all day, with these pinching and irritating, crackling and hissing when not passing messages on intercom or radio. The effect was like being 'in a camera obscura or a silent film – in that since the engine drowns all other noises except explosions, the whole world moves silently. Men shout, vehicles move, aeroplanes fly over, and all soundlessly: the noise of the tank being continuous, perhaps for hours on end, the effect is of silence.'[60] In the summer months it would be 2100 hours before the two sides drew apart and retired to their night laagers, entailing another couple of hours' driving. Maintenance and replenishment would then begin: a meal would be prepared; fuel and ammunition would be taken aboard and any minor running repairs would be made; grease and lubricants would be checked and topped up if necessary. It would be an hour after midnight before the crews could think about bedding down, but their slumber would be disturbed when it came to their turn to do an hour's 'stag', on sentry or radio watch. Thus three hours was the maximum sleep they could get, and senior officers reckoned a week was the most that tank crews could endure without their fighting efficiency being affected.[61] Yet, when Rommel swept all before him, tank units from both sides were in action continuously for up to three weeks. One officer noted 'with a shock how worn and tired the officers present looked. Red-eyed, haggard, bearded men with matted hair huddled around the map I had marked . . . Lack of sleep had sharpened features and lined every face into a sad caricature.'[62]

Besides, the little tin cans on tracks offered little protection to those within. Sometimes tanks were hit by shells which did not penetrate, the armour then glowing red and the tank rocking like a badly cast bell hit with a sledgehammer, while fear gripped the crew before being replaced by stunned relief. At other times the armour would glow red and then white as a shot reached through like a devil let loose, with dreadful implications for those inside[63] – 'The demented ricochet within the steel trap, the spattered brains, the torn entrails of a gunner impossible to extricate; the charred skulls and calcinated bodies of boys who seconds before were alive and beautiful'.[64] 'A tank cannot be readily fought with corpses or bits of them in it but one hesitates to tip a friend out into the unfeeling sand for the jackals to vandalize,' wrote Captain James Graham, 'and it was not uncommon for me to have to hold a gravedigging session after food and before sleep. The padre was a good chap but his place was with the main echelon which could be at bulkhead stores fifty miles behind. Usually some honest believer of an officer recited a garbled form of the committal service over the remains before we closed the shallow grave.'[65]

Nevertheless, heavy casualties were being inflicted across the Axis front – especially on the Italian infantry, whose fragility Auchinleck sought to exploit, forcing Rommel to stiffen their resolve by mixing them with German troops. Rommel wrote to his wife on 17 July that 'the enemy is using his superiority, especially in infantry, to destroy the Italian formations one by one, and the German formations are much too weak to stand alone. It's enough to make one weep.'[66] He was desperately short of men throughout his formations, although reinforcements arrived during July. First to come – by air from Crete – was 164th Division, which had been on garrison duties. Comando Supremo scraped together men and vehicles and pushed them to the front, including the Ramcke Parachute Brigade and much of the Folgore Parachute Division.[67] This decision was not universally welcomed. Ramcke's men were Luftwaffe personnel – 'Göring's agents' Rommel called them at first, although they would soon prove their worth. As for the Folgore, as parachutists they cost 45 times the amount of money to raise as an ordinary division.[68] 'We Italians are on the point of bankruptcy,' noted Sottotenente Eithal Torelli, 'but like good spendthrifts we wash the floor with champagne and eau de Cologne and build henhouses with the finest marble; now we are going to bury in the desert sand the parachutists who were trained for the invasion of Malta.'[69]

On 17 July, Auchinleck issued instructions for a renewal of the attacks on both enemy flanks around the end of the month, with constant pressure along the line in the meantime. The next day, however, he issued very different instructions: to attack as soon as possible (about 21 July) in the Ruweisat Ridge area against the main German positions, with a co-operating thrust in the south aimed at the enemy's rear. This would be Operation Splendour. There was no marked change in the situation to explain the sudden burst of optimism, but Auchinleck had received some reinforcements in the shape of 161st Indian Motor Brigade from Iraq and 23rd Armoured Brigade from Britain. Once more he had a superiority in armour, with 61 Grants, 81 Crusaders and 31 Honey tanks in 1st Armoured Division and another 150 Valentines and a few Matildas in 23rd Armoured Brigade against Rommel's estimated total of 31 (actually 38) German and 70 (actually 59) Italian tanks. Auchinleck also had a marked superiority in air support, artillery and infantry.[70]

However, 23rd Armoured Brigade had only just arrived and, instead of being used as a single formation, 50th Royal Tank Regiment was detached and sent to the Australians and replaced with a composite unit made up from the remains of 22nd Armoured Brigade, which Major Boyd Moss referred to as 'all-the-tanks-in-Egypt'. Tom Witherby of 46th Royal Tank Regiment arrived at Alamein after Auchinleck 'must have noticed 23rd Armoured Brigade busily trying to recover from the muddles' of its landing in Egypt on 12 July. 'Brigadier [Lawrence] Misa did not think we were ready for battle and protested at our being sent into action, but he was over-ruled.'[71] With an ignorant and impatient Churchill constantly asking why they could not be thrown into battle as soon as they arrived, fresh units were indeed committed practically straight off the ships: the tanks were not properly fitted up, but were released from workshops 'unexamined' on orders from GHQ – without their crews having time to acclimatize or train.[72] Sent to take part in what Witherby said 'must have been one of the most total disasters of the war', 23rd Armoured Brigade would charge forward with courage and naivety, exhorted all too prophetically by the commanding officer of 40th Royal Tank Regiment: 'Let's make this a Balaclava, boys!'[73]

The attack opened on the morning of 21 July, and once again the Kiwis found themselves counter-attacked by enemy armour but without the support of their own which they had been promised. They lost 700 men. Fifth Indian Brigade was to attack west along Ruweisat, and 23rd Armoured Brigade was to make a parallel attack south of it to El Mreir some 2 miles further west. At 0800 hours 23rd Armoured Brigade set off to win its laurels, all the while losing tanks to mines, anti-tank guns and tank fire, but pressing on to its objective some 3.5 miles west of where the Indian infantry were now held up.

Being in charge of the supply vehicles and not advancing over the ridge saved Witherby's life:

> I saw great clouds of black smoke. Then the wreckage of the attack coming back. The tank wounded, half-naked. Mortar bombs falling . . . there must have been a kind of madness at the Army Command, a feeling that there was a once and for all chance to drive the enemy back and that all risks must be taken in the hope of success. The kindest thing that can be said is that tired men do make mistakes.[74]

The operation had been controlled by Gott's XIII Corps Headquarters, but it was Misa, the brigade commander, who was sacked and sent back to handle replacements at Abbassia Barracks in Cairo.[75] Misa had obeyed his absurd orders after protesting, and was sacked for being proved right.

XIII Corps had put the enemy into confusion, but it had no more punches to throw and 23rd Armoured Brigade was withdrawn at midday, with just 7 from 87 tanks returning (although half of the remainder were later recovered). The day had been a disaster. Losses in 2nd New Zealand Division totalled 904, including 69 officers, and Inglis was 'angry almost beyond words and swore he would never again place faith in British armour'.[76]

XXX Corps had also been given ambitious tasks, including an advance on 22 July of some 6,500 yards west then 4,500 yards south to be carried out by 9th Australian Division following preliminary operations by the South Africans on the 21st. Morshead objected to Ramsden about the scale of these operations, and Ramsden complained in turn to Auchinleck, with the result that Auchinleck briefly became very angry; they then discussed it over tea.[77] The action proved to be desperate stuff. Companies that had already been in the line for over two weeks attacked into the teeth of ferocious artillery and machine-gun fire. In a two-company attack, 2/48th Battalion lost 49 killed and 61 wounded, with 3 men missing, and Private Stan Gurney won the Victoria Cross. In that week the battalion lost 270 killed and wounded and 50 missing – all the company commanders were dead, and their replacements had all become casualties. Nevertheless the division still made ground, although it could not secure the ambitious objectives assigned to it.[78]

Auchinleck wanted the XXX Corps attack renewed on the night of 24/25 July, adding 1st Armoured Division (less 4th Light Armoured Brigade) and the 69th Brigade from 50th (Northumbrian) Division to the corps, but the operation (codenamed Manhood) was put back to the night of the 26/27th at Morshead and Ramsden's request. When it went forward, the difficulties in launching and supporting a converging attack became apparent. An enemy counter-attack overran 6th Durham Light Infantry and 5th East Yorkshire Regiment of 69th Brigade, which had become disordered. The failure of the southern part of the attack left 2/28th Battalion (which had attacked from the north on to a feature known as Ruin Ridge) exposed. At 1030 hours the brigade commander received a signal saying simply, 'We have got to give in.' With tanks closing in from three directions, they had little choice. 'Many of the men of the 2/28th were in tears as they formed up into a column and marched off to captivity.' This abortive operation had cost the battalion 65 dead and wounded and 489 missing, while 69th Brigade had lost around 600 men plus another 32 tanks from 6th and 50th Royal Tank Regiments. Percy Lewis was with the tanks, whose first action this was. 'It was a frightening experience, we were green-horns and officers tried to comply with the training book as taught but it didn't work out.'[79]

Thus ended Auchinleck's last attempt to dislodge Rommel from Alamein. Criticism of the handling of operations was not confined to the Commonwealth divisions who bore the brunt but was widespread throughout Eighth Army, and this probably contributed as much as the state of the army to the decision to go on to the defensive.[80] Auchinleck knew that an operational pause to build up offensive strength was essential, and cabled London to that effect on the 27th. The men were utterly exhausted, having been under constant battle strain since May. 'For once we had sausages instead of A[rmour] P[iercing] shot for breakfast', noted the 9th Lancers' war diary without irony.[81]

Auchinleck called forward de Guingand to replace Brigadier John Whiteley as Chief of Staff at Eighth Army Headquarters, in spite of a complete lack of experience of the sort of staff work he was now being asked to undertake. De Guingand was unimpressed with the situation at Eighth Army and the proposed plans. The staff at Eighth Army 'were still looking over their shoulder. Other defensive positions far to the rear were being reconnoitred.' He also doubted the wisdom of the so-called 'OP' scheme, by which the artillery was to be controlled from the observation posts and concentrated against any threatened sector. 'There was,' he later wrote, 'a great danger of the guns being driven hither and thither and confusion setting in.'[82]

Oberst Fritz Bayerlein, Panzerarmee Chief of Staff, wrote later that Eighth Army 'very nearly succeeded in breaking through our positions several times between the 10th and 26th. If you could have continued to attack for only a couple of days more you would have done so. We then had no more ammunition at all for our heavy artillery and Rommel had determined to withdraw to the Frontier if the attack was resumed.'[83] The irony is that, in failing to drive Rommel back, Eighth Army avoided the trap that in effect befell Rommel – of winning an indecisive victory. Axis losses had been heavy: 2,300 Germans and 1,000 Italians killed, 7,500 Germans and more than 10,000 Italians wounded, and 2,700 Germans and over 5,000 Italians taken prisoner. But 9th Australian Division had suffered 2,552 battle casualties* during the four weeks' intense operations of July, and with overall Eighth Army losses over 13,000 Auchinleck would have had little strength to mount a pursuit.

---

*Between 17 and 27 July, 2/28th had lost 30 officers and 700 men killed, wounded and missing. There remained about 260 all ranks (including the left-out-of battle detachment for precisely this contingency). These reformed as other officers returned from leave, sickness or training, and in this way the battalion was rebuilt around an experienced nucleus. Where practical, Morshead also encouraged other units to transfer West Australians to 2/28th to maintain its character (Masel, *The Second 28th*, p. 89).

During July the DAF flew over 15,400 sorties. Nor had the Royal Navy been idle: four times it bombarded Matruh at night with the aid of flares dropped by Albacores, sinking two merchant ships and wrecking vital port installations. But the strain on aircraft was enormous. Another 113 had been lost, and Tedder's greatest need was for machines, not men. Many aircrew were forced to kick their heels for want of planes to fly, and those aircraft operating – often with alternating crews for up to eight sorties per day – were under colossal strain. But at least aircrew were spared the horror that the soldiers had continually to endure on the ground: bodies, unburied and putrefying among the minefields, covering the entire battlefield with the stench of death.[84]

5

Malta

Because of the revival of Malta as an air base and the numerous sinkings in the Mediterranean, supplies for the First Panzerarmee have fallen far below normal requirements. Unless Malta is weakened or paralysed once more, this situation cannot be remedied.

Count Galeazzo Ciano, 14 September 1942[1]

A month before Ciano made this observation, the Royal Navy had fought its way in to restore life to the beleaguered island, since when Malta had fought on with renewed and devastating vigour. At the crossroads of the Mediterranean, almost equidistant between Gibraltar and Alexandria, lying only 60 miles south of Sicily and 200 miles north of Tripoli, the small Maltese archipelago occupied a position of enormous significance in any Anglo-Italian conflict.

Phoenicians, Greeks, Romans, Byzantines and Arabs had all left their mark on Malta, but the last had had the greatest impact on the language. The distinctive Maltese tongue, with its numerous borrowings from French, Italian, Spanish and English, has an Arabic structure, grammar and essential vocabulary. The shipwreck of St Paul – traditionally in the harbour bearing his name – gave Malta its first church and a powerful Christian tradition, although one that was heavily overlain by Islam during centuries of Muslim domination. Attachment to the Roman Catholic church, together with the Maltese language, provided the basis of the national character, and their deep faith was of enormous significance to the resolution of the islanders during the trial they would face in the twentieth century.[2] In fact the people of Malta had been this way before. In 1565 the world's eyes had been focused on the Great Siege of the island by the Ottoman Turks, although in practically all accounts of that epic the ordinary people were overlooked – the chroniclers were interested only in the Knights of St John.[3]

By the end of the eighteenth century the rule of the Knights of St John – long decadent and inefficient – had collapsed with barely a murmur, even before a fleet from Revolutionary France bearing the young Napoleon Bonaparte on his Oriental adventure called in. The French swiftly took control, and just as swiftly antagonized the pious population with their atheist manners. By wantonly defacing the churches, they drove the people to rise up against the garrison that Bonaparte left behind. Led by their priests and the handful of educated upper classes, the Maltese besieged their own capital, willingly assisted by the British. By the autumn of 1800, after an occupation of just two years, the French were forced to leave. 'Brave Maltese,' said a British colonel who served with the islanders, 'you have rendered yourselves interesting and conspicuous to the world.'[4] Yet the British were curiously reluctant to add the island to the Empire, even when the Maltese sought their protection, and it was not until 1814 that the archipelago came under the British Crown. Over the next 125 years the union between the two island races who shared the same earthy sense of humour was cemented as the Royal Navy came to form the mainstay of the economy.

In a post-war essay, Vizeadmiral Eberhard Weichold, German liaison officer to the Supermarina, asserted that Germany's failure to understand the importance of seapower deprived her of the will to seize control of the Mediterranean that would have made it possible to supply Rommel, and furthermore that she was blind to the possibilities offered in North Africa. The Italian fleet might have managed to control the Mediterranean, but there was a 'silent admission' of British naval superiority in experience and achievement in battle, so that the Axis regarded the Royal Navy much as the British sometimes regarded the German Army.[5] This was just as well, since, had the Italians shown any determination whatever early on, then Malta must surely have fallen. They had plans to seize Malta as early as 1935, and its proximity to Italy led the Army and especially the RAF to discount the chances of successfully holding it. Fortunately for the British and the Maltese, Churchill and the Royal Navy believed in it, especially the Commander-in-Chief Mediterranean Station, Admiral Sir Andrew Cunningham. Malta possessed excellent dockyards and workshop facilities, which would enable it to support the submarines that would deploy there later.

The RAF was not similarly prepared. At the outbreak of war Malta had only *Faith*, *Hope* and *Charity* on which to base air defence. These were three Sea Gladiator fighters appropriated from their Royal Navy packing cases and flown by staff and administrative officers who happened to be on the island at the time.* They did enough to embarrass

---

*Flight Lieutenant George Burges DFC, who led them, was a flying-boat pilot then serving as ADC to the governor. None of them was a fighter pilot.

the Regia Aeronautica before being supplemented by Hurricanes and later Swordfish torpedo bombers to give the island an anti-shipping capability, but for a long time other support facilities were rudimentary to say the least.

By December 1940 Wellington bombers were operating from Malta against targets in Sicily and southern Italy.[6] However, the lion's share of the damage done to Rommel's supply lines early on was attributable to the submarines of 10th Submarine Flotilla, commanded by Captain G. W. G. 'Shrimp' Simpson, featuring such commanders as Malcolm Wanklyn VC and E. P. Tomkinson.[7] However, the Unity-class submarines that the flotilla mostly comprised had never been intended as operational vessels but were 'clockwork mice' for the training of surface vessels in anti-submarine operations.[8]

Over some eighteen months 14th Destroyer Flotilla and a cruiser squadron, Force K, also operated from Malta with conspicuous success that further underlined the Royal Navy's superiority over the Regia Marina. It was the complete destruction by Force K of a convoy including the German freighter *Duisberg* on 8 November 1941 that had goaded Hitler into sending Luftflotte II to Sicily. Soon the pressure was increased on Malta. In December 1941 there were 169 air-raid alerts – up from 76 in November – but these seemed light when the sirens wailed 263 times in January 1942.[9] Tedder sent Group Captain Basil Embry to report on the air situation, and without his incisive and accurate report it is doubtful whether the War Cabinet in London would have been sufficiently alerted to the Axis's favourable aircraft balance.

In March 1942 an RAF officer casually asked Air Vice-Marshal Hugh Pughe Lloyd, Air-Officer-Commanding, 'How goes the defence of the Island, sir?' He received a withering look in return. 'Malta is on the *offensive* and don't you ever forget it.'[10] But, with their bases constantly hammered and losses on the ground mounting, the Wellingtons were forced to evacuate to Egypt. Ammunition for the anti-aircraft guns was running low, and conditions for the submariners ashore – already bad – were becoming almost insufferable, while their losses were also mounting. When the Axis discovered that the submarines were operating from Manoel Island rather than Grand Harbour, it concentrated its efforts there.

It did not seem that conditions in Malta could get worse, but they did. An attempt to run in a convoy in March saw only 5,000 out of 26,000 tons of cargo landed. Thereafter all hope depended on the Allies' ability to supply Spitfires to the fighter squadrons on the island.[11] But Malta's trial by bombing was only beginning. The Axis air effort during the spring had been immense, with 2,850 sorties flown and 2,174 tons of bombs dropped in March. In April the island was assailed by an estimated 4,900 sorties, with 6,728 tons of bombs dropped and 11,000 buildings destroyed – though mercifully the shelters in the rocks saved all but 1,000 lives. Tedder visited the island in the middle of the month and found only six serviceable fighters. There were times when the defences rested on the anti-aircraft guns alone. Army and RAF personnel worked ceaselessly under constant attack, fortified only by a sense of humour. After attending an incendiary-bomb raid, a fire-fighting party met Pughe Lloyd, who asked what it was doing. 'To emphasize our story,' the team leader recalled, 'I handed him an incendiary bomb which we had extinguished before the case had melted. We, of course, had asbestos gloves on, and the look of surprise on the AOC's face as he quickly handed me back the still hot bomb was very amusing.'[12]

In the first four months of 1942 the absence of meaningful air reconnaissance was further hampering submarine operations, and 10th Submarine Flotilla was forced to evacuate to Alexandria. Malta's offensive capability had evaporated, and it seemed that Hitler's policy of bombing the island into submission was working: 150,389 tons of supplies destined for Rommel (99.2 per cent of those dispatched) arrived – an unprecedented figure, and one never surpassed.[13] Malta became the most bombed place on earth. Some 260 tons had been dropped on Coventry in November 1940, but in March and April 1942, some 6,700 tons were dropped on Valetta's Grand Harbour. The bravery of the Maltese – short of food and water, living in caves and shelters, surrounded by the stench of drains and sewers, with homelessness rampant and nothing but their faith to sustain them – was truly astonishing, and, if the award by King George VI of the George Cross to the entire island on 15 April 1942 was a stroke of genius in terms of sustaining morale, it was nothing less than the people deserved.[14]

Churchill personally telephoned Roosevelt and persuaded him to loan USS *Wasp*, which managed to fly in 46 Spitfires on 20 April, but these were all damaged or unserviceable within three days of their arrival. Churchill would not give up, however, and he persuaded the President to loan *Wasp* once more, and she and HMS *Eagle* were able to fly in more of the vital fighters. These began to arrive on 9 May, and were up and fighting within minutes of arrival. The following day Kesselring announced to OKW the neutralization of Malta; yet to the defenders this became 'The Glorious Tenth of May'. The gallant fast minelayer *Welshman*, having made many such runs previously, had escaped attack en route by disguising herself as a French destroyer and reached Grand Harbour once more with much needed ammunition. Soon the island was again under heavy attack, but with the aid of a smokescreen – and covered by furiously circling Spitfires – soldiers, sailors and airmen unloaded her precious cargo within seven hours: the guns could fire for a few more weeks. And 63 Axis aircraft were claimed destroyed. (Rome Radio, notoriously incorrect, admitted to the loss of 47.)[15]

For some weeks thereafter Malta was relatively free from attack but lacked an offensive capability. The real threat to the island, however, came not from bombs but from starvation; she was devoid of essential commodities, and it was vital that she be replenished. And Spitfires flown in would be useless without fuel to fly and ammunition to fire. 'The tempo of life is just indescribable,' reported a newly arrived pilot. 'The morale of all is magnificent – pilots, ground crews and Army, but it is certainly tough. The bombing is continuous on and off every day. One lives here only to destroy the Hun and hold him at bay; everything else, living conditions, sleep, food and all the ordinary standards of life have gone by the board.'[16] The situation was desperate: rations amounted to little more than a couple of slices of poor bread with some jam and a slice of bully per day. The 'Magic Carpet' service, by which submarines brought precious aircraft fuel and other essentials, could deliver only a small amount, and by the middle of August the island would literally starve unless supplies arrived.

An attempt to fight a convoy through from the east in mid-June – Operation Vigorous – was a failure. Flying in support, the torpedo-armed Beauforts of 39 Squadron, sent to intercept the Italian battle fleet, lost 7 out of 12 aircraft to fighters before they made contact with the Italian battleships *Littorio* and *Vittorio Veneto*. The Italians lost the cruiser *Trento*, sunk by a Beaufort-launched torpedo, and the *Littorio* was badly damaged. All of 39 Squadron's surviving aircraft were damaged in the process, but miraculously made it to Malta. Squadron Leader Patrick Gibbs, having just survived Me-109s and murderous flak that forced him to crash-land on a strange island, was greeted with the admonition 'We usually do this sort of thing *off* the runway!' However, he found Pughe Lloyd very receptive when he suggested his squadron could best operate from Malta rather than Egypt.[17] Tedder duly agreed and, together with 217 Squadron, the Beauforts became the new aerial strike force. Significantly, however, Italian fuel-oil reserves were now so depleted that Italy's battle fleet never again ventured out to dispute control of the Mediterranean. Hitler's optimism about seizing Soviet oilfields proved groundless, and the Romanian fields were reserved for the German war machine only.[18]

Meanwhile, from the western end of the Mediterranean, Operation Harpoon managed to get 2 out of 6 merchantmen into Valetta. The cost to the Royal Navy and RAF of these twin operations was a cruiser, 5 destroyers, 2 minesweepers, 6 merchantmen, and over 20 aircraft.[19]

On 21 June – the day of Kesselring and Rommel's discussion in the roadman's hut – 39 Squadron was sent to intercept the 7,744-ton German freighter *Reichenfels* and the 8,326-ton Italian tanker *Rosolino Pilo*. The former was sunk, but the latter got through. Significantly, however, the route to the west of Malta was now deemed unusable by the Axis, and future convoys had to use the Greek-coast route. This caused delays and cost yet more fuel.[20]

Sinkings of Axis ships attributed to Malta's submarines (13 between between 2 June and 6 November 1942, with several already stricken being finished off) often involved guidance by Ultra but were nevertheless the product of patience: their slow speed dictated that submarines must patrol and wait in likely places. A higher number of Axis ships were now lost to aerial torpedoes and bombs. For directing air operations Ultra was less important than the Malta outpost of the Photographic Reconnaissance Unit (PRU) established by Pughe Lloyd in 1941; this operated stripped-down Spitfires, and developed great skill in interpreting aerial photographs. The continuous coverage provided enabled the nature of cargoes, the state of loading, and hence accurately estimated departure times to be deduced – a task made easier when it was realized that most ships destined for North Africa were loaded at the same spot in Naples, christened 'Rommel's Quay'. Furthermore, by analysing wave patterns in a ship's wake, its speed could be calculated, enabling attackers to be vectored on to it. This skill, together with the assumption by both Italians and Germans that British anti-shipping success resulted from the reports of secret agents, also served to provide security for Ultra.[21]

On 15 July, Air Vice-Marshal Sir Keith Park – of Battle of Britain fame – replaced Pughe Lloyd as AOC. As a fighter-minded commander, he was happy to leave the strike element of operations to the likes of Gibbs, and he allowed the integration of 235 Squadron's Beaufighters into Gibbs's Beaufort wing.[22] By day, Beauforts of 39 Squadron – carrying a torpedo and escorted by Beaufighters and occasionally Spitfires – would seek out prey. Other ships were located at night by means of radar-equipped Wellingtons, usually operating from airfields in Libya and later Egypt. Anyone who questions Italian bravery should consider the risks the crews of these ships took for months on end, with perhaps a 50-50 chance of being burned to death in a sinking ship or a flaming sea. It is little wonder that Italian naval historians dubbed this period 'the hecatomb of the tankers'.[23] A mixed force of Beauforts and Beaufighters would take off from Malta, clearing the south-eastern tip of the island before coming down to under 100 feet to avoid Axis radar. When they reached the convoy the Beaufighters' task would be flak suppression, engaging the escorting destroyers and occasionally aircraft to give the torpedo bombers a clear run at the flammable merchant vessels. (To supplement the purpose-built tankers, many merchant ships also carried fuel in barrels or other containers.) Terence McGarry, who served with 39 Squadron, recalled that

> Success or failure depended on the accuracy of the interception, for without it the element of surprise was lost and the carefully briefed attack plan would be useless. A good interception also cut down our losses, for a bad one meant that the aircraft would be out of position, thus giving the enemy time to deploy. All therefore depended on a good recce (Wing Commander Warburton was the kingpin) and accurate navigation by the strike leader.

They were usually successful. Adrian Warburton, the star of Malta PRU, certainly never received the public recognition of a Douglas Bader, but then neither did the Malta-based aircrews.[24] Yet their contribution to the ultimate success of Eighth Army was phenomenal.

The arrival of *Unbroken* at Malta in mid-July, followed by *United* at the end of the month, heralded the return of 10th Submarine Flotilla to Manoel Island. Unfortunately, Malta was all but starved out; it lacked ammunition, gun barrels and other warlike stores – and, more importantly, food and fuel.* The flotilla's first operation would be in support of the vital Operation Pedestal, which would attempt to relieve the island. Upon this operation Malta would stand or fall, and with it a critical factor in the fate of the Nile valley.[25]

Having departed from Glasgow, 14 fast merchant ships (11 British and 3 American, including the tanker *Ohio*) passed Gibraltar during the night of 10 August. Once inside the Mediterranean, the convoy was guarded by the largest British naval force ever assembled during the Second World War: under the overall command of Vice-Admiral Sir Neville Syrfet, 2 battleships, 7 cruisers and 32 destroyers together with 7 submarines and numerous auxiliaries and refuellers were

---

* Medicines were also scarce. An airman who reported sick was asked which colour he preferred: blue, orange or green. He chose orange, and was given a dose from an orange-coloured bottle. 'What's in it?' he asked. 'Water,' replied the MO. 'We have no medicines but we give you a choice of colour' (Spooner, *Supreme Gallantry*, p. 208n).

divided into Force Z – comprising most of the heavy vessels, which would turn back at the Skerki Channel between Sicily and Tunisia, after which conditions became too risky for large naval units – and Force X, including the cruisers *Nigeria* (flagship of Rear-Admiral H. M. Burrough), *Kenya* and *Manchester* with 12 destroyers, which would proceed to Malta. But the main change to previous plans was the provision of extra carrier-borne air strength on *Victorious* (flagship of Rear-Admiral A. L. St G. Lyster), *Indomitable* and *Eagle*.[26] Kesselring loosed every available aircraft in Sicily and Sardinia against the convoy. There were some 146 German bombers (mainly Ju-88s, plus 16 Ju-87s), 72 fighters (nearly all Me-109s), 232 Italian fighters, and 139 Italian bombers including many of the effective SM-79 torpedo bombers.[27] On the morning of 11 August the convoy was sighted some 60 miles south of Ibiza and was ineffectively attacked by the Italian submarine *Uarsciek*. She also reported it to the waiting line of submarines and aircraft, and among these was Kapitänleutnant Helmut Rosenbaum's *U-73*. Skilfully avoiding the escorts, he fired at the carrier *Eagle* from 500 yards; struck on the port side by four torpedoes, she sank within eight minutes, taking 200 of her crew with her. Rosenbaum's escape was as skilful as his attack – it was an inauspicious start for the Royal Navy.

Through the rest of the day the destroyers followed up sonar contacts with pursuit and depth charges, and torpedo tracks were observed, but as evening approached the convoy neared the line on the chart where it would be within range of Sardinia's aircraft. At dusk, the first raiders came in through a storm of anti-aircraft fire. 'Tracers everywhere . . . the noise [was] deafening. Bursting shells and great white plumes of water shot into the air by near miss bombs. On top of all this din we had . . . sirens whooping, ordering emergency turns.'[28] Three raiders were shot down and no damage was inflicted on the ships. That night, Malta's Beauforts attacked the airfields in Sardinia.

At 0600 hours on 12 August (the start of the grouse season in never-never land) Martlets took off from *Indomitable* and shot down two shadowing enemies. A further eight Ju-88s were shot down in the first raid, and the rest of the morning was spent with submarine alarms.

Noon approached, when the heaviest air raid was expected. It began with Savoia bombers escorted by Macchi fighters. They were to break up the convoy using an ingenious new weapon, the *motobomba*. This was a parachute-dropped torpedo that ran on a circling or random course and would have been extremely hazardous if dropped within a convoy. Fortunately these aircraft were intercepted at a distance, and the convoy was able to sidestep this weird weapon. However, there soon followed

40 aircraft armed with conventional torpedoes – less threatening against a convoy able to retain its discipline, but dangerous nevertheless. The attackers were once more met by Martlets and Hurricanes and the full firepower of the fleet, including the sixteen-inch guns of HMS *Rodney*, and the enemy was driven off.

The respite was short. German dive-bombers attacked the *Nelson* and *Rodney*. Both of these survived near misses, as did the anti-aircraft cruiser *Cairo*, but the merchantman *Deucalion* was less fortunate. One bomb passed right through her, but near misses caused damage that forced her to drop back. Escorted by a destroyer, she turned towards the North African shore, hoping to make it to Malta independently; but she was found by torpedo-planes, and one hit was enough to touch off the petrol and kerosene on board. The crew had barely managed to abandon her when, with an almighty roar, she blew up – a sinister portent of what was to come.

Meanwhile the Italians were trying further ingenuity in the form of a radio-controlled pilotless flying bomb launched from a Cant seaplane. Intended for one of the capital ships, it malfunctioned and ended up exploding on the North African coast. The Italians' bad luck was then compounded when two Reggione fighters followed some Hurricanes (which they closely resembled) as the latter were landing on *Victorious*. Accepted as friendly by the anti-aircraft gunners, they each dropped a bomb; one just missed the bows, while the other landed square on the flight deck. The damage it might have caused was unthinkable, but to the astonishment of all concerned (and the justifiable disgust of the pilot) it fragmented without exploding. An eyewitness on *Victorious* described the scene below decks during the battle:

> The pilots snatched meals as they could and rushed back on deck to take their places on the revolving wheel of readiness. And in the hangar the maintenance crews worked like men possessed to make the aircraft serviceable as they were struck down. They were coming now with battle-damage to be repaired as well as the normal troubles of oil-leaks, coolant leaks, sprained oleo-legs and what-not. The hangar itself was a shambles as aircraft were ranged, struck-down, stowed, refuelled and rearmed at top speed; and the hangar-deck became more and more slippery with oil.[29]

Throughout the long afternoon the submarine alarms sounded. The Italian submarines *Emo* and *Cobalto* were depth-charged; *Emo* escaped, but *Cobalto* was forced to surface and was then rammed and sunk by *Ithuriel*, her crew being taken prisoner but the destroyer being forced to retire to Gibraltar.

As the exhausting day drew to a close, the convoy neared the Skerki

Channel. It was approaching the area where German aircraft from Sicily awaited and E-boats (motor torpedo-boats) prowled. Here Force Z, comprising the battleships, carriers and other heavy units, was to turn back. But before it did so German Stukas and torpedo-bombers had a chance to break through in one last daylight raid and achieve their first major success of the operation. In a maelstrom of fire and confusion a group of Stukas 'appearing suddenly from up sun out of the smoky blue sky' struck the carrier *Indomitable* with three hits on the flight deck, causing severe damage. 'Smoke was billowing out of her hangar lifts,' observed David 'Rocky' Royle from a neighbouring ship, 'and what I thought was the flight deck dripping molten metal' (actually blazing aviation spirit).[30] This forced her aircraft to divert to *Victorious*, leaving the latter – the only carrier still serviceable out of the three that had left Gibraltar – overburdened. Meanwhile another destroyer, *Foresight*, was also lost to the torpedo bombers. A torpedo 'just blew the stern away and we could see men spread-eagled flying through the air', recalled the horrified American Armed Guard gunners on board the US merchantman *Almeria Lykes*.[31] Then, as the cruisers *Cairo* and *Nigeria* led the way into the Skerki Channel, they were met by the Italian submarines *Axum* and *Dessie*, which opened fire at 1955 hours. Within minutes the darkening skies were lit by huge flashes as *Cairo* was hit aft and had her screws blown off and Burrough's flagship *Nigeria* was hit amidships by this brilliant salvo, as was the convoy's tanker, *Ohio*. *Nigeria* was forced to retire, and Burrough transferred his flag to *Ashanti*.

Suddenly, as the convoy altered its formation to enter the narrow channel, all coherence was lost. *Ohio* came to a temporary halt, forcing the merchantman *Empire Hope* behind to go hard astern in order to avoid a collision. Others were turning to avoid torpedo tracks, while destroyers were rushing hither and yon to give help. Worse, *Cairo* and *Nigeria* were the only ships equipped to control fighters from Malta and, as the last perfectly timed air attack by Ju-88s and Savioa bombers arrived, so Beaufighters from Malta also received an irregular and irrational fire from the Allied ships. ('If it flies, shoot it!') Simultaneously the Italian submarine *Alagi* fired and hit the cruiser *Kenya* in the bows, while the merchantmen *Brisbane Star* and *Clan Ferguson* were also hit by torpedoes from one source or another and lurched to a halt; when the ammunition on board *Clan Ferguson* went up she disappeared in a colossal roar. *Empire Hope* was hit by a dive-bomber, caught fire, and had to be abandoned. At 2113 hours Tenente di Vascello Sergio Puccini of *Alagi* noted that 'from 180 degrees around to 240 degrees we could see a continuous line of flame from the burning, sinking ships'; a little later he recorded, 'A burning ship blows up.'[32]

Yet *Ohio* managed to patch herself up and get under way again, slowly following the convoy, while *Brisbane Star* turned to hug the Tunisian coast and make her own way to Malta, which in a truly epic voyage she managed to do.

Some masters made their way alone or accompanied by a destroyer, and only a small group remained together, two fleet destroyers continuing with mine sweeps followed by the cruisers *Kenya* and *Manchester* with the merchantmen *Glenorchy* and the American *Almeria Lykes*. Waiting for them were E-boats, the prowling wolves of the sea, in perfect conditions for their night's work. As the night was split by the cracks of gunfire and the occasional searchlight beam, two Italian boats dealt with *Manchester*, leaving her immobilized to be scuttled the following day. *Almeria Lykes* went down, most of the crew being taken off on a destroyer. *Glenorchy* was hit and the crew abandoned ship – except for Captain G. Leslie, her master, and she sank taking him with her. Elsewhere E-boats had accounted for *Wairangi* and the American *Santa Elisa*. *Rochester Castle* had made as many as 11 emergency turns to avoid the attacking E-boats before finally her luck ran out and she was hit forward. But her bulkheads held, and she managed somehow to stay with the survivors as they plodded eastward towards the dawn which they both prayed for and feared. Burrough had now only the damaged *Kenya*, the light cruiser *Charybdis* and seven destroyers with which to protect the convoy should the Italians decide to finish it off. Then he heard from Malta that there was indeed a force of 6 cruisers and 11 destroyers bearing down on them through the Tyrrhenian Sea. Behind him trailed the remaining merchantmen, *Melbourne Star* and *Waimarama* and the damaged and priceless *Ohio*, and behind them *Dorset* and *Port Chalmers*. He did not know of *Brisbane Star*'s solitary fight to reach the island, nor that the threat of the cruisers was about to vanish.[33]

According to the official history, 'the RAF in Malta conducted a skilful and convincing bluff to deceive [the Italians] into the belief that strong air striking forces were on the way to deal with them'.[34] In fact Park had despatched three 'Goofingtons' (radar-equipped Wellingtons) with instructions to locate the Italian group and drop flares as if it were due to be attacked, while reporting to Malta on the radio in clear and calling on an imaginary force of Liberators to assist.[35] Park was also prepared to use his Beauforts, and the combined threat thoroughly alarmed the Supermarina which judged Malta's strike capability as considerable. Weichold supported the Supermarina's plea to Kesselring for fighter cover, but this was refused and Weichold believed that 'In this fashion, a splendid opportunity for a crushing victory . . . was thrown away.'[36] Kesselring, on the other hand, noted that the Regia Marina 'was regarded as a *pièce de résistance* and was therefore used sparingly . . . On top of this there were the extraordinary technical deficiencies which deservedly earned the Italian Navy the nickname "Fine-weather Fleet". Its doubtful seaworthiness called for increased air protection and that, with the limited strength of the Axis air forces in the Mediterranean, imposed ridiculous demands on the German Luftwaffe.'[37] Park's ruse made the Supermarina lose its nerve, and the Italians turned back – having burned several thousand tons of scarce and precious fuel oil to no purpose. Worse, they then ran into Adam Mars's 'pint-sized submarine' *Unbroken*. 'I was going to tackle twelve enemy warships all at one time,' wrote Mars. 'A story for my grandchildren – if the destroyers and aircraft let me live to tell it!' As the third destroyer swept past, 'I caught a glimpse of a scruffy-looking sailor smoking a 'bine as he leaned against the depth-charge thrower.' *Unbroken* fired two 'kippers' and turned to go. Diving to 120 feet meant that the 105 depth charges fired at her exploded harmlessly above her, but, some two minutes after firing her torpedoes, loud explosions were heard.[38] The next day it was reported that she had hit two cruisers with one salvo – a phenomenal achievement. Indeed, the heavy cruiser *Bolzano* and the light cruiser *Muzio Attendolo* had been put out of action for the remainder of the war.

Burrough had meanwhile to deal with the day's air assault. It began at 0800 hours, and *Waimarama* received a direct hit; she disintegrated in a colossal explosion that covered the sea around her with flaming aviation spirit and showered debris down on *Melbourne Star*. Worse, debris started a deck fire on *Ohio*, which the crew fought desperately. As if their plight were not already dangerous enough, she was now the focus of the next wave of attackers and was hit by a damaged aircraft that crashed on to her; she proceeded with parts of the plane covering her deck. *Rochester Castle* was also hit and a fire was started, but this was brought under control and she struggled on. *Dorset* was hit, and *Ohio* was straddled by bombs from Stukas, finally bringing her to a halt; Burrough sent two destroyers to watch over them. *Port Chalmers*, which had until now been miraculously unscathed, discovered a torpedo hanging in her starboard paravane (a mine-cutting device suspended from the stern). As she gingerly made way it exploded, but fortunately it did no serious damage and she could proceed.

Mercifully for the three merchantmen and *Kenya* (now dealing with an engine-room fire after another dive-bombing attack), they were now under cover of Malta's Spitfires (407 fighter sorties were flown that day to protect them). They were also met by the minesweeping squadron, so that Burrough and what was left of his force could withdraw to Gibraltar. *Ohio* still wallowed some 70 miles away, but *Dorset* had been sunk despite the defensive fire of the supporting destroyer *Bramham*. Desmond Dickens was a young apprentice from the *Dorset* who watched as 'that majestic-looking ship went lower and lower, and by 1955 *Dorset* was no more – what a pathetic sight that was – that great ship which had done so much to keep this England of ours full of food'.[39] At 1800 hours on 13 August most of what remained of Pedestal edged its way under the guns of Fort St Elmo at the entrance to Grand Harbour, to be greeted by thousands of wildly cheering Maltese, anxious at seeing so few ships when a large convoy had been promised and aware that there was no tanker. And at 1050 hours next day the fragile *Ohio*, still carefully shepherded by three destroyers, came under air attack once more. One bomb exploded under the stern and another in the engine room. For the second time the crew were taken off, and it seemed impossible that she could survive. Yet somehow the destroyers managed to get a tow on – despite her having only 3 feet of freeboard and slowly settling by the head. Her master, Captain D. W. Mason, thought she might last 12 hours.

Meanwhile *Brisbane Star*, having outwitted a U-boat, also somehow continued on her way at between five and nine knots, though she had lost her bows. Off Tunisia she had been boarded by the harbourmaster of Sousse and a French naval officer, who insisted she must be impounded. Captain F. N. Riley replied 'that I would not let him do it', to which the harbourmaster apologized but explained that those were his orders. Riley asked if he was a seaman and would 'he be a brother seaman, be kind to me, forget me and let me go'. After a pause the harbourmaster took Riley's hand and said, 'Goodbye, Captain, a safe voyage and good luck.'[40] On 14 August with Spitfires circling overhead she arrived to more cheers (and almost as many tears) in Valetta. The next day – the Feast of Santa Marija – *Ohio*, with a broken back and with parts of a bomber on her deck, finally made it. It was a sublime moment as the stupefied men were greeted by crowds 'cheering like mad' in what Lieutenant-Commander Roger Hill recalled 50 years later as 'the most wonderful moment of my life'.[41] She was nursed to a berth beside another sunken tanker, where, exhausted, she began to settle on the bottom.

When *Unbroken* also returned to Valetta on 18 August the wharf was again lined with cheering Maltese. 'They were happy,' wrote Mars. 'The convoy had got through, they had food to eat, and here was a submarine returning from a successful patrol. Our hearts went out to these valiant little islanders.'[42]

It had been a close-run thing. James Reid Forbes, who sailed in one of the escorts, HMS *Sirius*, as a young petty officer, remembered, 'The convoy never faltered, not even to pick up survivors. We brought an Italian submarine to the surface and massacred them all, didn't pick any of them up. It was a grim time in the war. Sink, burn, destroy. A kind of madness came over us at that time.'[43] Sir Andrew Cunningham noted that 'we paid a heavy price but personally I think we got out of it lightly considering the risks we had to run, and the tremendous concentration of everything . . . we had to face.'[44]

Strangely, as if admitting defeat, neither the Luftwaffe nor the Regia Aeronautica had attempted to interfere with the unloading of the convoy. Fifteen thousand tons of fuel (enough for about ten more weeks) and 32,000 tons of general stores had been brought in, but the people still faced months of hardship. The daily calorific intake of adult male workers was 1,690, and for women and children just 1,500 – enough to survive for several months, but only at the cost of loss of weight and physical powers.[45]

Naval historians tend to regard Pedestal (or the Santa Marija Convoy as it is known in Malta) as a turning point in the war, and it was indeed of major significance. If for the British it was a tactical defeat, it was also a strategic success of the first order. On it depended whether it would be possible to continue the strategic war in the Mediterranean. Malta might not necessarily have been forced to surrender for some months, but her aircraft and submarines would have been forced to abandon offensive operations and the Axis could have enjoyed supplies and re-inforcements largely unhindered, as at least some on the Axis side appreciated. Weichold wrote, 'To the continental observer the British losses seemed to represent a big victory for the Axis and they were accorded appropriate propaganda. But, in reality, the facts were quite different . . . [By the successful running in of supplies] the enemy had gained the strategic end of his operation . . . [It] was not the defeat it was made out to be by German public opinion, but a strategic failure of the first order on the part of the Axis, the repercussions of which would one day be felt.' And they were felt before very long: Malta's revival enabled a renewal of sustained anti-shipping operations, starting with the sinking of two large freighters – *Lerici* by submarine on 15 August and *Pilo* by the RAF on the 17th. The loss of these was reported just as Ultra revealed that Panzerarmee's consumption of supplies had been exceeding intake for two weeks and its stocks were sufficient to last only until the 26th.[46]

6

Enter Monty

The trouble about running this war is that there are too many
politicians who think they are generals and too many generals
who think they are politicians and too many journalists who
think they are both.

Notice on the Press Censor's Office, Cairo

During the summer of 1942, decisions were made in Washington
and London that greatly affected the war in Africa. When
Churchill and Brooke visited Washington in June, they tried to persuade
Roosevelt and the American Chiefs of Staff to defer a cross-Channel
operation (Sledgehammer) which the Americans regarded as the
obvious means to victory.[1] The Americans wanted to attack the
Germans as close as possible to Germany, and British opposition
caused considerable suspicion in Washington: the British seemed more
concerned with safeguarding imperial interests than with winning the
war as quickly as possible. But Churchill had insisted that 'no responsible British general, admiral or air marshal is prepared to recommend
Sledgehammer as a practicable operation in 1942 . . . I am sure that . . .
Gymnast [the invasion of North Africa] is by far the best chance for
effecting relief to the Russian Front in 1942.'[2]

Only after the US Army's Chief of Staff and the Commander-in-Chief
of the US Navy, General George C. Marshall and Admiral Ernest J. King,
visited London together with presidential adviser Harry L. Hopkins did
Roosevelt finally agree to an 'expanded Gymnast' and deferment of the
invasion of Europe until the Axis had been expelled from Africa – following an exchange of cables on 22 and 23 July. Planning to invade North
Africa now began under the new code name Torch. General Dwight D.
Eisenhower was appointed Supreme Commander for the operation, with
a combined Anglo-American staff; General the Honourable Sir Harold
Alexander became his deputy, and Montgomery – currently commanding

South-Eastern Army in England – was to command the British Task Force. But the Anglo-American agreement would be worthless without victory in the Middle East or should Malta fall.

Churchill was impatient at what he called 'the inexplicable inertia of Middle East Command'. In June, as Eighth Army fell back, he had told Auchinleck that 'you have 700,000 men on your ration strength in the Middle East . . . every fit male should be made to fight and die for victory'. He demanded that 'several thousands of officers and administrative personnel . . . swell the battalions on working parties'. How clerks, mechanics and quartermaster staff would reach the desert and then be supplied he did not say; but Auchinleck suffered these exhortations with patient forbearance.[3] Following the 1 July no-confidence debate, Churchill was visited by Julian Amery, son of his parliamentary ally Leo, and a friend of his own son Randolph. Amery had friends on the staff at GHQ and Eighth Army, and ignoring the frowns of Brooke, who was also present, he gave a gloomy picture of the state of morale in Eighth Army and urged Churchill to visit Egypt personally. Churchill, who was already considering visiting Stalin, liked the idea – despite having just been criticized in the House for spending too much time travelling.[4] 'It was quite clear,' wrote Brooke, 'that something was radically wrong' in the Middle East, and 'it was essential that I should go out and see what was wrong. But for this I wanted to be alone.' On 15 July he obtained Churchill's permission, but on 30 July, while he was en route in Gibraltar, Churchill cabled him to announce that he would come too and to say that he had also invited Field Marshal Smuts from South Africa and General Wavell from India for a conference, after which he would visit Stalin in Moscow. When Churchill arrived in Cairo on 3 August, Brooke reported that 'he is fretting that there is to be no offensive action until September 15th and I see already troublesome times ahead'.[5] Churchill was becoming obsessive: 'Rommel, Rommel, Rommel . . .' he paced up and down muttering, 'what else matters but beating him?'[6]

Churchill still held Auchinleck in high regard, and the subsequent cast lists that the Prime Minister bandied about indicate that he had not yet decided what changes to make. Over the next three days a 'circus of alternatives was discussed, proposed, countermanded and redrafted'.[7] The main problem was a new Eighth Army commander, it being agreed that Auchinleck could not combine the roles of Commander-in-Chief and operational command. Churchill proposed Gott, although he was doing so, as Brooke pointed out, without having seen him. Brooke knew that Gott was tired, having been in the desert from the beginning, commanding 1st King's Royal Rifle Corps (60th Rifles) in 1939 and now XIII Corps. Twice – in March 1941 and February 1942 – he had been involved in trying to save the day around Tobruk. His strength of mind, imperturbability and common sense made him the oracle to whom both high and low turned for advice and reassurance – he was always ready with a course of action when others faltered or were in doubt. It was little wonder that he was exhausted in both mind and body.[8]

On 4 August Churchill was astonished to find Corbett – Auchinleck's deputy – expecting to take over. Meanwhile Brooke, in conversation with Auchinleck, proposed Montgomery and Auchinleck agreed – as he also did to the sacking of Corbett. Churchill was not impressed by Auchinleck's explanations of delays in resuming the offensive, and when he heard of these proposed changes he was livid. The argument raged all night. On 5 August, Churchill and Brooke paid a visit to a fly-infested Eighth Army Headquarters which proved disastrous for Auchinleck. In the operations caravan, Dorman-Smith recalled later, Churchill demanded that Eighth Army attack again immediately, thrusting his stubby fingers at the map on the wall:

> Here, he said, or here . . . We were alone with him, as Brooke had gone up the line. It was a bit like being caged with a gorilla. Eventually the Auk said, 'No, sir, we cannot attack again yet.' Churchill swung around to me. 'Do you say that too? Why don't you use the 44th Division?' 'Because, sir, that division isn't ready and anyhow, a one division attack would not get us anywhere.' Churchill rose, grunted, stumped down from the caravan and stood alone in the sand, back turned to us. I wondered if he was thinking himself in Lincoln's shoes, when Lincoln dismissed McClellan at Harrison's Landing.[9]

Churchill also met Gott and was convinced of his suitability by this meeting, whereas Brooke had his misgivings confirmed when Gott confessed to him at tea that 'what is required out here is some new blood. I have tried most of my ideas on the Boche. We want someone with new ideas and plenty of confidence in them.'[10] The argument about a new Eighth Army Commander raged once again late into the night. The next day Churchill cabled the War Cabinet in London to propose that Middle East Command be reorganized into a Near East Command (covering Egypt, Palestine and Syria) and a Middle East Command (covering Persia and Iraq) and that Brooke take the former (and be allowed Montgomery as Eighth Army commander) while Auchinleck be offered command of the latter. Brooke, however, knew that as CIGS he was the only general capable of reining in Churchill's wilder impulses and directing his astonishing energy towards product-ive goals, and he courageously declined. A compromise was reached in which Alexander, due to command the invasion of North Africa, would be appointed Commander-in-Chief in Cairo and Montgomery would take his place, with Gott taking over Eighth Army. Ramsden, Corbett and Dorman-Smith would all be replaced.

Eventually Auchinleck was sacked not because of the failures of July – Dorman-Smith took the fall for those – but because he resisted Churchill's impatient demands for an immediate renewal of the offensive. The irony is that his successors would rapidly reach not only the same conclusion but that Auchinleck's proposed date of mid-September was in fact too soon and that late October was when the decisive action should be launched. He had to go because symbols are as important in human affairs as substance, and, like Wavell before him, he was compromised by the disasters that had occurred on his watch. In picking up an army on the run and turning it around he had saved Egypt, but he also had to take responsibility for Eighth Army's failures. The growing recalcitrance of the Commonwealth troops was symptomatic of these: due to a not unreasonable difference in perspective, what Auchinleck and Dorman-Smith saw as limited success, they, as national contingents rather than just small parts of a large army, saw as disasters.[11]

Then on an otherwise quiet day – 7 August – came the tragic news that Gott had been killed. He was flying back to Cairo from Burg el Arab in a transport on what was normally considered a safe route (it had been used two days previously by the Prime Minister's party), but the aeroplane was suddenly attacked by two German fighters and forced to land in the desert. Some of the crew managed to get out, but a further attack set the transport ablaze, killing all those inside.[12] Now, at last, Brooke got his way and, after a little more persuasion, obtained the Prime Minister's agreement to send Montgomery out to command Eighth Army.

Gott was widely mourned throughout Eighth Army, and many have since claimed that Montgomery's subsequent success was gained through implementing Gott's plans. This is patently untrue. Gott's virtues were his character, bearing and inspirational leadership, rather than his grasp of the strengths and limitations of the British military machine. As he himself admitted, he possessed no clear vision of how those strengths could best be employed.[13]

Churchill continued for a very long time to assume that Alexander – whom he regarded as 'Britain's finest fighting soldier'[14] – would be in operational control, not realizing that the very qualities that Alexander brought to the job of Commander-in-Chief meant that the forthcoming battles would be fought entirely by Montgomery. Harold Rupert Leofric George Alexander, third son of the Earl of Caledon, had long been destined for high command. When he and Montgomery had served as divisional commanders in France in 1940, Brooke as their corps commander had the perfect opportunity to assess their relative merits:

> Both of them completely imperturbable and efficiency itself, and yet two totally different characters. Monty with his quick brain for appreciating military situations was well aware of the very critical situation that he was in, and the very dangers and difficulties . . . acted as a stimulus . . . they thrilled him and put the sharpest of edges on his military ability. Alex, on the other hand, gave me the impression of never fully realizing all the very unpleasant potentialities of our predicament. He remained entirely unaffected by it, completely composed and never to have the slightest doubt that all would come right in the end.[15]

Montgomery clearly believed himself to be the military superior of both Auchinleck and Alexander. In Alexander's case this was a result of Montgomery's vanity and of their previous careers, in which Montgomery had been an instructor at the Staff College when Alexander was a student. But it is very difficult to understand the reason for Montgomery's deep antipathy towards Auchinleck. Montgomery's brother has suggested that it may have been jealousy of Auchinleck's Indian Army background, given that Montgomery had applied to join the Indian Army but had been turned down.[16] Fortunately he enjoyed much more cordial relations with Alexander, thanks to the latter's temperament, his refusal to concede in any way to the Germans, and his considerable charm. Alexander was 'The only man, yes, the *only* man under whom an admiral, general or air marshal would gladly serve in a subordinate position,' Montgomery once remarked.[17]

As Commander-in-Chief, Alexander brought no piercing intellect but he did bring leadership. He saw his job as the formulation of strategy – although he always discussed the plans and requirements of his subordinates before major operations, to ensure that they had the formations and logistical support necessary for victory. He would move heaven and earth to get these and to keep the politicians off his generals' backs, but he never sought to claim credit.[18] According to Charles Richardson, who saw a lot of him in Italy, 'he chose good subordinates and he was a leader. He got people to work for him enthusiastically, and they admired him, whether they were US, British, French, Indian, New Zealanders or whatever.' Major-General A. F. (John) Harding, who later served as Alexander's Chief of Staff, felt the trust that Alexander inspired in Churchill was a vital factor in the prosecution of the war, but that his tactical and strategic ability was dependent on his subordinates.[19] 'Bill' Williams felt 'this terrific stuff about Alex as a strategist was really tosh. He wasn't a strategist. He had some extremely able chaps working for him, but his real gift was his personal appearance on the battlefield, seeing what was necessary and getting it sorted out.' Montgomery was often incredibly rude, but the great thing about Alexander, according to Brigadier Sidney Kirkman, Montgomery's later artillery chief, was that he was 'very charming, very sensible and he saw Monty was likely to win this battle. He saw that he was saddled with Monty . . . There was no object in having a row . . . To the end they remained amiable, and laughing together. But in point of fact Monty had no respect for Alex, and Alex disliked Monty.'[20] Certainly Alexander was not inclined to dabble in the detail of Eighth Army's affairs, being prepared to leave those entirely to Montgomery – who would in any case have deeply resented any intrusion, especially had it come from Churchill. Instead, the Prime Minister's prodding, irritating notes were dealt with by the languid Alexander, who shielded Montgomery's back.[21]

On 8 August the Eighth Army staff officer Colonel Ian Jacob was given the unpleasant task of informing Auchinleck of his relief from command: 'I felt as if I were going to murder an unsuspecting friend,' he later recalled. But Auchinleck took the news with characteristic stoicism, refusing the move to Persia–Iraq, having always maintained that dismissed officers should not be re-employed.[22] He left Eighth Army Headquarters on 10 August, but then informed Alexander that he did not wish to hand over until the 15th. Alexander agreed, loth to be ungentlemanly, which meant that when Montgomery arrived on the 12th (Churchill having resisted his appointment on the basis that he could not arrive in time) he found he was three days early. Not that he was embarrassed in the slightest: he went to GHQ to meet Auchinleck, who spoke with the gravitas of Commander-in-Chief, which, he informed Montgomery, he would remain to the end of the week.[23]

Harding, who was then Deputy Chief of General Staff at Cairo, left an illuminating description of meeting Montgomery for the first time. Summoned on 12 August to meet the new Commander-in-Chief, he went into the office to find Montgomery in the chair and Alexander sitting on the desk drumming his heels. Montgomery introduced Harding to Alexander, and then asked in great detail about the army – down to brigade commanders – before asking if two desert-trained armoured divisions and a mobile infantry division could be assembled.

'And hold the front too, presumably?' asked Harding. 'Yes, of course.' Harding said he thought they could.[24] Only now did Montgomery realize he was in the invidious position of being unable to implement changes because his predecessor was still there. So, having bought some appropriate clothing, he decided to visit his new command the following day.

Montgomery later claimed that the plans he found in place were based on a withdrawal to the Nile. Admittedly, Auchinleck was determined to keep Eighth Army 'in being', and contingency plans for withdrawal existed, but he fully intended to fight whenever the Axis forces attacked again. However, Eighth Army was undoubtedly in a general mood of dour dissatisfaction. It was cynical of authority, and individual formations were doubtful of the martial abilities of any but themselves. News that Auchinleck was to be replaced was greeted by some with even more bitterness than already existed throughout the army. Few had heard of the new general coming out from Britain, who would not in any case have desert experience. No doubt the same mistakes would be made again, and paid for in Eighth Army blood.[25]

On 13 August Montgomery visited Eighth Army for the first time – the same day that Pedestal saved Malta. He was met by de Guingand, who was now Brigadier General Staff (BGS) of Eighth Army. Harding had suggested to Montgomery that Eighth Army was looking over its shoulder and thinking only in terms of retreat. Charles Richardson also thought so: 'If you'd spoken to the front-line soldier you'd have got the answer: "there's no question of retreat"; but, the higher up you got, the more the idea of a strategic withdrawal seemed probable.'[26] It was at these levels that Montgomery made his strongest impression.

Montgomery was at first unsure whether to retain de Guingand as BGS, especially as his preferred method was to employ a Chief of Staff after the German fashion, who would have absolute authority in the commander's name in his absence. His initial plan was to bring out Brigadier Frank Simpson, who had worked for him at 9th Infantry Brigade, V and XII Corps, if the War Office would release him. However, de Guingand impressed him – as Harding had done the day before – giving 'a first-class review of the situation and the causes of it – with nothing held back', Montgomery later recalled. 'We sat close together with a map on our knees and he told me the story; the operational situation, the latest intelligence about the enemy, the generals commanding the various sectors, the existing orders of Auchinleck for future action, his own view of things.'[27] De Guingand expressed his doubts about the policy of mobile brigades and battle groups and the lack of army/air-force co-operation. It was to prove the start of a long and fruitful partnership.

At Eighth Army Headquarters Montgomery was met by the acting commander, Ramsden, whom de Guingand had earlier referred to as 'bloody useless'. Montgomery was equally unimpressed with the harsh conditions, designed so that the staff would be no more comfortable than the men. His first action was to have the senior officers' mess – a wire cage designed to keep out flies – torn down. 'A meat-safe?' he said. 'Take it down at once and let the poor flies out.'[28] He then sent Ramsden back to XXX Corps. 'He seemed surprised . . . but he went.' Having assumed de-facto command, Montgomery sat down to lunch, 'during which I did some savage thinking'.[29] Afterwards he sent two messages: the first that the 'Army Commander requires best available soldier servant in Middle East to be sent . . . at once', and, by way of explanation, a second that 'Montgomery assumed command of Eighth Army at 1400 hours today.'[30] Having thus usurped his position two days early, he decided to make himself scarce and went to visit Freyberg, then acting commander of XIII Corps. He told de Guingand to send a message to all units cancelling all plans and orders for withdrawal and to summon the entire army staff for that evening.

Montgomery moved on to see 2nd New Zealand Division, where he commented on the lack of saluting. Freyberg replied that if he waved the men would probably wave back. He then wasted no time before pointing out that numerous senior officers had been 'sacked because they put their trust in "Jock" columns, the brigade group battle, and the Crusader tank'. Much to Freyberg's relief Montgomery agreed. In fact Freyberg expressed his absolute confidence in Montgomery precisely because the New Zealander had heard comments which were obviously intended to be critical but which made Montgomery appear to be of forceful if unorthodox character. Brigadier Kippenburger recalled Montgomery's first appearance among the hard-bitten Kiwis: 'He talked sharply and curtly, without any soft words, asked some searching questions . . . and left me feeling very stimulated. For a long time we had heard little from Army except querulous grumbles that the men should not go about without their shirts on . . . or things of that sort. Now we were told we were going to fight.'[31]

New Zealand was suffering a manpower crisis, and plans to form an armoured brigade were hampered by a serious need for reinforcements. When Montgomery learned this, he told Freyberg that as soon as possible 2nd New Zealand Division would be released from the front line for training and reorganization with a British armoured brigade until its own became available.[32] Consequently it was assigned 9th Armoured Brigade, which until a year previously had been 4th Cavalry Brigade, had only recently been mechanized, and had never seen battle. Commanded by Brigadier John Currie, it had spent the summer in arduous training near Cairo, without much equipment, which did little to make the new brigadier popular with his junior officers. But Currie had seen the results of untrained troops in battle, and he knew his brigade was destined for a difficult task. One of Freyberg's first acts after the reorganization was to hold a dinner in Alexandria for senior officers from 2nd New Zealand Division and 9th Armoured Brigade, and a great deal of reserve was broken down. The Kiwi fern-leaf emblem was painted on to the tanks, and from then on the two formations trained and exercised together.[33]

Montgomery, like Rommel, was a product of his First World War experiences, although these were very different from those of his opponent. If Rommel was an artist, Montgomery was an artisan. While Rommel lived off the memory of Monte Matajur, Montgomery had served most of the war on the staff – although at that stage he had not attended Staff College, so his experiences were entirely first-hand and unfiltered. His models for future operations were the meticulously planned battles of Sir Herbert Plumer – arguably the best British general of the First World War – particularly Messines Ridge in 1917, when artillery preparation was at its most thorough and well co-ordinated. The fundamental lesson implanted by Plumer was planning on a realistic basis: that if troops are well trained and given limited and identifiable objectives, and supported by the full weight of all available artillery intelligently brought to bear, then there is nothing that the enemy can do but withdraw. Plumer's three autumn attacks were models of this, and very successful (only later did the army become bogged down in the mud of Passchendaele).[34] Interestingly, de Guingand, who served Montgomery for longer and in a more intimate position than any other officer, felt that Montgomery was far more impetuous than is commonly supposed. His early life had been marked by rashness (he was nearly cashiered from Sandhurst following a serious bullying incident), but Montgomery had then imposed on himself an iron discipline and total professionalism which would ultimately take him to the top. However, if rashness overtook his studious application to detail (as at Arnhem in 1944), or his impulses overcame iron discipline, then the result was either failure or mediocrity.[35]

The German view was expressed by Rommel's intelligence officer, Major Friedrich von Mellenthin: 'Auchinleck was an excellent strategist with many of the qualities of a great commander, but he seems to have failed in tactical detail, or perhaps in ability to make his subordinates do what he wanted.' Indeed, if Auchinleck failed it was through being unable to impose a strict army plan on to his disparate force – a problem compounded by his staff being less than efficient. His offensives during July were 'costly, unsuccessful, and, from the tactical point of view, extremely muddled'. Montgomery on the other hand was 'undoubtedly a great tactician – circumspect and thorough in making his plans, utterly ruthless in carrying them out'.[36]

Certainly Montgomery was appalled by the state of affairs he found at Eighth Army Headquarters, writing in his diary that 'certain orders had been issued about the withdrawal, but they were not very definite and no one seemed clear as to exactly what was to be done. There was an air of uncertainty and a lack of "grip". Army HQ was completely out of touch with Air HQ Western Desert.'[37] He quickly grasped what others in less influential positions and many of the troops themselves had dimly perceived: that offensive operations were doomed until Eighth Army learned to fight as a single body with a common mission and clear, unequivocal orders.[38]

There soon came into existence a legend that, overnight, Montgomery transformed a beaten and dispirited army into a new model variety – like his hero Oliver Cromwell. A counter-legend also developed, particularly in the period after the war, that Montgomery was no more than a showman executing other people's plans. Neither is true. Certainly he was 'lonely, limited by the single-mindedness of his military obsession, jealous, suspicious or contemptuous of his contemporaries and seniors, [and] unable to show tenderness now that [his wife, who had died in 1937] was no longer alive'.[39] But that Montgomery immedi-ately made a strong impression, certainly on senior officers, cannot be denied. Another legend that has since grown to maturity is that by this time Eighth Army was hopelessly dispirited and had completely lost faith in its commanders. In fact few parts of the army had lost faith in themselves or even in their commanders. The army was not beaten or dispirited: it just wanted to be led to victory. Many blamed defeat on inferior equipment, but, while in some cases there was justification in this, in many there was not – certainly not to the degree popularly accepted then and since. The greatest tendency was to blame other arms or formations, and the total domination of the higher commands and staffs by British personnel certainly did nothing to smooth inter-Commonwealth relations.[40] Criticism of the armour by the infantry was fashionable if not always justified – not that the armoured formations in Eighth Army had performed well. Recently, the delaying effect of the extensive minefields meant that armoured formations were repeatedly late. Creating gaps in these obstacles was the responsibility of the infan-try formations that the armour was to support, and for clear command and control it was essential that the armour took responsibility for its

own minefield gaps and be given the trained men and equipment for the
job – something that Montgomery would in due course bring about.[41]

In the summer of 1942 Montgomery was an unknown quantity
outside the British Army and little known within it – certainly to ordinary soldiers – but at least he was untainted by defeat. But 'Monty', as he
would soon be known throughout the Western world, had learned a lot
about the public mood in the two years he had spent in the UK since
the debacle at Dunkirk, and the British Army was now dominated by
civilians in uniform. 'Such men are educated,' he wrote later, 'they can
think, they can appreciate. They want to know what is going on and
what the general wants them to do, and why; they want to see and
decide in their own minds what sort of person he is. I have never
believed in dealing with soldiers by a process of "remote control"; they
are human beings and their lives are precious.' So Montgomery
resolved to let his men see him as often as possible, and he would tell
them what he wanted them to do. He decided that the morale of the
army needed building up, and he consciously set about doing this, dis-
playing a less formal attitude to most senior officers and becoming less
concerned with parade-ground etiquette but instead giving short
punchy pep talks in his strange, high-pitched, yet earnest voice, when
his intense gaze left men with the strong impression that he meant
business.[42] On the evening of 13 August 1942 Montgomery stood on
the steps of his caravan and addressed his new staff for the first time.
Most of them were cynical of his chances of success. He had not 'got
sand in his shoes' – his long shorts revealed that his knees were certainly not yet brown – and he would be the fourth Army Commander
in the last twelve months. What he had to offer and how he would put
an end to the dreary series of defeats at the hands of the Germans was
not immediately apparent. Now, as the desert sun slowly started to slip
down the horizon, he laid it on the line. De Guingand remembered the
effect as 'electric – it was terrific! And we all went to bed that night with
new hope in our hearts, and a great confidence in the future of our
Army.'[43]

'I want first of all to introduce myself to you,' Montgomery snapped.

> You do not know me. I do not know you. But we have to work together;
> therefore we must understand each other and we must have confidence in
> each other. I have only been here a few hours. But from what I have seen and
> heard since I arrived I am prepared to say, here and now, that I have
> confidence in you. We will work together as a team and together we will gain
> the confidence of this great army and go forward to final victory in Africa . . .
> I believe that one of the first duties of a commander is to create what I call
> 'atmosphere' and in that atmosphere his staff, subordinate commanders and

troops will live and work and fight. I do not like the general atmosphere I find here. It is an atmosphere of doubt, of looking to select the next place to which to withdraw, of loss of confidence in our ability to defeat Rommel, of desperate defence measures by reserves in preparing positions in Cairo and the Delta. All that must cease! Let us have a new atmosphere . . . What is the use of digging trenches in the Delta? It is quite useless; if we must lose this position we lose Egypt; all the fighting troops now in the Delta must come here at once; and will. *Here* we will stand and fight; there will be no further withdrawal. I have ordered that all plans and instructions dealing with further withdrawal are to be burnt, and at once. We will stand and fight here. *If we can't stay here, then let us stay here dead* . . . [44]

War diaries are not necessarily the best indicators of plans and intentions. Nigel Hamilton in his biography of Montgomery goes to great lengths to show how contingency plans for withdrawal indicate Auchinleck's back-foot stance, although this is no means as clear-cut as he makes out – one could equally concentrate on the offensive ones. On the other hand, Correlli Barnett notes that when 51st (Highland) Division arrived in Egypt some time later than Montgomery it was deployed to protect the Delta and Cairo along much the same lines as in earlier plans.[45] However, at this stage, while it acclimatized and trained, the division was not under the command of Eighth Army and it remained an important responsibility of GHQ to continue contingency planning. Accordingly Lieutenant-General R. G. W. H. Stone, commanding British Troops Egypt, was instructed by GHQ to ensure that the defences were fully manned, and when the Egyptian government announced that it would not oppose enemy raiders he was forced to take over additional security responsibilities. Such precautions proved necessary: a raiding party of Italian marines was captured attempting to destroy the water pipeline and railway running west from Alexandria near the coast on 4 September.[46]

On 14 August Montgomery visited 9th Australian Division. At 24th Australian Brigade he called for and was issued with a slouch hat and a 'rising sun' badge – to which he was entitled, he said, because his father had been Bishop of Tasmania, where he was brought up until the age of 11. While Montgomery was talking to the others about hats, Morshead took Brigadier Victor Windeyer to one side and said, 'This man really is a breath of fresh air. Things are going to be different soon.'[47] Montgomery continued his tour, and on subsequent visits to units the slouch hat became festooned with badges. Eventually it was replaced with a black beret donated by Sergeant James Fraser of 6th Royal Tank Regiment, one of the crew members of his Grant command tank, with what became his trademark from then on: two badges – his general officer's cloth badge and a metal badge of the Royal Tank Regiment.[48]

News of the funny little general soon spread. When Lieutenant-Colonel Vladimir 'Popski' Peniakoff met McMasters, a regular regimental sergeant-major he knew, a somewhat blasé Popski heard Montgomery described enthusiastically:

> A short, wiry fellow with a bee in his bonnet about PT. The first thing he did when he took over was order half an hour's physical training for Army Headquarters before breakfast. Tubby brigadiers came out in their vests and *ran*! They heaved and they panted, shaking their fat paunches for everyone to see and when they couldn't make the grade they got the sack. Sacked them right and left he did, all the fat bastards!

The RSM chuckled ferociously, although his story was completely untrue – Montgomery did not make brigadiers go out for morning runs in the desert, and, although he sacked some very quickly after his arrival, it was not 'right and left'. But that did not matter: the 'Monty' legend was starting to be created, and the troops believed it. 'A general who has the courage to sack brigadiers from the Army Staff and who knows how to evoke enthusiastic devotion in the hearts of regular sergeant-majors,' Popski thought, 'will have no difficulty in defeating Rommel – *or even in winning the war*!'[49]

However, the replacement of one army commander by another meant little to many soldiers. 'Generals is generals' to Private Thomas Atkins, and Eighth Army had known too many changes to have immediate faith in another red cap band. What soldiers respond to is success, and the confused nature of war means that they little understand, or care, how it is achieved. Success would establish Montgomery's credibility, and he now had an opportunity to achieve it as Rommel's next attack was known to be looming.[50] Inevitably, he attracted an element of ridicule: after one address in which he invoked, as he frequently did, 'the Lord, Mighty in Battle', one young officer blandly inquired whether He could be presumed to be under command or merely in support.[51] But Montgomery's sincerity and clarity of purpose won the loyalty and enthusiasm of most. 'He told us everything,' McMasters had told Popski – 'what his plan was for the battle, what he wanted the regiments to do, what he wanted *me* to do. And we will do it sir. What a man!'[52]

It is not true that Montgomery merely took over Auchinleck's plans for the subsequent battle of Alam Halfa, nor that he simply modified them a little.[53] 'The essence of the defensive plan,' wrote Auchinleck later, 'was fluidity and mobility.'[54] Barnett claims that Montgomery adopted Gott's plan for XIII Corps, but Montgomery noted in his diary that Gott's plan 'was very bad and if it had been put into effect I consider the Eighth Army would have been defeated'.[55] In XXX Corps's area to the north, 'defended localities' were to have been held by two infantry battalions with one field and one anti-tank battery, between which 'battle groups' were to manoeuvre.[56] But the essence of 'manoeuvre warfare' is the manoeuvring of masses, not masses of manoeuvring – at which Eighth Army had already proved to be not very adept, for a variety of reasons. Unable substantially to alter the army's dispositions in the short space of time available, Montgomery's plan was the complete opposite: the army would stand firm in its positions and fight where it stood. Kippenburger noted that previously 'we did not know whether we would fight where we stood, or in the reserve positions, or run away'.[57] Now, with Montgomery's immediate issue of orders, they did. As early as the evening of 13 August, Montgomery had demanded the immediate release of 44th (Home Counties) Division from GHQ, although it had been in Egypt for only three weeks and was unacclimatized and not fully trained. 'If that's what Monty wants, let him have it,' said Alexander – setting a precedent he was to follow for many months – and the following day the New Zealanders were given orders to mine themselves in and be reinforced by one brigade from the new division, while the remainder of the division would take responsibility for the Alam Halfa area.[58]

Montgomery also began the process of introducing 'his' people into positions of command and staff appointments, with Lieutenant-General Brian Horrocks (who had formerly commanded 44th (Home Counties) Division under Montgomery in England) taking command of XIII Corps. This was a bold step, since Horrocks's last command in the field had been during the debacle in France in 1940 and he had since been commanding training formations in Britain. When Horrocks arrived in Cairo on 15 August he met Alexander, who was charming but vague, remembered Horrocks. 'All he said was, "Monty has some great plan for driving the Germans out of Egypt. I don't know what it is, but you are to take part in it, and I'm letting him get on with it." ' Alexander indicated that Horrocks was required for command of X Corps as and when the new American tanks arrived to equip it, but Horrocks declined this, according to his memoirs, on the basis that he did not have the experience or, coming from the Middlesex Regiment, a pedigree acceptable to the cavalry.[59] He was then summoned by Montgomery to Eighth Army Headquarters and appointed to command XIII Corps, which would have the decisive role in the forthcoming defensive battle. He was given instructions to defend Alam Halfa Ridge with guns and dug-in tanks. The cavalry were not to be allowed to run forward on to the German guns, but the panzers would be lured on to those of the British instead – a case, Montgomery told Horrocks, of 'dog eat rabbit'.[60]

7

Alam Halfa

Oh they've shifted father's grave to build a se-wer,
They've shifted it regardless of expense.
They've shifted his remains
just to lay some bloody drains,
To glorify some Toff's new res-i-dence.
Gor Bli-mey!

Eighth Army song

During August the Germans dropped leaflets on 9th Australian Division saying, 'Aussies! The Yankees are having a jolly good time in your country. And you?' These were eagerly gathered up as mementoes or posted home.[1] Other souvenirs included service records or booklets such as *Der Soldat in Libyen*, and even personal papers, and it was evident that the Germans had similar tastes – the British found many Russian items obviously taken from the Eastern Front.[2] A commonly collected souvenir among Eighth Army was paybooks. 'Germans set great store on their paybooks,' recalled Keith Douglas. 'Page four records all the essential details of their existence – if they lose page four they feel they have lost their hold on life.'[3]

In the middle of August Churchill visited Eighth Army Headquarters again, and was delighted by the new spirit. Montgomery made a presentation, insisting that the first week in October was the earliest he could consider opening the offensive; he was also at pains to stress that the battle would not be quick or easy, and that it would take some seven days to achieve the breakthrough. These two important timings would have serious repercussions later.[4] They became fixed in Churchill's mind, and he and Brooke departed on 23 August pleased with the changes they had made. However, once he had left Egypt Churchill's fears returned, and it seemed to Brooke that Montgomery – the antithesis of Churchill's romantic ideal of a soldier – would be tolerable to the Prime Minister only so long as he produced victories. Churchill would

103

always round on Brooke when 'your Monty', as he called him, took longer to achieve these than his impatience demanded.[5]

Before leaving, Churchill had visited a number of units – including the Warwickshire Yeomanry, as Captain Clive Stoddart reported to his 'dear Pa'. Churchill described his visit to Roosevelt, saying that he had asked 'for the very best toys', and ended his speech 'by bringing out an enormous cigar like an 88mm gun and after lighting it with great care and looking straight at everyone, speaking very slowly and deliberately, said "Gentlemen – you will strike – an unforgettable blow – against the enemy. The corn will be ripe – for the sickle and – you will be the reapers." '[6] It was a good speech, which Churchill also used to his old regiment, the 4th Hussars, and elsewhere – including the DAF.

By now the DAF comprised crews from ten different countries, including the USA. In July 1942 the American 57th Fighter Group embarked on the USS *Ranger* for transfer to Africa, while 12th Bombardment Group (Medium) prepared to fly across the South Atlantic as a first leg on a journey to Egypt. By early August both groups were in their new bases and preparing for their baptism of fire. While most DAF crews were wartime-trained, with only a small leavening of experienced and long-service personnel, the Americans were thoroughly trained regulars with many flying hours, albeit as yet no combat experience. Recognizing this lack, they were eager to learn and were accordingly attached to DAF units in the front line – 12th Bombardment Group in entirety to 3rd Wing South African Air Force, and 64th and 66th Fighter Squadrons to different RAF wings. These fighter squadrons flew their first operational sorties on 8 August, and the bombers eight days later. A third fighter squadron, the 65th, joined in September, and by the beginning of the offensive it was sufficiently experienced to fly as a group in its own right, while the B-25 Mitchells of the bombardment group took a regular hand in providing the formations of 18 aircraft that both sides found such a memorable feature of the battles.[7]

Montgomery was 'as fully insistent, as was Air Vice-Marshal [Arthur] Coningham, [AOC DAF] that [the headquarters of Eighth Army and DAF] should be together', and on 16 August he moved his HQ further back to Burg el Arab to collocate with Advanced Air HQ to ensure that 'the senior officers mess together in the same Mess'. As a result, 'Mary' Coningham (he was a New Zealander, and his nickname was a corruption of 'Maori') said that 'never before had he had such a clear and concise exposition of the military situation and needs during his experience in the Western Desert'.[8] A high standard of co-operation was achieved once more, and this had a considerable effect on future operations – and was to prove in sharp contrast to relations between Rommel and successive Fliegerführer Afrika, never cordial and now, with Generalmajor Hoffman von Waldau, positively acidic.[9] This was a feature of the war that would dog Rommel until his death, and already the strain was beginning to show. During a visit by Generale di Corpo d'Armata Giuseppe de Stefanis, commander of the Italian XX Corps, de Stefanis, who always accepted the danger of air raids with fatalistic calm, was astonished to see Rommel leap nervously to his feet and invite his guest to join him in a nearby dugout when anti-aircraft guns opened up nearby. Having admired Rommel's courage throughout the previous 15 months, the Italian, who was something of a psychologist, felt that Rommel had been driven to the brink of nervous exhaustion; he was obviously not cut out for this caravan-cum-office existence with papers floating everywhere and telephone calls constantly bringing bad news and frustration. If Rommel was to be himself again, thought de Stefanis, he should get back to real fighting.[10]

Rommel knew that this was the only theatre where British troops were actively engaged, and that they were being reinforced as quickly as the 45-day journey around the Cape of Good Hope would permit. The appearance of American equipment suggested that full-scale American involvement could not be far away, and he therefore decided he had no real alternative but to attack at the earliest opportunity. With typical energy, he set to work to create a strike force, and had no option but to accept promises of supply.[11] The situation in Russia may also have affected Rommel's thinking, by creating the prospect of a drive through the Caucasus. On 8 August, German troops occupied Maikop in the Caucasus oilfields, and on the 25th they planted their flag atop its highest peak, while on the 21st advanced guards had reached the Volga near Stalingrad – although it was not apparent at the time that this would prove the high-water mark of the advance.[12]

As the front grew more solid and defences became fixed on both sides, Rommel allocated sectors to Italian formations for administrative purposes and integrated German infantry tightly into their structure, almost to the point of a platoon per Italian company, so that he and his commanders could exercise close control. As Panzerarmee had been brought perilously close to its limit of endurance after Eighth Army's Manhood operation, a passive defence had to be adopted to enable a build-up of reserves, though this amounted to only a trickle of manpower with no quantities of heavy weapons, food, ammunition or fuel arriving.[13]

Axis reinforcement was provided by 500 transport aircraft that brought a total of 22,900 men for the army in April, May and June and a further 6,600 for the Luftwaffe (including anti-aircraft units). In July and August a total of 36,200 men arrived, including the 164th Division and the Ramcke Parachute Brigade. But even as the Pedestal battle raged few Italian merchantmen dared put to sea, and the heavy stores Rommel needed could only be brought over by ship.[14] Consequently, Ramcke's parachutists had to be flown in, and were then ferried to the front line crammed into whatever spare space they could find among the supply vehicles – an exhausting way to travel – arriving without artillery and even short of field kitchens, so that their daily supply and normal transport needs could be met only by constant improvisation.[15] The Italian Pavia and Sabratha Divisions, which had been rendered inoperational by the July battles (although they were retained in the order of battle as a deception measure), were replaced with the tough Folgore Parachute Division, and the Bologna Division marched 400 miles from Gazala in July heat that was like some biblical curse, being reviewed by Mussolini on the way. The Pistoia Division was also brought over, but was retained in Libya to protect communications, while Rommel growled at each new decoration or exhortation he received that 'I'd rather it was a fresh division, or tanks, or petrol . . .'[16]

Following Auchinleck's narrow failure to snap his extended and vulnerable line in July, Rommel considered whether to withdraw the mainly Italian non-mobile formations to Libya, to ease the demand for supplies. 'The British excelled at static warfare,' wrote von Mellenthin later, 'while in mobile operations Rommel had proved himself master in the field . . . But Hitler would never have accepted a solution that involved giving up ground, and so the only alternative was to try and go forward to the Nile, while we still had the strength to make the attempt.'[17] Besides, Rommel was unimpressed by the changes taking place on the British side: 'the situation is changing daily to my advantage', he wrote to his wife on 10 August. Convinced of the amateurishness of Eighth Army, he proceeded with his plans with a lack of reconnaissance that had been a hallmark of Panzerarmee operations from the earliest days. He planned to fight a decisive battle behind the British front, similar to the Gazala battle, 'in a form in which the great aptitude of our troops for mobile warfare and the high tactical skill of our commanders could compensate for our lack of material strength'. He heard from agents in Cairo that the British expected a great convoy to arrive at the beginning of September, and therefore held off until the last possible moment to give maximum time for preparations, unaware that every minute favoured the defenders with their new plan.[18]

*

For Rommel, August was a frustrating month made worse by poor health. However hard he tried, he could persuade neither the Italian nor the German High Command to improve his supply situation. In the past he had always achieved so much with so little that the German High Command, whose gaze was firmly fixed on the drive through the southern USSR towards Stalingrad, and among whom Rommel had no friends to plead his case, dismissed his demands as exaggerated. Hitler was the one man who could have solved most of Rommel's problems, but, now that the drive on Suez had stalled and the African theatre was overshadowed by the momentous events taking place in Russia, the Führer's personal interest in Africa had waned.

Rommel's constant complaints to Rome did, however, have some justification. For all that shipping losses in July had been light, only 6,000 tons had been landed – a fifth of his stated requirements. Captured ammunition was of use only with captured guns, and only limited amounts of German and Italian arms could be brought in through the port of Tobruk, which could handle only some 600 tons a day – a tiny fraction of his needs – and was subject to constant air attack. Also, the almost continuous battles of July had quickly used up the supplies he had captured at Tobruk. There were two Italians in the desert for every German, but during August the German element received only 8,200 tons of supplies (32 per cent of what had been asked for) compared to 25,700 tons shipped for the Italians.[19] Admittedly this figure included 800 tons for civilian requirements, and the Luftwaffe also received 8,500 tons. Nevertheless, the allocation disproportionately favoured the Italians and, while his own 164th Division was reduced to just 60 vehicles, Rommel must have been less than delighted to see the Pistoia Division arrive in Libya with nearly 400 vehicles when it was not even intended for service at the front.[20]

Rommel's view of the situation appears in his letters to his wife, 'Dearest Lu'. At the end of July he blamed Italian self-interest rather than inefficiency, and hoped for assistance from von Rintelen, who 'lets himself be done in the eye, for the Italian supplies are working excellently'. But, as liaison officer, von Rintelen was more concerned with political considerations than with supplies, and, as the Italians continued to promise much but deliver little, so did he. After receiving promises from Kesselring, Rommel proposed to OKW that Kesselring be given special powers to control Mediterranean shipping, although his suggestion was not acted on in the form he wanted. Many in Panzerarmee blamed Kesselring, the representative of the High Command, for the supply problems. 'Smiling Albert' was an optimist who has been accused of playing safe – offering no criticism while

Rommel was successful, so that he could share the glory, but not sticking out his neck for him so that he could avoid any blame should Rommel fail. Shortly before a conference with Kesselring and Cavallero on 27 August, Rommel wrote that Kesselring 'gets plenty of promises, but few are kept. His over-optimism concerning these blighters has brought bitter disappointments.'[21]

Ultra had revealed to the British that a comprehensive supply survey by Panzerarmee on 20 August showed that fuel consumption had exceeded receipts by 4,600 tons since the beginning of the month, and this inside information led to a policy of attacking supply lines on a scale not seen since the previous autumn.[22] The sinking of the tanker *Pozarica* by the RAF on 23 August reduced the Italians to begging fuel from the Germans, and an ambitious shipping programme was disrupted by an attack on the Corinth Canal after Ultra had provided details on the 26th.[23] Knowing, as he must have, that only a fundamental change in the strategic situation would raise Rommel in the High Command's priorities, Kesselring should perhaps have explained this to Rommel in plain language. Instead he prevaricated, and even promised to fly in 400 tons of fuel 'in an emergency' – another promise that Rommel ruefully noted he was 'unfortunately unable to keep'. He did try, however: the Luftwaffe lifted some 200 tons of petrol, but less than 50 was delivered – the balance being consumed on the journey, as Oberstleutnant Siegfried Westphal, the DAK operations officer, had noted it would be.[24] On 28 August, Ultra reported that the 5,077-ton tanker *San Andrea* was loading fuel for Panzerarmee at Taranto and would arrive at Tobruk on 3 September. The next message, recorded at 2139 hours on 30 August, was that she had been torpedoed and set on fire together with the transport ships *Picci, Fassio, Istria* (carrying the heavy equipment for 164th Division), *Dielpi* and *Camperio*.[25]

By the end of August, although Rommel's fuel situation remained critical, the tank strength of Panzerarmee had been carefully nursed back up. But no less than 85 per cent of his motor transport was of British origin, and naturally spares for this were extremely rare.[26] Indeed, even were his attack to succeed it remained doubtful whether he really could reach the Delta, even though he had always managed to get by somehow in the past. In fact at no other stage in the campaign were the odds so apparently evenly balanced. The Axis had some 500 tanks (of which 234 were German) against an Eighth Army strength of 478 (many of which were obsolescent – 117 Valentines, 139 Honeys, 136 Crusaders and 15 Matildas). However, Montgomery sat with a secure base behind him (for which he never gave his predecessors the slightest credit) and was steadily reinforced with manpower and equipment – including 6-pounder anti-tank guns. Through Ultra, he also had access to top-grade intelligence on the enemy's situation and thinking.

Montgomery had acted instinctively in choosing his means of defence, but on 17 August Ultra presented him with an appreciation of the situation drawn up by Rommel himself, including Rommel's plan to attack at the end of August using the traditional desert hook before the British could be properly reinforced.[27] The staff officer in charge of Ultra decrypts, 'Bill' Williams, later recounted how Montgomery 'had uncomfortably piercing eyes, and his questions, in a sharp spinsterly voice, were much to the point... He won [Alam Halfa] by accepting the intelligence with which he was furnished [and] because the intelligence proved adequate then, he believed it afterwards.' Thus Montgomery's talent was not the ability to read his enemy's mind but the more tangible application of professionally sound military judgement – although his ego would later prefer the legend.[28] Confirmation that his instinct was sound gave Montgomery the confidence to present what would be a modest tactical success as a strategic victory of the first order – the first step down the long path to hubris.

The Axis offensive was expected around the time of the full moon at the end of August. On 23 August Montgomery decided to launch a diversionary raid in the north towards the vulnerable Axis supply lines as soon as the offensive opened. It would be made by 20th Australian Brigade, which would secure a firm base from which an armoured force could raid the main tracks leading south from Sidi Abd el Rahman. The operation was code-named Bulimba. Its purpose was obscure, but one reason for it was undoubtedly to act as a 'test' before the autumn offensive, for it was to be launched in the area where on 15 August Montgomery had told Horrocks that he would make the main effort.[29] Meanwhile the DAF kept up an unbroken series of attacks – not only on the coastal road, where traffic was heaviest, but all over the desert.[30] When there ensued a delay beyond the full-moon period beginning on 26 August which British intelligence estimated would be Rommel's start date, additional armour and artillery was added to the southern sector, and this also enabled 8th Armoured Brigade from 10th Armoured Division to be brought up.

According to Lieutenant Brian O'Kelly, the newly arrived Horrocks looked like 'a country town family solicitor at a tennis party, with a gay silk neckerchief in the Desert Rat tradition and his knees already commendably brown. He exuded confidence and competence.'[31] But what followed was 'about the most difficult time I had in the war', recalled Horrocks. Freyberg queried every order he issued – resentful, Horrocks believed, at being passed over for another junior British general.

Furthermore, the armour jibbed at being told to act statically. When Major-General Callum Renton, commanding 7th Armoured Division – Eighth Army's only armoured division available for the battle – argued about who would give the order to 'loose' the armour at Rommel, Montgomery had to tell him firmly that armour was not going to be 'loosed'. Montgomery then backed Horrocks when the latter took 22nd Armoured Brigade from Renton and placed it directly under command of XIII Corps.[32] Christened 'Egypt's Last Hope' by Horrocks, it was equipped with the sum total of Grant tanks remaining to Eighth Army. The brigade's commander, Brigadier G. P. B. 'Pip' Roberts, was then ordered to prepare positions on Alam Halfa. Roberts cancelled the code words (typical hunting metaphors) and issued orders that his brigade was 'to take up an impenetrable position' reinforced with anti-tank guns, where 'it is hoped that for once the enemy may have to attack us in good positions of our own choosing'.[33]

At 1020 hours on 30 August, sentries from 2/17th Battalion found a British soldier with a remarkable story to tell. He was Private A. G. Evans of 1st Sherwood Foresters, who had escaped from Tobruk after its capture and had made his way eastward by surviving on scraps of food he found in searching old dugouts and helped by Arabs. 'Nobody took any notice of me,' he said, 'although on one occasion I went by mistake into a German camp, but I had an Italian water bottle and made a movement with my hands that I had seen Italians make, they did not stop me.' He had spent the previous fortnight in the area opposite 2/17th's positions trying to slip across, and had finally made it; he was now able to provide detailed information about the objective of Bulimba.[34] Montgomery spent the same day writing his general training policy for his own forthcoming major offensive, which was issued the next day. As the absence of the expected Axis attack seeming to indicate that this had been cancelled, he began considering the withdrawal of the New Zealanders, and went to bed as usual at 2200 hours. Later, when an Axis attack had begun and the BGS was convinced that this was indeed the offensive, not merely a series of raids, de Guingand went to inform the Army Commander that the battle had begun. 'Excellent, excellent,' murmured Montgomery, who turned over and went back to sleep.[35]

Had he attacked three weeks earlier, Rommel would have found Alam Halfa Ridge defended by two weak battalions of 21st Indian Brigade with 16 25-pounders and 16 6-pounders, while Eighth Army would have been engaged in withdrawing its front-line infantry and dividing into battle groups. He would not have been held up on unexpectedly dense minefields, and his original intention to drive beyond the ridge on to El Hammam might have been possible. Instead, the attackers were delayed by the need to clear mines, were bombed incessantly, and found 'a cockiness about the enemy's reactions that augured ill for us'.[36] In fact Eighth Army had been stood to from midnight on 24 August in expectation.[37] Rommel knew Alam Halfa had been fortified and expected a 'severe fight', but its capture would enable him to dominate Eighth Army as he had done by capturing the Knightsbridge box during the Gazala battle; it was 'the key to the whole El Alamein position'.[38] However, the DAF was now in a position to intervene in an unprecedented fashion and, while the sinking of fuel-supply vessels proved conclusive in halting his drive, the pounding he now received once he found himself limping through the minefields was something which would haunt the remainder of his career. The DAF flew 482 sorties on 31 August, 674 on 1 September, 806 on 2 September, and 902 on 3 September.[39] The continuous and very heavy attacks 'absolutely pinned my troops to the ground and made impossible any safe deployment or any advance according to schedule', recorded Rommel.[40]

During the night of 30/31 August, XXX Corps was attacked by the Ramcke Parachute Brigade. Elsewhere Commonwealth troops had clashes, but on XIII Corps's front there were three major enemy thrusts – north of Himeimat, at Munassib, and immediately south of the New Zealanders. Rommel's plan required a rapid penetration of the minefields in the area on the first night, so that the armoured formations would be through by 0330 hours and facing north, ready to drive forward at first light. Immediately the plan fell foul of minefields much thicker than Axis intelligence had anticipated. It was a bad night for the Germans. Their 3rd Reconnaissance Battalion reported being under air attack from 2130 to 0345 hours 'with a short respite from 0200 to 0215 hours'.[41] At around 0630 hours, as a lurid blood-red dawn rose laden with menace, the pioneers were still trying to create gaps as the DAF took swift action to bomb the struggling transport columns, and by 0800 hours Rommel knew his plan was in serious difficulty. Generalleutnant Walter Nehring, commanding DAK, had been wounded, as had Generalmajor Ulrich Kleeman, commanding 90th Light Division; Generalmajor Georg von Bismarck, commanding 21st Panzer Division, had been killed and Rommel's forces remained stalled under heavy fire. Rommel now directed his assault at Alam Halfa rather than to the east of it as originally intended. As the Axis armour debouched from the minefield gaps, they made little progress under constant air attack. Rommel knew that, with surprise gone, he had to bring the British armoured forces on his left flank to a decisive action.

At 1300 hours, after a refuelling stop, the panzers moved forward once more – this time covered by a sandstorm. They came on towards 22nd Armoured Brigade at the western end of Alam Halfa Ridge.[42]

'Pip' Roberts noted with alarm the appearance of Panzer Mark IV Specials,* bearing the new long-barrelled 75 mm gun. He had three regiments deployed, with 1st Royal Tank Regiment on the right, 4th County of London Yeomanry in the centre, and 5th Royal Tank Regiment on the left, supported by anti-tank guns of 1st Rifle Brigade. His fourth regiment, the Royal Scots Greys, was held in reserve 2 miles away. When the Germans drove into the centre of the position, a fierce battle soon developed and engulfed the Yeomanry. Major A. A. Cameron, commanding A Squadron, recalled that the Germans opened fire well before they had reached a line of telegraph poles that marked the limit of his own tanks' effective range:

> I saw tank after tank going up in flames or being put out of action, and this included my own when the big gun became unserviceable. However, the German advance had been momentarily checked and, although in the fog of battle it was difficult to know which of their tanks had been knocked out (German tanks seldom went on fire), the great thing was that they were not coming on in front.

He raced across to report that he had lost touch with all his tanks to his commanding officer, who sent him to report to Roberts, a few hundred yards to the rear.[43] Roberts now called up the Royal Scots Greys to fill the gap created by the destruction of the Yeomanry as the panzers began to edge warily forward again, approaching a sector held by the anti-tank guns of 1st Rifle Brigade. These courageously held their fire until the range was down to some 300 yards; then, as the panzers were about to overrun the riflemen, Roberts called on the radio, 'Come on the Greys, get out your whips!' The combined weight of the divisional artillery was brought crashing down upon the panzers and suddenly the Greys appeared over the crest of a ridge to the north to fill the gap. As the light began to fade the panzers drew off.[44]

The tank battle of 31 August was the climax of Rommel's efforts to reach the Delta.[45] Rommel knew this intuitively, although the following morning DAK made another attempt to take the ridge – this time using only 15th Panzer Division, owing to petrol shortages. Unaware that the offensive was already effectively over, Montgomery reorganized his defences between Alam Halfa and the sea, bringing forward 151st Brigade from 51st (Highland) Division. He directed 8th and 23rd

---

* PanzerKampfwagen Mark IVF2

Armoured Brigades to back up the 22nd, and began to plan, rather slowly, to counter-attack with 2nd New Zealand Division.[46] Throughout 1 September the German armour was 'under constant bombardment from guns and aircraft'.[47] Rommel himself was subjected to six air attacks, and his interpreter, Wilfried Armbruster, recorded in his diary that they had 'never experienced bombing that was anything like last night. Although we were well dispersed on Hill 92, the bombs came very close . . . Our combat echelon has had many men killed, three Flak 88s were hit and several ammunition trucks.'[48]

By 0825 hours on 2 September Rommel had had enough and he ordered a withdrawal to the start line of 30 August, moving stage by stage. Kesselring could not understand what had happened, and later blamed Rommel's health for what he saw as a failure of nerve.[49]

Meanwhile, Bulimba was launched on the morning of 1 September with 2/15th Battalion given the task of securing a position for 40th Royal Tank Regiment to conduct the raids. Elaborate fire-support measures were laid on, including the entire divisional artillery and 7th Medium Regiment Royal Artillery. At 0535 hours the assault infantry set out to cross the start line, from which its operations would be deemed to begin, but came under fire approaching it. Although they advanced with great dash, resistance was determined and well organized and the tank support was once more badly co-ordinated. Corporal Horton McLachlan's section was held up, whereupon he attacked the enemy post with the bayonet, killing three Germans. Then, taking a sub-machine-gun from a wounded mate, he destroyed another post and charged a third, where, out of ammunition, he used grenades and subdued another four Germans with the butt of his tommy gun and a well-aimed boot.[50]

With Lieutenant-Colonel R. W. G. Ogle severely wounded, by 0900 hours it was obvious to his second-in-command, Major C. H. Grace, that little could be achieved and a skilful withdrawal was completed. The raid cost 2/15th Battalion 39 dead, 25 missing and 109 wounded. German casualties are unknown, but 140 were taken prisoner. More importantly, several crucial lessons had been learned: the extensively mined and wired positions that the Germans were developing could be assaulted, but 'interlocking keys of co-operation were essential, as between infantry, artillery, and armour. Such keys would have to be cut to a precision-tool scale of efficiency not previously envisaged, if the combination of Axis minefield, defensive firepower, and rapidly counter-attacking armour was to be forced. Bulimba, following on

Ruin Ridge, taught that these bitter lessons could no longer be ignored.'[51]

By the morning of 3 September the Axis forces had withdrawn into a salient south of Alam Halfa, comforted because 'The impression we gained of the new British commander ... was that of a very cautious man, who was not prepared to take any sort of risk', but hoping the new Eighth Army commander would make an error that could be quickly turned into defeat.[52] However, Montgomery in fact proposed to drive the Germans from their positions with a setpiece attack – Operation Beresford – launched out of the New Zealanders' area by one of the Kiwi brigades and 132nd (Kent) Brigade from 44th (Home Counties) Division on an arc over 10 miles. Freyberg was not happy with this plan, and strongly expressed his concern to Horrocks. Freyberg was senior even to Montgomery in the Army List, but Montgomery insisted that the plan go ahead (leaving Horrocks to tell Freyberg this). While arguments over the size and composition of the attack proceeded – Montgomery was short of infantry reserves, having only one South African brigade free behind Miteiriya Ridge to reinforce the front line[53] – it finally became apparent that Rommel's offensive was over, even if he was not yet withdrawing.[54]

Operation Beresford was launched on 3 September and, as so often happened in this period, although the planning appeared to be sound the battle did not go according to plan. Both 4th and 5th Queen's Own Royal West Kent Regiment suffered heavy casualties and were driven back in confusion. (There were 700 casualties throughout the brigade – including its inexperienced commander, who advanced too quickly and was badly wounded.)[55] Fifth New Zealand Brigade fared slightly better, with 124 casualties, although 12 of the accompanying Valentines from 50th Royal Tank Regiment were lost to mines and anti-tank fire.[56] Sixth New Zealand Brigade lost 159, including their commander, Brigadier George Clifton.* Thereafter, both Montgomery and Rommel were left incapable of influencing the battle, and, having been counter-attacked continuously all through 4 September, Freyberg decided to withdraw his battered brigades towards evening, without consulting Horrocks or Montgomery. Rommel, fearing the New Zealanders had been success-ful, ordered 21st Panzer Division forward and 15th Panzer to stand by

---

*'The Flying Kiwi' escaped a day or so later, was recaptured, and was then sent to Italy, where he escaped four times before being recaptured near the Swiss border. He was then sent to Germany, where he also escaped four times – being badly wounded in the last of these. On his ninth attempt he succeeded (Clifton, *The Happy Hunted*).

to avoid his other forces being cut off, thus halting the withdrawal of DAK, although the Italians continued to pull back.[57] But the battle was effectively over.

German losses were 1,859 killed, wounded or missing, and 113 seriously damaged panzers, of which 38 had to be abandoned, alongside 400 precious lorries and probably another 1,000 damaged.[58] The Italians lost 1,051 men and 11 tanks together with 50 guns of 47 mm calibre or greater. The British lost 67 tanks and had 1,750 men killed, wounded or missing (of whom no fewer than 1,140 were lost in the ill-fated Beresford operation). Undoubtedly it was an overall British success, although whether it was the great victory that Montgomery unilaterally proclaimed it to be when he declared the battle over on 7 September is less clear. Nevertheless, it was an important boost to the morale of Eighth Army and, according to a tank gunner of the Staffordshire Yeomanry, 'it had been a very realistic exercise!'[59]

Planning for the offensive, which Montgomery had begun even before the defensive battle, could now continue apace. Unfortunately for the British, the mistrust between infantry and armour had resurfaced. The infantry had serious misgivings about the support they could expect to receive from the armour. Conversely, the armour felt that the infantry did not understand the limitations of tanks when operating close by anti-tank guns that effectively outranged them, and certainly units still equipped with tanks mounting 2-pounders had no effective high-explosive round and needed those guns neutralized. Clearly there was much training to be done.[60] However, von Mellenthin later described Alam Halfa as 'the turning point of the desert war'.[61]

It was a failure for the Axis for three principal reasons. First was the strategic success of Allied naval and air forces in constricting Rommel's supply line (three tankers were sunk in two days). Second was the tactical superiority over the battlefield of the DAF, which Rommel himself acknowledged had a 'paralysing effect' on mechanized forces and whose true significance had not previously been apparent.[62] Before the battle, large formations of British and American medium bombers led by flare-carrying Albacores had hammered targets behind the Axis lines, including Tobruk and the Luftwaffe landing grounds. The carpet bombing of ground formations by medium bombers was a new technique that caused high casualties and was to become dolefully familiar to the German Army over the months and years to come. It had reached a peak on 3 September, when a shuttle service of Bostons, Baltimores and Mitchells (The 'Boston Tea Party') had flown dawn-to-dusk bombing missions unmolested by the Luftwaffe. By the end of the battle, the German troops had nicknamed the bomber formations 'party rallies', since they closely resembled the displays normally reserved for ceremonial occasions.

Finally there was Montgomery's determination to stick to his plan and fight a static battle from prepared positions – something that suited the forces under his command better than the Germans.[63] On 7 September the diarist of the German 135th Flak Regiment noted that 'the main object of the operation had been to force the enemy to come out and come to grips in an open tank battle. The enemy had not accepted the challenge but fought a delaying action.' Rommel remarked to Kesselring on 1 September, 'The swine isn't attacking.'[64] The absence of a concerted British counter-attack also formed the essence of the story that both sides were happy to accept: it justified Montgomery's caution, while on the Axis side the battle had been merely a 'reconnaissance in force' – a description that went some way to saving Rommel's face and to justify this 'Six-Day Race',* although British propaganda was able to make much of it as a failed drive on the Delta (and Rommel's writings betray his true intentions). Rommel had not been on the receiving end of such concentrated air attack before, and this combined with the critical shortage of fuel to prohibit effective mobile operations and blunt his efforts. The British perimeter was not breached, and no supplies could be 'got from Tommy'. For Rommel, ever the gambler, Alam Halfa was a gamble that failed.

There was now the matter of Eighth Army's offensive. The first ships of the great convoy loaded with weapons arrived in Egypt in early September, and included the first 194 Sherman tanks; the question now was whether Rommel would remain in his position or retire to a less extended position such as Fuka or Sollum. This would relieve his own supply problem and could even jeopardize Torch if Panzerarmee were not comprehensively defeated before it began. But his gaze was so firmly held by the Delta that he chose to remain in his positions, improved as they were by control of Himeimat, which the British had not attempted to hold at the end of August. 'Looking back,' wrote Kesselring after the war, 'I see it was a mistake to remain there.' He thought the Fuka position more secure – though the decision to stay put was not a political one: Rommel's prestige with Hitler was such that 'neither OKW nor the Comando Supremo would have strongly opposed any serious intention of Rommel to retire. Rommel had hitherto always found the means to get what he wanted. But he believed in the strength of the Alamein line.'[65]

Montgomery has been criticized by many people for not following

---

*After a famous cycle race – the *Sechstagenrennen*.

up the Axis withdrawal more vigorously – in particular, for not driving Rommel off Himeimat. But Rommel repeatedly assured Kesselring that he could stop even a large-scale British attack and that at Alam Halfa it would have been better for the Axis if the British had attacked prematurely and had been bled white doing so.[66] There is no reason to believe that there would have been any other outcome at this stage, though this would not have been a decisive victory for Rommel. But had Montgomery succeeded then Rommel might well have chosen to withdraw. Furthermore, Montgomery had already decided to make his main effort in the north and intended to carry out only holding operations to keep the enemy in place in the south. Thus, with a deception plan in the south already in mind, he asked what would be the point of constructing dummies there 'if the Germans cannot see them? Leave them in possession of Himeimat. That is where I want them to be.'[67]

8

Lightfoot

Victory is the bright-coloured flower. Transport is the stem
without which it could never have blossomed. The eye is fixed
on the fighting brigades as they move amid the smoke; on the
swarming figures of the enemy . . . The long, trailing line of
communications is unnoticed. The fierce glory that plays on
red, triumphant bayonets dazzles the observer, nor does he
care to look behind to where along a thousand miles of rail,
road and river, the convoys are crawling to the front in
unnoticed succession.

Winston Churchill, *The River War*, 1899

Neither the British nor Axis gave serious thought to a wide
outflanking move south of the Qattara Depression. There were
serious logistical and organizational difficulties, and, although no plans
had been worked out in detail, Dorman-Smith and Auchinleck had
already selected the northern sector of the Axis defended line as the one
to be assaulted before Montgomery took over; Montgomery, for similar
reasons, then decided likewise.[1] The strongest argument against an attack
in the south was the likelihood of an Axis withdrawal before the enemy
could be decisively engaged. Montgomery was determined to break the
pattern of see-saw fights up and down the coast by forcing Panzerarmee
to fight – and be destroyed – where it stood. Planning was therefore a
matter of choosing in which sectors to make main or secondary assaults.

Montgomery wrote that 'whatever the military plan, it is vital that the
air should be brought in from the start; it is not sufficient to decide on the
plan and then ask the RAF how it can help'. Over 500 aircraft now
equipped the DAF, against some 350 of all types deployed by the Axis in
North Africa. These latter had the advantage of rapid reinforcement
from Italy and support from Crete, and none of the Allied fighters was a
match for the Me-109F or 109G, but the DAF was operating much closer
to its forward airfields. Following the successful co-operation with the air

forces during Alam Halfa, the army and air commanders agreed on a plan to take that co-operation a step further during the forthcoming offensive. The fighter and light-bomber forces would be given a period for rest and reorganization, while the medium and heavy bombers would develop a progressive programme against the Axis supply lines.[2]

There is evidence that, early on, Montgomery and his planners considered staging holding attacks to keep the enemy in the north, with a main assault in the vicinity of Ruweisat Ridge – similar in concept to the July battles, which then evolved into simultaneous attacks by the two British infantry corps to converge once the enemy's defences were pierced. But hard facts – particularly the supply of experienced troops and equipment – led Montgomery to decide to concentrate on a relatively narrow front with a subsidiary attack in the south as a diversion. This plan admitted some of the weaknesses of British training, while offering simplicity of aim and firm control to produce unity of action.[3]

Montgomery decided that there were three essentials: equipment, leadership and training. The first was well in hand, and he had full confidence that Alexander would provide all that he possibly could. As for training, although Eighth Army was composed of magnificent material, 'it had done much fighting, but little training . . . I was not prepared to launch the troops into an all-out offensive without intensive prior training.'[4] Dorman-Smith had recognized the need for training in an appreciation of 27 July, noting that Eighth Army was not 'sufficiently well trained for offensive operations'. This had produced the conclusion that no offensive could be launched before mid-September, which in turn had led to Churchill's intervention.[5] Montgomery now insisted that no offensive would be possible before late October. He assumed responsibility for training the army, and his policy was adopted throughout it.

When Lumsden, now commanding X Corps, issued his first corps training instruction, it stated that Eighth Army Training Memorandum No. 1 should be read once a week and be carefully studied by all commanders.[6] This memorandum was extremely detailed and thorough, covering the responsibilities of all arms in what was to come. Intense, rigorous and almost continuous training was instituted for units not in the line – a problem indeed, since the line still had to be held, so training could be done only by rotation. The men had to be taught the drills for a night assault through a heavily defended position disposed in depth, and be brought to full battle fitness – notoriously one of Montgomery's pet ideas. When troops usually went out of the line to a 'rest area', recalled one Australian, they 'cynically grinned whenever they heard the words. In a rest area you either dug holes all day and guarded dumps all night or you trained all day and guarded dumps all night. This rest area was different. You trained all day and then you trained all night. Not every day and every night – but almost.'[7]

Immediately Montgomery ran into objections. The first came from Churchill, who, when he heard the proposed date of 23 October, exploded; it took all Brooke's powers to calm him. Churchill also berated Brooke, who thought Montgomery's reasons for delay were excellent, and then bombarded Alexander with cables stressing the importance of Torch. Churchill later described September and October 1942 as his most anxious months of the war.[8] Alexander spoke with Montgomery, who dictated a reply laying out the need for training and for new equipment to be fully integrated and claiming that an October operation was assured of success.[9] Although written by Montgomery, this reply was sent in Alexander's name, and it was against Alexander that Churchill railed when he received it. As one of his secretaries put it to the Director of Military Operations at the War Office, Major-General John Kennedy, 'The mistake you people make is that you think what the PM wants is a logical reasoned argument. There is nothing he dislikes more.'[10] At Brooke's insistence, Churchill promised Alexander that 'we shall back you up and see you through'; but he was aware through Ultra of Rommel's dispositions and increasing minefields, and, seriously doubting whether Montgomery could blow a hole through them, pestered Alexander continuously. Churchill was certainly under immense pressure, having promised Torch to Stalin – and this was exacerbated on 21 September when Sir Stafford Cripps announced that he wished to resign from the War Cabinet in protest at Churchill's handling of the war. Churchill managed to persuade Cripps to wait until the offensive, and bought himself a breathing space.[11] There were also concerns about Montgomery's proposed superimposing of two corps on one sector of the front.

In the matter of leadership, Lieutenant-General Sir Oliver Leese Bt was now brought in to replace Ramsden at XXX Corps. A tall former Coldstream Guardsman who had commanded the Guards Armoured Division, Leese had an easy-going manner which was well suited to winning the confidence of the Commonwealth troops he commanded, and he soon became familiar in the forward areas in his open car, which he often drove himself – very fast.[12] But Alexander overruled Montgomery's desire to replace Lumsden, although Harding was given command of 7th Armoured Division. The appointment of Leese and Lumsden, to say nothing of the inexperienced Horrocks, stoked ill feeling among the Commonwealth generals, although Morshead for one claimed that he was too bound up with his own command to bother about personal feelings. Nevertheless, following representations to Alexander and his own Commander-in-Chief in Australia, General Sir Thomas Blamey, Morshead did raise the matter with Montgomery on 13 September. Montgomery said that, because he was not a regular soldier, Morshead did not possess the necessary training or experience for corps command. Morshead noted, however, that Montgomery 'admitted he did not know me or anything about my service and said if Leese became [a] casualty during operations I would then command [the] corps. Montgomery who has revitalised Eighth Army is quite friendly but he just doubts the capacity of any general who has not devoted [his] entire life to soldiering.'[13]

Montgomery's ignorance of the superb record of citizen soldiers at corps level during the First World War (notably the Australian Sir John Monash) meant that Blamey wrote with some justification of the 'unconscious arrogance' of the British High Command. However, Morshead's comment that Montgomery had 'revitalised' Eighth Army is significant, coming as it does just a month after Montgomery had taken over – and coming from a man not easily impressed, and who was in the process of receiving an adverse comment on his own abilities.[14] The strongest claims were made on behalf of Freyberg, who was also a former Guardsman and a regular major-general, but his only exercise of independent command had been at Crete in May 1941, and this was clearly marked against him. It was not until February 1944 that he finally received the recognition of promotion to corps commander, and then only after representations had been made on his behalf by the New Zealand government. But this belies the natural tendency for those at the very top, notably Brooke in the case of Leese's appointment, to choose men known to them. (Brooke almost invariably chose men who had previously served under him, and invariably chose well.)

It was more significant that Montgomery and Lumsden did not get on, since Lumsden commanded the armoured corps.[15] Lumsden was a 12th Lancer, and Montgomery regarded the cavalry as quixotic romantics who refused to take war sufficiently seriously and failed in the essential co-operation with other arms.[16] To complicate matters, on 28 May 1940 Montgomery's 3rd Division had been guarding the left flank of the British Expeditionary Force when the French collapse left an extensive gap on his left. Lumsden, then commanding his regiment (armoured cars), had filled the gap without waiting for orders and had held off German attacks for a vital six hours until reinforcements arrived. Montgomery had felt upstaged, and never forgave him.[17]

Lumsden was tall and always immaculately presented. He had a flair for personal leadership, and could inspire strong loyalty. Major-General Raymond Briggs, commanding 1st Armoured Division, felt he was 'the very model of a born soldier'. But Lumsden was on bad terms with his other divisional commander, Alec Gatehouse, and also with Freyberg. Gatehouse was perhaps Eighth Army's most experienced senior desert fighter. He was robust and independent of mind to the point of bluntness, with a high-pitched voice and a speech impediment as familiar to the German intercept service as to the British. But his Royal Tank Regiment background did not help in the clash of personalities with the cavalryman Lumsden; he was disparaging of 'the Staff' and 'Staff College types' (Lumsden was a former instructor), whose orders he interrupted and questioned almost to the point of insubordination.[18]

Montgomery wanted Lumsden replaced, but on this occasion Alexander felt he had to draw a line: that he could not make a completely clean sweep of old desert commanders. He was supported in this by his Chief of Staff, Major-General Richard McCreery, another 12th Lancer. Montgomery wanted Horrocks to command X Corps, and McCreery 'did venture to say that it would surely be very difficult for an officer straight out from home, no matter how capable, to command an armoured corps in the desert, whereas General Lumsden had had to control at least three armoured brigades and he was the one armoured commander in whom everyone had great confidence'.[19] Montgomery made no direct reply. 'I hardly knew [Lumsden] and so could not agree with complete confidence; but I accepted him on the advice of others.'[20] It was not to prove one of Alexander's happiest decisions, because Montgomery resented it and was not prepared to try very hard to make the arrangement work – and nor, it appears, was Lumsden.[21]

However, Montgomery was ruthless in his determination to make the army efficient, to keep things simple, and as far as possible to dispel the fog of war. If communications form the lifeblood of command, good staff work is its beating heart; officers who could not stand the pressure of war would be removed. He had shown after Dunkirk a determination to see 'the right man for the right job' in command of units and throughout the staff, and this often entailed appointing people he had previously earmarked. His belief in the 'stage management' of battles required that formations train and fight together, and one of his first orders in August 1942 had made this quite clear: 'Divisions must fight as divisions and under their own commanders, with clear-cut tasks and definite objectives . . . only in this way will concentration of effort and co-operation of all arms be really effective.'[22] Now he sacked numerous brigadiers and unit commanding officers – usually when he failed to receive a satisfactory answer to who was responsible for training officers.[23] This was not always fair: as Eighth Army's senior artillery officer, Brigadier Noel Martin had bitterly resented the dispersal of his guns among battle groups and boxes, but now found himself blamed for the policy. By a cruel irony, the senior gunner at GHQ Cairo, Brigadier W. Maxwell, confirmed Martin's fate when he tried to intercede on his behalf by assuring Montgomery that Martin was a delightful person and an amateur golfing champion to boot. Both men duly vanished.[24]

Officers are not 'worshipped' by their men: the bond is more fraternal or paternal with those officers in whom the soldiers have faith. Rommel undoubtedly inspired such a bond, but Montgomery's appeal for Eighth Army at this time was quite different. The 'desert club' of officers and men by no means accepted the interloper, especially when he began sacking so many of their own. For them, the 'little man' as they called him was an upstart, an ascetic with a crusading air.[25] When Major William Mather said that he would rather be a brigade major than one of Montgomery's liaison officers, Montgomery replied, 'Well may I tell you that I'm destroying the desert trades union. And the 1st Armoured Brigade's going to become a Tank Delivery Regiment!' Mather went on to recall that Montgomery had

> moved into what was a very tight trades union operation which was governed by the 'cavalry', the Guards and the Greenjackets, and all the old sweats who thought they were very superior people. They thought they could lick the hides off the Germans if they had the right equipment and the right generals – which was in fact true . . . We were very disapproving if people came out from England – Monty in particular. Of course he broke their trades union at once – which was not an easy thing to do.[26]

There had grown up in the desert a plethora of 'private armies', too many of which were commanded by men of great imagination but little professionalism. After the grim disappointments of the early months of 1942, these private armies were swelled by the volunteering for special duties of men who, while quite prepared to risk their lives, were not prepared to have them thrown away through incompetence at the top.[27] With so many of these outfits operating behind Axis lines, a command had been formed in Alexandria to control them. There the appearance of Lieutenant-Colonel John Haselden of the Long Range Desert Group with a plan to attack the fuel-storage facilities at Tobruk was met with great enthusiasm. Soon a bemused Haselden found himself saddled with an increasingly large and complicated joint operation – Agreement. Haselden's original idea had been for a raid by no more than ten men. It would involve a party of commandos travelling disguised as British prisoners of war 'under escort' by members of the secret Special Interrogation Group – mostly German Jews who had escaped to Palestine, who would act as drivers and guards. Now other operations were planned for the same night. The Special Air Service would capture Benghazi, sink all the ships present, and destroy the oil storage; the LRDG would attack the airfield at Barce. Since all parties would escape to Kuffra, 300 miles south of Tobruk, and would have to pass the fort at Jalo, this would be captured too. In a plan and appreciation for the forthcoming major operation, dated 19 August, Montgomery, who otherwise had nothing to do with it, noted the date when Agreement was to take place (9 September, though this was later changed) and pondered whether it might not be postponed to coincide more closely with the offensive.[28] Worries at the grandiose scheme were widespread. The Royal Navy had more important things to do than land the force to attack Tobruk. The SAS had been very effective attacking airfields in small independent groups of four or five men, but was planning to commit over 200, many of them inexperienced. Worse, there was an evident lack of security – to the extent that landings were practised before the interested gaze of the Royal Egyptian Yacht Club.[29]

On the morning of 13 September the commandos under Haselden penetrated the Tobruk perimeter. Thereafter everything went wrong. Haselden was killed, and the remaining commandos were forced to surrender. The SAS at Benghazi drove straight into an ambush and, after being badly shot up, was forced to withdraw. Only the LRDG at Barce was successful, destroying 32 aircraft. After a nightmare journey back across the desert its members discovered that the attack on Jalo was still in progress and the whole force was ordered to withdraw, reaching Kuffra by 23 September.[30] The cost of these operations had been prohibitively high, and no destruction of Axis supplies – the stated aim – had resulted. When David Stirling of the SAS subsequently went to see Montgomery to ask for a free hand to recruit in Eighth Army, he was received very coolly, although he was tasked with mounting raids on railways and landing grounds from 9 to 23 October before the major offensive, after which the SAS was to attack transport and administrative units in the rear areas.[31]

On 14 September Montgomery issued the operation order for the offensive. As half a million mines would dominate the start of the battle, the operation was code-named, 'with macabre flippancy', Lightfoot.[32] The order was issued in a 'Most Secret' document to corps and divisional commanders and senior staff officers, with the warning 'The battle for which we are preparing will be a real rough house.' Montgomery had no intention of allowing a battle of movement to develop, which would suit Rommel. Montgomery proposed 'to "trap" the enemy in his present area and to destroy him there. Should small elements escape to the west, they will be pursued and dealt with later.'[33] The infantry of XXX Corps would secure a bridgehead code-named Oxalic, through which a total of 18 lanes would be cleared by the engineers to form two 'corridors' for 1st and 10th Armoured Divisions. They in turn would advance to the 'bound' code-named Pierson, some 1 or 2 miles beyond, and thence to a 'report line' – Skinflint.* Time was limited and training must therefore concentrate specifically on the battle, neglecting other forms.[34]

As a preliminary, on the night of 29/30 September Horrocks launched Operation Braganza to capture an area of ground near Deir el Munassib for extra artillery deployment. This involved the unblooded 131st (Queen's) Brigade from 44th (Home Counties) Division, supported by armour from 4th Armoured Brigade, nine field regiments, and one medium battery of artillery.[35] On the northern side of the attack, 1/6th Queen's Royal Regiment met no effective opposition, but its sister battalion in the south – 1/5th – ran into positions held by the tough paratroops of the Ramcke Brigade and Folgore Division and were badly handled, losing 12 officers and 260 men killed, wounded and missing. Ernest Norris of 1/5th described how the supporting barrage suddenly stopped:

> You feel so naked you can't describe it. In a matter of seconds they were firing tracer bullets at us. It was still dark and I was aware of the tracer coming towards us – they seemed too slow to be bullets. But there were men getting killed and wounded all around. Captain Clark was mortally wounded and I heard him call out, 'Carry on, Mr Cole-Biroth, I've been hit.' Then my Bren-gunner screamed and went down. I mentally panicked. You don't know what's happening. By then it was almost daylight. We got down behind what cover we could find. I looked round. Captain Clark was dead. Mr Cole-Biroth was pretty badly wounded and Mr Whittaker had most of his face shot away. We had no officers left.[36]

Attempts to relieve the survivors and renew the attack broke down, and on the following day Horrocks called off the operation.

When 132nd (Kent) Brigade took over in the north it was found that, despite little fighting, there had been a great many casualties among 131st Brigade through heatstroke. It was evident that some formations were unfit for the coming battle, and Montgomery's expressed intention to keep divisions together had therefore to be modified somewhat;

---

*A 'bound' was a line or locality where tanks could gather stragglers and regroup; a 'report line' was a line on the map where they would pause to await further orders.

during the remaining period of training there was a sometimes bewildering interchange which created considerable additional difficulties for the command structure.[37]

Meanwhile Alexander, who hated his desk, visited regularly, and de Guingand usually attended. 'Monty would rattle out his requests – troops, commanders, equipment, whatever it might be. His Commander-in-Chief took short notes, and with the greatest rapidity these requirements became accomplished facts.'[38] The expansion and re-equipment of Eighth Army led to a parallel expansion and reorganization of the support services. Despite the disasters of Tobruk and during the summer, immediately before Alexander and Montgomery took over in the Middle East a highly organized and efficient base had been organized in the Delta under Major-General Wilfred Lindsell, one of the army's leading logisticians. It was equally fortunate that at Eighth Army Headquarters the responsibility for logistic planning fell to Brigadier Sir Brian Robertson, whose brilliance outshone even Lindsell's.[39] All captured German 'jerrycans' were called in from the infantry formations and handed over to X Corps, to ensure that its initial reserves of petrol carried by its own transport would not leak into the desert as was likely if the 4-gallon tins issued to the British were used. (These 'flimsies' were produced in their millions at a plant near Alexandria, and thoroughly deserved their nickname – a third of them were likely to leak.) Of particular significance was the quantity of transport available. Flexibility had been enhanced in the summer of 1941 by abolishing the RASC's rigid system of carrying fixed quantities of petrol, ammunition and other stores and by setting up a standard four-platoon organization for all transport companies on a general-transport (GT) basis (excluding technical transport – tank transporters, water and petrol tankers, and ambulance cars) to carry whatever was necessary as required. The formation of tank-transporter companies had been another notable innovation, speeding up the recovery and delivery of damaged or replacement tanks. They brought out some 200 repairable tanks on the retreat from Gazala that would otherwise have been lost.[40] Eighth Army now had the equivalent of 46 general-transport companies, with 6 tank-transporter companies and another 7 GT companies in GHQ reserve.

Reinforcements included 51st (Highland) Division. This was one of the best British divisions during the First World War, but had been the only division to surrender during the Battle of France in June 1940. Separated from the main British Expeditionary Force and sent to an eastern sector of the Maginot Line it fought valiantly, but when the French Army collapsed it was driven south, encircled, and trapped by Rommel himself. On 7 August 1940, 9th (Scottish) Division – formed as the original 51st's second-line formation when the Territorial Army was doubled in 1939 – was redesignated 51st (Highland) Division. The reformed division bore a legacy of pride, disappointment and desire for revenge. For most of its members the forthcoming offensive would be their first taste of battle, but in Major-General Douglas 'Tartan Tan' Wimberley they had a professional commander of long experience who understood the importance of morale to the infantry soldier.

Wimberley – a proud Cameron Highlander – assumed command in June 1941 and immediately set about creating divisional spirit. He went to great lengths to create a truly Scottish division, since the War Office's manning policy gave no guarantee that the drafts he received would come from Scotland, still less the Highlands. Increasingly, as happened during the First World War, the division became a Scottish symbol rather than a purely Highland one, as more and more men were posted from other Scottish regiments. When the War Office was determined to send him an English light anti-aircraft regiment, he appealed to General Sir Frederick Pile of Anti-Aircraft Command, who, being an Irishman, understood Wimberley's sensitivity. Pile exclaimed, 'My boy, I am with you, you shall have your Jocks somehow', and in due course he provided 40th Light Anti-Aircraft Regiment, which included two batteries recruited from northern Scotland. Montgomery, commanding South-Eastern Army at the time, was very sympathetic to Wimberley's aim and wrote to all his divisional commanders, some of whom in their turn were more helpful than others; a young officer sent to 53rd (Welsh) Division to recruit 25 Scotsmen returned in a week with 24, and the division began the battle comprising 70 per cent Scotsmen, with the figure at 80 per cent in the infantry battalions.[41] It would become known throughout the British Army as the 'Highway Decorators', as its members plastered their divisional sign of 'HD' everywhere they fought on a trail across nine countries and two continents before they finally ceased fighting at Bremerhaven in May 1945, their honour restored.[42]

The Highlanders were 'affiliated' to the 'friendly and very efficient' Australians to gain desert-worthiness and battle experience as soon as possible. Each unit of Jocks was assigned to one of Diggers, and the two sides greatly enjoyed the association. Wimberley put high emphasis on spit and polish, since in his view a Highland division proud of itself and its traditions should turn out properly. But he understood that a smart division unable to fight was useless, and when he visited Morshead's Australians in August 1942, finding them half-naked and brown as berries, he wrote, 'They took a bit of getting used to. I was dressed as a general and they treated me in the most matey way, but despite this it was easy to see that there was nothing wrong with their battle discipline.'[43] Indeed, the Australians 'had a very different type of discipline to ours', recorded the 51st's historian, 'but in the line our men learned very valuable lessons from these fine troops. The Aussies kept their weapons scrupulously clean and always free from sand. Their slit trenches were prepared with the utmost care, and each trench was equipped with such things as grenades.'[44] The Australians' superb patrolling skills were, as Captain H. P. Samwell of 7th Argyll and Sutherland Highlanders noted, highly unorthodox. 'They hardly bothered about compasses but went from point to point by means of battle landmarks, utilising everything from broken-down tanks to unburied corpses. One company had a skeleton whom they affectionately called "Cuthbert", who was propped up on his arm pointing to the gap in our minefield.'[45]

Montgomery has often been criticized for the abundance of material available to him, the suggestion being that he simply applied overwhelming strength. This both is simplistic and ignores the fact that every previous British offensive also enjoyed material superiority. Even during the July battles, as we have seen, Eighth Army vastly outnumbered Axis tank strength. The difficulty was bringing the force to bear and making it count. In this, Montgomery's plan was considerably different from those which preceded it in two important respects. First he realized, as perhaps did Rommel, that the battle would necessarily be a slogging match – all-in wrestling rather than twinkle-toes boxing. The former suited Eighth Army, with its superiority in infantry, while Rommel was the master of the latter. Rommel could roll with punches and return them given space, but the Alamein battlefield would deny him that space, exposing his shortage of infantry and their not being trained to attack at night. ('Followers of the armour by day and weapon holders by night' was Freyberg's assessment of Rommel's troops.)[46] Montgomery planned to get Rommel in a headlock and pummel him repeatedly until he could take no more. Second, Montgomery knew that to make those punches count he must make proper use of what would subsequently come to be regarded as his most effective weapon – the artillery. His guns would be concentrated in a way not seen since 1918, for he had long noted that what the Germans most disliked was intense artillery fire.[47]

One of Auchinleck's recommendations before his departure had been for greater concentration of this arm, with divisional and corps commanders of Royal Artillery being able to bring the greatest firepower possible on to a given target.[48] Montgomery now proceeded to make such arrangements. Brigadier Sidney Kirkman, who had been Montgomery's artillery commander in XII Corps, arrived from Britain 'armed', as he put it, 'with the immense authority of the new Army Commander' to put in place some essential reorganization.[49] Lieutenant-Colonel M. 'Stag' Yates was called in with an improvised staff to command the Medium Artillery of Eighth Army, which was allotted to XXX Corps for the battle. A composite survey battery and corps counter-battery staff completed the team. 'Even before the battle', a Royal Artillery report later noted, 'our artillery had achieved a moral superiority over the enemy's . . . the enemy was reluctant to fire at night, we fired whenever we wished. Our counter-battery measures were most effective, the enemy's singularly indifferent.'[50] Ammunition was pouring into the army area daily, and very large stocks were being built up. Detailed gunner planning began at the start of October, when the broad outlines of the army and corps plans were decided. The artillery of XXX Corps consisted of the divisional artillery of four divisions. In addition, three field regiments were lent by X Corps and were used to reinforce on a troop basis, instead of being employed as complete units, the idea being to reduce the number of reconnaissance parties wandering about, so improving security and the chance of surprise.[51]

One of the problems would be maintaining momentum over the long advance that would be involved – up to 3.5 miles. This was to be achieved by phasing the attack, bringing fresh troops forward at each stage. Thus XXX Corps's plan had a first-phase 'Red Line' some 2 miles from the final objective, where start lines would be secured for the second phase. Potentially the biggest problem of a night attack to be executed in depth is maintenance of direction. Most battalion attacks were planned on a two-company frontage, and guide parties were provided on battalion axes and on each company axis. Each group had to know the distance to be covered and the direction of each bound, marking the axis of advance both with tape and with pickets mounting rearward shining lights as the group progressed. Report and traffic-control centres would be established to control the movement of vehicles and prevent congestion in the minefield gaps.[52]

However, Montgomery soon found that there were widespread military objections to the plan, especially the need to push X Corps's armour through the infantry of XXX Corps. Planning took considerable account of the minefields, but Rommel's anti-tank guns received substantially less attention. It was expected that the initial infantry advance would neutralize these, but objections to the plan were not restricted to the armoured commanders. Leese was worried that for a

10-mile front he was short of both infantry and artillery. Two of his divisions were a brigade short and 'good' for only one attack, and another was untried in battle. He had 452 field guns and only 48 medium guns, and when he held his first corps conference the divisional commanders said they did not believe the armour would pass through as planned. 'Timings left very little margin for getting our essential vehicles through before it was time to clear the tracks for the armoured divisions,' noted a New Zealand report. As a brigadier remarked, 'even if it goes like an exercise it is virtually impossible'.[53]

Montgomery laid great store on the shock effect of massed artillery, but a 25-pounder concentration against well-dug-in troops could do little to physically damage them. It was therefore essential for the following infantry to 'lean' on the barrage – to keep close to the exploding shells in order to arrive on top of the enemy's position before he could recover from the shock of them.[54] That said, there were insufficient guns for a proper barrage across the entire corps frontage, and the fire plan instead relied on concentrations on known defensive localities, beginning with bombardment of artillery positions 20 minutes before H-Hour, when the infantry were due to cross their start lines, during which time command of all guns would be under corps command before passing to divisions for the five hours and ten minutes allowed for the infantry to seize their objectives.

At first Montgomery insisted that the plan would be followed: he had plenty of tanks, and did not mind how many were lost if the result was achieved. But he would have been in an untenable position had he persisted with a plan genuinely incapable of implementation. When the armoured commanders made their original protest, McCreery took it to Alexander, who returned him to the desert with a brief to explain the Commander-in-Chief's views, backed by a charming letter which enabled Montgomery to announce a change of plan as though it were entirely his own decision, uninfluenced by the reservations of the armoured commanders, and thus retaining his authority. This intervention by Alexander demonstrated his quiet ability to smooth the waters within his command, the ultimate responsibility for which was his alone.[55] Consequently, on 6 October Montgomery issued a memorandum outlining a change of plan, or at least of emphasis, in which the burden of the battle would move towards 'crumbling' by the infantry – attacking the enemy infantry from flanks and rear to cut off supplies – a much harder and more deadly battle than previously envisaged. Significantly, the 'dogfight' battle was now expected to take 10 to 12 days instead of seven, and it raised the importance of the artillery yet higher.[56]

Yet to the 9th Australian Division the plan was most inspiring. Eighth Army operations had so far seemed to the Australians to amount to 'sending a boy on a man's errand', consisting as they had of separate attacks on a one- or two-brigade frontage (or even less) and seizure of objectives which then had to be held with open flanks. An assault by four divisions in line abreast was something far more substantial. The most vulnerable part of the bridgehead would be the flanks, particularly in the north. Securing this area would be 9th Australian Division's responsibility, while similar responsibilities fell upon 1st South African Division in the south. Among the additional troops allotted to Morshead were 40th Royal Tank Regiment and 66th Mortar Company Royal Engineers. The latter was equipped with 18 4.2-inch mortars originally intended for chemical warfare, but which also fired a heavy high-explosive round. (In the subsequent operations supporting 24th Australian Brigade's feint attack, the entire Middle East high-explosive ammunition stock was fired.) In 9th Australian Division's plan, a Composite Force of a squadron from 9th Division Cavalry Regiment, machine-gunners, pioneers and anti-tank guns would cover 26th Australian Brigade's exposed right flank.

The Australians were better armed than ever before: 2/3rd Anti-Tank Regiment had received 64 6-pounders, and there were ample supplies of the Hawkins anti-tank mine/grenade; most battalions had a platoon of 8 2-pounders, and 9th Divisional Cavalry had 15 Crusaders, 5 Honeys and 52 carriers. The infantry, while marginally under strength, were also significantly better equipped with automatic weapons than their establishment prescribed. Machine-gun platoons had been reintroduced into each battalion, with 6 guns each, and there were 71 of the superb German MG-34s in the division, along with 63 Italian Bredas of various calibres from 6.5 mm to the 47 mm anti-tank gun as well as 15 81 mm mortars and 5 Besa machine-guns. (These latter were a British tank armament.) And on 10 October a draft of reinforcements had arrived from Australia which proved in due course to be far better trained than previous ones. The division was well set.[57]

The widest section of front to be covered fell to 51st (Highland) Division, and Wimberley planned to use seven battalions and his divisional reconnaissance regiment in the assault. He held four major exercises on a divisional scale, taking each brigade in turn with each battalion on a replica of the enemy defences created by his sappers, practising exactly what they were to do in the initial attack. Live barrages were fired and caused some casualties, including Major Sir Arthur Wilmot and five men killed from 1st Black Watch.[58]

The precise nature of the artillery support had not been specified in the original plan, and Freyberg suggested a creeping barrage – moving forward in timed 'lifts' – for 2nd New Zealand Division in First World War style. Brigadier C. E. Weir, his artillery commander, had been told while on a course some 20 months previously that 'a creeping barrage would never be used in this war'. Following an exercise, this had been practised nevertheless while the division was in Syria, and had been watched with interest by Leese, who now accepted Freyberg's proposal.[59] Timings were rigidly planned, and the advance was practised accordingly. Through the minefield it would be at 75 yards per minute, then at 100 yards every three minutes thereafter. At H-Hour plus 55 there would be a 15-minute pause to allow reserve companies to pass through those in the lead, and at H plus 115 a 30-minute pause to allow battalions to pass through.

Further south, 1st South African Division would also attack on a two-brigade frontage to secure the southern end of Miteiriya Ridge, while 4th Indian and 50th (Northumbrian) Divisions would contribute to the artillery fire plan and attempt to keep the enemy opposite interested. Far more significant were the plans for XIII Corps, which was to attack across the enemy minefields known as January and February in a feint operation as part of a deception scheme. They would then swing north behind the parachutists of Folgore Division and the Ramcke Brigade in order to pin down Axis forces, especially the armoured group of 21st Panzer Division and the Italian Ariete Armoured Division in the south.[60]

9

In the Line

Now father he was never called a quitter.
I don't suppose he'll be a quitter now.
And in winter and in heat
He'll haunt that bleeding seat
And only let them shit as he allows.
Gor Bli-mey!

Eighth Army song

Among many advantages over the Axis forces, Eighth Army enjoyed a distinct superiority in the matter of health. The Royal Army Medical Corps had long experience of service in tropical climates, and mastered the difficulties imposed by the desert with little real difficulty. Liberal use was made of AL63, an effective anti-louse powder, whereas Field Hygiene sections often remarked on the verminous condition of many prisoners. Being rotated from the front line more often than the Axis troops gave men more chance to get clean; laundry was often done using petrol – more plentiful than water – and bathing in the sea was greatly enjoyed when the opportunity presented itself. Indeed, many soldiers positively thrived on the hard but healthy lifestyle, although most men suffered desert sores, with any minor abrasion becoming infected and extremely uncomfortable, refusing to heal for weeks.[1] Axis soldiers suffered a far greater incidence of sickness, and were especially prone to dysentery, which proved a constant worry to the staffs. Rommel's Chief of Staff, Generalmajor Alfred Gause, was subject to violent headaches, and his operations officer, Westphal, was soon to go down with jaundice.

Rommel's own health problems were compounded by his not allowing himself time for rest. Professor Horster who was sent out specifically to look at him, insisted on a thorough examination. It revealed circulation and blood-pressure problems, chronic stomach and intestinal catarrh, and nasal diphtheria. In a temperate climate the last would have been enough to put most people in bed for several days, but in the dirt and heat of the desert the discomfort must have been excruciating and Rommel's will to keep going at all, let alone with the responsibility of commanding an army, was extraordinary.[2] But, with a heavy heart, on 23 September he left for home to recover, stopping en route at Derna, where he met Cavallero. He raised various points – including the presence of the Pistoia Division (why was it in Africa when he himself could not obtain proper supply?) – and, in turn, Cavallero asked in Il Duce's name how many of the combined German–Italian battle groups were commanded by Italians (a question Rommel sidestepped).[3] They then discussed transport problems at length, and the Italians promised to provide 3,000 workmen to repair the road surfaces that had deteriorated so much that they were wrecking Rommel's transport, that 7,000 tons of rails and sleepers would be brought forward to improve the railway, and that Kuffra would be eliminated as a base for British commando raids. (When he eventually returned, a month later, Rommel was not surprised to find that none of these tasks had been completed.)

In Rome he had similar experiences, with Mussolini saying, 'You have done the impossible before, Herr Feldmarschall. We are all sure you can do it again!' However, Mussolini was convinced the Americans would invade North Africa in 1943, and that it was essential to reach the Nile and consolidate before they did.[4] When Rommel reached the 'Wolf's Lair' – headquarters of the Führer – he found more unfounded optimism. He was showered with sycophantic praise, but his efforts to inject a little reality quickly foundered. Göring dismissed the American threat out of hand: 'Nothing but latrine rumours! All the Americans can make are razor blades and Frigidaires!' Only Hitler seemed to be genuinely sympathetic, promising multi-barrelled Nebelwerfer rocket launchers and Tiger tanks, and providing encouragement.[5]

In Berlin, Rommel was guest of the Goebbels family, and on the last day of the month he was presented with his marshal's baton at a ceremony in the Reich Chancellery, followed by a mass rally in his honour at the Berlin Sportpalast that was broadcast throughout occupied Europe and much of the neutral world. Three days later he was persuaded by Goebbels to attend another rally, at which he rather unwisely declared that 'we stand just fifty miles from Alexandria and Cairo, and we have the key to all Egypt in our hands. And we mean to do something about it too! We have not gone all that way to be thrown back again. You can take that from me. What we have, we hold.'[6] Then he left for rest and recuperation with 'Dearest Lu' at Semmering in Austria.

The absence of Rommel was keenly felt by Panzerarmee. However, he did not believe that the British attack would come for another six to eight weeks, by which time he would have returned; and in the meantime he had given detailed instructions to his deputy, General der Kavallerie Georg Stumme. Stumme – a short, good-humoured, 56-year-old Hanoverian – had been the first commander of Rommel's old 7th Panzer Division, and had commanded XL Motorized Corps in Greece. He maintained his high reputation into the USSR, until he fell into disgrace when his corps operation order fell into Soviet hands on the eve of Operation *Blau*, the 1942 summer offensive. Chronic high blood pressure gave his monocled face a permanent flush and earned him the nickname 'fireball' from his troops,[7] but he was, according to Kesselring, 'of a more even and genial temperament than Rommel [and] did much to relax the tension between officers and men, besides managing to create tolerable relations with the Italian Command'.[8] He was told by Rommel to expect attacks along the entire front until Montgomery had made up his mind which sector looked most promising and sought to reinforce it, and he faithfully followed Rommel's instructions for dealing with these. These instructions presumed that a frontal attack would be accompanied by landings from the sea, and included orders for early counter-attack and deployment of heavy weapons to engage the beaches.[9] During the pause in which Rommel expected any redeployment to take place – unduly long by German standards, but based on the slowness of British command – he could move his mobile armoured forces behind the most threatened sectors to counter the British advance. However, continuing fuel shortages forced a restriction of this plan as well as effectively preventing further plans for offensive action. That may explain the general mood of pessimism at Panzerarmee headquarters.

Rommel had shown great skill in mobile operations. Now, realizing that air power could decisively tip the scales in a war of movement, and aware that his desperate fuel shortage precluded such tactics in any case, he chose to build an ensnaring spider's-web defence scheme relying on the two weapons that would dominate the battlefield: the mine and the anti-tank gun. The British would have to attack frontally somewhere, and Rommel would fortify the desert with minefields – christened 'Devil's Gardens' – deeper and more fiendishly complex than ever seen before. These would delay and cripple the attack all the way to the main defence belt some miles further back. The forward minefields would be only lightly held, to delay attackers and create time for counter-measures.[10]

The outer edge of the defences followed the wire and minefields established during the fighting of July and, further south, by the recent Alam Halfa battle. South of Himeimat a continuous minefield was planned to meet the escarpment of the Qattara Depression, but was never completed. The outer edge of the minefield was to be wired and mined to a depth of between 500 and 1,000 yards, depending on the terrain. Weapon pits would be created in this belt mainly for machine-guns and light mortars. Beyond these minefields a second and wider belt was laid up to a mile and a quarter thick, and only beyond this would the main defensive position finally be encountered. Each battalion would man the outpost line with one company only, reinforced at night, while the bulk of the infantry and anti-tank gun emplacements would hold the second line. The guns in particular were carefully concealed so that even when firing (with flashless charges) they were practically impossible to spot.[11] Plans prepared by German engineers early in October indicate that lateral and flanking minefields were to be laid between the outpost and main belts to divide the front into sectors which would each accommodate two battalions. These sectors were designed as narrow isosceles triangles whose apexes rested on the front line, with mines along the two long sides but with the bases and centre portions left clear to permit the movement of counter-attacking forces. However, these plans had to be matched to local conditions, including terrain and shortage of engineers and equipment.[12] The entire defensive belt would be some five miles deep, and behind this the armour would be deployed.

In total, German engineers laid 249,849 anti-tank and 14,509 anti-personnel mines, which, with the captured British fields in the south, gave Rommel 445,358 mines of all types to stop a British advance. Kesselring later claimed to have had less faith in these minefields than his commander, though this would not have been typical of his usual optimism.[13] The vast majority were anti-tank mines,* but some thousands were German anti-personnel 'S' mines (Schuh or S Mi-35 – 'Jumping Jacks' to the Allies), especially in the forward areas. These were operated by a trip wire or remote control, and threw a bomb up to waist height, where it then exploded and scattered lethal ball bearings in all directions. Where the engineers had time to add finishing touches to their fiendish creations, they planted captured British large-calibre shells and aircraft bombs to be electronically detonated by the men in nearby defence posts, by trip wires or by the explosion of nearby mines.[14]

---

*The principal German anti-tank mine was the Tellermine, which could break the track of a tank or wreck a soft-skinned lorry but would not normally be exploded by the weight of a man.

The Axis now fielded four German and eight Italian divisions in Egypt. On 24 September Panzerarmee Afrika was officially renamed German–Italian Panzer Army. It still comprised Deutsches Afrikakorps (15th and 21st Panzer Divisions and 90th Light Division) together with 164th Division and the Ramcke Parachute Brigade. In the three Italian corps – X, XX and XXI – were Ariete and Littorio Armoured Divisions, Trieste and Trento (Motorized) Infantry Divisions, Folgore Parachute Division, and the Pavia, Bologna and Brescia Infantry Divisions. The Giovanni Fascisti Division garrisoned the Siwa oasis, and Pistoia Division guarded the lines of communication around the Libyan border based at Bardia. Panzerarmee fielded just over 500 tanks over half of which were Italian. Ninetieth Light Division was disposed in reserve with Trieste at El Daba on the coast in the north, with 288th Special Force and 580th Reconnaissance Battalion further back at Mersa Matruh. The forward positions were held from the north by XXI Corps (comprising 164th, Trento and Bologna Divisions and a battalion of the Ramcke Brigade), with X Corps (Brescia, Pavia, Folgore Divisions and two battalions of Ramcke with the German 33rd Reconnaissance Battalion) on the far southern flank.

Throughout the defensive plan, Rommel's doubts about Italian resilience led to the dovetailing of formations and even units. Wherever possible, Italian infantry were sandwiched between German units and headquarters were located near to each other to stiffen the Italians' resolve. This was symptomatic of the low esteem in which many Germans held their allies, although relations were generally cordial. It was Panzerarmee's view that Italian weakness stemmed from poor equipment and junior leadership, and that the Italians would fight well if given well-prepared defences and properly led.[15] Conversely, 'my own opinion of the Germans gets very confused,' wrote Capitano Piero Santini. 'The Germany of the panzergrenadiers is certainly warlike, but it preserves a basis of humanity, something of that romantic, sentimental, Goethe-like quality which no one can deny is a fundamental characteristic of the country. The Germany of the paratroopers on the other hand is 100 per cent Wagnerian – disquieting, grandiose and full of a sense of impending disaster.'[16] The sandwiching principle was also extended to the armoured formations. The armour was held in reserve in two groups disposed behind each corps: 15th Panzer and Littorio behind XXI Corps, and 21st Panzer and Ariete behind X Corps. Stumme wrote to Cavallero that when these deployments – ordered by Rommel – had been completed (by 20 October), Panzerarmee would be capable of meeting the expected frontal assault.[17]

Eighth Army gained detailed information on the Axis defences through patrols, aerial photographs and the Bulimba operation. Patrols were limited to the spiky outer edge of the position, but the highly skilled Army Air Photograph Interpretation Unit produced maps and overlays from the 10,650 photographs taken over all the enemy positions. These photographs were so good that there was a danger of believing that nothing had been missed, but many of the inner minefields were carefully concealed in camel-thorn and effectively invisible, especially after shifting sand had airbrushed out the clues.[18] Nevertheless Eighth Army Headquarters soon realized that Axis engineers were working to a pattern. In early October it issued a description of the defence works from the coast to as far south as Deir el Shein and, although many of the laterals were as yet incomplete, it correctly surmised the placing of artillery and anti-tank guns as being the purpose for the 'hollows' observed. In the extreme north, between the sea at Mersa el Hamza and Sidi Abd el Rahman, the garden pattern was not so clearly visible but the defences around the sand dunes and the coastal road and railway had evolved in a shapeless form thanks to the Australian assaults of July. Immediately south of Tel el Eisa, however, the pattern showed clearly, with four hollows between two belts of mines in the fairly level stretches down to the El Shein and El Mreir depressions, beyond which the pattern was again obscured by the remains of earlier fighting.

To the south of the Qattara box, where the pattern was unclear, it was assumed that the defences relied on strongpoints backed by positions held before the Alam Halfa advance. This was partially correct, although the double line of minefields was in fact laid as far south as Himeimat, absorbing British-laid fields. Shortage of troops in this area compelled the strongpoint system, although the intention was to man the line as strongly as in the north once sufficient troops were available. The British also detected traces of a massive minefield known to the Axis as the Qatani field, running west from the area of Deir el Dhib and eventually extended to the Rahman Track (which ran from Sidi Abd el Rahman on the coast behind the front line almost as far as Himeimat) and then south along it for a distance of 20 miles. Significantly, this was intended to insulate the northern front from the southern, and was the responsibility of DAK – whose enthusiasm for it was such that DAK had to be restrained from cornering Panzerarmee's supply of mines.[19] Further back the only major defences were along the coast, but it was difficult to discern anything among the paraphernalia of support services whose camps, transport parks and dumps overlaid the traces of previous campaigns. A plan to develop a second defence line at Fuka came to little.

*

On 6 September two Axis convoys out of Greece were attacked; a 10,000-tonner was sunk, and a 6,000-tonner was damaged and beached. So it would go on. Too late the Italians realized their mistake in agreeing to Rommel's drive on Alexandria. 'Unless we neutralize Malta,' wailed Cavallero that day, 'all is lost.'[20] Although by 15 September the continued airlift of reinforcements had boosted the German formations to around 75 per cent of their establishment, compared to 30 per cent on 21 July, supplies were another matter. As the head of the German Transport Staff twice pointed out, more troops meant fewer supplies.[21] Not only was Malta biting hard at the tenuous supply line from Italy, her anti-shipping effort was now strongly reinforced by aircraft from Egypt, including Wellingtons.[22]

The method of pathfinding at sea was for three Wellingtons of 221 Squadron loaded with parachute flares to fly with 50-mile spacing in parallel westward tracks supported by torpedo-armed Wellingtons of 38 Squadron. The combined side-search radars covered an enormous area, and when a searcher detected an echo it would turn 90 degrees in that direction, switch to forward-seeking antennas, and home in – sending out a continuous stream of signals for the others to follow. This aircraft would now become 'master of ceremonies', while the next search aircraft to arrive would fly some 10 miles east of the convoy and lay and maintain a path of flame floats. The third search aircraft would remain in reserve. The torpedo bombers would arrive and circle the flame floats at stepped-up heights until enough had arrived to launch an attack, whereupon the master of ceremonies would send an attack signal before dropping a single flame float at a point such that, if they aimed for it, the torpedo bombers would arrive at the target. He would then fly behind the convoy and drop a stick of parachute flares, followed by the second and third search aircraft to maintain the illumination until the bombers had completed their attack.

On 28 August 1942 a convoy had been sighted steaming west of Crete and was found later that evening by Wellingtons and Liberators that sank one of the main fuel-carrying storeships. The following day a second wave of torpedo-carrying Wellingtons also found the convoy. Squadron Leader Mike Foulis recorded that 'we sighted the ships at 0015 in the moonpath. There was no cloud and a bright moon. We could see the ship clearly, a vessel of about 8,000 tons or perhaps a little less.' He attacked, carefully avoiding the three escorting destroyers, but was forced to take violent evasive action to avoid anti-aircraft fire, which did not hit. The navigator reported two bright orange flashes on the vessel, stern and amidships. I swung the air-craft round and we could all see two great columns of water going above her masts. It was clear that both torpedoes had hit . . . Very quickly thick grey smoke began to come out of the ship. The destroyers closed in and within five minutes a heavy smoke pall lay all over the ships. We could plainly smell the smoke in the aircraft; it smelt oily and acrid.

Some ten minutes later the destroyers were still there, but nothing else. 'We sent another signal: "Tanker believed sunk, large oil patch seen." '[23]

In July only 6 per cent of Axis supplies were sent to the seabed, but in August 25 per cent of general cargo and 41 per cent of fuel was sunk – a total of 65,000 tons.[24] In September the naval staff and that of 201 Wing RAF (responsible for anti-shipping operations in Egypt) com-bined to collate Ultra and other intelligence and to prioritize targets, so that a ship taking rations (of which there were known to be large stocks in Africa) would be ignored in favour of a tanker, which would be engaged off the west coast of Greece by Malta-based aircraft (the limit of their range), leaving Alexandria to deal with ammunition ships sailing from Piraeus.[25] Such was the problem for the Axis that Kesselring tried once more to neutralize Malta during a ten-day blitz in October; but after losing 70 planes he had to acknowledge defeat. On 22 October Ultra revealed that only 90 serviceable aircraft were available for Axis operations in Egypt.[26]

Rommel was convinced of the treacherous nature of the Italian High Command. Captured British officers told him, he said, of an Italian who had betrayed his surprise attack at Alam Halfa. The sinking of supply ships was all the result of treachery in Italy. 'The ordinary Italian sol-diers are good,' he told his friend Kurt Hesse. 'Their officers are worth-less. Their High Command are traitors.' Making a gesture of frustration, he claimed that given three shiploads of fuel for his tanks he could be in Cairo within 48 hours.[27] The suspicion arose among the Germans that the Italians were consistently overestimating their own requirements to the detriment of their allies, owing to their officer corps' pernicious love of luxuries. Undoubtedly the Italian supply organization was corrupt and inefficient, but it was not traitorous.

Equally grave was the problem of delivery to the front of those sup-plies that did arrive. Unable to provide their own fighter cover and unable to persuade the Germans to do it for them, the Italians tried to avoid the ports of Tobruk, Bardia and Mersa Matruh, which were within easy reach of British air bases in Egypt, and preferred instead to run their shipping into Benghazi, or even Tripoli, and accept the long road haul to the front. But these ports were not free from interference either as long as Malta was in operation, and ships commonly had to sit in harbour for long periods – leaving them vulnerable to air attack. In any case, use of these ports put enormous strain on the transport system, mostly of captured British origin and deteriorating from overloading, overuse and want of spares, as well as using vast quantities of the fuel that was landed. Neither the coastal barge service nor the railway intended to relieve the pressure on road transport was reliable, lacking both capacity and maintenance crews. At any one time a third of the trucks held by Panzerarmee were under repair, and each failure in the system created further problems along the chain. One ship sent to relieve the fuel situation sat in Tripoli and another sat in Benghazi until well into October, awaiting transport to move their cargoes. While the British enjoyed the benefits of the desert railway, which enabled them to bring everything into the desert without need for a single drop of petrol before the dispersal to camps and dumps from the railhead, the Axis relied on lorries operating from sometimes as far west as Tripoli. Driving at a steady 40 miles per hour, the round trip from Benghazi to the Alamein line took a week.[28]

Rommel made urgent representations for more staff and coastal shipping – and air cover for it. In fact there existed in southern Europe sufficient of everything to mount several Malta-style convoys which, even accounting for losses, could have solved Panzerarmee's problems for some months. But, at a time when increasing numbers of escort vessels were being deployed to protect the merchant ships,* all using up precious oil,[29] Hitler denied Mussolini the fuel oil necessary. Thus the constant trickle of supplies across the Mediterranean made it easy for the Royal Navy and the RAF to interdict them. When eight of the new Nebelwerfers finally arrived in Africa, fulfilling one of Hitler's promises at least, they were completely useless – there was no ammunition for them to fire.[30] To add to this particular problem, the reinforcements Rommel had received had all come by air with practically no transport. He could clearly see that there was no chance of renewing the offensive or of fighting a defensive battle using mobile tactics, or even of easily withdrawing, because he did not have the transport. Even assuming that the two dictators allowed it, the British would not allow the extrication of his non-mobile formations.[31] The dimensions of the supply problem were illustrated by the appearance on Axis airfields of large Goliath cargo gliders. These engineless freighters needed to be towed by Ju-52, He-111 or He-177 aircraft, and were extremely inefficient: designed for air landing troops and equipment, they were useful only in a logistic emergency, such as supplying troops cut-off in Russia. For

---

*Up to six Regia Marina vessels were needed to protect one tanker.

maintaining an entire army across a sea they were a last-resort measure.[32]

Helmut Heimberg was flown to Africa via Crete after volunteering for a Luftwaffe field battalion. He flew low in a formation of 30 Ju-52s escorted by two Me-110s and arrived safely, only to find that the anti-tank guns that were to be issued to his battalion had gone down in a ship torpedoed by submarine. On 17 October 272 Squadron RAF, which operated Beaufighters, carried out an offensive sweep south of Crete. One flight intercepted an aerial convoy of 32 Ju-52s towing gliders, escorted by two Me-110s; it claimed two of the transport planes shot down.[33] Much precious mail went the same way. And those letters that arrived must have seemed to come from another world – from writers surrounded by trees and grass, where water came out of a tap and there was butter for the bread. Meanwhile the Axis troops spent their days – seemingly endless – caked in ash-grey dust, squinting out from their turrets and rifle pits under regular air attack.[34]

During September food throughout the German half of the army got progressively worse: one soldier described breakfast as being 'carbolic-flavoured coffee and mouldy bacon with *Dauerbrot*, the very thing for my stomach!'[35] The Italians were used to the climate and conditions and had rations that were basically adequate (as well as being sometimes lavishly supplemented by all sorts of fine delicacies imported from home), but the Germans fared very badly. Traditionally, the German soldier had subsisted on bread and potatoes. By the summer of 1942 he was in some cases getting the former from field bakeries where previously he had often to make do with biscuits. 'We called them "cement plates",' recalled one German soldier, Hans Schilling, 'and I felt sorry for the fellows who did not have good teeth because you had to grind it.'[36] Eventually the Italians, who both controlled the supply lines and had amassed large stocks in the rear areas, were persuaded to donate a quantity of bread, which was flown up to the front – a galling experience made worse by the magnanimity of individual Italian units in helping to feed hungry German troops. Olive oil replaced butter or margarine, and potatoes were replaced with tinned beans because it was thought that fresh potatoes would quickly become inedible in the desert. (There appears to have been no attempt to introduce tinned potatoes as the British did.) Apart from this, the Germans had nothing but a little cheese and the singularly unpopular Italian 'AM' brand of canned beef, known to the Italians as *Arabo Morto* (Dead Arab) and to the Germans as *Alter Mann* (Old Man) or *Asinus Mussolini* (Musso's Donkey).[37] The resulting deficiency in vitamin C fed the high sickness rate, and the craving for sweet items was reflected in the high regard with which captured British rations were regarded. A barter system had soon developed in which a tin of British potatoes was worth several bottles of sweet Derna water.[38]

Water was the biggest problem for both sides, but Eighth Army had a pipeline from Alexandria, run and maintained by South African and New Zealand engineers assisted by Egyptian civilians.[39] From its various branches, supplies would be drawn off by water trucks and taken to water points, to feed whatever containers were available there. These were usually 'flimsies' or captured 'jerrycans'. Major Philip Rainier, Eighth Army's staff officer responsible for water supply, managed to get the pipe as far forward as Tel el Eisa, where he informed the crew of an Australian machine-gun from a local unit about it. Disbelieving,

> one of them picked up all their water bottles and followed me. 'God's truth!' he exclaimed when he saw the little brass tap. 'Just like they put in a beer barrel.' Then he turned the spigot on full. Water spurted all over him from the pressure of the big pumps in the Alamein pump-house six miles away. He danced a wild fandango under the spray, waving his water bottles while the water sluiced off his naked bronze torso and soaked his khaki shorts. 'Whoooo-eeeeeeoo-ee,' he yelled so violently that heads popped up from all sorts of unsuspected holes where men were sleeping.[40]

The Axis forces, however, had to draw their water from old wells and cisterns along the coast, many of which were damaged or polluted. Already brackish, this water would be made worse by the chemical treatment necessary. 'Where would you find anybody in Germany who would drink water of this colour and taste?' asked Leutnant Joachim Schorm of his diary. 'It looks like coffee and tastes horribly of sulphur. But that's all to the good for otherwise it would stimulate one's thirst.'[41] Allied prisoners complained bitterly about the quality, often refusing to believe it was the same as given to Axis troops, and it proved another bone of contention between the Germans and Italians – as did the low standards of hygiene in the latter's defensive positions, breeding grounds for the flies that Eighth Army tried desperately to eradicate, and contributing further to the sickness rate.[42]

Eighth Army issued orders for each man to kill at least 50 flies per day. H. Metcalfe, an Eighth Army soldier, remembered the never-ending battle with them: 'eating and drinking became a work of art, one hand waving back and forth over the food, the other hand waiting, then a quick rush to the mouth before they pounced again. They were around mouth, eyes, face, anywhere there was moisture. They settled on the rim of hot cups of tea in dozens.'[43] Lieutenant-Colonel G. J.

Kidston, commanding 12th Lancers, once found 42 flies on his mug of tea, 'while myriads of others buzzed jealously around waiting for clearance to land'.[44] They seemed to behave as one fly, wrote a New Zealand historian:

> one horrible dark force guided by one mind, ubiquitous and immensely powerful, they addressed themselves to one task, which was to destroy us body and soul. It was useless to kill them for they despised death and made no effort to avoid it. They existed only in the common will, and to weaken that we would have to destroy millions of them. None the less we killed them unceasingly.[45]

With the end of Rommel's realistic ambitions of capturing the Delta, and as they prepared for the forthcoming offensive, many men could enjoy some leave. The men of the Panzerarmee could look forward to a couple of days at a rest camp by the sea – not that far from the front, but at least they would be fed by army cooks and might go swimming or play some sport and get the chance to scrape off their beards. Beer was also available, albeit limited to a couple of bottles of Löwenbräu per man.[46] Entertainments were organized at regimental level, and a group of comedians from 104th Panzergrenadier Regiment was very popular. Panzerarmee announced that 12 speakers were available for talks on many subjects, and distributed 1,200 sets of games; 21st Panzer Division received eight piano accordions, and soldiers papers were distributed – *Die Oase, Adler von Hellas* and *Kolonie und Heimat.*[47]

The Eighth Army soldier in possession of a four-day pass, however, could enjoy the thriving fleshpots of Cairo and Alexandria with their service clubs, welfare organizations and base camps all competing to persuade him to stay away from the less salubrious aspects of Egyptian civilization while enjoying a few precious moments of civil normality. 'To laze around doing nothing,' wrote Second-Lieutenant K. Waaka, 'to walk around without fear of getting blown sky high by shells; to sleep above ground in a comfortable bed; to sit at a table and eat every kind of delicious food.' Choice food could be enjoyed with few effects of rationing, whether at a café in town or in the cookhouses of the Maadi Base Camp near Cairo. At military canteens, almost any dish could be obtained: a breakfast of fresh pineapple followed by a brace of roast pigeon and bacon may have been unusual, but not excessively so. But to most fresh from the desert the demand was for egg and chips; then egg and chips again. Eggs were rare in the desert unless one was lucky enough to barter with a passing bedouin, and battalion cooks were notoriously unable to fry chips. Transport to town, beer ('by the any amount you like'), cinemas, cabaret and other amenities were also freely available. 'To know there's not a German within fifty miles of one; all these things seem to make life almost a dream,' Second-Lieutenant Waaka observed.[48]

New and clean clothing could be drawn from remarkably generous quartermasters, and after bathing and changing there was tea – without the taste of chlorine or petrol – then the raucous shouting of the streets. Conducted tours could be taken of places of interest.[49] To Gunner Tutt, Cairo was

> one of the great cities of the world. It is a great sprawl of a place . . . it bombards the eyes, the ears, the nose and the nerve endings with a plethora of experiences, all of them new, all of them exciting and stimulating. Its critics say it smells to high heaven in the summer. It doesn't. It smells to high heaven all year round. But the reek is of living people.[50]

The numerous cinemas included one with a sliding roof, providing cool, starlit darkness. Performances ended with the Egyptian national anthem, to which soldiers sang their own words, distinctly slanderous to the Egyptian royal family.[51] The gulf between British and Egyptians was wide and, in the 1940s, unbridgeable. Cabarets in the cities included the vast Pole Nord bar in Cairo and many other smaller places like it; Groppi's sold cakes and ice cream; for officers, the cool musty lounge of Shepheard's Hotel offered gin slings served by waiters in white galabiyas; and for those who wanted them, and could avoid the military police, there were the forbidden delights of Berka or Sister Streets in Cairo and Alexandria respectively. There was little other opportunity of feminine company, such Allied servicewomen as there were having long been appropriated by the base staff.[52] 'Up the line,' recalled a nameless soldier,

> we never had time to think about sex, and in the so-called rest areas we had to be careful with the bints who were out in the dunes. They were all Arab girls, and if you caught a packet your pay was stopped and all allowances home as well. So the family at home not only suffered financially, but were told why they were suffering. VD was considered to be a SIW [self-inflicted wound] and most men were scared of catching a dose. So we went without or relieved ourselves.

As an alternative to the cinemas, there were oddly administered clubs in Cairo called Pam Pam and Sweet Melody where there were girls – probably Coptic Christians trying to earn enough commission for a dowry. These would snatch a soldier's headgear, and when he approached her table to get it back they would clap their hands imperiously, whereupon a waiter would suddenly appear with two glasses of 'cherry brandy'. This would cost the unsuspecting soldier ten ackers (about two days' pay) every time she clapped her hands, and a month's pay could vanish down her throat in ten minutes – all for the merest hint of cleavage, but absolutely nothing else.[53]

In 1941, 80,000 tons of Middle East shipping space had been taken up with beer, and brewing had been improvised locally to reduce this. A famous Egyptian beer was 'Stella', 'with its vague and puzzling flavour of onions'.[54] Unsurprisingly, heavy drinking by large numbers of young men, often straight from the front line, led to regular and serious disturbances. Sweet Melody was noted for its fights. Fists, bottles and glasses would fly in all directions, but the band would continue playing, protected from the flying debris by wire netting. Little excuse was needed as troops argued over the fighting qualities of their regiments or their countries.[55]

Previously, the 'Poms' had been treated with a mild arrogance by the Australians, New Zealanders and South Africans, born partly from the latter's own sense of national identity and partly from British ignorance of their allies' homelands at a time when places on the far side of the world had not been made familiar by television or travel. The Commonwealth soldiers' countries were self-governing democracies and, while lacking in some of Europe's sophistication, were nevertheless civilized – with all the amenities this implies. Commonwealth troops were therefore scathingly amused by some of the enquiries they received.[56] However, the disasters of July had generated immense bitterness among them towards the British. For what had seemed good industrial reasons at the time, the Commonwealth had been asked only to contribute infantry divisions, while Britain would provide the armour. That Eighth Army was run by the British, however, rebounded on the ordinary British soldier when things went wrong and it was clear that the command was at fault. The increasing opprobrium that fell on the British armour tended to spill over to all British troops, with reference to 'Pommie bastards' taking a sharper edge than before.

Not that the British were alone in facing hostility: relations between Australians and South Africans were particularly strained. When a group of Springboks entered a bar in Cairo where a group of Aussies were sitting, an Aussie stood up and offered the leading Bok a chair. 'Sit down, cobber, and take a drink,' he said. 'You look all in. What's the matter – just run all the way from Tobruk?' What followed was one of the most spectacular bar brawls the Middle East had seen, even taking into account the destruction of Shepheard's during the First World War.[57]

Alas, leave was all too quickly over and the troops were soon back in the line. Aileen Clayton – a WAAF working in the RAF Y Service – was posted to 211 Group. Travelling in a light truck, she passed convoy after convoy moving towards the front. She did not object to the wolf whistles, 'which I always acknowledged with a wave, for I had the terrible heart-wrenching feeling that, for many of these lads, I would be the last woman they would ever see. They all looked so fit and so young, too young to die.'[58] Then, after a long march to their forward positions, life once more consisted of the old routine of boring guard duties and building defence works, bad food and little water, interspersed with bombardments and patrols. For much of the time – the unequal artillery duel notwithstanding – the hot days dragged for the men in the front line positions, with only perhaps some activity in the air to provide entertainment, although there was seldom more to watch than occasional groups of Allied fighters and the increasingly rare Axis reconnaissance aircraft.[59] Night-time provided little rest, however, for the classic BBC phrase 'Patrol activity continued' gave no indication of the nervous tension involved in the nocturnal routine.

10

Final Preparations

A general must know how to get his men their rations and
every other kind of store needed for war.

Socrates

Night was only marginally different from day. Every sound was menacing, and time seemed to last for ever. It was time for replenishment of water, food and ammunition; for bringing up reinforcements;
and for evacuating the wounded and the sick. Lorry drivers criss-
crossing the ground would peer through the gloom, straining to see
signs of minefields or slit trenches on the flat face of the desert. It was
time for the toiling improvement of defensive works: for digging –
usually accompanied by cursing – laying of mines and wiring. It was also
the time for patrols.

Patrolling was an intensely nerve-racking business, whether its
purpose was reconnaissance or fighting. Men would creep between
their lines and those of the enemy, the quiet being punctuated by mortar
bombs and bursts of machine-gun fire, possibly adding another corpse
to those already lying unburied and festering in no man's land. On 4th
Indian Division's frontage no fewer than 80 patrols were sent out
during September, each of which brought some additional information
concerning Axis dispositions and defences, culminating in a strong raid
on the night of 5/6 October by 1st Royal Sussex Regiment. Capturing
prisoners was a regular task for patrols. On the night of 11/12 October
a Greek patrol brought back a Slovenian deserter – the first of many
who were to fall into Greek hands from 20th Infantry Regiment of
Brescia Division opposite. 'At last we are among human beings again,'
said one deserter when he was brought in. 'If it was not for the fact that
we had been told that we should be brutally treated as [prisoners of
war], all of us would have come over.'[1]

A typical patrol report of the Durham Light Infantry recorded how a

148

reconnaissance patrol 'came under heavy fire when it approached the [target] area and had to dodge a strong enemy patrol on the way out. On the way back the patrol engaged an enemy patrol believed to be German, thirty yards south of west end of "Jarrow Gap", and had to make a detour through the "Don" minefield to get back to our lines.' A strong fighting patrol was then sent out to try to destroy the enemy ambushing party, but this had withdrawn.[2] Sapper F. Hesslewood accompanied some infantrymen on a fairly typical reconnaissance patrol. After seven anxious hours of creeping about in no man's land, he and his companions returned with a sample mine from an enemy field opposite, which he dumped disarmed on the table in the brigadier's tent.

> He wasn't there, of course, as it was still before reveille. Only the cooks were stirring. Captain Smith thanked me, a thing that pleasantly surprised me. I was not used to that sort of thing from an officer. On my way back to camp I did reflect on what the brigadier would have to say when he got to his table and found an anti-tank mine in front of him. At least he would know what sort of mine Jerry was using.[3]

Overhead might be heard the faint throb of aircraft engines passing unseen towards targets far behind the front – gunners, steadily and unhurriedly firing their harassment programmes on suspected enemy laagers and supply routes, would pause to listen for the first faint whisper of bombs that would send them scurrying for shelter. In other trenches, some of the infantry might have been fortunate enough to grasp a few hours' sleep in the cool night air, but most would be returning from some endeavour or other. At first light, both sides would 'stand to' against the possibility of dawn assault. One diarist noted that the flies stayed abed for twenty minutes before appearing in vast swarms to add to the misery of heat and dust. The British artillery – well supplied with ammunition – could afford to continue to fire all day on known or suspected targets, and with the sun rising behind them the Vickers medium machine-guns were also very active.

Other aspects of the plan that were being put in hand involved the whole of Alexander's Middle East Command, not merely Eighth Army. Much of the ability of the British to withstand disaster following the Gazala battles stemmed from the work of the base areas, where workshops, factories and the farms in the Middle East were able speedily to deliver munitions and other supplies that would otherwise have taken months to arrive from overseas. However, much of what was supplied was utter rubbish. The 'V' trade mark covered an astonishing array of

Indian goods in the Middle East and was, according to Keith Douglas, always a sign of the lowest quality and cheapest goods: ' "V" matches were in the proportion of about two good ones to eighteen bad ones in a packet. "V" ink was a foul greenish-grey liquid with lumps in it.'[4] 'V' cigarettes were especially bad. It was alleged that the manufacturers were annoyed that the troops believed the cigarettes were made from sawdust and camel dung, and had denied there was any sawdust in their product. Another equally horrific brand was Egyptian-made 'C-to-C' (Cape to Cairo).[5]

Although reserves were built up from the beginning of the war, the ever increasing ration strength – the total number of mouths to be fed – meant that the supply situation was far from satisfactory. From June 1941 to June 1942 the ration strength in the Middle East rose from 550,000 to 820,000, with 30,000 reinforcements arriving every month. GHQ was also responsible for the 40,000 troops and 250,000 civilians in Malta. Then in November 1941 Tenth Army in Iraq brought 140,000 men under command, and linked to this commitment was the evacuation of some 112,000 Poles from Russia including 35,000 civilians. Among the nationalities represented in Middle East forces were Czechoslovaks, Yugoslavs, Greeks and Cypriots. All these required over 30 different ration scales.[6] Neglect of the economic potential of the periphery of the Empire both increased the pressure on Britain's industry and added to the shipping crisis created by the fall of France and submarine sinkings. According to Churchill, shipping became 'the stranglehold and sole foundation' of British strategy. When it further emerged that precious shipping was wasted on civilian, non-essential and surplus cargoes – a problem compounded by the limited capacity of the ports in the region – the Americans protested when asked for help. Total port capacity in the region in 1940 amounted to around 5.5 million tons, but by the summer of 1942 the military programme alone required 5 million tons. It was essential that local resources be exploited to the utmost.[7]

The delicate balance of trade and political considerations involving Egypt, Iraq, Persia and the USSR meant that civilian imports needed to be compressed rather than suppressed, and so on 1 April 1941 the Middle East Supply Centre was created at the behest of Wavell and the British ambassador, Sir Miles Lampson, to mobilize and co-ordinate the economic potential of the region – at this stage only unreliably exploited. Commander Robert Jackson of the Royal Australian Navy was appointed director-general and set about licensing imports, collecting and distributing cereals to prevent hoarding and profiteering, and stimulating local production to conserve shipping. In due course

MESC's success became 'an indispensable condition both to achieving the necessary flow of supplies to Soviet Russia and to winning the battle of El Alamein'. An Egyptian factory manufactured spares for the RAF at short notice when stocks approached exhaustion; a Tel Aviv workshop switched overnight to the production of bolts whose shortage had stalled numerous tanks; research at universities in Jerusalem, Cairo and Beirut produced drugs to avert epidemics. At the same time reinforcements and *matériel* – particularly from America – could be quickly unloaded and forwarded from uncongested ports free from the threat of riots or rebellion because civilian requirements had also been considered.[8]

Nevertheless, security at ports and dumps and in the base areas remained a problem, it being necessary to guard against both theft and possible sabotage. Apart from vast quantities of *matériel*, between 1 August and 23 October Eighth Army received over 41,000 reinforcements in addition to new formations and units.[9] These all had to be accommodated, watered and fed while they were prepared to be sent into the desert. Vehicles, including the new Sherman tanks (called 'Swallows' for security purposes), required modifying with sand filters and desert paint. The DAF also received reinforcements. The 'West African Reinforcement Route' developed from a mail service originally set up in 1936. From July 1940 Longmore, as AOC-in-C, expanded this into a huge operation involving many thousands of aircraft. Those built in Britain were dismantled, boxed and transported by sea from the Clyde to Takoradi in the Gold Coast (Ghana), where they were reassembled and flown in convoy via Nigeria, French Equatorial Africa (Chad), Sudan and Egypt to Cairo. American aircraft – mainly Maryland, Marauder and Baltimore medium bombers – were flown across the southern Atlantic route from British Guiana via the Azores to Accra by British and American crews, thence to Cairo by the RAF. Some 3,500 aircraft had arrived this way, and in the month before Alamein over 700 aircraft of all types were flown in. It was no exaggeration to say that 'victory in Egypt came by the Takoradi route'.[10]

Signals preparations – both administrative and operational – were extensive. A massive buried-cable network was laid to all formations and units in Eighth Army to provide administrative communications, and vast quantities of line were also laid for tactical control. For example, 1st South African Division Artillery Signals Company laid 90 miles of line for 1st and 7th Field Regiments, 4th Field Regiment laid 54 miles, and 1st Light Anti-Aircraft Regiment laid 19 miles.[11] During Crusader some British commanders had begun to eavesdrop on their own command's operational traffic, to get an idea of the situation as it developed rather than waiting for formal reports.[12] At Alam Halfa, this process was systematized in the form of the 'J' service, developed by Lieutenant-Colonel Hugh Mainwaring, GSO 1 (Operations) at Eighth Army, and this brought to light serious lapses in the command and control system. After the battle the 'J' service was established on a permanent basis alongside the parallel development in the United Kingdom of 'Phantom', the GHQ Liaison Regiment.[13]

Eighth Army's transport services were of enormous significance. Some 8,700 vehicles were issued to Eighth Army between 1 August and 23 October, out of 10,300 landed in the Middle East.[14] When broken lorries returned for repair or overhaul to a vehicle-replacement depot, as they frequently did, they were immediately de-kitted. (This often did not take long: one unit reported that a 30-cwt lorry from the desert had as its complete kit one 7-pound sledgehammer with broken helve, one Italian officer's paybook, and half a tin of dehydrated potatoes.)[15] Thereafter the workshops' inspection and reissue of repaired vehicles, as well as the provision and servicing of all new vehicles (apart from those of the RASC, which had its own arrangements), was the responsibility of the Royal Army Ordnance Corps (RAOC).

However, early in 1942 the Army Council had announced the formation of the Royal Electrical and Mechanical Engineers to take over the repair responsibilities, with handovers and transfers to take place officially by 1 October. In the event this major reorganization took place smoothly, with no interruption to maintenance, and the shortfall of skilled artificers was made up from technical units elsewhere in the Middle East. Third-line workshops of the newly formed corps were retained under Eighth Army control, as was third-line transport (that not belonging to units or specifically assigned to brigades). An attempt was made to reduce congestion in the divisional areas by centralizing all tank output under the newly formed Tank Reorganization Group based on 1st Armoured Brigade. The purpose of this group was to streamline the replacement of tanks so they could be provided to regiments complete with crew, rations, ammunition and water. It included a personnel reinforcement and training unit provided by the Royal Armoured Corps (carrying stocks of all the different coloured berets and cap badges of the corps), a kitting-out section from the RAOC, a Royal Signals detachment to ensure that communications were in order, and RASC tank transporters to deliver tanks and their crews, to the units. When a regiment changed its armoured fighting vehicles to a different type it was found expedient to send the entire unit to the group, and if it lost a squadron one was provided complete and fully trained.[16]

With short lines of communications after arriving in the Alamein line the administrative problems were fewer, and of a different nature. The demand for fresh rations had increased at a time when the quantity and quality of vegetables available were at their lowest, and a massive redistribution of stocks was necessary – during the retreat it had been practically impossible to plan maintenance dispatches. The railway was heavily congested with backloaded stores, and every form of transport had been used by day and night in the early stages of the Alamein fighting. Thereafter the problems of supplying Eighth Army and of stockpiling for future operations put great strain on the railway organization. Up to 600 tons a day were handled though the main railhead at Burg el Arab. After the Alamein position had been occupied the troops were on full rations, with approximately 80 per cent of the forward troops eating bread, and varying amounts of hard equivalents making up a different scale for the remainder. The full scale included 'bully', onion and tinned vegetables or 'M and V' and tinned potatoes issued on alternate days. Both scales included tinned fruit, margarine, cheese, fish and sausage.[17]

Within units there were two main methods of cooking: centralized, with the food being brought up in insulated containers by 'B'-echelon transport, or by vehicle or section. If transport could not get forward or if crews did not laager early enough they might not get a hot meal, and having to break laager before dawn precluded a hot breakfast. As a result, a mobile cookhouse was developed and issued on a squadron basis to armoured regiments, and proved very successful.[18] During the retreat the strain on the front-line troops and the tendency to 'live out of a tin' – especially in armoured regiments – made it essential to supplement the normal rations and to modify the battle ration, both of which played their part in maintaining morale.

Medical arrangements had been in place for some time, but modifications were necessary for the offensive. Being somewhat isolated, XIII Corps in the south formed its own medical concentration area with two casualty clearing stations (CCSs), while the divisions of X and XXX Corps all established main dressing stations close to the coast road. An army CCS was established at Gharbaniyat, east of El Hammam. Desert conditions had evolved the field surgical unit (FSU), consisting of a surgeon, an anaesthetist and support personnel all mounted on a three-ton truck and a staff car. Highly mobile, FSUs could be attached to CCSs or field ambulances so that emergency surgery could be undertaken to render the wounded fit enough for evacuation to base hospitals in the Delta. On 18 October Montgomery informed Eighth Army's Deputy Director Medical Services that he expected the battle to last about seven days and to result in 10,000 casualties (excluding killed, missing and sick). The latter figure would prove remarkably accurate.[19]

Given that various Axis commanders later claimed that the odds were heavily stacked against them, one might question their satisfaction with the poor quality of the intelligence on which they based their plans, yet they seem to have been so busy with their own schemes that little effort was made to improve the flow of information regarding what Eighth Army was up to. Axis patrolling was patchy or often non-existent, and air reconnaissance, which had previously been relied on, was now proving singularly hazardous in the face of Allied air superiority. Low-level flights could not easily be accomplished in the face of DAF fighters and became increasingly sporadic, and in any case, were unable to distinguish between real and dummy equipment. In an attempt to get above the fighters, extremely high-level flights were made by Ju-86s capable of flying at over 45,000 feet, and Tedder had been concerned about these for some time. To counter them, two specially stripped down Spitfires were deployed which would work together – one with no armour or radio and only two machine-guns, the other with armour, radio and four machine-guns. The first victory was a solo effort by Flying Officer G. W. H. Reynolds at 49,000 feet on 24 August, and thereafter only five more Ju-86 sorties were reported, in which two planes were shot down. The last known of these sorties took place on 15 September. Meanwhile the DAF's 208 Squadron minutely mapped Axis positions.[20] Air superiority greatly assisted the major deception plan – Operation Bertram – that would cover the offensive. Eighth Army's deception techniques were not original but the staff co-ordination of these techniques and their incorporation into the plan from the beginning was new.[21]

Over the years, much has been made of the 'going-map' ruse at Alam Halfa, in which a marked map left in an abandoned vehicle showed areas of good 'going' where in fact it was bad. But such isolated expedients seldom work. In fact faked details started east of the point that Rommel's troops reached on 31 August, while it should not be forgotten that, to Panzerarmee's commanders, 'going' was simply another form of opposition – treated in the same way as minefields or points of resistance, to be avoided or overcome as necessary. What the 'going map' and the emphasis placed on it indicate is a poor understanding of German methods.[22]

The Germans also made extensive use of dummies, though they never attempted anything as comprehensive as Operation Bertram.

When they were threatened with immediate counter-attack on 5 July, 21st Panzer Division's war diary noted that 'the enemy must be cured of his zest for the offensive'; playing on British fears of the 88 mm gun, they had therefore created a number of dummies out of telegraph poles while mobile 88s would fire from their positions. Only three weeks later, when Allied patrols finally reached them, were two Bofors guns with poles wired up to resemble 88s revealed for what they were – and then, the patrol report noted, only when 5 yards away from the dummies.[23]

General Tuker of 4th Indian Division took great pleasure in the use of dummy figures which forward sentries pulled up and down. 'We kept the Italians amused in the moonlight,' he said. 'The next day the dummies are pulled up so that [the enemy] know they are dummies. The next night they are attacked where the dummies were shown the night before.'[24] Indeed, raids and dummy attacks would be the division's main contribution to the forthcoming offensive; responsible as it was for holding Ruweisat Ridge, it was important to keep the enemy anxious over this important ground. But Bertram was on another scale.

The breaking of the Abwehr Enigma cyphers in December 1941 extended Ultra into Axis thoughts on British intentions, enabling deception to be tailored accordingly.[25] In March 1942 'A' Force (the GHQ deception unit) had begun Operation Cascade, a comprehensive order-of-battle deception plan covering the whole Mediterranean theatre. By renaming base units and sub-areas, it created a bogus armoured division, seven bogus infantry divisions and a bogus corps to add to two bogus corps previously created. False radio traffic added realism to the information the Axis gathered from civilian sources in Egypt, but the Axis could not know that these sources were mostly controlled by the British through the Cheese double-agent network run by 'A' Force.[26] Montgomery summoned 'A' Force's commander, Colonel Dudley Clarke, to see him on 19 August. De Guingand told Clarke, 'Well, there it is. You must conceal 150,000 men with a thousand guns and a thousand tanks on a plain as flat and hard as a billiard table, and the Germans must not know anything about it, although they will be watching every movement, listening for every noise, charting every track . . . You can't do it of course, but you've bloody well got to!'[27] The Bertram plan, written by Clarke and implemented by Charles Richardson, included subsidiary plans code-named Diamond, Brian, Munassib, Martello, and Murrayfield, while, on the night of the assault 24th Australian Brigade holding the front near the coast would mount diversionary operations designed to draw enemy artillery fire into its area by means of so-called 'Chinese' attacks using wooden figures similar to Tuker's.[28]

The plan set out to suggest that the attack would not take place before the end of the first week in November.[29] Clarke therefore instituted Operation Treatment to create an atmosphere in Cairo suggesting that nothing serious would happen earlier: some of the better-known generals in Eighth Army were booked into Cairo hotels at the end of October, the staff college at Haifa had its term extended to include a major combined-operations exercise, and local rumours were given substantiation by Cheese. In Persia a bogus summit conference between Alexander and Wavell from India was arranged for 26 October.[30] A comprehensive radio programme (Canwell) was devised to support the visual illusion designed to conceal the huge build-up of forces in the northern sector of the Allied line while simulating a build-up in the south.[31] Martello and Murrayfield were complementary plans forming the most important aspects of the overall scheme, enabling the stationing of the armour of X Corps in assembly areas close to its start lines. Meanwhile a force equivalent to X Corps would be concentrated in an assembly area near El Imayid, to accustom the enemy to their presence. An air-force bombing and strafing programme similar to the one designed to precede the offensive was ordered in September, so that when the real one was started it would not arouse suspicion.[32] However, nothing could disguise the gathering of thousands of vehicles from those Axis reconnaissance aircraft which managed to penetrate the fighter screen.

The GHQ Camouflage Section was given the task of concealing the huge dumps of rations, ammunition, fuel and stores that would be accumulated in the north and making it appear that preparations were proceeding in the southern sector. The first problem was concealing the huge quantity of stores necessary for so large an operation. Fortunately 100 sections of slit trench were found near El Alamein station, beautifully lined with masonry. Into these were put 2,000 tons of petrol, which air observers tried and failed to locate.[33] A new field maintenance centre was sited on the ruins of a desert castle and village. Stocks were built up on partially demolished walls, and existing walls were demolished and rebuilt with stocks. These proved very realistic when viewed from the air, but the disruption of normal operations caused something of a headache for those running the FMC.[34] Food delivered at night on ten-ton lorries was stacked in the shape of 3-ton lorries and suitably camouflaged under nets, with any overflow stacked beside it in the shape of a driver's 'bivvie'. Similar methods were used for ammunition, engineer and ordnance stores.

In the southern sector there were real troop concentrations, including 44th (Home Counties) Division and 7th Armoured Division as well as 4th Light Armoured Brigade, detailed to carry out a diversionary attack which would also protect double-agents supporting the deception plan from accusations of deliberately sending false reports. The 44th (Home Counties) Division was the unluckiest in Eighth Army: units fresh from the United Kingdom had been decimated in attacks during Alam Halfa; one brigade had been removed and sent to 10th Armoured Division (without a proper chance to convert to its new lorried role) and 2nd Buffs had then been removed from 132nd (Kent) Brigade, leaving the division with just five battalions instead of nine. Now the remaining units spent the weeks preceding the battle driving back in darkness and forward in daylight to enable Axis observers to see the 'build-up' in the south.[35]

Plan Brian was a scheme to complete the impression that the southern area was being filled with strategic reserves of maintenance stores by creating three large dummy camps for (dummy) administrative personnel – counterparts to those in the north. Since it was to be suggested that stockpiling of stores was taking place at night, this did not require a lot of simulated lorry movement during the daytime and was carefully planned so that completion appeared to be due for November.[36] Major W. F. Abercrombie, commanding 1509 (Seychelles) Company Pioneer Corps, regarded his unit as the 'cheese in the mousetrap', recalled Lieutenant G. Raphael.

> The dummy camp and vehicle sites were erected at night with the help of moonlight and during daylight gave every appearance of busy military areas to very high-flying enemy planes. Vehicles travelled around and about creating dust and in the early morning every encouragement to brewing up in amongst the dummy bivouac was given, and of course round the vehicles or tanks, outlined in hessian, supported by thin wooden poles and 'cats' cradles of strong twine.[37]

Diamond was a scheme to build a 20-mile fake water pipeline, ostensibly to supply the large 'build-up' in the south. The dummy pipeline made use of three dummy pumphouses, two 'overhead' water-storage reservoirs, and a 'dish' reservoir.[38] The trench to carry it was dug conventionally, and fake railway line (itself made from 'flimsies') was laid in the trench to simulate the pipe. Before each stretch of the trench was filled in, the dummy pipe was removed at night for use further along the trench and traffic was diverted and driven alongside it to add veracity.[39] Significantly, it was built at a rate that suggested that the D-Day of any subsequent operation would not be until at least ten days after the real one.[40]

Plan Munassib involved digging gun pits with dummy guns at the eastern end of the Munassib depression (south of the sector where the main attack would come) to represent three and a half field regiments. They were left without any sign of normal movement around them, in order to convince the Germans they were dummies. Shortly before the attack was due to start real guns moved in and joined the assault – a ploy that was also intended to reinforce the German belief that the main assault was still due to come in the south.

The initial attack by XXX Corps was planned to go to a depth of some 6,000–7,000 yards and, in order to be able to bring down defensive fire in front of the infantry on their objectives, it was essential to deploy field guns within 1,500 yards of the defended localities. The problem that immediately arose was how best to conceal the necessary large concentration of guns from the enemy. It was solved in variety of ways, but one of the best methods, used to hide much of the supporting artillery, was 'cannibalization'. A 25-pounder and its limber, and also its distinctive tractor, would be hidden under covers called Cannibals designed to resemble a lorry. No fewer than 360 guns were concealed this way in preparation to launch the attack on 23 October.[41] This worked very well except on one occasion when a strong wind sprang up and a large number of supposed 3-ton lorries were seen swaying like willows in the breeze. Luckily the enemy did not spot this curious phenomenon.

Major R. Gordon-Finlayson of 128th Field Regiment Royal Artillery was in M Training Area on 14 October when his commanding officer gave orders to the battery commanders for Operation Lightfoot. Reconnaissance parties, digging parties and ammunition-dumping parties were called for, the cover plan was explained, and security was stressed. There would be total radio silence, and a carefully prearranged timetable would ensure that the guns and vehicles moved forward at night to hide under covers which had been set up some time before lest air photographs show a change in vehicle density behind the front and the enemy suspect the imminence of the attack.[42]

Early planning required each unit to state the number of vehicles it would require for an attack and a short advance. From 1 October these numbers were fixed, and any shortfall in numbers or change in arrangement as vehicles moved back and forth was hidden by the erection of dummies, which in turn could be used to shelter real vehicles when they were actually on a position. Each formation appointed officers to ensure that its dummies could not be seen spotted as such from the air, for which purpose they were interspersed with real vehicles, realistic track patterns were produced, and some real and dummy vehicles swapped position at the end of each day.[43]

Montgomery's change of plan on 6 October naturally had a knock-on effect on Bertram. The original Martello area was expected to be some 15 to 20 miles south of a series of tracks that led both south and north. The new area could only portend an attack in the north, and an additional deception was required. Three staging areas – Murrayfield (North), Murrayfield (South) and Meltingpot – were established astride a series of tracks tending towards the south. To bring the armoured formations forward, the engineers had to bulldoze tracks from Martello through Cannibals 1 and 2 (where the concealed guns were located) to the front line. These tracks were built by South African road-construction companies using American equipment, and, owing to the postponement of work for deception purposes, some 120 miles of track had to be completed in a very short space of time. This had to be organized so that the tracks followed the least conspicuous course, and began from different places so as not to appear as a coherent track scheme until the last minute.[44]

The purpose of Plan Murrayfield was to conceal that the guns and tanks had moved from the rear. Accordingly, 1st Armoured Division and 74th Armoured Brigade (Dummy Tanks) moved forward from Wadi Natrun to El Imayid in two stages. The first, to a staging area south of Burg el Arab, was carried out openly as a training exercise; then the units moved to the forward positions at night and were immediately replaced by dummies. This involved 1,500 vehicles from 2nd New Zealand Division, 1,370 dummy trucks, 64 dummy guns, and 30 dummy tanks occupying the space vacated, although no move was apparent to aerial reconnaissance.[45] Plan Meltingpot saw 10th Armoured Division move from Wadi Natrun by day to a staging area far to the south, then return at night to the main assembly area in the north, having left behind a mixture of dummy and real equipment.

From 18 October the emphasis was firmly on Bertram. The first move was to send 9th Armoured Brigade to 1st Armoured Division's staging area during the day, then after dark it returned to the corps assembly area, where it took its place under Sunshields. These were originally an idea of Wavell's – covers fitted over tanks to make them appear like lorries. Thus no difference in the dispositions in and behind the Alamein line would appear from the air. In fact 24th Armoured Brigade was now in the positions vacated by 9th, and during the day Headquarters 1st Armoured Division with 2nd Armoured Brigade moved up to their staging areas, as did 10th Armoured Division to the south. This presented the Camouflage Section with a difficult and unforeseen problem, as there would now be gaps left by the tanks moving forward. Fortunately, Captain John Baker from the Camouflage Development Centre at Helwan, near Cairo, made 'tanks' from the plaited panels of split palm that the local fellahin (farm workers) used as beds. By a remarkable piece of improvisation, thousands of such panels were made by local workmen and knocked together in rudimentary form by three pioneer companies (one East African, one Mauritian and one from the Seychelles) together with No. 1 Camouflage Company Royal Engineers. Obscured under camouflage nets, they were all that was necessary to create three large 'armoured formations' apparently camouflaged and awaiting movement orders, probably to the south.[46]

The final stage of the concentration took place between 20 and 22 October, when all movement was at night until the whole of X Corps was in position near the coast behind El Alamein station. This required a massive effort by engineers, pioneers and transport, and the labour of several infantry battalions. It involved 722 Sunshields, 560 Cannibals, 500 dummy tanks, 150 dummy guns, and nearly 5,000 dummy transport of various kinds.[47] Other, seemingly trivial, details also needed attention. Major N. P. MacDonald of 41st Royal Tank Regiment recalled that 21 October was notable for last-minute 'flaps'. Many of the tanks were new, and the crews had to learn operating procedures and thoroughly check equipment and weapons. Also, a camouflage painting unit arrived and in less than 12 hours had transformed all his unit's tanks into peculiar shapes – if seen from a distance. Close up they seemed a mess of ochre and black paint, the latter being very wet and sticky.[48]

Panzerarmee was aware of the existence of dummy equipment behind the British lines, but assumed that this was to misdirect air attacks, as both sides had used decoys for this purpose for some time. Certainly the changes from dummy to real went unnoticed by Axis air reconnaissance, which day after day reported no changes of any significance either in British positions or in their density of occupation. Gale-force winds on 16–17 October caused the destruction of many dummy vehicles and brought the fear of the plan being blown, but hard work by the camouflage units under extra fighter cover repaired the damage in short order.[49]

Rommel left no clear record that he expected Eighth Army's offensive to take any particular course, except that he expected a battle of *matériel* and attrition similar to what transpired. 'In this form of action,' he noted, 'the full value of the excellent Australian and New Zealand infantry would be realized and the British artillery would have its effect.'[50] However, it is doubtful that he saw the issues and their consequences clearly before the battle: his intelligence staff practically wrote off the New Zealanders after Alam Halfa, reporting them as weak and low in morale, and did not even bother to record their disposition clearly within Eighth Army. In Panzerarmee's records and the plans issued before the battle, the positioning of troops and especially reserves, and several minor instructions, all indicate that the British attack was expected to take the broadly conventional form of a breakthrough and an outflanking movement through the southern half of the line. An intelligence summary issued on 10 October deduced from British reconnaissance activity that the main thrust could be expected somewhere south of Ruweisat Ridge, with the possibility of an attack along the coast road as either an alternative or a diversion. The mining of the southern sector had been given priority by Rommel before his departure in September, but lost out to the northern sector early in October primarily because the shortages of transport, fuel and infantry precluded ever making the southern sector impregnable. The plan was to absorb the assault and weaken its impetus before swinging back on the hinge of El Mreir or El Dhib on to the massive Qatani minefield.[51]

The Germans expected the method of attack to follow the pattern adopted during the two British offensive phases of the Alam Halfa battle, in both of which the infantry advance had been allowed to peter out before the arrival of armour, to which the Germans were confident their own armour could react more quickly. A touch of complacency is even evident in the records. While Stumme and Panzerarmee were expecting an attack to take place during the full-moon period (Westphal issued a report predicting 20–25 October), on 21 October Oberst Ulrich Liss, head of Fremde Heeres West (the intelligence branch of OKW), visited Panzerarmee and expressed the opinion, based on various pieces of information regarding the Allied invasion of North Africa, that the British attack would not start before the beginning of November; he also reported this to Berlin.[52]

Panzerarmee intelligence, however, was convinced that an attack was imminent. But it was also confident that the assembly and concentration of the assault forces would provide warning. 'An assembly of attacking troops and artillery will take at least one or two days, our own troops cannot be taken by surprise provided they keep their eyes open and make use of every means of observation.'[53] As early as 1 October the intelligence officer of 15th Panzer Division had predicted the British use of deception with some accuracy, but his forecast of the attack methods was less perceptive. He too expected warning of an impending assault, and later criticized the quality of reconnaissance by both land and air. He made no attempt to predict the date, and the only warning Panzerarmee did receive came from an Italian naval intelligence message on 22 October warning that British naval operations were imminent and would possibly include an assault landing near the coast.[54]

However, the lack of obvious preparations continued to suggest that the British were not yet ready but would follow the pattern set the previous year and open their attack in November.[55] The double loss of Fellers and Seebohm was a considerable blow to German intelligence and, although a replacement radio-intercept company was sent from Germany, this never achieved the efficiency of Seebohm's unit. With a general improvement in Eighth Army's radio procedures and with air reconnaissance extremely difficult in the teeth of an aggressive and dominant DAF, intelligence had virtually dried up. What information the Axis did have suggested that logistic build-up and the forward movement of troops gave it until the middle of November to prepare.[56] But in the first three weeks of October sea and air attacks sank no less than 45 per cent of Italian and 59 per cent of German tonnage dispatched, and 65 per cent of the latter was fuel.[57] This halved the potential endurance of Panzerarmee's armour and transport from 21 days to 11.[58] Thus Stumme commented on 22 October that his troops were 'living from hand-to-mouth; we fill one gap only to see another open. We cannot build up the basic supply which would enable us to overcome critical situations through our own resources and which allows operational freedom of movement, which is an absolutely vital necessity for the army.'[59] Red-faced, almost bursting out of a uniform a size too small for him, with a monocle positively screwed into his eye socket, he hissed the word *Pflicht* (duty) almost as a threat, and made it clear that the testing time was close at hand.[60]

PART II

The Battle

11

Barrage

It is not a field or a few acres of ground we are defending, but
a cause, and whether we defeat the enemy in one battle or by
degrees, the consequences will be the same.

Thomas Paine

'I felt different from the rest in that for the life of me I could not see
the sense in grown men hurling chunks of red hot metal at each
other, the only direct object being to mangle and maim,' recalled
Bombardier Louis Challoner of 3rd Royal Horse Artillery.

> I remember Len Chandler alluding to one conscientious objector who had
> volunteered to become a medical orderly and who had seen more action,
> danger and death than most of us. 'I wish I'd had the guts to do what he's
> done,' said Len, 'but I'm not that kind of conchie. With all my conscience, I
> object to Hitler and all his brood; I object to his ways and I object to his
> means, but just objecting, however conscientious we are about it, is not
> enough. We have to do something about it, and this is what we can do.'[1]

Since for the most part the barrage would comprise concentrations
on known enemy positions, these had to be carefully and accurately sur-
veyed. V. L. Bosazza of 46th Field Survey Company SAEC described
his work in the build-up:

> In September our artillery drew attention to the fact that the Axis guns, par-
> ticularly their 88s, either did not have alternative positions or did not use
> them. A British survey company officer came up and helped us with
> unmarked triangulation stations far forward. At the same time four tubular
> scaffolding towers were erected to observe enemy positions. With help from
> aerial photographs we gradually built up an accurate plot of the order of
> battle of almost the entire enemy artillery.[2]

The essence of counter-battery work was determining the locations of
hostile batteries. While photo-reconnaissance by the RAF was essential,
the unsung heroes were 4th (Durham) Survey Regiment Royal Artillery.

Sound-ranging was useful, but never as effective or as accurate as flash-spotting, which was done mainly from towers such as Bosazza described at intervals on the front.

Designed by Major L. Kellett and first used at the siege of Tobruk, these towers were erected in accurately surveyed locations and gave useful landmarks in the featureless desert. The flash-spotters, protected by a few sandbags, lay on the tops of them with their binoculars, theodolites and telephones and could pinpoint an active hostile battery, whose presence could then be confirmed from air photographs. Efforts were made to decide if a battery was German or Italian and whether to 'strop it up' there and then or to leave it in blissful ignorance until H-Hour. If German it would receive a heavier blow, and often it was decided to give it a second 'strop' after an interval of 15 minutes, when any survivors would have recovered their breath and be back on the gun position. Eventually some 250 hostile battery positions were located, of which 140 were targeted on the opening night of the offensive.[3]

Although the flash-spotting towers were invaluable, and subject to much harassment from the enemy, K. A. Nicholls of 7th Medium Regiment could later recall only one attempt to copy them. A tower appeared overnight, and soon after dawn a single gun was moved out of one of the troops to engage this 'one-gun' target. Difficult though it was to hit, it was not long before the scaffolding collapsed. 'This seemed to dissuade the enemy from trying again, although he had not succeeded in destroying any of our towers.'[4] The gunners would be crucial to help the infantry forward, but the responsibility for breaching the Devil's Gardens and enabling the infantry's transport and support weapons to join them, and crucially the armour, would fall to the engineers.

British minefields were marked with perimeter fences of one or two strands of barbed wired, from which hung tin triangles that glinted in the sun. Between these fences would usually be at least some mines, but the fences themselves became effective obstacles to the Axis once their significance was known. British Minefield D was among those captured by the Germans in the south after the Alam Halfa battle, but it had no mines in it whatever. As the offensive approached, engineer recces were ordered which revealed that the paucity of mines had not been discovered. Three times it was reported that there were 'no mines in the minefield, but the gaps are now heavily mined'. The tin triangles had worked. (All too well it seems: during the assault, the lead vehicles of one British battalion made straight for the marked gaps and were promptly blown up.) While the British used minefields as deterrents and a delaying technique, the Germans used theirs as weapons, leaving them unmarked on the British side so that it was possible to know where they began only by reconnaissance or destruction.[5]

A School of Mines was set up when Eighth Army's chief engineer, Brigadier F. H. Kisch, gave Major Peter Moore some papers on breaching minefields and said, 'I'm sure there should be a *drill* for this.' Based at Burg el Arab and using the first Polish mine detectors* to arrive in theatre, and assisted by the Royal Engineer commander of 1st Armoured Division, Lieutenant-Colonel Kenneth McKay, the school evolved a drill for a troop (or platoon) of two officers and some forty men to clear a gap some 16 yards wide. This drill was then taught throughout Eighth Army. It included everything from the plotting of minefields to location and marking of individual mines within gaps.[6] Despite the widespread use of aerial photographs and other methods, the only really effective way of discovering enemy minefields was for a sapper officer to go 'snooping around'. Armed with a compass and binoculars, he would wander into the afternoon haze, which provided ample cover, when the enemy was apt to lie low. As the haze cleared in the early evening, he could take bearings of whatever was visible and lie up until dark before returning.[7]

Eighth Army received a total of 403 mine detectors of various types. However, there was only one sure way to locate mines, as Sapper B. Easthope of 577th Field Company recalled:

> We used bayonets. Mine detectors were not satisfactory. Besides there were wooden mines. You probed lightly – if you struck something solid you explored gently around it with your hands. If a wire, where did it lead? Don't cut it, don't lift it. Expose it and find where it goes to. You had to take your chance when clearing mines. One chap from an 'S' mine got a pellet in the jaw which came out by his neck behind the ear. There were 348 ball bearings in an 'S' mine, which would jump about three feet out of the ground before exploding.[8]

Another new development was a special flail tank called a Scorpion,† comprising a Matilda fitted with a rotating drum wielding chains to explode the mines in its path. Largely developed by 21st Field Park

---

* Invented in Scotland by Captain J. S. Kosacki and Lieutenant Kalinowski, and the forerunner of modern metal detectors, these would send a 'ping' to headphones whenever they passed over a metal object buried in the ground.

† Brigadier Kenneth Ray, chief engineer of XXX Corps, suggested the name 'Scorpion'. Montgomery was said to be delighted and quoted from the Bible, 'My father also chastised you with whips, but I shall chastise you with scorpions' (1 Kings 12:14) (Orpen, *South African Forces, World War II*, vol. III, p. 405).

Company SAEC, it was demonstrated to Morshead on 12 September and to Montgomery on the 16th. While most of 1st Army Tank Brigade were sent to southern Palestine, a party from 42nd Royal Tank Regiment and 6 officers and 39 soldiers from 44th Royal Tank Regiment would man the 24 Scorpions available by 16 October.[9] The flails were driven by an auxiliary Ford V-8 engine which was housed with a sapper driver in an armoured box outside the tank hull. It flailed at about 1 mile per hour. The dust cloud this produced 'had to be seen to be believed', and the machine had to be driven practically 'blind', with the driver in his gas mask. 'If the flail driver looked out he would be deluged in sand and bombarded by stones, scrub and the occasional mine!' An Italian prisoner was later reported as saying that the slowly advancing pillar of dust out of which emerged dreadful noises of clanking, grinding and rattling of chains was more frightening than the artillery barrage.[10] Sappers had to follow the Scorpions on foot, to ensure the lane was clear and marked, and each gap, however cleared, would need to be driven through the entire depth of the enemy position. Since at least three or four fields might be encountered, each at least 400 yards deep, the total depth to be cleared was considerable. In the event, fields were found to be perhaps half as deep as expected, but more numerous and very ill-defined, with many patches of mines laid between them in no particular pattern, which greatly complicated and slowed the work.[11] Apart from preparing to clear lanes in enemy minefields, the sappers had also to clear lanes in Eighth Army's fields and to assist in many of the other preparations.

The security of the plan was meticulously controlled, with briefings for the top down beginning on 28 September for brigadiers and the crucial Royal Engineer commanders. On 10 October commanding officers of units were informed, many attending the Amariya cinema near Alexandria for briefings by the Army Commander. Although warned to expect a 'dogfight' lasting up to 12 days, most, such as Lieutenant-Colonel Victor Turner, commanding 2nd Rifle Brigade, found the briefing 'absolutely thrilling'. For the first time they experienced the complete assurance of ultimate victory, and left Alexandria and Cairo for ever when they left the cinema.[12] They were allowed to divulge the plan to their company, battery and squadron commanders a week later, but only on 21 October were they in turn permitted to brief their junior officers, NCOs and soldiers. Meanwhile units had extensive preparations to make.

Lieutenant-Colonel William Roper-Caldbeck of 1st Black Watch described how

I had been told of the attack but I could not pass on the information. Eventually the whole Division was to assemble and attack from the area held by the Battalion so there was a lot of preparations to make. We dug slit trenches for the whole B[attalion] back in the reserve c[ompany] areas and buried I have no idea how many tons of food, ammunition and water. On 19 October, we handed over to 5th Seaforths and moved back to 'E' Box where we made our final preparations.[13]

Neil McCallum was manning a traffic control point on 23 October when

a colonel came up in a jeep. 'It starts tonight,' he said. Then he smiled. 'I dare say you have guessed it is not a scheme this time.' This was slightly untrue, because everything in the army is a 'scheme', only this scheme was to have a real enemy. Sure enough, when the final orders were brought by dispatch rider, they were headed 'Scheme Three'. The rehearsals had been schemes one and two.[14]

Montgomery insisted that every man should go into battle thoroughly briefed on both the overall plan and his part in it. This might seem an obvious necessity, but too often soldiers have been led into operations with only the sketchiest idea of the 'big picture' and with no more than a 'Follow me' from an equally baffled officer. At Tel el Eisa in July, Lieutenant Stuart Hamilton of 8th Royal Tank Regiment had witnessed the Australian style of orders group when he noticed a group of infantry gathering around an empty oil drum. 'They were an incredibly scruffy crowd with no one appearing to be dressed the same: some stripped to the waist with dirty ragged shorts and scuffed boots; others in dirty slacks and equally dirty singlets: some wearing slouch hats, others with tin hats or bare headed: talking, smoking and laughing amongst themselves.' Soon a regimental sergeant-major appeared; he was tall and immaculately dressed, with clean and polished kit that would have done credit to a Guards battalion. 'He stood on the drum with his hands on his hips, and bellowed "Friends, Romans and Countrymen" – this is going to be good I thought – "lend me yer fuckin' ears you heap! You lucky bastards are going to have the chance once more of putting the shits up the fuckin' Jerries! Aren't you the lucky ones . . ."'[15] Now Morshead wrote to his wife, 'A hard fight is expected, and it will no doubt last a long time. We have no delusions about that. But we shall win . . .'[16]

Evan Thomas was an volunteer serving with the American Field Service* as an ambulance driver attached to the New Zealanders.

---

* The first AFS unit – comprising 100 men aged 19 to 55, recruited from across the USA and serving without pay – assembled in New York and entrained for Canada on 6 November 1941.

'Everyone knew that an end had come to the old business of squirting a garden hose at a four-alarm fire. As one New Zealander put it: "We've got the men; we've got the equipment; and here we go – rip, split, or bust!" '[17] Among those preparing to take part were American officers of the King's Royal Rifle Corps (known to its members as the 60th Rifles, having been raised as the 60th Royal American Regiment in 1756). In total, 17 American volunteer officers served with the regiment during the war, all eventually being either killed or wounded. Lieutenant Charles Bolté recalled a year spent training in England, where 'we learned how to stand up straight, how to shoot straight . . . and all the problems of training men and looking after them in barracks, in the field, and in battle. We learned to salute with a quivering hand, to say "petrol" for "gas" and "wireless" for "radio", to drive on the left and to mistrust Americans who talked about the natural superiority of everything American.' Now, 'we all cheered when we heard the news: action at last, a big battle that promised to be the turning point of the war'.[18]

The men of Eighth Army were fortified in the knowledge of their superiority: 'This thing can't go wrong,' Sergeant J. A. Brown of the Transvaal Scottish told his diary, 'we know it can't – and because of this the spirit of aggression is swelling in us like a dark, strong tide.'[19] Nevertheless, as Peter Jones noted when sent to 2/48th Battalion on 22 October, there were ominous portents. Passing a hospital tent he saw a large sign with the silhouette of a vampire bat and the words 'Advanced Blood Bank'.[20]

Despite the growing feeling of confidence in Eighth Army, deserters were still quite numerous, although soldiers had little chance of blending into the life of the cities, where the military police were vigilant. Deserters included officers lurking in Cairo, impeccably dressed scroungers who would ask newcomers from the desert for a loan of money, always because their 'wallet had been stolen by pickpockets'.[21] Interestingly, many front-line infantry units, having been made up to strength with reinforcements, now found themselves over strength: either the news of Alam Halfa or the possibility that the Army Commander might know his job had combined to persuade some absentees that the time was ripe to return to their units. Most commanding officers were content to impose extra duties by way of punishment rather than refer the matter to authorities who might feel it necessary to take more drastic action.[22]

On 23 September, Gunner R. H. Roper returned to 57th Light Anti-Aircraft Regiment, having been missing believed captured since 2 February. He had been injured in the knee in Cyrenaica, and had spent five months lying up in caves, cared for by local Senussi Arabs. Shortly after the fall of Tobruk he was joined by some South Africans who had escaped from the fortress, and with Arab guides the party made a journey of 60 miles to reach a patrol of the LRDG. He was awarded a Distinguished Conduct Medal for his fortitude and bravery.[23]

Major Gordon-Finlayson's battery now moved forward.

> The digging party had arrived in the gun area by Tel el Eisa Station on the night of 17 October. Each day the men and vehicles had to be well clear of the forward area before first light, only to return to their labours each night after dark. Gun platforms were selected, pits marked out, ammunition trucks met and their loads man-handled into shallow holes until each gun-pit had 750 rounds hidden beside it. Ammunition pits were marked with stakes to avoid total obliteration by drifting sand. Command posts were dug, alternate positions were chosen, survey checked and re-checked, cable duplicated and buried, slit trenches prepared. Smoking was forbidden, but the men worked with a will; they had looked forward to this moment during the years of training at home. All round us other units did similar jobs in the darkness, the clink of shovels, furious whisperings and revving of trucks axle-deep in sand disturbed the night until one felt that Rommel himself would hear us.[24]

Lieutenant R. G. W. Mackilligin, another Highland gunner, recalled that the

> prelude to the battle was a nightmare . . . we worked from dusk to dawn each night, and as the flies and heat made it virtually impossible to sleep during the day, we entered the battle in a fair state of exhaustion. Working conditions were appalling: the Alamein position had been fought over several times and the whole area was littered with decomposing corpses, some unburied and others whose graves had been uncovered by the wind. The stench of putrefaction was all-pervading and the air thick with dust and horrible desert flies.[25]

From as early as 6 September through to 22 October, flights of 20 to 30 bombers flew over Tobruk almost every night, while others attacked Matruh, Sollum, Bardia, Benghazi and even Suda Bay in Crete and Navarino (Pilas) in south-west Greece as and when intelligence reports suggested shipping movements there. In this respect the recently arrived Liberators of the USAAF proved immensely useful. Once their rest period after Alam Halfa was complete, the light bombers, fighter-bombers and fighters were able to start attacks on landing grounds, supply columns and concentrations in the immediate rear of Panzerarmee. When, on 9 October, it was learned that heavy rains had rendered many of these landing grounds unserviceable, a particularly heavy raid was organized which, for the loss of 19 aircraft, effectively crippled the Axis air defence to such an extent that it never fully recovered. From that day on the Luftwaffe was never again a serious threat to Eighth Army operations.[26]

On the night of 19 October the air offensive in direct support of the forthcoming land operations officially began, with light bombers and fighters joining in with the medium and heavy bombers and concentrating on the airfields around El Daba. The next day Coningham announced that the 'Allied Air Forces have today started the battle. The whole of our air and ground personnel is involved. The victory you are going to win will be decisive in the land battle.'[27]

On 20 October an Italian supply convoy was mauled and the tanker *Panuco* was sent to the seabed by a Wellington. Westphal demanded a replacement, and a helpful reply arrived on the Enigma machine: 'Tanker *Proserpina* ... arriving Tobruk early 26th ... tanker *Luisiana* will set sail with tanker *Portofino* from Taranto evening 27th, put into Tobruk approximately 31st' – helpful to both sides, although the Axis did not know it.[28]

Throughout the following five days and nights the assault was maintained with barely an hour in any 24 in which Allied aircraft were not over Axis lines. During these five days the DAF flew 2,209 sorties and the Americans 260 for the loss of 13 British and 1 American aircraft, and a continuous fighter patrol was maintained over the Axis forward airfields to force them on to the defensive.[29] At the same time, fighter cover over Eighth Army was gradually thickened. This increased air activity did not go unnoticed by Axis headquarters, but the ground commanders remained lulled by the apparent lack of corresponding activity in the lines opposite, and the air commanders were utterly preoccupied trying to repair the damage already caused.[30]

By ferrying forward over a number of nights before D-Day, each XXX Corps division with a part in the initial assault took over the portion of front that would form its start line. Only 2nd New Zealand Division had to move forward in entirety, although the other formations had to bring forward reserves and extra artillery. During darkness on 21 October the two New Zealand infantry brigades were brought forward by 4th and 6th Reserve Mechanical Transport Companies to an area about 10 miles behind the front, where they were dispersed to ready-made slit trenches and instructed not to show themselves above ground during daylight. The following night they moved forward again, many of the infantry having to march. These complicated movements took place along a series of parallel tracks starting some 8 or 10 miles behind the front line, some of which had been used for routine supply purposes. Others – especially in those areas close to the front line – had been camouflaged by allowing wire, minefields and other defences to appear to cut across them. At night, all these obstacles had to be removed and traffic kept flowing by control points manned by provosts linked with 18 telephone posts so that they could report any accidents or breakdowns which might impede the flow or disclose the use of the tracks in daylight.[31]

The Australians were served by their own tracks called Diamond, Boomerang, Two Bar and Square, manned by 9th Division Provost Company; 51st (Highland) Division by Sun, Moon and Star; 2nd New Zealand Division by a short branch leading off Star and by Bottle and Boat; and 1st South African Division by Hat. The tracks were marked by cairns of stones with the side facing the driver painted white. Two provost sections from 501st Traffic Control Unit (formed only on 7 October) policed each track, while another manned a 24-hour straggler post on the Matruh–Alexandria road. One of the many duties performed by the traffic police was maintaining dozens of hurricane lamps which they had improvised inside 'flimsies', each with a shape appropriate to the track name cut out of it. Indeed, it would be the sappers, signallers and military policemen who led the armour into battle, and for the last of these it was, as the Deputy Provost Marshal declared, 'both operationally and administratively a bigger job than Military Police have ever tackled before'.[32]

This complicated and difficult movement plan over three or four nights was carried out very successfully, despite some units reporting problems in preventing unauthorized movement or in keeping their men from appearing above ground. Although the western ends of all the tracks were well within Axis artillery range, they received only the usual random and sporadic shelling. A recurring problem would be created by the overlaying not only of units and formations, but of two corps over the same area of ground, leading to considerable confusion for those charged with traffic control or administration and supply. Map-reading on such featureless terrain was difficult enough at the best of times, and in the confusion created by battle and its attendant dust, smoke and noise (to say nothing of night-time movement) units would claim to have arrived on an objective only to have their claims disputed by others. Since questioning an officer's map-reading is akin to questioning his personal honour, this would often result in some very heated arguments.[33]

Final preparations involved loading vehicles. In the armoured regiments this was complicated by the variety of tanks employed. Most such regiments had a squadron of Crusaders and two of Grants and Shermans in their fighting or 'F' echelons. This extraordinary mix of equipment – with three different fuels and weapons of nine different calibres (further complicated by high-explosive and armour-piercing rounds) – created a considerable headache for quartermasters. Immediate replenishments of ammunition and fuel were carried by soft-skinned lorries in the 'A' echelon, which also included fitters from the light aid detachment to make running repairs and the regimental aid post for immediate treatment of casualties. Two gallons of water and three days' rations per man were carried on each vehicle for the first three days of battle, plus three days' reserve (for emergencies only).[34]

On the morning of 23 October, 21st Field Squadron Royal Engineers was briefed by a senior officer:

> I know I'm speaking to young men only 20 or 21 years old, but I have to give it to you straight: right behind you is a whole division relying on you sappers to open the lanes for the tanks and infantry to pass through. Also behind you are a thousand guns. They will put up a terrific barrage as you sappers go in. Some of you will be killed, or lose an arm or leg, because Jerry will be trying to stop you. There will be mortaring, Stuka dive bombing and the rest.

Sapper A. Rowlands thought he must have smoked about 20 cigarettes in ten minutes. 'I was shaking, saying my prayers and wishing it was only a dream.'[35] Ewen MacDonald of 5th Cameron Highlanders had just returned from a few days' leave in Cairo. He asked his friend Kenny MacDonald, a shepherd on the Lochiel estate at Achnacarry, 'Kenny, have you felt fear?' 'No Ewen I haven't,' Kenny replied. 'But I myself felt a twinge of fear,' wrote Ewen years later, 'because I had seen round about in the lines graves which reminded me of the potato pits which my father used for the local crofters in the sand. The graves each had a rifle upside down with a helmet on top of it. And I thought, this is what might happen to me.'[36]

By 23 October, Eighth Army had a powerful superiority, with 1,029 tanks ready for battle (including 267 Shermans, capable of mixing it with the German Panzer Mark IV 'Specials' but still largely unknown to their crews) and about 200 replacements standing by. It also fielded 832 25-pounders, 32 4.5-inch, 20 of the superb new 5.5-inch guns, and 24 'Priests' – 105 mm howitzers mounted on Grant chassis – plus 735 6-pounders (including a few self-propelled and lightly armoured, called 'Deacons') and 521 2-pounders. The Germans could field only 218 serviceable tanks at this time, with another 21 under repair and some 50 light Mark IIs, while the Italians fielded 278. Thus British superiority amounted to around 2 to 1 – still less than the 3 to 1 generally accepted as necessary to assault prepared positions.

A printed address to the soldiers from Montgomery, with a facile cricket metaphor and a final theatrical exhortation, formed the last, carefully timed line of the prologue for the drama about to unfold:

> All that is necessary is that each and every officer and man, should enter this battle with the determination to see it through – to fight and to kill – and finally to win. If we do this, there can only be one result – together we will hit the enemy for 'Six', right out of Africa ... Let us all pray that 'the Lord mighty in battle' will give us victory.[37]

The day of 23 October passed quietly enough – if mortars and machine-guns can be said to be quiet – just like every other day for weeks previously. As the afternoon drew on, with the wind blowing the dust about like flour, the RAF could be seen operating way above, and not a single Axis aircraft was reported over Eighth Army.[38] At dusk, 212 Group RAF and 7th Wing SAAF moved with their Hurricanes to forward airfields from where they could operate more intensively against Axis landing grounds.[39] When the hour for action was drawing near, a throbbing, at first half-imagined then faintly heard, stole through the night and grew into a rhythmic surging sound as bombers approached from the east and passed over. Major Gordon-Finlayson's battery moved forward as it had 'so carefully repeated many times over similar ground in M Training Area' to occupy its carefully prepared battle positions.

> All that day, whilst the Jocks who were to attack were hidden in slit trenches around us, forbidden to emerge until nightfall, command posts worked out gun programmes and checked interminable details; numbers one unearthed their ammunition and piled it round their gunpits in stacks according to targets to be engaged. I visited all the men, explained the plan and read to them the Army Commander's message.[40]

Panzerarmee sent a situation report to Berlin: 'Quiet day. No change.' Despite the flatness of the ground and the absence of cover, Eighth Army's deception schemes had achieved operational surprise.[41]

As dusk fell, most men were glad just to get the chance to finally stretch their legs. In 3rd South African Brigade's area the hush that descended, as it did along most of the line, was broken only by the solemn notes of 'Abide With Me'. Men stood to attention as Sergeant John Summers, following a tradition of the 1st Royal Durban Light Infantry and adopted now by the 1st Imperial Light Horse and Brigade Headquarters, played the hymn on a trumpet.[42] 'Perhaps the worst of the suspense was over,' recalled the Rifle Brigade's historian:

> We were now committed: no luck, no accident had transported us to the base. It was no good wishing we had spent more time maintaining the carrier or learning to read a map or had written more punctiliously home or behaved a

little better in Cairo. In a quarter of an hour we would advance through the minefields which we had sat opposite for the best part of two months. It was better to concentrate on what was important at the moment – was there time to have a 'brew'.[43]

When the sun went down, the Axis troops climbed out of their trenches, stretched luxuriously, waited for and ate their evening meals, and began once again the monotonous night routine of reliefs and of digging, wiring and laying mines.

For the crew of HMS *Belvoir*, a Hunt-class destroyer, 23 October was much like any other day; orders to sail that afternoon were probably for a run down to bombard Matruh. However, when the ship was making for the harbour entrance, four or five landing craft joined in line ahead, which aroused the interest of the crew. 'Were we to invade some small port or take some soldiers from the beach?' wondered F. Goldsmith. 'The latter seemed more likely when it was realized that the landing craft were empty. But there was something strange, as there was no sense of urgency and we were in sight of the shore for all to see.'[44] In fact it was another deceptive display: rafts were to be deployed out to sea between El Daba and Sidi Abd el Rahman and to simulate an amphibious assault by a combination of noise and smell. Behind a smokescreen, the reek of cordite and diesel would be combined with confused shouting and the firing of flares.

Contrary to popular opinion, the guns did not all open fire at once along the line. The first shells sent over were high air bursts at about 2030 hours, fired by 7th Medium Regiment to test the meteorological conditions to ensure accurate shooting. All guns had been carefully calibrated during October, and careful arrangements had been made to ensure that predicted fire would be accurate without the need for registration by shooting before H-Hour.[45] At 2115 hours 15th Panzer Division reported to DAK Headquarters that they had been under heavy fire for three minutes, which was part of 24th Australian Brigade's diversion.[46] Tuker of 4th Indian Division telephoned 149th Anti-Tank Regiment to say he did not like the quiet and could something be done about it since his forces were not taking part in the barrage. A fire order was given for a few guns with flash cover: 'AP – towards the enemy – well cocked up – five rounds gunfire – five minutes.' At 2120 hours they signalled back 'Guns now firing' as the whip-like crack of solid shot shattered the silence Tuker found so oppressive.[47] In the south at 2125 hours XIII Corps began a neutralization shoot with 136 guns.[48] Thereafter there was silence until 2140 hours.

A few distant points of light then flickered unimpressively from the desert on the British side; they came from the muzzles of the long-range guns opening up in advance of the shock moment, so that their first shells would fall in the same split second as those of the massed field artillery. Bombardier Challoner was tense with expectation. 'Men stood at their stations, strained and silent, as they waited for the two words which would trigger off the holocaust – "Take Post!" – and then a further three minutes of quivering tension had to elapse before the synchronized command rapped from a thousand throats – "Fire!" ' In an instant, at the stroke of 2140 hours, flashes from hundreds of guns were seen sparkling in a long line across the desert. The 'minimum' treatment accorded to an enemy battery was a concentration of 10 guns to 1, and the 'maximum' 20 to 1. On XXX Corps's front of about 7 miles, 432 field and 46 medium guns engaged accurately located hostile batteries for 20 minutes at intense rates. In total, 882 field and medium guns opened fire.

'The roar from the massed guns defied any description,' continued Bombardier Challoner:

> No fury of sound had ever assailed our ears like that before, it cuffed, shattered and distorted the senses, and loosened the bowels alarmingly. I was more than startled, I was shocked, and needed to know that everyone else was there. When I could focus, the faces I saw first looked blanched and then flushed brightly in a kaleidoscope of passionately flickering hues as every line and detail was etched into relief by the flashes from the muzzles of the guns . . . hundreds of guns almost hub to hub, all bucking, recoiling, spitting fire and snapping like a pack of vicious terriers, all at once, it was sheer horror . . . The constant drill by which our army life had been ruled was now our saving grace, and even before the initial shock had been fully absorbed we fell into the routine of performing all our tasks automatically.[49]

As a quiet interval follows a lightning flash before the thunder is heard, so the sound of the guns took time to reach the infantry. A gunner in 2/8th Field Regiment noted that so many guns firing combined with aerial bombardment 'made it difficult to breathe. It seemed that the air was on the move; it would gradually take a loose blanket from the body of anyone lying prone.'[50] Watching from a water tower behind the line, Philip Rainier could distinguish two separate lines of flickering flames. 'The nearer line of gun flashes was yellow while the farther line of our shell bursts was red. But the sound of the bursting shells was drowned in the nearer roar of the angry guns which were hurling them.'[51] Kenneth Slessor, war correspondent and poet, described 'the sob and clubbing of the gunfire'.[52] For fifteen minutes the counter-battery bombardment continued unabated; then suddenly the guns were silent. There was a breathless stillness as if their force was spent, while above Eighth Army's hidden array two searchlights pointed long, still fingers into the sky. Five minutes passed.

At 2200 hours the two beams swung inward, intersected and stopped, forming a pointed arch dimly seen in the moonlit vault, like a remote symbol of crossed swords. At that instant the British guns opened a barrage of unimaginable intensity, eclipsing their first performance, and to the urgent drumming of the guns the infantrymen stepped out from their start lines in slow, measured paces at the even rate of 75 yards per minute.[53] Now all the artillery engaged targets on their immediate front. No barrage as such was fired in this initial attack, as the line was long and it was known for certain that some areas had no enemy in them. The infantry relied for support on a large number of concentrations fired on all known and suspected Axis company areas – strongpoints, anti-tank guns, slit trenches – which had been fixed in the same way as the hostile batteries. Nevertheless, such was the intensity of the artillery effort that for the rest of the war 'Alamein barrage' became a term widely used throughout the British Army for any artillery programme that someone wanted to seem impressive.[54]

That evening Ralph Ringler of 104th Panzergrenadier Regiment had been attending a party for his battalion commander's birthday in a tent erected by the adjutant. There had been a happy atmosphere, with songs and alcohol which

> raised our spirits. In the desert only a little wine is needed to warm the heart. Perhaps for many it was their last happy evening. Outside it was peaceful – too peaceful . . . Unteroffizier Monier told me for the umpteenth time about his wife and children at home in the Palatinate; he proudly showed me their photograph. 'If I could see them once more at home, Lieutenant, just once more.' . . . The 'inferno' came with a bang – with an inhuman relentless series of explosions. The whole desert horizon seemed to burn and to shudder. As I surfaced from a deep sleep, the shock raced through my limbs . . . The shells howled overhead and exploded, the ground rocked and the detonations shook me into confusion.[55]

Martin Ranft was in a German artillery battery equipped with French guns between the coast and the main road when suddenly the sky lit up. 'Look at that!' he shouted. There was a pause of six or seven seconds, then came the sound: 'Fantastic. Never experienced anything like it. We were on the receiving end of artillery concentrated on a half mile square. Next morning when we looked out of our holes all was different.'[56] Sergente Riccardo Poletto had just settled down to sleep when 'shells suddenly fell all around. There was choking smoke. It seemed an avalanche of fire . . . massed enemy artillery firing non-stop for hour after hour.'[57]

The original programme was divided into five phases, any of which could be repeated according to the progress made. Once they had started firing, the gunners continued at varying rates for the next three and a half hours on a timed programme, and then as required by the infantry. The gun detachments got no rest that night or for some nights to come, because when not firing on their own immediate front they were either engaged in defensive fire tasks for other formations or firing standard concentrations (stonks) arranged by corps or divisional headquarters. During the next week there was little opportunity for anyone to get any rest, because attacks were launched on different parts of the front each day – particularly in the north – and each one was supported by all the guns that could be brought to bear. Very often if guns could not reach the target they had to move to a position from which they could.

German records show that, although the casualties inflicted by the artillery programme were not heavy and many weapons in fact survived, communications with the front line were very badly disrupted, so that for some hours Axis commanders at all levels were unable to tell exactly where or to what depth the defences had been penetrated.[58] Erich Stoch was with 90th Light Division in reserve near the coast. 'The noise and the spectacle of the "drum-fire" woke us. It was not so much the sound of the explosions, but rather a strange throbbing and trembling in the earth. The sky was alight along the whole length of the Front.'[59] Nearby the crew of HMS *Belvoir* were amazed by the bombardment: 'It reminded me of electric storms we had seen at Freetown,' said F. Goldsmith, who had returned with his dummy invasion fleet and was told that it had kept a German division on the coast. 'Come to think of it, if by this they evaded the awesome bombardment it also did them a good turn.'[60] At DAK Headquarters reports were coming in, but the situation remained confused. 'The great weight of shell fire made it seem possible that the enemy was beginning an offensive. At midnight it seemed that the enemy had penetrated the outpost line in a few places and was advancing towards the main defence line.'[61] In fact they were already deep inside it. The moon shone down. The fight was on.

12

The Assault

You could not be successful in such an action without a large loss. We must make up our mind to affairs of this kind sometimes, or give up the game.

Arthur Wellesley, Duke of Wellington

On the far north of the line, 24th Australian Brigade laid on its diversion. Dummy figures were raised and illuminated, and strong raids were put in on enemy posts. Lex Gardiner recalled that to 'supplement the bull's wool, a Bofor[s] is firing red tracer over the heads of the dummies and a searchlight of ours is shining on them, the dummies are swaying in the light sea breeze and they give the appearance of our troops advancing over undulating ground'.[1] Axis prisoners later captured in the sector claimed to have defeated part of the main attack, and for four hours the brigade area was heavily shelled.

Meanwhile the main attack was in fact going in to the south. Well practised at keeping the pace, the infantry were advancing in straight extended lines on either side of their company guide groups. The battalion guide parties were marking the centre lines of the advance with stakes driven in at 100-yard intervals, each with a coloured rearward-facing light, a different colour for each unit. The signallers were running forward with their line well to the right of the route, to be clear of later vehicle movement. Quickly following behind were the engineer mine-clearing parties, while further back again came the traffic-control groups and administrative personnel. The infantry were not the lightly dressed men carrying rifles across the chest at the high-porte as in popular image. Each carried well in excess of the standard scale of ammunition, plus grenades, a pick or shovel, four sandbags, personal kit, full water bottles, two days' rations and an emergency ration.

On the extreme right of XXX Corps's advance, 2/24th Battalion of 26th Australian Brigade advanced with two companies forward, and after passing through the forward minefield it began to reduce the enemy posts it encountered one by one, securing its objective by 2310 hours. The follow-up companies then passed through and took the battalion's final objectives by midnight, having met little serious opposition. They had sustained 4 dead and 39 wounded, but took 43 German and 35 Italian prisoners, 6 light guns and 16 machine-guns. Once they were consolidated, the Composite Force moved up behind them to secure their right rear and fill the gap between them and 24th Australian Brigade's position. To the south, 20th Australian Brigade's advance began with 2/17th Battalion on the right with three companies forward and 2/15th Battalion on the left with two. Some stiff opposition caused 2/17th to sustain 15 killed and 47 wounded, with 14 missing, but 2/15th was able to secure both its intermediate and its final objectives relatively easily, losing 5 killed and 40 wounded.[2]

Thus far 9th Australian Division had achieved success, but the minefields were still to be cleared in order to allow the passage of essential support weapons and other transport. An Aussie engineer later described his less than orthodox approach: 'I walk along like this, and I give a kick here and a kick there . . . They were as thick as thieves, these mines, and booby-traps in between them . . .We had a bit of shelling, of course, but that's not the trouble you think it is. No; it's the machine-guns on fixed lines. They're unhealthy.'[3] Australian sappers had built mine-detector perambulators, and Andy Dowd noticed several of his fellow sappers having what looked like a Chinese rickshaw race with their equipment to get clear of enemy observation.[4]

It was soon found that the first phase had been launched against only the crust of the defences, behind which lay the main line in considerable depth. At 0038 hours 2/48th Battalion of 26th Australian Brigade crossed its start line, also with two companies forward. These ran into strong resistance, during which Sergeant William Kibby, originally from County Durham, took over his platoon when its commander was hit and rushed forward against a troublesome enemy post with his tommy gun. He silenced it and took a dozen prisoners.[5]

The advance continued until the lead companies had covered over 2,000 yards, whereupon the rear companies passed through to the final objective 1,300 yards beyond. In the swirling smoke and dust, it was found that the Bofors guns, firing four rounds every five minutes along the boundaries of the advance,* were of considerable help in maintaining direction. The success signals indicating objective achieved were fired at 0345 hours, some 7,000 yards beyond the brigade start line, as

---

*A method adopted from a suggestion by Captain J. C. White NZA (Murphy, *2nd New Zealand Divisional Artillery*, p. 374).

the brigade began to reorganize for defence, pushing companies into the gaps between the units while the Composite Force moved into the gap between 2/24th Battalion and 24th Australian Brigade.[6]

The second phase of 20th Australian Brigade's role involved 2/13th Battalion with 40th Royal Tank Regiment in support. As with other battalions, there were also attached elements of Royal Australian Engineers (2/13th Field Company), 2/3rd Anti-Tank Regiment and 2/2nd Machine Gun Battalion. 'All but 40th Royal Tank Regiment were already well known and trusted cobbers. The tank wallahs were soon blood brothers too, and later the friendship that now sprang up was, indeed, cemented in blood.'[7] Without open flanks to worry about but a considerable area of ground to cover, strongpoints had been selected from map overlays and assigned to platoons and fighting patrols as individual objectives. The tanks were regarded as necessary to cover so wide an area, but so many secondary minefields were encountered that, even though reinforced, 2/13th Field Company had been unable to clear a way in time and the infantry attacked alone.

At first the defenders from the Italian 62nd Infantry Regiment made off.[8] The rear companies passed through, but they were still unsupported by the tanks when they ran into heavy crossfire which caused serious casualties, especially among the officers and NCOs. They dug in where they were, but when daylight came they found themselves skylined on a crest and were forced to retire under heavy shellfire. At least by now the tanks had been able to get up to them, and these quickly destroyed all the remaining troublesome posts in the area.[9]

So far the Aussies had taken 127 German prisoners from I Battalion 382nd Infantry Regiment and 264 Italians from I and III Battalions 62nd Infantry Regiment. To their left, 51st (Highland) Division had a much more difficult task, with a wider frontage to cover requiring seven battalions and its reconnaissance regiment attacking 'six-up'. Only on the flanks was a second battalion to pass through to reach the final objective. From a start line of a mile and a half, they would move through an expanding funnel to a final objective 3 miles wide. To aid control, Wimberley had inserted report lines, named after various colours, and the objectives were all given names of towns from the appropriate regimental area: thus the Gordons and Black Watch would attack Arbroath, Montrose and Dundee; the Argylls would storm Paisley, Greenock and Stirling. As the infantry filed forward, Wimberley stood watching from outside his battle headquarters. 'There was nothing more I could do now to prepare them for the battle, it was only possible to pray for success, and that the Highland Division would live up to its name and the names of the very famous regiments of which it was composed.'[10]

Every man went into action with a St Andrew's saltire on his back to aid identification and as a proclamation of nationality, every platoon officer was accompanied by his piper, so that throughout the night in this central portion of the line 'the wild skirls of the most eerie, exhilarating and frightening music the battlefield knows would pierce the din of shell and mine exploding and the hoarse racket of gunfire'.[11] According to one Highland soldier, Bob Scott, the pipes were 'made for the desert. During the lulls in the barrage you could hear them all along the Front,' although 'this is a long way from Loch Tummel and Loch Rannoch.'[12] 'All my thoughts were pleasant thoughts,' said Robert Weir of 5th Cameron Highlanders, 'and when our piper played "The Road to the Isles" I asked myself: "I wonder if it is." ' He knew the 'Isles' were the celestial isles of the Blessed, whence none returned.[13]

On the far right of the division was 5th Black Watch of 153rd Brigade. One company encountered wire, and the company barber had the wire-cutters. 'Get a bloody move on, Jock,' came a voice in the night, 'you're no cuttin' hair now.'[14] Nineteen-year-old Piper Duncan McIntyre played at the head of C Company as it advanced and men fell all around him. When the time came to assault the objective he broke into the regimental march 'Hielan' Laddie', and 'by his complete disregard of personal danger and by his fine example he inspired his comrades to advance to the objective, which was captured'.[15] Quickly hit twice he continued to play, but a third hit brought him down. He continued to play as he died, and was found the next morning with his fingers still clutching the chanter.[16]

Following 5th Black Watch, which cleared its objectives on time, came 1st Gordon Highlanders, which launched its attack from the Red Line with A and C Companies towards Braemar and Kintore. The latter was soon taken, but contact with both companies was lost when the radio failed and runners could not get through. B Company was sent forward to make good the ground, and at around 0200 hours D Company followed on, mounted on the tanks of a supporting squadron from 50th Royal Tank Regiment, joining B Company for the advance to the final objective, Aberdeen. However, they encountered a minefield in which five tanks were lost some 1,600 yards short of the objective. With daylight fast approaching it was decided to consolidate around Kintore. A carrier patrol failed to make contact with A and C Companies, which had fought their way forward with great difficulty, been caught in crossfire, and lost most of their officers. They had accounted for every enemy post except one with bayonet and grenade, but paid a heavy price, mustering barely 60 all ranks between them by daylight.[17]

To begin with, 5th/7th Gordon Highlanders met little opposition as it made for Elgin and Cruden, most of the defenders having fled leaving only a few machine-guns in action. The Green Line was reached, but the supporting sappers suffered heavily and wire and mines were encountered around midnight with A and B Companies reaching the Red Line and securing Insch and Turriff, having advanced some 4,000 yards. C and D Companies then took the lead under shellfire, and were held up by more machine-gun posts. Captain J. Sharp's D Company tried to move around to the left to cover C Company's attack, but disappeared into the dust and smoke and was never seen again; Captain Sharp was found two days later with many of his men lying dead in a minefield. C Company was unable to make further progress and dug in where it was, being joined by mortars and machine-guns from 1/7th Middlesex Regiment.[18] Their commanding officer was Lieutenant-Colonel J. W. A. Stevenson, an Essex and England cricketer, who exhorted his men to throw cricket balls at the enemy should they exhaust their ammunition.[19]

First Black Watch of 154th Brigade kept so close to the barrage that it had to pause several times to wait for it to lift. Its third objective was some 6,500 yards from the start line – a distance far greater than it had ever previously considered for night attacks. 'Control over such distances was hard, but direction was much harder,' wrote Lieutenant-Colonel Roper-Caldbeck, 'it was an awful problem to know where you were. We were working on dead reckoning by compass, pacing and taping our distances, but even so it was not easy because members of the navigating party kept getting hit.'[20] The battalion was on its objective precisely on time and made short work of the defences. But as Roper-Caldbeck was congratulating Hughie Rose, the youngest officer in the battalion, Rose was struck in the neck and killed instantly.[21] Later, while visiting this battalion, Wimberley had a narrow escape when his jeep was blown up by a mine which killed his driver.

The following sapper mine-clearing parties soon discovered that the opposition was far from subdued. Finding itself ahead of the infantry, John Chartres's column from 7th Field Squadron had to make a careful U-turn.

Somehow a provost 3-tonner loaded with MPs in smart white belts and red caps with mine-gap torches already lit also managed a U-turn with its tailboard towards the enemy . . . It had all the appearance of an illuminated float in a carnival procession! Arthur Barwell and I watched fascinated as tracer rounds of every imaginable calibre spattered around it – and somehow missed. I distinctly remember that Arthur and I both laughed hilariously.[22]

Seventh Argyll and Sutherland Highlanders attacked with C and D Companies leading and its pipers playing 'Monymusk'. It encountered little opposition but many mines and booby traps, and took its initial objectives of Mons, Meg, Paisley, Renfrew and Falkirk by 2300 hours, then set off for the Red Line, which was secured by midnight. After a pause, it moved off from the Red Line towards Greenock at 0100 hours, but was by now much reduced.[23] Captain Samwell found himself amid a group of Italian prisoners. 'Suddenly I heard a shout of "Watch Out!" and the next moment something hard hit the toe of my boot and bounced off. There was a blinding explosion, and I staggered back holding my arm over my eyes instinctively. Was I wounded? I looked down rather expecting to see blood pouring out, but there was nothing – a tremendous feeling of relief.' Unhurt, he looked around for the sergeant who was with him, who lay sprawled on his back groaning, his leg a tangled mess. One of the enemy in the trench had thrown a grenade as he came out with his hands up. Samwell

> suddenly felt furious; an absolute uncontrollable temper surged up inside me. I swore and cursed at the enemy now crouching in the corner of the trench; then I fired at them at point-blank range – one, two, three, and then click! I had forgotten to reload. I flung my pistol away in disgust and grabbed a rifle – the sergeant's I think – and rushed in. I believe two of the enemy were sprawled on the ground at the bottom of the square trench. I bayoneted two more and then came out again.[24]

Although rare, this type of incident did occur – occasioned by high passion where vengeance was desired.

Captain Charles Barker's experiences were more typical. Trying to reach 5th/7th Gordon Highlanders in the ever increasing confusion, noise and acrid choking gunsmoke, armed only with a pistol and 18 rounds of ammunition, he 'ran straight into hordes of Italian soldiers fully armed. Any one of them could have shot me without trace. I quickly realized there was no point in doing more than encourage as best I could this host of prisoners to follow me down the tape.' But they followed the solitary British officer willingly enough, although by the time the shelling from both sides had taken its course only seven of them were left.[25]

With the Argylls' companies now reduced to around 30 men each, the commanding officer, Lieutenant-Colonel Lorne Campbell, called off a further advance and the battalion prepared a defensive position to await the dawn.[26] To the left, 51st Reconnaissance Regiment had been organized into a composite squadron and an infantry squadron and by 2330 hours it was moving through the minefield gaps under heavy fire. Fiftieth Royal Tank Regiment was to attack Nairn supported by the reconnaissance regiment, but soon ran into heavy anti-tank fire and withdrew firing smoke shells to provide cover, and the recce men dug in where they were when first light came.[27]

On the far left of the division, 7th Black Watch was to pass through 5th Camerons (which advanced to 'The Inverness Gathering') once the latter had taken the Red Line; then it was to capture The Ben, which rose some 30 feet above the desert and was therefore very prominent. By the time the battalion was ready to cross its start line it had already suffered heavily from enemy shelling and had to be reorganized into two composite companies.[28] Indeed, 7th Black Watch made perhaps the most hard-fought and successful battalion action of the night in taking the final objective at the north-west extremity of Miteiriya Ridge. As soon as it passed through it came under heavy shellfire. Of six navigating officers detailed to take over if necessary, one was killed and the others were wounded. Few enemy were encountered while approaching the Black Line, though fire was intense, but on the Black Line the enemy's withdrawal was found to have stopped and there was heavy fighting on the top and forward slope of Miteiriya Ridge.[29]

By 0240 hours 51st (Highland) Division had overrun positions of the Italian I and II Battalions 62nd Infantry Regiment and the German I Battalion 382nd Regiment. Italian II Battalion 46th Artillery Regiment was surrounded, leaving the Scots facing III Battalion 115th Panzergrenadier and III Battalion 382nd Regiment.[30]

In 2nd New Zealand Division's sector the first phase began with two battalions only. In the north, 5th New Zealand Brigade was led by 23rd Battalion, which crossed its start line before the barrage began at 2135 hours with two companies leading. Brigadier Kippenburger wished each section good luck. 'The responses were very stirring: "We'll do it, Sir"; "We won't let you down, Sir"; "The Twenty-third will do it, Sir" ... Pat Lynch, one of the company commanders, who was to die within an hour, said it was time to go. Reg [Romans] blew his whistle and as one man the battalion stepped off. I watched till they had disappeared.'[31]

Marching on a compass bearing for a set distance, they felt the impact of the corps artillery as it opened the counter-battery programme, and they halted some 500 yards behind it. When the barrage proper opened at 2200 hours they crept forward to be close behind it, and when smoke shells indicated the first lift they pressed on. They followed the barrage closely for several hundred yards without meeting opposition before A Company on the left came under machine-gun fire. The historian of those honorary Kiwis the Royal Wiltshire Yeomanry described the

> irregular rattle of the machine-guns which swing from time to time into a rhythmic cadence as two or more hit a periodic synchrony. Tuttle-uttle-uttle-uttle-tut-tut-tut-tut . . . They chatter, those machine-guns, like monkeys, scolding, answering in different keys as the wind takes their sound. Bop-op-op-op . . . tat-at-at-at-at . . . The sulky one throws in his ill-tempered comment from a distance. Bop . . . op-op-op . . . op . . . op-op. And through it the infantry walk steadily forward, taking an occupied enemy post here, passing an abandoned one there but always forging slowly ahead.[32]

In a series of short rushes, A Company cleared a number of enemy posts but lost Pat Lynch and two other officers as well as a number of men. Having subdued the enemy position, under the command of its surviving platoon commander it joined 24th Battalion on its first objective to the left. The rest of 23rd Battalion cleared several other posts and arrived on its objective in good order, but now had no contact with 24th Battalion or with Brigade Headquarters, since the jeep carrying the rear-link radio was held up in the minefield. Unsure of their exact position, but judging it by the fall of shells to their front, Lieutenant-Colonel Reg Romans called on his three companies to press on, and with great spirit they did so on to the final objective, Miteiriya Ridge. Romans found that the battalion, now somewhat disorganized, had passed beyond the barrage, and it drew back to its proper objective where it finally established contact with A Company and 24th Battalion on the left, although they had no contact with 5th Cameron Highlanders on their right. In one night they had lost 33 dead, 143 wounded and 1 missing.[33]

To their left, 24th Battalion of 6th New Zealand Brigade advanced with two companies leading and one in reserve. They too met considerable opposition, but the Bofors tracer helped both companies to keep their course until they reached their objective and cleared a strongpoint some 200 yards beyond it. Opposition caused some confusion and forced Battalion Headquarters to get involved, but the companies were able to form a defensive line, although there was no contact with any friendly troops to their immediate south, where the South Africans were in a fierce struggle.[34]

Following up both brigades was 28th (Maori) Battalion, with the task of clearing any isolated enemy posts. The two companies behind 5th New Zealand Brigade suffered some casualties from fire sweeping in from the north, but only D Company met any serious opposition untouched by 24th Battalion. Major C. M. Bennett's B Company was opposed at one point 'by a wall of enemy firing at us with all they had. We all broke into the haka "Ke mate! Ke mate!" and charged straight in with the bayonet . . . It was the most spirited attack that I myself had taken part in.' That night the battalion suffered 22 dead and 72 wounded with 4 missing.[35]

Throughout the battle, headquarters had only the sketchiest idea of progress, usually passed back by various parties of sappers and signallers supporting the infantry. At division, however, with the situations on the flanks being equally vague, Freyberg saw no reason to delay the second phase, for which his four remaining battalions were approaching their start lines. For this phase the artillery barrage was to resume at 0050 hours and move forward in 100-yard lifts every three minutes. In 5th New Zealand Brigade's sector, 21st Battalion on the right and 22nd Battalion on the left would pass through 23rd Battalion, each with three companies forward and one in reserve. Navigating by compass amid intermittent shell and mortar fire, with their attendant smoke and dust, the intelligence and provost sections had difficulty laying the guide tapes and lamps, and Lieutenant R. B. Abbott of 21st Battalion was awarded the Military Cross for his efforts. These enabled the line to advance, leaning hard against the barrage when it resumed on schedule, and catching the defenders of several posts still desperately hugging the bottoms of their trenches as the infantry passed. Still other posts were missed altogether as the lead men bunched either to attack points of resistance or to avoid booby-trapped minefields. The latter were sometimes of diabolical ingenuity. A favourite booby-trap concoction was to link the so-called Italian 'Red Devil' grenade to anti-tank mines; these in turn were linked to shells or a mine, and finally to air-force bombs, the whole thing being connected up with trip wires and instantaneous fuses, each 'distinct damnation' being certain if the other failed.[36]

As the advance progressed on its diverging course, contact between units and even companies was lost, so that all the battalions approached the final objectives thinly spread, but they nevertheless managed to keep up with the barrage. On the extreme right, 21st Battalion encountered men of 7th Black Watch, with whom they had made a treaty to shout 'Jock!' or 'Kiwi!' if in doubt about identity.[37] Here the Kiwis had to overcome a strongly defended German strongpoint, but they cleared their objective within 20 minutes of the end of the barrage, although they lost two company commanders killed and one wounded. A patrol led by Lieutenant P. Robertson then went forward and captured a battery of field guns, bringing back over 100 prisoners, mainly Italians.[38]

To its left, 22nd Battalion also met opposition, which left few survivors in C Company. The reserve company replaced it, but by the final stages of the advance the battalion was so extended that all four companies were in the line and there was no reserve. An extensive position was cleared so that the objective was taken by 0315 hours, but it had cost the battalion a third of its number – 101 men – a price in blood which fortunately left little for the following companies of 28th (Maori) Battalion to do. 'To be advancing,' recalled Mike Kenny, 'and seeing tracers coming towards you, hissing past, shells bursting around, being met by whizzing dirt, seeing comrades blown over, challenging dugouts, getting Ities out at bayonet point, over-running dugouts and to be fired at from behind – what a night!'[39]

'It was some scrap this time, believe me,' E. M. Scott wrote home afterwards:

> The Masterton boys [where 22nd Battalion recruited] came through fairly well. Went in that night with twenty-five in that platoon and reached the objective with twelve. It is remarkable the stuff we went through that night without sustaining a great number of casualties. Some of course were unlucky and some grand soldiers and great mates are no more . . . the rotten part about an attack is that it must go on, and if your best mate goes down beside you, you can't stop. It seems hard and callous, but it's unavoidable. The stretcher bearers and the lightly wounded following up attend to them.[40]

The New Zealanders had penetrated the position of Italian II Battalion 62nd Infantry Regiment and were now facing the German II Battalion 115th Panzergrenadier and Italian XII Battalion 133rd Armoured Regiment.[41]

On the far left, where 6th New Zealand Brigade had the same width of frontage but a shorter distance to cover, its two battalions advanced with two companies forward and one in reserve – 26th Battalion on the right and 25th Battalion on the left. Meeting little opposition, the former made good progress – although at one stage it overran the barrage and took a number of casualties from it – and by 0300 hours it was digging in on its objective, where an enemy headquarters area including an aid post with a German doctor and several patients was captured. Thereafter the battalion was heavily shelled and mortared until well into daylight, suffering almost 100 casualties, including 24 dead.[42] To its left, 25th Battalion advanced, only three companies strong, without encountering any men from battalions that had preceded it, and no contact could be made with the South Africans to the south. Reaching Miteiriya Ridge without serious opposition at about 0200 hours, the infantry promptly began to dig in. Patrols sent to right and left contacted 26th

Battalion's headquarters some 600 yards away, and when men from C and D Companies of 28th (Maori) Battalion arrived they were sent to cover the exposed left flank. D Company, however, immediately ran into opposition, in the subduing of which it lost 17 men.[43]

In the South African sector, while the bombardment of Axis positions proceeded, the infantry moved to their forward prepared positions without incident. A firm base including fire positions for the Vickers machine-guns of Regiment President Steyn and Die Middellandse Regiment was secured by 1st South African Brigade, and from there they were to establish and hold a line from what would be the left flank of the divisional objective to a point in an area known as Duke's Ridge.[44] Before that, however, the other two brigades had to make an assault. As they crossed their start lines they faced serious opposition, having major strongpoints to subdue in their sector.

Closest to the New Zealanders was 1st Cape Town Highlanders on the right of 2nd South African Brigade, which advanced just over 400 strong. Immediately the Highlanders came under heavy fire, and the battalion mortars were shelled. However, within 40 minutes C Company had secured its objective, although A Company was caught by its own artillery fire and the company commander was wounded. Murray Reid of 8th Field Company New Zealand Engineers came across them: 'It appeared this company had swung too far north and become mixed up in the barrage.'[45] It resumed the advance when the fire lifted, and B Company and support weapons were ordered forward as the engineers began gapping the minefields. They were ordered to continue the advance at 0030 hours, and, although clearing the minefield took longer than anticipated, by 0800 hours the battalion had managed to get two companies dug in with support and anti-tank weapons. They had suffered 40 casualties.[46]

On their left, 1st Natal Mounted Rifles were held up briefly by artillery fire but were soon clearing enemy dugouts with Bren guns, bayonets and grenades and reached their first objective by 2350 hours. By dawn they had consolidated their position – but at the cost of 9 dead and 96 wounded from 337 who had crossed the start line. B Company, which had been forced to assist the 1st/2nd Field Force Battalion, was reduced to 1 officer and 28 men.[47] The Field Force Battalion had been delayed early on by anti-personnel mines and was already behind schedule when it came across a strongpoint, identified in photographs as a dump, which had received no attention from the supporting artillery. In an attempt to outflank this position, A and B Companies managed to penetrate the enemy forward defended localities, but continued to suffer heavily. Lieutenant R. A. Edwards's platoon was reduced to himself and just four men, and three-quarters of Lieutenant B. J. Grobler's platoon became casualties. It was Corporal J. M. Maritz of this platoon who managed to reach 1st Natal Mounted Rifles and alert them to the serious situation his mates were in. Lieutenant W. A. van Heerden, serving in his first action and already wounded, led a bayonet charge which overran a mortar and a machine-gun position and took eight German prisoners. He was wounded twice more, while all but four of his platoon become casualties. C Company was reduced to just 11 men, B Company to 18, and A Company to a platoon while Edwards was still reporting back from the minefield.

With the assistance of support fire and B Company from 1st Natal Mounted Rifles, an assault was put in once more on the strongpoint which had caused such grief. Casualties were again horrific, and all the officers were among those hit, but it was finally overcome. Throughout, the selfless courage of the stretcher bearers was noted by the Field Force Battalion. In the South African Army, many of the ancillary tasks were carried out by 'non-Europeans' – the Cape Corps, Indian and Malay Corps, and Native Military Corps. Locas Majozi of the last of these, although himself wounded by shell splinters in the leg, hip, buttock and neck and told repeatedly to return for medical attention, continued to carry out other wounded men until he collapsed from loss of blood. In one night of bitter fighting the battalion lost 41 dead and 148 wounded.[48]

All three of 3rd South African Brigade's battalions took part in the initial attack. The lead companies of 1st Rand Light Infantry set off quickly, but were caught by enemy artillery which inflicted casualties. They fought their way on to their objective, a group of strongly fortified hillocks called The Pimples, taking further casualties, and, as the battalion consolidated, 1st Royal Durban Light Infantry moved through and cleared pockets of resistance that had been missed. Axis defensive artillery fire which was overshooting the rapidly advancing forward troops caught them, but by 0030 hours they had reached their first objective. Their vehicles got through the minefield gaps, and 1st Imperial Light Horse was soon up in line with them on their left, although 1st/2nd Field Force Battalion to their right was still struggling to get forward.[49] This led to delays while Brigadier R. J. Palmer ordered 1st Rand Light Infantry to try to cover the exposed right flank. But at 0205 hours Pienaar decided to accept the risk involved and allow the advance to continue. Palmer told 1st Rand Light Infantry to send a company to cover the flank, and the remainder of the brigade advanced another 400 yards.

Prisoners captured so far indicated that the opposition was being provided by the Italian Trento Division, although a number of Germans had also been brought in. Pienaar now ordered the armour of the divisional reserve group to cover the 'Banana' position that was still causing 1st/2nd Field Force Battalion trouble, although it had to come through 3rd South African Brigade's gap to do so and did not succeed until 0330 hours. At the same time 1st Royal Durban Light Infantry and 1st Imperial Light Horse pushed on to the final objective, which was secured at 0404 hours. That success had cost the former 7 killed and 42 wounded, with 4 of the attached signallers also killed and 9 wounded.[50]

South of the main assault, 4th Indian Division had been detailed to hold the important area of Ruweisat Ridge in a static role, and had handed over to Eighth Army no fewer than 382 vehicles for issue to other formations.[51] In this sector there was no roar from the cannonade – 'at least none that we heard as the sound came through the muffling sands below Ruweisat – not even from our divisional guns hard by', recalled Tuker. 'Wide to the north and south played the swift flickering lightning flashes, dead white, as if giants danced a Khuttack war dance whirling their swords about their heads under the moon.'[52] At 2215 hours the artillery of 4th Indian Division, which had been firing in the general counter-battery programme, switched on to Point 62, a fortified position on the north-west extremity of Ruweisat Ridge where several stone sangars had been built on the slope of a small hillock which was well known to the Indians, who had reached it on several occasions but had been unable to hold it. At 2300 hours C Company 1st/2nd Gurkhas with three carriers and an engineer detachment from 12th Field Company Indian Engineers raided the position and cleared the sangars before withdrawing, although they lost 8 dead and 17 wounded in the process.[53] A similar raid by 1st/1st Punjab Regiment from 161st Indian Motor Brigade failed to close with the enemy but, together with dummy attacks, succeeded in helping to confuse and pin the enemy to their front, drawing considerable fire.[54] Similar operations were carried out by 50th (Northumbrian) Division in XIII Corps. In the centre, 1st Greek Brigade launched a raid with a reinforced company that it claimed resulted in 50 enemy dead.[55] While this was certainly exaggerated, 18 Italian prisoners were brought in from I and II Battalions 20th Infantry Regiment of Brescia Division.[56]

Horrocks's assault plan for XIII Corps was to make four gaps in the British minefields (Nuts and May) the night before the battle was due to start, through which the advance guard would advance to the German minefields January and February. There the sappers would make four gaps corresponding to those made in the British fields – a pair about 200 yards apart in the north, and another pair similarly spaced around 1,000 yards to the south. On the right, 1/7th Queen's Royal Regiment had to breach January, keeping level with 7th Armoured Division on its left. The other battalions of 131st (Queen's) Brigade would move forward to the February minefield and take control of the minefield gaps from 1st/60th Rifles of 22nd Armoured Brigade, who would lead 7th Armoured Division with 44th Reconnaissance Regiment and the Royal Scots Greys. Artillery support would be generous – being supplied by the combined divisional artilleries of 7th Armoured and 44th (Home Counties) Divisions, plus a corps field regiment – but not comparable in intensity to that in the north. Thereafter, 44th (Home Counties) Division's task was to take over the minefields and the bridgehead running west from 7th Armoured Division and hold the area 'at all costs' – a vast area for a division at full strength, let alone one heavily depleted.[57]

It was also incumbent upon the Home Counties engineers to help the armour forward. For this they developed devices – appropriately named 'snails' – that dripped heavy oil on to the rear wheels of a lorry so that it would leave a clearly visible track on the ground for those following behind.[58]

At 1845 hours 22nd Armoured Brigade advanced, and by 2100 hours it was through the minefields and in no man's land, then locating the forward edge of January at 2300 hours. Unfortunately it encountered a solitary mine some 800 yards from the real edge of the minefield and the Scorpions starting flailing. The resulting delay had unfortunate repercussions later.[59] With little room for manoeuvre and immediately under heavy fire, casualties were suffered from the beginning. On the right of the operation 1/7th Queen's Royal Regiment became badly disorganized in the swirling dust and smoke, which reduced visibility to ten yards. However, the attached engineers managed to clear No. 1 gap, and 5th Royal Tank Regiment was able to get through.[60] Sapper Rowlands turned round to see the barrage and could 'see the flashes from our guns spewing out death. I wanted to lie down or run off, but before I knew it I was inside the minefield, knocking the iron stakes into the sand with a heavy hammer . . . Screams, shouting, blood, being strafed and mortared by Jerry. It was a terrifying experience . . . My hands didn't stop shaking for nearly eight weeks.'[61] The cost was fearful: 1/7th Queen's lost 10 officers (including their commanding officer) and 179 men killed, wounded or missing. The delay meant there was then not enough time nor the equipment available to clear February, and 1/5th and 1/6th Queen's were not brought forward.[62]

Further south, 1st Rifle Brigade had to take on not only the local protection of the sappers but also command and control of all troops in the
immediate area and, in the initial stages, traffic control. It was fitted for
this by reason of the large number of radio sets in the battalion. Behind
it came signallers laying line. The minefield gaps were soon fearfully
congested, and the enemy concentrated every available weapon – from
machine-guns to anti-tank and field artillery – on anywhere they suspected a gap was being made.[63] Lieutenant Peter Luck's truck got stuck
in some soft going right at the entrance of one of the minefield gaps. He
was greatly embarrassed when his company commander roared at him
to get out of the way. Rushing forward on foot, he found his company
commander next to a knocked-out Scorpion with one of his own
machine-gun trucks behind it.

> Hugh pointed out the muzzle flash of the anti-tank gun as it fired again and
> almost instantaneously something like a very fast ball on a dry wicket
> bumped on the ground near the tank and bounced off into the air in a whir-
> ring long-hop. 'Get onto that bloody gun before they hit the Scorpion's petrol
> tank and light up the whole gap.' 'Okay Hugh,' I said, confidence restored
> with the prospect of making myself, at last, effective.

He jumped into the machine-gun truck and was about to set off when
the company commander mentioned something about manhandling
the guns because of the threat of mines, but in the pandemonium of fire
Luck just waved ambiguous acknowledgement as he set off. 'The next
thing seemed to be a great concussion that occurred almost simultaneously with my biting, literally, the dust. It so winded me that for a
moment I could not breathe. In this condition I realized that we had
gone over a mine.'[64]

The Scorpions proved of only limited usefulness.* They overheated
so quickly that petrol vaporized after 200 yards, and most minefields
were deeper than this. Their air filters were inadequate to deal with the
dust thrown up by the flails and, although modifications and training
had taken place until they went into action, they continually broke down
in the minefields and had to be repaired and worked on under fire.[65]

After half an hour No. 3 Gap was reported as impassable because of
soft sand, but 20 minutes later, after a troublesome Italian anti-tank gun
had been engaged by a platoon of Vickers machine-guns, No. 2 Gap
was secured and the motor infantry began to try to clear the western

---

*After further development they went on to prove extremely useful later in the war.
In 1948 the Royal Commission on Awards to Inventors recommended awards total-
ling £20,000 tax free to 11 people, including five from the Union Defence Force of
South Africa, for their work on them (PRO CAB 44/101).

ends of Nos. 3 and 4. However, it was already apparent that the second minefield would not be breached that night, and the lead companies were ordered to gain as much ground as possible before dawn. They overran three strong Italian posts, and by first light they were some 3,000 yards short of Himeimat. The anti-tank gun which had caused so much trouble was found abandoned with many dead around it; it was then turned about and its entire stock of ammunition was fired at another strongpoint, with considerable effect. The riflemen took over 300 prisoners, but casualties had been heavy and the two lead companies of 1st Rifle Brigade had to be amalgamated.[66]

At the southernmost part of the line, the Fighting French were divided into two groups. Soft going and several deep wadis slowed the entire force, but they reached their forming-up points south-east of Himeimat in plenty of time. At 0230 hours, supported by what little artillery had been able to move forward with them and covered by a smokescreen, they advanced against strong opposition – particularly the group on the far left, which was counter-attacked by eight captured Honey tanks. Lacking anti-tank guns, this group was forced to pull back.[67]

In a letter to his wife, Lieutenant Les Symonds of 44th Reconnaissance Regiment recalled his friend Mike Day approaching him during the advance. Day seemed oblivious of the machine-gun fire, 'as though he is on an afternoon stroll. He must get hit. Oh, the bloody fool, the brave bloody idiot. He is by my side now. "Hello, Les. The tank's been hit – knocked out." ' Symonds asked why the gun was not firing.

> 'He can't. It's jammed in the recoil . . .' Mike's sentence ends in a scream as he falls beside me holding his stomach with both hands. I lay him out in a comfortable position, but he does not seem in pain now, after a minute he speaks. 'This is mine Les . . . The bastards have got me in the guts. No chance. There is a letter for my mother in my pocket. Will you see she gets it?' I find the letter in his breast pocket. It is already soaked with blood. 'Okay, Mike, I have it.' He is silent for a few minutes while the battle continues around us. Then he says: 'Are you still there, Les?' I hold his hand and he says melodramatically: 'The gap must go through you know.' Then a pause and then, 'Good luck, Les.' A few more seconds and he says, 'Goodbye, Les.' Mike Day is dead.

'I must do something, I must, I must, I must,' thought Les Symonds.

> I again stand to my feet grasping my Tommy-gun – a useless weapon at this range; I am not sure what I intend to do. There is a crash. The world is coming to pieces around me. The Tommy-gun flies through the air. I am hurled to the ground. I hear a voice filled with despair calling out: 'They have got Mr Symonds.'[68]

13

The Armour Stalls

War is at best barbarism. Its glory is all moonshine. Only those who have neither fired a shot nor heard the crying of the wounded could think otherwise. War is hell.

William Tecumseh Sherman

'Once a man is wounded he suffers a psychological blow as severe as the physical one,' noted Captain James Graham.[1] Les Symonds was lost on the battlefield:

What is wrong with my arm? I look down at my middle where it feels to be. It is not there. It is lying twisted up above my head. God! It is knocked off. No. It is still joined and only as I lift it down do I feel the agony of it. The sand is stained with blood in the moonlight. I am bleeding very badly. I raise my head and look around. No longer is anyone in fire positions, a few are groaning. There is nothing I can do now. I needn't think now. I am so tired – so tired. I pray a little. I think a little of you, darling Peg. There seems to be no small-arms fire now, but the mortar bombs are dropping still, but only occasionally.

I am not sure whether I am conscious or unconscious, but after a while I realize someone is cutting off the arm of my shirt. I see a white armband with a red SB. Stretcher-bearers. Brave lads armed only with a medical satchel. My arm is bandaged and a tourniquet is fixed. I am laid on a stretcher and lifted onto a Red Cross carrier with the stretcher horizontally across it. Three, four more stretchers are loaded onto the vehicle. There is another cluster of falling bombs, and the stretcher-bearers lean over us with an instinctive idea of protecting us. As the overloaded ambulance Bren-carrier turns and heads back over the stony, uneven desert, the pain in my shattered, unsplinted arm is something that cannot be described – only experienced.[2]

At the regimental aid post the medical officer told Symonds there was little he could do, and Symonds was evacuated to an advanced dressing station. James Graham spent four days working at one such station provided by 2nd Light Field Ambulance:

Into the campus, marked with a few whitewashed stones and red cross flags at the corners would come an ambulance or a truck at narrow intervals of time; sometimes crowded with sitting wounded, tired, dirty, thirsty, shocked and subdued; an arm in a rough sling, a bandage round the forehead or over one eye, some hobbling, some reeling as we helped them from the tailboard. We watered them, inspected their wounds, replaced the crude padded field dressings that had been applied by their comrades an hour before with a sterile surgical dressing, tried to relieve the few who complained of pain, sorted them according to the urgency of their need, docketed them and sent them off to the rear.[3]

Among them was Les Symonds:

I can feel my heart pumping in little bursts. I am cold – freezing cold. A doctor stands beside me – feels my pulse. On his instructions I am piled with blankets, and a half-grain of morphia is prepared. A prick in my arm. A voice saying: 'This will ease it, old chap.' A cup of tea. A cigarette between my lips. The pain has gone, or at least if it hasn't it doesn't matter any more. I am awake and asleep at the same time.

Symonds's arm was splinted and he was put into another ambulance and sent to the main dressing station.[4]

Evan Thomas was at the New Zealand main dressing station, which

looked like a scene from *Gone with the Wind* (station scene, siege of Atlanta) since there wasn't enough room inside the tents to hold all the patients awaiting treatment. However, the general atmosphere was cheerful enough and the doctors were doing a remarkable job of rushing things through and at the same time seeing to it that no man was deprived of his right to the best available care![5]

Bernard Williams was the surgeon of No. 6 Field Surgical Unit, deployed well forward:

It was a few hours before the first casualties reached us, and they soon became a flood. Much of the work was 'life and limb' surgery which meant dealing with chest and abdominal wounds, amputating hopelessly mangled limbs and trying to preserve others. Our facilities were limited [but] we enjoyed an excellent transfusion service. Troops were bled back at the base, each donor being given a pint of beer in exchange for his blood. But for ten days we were overwhelmed. Many were pretty seriously smashed up. Young men shattered, legs, eyes, arms gone. One never gets over seeing this. It gave me tremendous admiration for our soldiers – they were tough, resilient and brave.[6]

Les Symonds was operated on, and when he came to he found he had been further evacuated to a casualty clearing station. 'A long tent ward

with beds. A nursing sister comes to my bed. I drink a little. Again the
needle and I sleep.'[7]

Among the hundreds of other casualties that were now passing along
the evacuation chain in hospital trains back to Cairo and Alexandria was
Major Hew Blair-Imrie from 5th Black Watch, who compared the
difference in attitudes he encountered. Outside the regimental aid post
'there were so many shell splinters lying about that the wonder was that
anyone had got through alive'. When he arrived at the advanced dressing station the orderly fussed over a wounded Italian and a German
'like an old hen, while a bevy of padres of various denominations
descended on me and started being sympathetic. Actually what I
wanted at that moment was not sympathy (although I quite like the
wounded hero role!) but a stimulant . . . well I got my stimulant in the
form of hot sweet tea!' The Royal Army Medical Corps were 'so kind
and eager to help and do all they possibly could for the wounded. I was
most impressed.' On the hospital train, however, 'the kindly orderlies
pinched my boots, puttees, T.O.S. Binoculars and various other things',
and arriving at the general hospital Blair-Imrie got the impression that
'we were really rather a nuisance . . . some time later a cup of stone cold
tea was brought. The chap knew it was cold but it didn't seem to
worry him . . . the difference between the chaps at the front and at
the hospital stuck out a mile. In one case it was the casualties that mat-
tered, in the other the hospital routine.' Fortunately he was moved to
another hospital near Suez with Italian orderlies who were much more
pleasant.[8]

Both sides treated the wounded only according to clinical need.
Susanna Agnelli, the 20-year-old daughter of the owner of Fiat, had
chosen to become a nurse rather than be idle in wartime. The Regia
Marina, she said, had better equipment and a superior style to the other
services; the nurses were smartly turned out and strictly chaperoned.
On her first trip, long before the African shore was visible from her
hospital ship (which ran like a liner from Naples to Benghazi, Tobruk
and Matruh) she was on deck with the hot wind blowing from the shore
as casualties were swung up in large nets and categorized by rank and
the nature and severity of wounds. There were all sorts of men: one
could recognize the Italians, she wrote, by their darker skin; the
Germans were blond and proud, and the British laughing but very
creamy and vulnerable-looking. Other than air raids, this was her first
experience of war: 'Flesh torn up, despair, pain, missing limbs, young
eyes questioning, utter nonsense, medals, pride, adventure.'[9]

*

At the front on 24 October a 'nauseous slimy morning crept up' for Ralph Ringler. 'In the sky there stood a black-brown smokescreen, the sweet suffocating vapour of gunpowder that hung stubbornly at a uniform height above the ground. The acrid smell mounted horribly in the nose, the heavy pressure pressed on every ear and lung, so the rising sun cheered us up.'[10] 'When the sergeant gently shakes me by the shoulder,' wrote Rifleman R. L. Crimp in his diary, 'it's first light, eerily quiet. Skeins of smoke drift in the lustreless sky. There's a reek of cordite, stale and damp.'[11] Not until 0400 hours had the Axis artillery showed any significant ability to retaliate.[12] Then with daylight the front erupted with fire of every kind into a pandemonium that was to continue with periods of increasing intensity for several days. First-light recces flown by 208 Squadron RAF – one in the north for XXX Corps and one in the south for XIII Corps – revealed that there had been no appreciable change in Axis dispositions.[13]

The major concern at Panzerarmee Headquarters throughout 23 October had been the critical fuel situation, which robbed the armoured forces of the mobility essential to meeting an attack, and on the first morning of the battle the headquarters knew nothing of the current situation.[14] Specially equipped Wellingtons from 162 Squadron RAF were jamming Axis radio communications, while since the bombardment land-line communications had been 'smashed by this drumfire, and reports from the front virtually ceased'.[15] Stumme had set off to find out what was happening, accompanied by Oberst Büchting, but his car had returned without its passengers. The corporal driver was safe, but in a severe state of shock and unable to give a clear explanation of what had happened. 'They told me to get out of the firing area as quickly as possible,' he stammered, 'and when I looked round the car was empty.'[16] Panzerarmee was now leaderless, and except in the northwest, where II Battalion 125th Panzergrenadier Regiment and Italian III Battalion 61st Regiment held out, chaos reigned: the assault had partly or completely overwhelmed the Italian I and II Battalions 62nd Regiment and II Battalion 61st Regiment and the German I and III Battalions 382nd Regiment. But a conference at DAK Headquarters confirmed orders not to prepare or launch any large-scale counter-thrusts, in accordance with a decision made in conference with Stumme on 14 October. It was decided to concentrate on the main task of holding the front.[17] In the shrewd judgement of Tedder, the Axis forces had already lost the battle.[18]

However, it was not going according to Montgomery's plan. The infantry had not secured the Oxalic line, and the armour was not ready to exploit beyond them. The armoured formations making their own minefield gaps relied for this on their infantry components. In 1st Armoured Division, behind the Australians, this infantry component comprised 7th Motor Brigade, containing two Rifle Brigade battalions: 2nd – a regular battalion – and 7th, formerly 1st London Rifle Brigade – a Territorial unit. The former had been organized as a 'minefield task force', training with the sappers and supporting tanks to protect and control the gaps; the London Rifle Brigade was to pass through these gaps once they had been made and deal with any resistance that hindered further progress as the armour came forward. Instead it spent 24 October in its assembly area near the beginning of the Sun track awaiting orders to advance, drinking tea and discussing the latest 'developments': either the New Zealanders were in El Daba or the Germans were in Cairo; Monty was either dead or had been spotted in his tank in the battalion area. Close by, the full congestion of the battlefield could be observed, with endless streams of lorries moving forward and ambulances and columns of bedraggled prisoners moving back. The occasional shell-burst would land alarmingly close, or a Messerschmitt would appear out of the low cloud of powder-fine dust to strafe or bomb the crowds of vehicles, answered by the thump-thump-thump of the Bofors guns. More often, formations of Boston or Maryland bombers would be seen heading towards the front to deliver their more concentrated attacks.[19]

The first large day-bombing task for the DAF was in the Australian sector, aiming at a headquarters some 1,500 yards to the north and due to be indicated by smoke shells. Unfortunately, flying at 18,000 feet, the formation of 18 aircraft (which the Aussies called a 'football team', from the number in an Aussie Rules side) dropped its 2,000 lb bombs on 2/13th Battalion, some 2,500 yards south of the target. Mercifully for those below, only four men were hit. It transpired that the blue smoke used for target indication was invisible above 9,000 feet, and in future missions the aircraft came in much lower – although this rendered them vulnerable to anti-aircraft fire.[20] The waves of bombers soon became the 'ferry service of the boys in blue'.[21] 'Our bombers flew in tight formation, fairly low and with the most awe-inspiring intentness of purpose,' wrote Lieutenant-Colonel Roper-Caldbeck. 'Nothing made them break formation – nothing made them hurry. Almost solemnly, they approached their targets on an even keel and course; unloaded their terrific bombloads and solemnly wheeled away again. It was most impressive and must have had the greatest effect on the enemy.'[22] However, they did not operate unscathed: Rifleman Crimp saw a Boston receive a direct hit – 'fatal conjunction in time and space of plane and shell, almost predestined in its precision. There's an explosion inside – shell, bombload and petrol in single flash – the plane breaking up and falls in a thousand fragments while the rest forge on.'[23]

But still the bombers kept coming, providing immense reassurance to Allied soldiers hugging holes in the ground. R. Scott, a Highland anti-tank gunner, saw a squadron of Bostons fly over

> in perfect formation. Then about an hour later a dozen Baltimores arrived just as Jerry reorganized . . . and that went on all day. On one sortie a Boston or Baltimore began to lose height and smoke poured from its tail. One crew member jumped, then another and as the last man got out a mighty roar went up. Up till then I thought we were the only ones around.[24]

The feeling of isolation was a common one, especially when Stuka raids began to come in.

In the Highlanders' area, the immediate task was consolidation. They had bitten deeply into the Axis defences, and around and in front of them a tank battle would rage all day, over the heads of the infantry, while they themselves were subject to constant and heavy mortar and shellfire. In the northern corridor, behind the Australians and Highlanders, 2nd Armoured Brigade was attempting to deploy as it grew light, with the Queen's Bays leading and 10th Hussars and 9th Lancers in reserve. With the approach of dawn, John Chartres in 7th Field Squadron withdrew past the Queen's Bays, drawn up ready to advance. 'A sergeant in the turret of the leading tank saw our rather battered little column approaching, whipped his beret off and called for "a cheer for the Sappers". It was an incredibly emotional moment driving down the line of tanks cheered at dawn on the morning of 24 October 1942. A moment in life which I will never forget.'[25]

The armour passed through the first minefield without incident and began to deploy with Aussies on their right and Highlanders on their left.[26] When aircraft came over, they saw the barrels of Axis 88s facing them rise skyward, giving them a chance to engage them.

By 0715 hours 15th Panzer Division was launching its first probing local counter-attack against the Australians, but it was driven back by intense artillery fire as well as by supporting fire from 2nd Armoured Brigade's Shermans and the Priests of 11th Royal Horse Artillery firing over open sights. Behind them came military police, who were to mark the routes with no fewer than 88,775 lamps – under fire and with the constant risk of stumbling upon concealed enemy positions within the minefield.[27] However much soldiers may have disliked the military police in the cities, the work of the divisional provosts earned nothing but praise now. Corporal Eyre of the RASC remembered how his feelings changed. 'Before Alamein I used to think of them as officious and bullying, but when I saw those Redcaps standing in the middle of the minefields directing traffic through I realized what a tough job they were doing.'[28]

Twice 1st Gordon Highlanders was attacked by tanks, which each time were repulsed by the anti-tank guns of the neighbouring 2nd/60th Rifles. Charles Bolté had made it through the night, but 'in the morning a shell landed behind me when I was looking back to see if our tanks would get up before the Jerries did. A fragment went through my right thigh, high up. The blast knocked me down and after a while they carried me away.'[29]

Early in the afternoon the commanding officer of 50th Royal Tank Regiment ordered an attack on the northern end of the Nairn area, to be supported by a troop from 51st Reconnaissance Regiment riding on his Valentines. They were within 250 yards of the objective when the six leading tanks were hit and immobilized and the rest withdrew. For over an hour a firefight ensued, with the tanks repeatedly hit by light anti-tank shells. When they began to run out of ammunition the crews withdrew to where their still mobile brethren were sheltering out of range.

Eventually the squadron commander and the recce men withdrew at 1600 hours, having at least succeeded in drawing German attention from an attack by 2nd Seaforth Highlanders on their right.[30] With tank support, this cleared Stirling at about 1600 hours, but cost B Company all its officers and the company sergeant-major. Thereafter,

> [an] armoured brigade tried to make some gaps through [the minefield] just by B[attalion] HQ but having failed, it sat back just behind us with all its tanks in full view of the enemy. To make matters worse, our own B[rigade] HQ moved up to join the throng. There is a good expression in the desert, 'a Stuka's delight'. The area we were in became a real Stuka's delight and the one saving grace for some time was that the RAF kept the Stukas too busy, but every enemy gunner had their innings.

The Highlanders sat there for four days:

> One could do nothing but sit still and be shelled. By day the opposing armour slogged at each other in stationary battles and we collected most of the shells. It was very wearying and bad for the temper – and we were losing too many men, and too many officers.[31]

To their immediate south, in the morning 7th Black Watch had found enemy between its forward and rear positions, and movement forward of Miteiriya Ridge proved impossible in daylight.[32]

Lieutenant Norman Craig was at 133rd (Royal Sussex) Lorried Infantry Brigade Headquarters, where he and Lieutenant J. Howe were to act as liaison officers. Soon, however, they found themselves posted to different battalions of the brigade, and as Craig jumped into a truck he 'bade a hasty farewell to Howe who was sitting on the edge of a slit trench'.

There was a sudden violent explosion as a shell landed, miraculously leaving the truck unscathed.

But as the sand cleared I heard a frightened, ghastly whimpering from beside the command vehicle. It was Howe. He was half kneeling, half hanging out of the trench, clutching his stomach. A sharp red stain had appeared on his shirt front. He was bending forward, writhing in agony and his eyes were wild with pain and terror. 'It's my guts . . . oh my guts!' it was a startled, hopeless cry, like an animal's; there was something deep and incommunicable about the extremity of his suffering . . . He was sobbing deliriously.

Although Craig tried to get help from a nearby unit, Howe died soon afterwards.

The reality of death in battle had touched me for the first time. The incident seemed to typify all the incalculable perversity of the battlefield whereby abruptly and at random a human being is struck down – always when one least expects it and usually the individual who least deserves it.[33]

The New Zealand front was perhaps the most ordered within XXX Corps, and the Kiwis – although short of the objective on the left – maintained a continuous line held by four battalions. Once on their positions, all commanders had looked for ways to signal their success, but none of the flares sent up was picked out by watchers in the rear from the myriad flashes of gunfire and tracer. Eventually runners and radio contact enabled Division Headquarters to gain a picture of the night's results. Altogether some 250 prisoners had been taken, and, as these were moved back, so the traffic of the support columns moved forward through the minefield gaps – mortars, signals detachments, anti-tank guns and 'A' echelons. Following these came the Divisional Cavalry Regiment and 9th Armoured Brigade, creating a potentially vast traffic jam. But discipline was good, and most of the battalion support vehicles had been able to get forward, deliver their loads, and get off the ridge before dawn broke – otherwise they would have been horribly exposed.[34]

Throughout the night, 9th Armoured Brigade had struggled through the dust. 'We moved forward through the gun positions, soon after the artillery barrage had opened up, observing strict wireless silence,' wrote Trooper J. M. 'Maxie' Day of the Warwickshire Yeomanry. 'The only thing visible was the backside of the tank immediately in front. The wireless silence was suddenly broken by "Charlie Two, Charlie Two, I have lost the column." ' Desperately and in total confusion, Day's troop tried to close up and then saw a New Zealander near a 6-pounder frantically waving his hat.

> I swerved to miss him, there was a bloody great flash and the New Zealander floated through the air over the gun. The tank seemed to lift off the ground about six feet and clouds of dust filled the inside. The offside track had been blown off by a mine. I got out with the tank Commander to see what we could do for the New Zealander – the rubber of the tank track had pitted his face like shrapnel.

They were not alone: five or six other tanks sat around having struck mines, and when dawn arrived they came under attack from Stukas – although most of these attacked the gun lines behind them.[35]

On the route following 22nd Battalion came the Royal Wiltshire Yeomanry on a mine-free track cleared and marked by the Kiwi infantry. 'Lurch, clank, bump. Up comes the dust again and before we've gone a few yards we're back in the "pea-souper" once more,' recalled the Yeomanry's historian as the precious protecting darkness dissolved. At 0600 hours the lead squadron was well forward of the infantry and thus became the only armoured regiment to break out beyond the infantry on the first day of the battle. But it was at a heavy price. 'Those in the rear of the column have been speculating about the origin of a new addition to the carnival of noise which is going on around them. Something different, this one. Deeper and more earth-shaking than the rest. Woomph! This is quite unmistakable. A very sinister sound.' Mines – despite the declaration that the lanes were clear. The armour ought to have been clear of the minefields, but 'Woo-umph! There it goes again. And this time there is no mistake. A spurt of flame appears in the distance through a gap in the fog and quickly grows into a flaming mass. Little figures jump out and run for their lives as the sand spurts up around them in the eerie light from the burning tank.'[36]

Behind 6th New Zealand Brigade's sector a support column for 26th Battalion set off led by a small detachment of engineers manning two Scorpions. But these soon broke down, and several following vehicles were damaged by mines. The route was eventually cleared by 8th Field Company, while the route for 25th Battalion, which had been cleared quite quickly, also served the heavy squadron of the Warwickshire Yeomanry and the Honeys and carriers of the Divisional Cavalry Regiment. These, however, were unable to penetrate the minefield over the ridge and had to halt in hull-down positions along the brigade front.

With A Squadron caught in an uncharted minefield, the Royal

Wiltshire Yeomanry was in trouble. The intelligence officer drove up and down in a scout car trying to bring the remainder through the gaps

> like a mechanical sheep dog. He hands a report to the Commanding Officer and then goes roaring back in the dust and muck towards the stricken front of the line. What did he say? He was going to try and find a way through the uncharted minefield? He must be crazy. But he has gone and nobody seems to be stopping him. They see him climb up the ridge to where more and more of our tanks are blowing up. He becomes a tiny speck as he nears the crest. Then that tiny speck bursts into a sheet of flame. One more sickening 'woo-umph' and it seems to those watching that there is momentary silence. But the unholy din carries on, just as it did before.[37]

The field artillery also had to move well forward in order to support the infantry. Such was the press of traffic that, in trying to find space in which to deploy, the advance party of 4th New Zealand Field Regiment, which was to move forward in support of 9th Armoured Brigade, ended up doing so in the South African sector. The state of the ground which had been captured and on which the guns were deployed was astonishing. The sappers had cleared gaps through the maze of minefields, and every gun, tank and vehicle had to stick rigidly to these paths. The result was that the paths rapidly became a deep trough of loose sand which flew up in clouds when a vehicle or pedestrian came along. There was a stifling cloud of fine dust in the air at all times. Once the battle had started, the gun areas were in any little clearings beside the tracks.[38] Gunner Bruce McKay Smith recalled being in the gun positions and the dust as 'a horrible experience. We had several vehicles blown up on mines, and I happened to be in one vehicle which was blown up, but never got hurt.' Smith, like many other field gunners, found himself on the morning of 24 October

> in a very confused state in the middle of a tank battle. We were in just a slight depression and reasonably safe until a German high-powered machine-gun opened fire on us, which created some havoc and a few casualties. The anti-aircraft Bofors gun which was with us suddenly found where this machine-gun was and fired about five rounds into it, and they surrendered very quickly after that. Among those who surrendered was an Austrian doctor who stayed with us for quite a few days.

The doctor tended the sick and wounded until Field Security took him away as a prisoner of war. 'We were sorry to see him go,' said Smith.[39]

Whereas 1st Armoured Division formed strong task forces to tackle the minefields, 10th Armoured Division, which was to push beyond the New Zealand objective, was content for this task to be left to engineer parties, with only a small covering patrol for each lane. Major Peter

Moore, once more commanding 3rd Field Squadron,* recalled that 'we felt rather lonely and naked'. When they came under machine-gun fire, Moore had to detach a group under Lieutenant John van Grutten to deal with it using rifles and grenades as they pushed through the first minefield. Pressed for time, he anxiously awaited the military-police detachment due to mark the route forward, but its two vehicles had been destroyed. Lance-Corporal Eeles, the only unwounded survivor, appeared staggering under a load of pickets. 'Good God, what are you doing here? Where's your lorry?' asked Moore. 'Sorry to be late, sir,' said the little lance-corporal with apparent unconcern. He explained the situation and that he had carried as many pickets forward as he could. 'I'll be right back for some more, sir.'[40] Lieutenant-Colonel Gilbert McMeekan, the Royal Engineers commander, told him he must get on with the job of marking the routes, and with help from some sappers he 'completed their gap under heavy fire of all descriptions', so that McMeekan found the route completely marked and lit by dawn. Eeles was awarded a Distinguished Conduct Medal.[41]

While 10th Armoured Division's sappers managed to clear the necessary gaps as far as 5th New Zealand Brigade's objective behind 26th Battalion, to the south they encountered opposition near the boundary between the New Zealanders and South Africans. Here the enemy was too strong for the small covering parties to deal with, and they had to wait for the South Africans to do it for them. They then found themselves in an extremely complicated mine garden stretching some 750 yards.[42] Consequently, most of the armour was backed up in the New Zealand sector, and some of the infantry went so far as to rig up dummy minefields in order to stop the tanks milling about their slit trenches.[43] To their front, however, the British tanks caused consternation among the Italian infantry, who streamed to their rear shouting 'Front kaput! Front kaput!' Von Thoma, commanding DAK, responded by directing Oberst Willy Teege's 8th Panzer Regiment to drive the British armour back into an intact sector of the minefield. In the south he was forced to commit combat groups from 21st Panzer and Ariete Divisions, being still unsure which was the main assault.[44]

Behind the Royal Wiltshire Yeomanry came the Crusader squadron of the Staffordshire Yeomanry from 8th Armoured Brigade of 10th Armoured Division. Unfortunately, nine of its tanks had been immobilized on mines, and when daylight came they drew heavy fire and a

---

*10th Armoured Division's three engineer units – 2nd and 3rd Field Squadrons and 141st Field Park Squadron – were all Cheshire Territorials whose recruitment was largely based on New Brighton Rugby Club.

number were set alight. The rest of the regiment was deterred by this and remained behind the ridge. McMeekan's sappers had struggled forward through the night, and, despite being wounded himself, McMeekan had found the enemy's own gap through the fourth minefield. But, maddeningly, he was unable to establish communications with 8th Armoured Brigade until eventually he was brought to see its commander, Brigadier Neville Custance. But it was half an hour too late: one of the brigade's regiments, the Sherwood Rangers, had already been halted by the enemy.[45]

They had approached 26th Battalion's area as dawn spread behind them. 'I looked down into the face of a man lying hunched up in a pit,' wrote Keith Douglas:

> His expression of agony seemed so acute and urgent, his stare so wild and despairing, that for a moment I thought him alive. He was like a cleverly posed waxwork, for his position suggested a paroxysm, an orgasm of pain. He seemed to move and writhe. But he was stiff . . . The picture as they say, told a story, it filled me with useless pity.[46]

The Sherwood Rangers also drew considerable fire. 'Every kind of tracer came flying towards us from all directions,' wrote Major T. Martin Lindsay. 'The tank crews waiting behind in the packed gaps through the minefield saw armour-piercing tracer shells screaming from all over the place – then the explosions of tanks blowing up, sheets of flame as they caught fire and the dull-cherried glow of red hot tank turrets.'[47] Bart Cox of New Zealand 22nd Battalion saw a tank hit. It 'brews up over the ridge. The crew bale out and stumble back to safety, their hands and faces burnt horribly . . . They do not say much – just stand mute – shocked – in agony.'[48] Elsewhere, Corporal H. J. de Stigter of 21st Battalion had his captured Axis trench shot up by a Crusader tank. 'The Tommy officer was very apologetic,' he recalled, 'but he was quite sure all our area was held by the Hun . . . found quite a bit of loot including a piano accordion and a Luger [pistol] or two.'[49] Much to the infantry's relief, the armour soon withdrew.

In the South African sector, from dawn onwards on 24 October, tanks, guns and transport had rumbled down the Qattara Track.[50] With daylight, it could be seen that 3rd South African Brigade was firmly on its Mango objective but 2nd South African Brigade, although on Miteiriya Ridge, was short of Lemon. Patrols that went forward made no contact with 3rd South African Brigade's front, but three Germans were brought in to 1st Cape Town Highlanders' lines at 1050 hours and turned out to be from 433rd Infantry Regiment of 164th Division. Across the divisional frontage, the infantry dug in and the artillery provided support by firing on any Axis positions or possible concentrations. The 1st/2nd Field Force Battalion, which had had the most gruelling of nights, was surprised during the morning by 14 Germans who had lain concealed in its area and suddenly started a private battle of their own. They were swiftly wiped out. There were no other major actions during the day, and it might have seemed to the South Africans that the battle was virtually over.[51]

Things remained similarly quiet along the central front held by 4th Indian and 50th (Northumbrian) Divisions, but further south the battle raged fiercely. In XIII Corps's area confused masses of vehicles had provided rich targets for the Axis artillery. While the tanks were largely immune, the Greenjackets of the 1st/60th Rifles and 1st Rifle Brigade suffered heavily, having to sit wedged between two minefields under constant and heavy shellfire throughout the day. Two companies were ordered to form strongpoints behind the first minefield, while the remaining two were tasked to help 44th Reconnaissance Regiment clear the gaps between the minefields and consolidate the night's gains.[52] The padre of 1st Rifle Brigade was killed conducting a burial service in view of the Italians, and the medical officer of the 1st/60th Rifles was wounded. Another attempt was made to breach the February minefield, and 4th County of London Yeomanry managed to get a squadron through but lost 14 tanks in the process.

The failure of the Fighting French to capture Himeimat meant that the riflemen had to spend the day under its baleful shadow until relieved that night. The bulk of 7th Armoured Division was withdrawn during the night of 25/26 October to reorganize, before moving up to the northern sector on the 31st, leaving the Fighting French, elements of 44th (Home Counties) Division and 4th Light Armoured Brigade to form a very thin defensive line in front of Himeimat.[53]

At 0700 hours Freyberg thought there was still an opportunity for the armour to break out as planned if a supreme and immediate effort were made. From his own command tank – a stripped-down Honey in which he had been touring the area since 0500 hours – he ordered Brigadier John Currie of 9th Armoured Brigade to gather his regiments and to reconnoitre a route to the gap behind 22nd Battalion to join the Royal Wiltshire Yeomanry, and through his Chief of Staff he passed exhortations to 10th Armoured Division to press on. When the latter replied that they could not because of congestion in the New Zealand area, Freyberg was singularly displeased, convinced that any congestion could be overcome by determined leadership. He told Currie to press on, and at the same time he informed 10th Armoured Division that routes were available with guides, that 9th Armoured Brigade was preparing to break out over the ridge, and that 8th Armoured Brigade was well placed to support it and awaiting orders from 10th Armoured Division. However, all these communications were being handled by the chiefs of staff of the divisions concerned, and all efforts to get in touch with either Major-General Alec Gatehouse of 10th Armoured Division or Lumsden of X Corps – both of whom were on the move visiting subordinates – failed.

Lumsden had warned his divisions that they must on no account 'rush blindly onto the enemy anti-tank guns or try to pass through a narrow bottle-neck which is covered by a concentration of enemy tanks'. In such cases, 'a proper co-ordinated plan must be made' and the enemy anti-tank guns be engaged by field artillery and machine-guns.[54] The sequence of orders and moves that now ensued is very difficult to follow. According to the British official history, at 0730 hours orders were given by Lumsden to 24th Armoured Brigade, which then sent 47th Royal Tank Regiment up on 8th Armoured Brigade's left; but there appears to be no mention of this in New Zealand records. 'We were on Miteiriya Ridge by dawn on the 24th,' recalled Frank Compton of 47th's A Squadron. 'The scene as the light became good amazed our crew. There were tanks as far as the eye could see, all jockeying for position so that they could "hull down" on the ridge, which was by now under heavy shell fire, for Jerry had got over the shock of our barrage.'[55] The British narrative then notes that at 0935 hours Lumsden called on 24th Armoured Brigade to advance north-west behind the New Zealand front and attack the enemy holding up 1st Armoured Division. This led to a movement of armour in the rear of the New Zealanders, but it did not cross into 51st (Highland) Division's front.

There is no doubt that Lumsden himself was an inspirational leader, but efforts to get the armour forward were not helped by the anarchic command methods within X Corps. Lumsden was apparently giving orders to 10th Armoured Division's brigades directly because Gatehouse was off the communications net. Edward Boulton was on the staff of 10th Armoured Division and found himself acting as a communications link between Lumsden and X Corps Headquarters, relaying commands

> which I had the greatest difficulty in trying to pass on, and with Corps HQ who wanted to know what Lumsden was doing and saying and what was happening. Like many ex-Cavalry officers, he never used codes but gave orders in parables to confuse the enemy and often ourselves. The first command was entirely phrased in terms of an eighteenth century battle, the history of which

I did not know, and although I assumed what he meant I was unable to reach any of our op[eration]s staff as they had not informed Harry [Llewelyn, the sole staff officer left at 10th Armoured Division Headquarters] of their whereabouts. The second command was simpler as it was all about tarts walking down a street and being picked up by one brigadier or another, identified by Christian names. Lumsden became restive at not being able to get through to Gatehouse and ordered me to commit the division or otherwise to carry out various tasks and would not wait for an answer. I compromised with 'yes' and 'no', and managed to get word at last to Gatehouse, who quickly sent back his [Chief of Staff].'[56]

Eventually it was relayed through XXX Corps that Lumsden had decided that 10th Armoured Division was not in a position to support 9th Armoured Brigade and that no further armoured advance would be made for the time being.

As the morning wore on and these messages passed up and down for some three hours with no action, Leese at XXX Corps had become concerned. At 1045 hours he went to visit 2nd New Zealand Division Headquarters,where he learned that an enemy counter-attack thought to be imminent on to 5th New Zealand Brigade's front had been broken up by artillery and tank fire. His reaction was that Miteiriya Ridge should be made more secure, and a plan for the two corps was made for the afternoon, whereupon he joined Freyberg for an inspection of the area as far as the ridge. After they had departed, a long message arrived from 10th Armoured Division claiming that two regiments of 8th Armoured Brigade were on the ridge but not in contact with 9th Armoured Brigade and that 1st Armoured Division was held up by mines further back than originally reported. Gatehouse now proposed bringing 24th Armoured Brigade across the rear of 8th Armoured Brigade to make contact with 1st Armoured Division and cover the right flank of the New Zealand sector, where Lumsden had ordered him to provide support. He did not want to continue the advance until this was secure, fearing heavy tank casualties unless or until the enemy's anti-tank defences were dealt with by artillery fire in a new operation either that night or the following day.

Freyberg and Leese had no idea what the armour was planning until they encountered Gatehouse personally at around midday.[57] At 1040 hours Montgomery had spoken to Lumsden's BGS and agreed that for the armour to cross Miteiriya Ridge would require full artillery support.[58] However, despite Lumsden having started his career in the Royal Artillery, according to Sidney Kirkman, the chief gunner, he had absolutely no understanding of artillery co-operation and did not even have his corps's Royal Artillery commander with him. Returning to

Freyberg's headquarters, Leese spoke to Montgomery, who insisted that the armour push on. Lumsden then appeared, and the two corps commanders agreed that if the Army Commander wanted a further tank advance then the sooner it took place the better. However, a message now arrived from Freyberg, who had gone forward to speak to Currie and Kippenburger (Freyberg would seldom make a decision without first consulting his brigadiers), that this should take place after dark. Montgomery noted in his diary that 'I was beginning to be disappointed somewhat in Lumsden, Briggs [1st Armoured Division] and Fisher [2nd Armoured Brigade] and also in Gatehouse.'[59]

14

Crisis Conference

And here upon the turret-top the bale-fire glowers red,
The wake lights burn and drip about our hacked disfigured dead,
And many a broken heart is here and many a broken head;
But to-morrow,
By the living God, we'll try the game again!

John Masefield

The infantry were not impressed by the armour's performance. Before Alamein, X Corps had practised effecting a passage through deep minefields, putting special emphasis on preparing rapid artillery fire plans to overcome anti-tank screens.[1] However, a liaison officer from 4th Indian Division who was, according to Tuker, 'an observant and expert lieutenant-colonel with a tactical capacity above the ordinary' reported the confusion on 10th Armoured Division's corridor:

> Progress not as quick as expected. Lanes through minefields nowhere nearly through. Appalling congestion in lanes. Armour head to tail in single file in both lanes, treading on heels of infantry (and suffering from considerable shelling) . . . Not much fun for leading tanks as they got to end of cleared lane . . . At once came up against anti-tank screen. Even Italian anti-tank guns made good shooting. Artillery busy being organized to help infantry forward. None seemed available or under command of armour to get them forward. New units untrained to do own fire and movement . . . All kept engines running whole time even when not in action and soon ran dry. Troubles of getting petrol convoy up to them through congested lanes. A petrol convoy did arrive eventually behind Miteiriya, did not disperse and got bombed. One of best Hun air actions of the battle.[2]

Montgomery's orders for the continuation of the battle were for XIII and XXX Corps to carry out by the morning of the 25th – with modifications – those tasks not completed on the 24th. The remainder of Oxalic would be secured by 9th Australian and 51st (Highland)

Divisions, and the armour was to debouch by night and move to the Pierson bound. Significantly, the armour was not to wait on the infantry but to press on – 1st and 10th Armoured Divisions moving westward, 9th Armoured Brigade and 2nd New Zealand Divisional Cavalry Regiment southward, with all four armoured brigades linking up on the Pierson bound. These orders were not to Lumsden's liking, and he queried them: he was, according to de Guingand, 'not very happy about the role his armour had been given'.[3] Montgomery was not pleased and again spoke with Lumsden's BGS, stressing the need to get forward; then at 1415 hours he sent for Lumsden 'and told him he must "drive" his divisional commanders, and if there was any more hanging back I would remove them'.[4] Lumsden emphasized that the operation would certainly be costly in tanks but that he was willing to try it.[5] Later he told Freyberg that 'playing with armour is like playing with fire: you have got to take your time about it. It is like a duel. If you don't take your time you will get run through the guts. It is not for tanks to take on guns.'[6] Most of the infantry commanders agreed, and would have preferred a repeat of the previous night's plan, had the time and the infantry reserves been available – which they were not.

A major problem was maximising recovery and repair of tanks on a congested battlefield. The light aid detachments of the armoured regiments had been brigaded to form first-line repair workshops sited on brigade axes of advance, and early equipment casualties could be brought quickly to these, minimizing the demand on recovery resources. These first-line brigaded detachments proved very successful, repairing no fewer than 66 of the first 113 tanks recovered. Each armoured division also formed a skeleton armoured workshop which could move up to the assembly area vacated by the tanks once they moved forward, and would thus be available for work before any battle casualties were back-loaded.[7] For example, by 7 November 29 Valentines of 23rd Armoured Brigade had been recovered to third line 14 miles away. (It was noted that this was too far, but there was no space to bring the third-line workshop closer during the battle.) During the battle as a whole, 68 tanks belonging to 23rd Armoured Brigade were repaired and returned – the equivalent of more than a battalion, enabling units to remain in action when they would otherwise have been unable to. (Another 55 tanks awaited recovery, and only 19 were completely destroyed.)[8] Nevertheless, even at this early stage of the battle the Royal Wiltshire Yeomanry of 9th Armoured Brigade had to be withdrawn shortly after midday, when its four remaining operational tanks were handed over to the brigade's other regiments. It had lost 10 killed and 32 wounded (including its commanding officer and 7 other officers).[9]

The exposed tanks had drawn a lot of fire on to 5th New Zealand Brigade's positions, and the infantry were somewhat relieved to see them go to the rear. As the commanders tried to co-ordinate their future moves, there were several alarms of impending counter-attack on the New Zealand front – particularly during the morning, when, as Leese reported to Montgomery, 'there was a lot of hate'. During the afternoon, enemy fire on to the ridge slackened and any perceived counter-attacks received heavy artillery concentrations from the combined British guns before they could develop. Orders had indeed been given by Panzerarmee to recover positions lost overnight, and at 1540 hours DAK recorded that von Thoma gave orders to recapture the main defence line 'as quickly as possible, whatever happened'. Then, with Stumme still missing, he assumed command of Panzerarmee, although he remained at DAK Headquarters.[10] Two companies from 8th Panzer Regiment did advance from the south towards the New Zealanders and claimed to have taken back some positions, but these could only have been those taken and then abandoned during the night. By mid-afternoon this force was in contact with some of the unsubdued posts in front of the Highlanders, and this appears to be as far forward as it got, but the claim to have recaptured positions demonstrates the chaos prevailing throughout the Axis command due to disruption of its communications. The German attack had been directed to try to close a gap caused by 5th New Zealand Brigade's overrunning of the Italian II Battalion 62nd Regiment, which had been sandwiched between II and III Battalions of the German 382nd Regiment. The former of these had been pushed back but had reformed, while the latter still held most of its main defence area in front of the Highlanders.[11]

Von Thoma regarded the situation as serious but not critical. 'There was no great cause for alarm in the southern sector, but it was possible the enemy might continue his attack, perhaps in greater strength. In the northern sector, the situation seemed to be firm again in the meantime since 15th Panzer Division had entered the fight but the enemy was expected to continue the attack.'[12]

On the afternoon of 24 October Rommel received a priority telephone call to his hotel in Semmering. It was the chief of OKW, Wilhelm Keitel, saying the Allied offensive had started and Stumme was missing and was Rommel fit enough to return to Africa? Rommel replied that he was, and Hitler himself then called: Rommel was not to interrupt his rest unless the situation was really serious. Hitler then called again at midnight in the unusual role of someone asking a favour – the situation really was serious.[13] 'Rommel, the news from Africa sounds bad. The situation seems somewhat obscure. Nobody appears to know what has happened to General Stumme. Do you feel capable of returning to Africa and taking command of the army again?' Rommel said he would leave at once.[14] Overnight, Stumme's body was found by troops from 15th Panzer Division. He appeared to have suffered a heart attack while trying to cling on to his moving car. Büchting had been shot through the head.

In September Tedder had written to Portal about the value of the Fleet Air Arm's obsolescent Albacores, which were due to be replaced. 'The point is that the Albacore flies slowly, and the pilot can put his head out and get clear vision, and in consequence, can amble about the countryside looking for targets with the help of the moon and/or flares, until he finds something appetising on which to direct the Wellingtons.' Admiral Sir Henry Harwood, who had replaced Cunningham as Commander-in-Chief Mediterranean Station, had therefore agreed to retain their services until after the offensive. On the night of 24/25 October the bombing programme of 205 Group involved 84 Albacore-directed Wellington sorties between 2200 and 0500 hours targeted exclusively at 15th Panzer Division.[15]

The renewed attack on the Oxalic line was due to begin at 0200 hours on the 25th. In 9th Australian Division's area it would be conducted by 20th Australian Brigade with 2/17th Battalion on the right and 2/13th Battalion on the left, whereupon the London Rifle Brigade would pass through and secure Point 32 to form a bridgehead for 1st Armoured Division to debouch towards the Pierson bound.

Major George Colvin had come forward to take over command of 2/13th Battalion following the mortal wounding of Lieutenant-Colonel Bob Turner, and he found the battalion practically without officers. Morshead agreed that all the left-out-of-battle officers be sent forward, and when a patrol indicated no sign of 1st Gordon Highlanders on the left, nor of enemy posts, it was decided to attack silently, without artillery support but with that of 40th Royal Tank Regiment. The attack proceeded according to plan, and only after it began to dig in on its objective did 2/17th Battalion begin to receive harassing fire from artillery and machine-guns. On the left, 2/13th Battalion encountered machine-gun fire after 500 yards but advanced through it, and by 0315 hours it was also digging in on its objective.[16] It spent the rest of the day – 'Black Sunday' – under counter-attack. Among those killed that day, noted Arthur Newton of 2/13th Battalion, was Sergeant Darby Green – 'A wonderful man who was killed, as he had foretold in a poem he once wrote, by a spandau [machine-gun] burst.'[17]

The London Rifle Brigade received its orders to move forward at 1700 hours on 24 October, although it was not until 0400 hours the next morning that it cleared the foremost minefield. In the dark, the Australians were apparently dealing with a counter-attack. Only the brigade's commanding officer, Lieutenant-Colonel Geoffrey Hunt, was confident of its location in a gap to the left of the Australians and to the right of 51st (Highland) Division. He hurriedly arranged defensive localities for his companies and they began to scratch at the rocky surface, managing to get reasonably well dug in before dawn. This proved very necessary: heavy shellfire forced the battalion's carriers to withdraw soon after, and throughout the morning there was a steady drain of casualties.[18]

Wimberley wanted 1st Gordon Highlanders to secure Aberdeen with an attack after dark, in order to conform with the Australians. Throughout 24 October, A and C Companies had been exposed and isolated. Twice Lieutenant Harry Gordon, commanding the remnants of C Company, sent runners back to inform battalion of their situation; twice he saw them killed. Finally he sent Sergeant-Major Thompson, saying, 'You have got to get through.'[19] He did, and at dusk on 24 October B and D companies relieved A and C, which withdrew into reserve as a composite company. D company then advanced on Aberdeen, which it secured without opposition, and managed to make contact with the London Rifle Brigade from 1st Armoured Division.[20]

At 2300 hours 7th Argyll and Sutherland Highlanders made a silent attack on Nairn, a low ridge comprising three different objectives about a mile in front of Greenock. The Argylls were now reorganized into three companies, which formed up from right to left in order A, D and B but were heavily shelled and machine-gunned on the start line. Nevertheless, they pressed on. In the moonlight they could see groups of the enemy moving about, and when these began to retreat they chased them with the bayonet. They consolidated on the reverse slope of a shallow depression, and A and D Companies – having no officers left of their own – were again reorganized, into one company. They held this isolated position largely out of touch with battalion until relieved by 2nd Regiment Botha from 1st South African Division on 30 October.[21]

The armour was due to attack at 2200 hours, supported by 300 guns. Tenth Armoured Division would move through the New Zealanders' positions with 8th Armoured Brigade on the left and 24th Armoured Brigade now on the right. Ninth Armoured Brigade would advance through 26th Battalion's positions to an area to the south and link the left of 10th Armoured Division's objective to the infantry positions.

When 26th Battalion learned of the plan, it discovered that the opening barrage was due to fall on its forward companies, and runners were hastily sent to order their withdrawal. But they were still partly caught by the barrage and by a later bombing raid. Amazingly, only one man was killed and another was wounded, and fortunately things had calmed down by 0100 hours.[22]

It was also proposed that 133rd Brigade should take over from 5th New Zealand Brigade so that the latter could follow up 9th Armoured Brigade, but Freyberg held up the orders for this relief. He was doubtful about the armour's ability to complete its task, and told Leese so quite bluntly. Gatehouse kept a tactical headquarters well forward, but his divisional main headquarters was a long way back and communications between them remained very poor. Freyberg was annoyed that he could not co-ordinate his own 9th Armoured Brigade with the actions of the armoured division it was supporting, being in touch only with the staff, who were themselves in frequently out of touch with their commander. Meanwhile, for the men of 9th Armoured Brigade the 24th had been a long and frustrating day. 'We continued to engage the enemy without making the required gap, and luckily without too heavy losses . . .' recalled Clive Stoddart of the Warwickshire Yeomanry. 'As darkness fell we were still on the ridge.'[23]

Soon after dark, men and vehicles were milling about – bringing up supplies, improving defensive positions, and preparing for the advance. On the Axis side, measures were also being taken to receive the next phase of the attack. Sent forward to hold a gap in the minefield, Ralph Ringler's 10th Company of 104th Panzergrenadier Regiment set off under heavy shelling. He recalled that

a terrible shock tore the wheel from my hands and threw the car forward . . . Monier! I ran back, the vehicle carrying the anti-tank gun was undamaged, the driver lay near the lorry unhurt. 'What happened,' I called to him, 'where is Unteroffizier Monier?' . . . A moan came from a dark patch near the marker poles of the minefield. 'Monier, are you all right?' 'I knew it would happen,' he whispered faintly, 'please, my wife . . .' Monier was dead.[24]

On the British side congestion was appalling, and Panzerarmee – expecting a repetition of the previous night's operations in the absence of strong armoured forces during the day – began directing harassing fire from artillery, mortars and machine-guns on fixed lines into the area behind the ridge. This caused some disruption to the sappers clearing gaps in the minefields, but the two squadrons of Honey light tanks and Bren carriers of 2nd New Zealand Divisional Cavalry Regiment made it through. C Squadron was then held up by anti-tank fire, but B Squadron advanced for nearly 2 miles, followed by 9th Armoured Brigade. At first light they withdrew, having lost 23 men, 5 tanks and 4 carriers, but having overrun several posts and taken a number of prisoners.[25]

Next on to the ridge were the Staffordshire Yeomanry of 8th Armoured Brigade, followed by the Sherwood Rangers. Shortly after midnight, one of the Sherwood Rangers' soft-skinned support vehicles was set alight by a shell near the close-packed convoy carrying infantry, petrol and ammunition. It was immediately the subject of bombing attacks by Axis aircraft that had been lurking since dusk hoping for just such a target. Desperate attempts were made to save the column as shells also began to land, but few vehicles could be got clear of the mass before flames swept throughout the entire convoy. Casualties numbered some 50, being especially heavy among the lorried infantry company of 1st Buffs, and this disaster disorganized the advance not only of the Sherwood Rangers (who lost 20 soft-skinned vehicles loaded with petrol and ammunition) but also of the whole brigade. The commanding officer of the Sherwood Rangers called a halt, which affected 3rd Royal Tank Regiment following behind, and these dispersed with permission from Brigadier Custance, who also called Gatehouse proposing that the whole advance be postponed.[26]

Montgomery had gone to bed early as usual – happy that at least 1st Armoured Division was on Pierson, if somewhat annoyed at the delays in 10th Armoured Division's operation. His armour was 24 hours behind schedule, but once the two divisions were 'out' he could begin 'crumbling' and he felt that he still held the initiative. Meanwhile, the request made by Custance for a postponement was passed back by Gatehouse to Lumsden, who in turn telephoned de Guingand and recommended that permission be granted. De Guingand decided that this was one of those rare occasions when he had no alternative but to wake the Army Commander, and at 0200 hours in the morning of 25 October, while Gatehouse's lead units were struggling to the forward edge of the minefield, he did so.[27] It was a conference charged with high drama. The two corps commanders arrived at 0330 hours: Leese the burly, genial, red-faced Guardsman and Lumsden the tall, good-looking cavalryman who always appeared, as Richard McCreery recalled, 'in a perfectly clean, well starched collar no matter how many sand storms he had to pass through'.[28] William Mather, who acted as liaison officer between them, noted that Lumsden

> had his own tank which was painted white and which he drove by himself, because he had the most remarkable sense of location. What he did was quite wrong: he'd swan all over the place by himself in his white tank. He had beau-

tifully pressed cavalry trousers, immaculate bush shirt and white silk scarf and everything else – and he was very morale-raising because he'd suddenly appear, this immaculate creature, like someone from the Gods.

But, although he undoubtedly had great abilities, 'Monty saw right through him – this tremendous sort of surface glaze on Herbert Lumsden. He wasn't as good as he was made out to be, but he had such tremendous polish, always had the answer to everything, always had such charming manners. And Monty saw right through this – and it made Herbert collapse.'[29]

Montgomery received his corps commanders in his caravan seated on a stool while studying a map – probably the best way for a general of small stature to receive two lanky subordinates, especially in circumstances akin to a headmaster summoning unruly schoolboys. He was well aware of Lumsden's reservations about his plan for X Corps, since the latter had been less than discreet in letting this be known – and in criticizing Montgomery for wearing the black Royal Tank Regiment beret. Freyberg had expressed the view that 'the tanks won't do it', but Montgomery was not someone who regarded his orders as a basis for discussion, whatever the opinions of tank commanders who believed he was misusing their armour. According to de Guingand, he listened intently to what each had to say, including Lumsden's opinion that the armour had been given an impossible task. Then he saw Lumsden alone, stating clearly and firmly that the tanks could and *would* go through.[30] At this bleak hour, with doubts being cast on his stewardship of the battle, Montgomery rose to the challenge of high command and showed a steely resolve. Leese wrote to his wife later that day, 'I'm convinced the armour could have gone through and exploited that critical time immediately, after a successful attack. But I'm afraid they've no stomach for a fight – and are not given the lead or have the will to succeed . . . All my infantry think nothing of them.'[31]

Both armoured brigades of 10th Armoured Division continued to advance beyond Miteiriya Ridge, 24th on the right and 8th on the left, although they were now authorized to advance with just one regiment forward – the Staffordshire Yeomanry. Meanwhile, Currie had personally reconnoitred a route over the ridge on foot for 9th Armoured Brigade before ordering 3rd Hussars to advance. Although the Warwickshire Yeomanry which was following up was delayed, it too managed to get forward. Encouraged by its appearance on the left, the Staffordshire Yeomanry pressed on, its attached company from 1st Buffs overcoming some anti-tank guns. But then it encountered devastating fire from anti-tank guns on either flank. John Lakin of the

Warwickshire Yeomanry witnessed their tanks 'go up in sheets of flames one by one, just as if someone had lit the candles on a birthday cake', and they had to withdraw, inducing 9th Armoured Brigade to follow.[32]

Behind them, Tuker's liaison officer reported that the armour was still 'grinding through the lanes and gingerly deploying'.[33] It was the first time in battle for Trooper Philip Foster of the Sherwood Rangers as he followed the tanks with the 'A' echelon:

> We were nearly choked and blinded by the flour like dust. The night was nearly over. The column was now winding through lanes in the minefields. As dawn broke, the flood of battle burst with staccato fury. The tanks in front of the Echelon had fallen foul of savage crossfire from 88 mm guns and machine-guns. The whole column had been forced to halt. Tanks began to 'brew up' right and left. Armour-piercing thermite shells ricocheted close to the Echelon and the order was soon given to withdraw.[34]

'In the half-light,' recalled Sergeant Buck Kite of 3rd Royal Tank Regiment, 'we were nose to tail, unable to move and came under artillery and anti-tank fire without being able to do much about it. Several tanks in front of mine were hit and I thought it was going to be my turn when somehow we were able to push on and deploy on the ridge though we didn't get far.'[35]

With the tanks firing from hull-down positions, the sappers began clearing mines again and tank crews started to repair damaged tracks. Kite's commanding officer, Lieutenant-Colonel Peter Pyman, recalled grimly that 'I lost most of my engineers in their gallant attempts to clear the minefield. It was a most desperate day.'[36] Another observer from an armoured unit, J. Ruane, said:

> the sight of sappers lining up and going over a ridge to probe for mines with bayonets was terrible and awe-inspiring to watch. Every one of them deserved a medal, as they seemed to go to a certain death. They no sooner 'went over' than bursts of enemy machine-gun fire seemed to wipe them out; then another line would form up, stub their cigarettes out and move over the top. It was a privilege to be in the company of such men.[37]

Tuker's liaison officer noted the 'lesson surely is lack of artillery to help them. Counter-attacks by 15th Panzer [were] held by 1st Armoured sitting and shooting and *not* charging about like untrained formations.'[38]

Brigadier 'Pip' Roberts later noted that Montgomery

> expected much more than [the armour] could possibly achieve – *much* more. I mean whenever you attack with tanks – and this was on a really detailed, pre-conceived plan – you get heavy casualties. When you give the enemy

casualties is when he attacks you. Now whenever the Germans attacked during Alamein – which they did, because they put in counter-attacks – *they* had heavy casualties.[39]

Indeed, 'the German anti-tank gunners blazed away at us all day', according to Major Lindsay of the Sherwood Rangers, until the Germans counter-attacked in the evening, coming

> towards us out of the setting sun – a favourite German trick. Their shelling was intense. They put down patches of smoke and in this cover small groups of their tanks manoeuvred from ridge to ridge. The Regiment blazed away at them with every gun available and large fires on the enemy side showed we were doing damage. After a time the Hun had had enough and withdrew.[40]

Gatehouse's orders finally reached 8th Armoured Brigade at dawn: it was to withdraw leaving one regiment – the Staffordshire Yeomanry – forward of the ridge. Instead, the entire brigade pulled back, leaving the New Zealanders exposed. As the last of the British tanks returned through 6th New Zealand Brigade's position, a solitary Grant tank followed up and drove among the men of 26th Battalion's C Company, many of whom were out of their trenches making the most of the freedom of movement provided by the half-light. Seemingly in no time, 34 were lined up under the guns of the Grant and were then being marched back towards the Axis lines by its German crew, the audacity of whose feat was at first disbelieved at Battalion Headquarters before a belated rescue attempt failed.[41] At least 24th Armoured Brigade had made some progress to the north, with all three regiments reported as on the Pierson bound at 0615 hours – in contact with 2nd Armoured Brigade of 1st Armoured Division and deploying among the Australian infantry in their bridgehead.

Dressed in their colourful cravats, the tank commanders surveyed the scene and became the subject of a vigorous counter-bombardment, but they failed to advance. 'However hard and however often the "GO" button had been pressed on the army control panel, its impulses were not motivating these tanks whose commanders, though as brave as they were bizarre, evinced no intention to advance "at all costs" to the Pierson bound,' wrote the Australian official historian.[42] Perhaps this was hardly surprising, since even the new Shermans were prey for the anti-tank guns because they burned easily. Later the British would christen them 'Ronsons', after the reliable cigarette lighters. Their engines ran on high-octane petrol, and a white-hot round would send them up in seconds. Gunner L. Wink saw a tank slewing around. 'Its turret swung round and then it suddenly shook and vibrated. Then there was a loud explosion and flames burst through the hatch like a blow-torch. All I could think was "Christ help those poor sods inside it." I tell you I was very glad I was below ground. Those things were absolute death traps.'[43]

As daylight broke, 9th Armoured Brigade found itself abandoned by 10th Armoured Division in a slight hollow with little cover some 1,000 yards in front of 22nd Battalion. To the south-west the Divisional Cavalry had moved some 2,000 yards, having overrun a number of posts and collected many prisoners. It was now in a shallow valley over-looked by strong enemy posts to the south and west, with 3rd Hussars on the right facing south-west and the Warwickshire Yeomanry on the left facing south. Here they provided a screen against a counter-attack that never developed. They saw little enemy activity to their front, and stayed mainly in hull-down positions for protection, although during the day they did round up a number of prisoners. Brigadier Currie wanted to advance, but needed first to withdraw to refuel. Freyberg, fearing that if he did so Lumsden would not allow him back, refused to permit this, and Currie – an eternal subaltern – had to content himself with a forward recce in his Crusader. His tank was hit and lost a track. After being brought back, he took forward a troop to deal with a battery of 50 mm anti-tank guns, which were driven off without actually being hit.[44] Behind 9th Armoured Brigade the infantry continued to improve their positions, but 133rd Brigade – which was crowded in rear of 5th New Zealand Brigade without being properly dug in – lost some 60 casualties and several trucks before new orders arrived allowing it to move further back.[45]

The true situation was, however, unknown to Montgomery. Gatehouse did not report that the Staffordshire Yeomanry had with-drawn east of the ridge, merely that they had been 'forced to retire a little'.[46] Montgomery's conference had not 'galvanised the whole show into action', as de Guingand thought, but had stung Lumsden into resentful silence and Gatehouse into suppressing the truth. Thus, far from being in a position to threaten Panzerarmee's lines of communica-tion and protecting the XXX Corps crumbling operations, X Corps was mired on Miteiriya Ridge, while XIII Corps was also stalled in the south. Although Montgomery now expected to begin 'crumbling' oper-ations to the south-west, using 8th Armoured Brigade as a hinge while 24th Armoured Brigade would come under command of Briggs's 1st Armoured Division, the 'Masterplan' had in fact failed.[47] The armour could not advance in the face of determined anti-tank defences.

Shortly before midday Montgomery visited 2nd New Zealand Division Headquarters to assess the local situation before conferring once more with Leese and Lumsden. Freyberg was extremely angry with the caution of Gatehouse's armour, and now considered the planned 'crumbling' operations impossible. Instead, he proposed a further artillery-supported infantry attack that evening to gain the Pierson bound for the armour, which could then follow up. Lumsden agreed, but Montgomery did not. For a man with a logical, rational approach to war, this was an intuitive decision: any further failure in this sector would effectively mean that the battle was lost, so he chose instead to withdraw 10th Armoured Division and rest the New Zealanders, who were too precious to future plans to be wasted now, and he issued orders to alter the direction of operations to the north-west through 9th Australian Division's area. This second conference marked the first turning point of the battle. If it demonstrated Montgomery's ability to alter his plans while maintaining his original aim, it also exposed the errors in his original plan to superimpose the operations of two corps in the same area. Far from demonstrating a cautious approach, this had been revealed to be over-optimistic in expecting a breakthrough and pursuit so early in the battle.[48]

At a range of about 800 yards Ralph Ringler tried to make out the type of tank approaching his position: 'it was almost impossible in the midday heat haze . . . their guns are pointed at us – now it doesn't matter which side they're on! "Fire!" ' His gun knocked out three of them. 'Gradually the rest of the "Bandits" disappeared behind the dunes. In front of us, in the sand, there died a number of English soldiers, agonisingly, thoughtlessly – men like us.'[49]

In the early afternoon of 25 October an Axis counter-attack came in on the London Rifle Brigade's front, led by a dust cloud that swirled in front of a mixture of Italian M13s and German Mark IIIs. But the battalion's anti-tank gunners were well placed, and the continuous stream of small-arms fire forced the approaching tanks to close their hatches, restricting their vision. Then, as enemy tanks were hit, the crews tried to escape. 'One Italian officer was hoisting himself out when a 6-pounder shot hit him in the chest and he literally disintegrated,' recalled Sergeant D. A. Main.

> From the right came cries of 'You rotten Pommie bastards!' The Australians strongly objected to our knocking out the tanks with our 6-pounders before they came within range of their 2-pounders. Finally, as the barrage had now died down, my platoon commander suggested a bayonet counter-attack. As there was no future in this I asked him if he had a touch of the sun.[50]

Unable to make forward progress, the Axis tanks soon withdrew, leaving 14 of their number behind. The significance of this short, sharp engagement was that it demonstrated Panzerarmee's determination to use armour to drive the intruding infantry back out of the minefields before they could consolidate. However, in attacking dug-in infantry well supported by effective anti-tank guns, that armoured strength would inevitably be written down, and tank losses incurred in this fashion would be far more important than any amount of ground gained.[51] At 1525 hours von Thoma discussed the situation with Bayerlein and Kesselring, who had arrived there. Plans were made to seal off the penetration that day at all costs, and to commit XXI Corps and Kampfgruppe Värst the next day to roll up the enemy from the north, where it was now apparent the British main effort was directed.[52]

The arrival of the London Rifle Brigade, whose vehicles had insufficient space between the minefields for proper dispersal, soon brought more fire down into the general area. 'The enemy gunners were not too proud to shoot at sitting ducks. The carnage was terrible to watch,' recalled 2/13th Battalion's historian. 'It was not long before a flood of casualties swamped the 2/13th R[egimental] A[id] P[ost] which was already working at full pressure to cope with the unit's own casualties. Captain Phil Goode and his men were equal to the occasion.'[53] Probing attacks rather than hammer blows were made by the Axis armour throughout the day. Panzers approached 2/13th and 2/17th Battalions' positions, but were brought to a halt short of 2-pounder range by a remarkable firestorm. The anti-tank guns were under strict orders to hold their fire while the attackers put down a smokescreen through which they advanced, and they kept their cool so well that Sergeant A. R. Bentley did not open fire until the lead tank was 40 yards away. Immediately the cracks of other guns joined in, and soon 17 panzers had been destroyed. Bentley claimed five, Private J. D. Taylor claimed two, while Lieutenant A. F. Wallder's D Troop from 2/3rd Anti-Tank Regiment claimed nine. The remaining panzers withdrew while their supporting infantry prepared to assault. The attack was pressed for another hour and a half and caused many casualties: by day's end, 2/17th Battalion had lost 12 dead and 73 wounded.[54]

Having spent 24 October under all sorts of fire, the infantry holding the XXX Corps line spent 25 October in much the same situation. Fifty-first (Highland) Division continued to clear up its area. In the afternoon, 5th Black Watch was tasked with securing Stirling after tanks from 50th Royal Tank Regiment had failed in the morning. It threatened to be a tough battle, but when the attack went in, at 2115 hours, it was a walkover, the Germans having already withdrawn. They had left so precipitately that a couple of German vehicles, including an armoured car, drove casually on to the position and were captured.[55]

1. Seen here shortly after his arrival in the desert (note the impractical breeches and boots), Erwin Rommel soon became synonymous with it as the 'Desert Fox'

2. Generalfeldmarschall Albrecht Kesselring was the senior German officer in the Mediterranean, but his power – even his influence – over Rommel was severely limited

3. Eighth Army crisis conference: (*left to right*)
Lieutenant-Generals Willoughby Norrie, Neil Ritchie
and 'Strafer' Gott. Gott was Churchill's preferred
successor to Ritchie

4. Cairo, 4 August 1942: (*left to right, rear*) Air Marshal
Sir Arthur Tedder, General Sir Alan Brooke, Admiral Sir Henry
Harwood, Richard Casey; (*front*) Field Marshal J.C. Smuts,
Sir Winston Churchill, General Sir Claude Auchinleck and
General Sir Archibald Wavell

5. The new Commander-in-Chief Middle East, General the Honourable Sir Harold Alexander, and the Eighth Army Commander, Lieutenant-General Bernard Law Montgomery

6. Montgomery (bareheaded) confers with the Commander XIII Corps, Lieutenant-General Brian Horrocks (behind his arm), and Brigadier G.P.B. 'Pip' Roberts (in beret) of the 22nd Armoured Brigade, which would bear the brunt of the armoured battle at Alam Halfa

7. An Australian soldier inscribes his feelings on the wall of Alamein station. During sustained operations throughout the summer and autumn of 1942, the 9th Australian Division poured its blood into the sand

8. The sign on this YMCA van says it all. For Tommy Atkins and his brother Jock, nothing was more important than tea

9. Had Malta not been relieved, the entire British position in the Middle East might have been compromised. Air attack was always terrifying, and at sea, with seemingly nowhere to hide, even more so

10. Formations of eighteen bombers were a memorable feature for both sides – reassuring for the Allies, but dreadful for the Axis, and a constant drain on nerves and willpower

11. The Scorpion flail tank proved of limited value during the battle, being prone to break down in the exacting conditions, but it was the forerunner of many successful similar devices

12. Although radio provided greater flexibility in communications, the need for security and reliability meant that communication by cable was extensively used. Here armoured signals cable is laid in preparation for the offensive

13. The infantry commanders in conference before the battle: (*left to right*) Lieutenant-General Leslie Morshead, Major-General Douglas Wimberley, Lieutenant-General Sir Oliver Leese and Major-General Dan Pienaar

14. X Corps armour commanders in conference shortly before the battle: (*left to right*) Major-General Raymond Briggs, Lieutenant-General Bernard Freyberg, Major-General Alec Gatehouse, Lieutenant-General Herbert Lumsden and Major-General C.H. Gairdner

15. A dummy pumping station with a dummy soldier on the dummy pipeline that was part of Operation Bertram, the deception plan for the battle

16. The vast quantities of stores being collected in the north of the Alamein position were hidden from view. Crude covers like this were sufficient to fool Axis air reconnaissance

17. Tank transporters were only one of many types of vehicle driven by the Royal Army Services Corps, here recovering a Matilda. Their work effectively helped to increase British combat strength

18. Linesmen repairing telephone communications. Though the Royal Corps of Signals lacked the glamour of other branches of the army, its work was nevertheless fundamental to the success of the battle

19. In the Sherman, the British finally had a tank that was a match for anything in the German inventory. It was, however, still vulnerable to German anti-tank guns

20. Despite the introduction of new equipment, many British armoured squadrons still only possessed inadequate tanks like the under-armoured and under-armed Crusader

21. Gunners manning a 25-pounder, a phenomenally effective weapon that Axis soldiers dreaded and that provided the basis of the Royal Regiment of Artillery's dominance of the battlefield

22. The efficiency and flexibility of Allied air commanders Air Marshal Sir Arthur Tedder (*left*) and Air Vice Marshal Arthur Coningham made a vital, and neglected, contribution to the winning of the land battle

23. An air gunner's view of a Baltimore bomber flying yet another sortie to attack Axis positions. Bombers were very vulnerable to both ground fire and fighters

24. A soldier prepares to advance as the skyline behind him is lit up by the barrage. Few who experienced it would ever forget its intensity

25. Royal Engineers waiting to advance in the light of the barrage. Although two men can be seen carrying mine detectors, these were of limited value, and the only sure way to locate mines was by hand, usually under fire

26. British infantry attempting to advance under artillery fire. For days on end, infantrymen of both sides endured constant shell and mortar fire

27. Italian troops run for cover as RAF bombs rain down on Axis positions

28. While the battle raged on land, anti-shipping operations continued to sink Axis ships.
It was a war with no quarter given

9. Men of 2/3rd Pioneer Battalion sheltering under the railway embankment following a series of punishing assaults on German positions near the coast. The strain of battle is self-evident

30. The qualitative advantage of German armour had been negated by the time of the battle, and for this crewman, like so many others on both sides, the end was grim

31. Montgomery welcomes
von Thoma to his
headquarters by the sea.
Like von Thoma, Rommel
knew the end in Africa was
inevitable

32. Earlier on, much had been made of Italian soldiers surrendering in droves, but the
only alternative in the desert was death through thirst. These prisoners are German

To the south of the New Zealanders, the South Africans had taken the opportunity of the previous night and the day of 25 October to organize their defences and clear mines. They also sent out numerous patrols to try to ascertain the enemy's new defence line. Visiting the front during the day, Pienaar watched some premature bomb releases by the DAF, which was pounding Axis positions whenever the opportunity occurred. Visibility was poor throughout the day, hampering both the aircraft and artillery observation. However, there was little activity in the South African sector.[56]

Overnight diversionary actions by 4th Indian Division and a harassing fire programme by 50th (Northumbrian) Division in XIII Corps's sector were carried out to keep the enemy guessing about future intentions, but from observations during the day it was apparent from all three divisions' fronts that the enemy was not thinning out his defences to provide reinforcements elsewhere.

For Horrocks's corps, the task for the night of 24/25 October had been a modification of the original plan which had called for 50th (Northumbrian) Division to attack on the night after 44th (Home Counties) Division. But, since this had assumed that the enemy line would be breached and that 7th Armoured Division would have already passed through to exploit into the area facing the North Countrymen, the plan now meant combining the two attacks. Two battalions of 44th (Home Counties) Division under command of 7th Armoured Division were to break through the second mine barrier to form a bridgehead for 22nd Armoured Brigade followed by 4th Light Armoured Brigade to sally forth with the intention of swinging north across the front of 50th (Northumbrian) Division, which was to step forward and clear the area between it and the armour. The first objectives were a strongly held area in the Munassib Depression code-named The Moor and another isolated strongpoint, The Cape. The second objective was a line of defences some 300 yards to the rear of The Moor, and it was anticipated that a third objective would exist in ground between the second and that due to be taken by 7th Armoured Division. The attack would be carried out by 69th Brigade, with 6th Green Howards on the right and 5th East Yorkshire Regiment on the left. To the north, 151st (Tyneside) Brigade would silently push a battalion group forward to occupy positions north of the depression and dominate it when dawn broke. The division would then hold these positions as a firm base for future operations.[57] Throughout the day, the Axis defenders of The Moor were subjected to heavy artillery fire. At 2230 hours a smokescreen was put down in front of them, and under cover of this 6th Green Howards crossed their start line at 2305 hours with two companies leading.

The attack began well: Lieutenant D. Cox of 2nd/22nd (Cheshire) Regiment had an excellent view from where his Vickers machine-guns were providing supporting fire, with the Green Howards breaching the wire and crossing the minefield. But they then ran into intense mortar and machine-gun fire and took heavy casualties, especially on the right, and, when the Vickers fire switched from the objective to allow the assault, instead of rushing from one wadi to the next they hesitated and the attack came to a standstill.[58] On the left, B Company managed to secure the high ground of Point 94, where they were held up and began consolidating shortly after midnight. At 0140 hours A Company was launched against those strongholds still holding out on The Moor, but it had a difficult fight over 300 yards without artillery support to reach its final objective.[59]

To the left, 5th East Yorkshire Regiment had a much harder time of it. After advancing some 1,300 yards to the objective, two of the three carriers allotted to breaking down the wire with grappling hooks were destroyed by mines. By a mischance, the British artillery barrage fell short on to the Yorkshiremen, forcing them to retire, and a breakdown in communications meant that an officer had to be sent to Brigade Headquarters for instructions. The artillery programme was repeated twice, and after a third attempt to penetrate the booby-trapped and heavily mined wire defences, but with not enough time before dawn to prepare a fresh assault, the battalion was ordered to withdraw to a reverse-slope position some 400 yards away and dig in there.[60]

Casualties in these operations had been heavy, amounting to some 100 in 6th Green Howards and 150 in 5th East Yorkshire Regiment. An attempt by A Company 6th Green Howards to renew the attack on to Point 92 at 1430 hours on 26 October was repulsed by heavy artillery fire, causing another 60 casualties, reducing that company to one-third strength.[61] Lieutenant-Colonel D. A. Seagrim praised the support of Cox's machine-gunners, saying that none of his men would have got back without it.[62] There was little point in continuing these operations, and they were subsequently suspended and 69th Brigade spent the next few days mortaring the enemy as hard as possible.[63]

For its task, 7th Armoured Division chose 1/5th and 1/6th Queen's Royal Regiment. The sound of tanks forming up led to an intense bombardment of the bridgehead area, which coincided with the arrival of the petrol and ammunition lorries of the Royal Scots Greys' 'A' echelon, but fortunately replenishment was completed without casualties.[64] Passing through the minefield went well at first, with both Queen's battalions advancing two companies up on a frontage of 400 yards and pushing some 800 yards beyond the minefield before starting to dig in. 'Eventually our leading platoon and the 1/6th Queen's on our left arrived in the middle of the Italian positions and some twenty or thirty Italians cheerfully gave themselves up and remained for the next twenty-four hours, withdrawing with us at the end of that time,' recalled Lieutenant D. J. Watson of 1/5th Queen's. Behind, the sappers cleared the gaps and 4th County of London Yeomanry began to advance, but soon began to take casualties from anti-tank guns beyond the forward edge of the infantry's positions. Harding, well aware of the need to pre-serve his armour, stopped any further attempts to negotiate February and ordered the armour's withdrawal, thus leaving the infantry in the open for the following day, where they were subjected to intense fire of all kinds.[65] Once again the lead elements of 7th Armoured Division were caught between minefields and exposed. The men of 1/5th and 1/6th Queen's Royal Regiment were unable to lift their heads above ground in most areas. Lieutenant Watson recalled that the Folgore Division

> proceeded to inflict heavy casualties on us, using mortars and machine-guns, firing from entrenched positions. I remember young O'Connell, both legs severed by a mortar-bomb, screaming for help and then for his mother before he mercifully died. Major Capper, who led the advance, was hit and disappeared from sight, but called out deliriously at intervals during the day before he too fell quiet.[66]

Private S. Gray spent a long while lying in the open not daring to move.

> It was on the point of getting light. So I said to the officer, 'It's coming up to sun-up. Then they will pick us off.' He said, 'Pass the word around, every man for himself, and find a hole to get into.' Strange as it seems, a cloud came over the moon, which gave us the chance to move. But as we did so, over came mortars and shells and got some of the chaps. I and another chap found an empty German trench. Mortars and shells kept coming in our direction.

Eventually, Gray got back to British lines, and during the day Montgomery gave XIII Corps permission to break off the attack. Once more, casualties had been severe: 1/5th Queen's had lost 8 officers and 110 men; 1/6th Queen's 10 officers and 189 men. Forty-fourth (Home Counties) Division had indeed been dogged by bad luck, and it came as little surprise when it was later broken up to provide infantry for other formations, though it was a pity, since, as a sapper lieutenant wrote later, 'I met a lot of them before they went. Home Counties blokes, quiet and with no swank, and believe me they can fight.'[67]

15

Crumbling

Here dead lie we because we did not choose
To live and shame the land from which we sprung.
Life, to be sure is nothing much to lose;
But young men think it is, and we were young.

A. E. Housman

An Australian diarist summarized Alamein thus far: 'Shocking three days of noise, death and fear.'[1] For the troops on the ground there was at this time a tremendous feeling of uncertainty which affected even the most hardened soldier. While they could assess the situation on their own small sector, there was no news of the general progress of the battle. Fighting seemed to be taking place in every direction, including to the rear.[2] Conditions in many of the positions were dreadful: the machine-gunners of 12 Platoon 1/7th Middlesex Regiment, on the Aberdeen position with D Company 1st Gordon Highlanders, were so desperately short of water that they had to use the foul coolant from a couple of their guns' radiators, replacing it in the 'traditional emergency manner'. Lance-Corporal H. Sleeth volunteered to go back and report to battalion. He had already been hit twice and it would be a mission of great danger, but he made it to his Company Headquarters despite being blown up. Refusing to be evacuated, he then guided a relief patrol with food, ammunition and reinforcements that evening.[3]

While some peered uncertainly out of their holes, many were kept busy. All day and all night throughout the battle, signallers – 'bolstered by courage and tradition' – would run along their lines searching for breaks and, having located them, fixing, testing both ways, and then running forward or backward as necessary. 'Sitting ducks we exposed linesmen.' V. J. Walshe of 2/17th Battalion saw a signaller mending a line with his back turned. Then he realized 'he was not moving, went closer and found it was Bruce Weary – no apparent mark on him, sitting upright, but he was dead'.[4] Company orderlies faced similar risks. An equally important and dangerous task which fell to the sappers was the destruction of bombs and booby-traps and of damaged enemy tanks and equipment, to prevent their recovery and repair. Since many of these tanks and guns had been knocked out early on by long-range fire, they often remained covered by the enemy, making it dangerous work.[5] After Lieutenant B. S. Jarvis destroyed his first 88 with a charge, he felt very satisfied. 'It is grand to think of the Boche making these weapons, running them over to Sicily and then transporting them all the way to Alamein only to be destroyed in a twinkling by a British sapper.'[6]

Montgomery's decision to switch north has often been portrayed as a calculated one which had been made necessary by the peril in which 8th and 9th Armoured Brigades had found themselves. In fact it was more a result of the constant murmuring of the armoured commanders and their failure to break through.[7] Although XXX Corps had now captured all its objectives, this had been done only at great cost, especially among 51st (Highland) Division. By the morning of 26 October, XXX Corps had already suffered 4,643 casualties while Lumsden's X Corps had suffered only 455 – less than half those incurred by XIII Corps' feint operations in the south. According to Leese, 'we were within an ace of losing our grip on the battle'.[8] There was also apparent tardiness in the north, where 1st Armoured Division had failed to push the armoured shield right on to the Kidney Ridge feature – though its navigation was so poor that it at first refused to admit this and would not assist the Royal Artillery in surveying-in as the infantry did, showing no understanding of corps artillery co-operation. When Kirkman reported that Lumsden 'wanders about the country by himself and the CCRA [Corps Commander Royal Artillery] doesn't know what's going on', Montgomery was furious. In his diary he wrote 'there is no doubt these RAC Generals do not understand the co-operation of all arms in battle. I have had many examples of this since the battle started. Lumsden is not a really high-class soldier.'[9] Indeed, only now was 2nd Armoured Brigade able to close up with the Highlanders on the Pierson bound. But during the previous two days it had been constantly in action; the tanks had needed replenishing with ammunition two or three times a day, with the drivers of soft-skinned 'B'-echelon supply vehicles and their mates coming right up to the battle positions to do this, showing great courage and calmness.[10]

Rommel returned on the evening of 25 October and was very welcome to his army, although there was little but gloom to greet him. On the way, in Rome, he met von Rintelen, who told him that Stumme was still missing (although he had by now been found) and that only three issues of fuel remained (an issue being the amount required to move the army 100 kilometres). Rommel had considered his minimum requirement to be 30 issues, and had built up eight before going on leave. What, he asked, had become of the other five, and why had stockpiles not been built up? Although he might not unreasonably have blamed the RAF and the Royal Navy, von Rintelen apologized, having also just returned from leave. 'Insufficient attention was paid to the supply situation in my absence,' he said. 'Then the Italians must use every possible means, including their submarines and navy, to rush supplies to Panzerarmee,' Rommel yelled at the attaché. At Crete he learned that Stumme was dead and von Thoma temporarily in charge. He then flew to Qasada airfield, transferred to his Storch, and flew eastward until dusk before transferring once more to his car and arriving at Panzerarmee at 2330 hours.[11]

He received discouraging reports from von Thoma, who explained that the overwhelming British artillery had destroyed the Devil's Gardens and that the Axis had been able to halt the enemy but not repulse him. 'The fuel situation permitted only local counter-attacks by our panzer units which were standing ready immediately behind the threatened sectors of the front.' Allied artillery fire and repeated bombing attacks had decimated the troops, and only 31 panzers were battle-worthy in 15th Panzer Division. 'Only small supplies of fuel remain close to the front.'[12] Bayerlein said later that Rommel 'took over a battle in which . . . no major decisions which could alter events were possible', and Walter Warlimont of the OKW operations branch also described the battle as simply one of *matériel* in which nothing could make up for 'the failure of the overseas supply lines'.[13] But Rommel was not completely at the mercy of circumstances – which had, in any case, to a large extent been shaped by him.

He later reflected that he 'could have made the action more fluid by withdrawing a few miles to the west and could then have attacked the British in an all-out charge and defeated them in open country. The British artillery and air force would not have easily intervened with their usual weight in a tank battle of this kind, for their own forces would have been endangered.'[14] Perhaps he could have done that, but in fact he sat waiting for the next blow to fall. However, he at least felt able to begin to move his armoured reserve up from the south, and 21st Panzer Division was ordered to move its northern battle group at 1455 hours on 26 October.[15] As early as the 24th, radio direction-finding had indicated that the main British effort was indeed in the north, and now a

prisoner regarded as 'trustworthy' confirmed the suggestion of reconnaissance by insisting that the main thrust would come there.[16]

Rommel also decided that he must concentrate Panzerarmee to
block any further advance by Eighth Army, and decided to reinforce the
coastal sector. He felt sure that Montgomery planned to break through
to the sea between El Daba and Sidi Abd el Rahman, and hoped to concentrate sufficiently to delay or prevent such a breakthrough.[17] He
immediately realized the significance of a feature known to the Allies as
Trig 29, then held by 125th Panzergrenadier Regiment. Later, when Trig
29 had changed hands, he wrote, 'Attacks were now launched against
Hill 28 [Trig 29] by elements of 15th Panzer Division, the Littorio and a
Bersaglieri battalion. The British [sic] resisted desperately. Rivers of
blood were poured out over miserable strips of land.'[18] But Rommel
was not one to waste men's lives on miserable strips of land if they had
no tactical significance: Trig 29 was to prove of enormous importance
to Montgomery's ability to crush Rommel's forces in the vice of his
artillery over the following week.

The instructions given to 9th Australian Division were to begin
attacking north towards the sea with the ultimate objective of destroying the Axis forces in the salient formed by the advance of Eighth
Army's flank. The tactical importance of Trig 29 had been appreciated
before the battle opened: despite being no more than a rise of some 20
feet, Trig 29 was the highest ground in the area and dominated everything around it. The plan now involved 1st South African Division
firing a concentrated artillery programme to suggest an attack in their
sector and the area around Trig 29 (including the spur and forward
slopes running to the east) being seized that night. The entire northern
front of 26th Australian Brigade would be advanced to the edge of the
Axis defence line on its right, with 2/24th and 2/48th Battalions being
used to seize Trig 29 and the nearby Fig Orchard, a feature easily recog-
nizable on the ground.

Lieutenant-Colonel H. H. 'Tack' Hammer, who had commanded
2/48th since January, had given his battalion a motto – 'Hard as Nails' –
and the battalion had swiftly lived up to it. Now he produced a bold and
original plan. He would advance towards Trig 29 with two companies
forward under cover of a barrage; then, just as the barrage lifted, he
would rush a third company on to the objective, using the 29 carriers
and other vehicles he had assembled. Ten carriers from the battalion
carrier platoon would carry two platoons of this third company, while
four more carriers would quickly follow towing 37 mm anti-tank guns (a
Bofors weapon roughly equivalent to the 2-pounder). The third platoon
would be carried on the gun lorries (portees) of a troop of 6-pounders

from 2/3rd Anti-Tank Regiment, which would follow on last. Once 2/48th had completed its part of the operation, 2/24th would form up in the area secured and move north-east in order to roll up the Axis defences along the flank of a switch line they had formed up to Thompson's Post at an angle to the main line, as a second line against a frontal assault from the area of Point 23 (2/15th Battalion's Bulimba objective).

At dusk the Aussies had a piece of great good fortune: an encounter with some Germans led to the capture of the acting commanders of 125th Panzergrenadier Regiment and its II Battalion. On the battalion commander was found a map of the objective showing enemy dispositions and minefields: the track which Hammer's carriers were to use was shown as free from mines. Alterations were thus made to the plan, to reduce the minefield-gapping task of the sappers from 1,000 yards depth to just 200. The map also showed that Trig 29 had been recently reinforced.

When the barrage opened at midnight, the lead companies pressed forward on foot through heavy defensive fire to their intermediate objective some 200 yards short of Trig 29 and halted. Then, just as the barrage stopped, the carriers, moving four abreast, charged straight through the smoke- and dust-filled air on to the objective and the infantry leaped down and charged. There was a sharp hand-to-hand fight with the confused and surprised defenders, but the Aussies were unstoppable. Further back, the companies that had led the attack on foot were still fighting their way forward. It was here that Corporal B. W. A. Lindsey and Private P. E. Gratwick found that their platoon had been reduced to just seven men. Undeterred, they jumped up and raced forward. Gratwick assaulted two posts with bayonet and grenades before being killed by a burst of machine-gun fire; but the enemy was completely unnerved, and when the remainder of the company followed up the position was quickly secured.*

By first light, despite a stray shell having destroyed six mine-laden lorries with a devastating detonation, over 2,000 mines had been laid and the companies were reorganized and ready for defence, albeit in rather shallow trenches.[19] Meanwhile, the Composite Force formed to guard the northern flank had conformed to the new line, and 2/24th Battalion ('Wangaratta's Own') had advanced to the north-east towards Fig Orchard. The line of posts encountered was held not by Italians, as had been expected, but by Germans, and proved correspondingly difficult to destroy. Nevertheless, a number of posts were reduced, and

---

*Gratwick was awarded a posthumous Victoria Cross for this action.

when the rear companies passed through they each took care of another three. Unfortunately, the cost was such that when the commanding officer, Lieutenant-Colonel Charles Weir, went forward at 0400 hours he decided that his companies were too depleted to hold the extended front on which his men were digging in and he withdrew them 1,000 yards. Twenty-sixth Australian Brigade had taken 173 prisoners from the three battalions of 125th Panzergrenadier Regiment and 67 Italians from Trento and Littorio Divisions, while losses that night amounted to 55 dead and 256 wounded and missing.[20]

Throughout 26 and 27 October 2/48th and 2/24th Battalions were subjected to violent and prolonged bombardments. 'Those who were there may recall the extraordinary rising and falling in waves of sound. All the different weapons appeared to be coordinated to produce a definite rhythm ranging from diminuendo to deafening crescendo and it went on for hour after hour.'[21] But when the Axis forces tried to marshal infantry for a counter-attack they were met by the crushing weight of fire provided by the division's three field regiments and 7th Medium. These were also able to fire counter-battery missions against many of the Axis guns – all as a result of controlling this piece of ground which gave observation for 2 or 3 miles in every direction.

Although the bridgehead originally planned had now been seized and extended to the north, the Axis forces nevertheless maintained an unbroken front. However, by the morning of 27 October, III Battalion 382nd Regiment had been reduced to 1 officer and 10 men, II Battalion 115th Panzergrenadier Regiment to 3 officers and 40 men, and the entire Italian 62nd Regiment to 150 all ranks.[22] It was, according to the Italian soldier and writer Paolo Caccia-Dominioni, as if 'the little rectangles on the map, each one representing a battalion, were like ice-cubes laid out on a metal shelf over a kitchen stove: they spluttered and melted away one after the other'.[23] The pressure on the Axis positions in front of XXX Corps was such that according to the DAK war diary, DAK was being committed from the outset

> to bolster up the northern sector. Pitifully small reserve groups composed of tanks, anti-tank and parts of the artillery, were stationed behind the front-line as mobile counter-attack reserves. These parts of the Afrikakorps thrown into counter-attacks several times daily – often against superior tank forces – and also the Grenadier battalions of the panzer divisions, engaged in desperate struggle for several days, had suffered heavy losses.[24]

Not only were the infantry in the defensive line melting, so was Rommel's only effective mobile formation, which found itself constantly attacked from the air.

*

All over the battle area the DAF was active, pounding Axis concentrations wherever they could be located. 'Dickie' Richards, a radio operator serving on Baltimores with 223 Squadron RAF, described a typical sortie. Climbing to 15,000 feet and joined by a fighter escort which flew higher and to the right to prevent their being jumped by 'the Hun in the Sun', they would cross the coast and fly parallel for a while before recrossing it, dropping height, and heading for the target. The whole formation would weave to fox the anti-aircraft predictors who were trying to calculate their height, but this would cease over the target. Each bomber would then fly straight and level for the benefit of the bomb aimers – the most hazardous time, as the Axis flak gunners could get a fix. The radio operator would go to the lower fuselage to open the winding hatch and pull out a pair of Vickers guns in case of attack from below. The top gunner immediately above would be rotating four Browning machine-guns in readiness.

> When all guns were firing the row in the cabin was horrendous! Over the intercom the observer would announce the release of all the bombs in succession. Then I would have to poke my head out of the hatch and confirm the release of each bomb until all six were off. I had a perfect ringside view of what was coming up at us, seeing the flashes of all the guns firing below. I was not very keen on this part of the operation!

Each aircraft would execute a steep diving turn as it left the target area and tried to regain formation quickly for the flight home. Frequently the bombers would be interrupted by Me-109s and there would be a running dogfight.[25]

However, the heaviest blow from the air was dealt at sea. With little petrol, the Axis armour was being committed piecemeal in a manner quite against its usual practice. Equally, any thoughts of pulling back to create the conditions for mobile warfare were stymied, while any attempt to concentrate was pounded by artillery and from the air. Rommel reported to Hitler that unless the supply position improved immediately the battle would be lost.[26] But if the Australian attack on the night of 25/26 October brought trouble to the Axis, the following day was to bring considerably more, thanks to the Allied air force.

On 25 October an enemy ship had blown up after an attack by Bisleys (Blenheim Vs) of 15 Squadron SAAF and Beauforts from 39 Squadron RAF. On 26 October the 4,869-ton tanker *Proserpina*, laden with fuel, was heading for Tobruk in company with another merchantman of 5,000 tons and a smaller vessel of 600 tons escorted by four destroyers. She was expected by the British: her route had been plotted by Ultra and sent to the Middle East the day before.[27] Five South

African Bisleys led by Major D. W. Pidsley supported by eight torpedo-armed RAF Beauforts and nine Beaufighters were sent to intercept. Flying close to the shore at just 100 feet, they flew over about ten E-boats some 15 miles from Tobruk and one Bisley was shot down by intense anti-aircraft fire. Tobruk also provided a powerful barrage, but at 1528 hours two of the merchantmen and two destroyers were spotted and attacked by part of the air group. Shortly afterwards the remainder of the convoy was spotted, and Pidsley swung round through desperate anti-aircraft fire from the destroyers to attack the tanker. His number two, Lieutenant E. G. Dustow, dropped his bombs across the tanker's bows, narrowly missing it; but his aircraft clipped the tanker's mast and, hit hard by anti-aircraft fire, crashed into the sea and the crew were lost. Seconds later Pidsley screamed in at 20 feet and scored a hit on the bridge before a torpedo from a Beaufort struck the bow.[28] 'We left the convoy with great clouds of black smoke enveloping the tanker and rising high in the sky,' remembered Jack Trotman, who was part of a Beaufighter crew from 272 Squadron RAF. The fire was later visible up to 60 miles away.[29] Of 22 aircraft that started the raid, 6 failed to return. Pidsley received an immediate Distinguished Flying Cross, and all the aircrew were commended for their part in this outstanding and immensely significant success. That evening Rommel signalled Comando Supremo and Berlin that 'now *Proserpina* has been burnt off Tobruk, Panzerarmee has petrol for only two or three days' current consumption. Therefore it is impossible at present, to initiate mobile operations.'[30]

To the left of 9th Australian Division, in 51st (Highland) Division's area, the fighting had largely subsided but there was plenty of shelling and mortaring. Neil McCallum was sent as a reinforcement to a battalion of a different regiment, where he was astonished to find 'in a twentieth-century Armageddon a Highland Lieutenant-Colonel, desperate for reinforcements to replace his killed and wounded officers, who would not allow Lowland Scots to fight beside him. And the half-colonel spoke with the accents of Mayfair.' The second battalion he was posted to, however, was entirely welcoming.[31] A German captured by 5th Black Watch turned out to be an old acquaintance of the commanding officer, Lieutenant-Colonel T. G. Rennie: they had been members of the same Shanghai club in 1936. Rennie insisted on a drink before the prisoner was escorted to Brigade Headquarters for interrogation – much to the annoyance of the intelligence officer, as they drank his whisky.[32] Major Gordon-Finlayson's battery moved at daybreak up to a position in the former no-man's land now crammed with tanks, guns and vehicles, HQs and signboards. One felt that a single bomb would do untold damage, but only our Bostons and fighters were to be seen by day. We were in a central position from which we could support our Jocks or the Australians, New Zealanders, South Africans and Indians on our flanks. Each night we fired big programmes in support of one formation or another; by day we answered other calls for fire.[33]

Having been shot through the thigh, Captain H. P. Samwell spent 26 October in a trench with a wounded Austrian under heavy shell and mortar fire, talking about skiing. Later, 'I thought of his wife and children, of our talks about Austria, how damned stupid the whole thing was. First, he shoots me, then I shoot him, then we talk together as friends and share a trench where he is further wounded by his own side. Why were we fighting each other? Did it make sense?' wondered Samwell. 'Then I thought of the massacres in Poland, France, Belgium. Yes, I suppose it was necessary.' Lieutenant Sills appeared and made a joke about the position of Samwell's wound. ' "I'm off to bring in our carriers; they are lost over there." He passed on – a bullet whistled after him. God, how strong the sun was!' Samwell heard some explosions in the direction Sills had gone. 'I heard a faint shout, "Up the Argylls!", and then silence. He never came back.' At about midday armoured units arrived and began firing over the heads of the lead companies and drawing heavy return fire. 'A tank rumbled into view: one of ours – I shouted, but it was hopeless . . . The next moment it went partially over a trench in which some wounded of our own and Germans were lying. I sank back into the trench.' Samwell was finally evacuated that night.* 'The last I saw of my Austrian he was lying on a raised stretcher having a blood transfusion. I wonder if he lived. I still have his papers.'[34]

The New Zealanders and the tank crews of 9th Armoured Brigade (totalling 59 tanks in two regiments) spent 26 October under intermittent shellfire with little enemy activity to observe close to Miteiriya Ridge, but considerable traffic moving some 2 or 3 miles to the west. Towards evening, after the artillery had laid some heavy concentrations on them, these vehicles appeared to withdraw. However, this artillery activity drew a response: aircraft bombed 6th Field Regiment's gun line, causing some casualties and damage, and these attacks also hit 2nd New Zealand Divisional Cavalry Regiment and 28th (Maori) Battalion's positions. During the day, plans had been prepared for reorganizing and

---

* Sills's grave was later found at Tobruk, where he must have died of his wounds while in German care. Samwell was killed in the Ardennes in January 1945 while still serving with 7th Argyll and Sutherland Highlanders.

strengthening the division's front. This entailed relieving 21st Battalion in 5th New Zealand Brigade with 28th (Maori) Battalion and reorganizing 22nd Battalion's sector now that 133rd Brigade had departed, as well as the laying of a defensive minefield across the brigade front. To its left, 6th New Zealand Brigade would advance in conjunction with 2nd South African Brigade to the original final objective – a seemingly pedantic move, since the ground to be taken was of little tactical value and would be more difficult to defend than the crest of Miteiriya Ridge.[35]

During the previous night, 1st/3rd Transvaal Scottish had sent a patrol some 500 yards forward of the divisional objective to a reported enemy position which was discovered to be unoccupied. Other patrols furnished by 1st Royal Natal Carbineers and 1st Duke of Edinburgh's Own Rifles were fired upon. Early the following morning, 1st Cape Town Highlanders saw two companies of the enemy advancing towards them, but by 1130 hours these were pulling back – sped on their way by artillery fire as they drew out of range of the Vickers machine-guns. During the afternoon a company of 1st Cape Town Highlanders and a company from 2nd Regiment Botha were sent to deal with some 60 enemy who had reoccupied a strongpoint aptly named The Beehive, which lay on the boundary between the South African and New Zealand objectives. This would form part of a forward move by the whole of 1st South African Division to occupy the general area of its previous defensive-fire tasks some 1,000 yards beyond the original objective. The 1st/2nd Field Force Battalion had by now moved on to Miteiriya Ridge to conform with 3rd South African Brigade on its left and 1st Cape Town Highlanders on its right.[36]

The reorganization and extension of the left flank of 2nd New Zealand Division was completed that night in spite of 6th New Zealand Brigade's attack drawing heavy fire down on itself. By 2200 hours 28th (Maori) Battalion had completed its relief in place of 21st Battalion and the divisional engineers were busily sowing mines when, with strong artillery support, 26th Battalion stepped out to advance its right flank a short way to conform with 22nd Battalion and to swing its left about 400 yards in conjunction with 25th Battalion. They suffered a number of casualties from a heavily booby-trapped minefield and were subjected to some mortar and machine-gun fire but met no serious opposition before digging in, remaining some way short of the objective on the far left.[37] At the same time, 25th Battalion had advanced behind a barrage with three companies forward – now so perilously weak that they could not form a solid front and had to operate independently. C Company lost some men to booby-traps in a minefield and overran some Italian-held posts; detaching men to escort the prisoners to the rear then cost it as many again and left the company very low in numbers. When a patrol moving further west encountered German machine-guns, it dug in where it was in a position which daylight revealed was overlooked by enemy to its front and on both flanks, with only a very exposed route to the rear.

To the left of the patrol, D Company had been delayed. Captain C. S. Wroth recalled:

> we had not covered more than a quarter of our 800 yard advance . . . before prisoners began appearing in large numbers and the difficulty was to maintain momentum and the effect of the barrage and still deal with the prisoners. A man at a time was quickly detached from a section for every twenty or so prisoners but even with only hurried search it was apparent the barrage would get away from us if we did not hurry.[38]

Still further to the left, B Company advanced without contact with the South Africans to its own left.

Although 6th New Zealand Brigade could claim to have secured most of its objectives by midnight, strong machine-gun and mortar fire hindered its efforts to establish communications among its units and with the South Africans. But by dawn it had managed to bring forward mortars, anti-tank guns and machine-guns, and had formed a line of sorts – albeit with wide gaps between companies and exposed routes to the rear. However, with good observation for its artillery and 9th Armoured Brigade's tanks in support, it could hold all but the very strongest counter-attacks, and none was forthcoming. Although the brigade had suffered 60 casualties, it had taken 70 prisoners – almost all Italians from II Battalion 62nd Regiment, including the Battalion Headquarters.[39]

At 2200 hours B Company 1st Cape Town Highlanders advanced behind an artillery barrage to which the enemy swiftly replied. Despite badly disrupted communications and casualties, it reached its objective, only to find itself unsupported. Nevertheless, 2nd Regiment Botha reported at 2315 hours that it had secured The Beehive next to the Kiwis, and shortly after midnight it made contact with the Highlanders, whose commander, Major W. Sholto Douglas, was awarded the Military Cross for his night's work.

At dawn, prisoners came trickling back: 3 British soldiers had been released from captivity, and 1 German and 4 Italian officers and 75 men – 4 of whom were German – had been were captured. However, a gap remained between the two divisions, and Valentines from 8th Royal Tank Regiment were called up in order to clear this. They were successful, but five tanks were lost to mines. Second Regiment Botha had suffered 17 casualties, including 2 dead, but claimed to have inflicted 40 killed on the enemy. For the remainder of 27 October, however, the newly won positions were heavily shelled and machine-gunned.[40]

While this operation took place on 3rd South African Brigade's front, the remainder of the division had a difficult move to make. Leese called his divisional commanders together after dark on the 26th to outline how the Army Commander intended to regroup in order to form a fresh strike force to break out. He repeated what Montgomery had told him a few hours previously: that 'as long as you can make a German commander dance to your tune, you have nothing to fear; but once you allow the initiative to pass into his hands you are liable to have plenty of trouble'. Montgomery had decided that 2nd New Zealand Division and 10th Armoured Division would withdraw into reserve for regrouping and future operations and that the South Africans would relieve the New Zealanders, with 4th Indian Division taking over from the South Africans and coming under XIII Corps. At the same time, XIII Corps would furnish all the infantry it could spare and 51st (Highland) Division would take over from 20th Australian Brigade in order to free it for future attacks. There would be only 48 hours to arrange this complicated manoeuvre, and Pienaar raised objections, saying he had not enough transport for such a move. Quickly ascertaining his own transport situation from his Chief of Staff, Freyberg commented, 'Good! Then I'll spike his guns; he doesn't like accepting help.' He said aloud to Pienaar, 'Is it only transport that's worrying you, Dan? No other difficulty?' When Pienaar declared that this was so, Freyberg added, 'Can we help you then? I'll give you any transport you need.' With that, nothing more was heard of the lack of transport.[41]

Thus throughout the night of 26/27 October and the following day the military police oversaw the repositioning of 60,000 men. Relief-in-place is a most difficult phase of war, and in the desert, with the inherent difficulties of navigation, it was a mammoth task. Individual units complained about others being in the wrong place or being late, but the moves were accomplished without serious problems. Fourth Indian Division was most concerned with reliefs due to begin on the 27th, in which 2nd Fighting French Brigade under command of 50th (Northumbrian) Division would relieve 161st Indian Motor Brigade, which would in turn take over from 1st South African Brigade, while 5th Indian Brigade – currently in XXX Corps reserve – would relieve 2nd and 3rd South African Brigades after dark. With 7th Indian Brigade remaining in position, by the morning of 28 October this would leave 4th Indian Division with all three brigades in the line holding no less than 13 miles of front. The following day, after careful survey, Tuker reduced this by 3 miles.[42] Meanwhile, XIII Corps passed a quiet day on 27 October, apart from showing dummy tanks and the employment after dark on the 26th of the 'sonic unit'. (The latter was an armoured gramophone with one record: on one side was an armoured division moving up to attack, and on the other a divisional artillery firing a barrage.)[43] Although Horrocks instructed 44th (Home Counties) Division's engineers to keep gapping February 'by stealth', the main concern was covering the extended front with its infantry and releasing 7th Armoured Division for regrouping in the north.

In only a few days fighting, the strain had been colossal. Battle fatigue (previously known as shell shock) was not exceptional. Rifleman Suckling of 2nd Rifle Brigade described one man who 'every time he saw something flying would run across the area shouting, "Collapse your bivvys, they're on you!" We lost many a brew over him. To him anything that flew was an enemy plane.' Men fought for day after day on nothing but tea and cigarettes, sleeping soundly as soon as they lay down, but waking at the first sound of the wireless chattering or the whispered order 'Stand to!' 'After two days I could sleep through noise,' said gunner subaltern D. Elliott, 'except the executive command "Take Post!" '[44] Clive Stoddart was fortunate enough to be pulled out of the line with 9th Armoured Brigade so that it could refit. To his 'dear Pa', he wrote that certain things stood out:

> Firstly the wonderful feeling of being able to lie down and to sleep and not have to fight it, which was one of the greatest battles of all. Secondly, the feeling which to me was something I will never forget – because I'm a coward and always feel very frightened – of being safe and away from the shells and all the other hell, anyway for 24 hours. It really was heaven, that feeling of security, if only for a short while made one really want to go down on one's knees and thank God. A great many of us did.[45]

16

The Defence of Outpost Snipe

Was none who would be foremost
 To lead such dire attack;
But those behind cried 'Forward!'
 And those before cried 'Back!'
And backward now and forward, wavers the deep array;
 And on the tossing sea of steel,
To and fro the standards reel;
And the victorious trumpet-peal
 Dies fitfully away.

Thomas Babington Macaulay

Although the remaining centres of resistance about the Oxalic line had been cleared up, on the night of 26/27 October Montgomery instructed that more ground was to be secured around the boundary of 51st (Highland) and 9th Australian Divisions and 1st Armoured Division was to secure two features in the Trig 33 – Kidney Ridge – area. Kidney Ridge faced the extreme right of 51st (Highland) Division's sector and was a conformation shaped, on maps at least, like a kidney bean – although it was by no means so easily discernible on the ground, and opinion varied as to whether it was a ridge at all. About half a mile to the north-west and a similar distance to the south-west were two localities named Woodcock and Snipe. These were given as objectives for 7th Motor Brigade, commanded by Brigadier T. J. B. 'Jimmy' Bosville, despite some difficulty in deciding precisely where they were – a dispute that could lead to chaos in planning a set-piece attack.

The plan was to put a battalion on each of these objectives, supported by all the available guns of both X and XXX Corps, with attacks to be made at 2300 hours on 26 October. At dawn the following morning 2nd Armoured Brigade would pass round to the north of Woodcock and 24th Armoured Brigade would pass round to the south of Snipe.[1] Lumsden was attacking widely separated and deep objectives

241

with only a weak brigade of motor infantry, but apparently he intended to relieve this with 133rd Brigade later. However, the latter was not warned until it was too late to influence the battle.

As the infantry element of 1st Armoured Division, 7th Motor Brigade's two battalions – 2nd/60th Rifles and 2nd Rifle Brigade – were not standard infantry battalions with four rifle companies and assorted support platoons. Instead, they included a complete anti-tank company equipped with 16 6-pounder anti-tank guns, three companies each including a scout platoon manning a total of 33 tracked carriers, a platoon of 3-inch mortars, and a machine-gun platoon with Vickers medium machine-guns. Consequently, although possessing no more than 90 riflemen, such a battalion could deploy considerable firepower.

The commanding officer of 2nd Rifle Brigade, Lieutenant-Colonel Victor Buller Turner, reported to Brigade Headquarters at 1600 hours on 26 October and was given Snipe as his objective. He sent Lieutenant Dick Flower and his carrier platoon to reconnoitre a start line, and prepared to give his own orders. The plan involved an artillery fire plan from five minutes before H-Hour until 25 minutes past. He was told that the supporting barrage would be fired on a bearing of 233 degrees, but that this might vary and in that case he should conform to it. Flower returned having reconnoitred a route into a space approximately 300 yards wide between two Highland battalions which was the only possible start line by 1st Armoured Division's reckoning.[2] It seemed simple enough, and Turner went forward to reconnoitre the ground, sending his second in command, Major Tom Pearson, to attend to the preparations. To his front, Turner found a featureless waste on which it was impossible to be sure of one's position. Indeed, the staff of 1st Armoured Division had incorrectly positioned the neighbouring 51st (Highland) Division by about 1,000 yards.

Having formed a minefield task force during the early stages of the battle, 2nd Rifle Brigade had sustained losses which meant that it now fielded only 22 carriers and 76 riflemen, but these were tough and experienced, having been in the desert since the beginning of the campaign in June 1940. Mostly from London, they had taken part in the epic defeat of the Italians at Beda Fomm in February 1941 and had seen a considerable amount of action. Now they were reinforced by G and H Troops from 239th Battery, 76th Anti-Tank Regiment.* Commanded by Lieutenant Alan Baer, a tall, slim Oxford undergraduate, these

---

*Another experienced unit converted to the anti-tank artillery role from the pre-war 5th (Flintshire) Battalion of The Royal Welch Fusiliers (TA), its members still wore the flash of five black ribbons on their tunics that marked their previous existence.

brought with them another six 6-pounders.[3] Together with 16 sappers under Lieutenant N. Graham from 7th Field Squadron, Turner had almost 300 men. Before Baer had left to join Turner, Major R. A. Wyrley-Birch, the hugely experienced Rhodesian second in command of 76th Anti-Tank Regiment, had warned him that 'from all the signs, I should think it highly probable that you are in for a death-or-glory affair'. Indeed, when Turner briefed his officers he in turn gave a prophetic warning that it would probably be a 'last man, last round' job.[4]

From the beginning 2nd/60th Rifles found the way to Woodcock extremely difficult, meeting some opposition and having great difficulty navigating in the darkness, which was exacerbated by dust from shells and vehicles. After crossing the start line, they encountered an enemy post and took a dozen surprised Germans prisoner. They then approached the barrage and were enveloped by its dust. The order was given to de-bus, then suddenly the lead vehicles found themselves under fire at a range of 75 yards. B Company tried to work around to the left flank, but was held up by machine-guns firing on fixed lines. However, A Company managed to slip around to the right and on to the objective – scattering defenders in the process – and the remainder of the battalion followed up.[5] At first light C Company appeared to be on the objective and it could at least claim 6 anti-tank guns and 100 prisoners taken.[6] However, its position was impossible to verify, although it had certainly not reached Woodcock and was probably south and east of it in a position that would be untenable in daylight. It therefore moved to a better defensive location and began to dig in, remaining there all day.[7]

Further south, 2nd Rifle Brigade found the going equally bad and the dust stifling, lying as it did 18 inches deep in the minefield lanes. More startling was that the British artillery was firing on a bearing of 270 degrees rather than the 233 degrees as expected. The advance was therefore altered to follow the southern end of the barrage, which delayed the crossing of the start line until ten minutes after H-Hour at 2310 hours. The advance then passed through the right of 5th Black Watch and a column moved into 1st Gordon Highlanders' area at around 0200 hours, where it seemed to the Jocks to 'mill about'.[8] With the carriers leading, followed by the dismounted riflemen, the battalion advanced over the first 1,000 yards from the start line. Enemy fire was spasmodic, but a dummy minefield caused a brief delay. Some 20 Italian prisoners were taken, and other groups of enemy were seen fleeing westward.[9] Turner, dressed in corduroy trousers and a leather jacket against the biting cold, rode in a jeep followed by a 15-cwt radio truck from which the adjutant, Captain Tim Marten, kept Brigade Headquarters informed of progress by keeping a careful eye on his odometer. 'We have just done the Cambridgeshire distance,' he reported. 'Getting on for Cesarewitch now.' 'Just running up to the winning post.'

After some 3,000 yards Turner asked Captain Ralph Noyes from 2nd Royal Horse Artillery, his artillery forward observation officer, to call in a smoke shell accurately on the objective. When this landed 300 yards away he was satisfied that he was where he should be and moved on to a former German engineer store covering an oval depression about 800 by 400 yards in area. It was 0015 hours, and the soldiers began to dig in. A small German dugout became Battalion Headquarters. There were excreta and a few German bodies lying around, and the smell was none too pleasant as Turner signalled that he had occupied his objective, unaware that he was in fact, some 800 yards too far to the south-east.[10]

Only now were the anti-tank guns and ammunition lorries called forward, having been left at the start line under Pearson. Two of the portees collided, and neither they nor the guns they carried could go any further; then, at about 2330 hours,the column was partially hit by a stick of bombs from a solitary enemy aircraft that dropped a parachute flare, hitting two vehicles and setting them alight. The ambulances and the medical officer, Captain Arthur Picton, remained behind to treat the wounded and were later unable to reach the position. Fortunately, Picton's orderly, Rifleman S. H. Burnhope, who combined his duties with those of company barber, was one of those who went forward, where he performed prodigious feats to succour the injured with his meagre supplies. Eventually, after a torrid time in the soft sand, involving a number of extractions using spades and tow ropes, 13 battalion anti-tank guns and 6 of 239th Battery were offloaded from their Chevrolet portee mounts by 0345 hours and were placed to defend the perimeter. Also brought in were supplies of rations, ammunition and water.

The anti-tank guns of S Company were divided among B Company to the south-east and C Company to the west, with 239th Battery's guns under A Company holding the north-east sector. C Company's carrier platoon under Lieutenant Dick Flower was sent west to reconnoitre. It captured another group of 14 prisoners and found about 150 in a huddle apparently willing to give themselves up. But, before riflemen could arrive to assist, Flower encountered the laager of a mixed German/Italian battle group called Gruppe Stiffelmayer, including some 35 tanks and tank destroyers. The carriers engaged these monsters with their Bren guns, and succeeded in setting alight three supply trucks before beating a hasty retreat. The flames of a nearby derelict truck exposed them to the rage of the tanks and they were forced to withdraw, losing one carrier. Many of the prisoners bolted, but some 35 remained from 220th and 33rd Pioneer Battalions of 164th and 15th Panzer Divisions respectively.[11]

Turner did not now need Flower's contact report to inform him that his position lay inside the enemy front line. Camp fires could be seen to the south-west and – more significantly – 1,000 yards to the north, where there was another major tank laager, this one belonging to 15th Panzer Division. When Gruppe Stiffelmayer was seen moving out soon afterwards, it split into two, one part heading towards 15th Panzer Division's laager and the other moving in line ahead directly towards Turner's hollow. The lead vehicle was a Panzer IV Special – DAK had just 30 of them. Unaware of the British presence, it drove to within 30 yards of the position before bursting into flames as a 6-pounder round from C Company hit it. At the same time, A Company hit a self-propelled tank destroyer (mounting a Russian 7.62 cm gun), and the remainder of the column turned away in alarm to await first light. The shallow depression and scrub provided good concealment for the small anti-tank guns and accompanying infantry, who saved themselves from a great many casualties through the skill with which they dug themselves in against what Turner later described as the 'deluge of fire that poured down on us for the rest of that day'.[12]

The gunners derived considerable confidence from the 6-pounder's stopping power, which turned out to be crucial in the ensuing action, since at 0400 hours Captain Noyes, the forward observation officer, went out on a recce and was not seen again. It later transpired that he had ended up in the London Rifle Brigade's position, and, although he made an attempt to walk back to Snipe in daylight, he would have had to cross the strong German position at Woodcock, so the garrison spent the remainder of their stay without adequate artillery support. For a while things remained quiet and this was not too much of a problem. At 0545 hours Pearson left for 51st (Highland) Division lines with the non-fighting transport, taking the prisoners with him. Half an hour later the sky began to grow pale, and in this half-light just before dawn the enemy armour began to break laager and move towards its missions for the day. The riflemen were surprised to see that these were in a westerly direction.

Then, at a range of about 800 yards, some panzers that had been lurking in dead ground since the night action suddenly appeared. The anti-tank guns were able to engage them very effectively, helped by the panzers moving across them and presenting the more vulnerable sides and rears of their vehicles. Capitano Preve described things at the receiving end: 'Suddenly there is the most violent fire from another eight or ten anti-tank guns hidden on our left and in depth . . . The survivors then give incredible proof of valour. Second Lieutenant Camplani from outside his turret urges his own tanks to the attack at the head of them, drives his own tank at full speed on the most forward anti-tank gun.'[13] Sergeant Charles Calistan later recalled, 'I let go at 150 yards. You couldn't miss. All our guns seemed to be firing at once. My target burst into flames but came on for another fifty yards before it halted. Suddenly the night was bright with burning tanks.[14] Soon, eight more from each of the two groups were knocked out or destroyed completely, their escaping crews chased across the open ground by streams of bullets from the Vickers guns. But the cause of such destruction could not be concealed for ever, and the defenders of the outpost were now to be subject to direct and indirect fire that caused immediate casualties – particularly as the improving light revealed that some guns needed resiting, making them and the carriers involved very vulnerable. Marten, reporting events to 7th Motor Brigade, asked Turner, 'Have we come to the right place, sir?' 'God knows,' replied Turner, 'but here we are and here we'll stay.'[15]

Turner was worried that 24th Armoured Brigade was nowhere to be seen. It was by now long overdue. He was unaware that 2nd/60th Rifles had failed in its attempt to seize Woodcock and that, in consequence, uncertainty had crept into the remainder of the operation. When at around 0730 hours the lead Shermans of 47th Royal Tank Regiment appeared on the nearby crest, nobody imagined that they would then engage the Snipe outpost, but the appearance of a strongpoint with Axis armour scattered liberally all around deceived the approaching tankies that here was the main enemy laager rather than their own 'pivot of manoeuvre', and they opened a galling fire. Most of it landed on 239th Battery, and immediately the battalion intelligence officer, Lieutenant Jack Wintour, jumped into his carrier and raced to warn the approaching tanks of the situation. However, it took half an hour for the 'friendly' fire to cease.

At about this time Turner became aware of approximately 25 enemy tanks taking up hull-down positions some 1,000 yards to the west. The anti-tank gunners managed to set fire to three of them, and 47th Royal Tank Regiment now came on to the position. Turner recalled that when the leading Shermans entered the Snipe position at 0830 hours, the battle became intense. Smoke screens were laid by both sides which had the general effect of entirely obscuring any possible targets from our tanks. The enemy, however, made effective use of his tanks and 88 mm guns. Within fifteen minutes seven Shermans had been set alight within our area and the 24th Armoured Brigade very sensibly started to withdraw.[16]

The enemy reacted with a storm of fire from tanks north of Woodcock and medium artillery. 'For the next half hour we got a concentrated dose,' noted Rifleman Crimp in his diary:

It's most unpleasant crouching in the bottom of a pit, packed tight with even more chaps now whose single objective is to keep their 'nuts' down as low as possible, silently braced and wondering whether the next one's coming our way. The shells scream down in inexorable succession, and all around us is the driving rending crash of high explosive. Several times my tin hat is crushed onto my head by the impact of nearby detonations, and once my lungs are filled by a rush of sand. Everyone lies still. You can't do a thing – it just has to happen. If one lands in the trench – well, we shan't know much about it.[17]

Within half an hour 47th Royal Tank Regiment had been reduced to 5 Shermans and 6 Crusaders, and retired together with 41st Royal Tank Regiment from 24th Armoured Brigade, which had lost 12 tanks. Sergeant R. W. Binks of 239th Battery managed to knock out a Panzer IV at the extreme range of a mile, but two of the battery's guns were also knocked out. That of Sergeant Bob Smith took a direct hit, and all the members of his detachment were either killed or wounded. Smith himself was blinded for several hours, but this did not prevent him from moving to join his friend Sergeant Ronald Wood.[18] The remaining infantry were glad to see the tanks go after suffering in the storm of shot and shell that accompanied their presence, but their departure signalled the end of the plan to swing 24th Armoured Brigade around to the south and into the open ground beyond, and left 2nd Rifle Brigade in the outpost alone and unsupported.

As the dust from the retiring tanks settled, so Italian infantry could be seen forming up to launch an attack from the south. At 0905 hours a message was sent to 7th Motor Brigade that 'our crying need is for a gunner'. One was promised but never arrived, being unable to cross the mile-wide void that now existed between the outpost and 24th Armoured Brigade.[19] Instead, much British fire landed in and around the perimeter throughout the morning, which made Turner 'hopping mad' until Pearson was able to contact the guns personally at 1230 hours. Meanwhile, Turner sent Flower and his scout carriers to deal with the infantry threat – which was quickly managed, inflicting heavy casualties in the process and knocking out two Italian vehicles towing captured British 6-pounders. 'During the next half hour,' recalled Flower, 'many excellent sniping targets were offered by small groups of Italians as they tried to run away.' Given a shortage of ammunition, however, only rifles were used to engage them. Captain Peter Sheperd-Cross made a dash with three carriers to fetch more ammunition, taking some severely wounded with him. He made it back to the ridge despite taking a direct hit on his carrier from a 75 mm, but all attempts in the opposite direction were met with such withering fire as soon as he breasted the crest that he was unable to return. The garrison was now truly cut off.[20]

Soon after his departure, Italian M14 tanks appeared and launched an attack from the south-west. Thirteen M14s from XII Battalion 133rd Armoured Regiment of Littorio Division under Capitano Preve posed a serious threat to what was a relatively weakly held section of the perimeter, and Turner hurriedly attempted to redeploy two of his guns to meet it. Manhandling the weapons across the soft sand was a difficult task, and four of his men were killed in the process. Ultimately it proved unnecessary, since the Italians were reluctant to press forward to assault. Although classed as a medium tank, the M14 was poorly armoured, and four of the group were swiftly penetrated, causing the others to withdraw. This action had been intended to cover 25 to 30 German tanks from Gruppe Stiffelmeyer as they moved to counter-attack 24th Armoured Brigade. The failure of the Italians, however, caused the German group to detach a part of its strength to deal with Snipe while advancing against the British tanks. Consequently those advancing towards Snipe exposed their side armour to the British tank gunners, and those advancing against the tanks exposed theirs to the anti-tank gunners. In rapid succession, eight were left burning in what Turner described as 'cross-trumping', and the remainder hurriedly withdrew.[21]

With the time approaching 1100 hours, the situation within Snipe was deteriorating. Casualties had been mounting all morning, and ammunition was beginning to run low, particularly for the 6-pounders. The flies were starting to gather in thick black clouds and the heat began to intensify, while smoke and dust swirled everywhere. Six more carriers had been hit, and only 13 guns were left in action, mostly manned by scratch detachments, due to casualties. Major Mike Bird, commanding S Company, together with Corporal Francis, drove about the position in a jeep delivering the heavy green boxes of ammunition, drawing fire wherever they went. Three of the remaining carriers were sent out ferrying wounded. Unfortunately, one of these was hit. Pearson, observing from the ridge, drew a storm of fire every time he showed any inclination to attempt a resupply. The outpost was battered and beleaguered and strewn with wrecks and very much alone. Major-General Raymond Briggs, the divisional commander, listened to the battle's progress on the radio and to appeals for tank assistance.

> News had just reached me that the 21st Panzer Division was on the move from the south to join the 15th Panzer Division opposing us. I knew that every tank would be needed at short notice, as indeed they were a few hours later, to take on the two divisions. I had to balance the possible destruction of the Rifle Brigade against the necessity to conserve my tank state. My reluctant decision was that I must leave the infantrymen to fight it out themselves.[22]

Fortunately, despite a constant rain of harassing fire from artillery and mortars, they were otherwise largely left alone by the enemy for a while. But radio intercepts showed that the enemy was very concerned about the location of this fierce resistance, which lay directly across the path of a proposed counter-attack. At 0740 hours on 27 October orders had been issued by Panzerarmee that DAK would go into action at 1500 hours.[23] This was to be Rommel's major attack in the old style, with artillery and Stuka support – but it would be dashed against a rock of anti-tank guns. Apparently convinced that the lack of fire emanating from the position for a while indicated a slackening of resistance, at around 1300 hours Italian infantry again attacked the position, moving in against the south-western section and once more supported by eight tanks and a Semovente assault gun mounting a 105 mm howitzer.[24] They came on with great determination and regardless of loss, and only one 6-pounder could bear on the attacking armour. Turner, seeing that Sergeant Calistan was alone on this gun, with the remainder of his detachment wounded or fetching ammunition, ran to join him along with the platoon commander, Lieutenant Jack Toms. Acting personally as loader, Turner ordered Calistan to hold his fire until the range had closed to 600 yards. Six enemy vehicles were hit in rapid succession, and all began to burn, but the others kept coming and the gun had only two rounds left.

Calistan later recalled:

> Our colonel kept going from gun to gun. How he inspired us! The enemy tried to shift us with an infantry attack but we soon sent them on their way with our Bren-carriers and our infantry, who were in position in front of us. When the next attack came in the colonel was acting as loader on my gun. He got wounded in the head – a nasty wound and we wanted to bind it up but he wouldn't hear of it. Keep firing – that's what he wanted and we didn't pause.

When the guns ran short of ammo he got it from one of the others . . . Two of my gun crew crept out on their bellies – right into the open to get some ammo. They were under enemy fire the whole time and their progress was terribly slow. Then our platoon officer [Toms] decided to reach his jeep which had four boxes of ammo aboard. God knows how he got to it – they were machine-gunning the whole way. He started coming towards us and then they hit the jeep and it caught fire, but he kept on coming. We got the ammo off and then I had an idea. We hadn't been able to light a fire but here was a perfectly good one. So I put a can of water on the Jeep and it brewed up well enough for three cups of tea! . . . When the colonel was too weak to refuse attention we bound up his head and put him behind some scrub. He called out that he wanted to know what was happening and my officer kept up a running commentary. We hit three tanks with three successive shots and the colonel yelled out: 'Good work: a hat trick – a hat trick!'[25]

The enemy had been held off just 200 yards from the perimeter. Turner's helmet had been penetrated with a shell splinter, but after his wound had been carefully dressed he continued his tour of the guns. The strain was too great, however, and he was led to the headquarters dugout, where he began hallucinating that he was defending a harbour against enemy ships. 'Open fire on that destroyer!' he cried, and eventually he had to be restrained.[26] Most of the officers were now either dead or wounded, including Bird, Toms and Flower. No officer remained on the western part of the perimeter, and when Lieutenant J. F. M. Lightly was sent to take over he was captured while trying to get forward to obtain better observation, with command subsequently falling upon Sergeant G. H. Brown. Fortunately, with the heat of the desert afternoon at its peak, the garrison was spared any more major assaults for a few hours, though subjected to constant mortar and shellfire, with little water and tormented by flies.

Meanwhile, the DAK operation due for the afternoon of 27 October was to be heralded by a five-minute bombardment and Stuka raid. As the Stukas approached, they were attacked by Warhawks of the USAAF's 64th and 65th Squadrons. Sixteen of these (eight carrying 500 lb bombs to attack the landing grounds at El Daba) met the strong force of some 20 Ju-87s, 20 CR-42s and 20 Me-109s. The Warhawks dropped their bombs on Landing Grounds 20 and 104 and gave chase, claiming three Me-109s and three CR-42s. Henry Ritchie of a nearby artillery unit felt completely exposed. 'Every passing second seemed a lifetime as we lay next to a gun or a lorry wheel, or curled up in a shallow shell crater.' Suddenly the Axis formation was intercepted by 12 Hurricanes from 33 Squadron and 12 from 213 Squadron, who claimed a further two Ju-87s, four CR-42s and three Me-109s. 'Glory, glory be.

So great was our surging relief that it was like a resurrection, a rallying call moment of rebirth and thankfulness.' Ritchie counted eight enemy planes destroyed, but three Hurricanes were also lost.[27] This was the Axis's main air operation for the afternoon and, because of its timing, clearly of great significance to Rommel's counter-attack. Yet the pattern of dive-bombing that had always previously preceded an armoured thrust had completely broken down.[28]

At about 1600 hours 2nd Armoured Brigade appeared on the ridge to the east and shelled Turner's position intensely. 'During an unpleasant day,' said Turner later, 'this was the most unpleasant thing that happened.'[29] At the same time some 70 German and Italian tanks and self-propelled guns could be seen forming up in the area of Kidney Ridge facing east towards the British lines, in two groups one behind the other some 1,200 yards away to the west. The larger group, consisting of 40-odd vehicles moved against 2nd Armoured Brigade. They must have been new arrivals, for they moved immediately in front of 239th Battery, of whom they appeared to be blissfully unaware. As Turner remarked, 'it is inconceivable that the tanks which had been engaging us all day should have been so unwise'.[30]

It was what 239th Battery had been waiting for. As Rommel himself later wrote, 'a murderous British fire struck into our ranks and our attack was soon brought to a halt by an immensely powerful anti-tank defence, mainly from dug-in anti-tank guns'.[31] Indeed, the myth – oft repeated among tankies – that the best anti-tank weapon was another tank was firmly laid to rest. Instead, here was further proof of the stopping power of the anti-tank gun when carefully sited and steadfastly manned. Rommel was now learning the bitter lesson that he had so often inflicted on the British. Superbly concealed, 239th Battery could not see the Rifle Brigade's guns from a kneeling position. Reduced to four guns and facing 40 tanks the battery held its fire until the enemy's side armour was fully exposed at a range of just 200 yards. The gun of Sergeant D. Newman of S Company could be heard barking on the left. He later claimed four hits, including a 7.62 cm self-propelled gun and a Panzer Mark II from which a man wearing a three-quarter-length white jacket baled out.[32] Then, as a panzer turned to attack Newman, Sergeant F. E. H. Hillyer engaged it of his own initiative and scored a hit. Lieutenant Baer now gave the order to open fire, and when the breech of one gun was fouled by sand it was so vital to keep the rounds flying that Baer repeatedly banged it shut with an empty shell case. In two minutes a dozen enemy tanks had ground to a halt, half of them burning fiercely. All four guns were now scoring hits and held their ground trading shot for shot. A Panzer Mark IV bore down straight upon Sergeant J. Cullen – both he and Sergeant Binks hit it together. A minute later, Binks's gun took a direct hit which killed or wounded all the detachment except himself. But these few guns had halted Rommel's attack and, now assailed in the flank by 2nd Armoured Brigade, the Germans withdrew to take cover in low ground near Kidney Ridge.[33]

Although the attack was stalled it was not finished. Fifteen panzers detached from the second wave to attack A Company. They moved carefully forward, their machine-guns hammering to cover each other, and making use of every fold in the ground. Only three 6-pounders could be brought to bear, and these could muster only about ten rounds each. It was the most clinical and determined Axis attack of the day, and Turner – somewhat recovered from his earlier distress – told Marten, the adjutant, to burn the maps and codes. With bullets rattling on the gun shields and kicking dirt into their faces, the Riflemen patiently awaited the final confrontation as the panzers advanced inexorably. Sergeant-Major Jack Atkin watched in fascinated horror as the anti-tank guns followed their targets: 'Why don't they open fire?'[34]

Sergeant H. Miles was hit and his detachment was forced to the ground. Rifleman Suckling was part of a nearby rifle platoon and knew there was an anti-tank gun to his right, but its silence suggested the detachment had been knocked out or was out of ammunition. 'If one of us were to crawl to it, perhaps we could have a go at the panzer. We did a John Wayne, raising a tin hat above our slit trench. We did this and the tank gave it a burst from his machine-gun. It would have been suicide for any of us to get out and have a go.'[35] Nearby, Rifleman Crimp watched as

> one of our [anti-tank] chaps crawls from his trench and with bullets ripping into the sand around him, runs stooping over to a 6-pounder fronting north, extracts a shell already in the breech and creeps back with it to his own gun which faces the panzer. It's amazing how the [machine-gun] stream misses him, but he calmly puts the shell in, takes steady aim, and fires. Immediately there's an explosion from the panzer.[36]

Rifleman Suckling 'thought this was the tank firing at us with his 75. Deeper we crouched in our position', but Rifleman Crimp noted that the machine-gun cut out 'and the tank stays still. A strand of smoke issues from the turret.' When Rifleman Suckling and his mates noticed the smell of burning rubber, 'we looked over the edge of our trench . . . the panzer was burning'.

Jack Wintour, who watched this from the battalion command post, leaped up and down shouting, 'He's got him! He's got him! He's got him!' Colour-Sergeant J. E. Swann, whose own gun had been knocked out, had crawled 30 yards in order to take over from Miles. Swann had loaded and fired single-handedly until Miles's detachment, inspired by his devotion, sprang forward to help him. Suddenly, at a range of just 200 yards, the other 6-pounders opened fire, and within minutes six tanks were pouring flames and smoke – one a mere 100 yards from Swann's muzzle. The remaining panzers quickly retired to a depression some 800 yards away, where they remained, keeping a steady fire on Snipe for the rest of the day, unaware that the guns they faced now had just three rounds each.[37]

The wreckage that littered the area gave testimony to the devotion of the defenders. Some 70 tanks and self-propelled guns had been knocked out, together with soft-skinned vehicles. But the cost had also been high – including 16 carriers and 10 guns, with another 5 damaged. Shortly after, at 1740 hours, Bosville spoke to Marten, the senior unwounded officer, but now without the help of codes. 'Friends will come and take your place at dinner time,' he said. 'You are to wait until they are happily settled in your place. Your carriages will then arrive and take you home.' 'Will it be an early dinner or a late one?' asked Marten. 'The fashionable time' – which meant around 2100 hours. The defenders contracted their perimeter as it fell dark, but the problems of navigation combined with communication difficulties made the relief impossible. Instead, 5th Royal Sussex Regiment advanced to what it believed was the correct location and dug in.[38]

At 2300 hours Marten was given permission to withdraw. Both sides were out collecting wounded, and neither interfered with the other. Unfortunately, shortage of serviceable transport meant that the dead would have to be left behind, but the worst of the garrison's wounded were loaded upon three jeeps and six carriers and sent ahead. Out of 19 guns that had started the action, only Ronald Wood's gun from 239th Battery could be removed, loaded on to a bullet-riddled portee. The rest of the battalion had to form a column and march. Sergeant Calistan recalled that

> we had to go the whole way back to our own lines as best we could. We had to go the whole way under fire for two and a half miles. We removed the breechblocks and sights of our guns. We had men with tommy-guns leading and we carried the wounded in the centre. Before we moved off I did something you may think rather stupid – I went back and kissed my gun. I carried one of our wounded on my back. Freddie – that was his name. He had volunteered to come out here. Been out only a few weeks. He had a wife and four

children. He had been wounded trying to help someone else. They got him on the way back – shot him through the head.[39]

News of the action spread rapidly around Eighth Army; and a committee of investigation examined the site a month later to determine what had happened there. Many of the less severely damaged vehicles had been recovered by the enemy, but the committee eventually decided that 21 German and 11 Italian tanks had been destroyed, plus 5 self-propelled guns, with between 15 and 20 estimated to have been knocked out and recovered, giving a total of 52–57, of which 19 were claimed by 239th Battery. Personnel losses on the enemy side were difficult to assess, but certainly far higher than the 72 suffered by the defenders. Lieutenant-Colonel Turner received a Victoria Cross for his outstanding leadership, and many other awards were made – including Distinguished Conduct Medals for Calistan* and Swann.

Elsewhere the battle continued to rage. German reinforcements – advanced elements of 47th Infantry Regiment – were flown in from Crete and put straight into action; but it was apparent from signal intercepts that other valuable units – including 288th Special Group, 33rd and 580th Reconnaissance Battalions, and much of Trieste Division – were being held near the coast because of continued fear of seaborne or airborne landings in the rear.[40] The DAF remained heavily engaged. In 9th Australian Division's area, with pressure increasing upon 2/48th Battalion, an air strike was brought up when a large formation of enemy vehicles was seen assembling near the Sidi Abd el Rahman mosque. 'Our bombers came in and straddled the area, leaving spirals of black smoke curling skywards,' recalled the battalion historian.[41]

When, late in the afternoon, an infantry attack was finally launched by the German 155th Regimental Group towards 2/48th Battalion, 'a great wall of fire was put down by our three regiments of artillery to check them, and the battalion joined in with mortars, machine-guns and rifles'.[42] At 1715 hours the attackers reported to 15th Panzer Division Headquarters that the position had been taken at 1630 hours with heavy casualties. In fact the German had been forced back and had dug in some 800 yards away, although this was not reported to division until 2000 hours.[43] 'Very heavy casualties had been inflicted,' noted the Australians. 'The night was filled with the cries of the wounded. Patrols

---

*Sergeant Calistan was later commissioned. He was killed in action in Italy while serving with the London Rifle Brigade.

sent out later reported that the battlefield was strewn with enemy dead.'[44] Panzerarmee ordered the attack to be resumed the next morning at 0900 hours, which it was – only to be halted once more with heavy casualties.[45]

The task of 51st (Highland) Division for the day was to clear up any remaining resistance within its boundaries, while 2nd New Zealand Division was to push up to the corps's final objective. Early on 27 October, ZZ Battery of 76th Anti-Tank Regiment had moved forward in its self-propelled Deacons through B Company 1st Gordon Highlanders towards an enemy post that at once yielded 30 prisoners, finally enabling the whole battalion to move forward to Aberdeen. This meant that 26th Battalion had to mount an advance of 800 yards, and 25th Battalion an even longer one. Although they took over 60 prisoners in the process, this cost the Kiwis another 60 casualties of their own.[46] Otherwise, although the move of infantry formations northward during the night of 27/28 October was not easy, it went off without mishap. The 1st South African Brigade took up position on the right of the new sector, with 3rd South African Brigade on its left and 2nd South African Brigade pulling back into divisional reserve.[47]

17

Thompson's Post

Let us be clear about three facts. First, all battles and all wars are won in the end by the infantryman. Secondly, the infantry man always bears the brunt. His casualties are heavier, he suffers greater extremes of discomfort and fatigue than the other arms. Thirdly, the art of the infantryman is less stereotyped and far harder to acquire in modern war than that of any other arm.

Field Marshal Earl Wavell[1]

While the tactical plan of the Allies had not worked as intended, the effect of the Snipe action was possibly more useful. Rommel's armour had been seriously written down and the German fighter defences had been almost eliminated, so the DAF was now free to make continuous bombing raids by day and night. While the weight and frequency of the air effort exceeded that at Alam Halfa, it was less destructive – due to Axis dispersal and digging – but the effect on morale would be increasingly felt.[2] Rommel had also burned a great deal of precious fuel to no purpose, and had missed his only real opportunity of preventing the Allies from crushing him.

His situation was made worse by events at sea: 'Big topic of conversation is still yesterday's strike,' noted RAF officer Ralph Manning on 28 October. 'The Wellington boys last night found the convoy. The small MV [motor vessel] was missing; the big MV was stationary, and farther east was the red glow which was all that was left of the tanker. They hit the big MV with two torpedoes and it went sky high. They only lost one aircraft.'[3] The *Tergestea*, carrying 1,000 tons of fuel and 1,000 tons of ammunition, had been caught at dusk as she tried to enter Tobruk harbour. Panzerarmee had been dealt another crippling blow. And Rommel was not alone in his anxieties. In Rome, Mussolini told Cavallero that Panzerarmee's fuel problem 'gnawed at his liver, day and night'.[4]

Nevertheless, for all the heroics of 2nd Rifle Brigade, Kidney Ridge remained in Axis hands. The British tactic of sending out battalions unsupported to hold localities with open flanks was not sustainable in broader terms. An advance across a wide frontage was required.[5]

As a first step, 133rd Brigade had been ordered forward to take over the tasks of 7th Motor Brigade on the evening of the 27th. This meant it would have to relieve 2nd Rifle Brigade in place on Snipe (which, as we have seen, did not happen) and capture Woodcock – difficult tasks in any circumstances, and made more so since both positions were quite unrecognizable on the ground.[6] In fact the map showed a contour in the shape of a kidney bean between the 25 m contour and the 30 m contour defining the ridge, and 1st Armoured Division when studying the actual ground concluded that the highest visible point was the kidney ring contour, when in fact this contour indicated a deepish depression which was occupied by 1st Gordon Highlanders on 27 October as the final objective on Aberdeen. It was this confusion that led 2nd Rifle Brigade to end up too far left of Snipe, and why 5th Royal Sussex Regiment also failed to occupy it. It would also lead to tragedy for 4th Royal Sussex Regiment.[7]

The task was further complicated since 133rd Brigade had been an ordinary infantry brigade until 8 September, and its battalions had barely completed a major reorganization. However, as there was no settled or agreed War Establishment or scale of equipment for a lorried infantry brigade, no extra staff or signals had been provided. The brigade was short of transport, and what it had was entirely unarmoured – unlike the motor battalions' large scale of carriers.[8] Requests for armoured vehicles to carry the radios had been refused, and it had to use 15-cwt trucks, 'which stood out like pyramids on the desert'.[9] The anti-tank gunners returned from their courses only just before the battle, so there was no time for battalion or brigade training. Exercises including divisional schemes had been held, but none included practice in close co-operation with armour, and Gatehouse did not seem to accept the brigade fully into the divisional 'family'. 'We did not expect to play any part in a battle of attrition,' recalled Captain John Stanton, 'but were geared to the breakout and pursuit.'[10] Thus, seriously handicapped and arriving on its start line at night on short notice and on ground occupied by elements of three other divisions, the brigade was bound to experience confusion. Brigadier Alec Lee had been warned that he was to relieve 7th Motor Brigade during the morning of 27 October, but could get no information from 7th Motor Brigade Headquarters and it seems that the divisional chain of command had broken down, since the instructions came direct from Lumsden himself, although Gatehouse was present. Lee was told that all he had to do was 'walk through' with ample artillery support, and that two further armoured brigades would follow him at first light. Lee did not like the sound of this at all, and said so, but was told that risks had to be taken.[11]

Severe congestion through the minefields meant the brigade reached the start line 20 minutes late of H-Hour at 2230 hours. Here it found its way blocked by 1st Gordon Highlanders, across whose newly won position it had been falsely directed, and it opened fire, tragically causing several casualties and setting alight a petrol truck.[12] Having reoriented itself, the brigade resumed its advance and came under fire from the left. The reserve company had to be dispatched to deal with this, and was nearly annihilated in the process. They now knew they had a fight on their hands, as Lieutenant Douglas Sladden remembered. 'We had been in action before, at Alam Halfa, but a set-piece night attack was "something else".'[13]

In due course Lieutenant-Colonel Ronald Murphy of 4th Royal Sussex Regiment judged that he must have reached Woodcock, and halted to consolidate. At 0529 hours he reported that he was in possession of the objective, when in fact he had halted on its eastern edge – between II and III Battalion 115th Panzergrenadier Regiment and right in front of the German II Battalion 33rd Artillery Regiment.[14] Half an hour later he reported that enemy tanks could be heard moving nearby (the Italian IV Battalion 133rd Armoured Regiment and German 33rd Anti-Tank Battalion), but soon afterwards both his radio and that of his forward observation officer from 104th Royal Horse Artillery fell silent.

The battalion was seen by 2nd Armoured Brigade to be attacked and overrun. It lost 47 dead (including Murphy) and 342 missing, and at a range of 2 miles the 10th Hussars later saw a sorry column of prisoners being marched away.[15] Eric Laker described the shock of capture:

> I looked up and saw some of our fellows climbing out of their slit trenches with their hands up! One even had a white handkerchief tied to his rifle. I saw a tank that had come over the ridge with others to the right of it. A fellow was sitting on the top with a nasty looking LMG [light machine-gun] which he was waving around in a most unfriendly manner, and walking beside the tank was a chap with a revolver. He was waving his hands around indicating to our fellows that they were to come to him and surrender. Then to my horror I saw a black cross on the front of the tank. I am convinced that no man living can put into words what my feelings were at that moment.[16]

Lee later complained bitterly that some armoured commanders 'thought that as tanks were scarce they must be conserved at all costs, and that infantry were expendable'.[17] His brigade was completely unsupported by armour, however. Having absorbed the remaining 'runners' from 41st and 47th Battalions, 45th Royal Tank Regiment had been ordered to support 133rd Brigade, which was reported as being 2,000 yards ahead. But it found the route blocked by a recently laid enemy minefield, and by the time an alternative route had been arranged it was 0700 hours. One squadron moved towards Snipe, while the remainder protected the infantry's left flank. Soon afterwards they came under heavy fire from enemy tanks and received belated information that the ground to their front was mined, Snipe was still in enemy hands, and 133rd Brigade was now to their rear. They were ordered to retire, and by 1100 hours – now down to eight tanks – were back behind their start line.[18]

To the south, 2nd Royal Sussex Regiment was also pinned down by heavy fire, but was generally, all right although its commanding officer was killed. Lieutenant John Montgomery 'felt lost. I had been with the colonel all the time and now that he was gone there seemed a great change in the battle. I could not realize for some time afterwards that Kenneth Hooper, whom we had all known so well . . . an extremely young and energetic battalion commander was dead.' He had been leaning out of a trench to observe the enemy's positions when he was shot through the forehead by a sniper.[19] At 32 years old, he was not especially young for a battalion commander – and they would get younger still as the war went on.

Early on the morning of 28 October, Montgomery gave orders for the Kidney Ridge sector to go on to the defensive and for 1st Armoured Division to withdraw for rest and reorganization. Rommel had meanwhile decided to move more German forces up from the south to counter the constant British attacks and cover his heavy losses. By the end of 28 October, 15th Panzer Division was reduced to 21 serviceable Mark III and IV panzers, while 21st Panzer Division had only 45; the Italian total was 196 mediums. The number of Germans posted as missing was 1,994, and of Italians 1,660. In 164th Division, two battalions of 382nd Regiment had been destroyed and the third reduced to quarter-strength, while III Battalion 115th Panzergrenadier Regiment was only 40 men strong.[20]

That night, 5th/7th Gordon Highlanders was tasked to cover the tank-recovery section of 24th Armoured Brigade, during which time it traversed 1,000 yards of desert only to find seven of the eight tanks already burnt out before withdrawing under heavy machine-gun fire; all agreed it was a very unprofitable excursion.[21]

On 30 October it was agreed between the War Office and Alexander that operational requirements to keep units up to a minimum effective strength required certain formations be disbanded – a bleak reward for

24th Armoured Brigade and the unfortunate 44th (Home Counties) Division – and 45th Royal Tank Regiment handed over its remaining tanks to 10th Hussars from 2nd Armoured Brigade. Most of its personnel were posted to 6th Royal Tank Regiment, now in Palestine, where at least they could look forward to a swim and a sleep and some respite from the flies and the dust.[22]

North of 9th Australian Division, Axis positions were held by I and III Battalions 125th Panzergrenadier Regiment, behind which was grouped 90th Light Division. This formation was now to take command of the northern sector, taking 125th Panzergrenadier Regiment under command, and was to dig a new defensive line. Steadily, the losses suffered by XXI Corps were compelling Rommel to commit DAK to the northern battle in piecemeal fashion. These panzergrenadiers would now be engaged in the most bitter and costly fighting of the battle – over a defensive complex known as Thompson's Post to Eighth Army and 'the hut' to Panzerarmee. By the time they abandoned it, the entire area would be carpeted with Australian dead – an astonishing example of sacrifice and devotion to duty.

While Montgomery's new offensive was being prepared it was essential that the momentum of attacks be maintained, and this fell to the Australians. Rather than driving the New Zealanders through the 'thumb' which the Australian attacks had created, Montgomery instructed Morshead to 'attack north' again. Morshead in turn proposed an ambitious plan. In subsequent phases, all three of his brigades would be involved, supported by tanks from 23rd Armoured Brigade and the entire XXX Corps artillery. In the first phase, 20th Australian Brigade would secure the flanks of the northward advance, with 2/13th Battalion moving along the Axis switch line to a position south of Thompson's Post and 2/15th Battalion striking north from Trig 29. Thereafter, 26th Australian Brigade with 46th Royal Tank Regiment in support would strike north-east from Trig 29 to cut the coast road. From the firm base thus established, 2/48th Battalion would move east along the road to take the front-line positions in rear, with 2/24th Battalion coming down to take Thompson's Post itself from the north. Meanwhile, 24th Australian Brigade would maintain a firm base in the original coast defences and also capture the Axis post and area north of 2/48th's breach. However, despite the liberal provision of fire support, the guns were not in good positions to provide it and would have to fire concentrations in enfilade; for those attacks heading east, they would be firing into the faces of the infantry. Thus the plan called for timed concentrations receding ahead of the infantry and requiring a safety margin of some 400 yards much reducing the protective value of the fire.[23]

The relief of 26th Australian Brigade by 20th Australian Brigade on 27/28 October in order to be in position to attack on the night of the 28th was made all the more difficult by strong counter-attacks directed against both 2/24th and 2/48th Battalions at the time set for relief. Still, this most difficult of the phases of war was completed by dawn, and 20th Australian Brigade was ready to open its attack at 2200 hours on 28 October. During the evening, 10th and 12th Batteries of the Italian 4th Group 46th Artillery Regiment opposite were ordered to retire. 'The withdrawal was carried out during the night,' wrote Capitano Luigi Bolner, 'the men abandoning even their blankets and personal possessions and dragging the guns out from under the very noses of the enemy who surrounded them on three sides. We set up shop again about a mile to the west – but we had no ammunition and no communications.'[24] Then at 2105 hours the barrage opened. 'In a few minutes the northern sector was under a barrage reminiscent of Great War days,' noted 15th Panzer Division's war diary. 'The horizon was ablaze with the flashes of enemy guns.'[25]

The Australian ranks were already severely depleted; 2/13th Battalion's companies were only of platoon strength and, having attacked on two nights, been counter-attacked on two nights, and moved the night before, were understandably exhausted. Captain Cal Vincent arrived to take command of B Company after the battalion orders group, which had been attended by Lieutenant Frederick Treweeke. For his company orders group, Vincent, Treweeke, another officer, a corporal and two privates assembled in adjacent holes in the ground and Treweeke shouted the orders out between shell bursts – until one killed him. Vincent managed to decipher the rest from the scribbled notes, and led his emaciated company of two officers and 30 men to the start line.[26] As they crossed it they 'seemed to be continuously walking through our own artillery, or else it, catching up, was going through us. We heard afterwards that it was Jerry firing into our shell bursts, but I couldn't see any great difference.' The defences were stubborn, and many anti-personnel mines were encountered, but the enemy posts were systematically reduced and eventually an area some 800 yards south of Thompson's Post was secured.

Attempting to consolidate, the battalion was under fire from machine-guns and mortars 800 yards away. Lance-Sergeant Reginald McKellar was detailed to lead a patrol to deal with them. 'The company commander handed me a compass, gave me a bearing and wished me luck. Luck! – my platoon consisted of ten men plus Lady Luck!' They crossed a minefield and approached the post, where they were pinned by machine-gun fire. 'I gave the order for the patrol to let fly with their grenades, of which we carried four apiece. They fell thick and heavy. The Germans were rattled and put up a feeble resistance. We took four prisoners with the guns.' The patrol then rushed the mortars and overcame the defenders – after one Aussie had a fist-fight with a German twice his size. Under fire from another post, they then made their way back to the company, taking their prisoners and the mortars with them.[27] By the end of the night the four rifle companies had been reduced to fewer than 100 men and Major Colvin – in command for just four days – was among the casualties.

On the left, 2/15th Battalion attacked northward from Trig 29 and, despite being shelled in its forming-up place (the adjutant and commanding officer, Lieutenant-Colonel C. K. M. Magno, were both wounded), it put in a vigorous and skilful attack. The troops advanced through machine-gun and mortar fire against a line of posts, killing some 89 Italians and taking 130 German and Italian prisoners. When two tractors approached at first light, towing anti-tank guns, they took these and captured the accompanying 22 Germans. But the attack cost 6 dead and 39 wounded or missing. Lieutenant-Colonel Magno was found by his driver, Perc Lyall, 'lying in a shallow depression in the ground. As I dressed his wounds he told me he had been wounded in the leg earlier in the night. Now the CO had lost an arm and had a bad head wound, but he was most concerned with the wound he had taken in the stomach.' With help, Lyall managed to get Magno to a British aid post. Magno 'was still worried about his Battalion, instructing me to get back as quickly as possible, as I had the Brigade wireless set on board [his carrier] and must maintain contact with Brigade. Lieutenant-Colonel Magno, who was very calm through this ordeal grabbed my arm and thanked me for what I had done, saying "I'll never forget you for this". My CO died . . .'[28]

The next stage of the advance was to be made by the fresh 2/23rd Battalion of 26th Australian Brigade, supported by 46th Royal Tank Regiment. To increase mobility, Lieutenant-Colonel Bernard Evans had arranged to mount one company on the tanks and two follow-up companies on carriers from his battalion and 2/24th. Unfortunately, as the battalion waited in the forming-up place for the 20th Australian Brigade success signal, the Axis defences were alerted and waiting, and the Australians crossed the start line into a torrent of fire from every conceivable weapon. Furthermore, the tanks struggled to find the minefield gaps, and command broke down within 46th Royal Tank Regiment (whose commanding officer and all of whose squadron commanders were wounded). Eventually the attack was reset and relaunched at 0055 hours. But the tanks soon ran into fire from anti-tank guns, and casualties once more began to mount. At 0300 hours a dismayed Evans lit a cigarette without bothering to hide the match. 'Well boys,' he declared, 'this looks like the end of 2/23rd Battalion!' Calling on the survivors to form a single line, he led some 60 men in an attack against the main enemy position at 0315 hours. Renewed mortar and machine-gun fire halted them, and they began to dig in. But before daybreak their tenacity was rewarded as they saw men running away from the positions that barred their way. They moved forward once more, having covered some 800 yards from the start line, and took the main German position, capturing 13 guns and 158 prisoners. They had lost 29 dead and 178 wounded and missing.[29]

Brigadier David 'Torpy' Whitehead of 26th Australian Brigade now made a new plan: he would attack with 2/24th and 2/48th Battalions from the ground firmly held by 2/15th, and Morshead released 40th Royal Tank Regiment to support him. However, when it became apparent that there would not be enough time to implement this plan before daylight, it was postponed and instead the area already taken was secured. The remaining eight tanks of 46th Royal Tank Regiment were withdrawn.

From 0700 hours on the morning of 29 October, 2/13th Battalion was in an isolated position which was fortunately covered on the left flank by an Axis-laid minefield. The strain was enormous, as Corporal Jack Craig noted: 'Why can't our chaps be relieved? Human endurance can stand so much. This cannot go on much longer. I wonder what the top brass really want from a human being. It is about time the Poms had a go.'[30]

Although heavy shelling wounded 2/13th's commanding officer and adjutant, it was against 2/15th and 2/17th Battalions that counter-attacks were directed by 200th Panzergrenadier Regiment, heading for the critical height at Trig 29. 'I was in France in 1918,' remarked Tony Scott of 2/2nd Machine Gun Battalion to his mate, 'but I didn't see as many Germans as all those bastards comin' this way!'[31] Once more, control of this position enabled the divisional artillery to pound Axis troops forming up to attack, and to devastate them once attacks were under way. Three attacks came in during the day, but all were repulsed – though at a cost of six Australian anti-tank guns. Australian training in quick and thorough consolidation of a position meant, that unless they could dislodge the Australians within a couple of hours of taking a position, Axis forces could not hope to budge them after that; they had not the strength nor the ability to launch the effective set-piece operations then necessary.[32] Pressure on I Battalion 115th Panzergrenadier Regiment during the afternoon of 29 October had led DAK to direct the panzers of Teege Group to counter-attack, but 15th Panzer Division's suggestion that 36th Bersaglieri Battalion be brought in to fill the gap of about a mile between I Battalion 115th Panzergrenadier Regiment and its neighbour, I Battalion 104th Panzergrenadier Regiment, had to be refused – the Trieste Division was about to be committed in DAK's sector, and filling the gap would take too long as 36th Bersaglieri was too far south.[33]

Far away in London, the repercussions of Montgomery's decision to withdraw the remainder of the armour were being felt. On the evening of 28 October, Anthony Eden, the Foreign Secretary, went for a drink with Churchill at 10 Downing Street, and much to Brooke's consternation he left the great man with the impression that the offensive was petering out. Montgomery had told Churchill it would be a seven-day battle, yet now he was regrouping. 'Before I got up this morning,' wrote Brooke the next day, 'I was presented with a telegram which [Churchill] wanted to send Alexander. Not a pleasant one!' Brooke was forced to field angry enquiries from Churchill. 'What was *my* Monty doing now, allowing the battle to peter out?' When Brooke learned that the mischief-maker was Eden, architect of the disaster in Greece the previous year, he lost his temper. At 1230 hours there was a Chiefs of Staff conference under Brooke's chairmanship, attended by Field Marshal Smuts. Churchill produced the proposed telegram and recounted his fears over the depth of Axis defences and many other points. His political position was at stake, and, with Torch looming, a failure at Alamein would cost him his head. Brooke was in a similar position, since failure would cost him his position as CIGS, but he expressed complete confidence in Montgomery. However, it was Smuts who calmed Churchill down. 'You are aware,' he said, 'that I have had no opportunity of discussing the matter with the CIGS, but I am in entire agreement with all the opinions he has expressed.' It was, said Brooke, 'as if oil had been poured on troubled waters', although his own anxieties were by no means assuaged.[34]

Although Brooke had managed to scotch the telegram, Eden had insisted that Richard Casey, the Minister of State in Cairo, be cabled to go up to the front and report on the situation. Casey turned up at Eighth Army Headquarters, and at first was so alarmed by the apparent stalemate that he showed de Guingand a draft signal he was preparing to send to Churchill in case of a possible reverse. 'Bill' Williams saw de

Guingand have an 'incredible burst of temper, saying: "For God's sake don't! If you do, I'll see you're drummed out of political life!" ' – de Guingand not realizing that Casey was not actually in political life. Nevertheless, Montgomery took the pressure from Churchill and Casey seriously, and recorded in his diary that 'we must make a great effort to defeat the enemy, and break up his army, so as to help Torch. I have therefore decided to modify my plan.'[35]

Alexander and Tedder also felt it necessary to visit Eighth Army Headquarters on 29 October, to discuss a final big push to break the enemy line. Tedder tried to impress on Montgomery the need to speed up operations.[36] Montgomery asked for a field survey company of Royal Engineers and for 51st (Midland) Medium and 95th Anti-Tank Regiments Royal Artillery; he received authority for these and for the Greek Armoured Car Squadron to join 1st Greek Brigade (although it had no armoured cars, only machine-guns).[37] In XIII Corps's sector, since it was clearly impossible to carry out large-scale offensive operations with troops being dispatched northward, it was decided to arrange a demonstration against Qaret el Himeimat on the night of 29/30 October. For this, 118th and 124th Royal Tank Regiment were deployed during the day with dummy tanks in menacing positions where it was hoped they would be observed and noted.[38]

Morshead now boldly decided to try both to open the main road from the Axis front line, as had been called for in the previous plan, and to strike north from 9th Australian Division's already pronounced salient towards the sea, in an attempt to cut off all those Axis forces to the east of it – an even more ambitious attack than the last, although the method of execution would be similar. This time, however, once one battalion had cut the road, there would be two battalions turning back eastward and a third would advance north to clear the way to the sea. Once again Whitehead was put in charge of the attack with 26th Australian Brigade – less 2/23rd Battalion, but with 2/32nd and 2/3rd Pioneer Battalions under command and 40th Royal Tank Regiment in support. The lead would be taken by 2/32nd Battalion, which was to capture Barrel Hill (which was identifiable by a navigation beacon sited there). Forming up behind it would be 2/24th and 2/48th Battalions, which would pass through to take Thompson's Post from the southwest, with 2/48th then pushing through to the coast. Finally, 2/3rd Pioneer Battalion would pass through 2/32nd, moving from Barrel Hill to near the coast to mop up and reorganize facing east and west. Extra engineers in the form of 2/3rd Field Company were allotted to the operation, and fire support would include no fewer than 12 field and three medium regiments with a total of 360 guns. At 1700 hours on the

29th, Morshead issued outline instructions for the operation to start on the night of 30/31 October, with final orders to be given at 0700 hours the following morning. In his notes he recorded that 'Whitehead doesn't want any tanks.'[39]

During the course of the nightly replenishment and patrol routine, a soldier from 2/17th Battalion took a prisoner while armed with nothing more lethal than a dixie of stew. The prisoner was handed over to 2/23rd Battalion, and the stew to its rightful owners. In all, 23 Germans were captured from I Battalion 155th and I Battalion 361st Regiments.[40]

That same night, demonstrations continued to try to pin down Axis forces. Three Hunt-class destroyers with eight motor torpedo boats and nine tank landing craft launched one from the sea that drew fire and enemy aircraft over the smokescreen they created. In the south, XIII Corps continued its demonstrations with 7th Armoured Division firing a timed artillery programme and the Royal Scots Greys and 4th/8th Hussars carrying out a feint attack using the sonic deception car. However, despite their best efforts, the dummy attack appeared to be a complete failure – there was no reaction from the enemy whatever.[41]

A *khamseen* on the morning of 30 October passed 'like a great shroud over Egypt, half-burying the dead and hid for a brief moment the hate and passion of war'.[42] But not for long. During the morning, 2/15th Battalion was attacked four times between midnight and dawn. One attack made a penetration and almost reached the anti-tank guns, but eventually all the attacks were driven off. It was obvious that the Axis forces were reinforcing heavily opposite the place where 2/32nd Battalion was to establish the base for Morshead's operation. The German defences were also being strengthened with both real and dummy minefields, but only captured mines and unsafe Italian V3 mines were available for the former. An accident involving V3s cost 33rd Engineer Battalion 31 men in one night, and Axis weakness combined with constant shelling made the process of mining very slow. Nevertheless, by regrouping and bringing up more reserves, a continuous front was again formed; 15th Panzer Division sent I Battalion 104th Panzergrenadier Regiment back to 21st Panzer Division, and I and II Battalions 115th Panzergrenadier Regiment (reduced to 120 and 70 men respectively), together with 23rd Bersaglieri Battalion, went back into the front line; 8th Panzer Regiment with the Italian 133rd Armoured Regiment and 27th Light Tank Battalion were assembled as a mobile reserve.[43]

Meanwhile Morshead decided that, with both 2/24th and 2/48th Battalions already severely depleted and 2/32nd Battalion under threat, any of these three might need help. He therefore altered his plan so that only if help were not needed was 2/3rd Pioneer Battalion to attempt to cut Axis communications north of the coast road. The resulting orders became known as the 'IF' plan – the Pioneers were to help any of 2/32nd, 2/24th or 2/48th Battalions if required; if not, they would carry out their original instructions. This change led to the support weapons previously allocated to the Pioneers (anti-tank guns and machine-guns) being directed elsewhere. The situation was not an easy one for a unit about to undertake its first infantry task, already reduced to three companies (the fourth being detached to the Composite Force), and in any case, without the normal scale of support weapons of an infantry unit.

The main air effort was throughout directed in support of the Australians. A programme for 'softening-up' the enemy defences involved over 150 light and fighter-bombers dropping 85 tons of bombs – the most intense operations being during the afternoon, when 54 Bostons and Baltimores from 21 and 24 Squadrons SAAF and 55 Squadron RAF, escorted by fighters from 233 and 239 Squadrons (each also carrying 500 lb bombs), attacked strongholds and concentrations just north of the Australian salient.[44] The artillery barrage opened at 2200 hours, and the lead companies of 2/32nd Battalion, crossing the start line ten minutes afterwards, soon caught up with it. This was a proper barrage, advancing at 100 yards every three minutes, on which the infantry could lean. They were normally expected to stay some 100 yards behind the falling shells, but could get closer if the artillery was firing from behind them, since the blast was thrown forward. Huddling in their trenches amid the choking dust and swirling smoke, and stunned by the concussion of dozens of shells, with ears ringing and heads throbbing, if not cruelly cut about by the flying metal or sub-merged under collapsing parapets, the defenders were then faced at short range by a line of men almost upon them with bayonets they were known to be ready to use. The railway line was quickly taken, along with 175 prisoners – nearly all German, from I Battalion 361st Regiment.

Following a reorganization the advance resumed, but now Australian casualties began to mount. The Australians were reaping an unexpect-edly bitter harvest from the fake attack of 23 October, as the Germans in this sector thought they had repelled a major assault and their morale was high.[45] After the lead sections crossed the railway line, Lieutenant-Colonel John Balfe of 2/32nd Battalion and his radio operator were confronted by six Germans, apparently wanting to surrender. But one of the Germans drew a pistol and shot Balfe in the arm, whereupon Balfe emptied his revolver in return and made off.

When the battalion reorganized on its final objective, a blockhouse was discovered with three German medical officers and their orderlies. True to the spirit in which this war had been fought, these remained and worked ceaselessly throughout the remaining days of the battle, tending all who were brought to them according only to their needs, and soon being joined by 2/32nd's medical officer and a section of 2/11th Field Ambulance.

The other three battalions set off in the wake of 2/32nd, and each had some action on the way. Two platoons from separate companies of 2/3rd Pioneer Battalion were saved from assaulting each other only by the inimitable profanity of their language. Instead they took a troublesome post to the left of the track leading to 2/32nd's position, along with some 50 prisoners.[46] Others assisted the engineers and 2/32nd Battalion in their efforts to clear the area. Further forward, Balfe was hit again and had to be evacuated, and an Axis anti-tank gun shot up many of the support vehicles trying to bring up ammunition and defence stores. By 0345 hours the lead elements of 2/32nd had occupied an area which became known after daylight as The Saucer, but they could not establish contact with 2/15th Battalion on their left as the fire being poured into the gap began to increase. For the next two days The Saucer would be the focal point of the battle.[47]

Mustering barely 450 bayonets between them, 2/24th and 2/48th Battalions set off for the sound of the guns on an eastward march of some 2,000 yards. All along the way they sustained casualties, but kept moving towards the barrage – although it was receding, so they did not receive its full benefit. Confusion on the start line between the two battalions did not help, and they took heavy fire from mortars and machine-guns as the two lead companies of 2/24th Battalion reached their intermediate objectives. Beyond this, as the rear two companies passed through, the fire increased. Reformed on a two-company basis, the battalion continued south of the railway line, where no enemy posts were encountered but two 1,000 lb aerial bombs were exploded by trip wires, with catastrophic results. 'When the survivors recovered from the blast it was to be confronted with a sight of horror. The dead and wounded were scattered over a large area and even in the fading moonlight we could see that most of our mates who were still alive had been severely wounded. The survivors rushed to their aid and did what they could.' Casualties in this one incident were 11 dead and 16 wounded.[48]

As 2/24th continued to advance, its numbers dwindled and groups from different companies helped each other. But its losses were too great, and it could go no further. The 84 men remaining dug in due north of Thompson's Post. This was an extended Axis defensive locality, and, when a patrol from 2/13th Battalion reported it as unoccupied, Lieutenant-Colonel Weir personally led a patrol to investigate.

To the west and north, 2/48th Battalion had a no less arduous battle: struggling forward into the teeth of sustained fire for some two hours, the reserve companies had to fight their way to the intermediate objectives, dealing with unsubdued posts left in the depleted lead companies' wake. With most of the officers and senior NCOs already casualties, Sergeant Kibby took command of his company – now barely a dozen men – and organized an attack on its objective. When they were forced to ground 20 yards away, Kibby leaped up and charged – hurling grenades which silenced the post, but at the cost of his life. For his actions since the start of the battle he was awarded the Victoria Cross. Johnny Ralla recorded in his diary:

> I went to the assistance of Hal Laughton a little higher up the ridge. He had been badly wounded. From that time on we of A Company began to lose men at a fast rate. Lieutenant B. Y. Hamilton was killed by a burst from a spandau and Captain Shillaker severely wounded. Sergeant Derrick took over and the advance continued until we were forced to ground near the objective. C Company came to our assistance and did the trick with bayonet and grenade, but not before Frank McMillan had been hit.

Ralla was then himself severely wounded. 'Back in hospital I ran into a lot of my mates.'[49]

Lieutenant-Colonel Hammer held a conference of those who now commanded the remnants of his companies. He decided to try to make contact with 2/24th Battalion and see if it could hold the ground already taken. Handing over command to the adjutant (who had already been wounded three times), he set out alone armed only with a revolver, and returned having been shot in the face but with two prisoners. Although he had reached 2/24th's headquarters, Weir had not been there. Hammer therefore ordered a withdrawal to the blockhouse, believing that 2/24th would also have to withdraw. Meanwhile Weir's patrol had soon revealed Thompson's Post to be strongly held, and Weir returned to headquarters to learn that Hammer proposed to withdraw, which he also decided to do. Shortly before dawn, both battalions returned to The Saucer.

Weir was also wounded, and command passed to a temporary captain of three months' standing, who led the 54 survivors into 2/32nd's perimeter. Of 206 men from 2/24th Battalion who had gone into the attack, 42 were dead and 116 had been wounded (some carrying on); another 2 men were missing. They in their turn had taken 48

German and 11 Italian prisoners, an 88 mm, two 50 mm and two 20 mm guns, 12 machine-guns, a medium and a light mortar, and 7 howitzers. Hammer's men had also now withdrawn, bringing some 200 German prisoners, having lost 47 killed and 148 wounded. Only 14 out of 18 officers were alive and unwounded, and 2/48th Battalion had lost two-thirds of its officers and half of its men since the battle's opening.

In total, the division had taken 544 prisoners during this operation, including 421 Germans. While the crumbling operations had maintained continuous and direct pressure on the Axis defences, this had been achieved at the cost of crumbling two fine battalions – there were none better in the British or German armies. Nevertheless, important reinforcements had also arrived: 9th Battery from 2/3rd Anti-Tank Regiment and the Rhodesian-manned 289th Anti-Tank Battery Royal Artillery.[50]

Throughout this period 2/3rd Pioneer Battalion had been sitting on its heels awaiting orders. At 0430 hours a signal was received to begin its original attack at 0425 hours – the barrage had already begun. Compelled to hurry, the battalion advanced through heavy fire to its first objective some 1,500 yards away, taking 30 prisoners and 3 machine-guns. Shorn of communications and without a forward observation officer (his truck had been blown up), the battalion found itself held up by its own barrage as daylight filtered across the desert. Having no anti-tank guns or extra machine-guns, the Pioneers were in greatest need of artillery support and ammunition. However, their vehicles were held at Tel el Eisa, and would remain there until called forward – though there was no way to call them forward.[51] With light revealing both to the Pioneers and to the surrounding defenders that the former were in another saucer, the Pioneers found themselves 'with no support and little ammunition, shooting at targets which mostly they could not see whereas the enemy could see every move and almost every man'.[52]

The Australian attack had come in at the junction of the German 361st Regiment (90th Light Division) and 200th Panzergrenadier Regiment (90th Light Division), while 2/24th and 2/48th Battalions had attacked 125th Panzergrenadier Regiment. The carriers that brought up Australian ammunition and evacuated the wounded had led to Axis reports that a 'strong force of British armour' had participated in the attack – an impression reinforced by further reports that morning of British armour attacking 361st Regiment – so that Rommel himself 'immediately drove up to Sidi Abd el Rahman and set up my command post east of the mosque'.[53] He then ordered 21st Panzer and 90th Light

Divisions to counter-attack the Australian wedge, putting von Thoma in command of this.

As Montgomery had hoped, the enemy was reacting violently to the northward moves by the Australians: once the latter got in behind 125th Panzergrenadier Regiment, it appears that Rommel lost his grip on the battle. At 0740 hours on 31 October, DAK was ordered to assume responsibility for the counter-attack in the coastal sector, and to this end von Thoma had to leave for 90th Light Division Headquarters immediately. 'This step,' said the DAK war diary, 'is all the more incomprehensible since the Corps Commander has to leave his main front in order to direct a counter-attack on an unfamiliar front some distance away.' Rommel was faced with either withdrawing 125th Panzergrenadier Regiment – which could be done that night – or having to push the Australians southward, from the railway. Von Thoma was of the opinion that the position was untenable and that this was the most favourable time for a withdrawal, but Rommel insisted on the counter-attack. It was a decision which had a profound effect on the course of the battle. The Axis forces were being drawn into the area which best suited Montgomery's plans, and devoting their energy to wasteful counter-attacks against the Australians.[54]

If Rommel was lacking accurate information about the nature of the threat in the north, neither Morshead nor indeed Whitehead had an accurate picture of the situation that confronted the four weak Australian battalions. With daylight they discovered various trenches and enemy outposts overlooked during the night, and another 200 prisoners were taken and sent back by 2/32nd Battalion, while the Pioneers' rear company sent back 47. Their two lead companies, however, were receiving Axis attention. At 1030 hours a German officer approached under a white flag to advise surrender rather than annihilation. 'If you want us, come and get us' was the politest suggestion among various remarks. For the rest of the morning the Pioneers were lacerated with all types of fire. Further south, The Saucer was also under increasing pressure as DAK tried to relieve 125th Panzergrenadier Regiment. Fortunately, 40th Royal Tank Regiment – less one squadron – had been able to make its way forward as sappers from 295th Field Company systematically cleared the obstacles between it and the beleaguered infantry.[55]

At about 1130 hours the first German counter-attack was delivered – some 15 tanks manoeuvring north of the railway, where they were met by the 6-pounders of the Rhodesians and 2-pounders of the Valentine tanks, deployed in hull-down positions. The German tanks withdrew, with their accompanying infantry pasted by every available gun and mortar. But the pressure on the Pioneers had increased, and first one and then the second of the forward companies was forced to withdraw, yielding prisoners as they did so, having long exhausted their ammunition. During this action there were noted several instances of the Germans withholding fire from men carrying or helping the wounded.[56]

With the outstretched arm of the Pioneers withdrawn, the main assault on The Saucer came in the early afternoon. The air reeked of high-explosive and the stench of dead bodies. Some 15 panzers plus self-propelled guns led the way. The 6-pounders busily engaged the German tanks, knocking out four for the loss of two guns, but the panzers pressed on, knocking out 18 Valentines and overrunning a company of 2/32nd whose positions they drove over, and capturing most of the survivors. With more Valentines than panzers being knocked out, it was decided to call up the reserve squadron of 40th Royal Tank Regiment; but before this arrived it was the Germans who had withdrawn. Soon afterwards 40th Royal Tank Regiment was itself withdrawn altogether from The Saucer, having earned the undying admiration of the Australians by its bravery. At 1600 hours the Germans renewed their assault from the north, and the Pioneers were now forced to withdraw to the south side of the railway embankment. But by 1900 hours the counter-attack had stalled, although 90th Light Division now reported that it had re-established contact with 125th Panzergrenadier Regiment and 10th Bersaglieri Regiment on the coast.

During the afternoon, it had become apparent to Morshead just how weak were his battalions holding The Saucer. Furthermore, an intercepted message from DAK to 90th Light Division instructing the latter to wipe out the salient convinced him of the need for a relief – a decision that would save the right flank, and possibly the battle.[57] The 2/24th had been reduced to just 140 men, who had been in continual action for nine days without sleep; their main ration item was Benzedrine tablets. But to give up the ground taken would have gone against both the Army Commander's plan and Morshead's own character. Instead he decided to relieve 26th Australian Brigade with the 24th; 2/32nd would remain behind to join its parent formation. Orders were issued at 1930 hours and, using a circuit of transport that reflected a high standard of staffwork, completed by 0330 hours on 1 November. The Axis forces were too exhausted to interfere. As the weary survivors of 2/24th and 2/48th Battalions – who had suffered further casualties during the day – climbed aboard the transports to move to Tel el Eisa, they said farewell in typical Australian language: 'Start digging you bastards, or you'll be sorry!'[58] They were taken back to the original front line near the coast, to sleep the night and muster next morning for their saddest roll calls ever.[59] Understandably exhausted, Sergeant F. Legg noted in his diary that he was 'So "done" that I trembled uncontrollably for ½ hr.'[60]

With the greater part of Eighth Army now regrouping for Montgomery's revised plan – code-named Supercharge – Rommel continued to waste resources in a vain attempt to restore the situation in the north. In the early hours of 1 November the commander of 125th Panzergrenadier Regiment arrived at 90th Light Division Headquarters to report that only a remnant of his formation remained. When Rommel heard that it still held some of its original positions and had especially distinguished itself, he decided to renew his full-scale efforts to relieve it. Dawn on 1 November, revealed to the newcomers of 24th Australian Brigade the enemy all around at a range of 800–1,000 yards. The Germans opened fire with everything they possessed, but in the ensuing artillery duel, they fared the worst, having both fewer guns and, more importantly, less ammunition.

Then, at 0840 hours, 30 Stukas were seen heading towards the Australians, escorted by 15 fighters. But before they could launch their attack they were caught by fighters from 112 Squadron RAF and 66 Squadron USAAF, and seven were shot down. In their panic they jettisoned their bombs, most falling on their own positions.[61] A second sortie by 112 Squadron just before noon encountered more Stukas and claimed 5 destroyed, 1 probable and 2 damaged.[62]

At 1000 hours German infantry had been observed assembling, and a report came in from Eighth Army that a signal had been intercepted ordering 21st Panzer and 90th Light Divisions to attack the Australian salient from the north-west. Morshead drove over to confer with Brigadier Arthur Godfrey of 24th Australian Brigade, who he decided was in a position to continue as he was. The remainder of the afternoon saw a sustained and desperate assault directed at 2/28th and 2/43rd Battalions, both units far stronger than those they had relieved.[63] Lieutenant Roger Price of 2/28th Battalion recalled that the Germans came forward in small groups, rifles slung, 'for all the world looking like spectators drifting away from a minor football game'. Still, they were engaged at close range with every weapon the Australians could bring to bear:

> Our automatics and riflemen were firing like mad, and the advance was checked. A flight of our fighter-bombers swept in to give us close support. They came over at a few hundred feet and we could see the bombs leave the aircraft and follow them down. Next came our artillery, and the enemy attack wilted. The enemy countered by shelling us viciously with artillery and mortars which were ranged on us from three sides. It seemed impossible that

anyone could live through such a storm of fire. Every time I lifted my head the dirt was spurting everywhere from flying shrapnel.

Surprisingly few men were hit. Nevertheless, 12 6-pounders (including 8 belonging to the Rhodesians) and 2 2-pounders were knocked out.[64] But by 1430 hours the panzers appeared to realize that their infantry could not get through, and they backed away.

The attack was resumed an hour later from the north and managed to overrun Barrel Hill, and some of the panzers pushed past towards Thompson's Post. But the supporting infantry was effectively halted by artillery fire, and by 1700 hours appeared to have given up. Then half an hour later another attack was forming up and had to be halted by the guns once more. From 1915 hours Brigade Headquarters came under intense shellfire which mortally wounded Brigadier Godfrey and wounded other members of the staff. At dusk, adopting the traditional German tactic of advancing out of the setting sun with panzers and infantry concealed in smoke and dust, another assault was made but failed to penetrate the position.[65] Allan Jones of 2/43rd Battalion remembered the day

> as a collection of scenes as indelibly vivid as any film could be. The dust and smoke of bursting shells, the distinctive sharp crack of 6-pounders, the yells of men, and the irregular crackle of small-arms fire, and the cheers whenever a tank or mobile gun was knocked out. . . I hugged the gritty bottom of my doover [trench] and listened with terrified fascination to the report of shells leaving the barrels of guns, screaming through the air and arriving to burst with teeth-jarring detonations, some of them only feet away.[66]

Further attacks were made at 2030 and 2130 hours, but were held. Corporal John Lovegrove later recalled the bloody fighting:

> I am totally shattered and could weep as I look back now and feel so strongly for my men . . . We had virtually all been together since enlistment 2½ years ago and entwined with a bond of respect and comradeship that mere words can't adequately describe – every bit as strong as a family 'blood' relationship and the horror of that night will live with those of us who survived for the remainder of our days.[67]

The Australians had fought continuously since the opening day. In his subsequent dispatch to the War Office, Alexander would say, 'They fought until flesh and blood could fight no longer. Then they went on fighting.'[68]

The fire continued unabated around The Saucer, then at 0230 hours the next morning it was drowned by a new sound to the south: Operation Supercharge had begun.[69]

18

Supercharge

Ubique means that warnin' grunt
The perished linesman knows,
When o'er his strung and sufferin' front
The shrapnel sprays his foes,
And when the firin' dies away
The husky whisper runs
From lips that haven't drunk all day
'The guns, thank God, the guns.'

Rudyard Kipling

The proximity of enemy on three sides of the Australian salient guaranteed constant heavy exchanges of fire well into the night, even after the infantry advance of the new offensive Supercharge had begun. At one point the Australian field gunners had to switch from their task in support of the offensive to deal with urgent calls for defensive fire from 24th Australian Brigade.[1] Casualties were heavy – the 450 casualties suffered being equal to the total strength of 26th Australian Brigade.[2] That evening 2/3rd Anti-Tank Regiment received seven reinforcement officers from the Middle East Officer Cadet Training Unit. One of these, on introduction to his new battery commander, was gazing somewhat awe-struck at a dead German officer and asked what had killed him. The major quickly replied, 'I don't know and I don't care; all that I'm concerned with is that he is bloody well dead.'[3]

Conferences had been held at all levels over the previous three days to prepare the new offensive. The original plan was to thrust along the coast road to the north, but this was later modified to a drive further inland. McCreery later claimed, backed up by Alexander, that it was he that pressed Montgomery to alter the direction of the new offensive. But Montgomery disliked McCreery, and it was de Guingand who succeeded in persuading the Army Commander to make the change. Charles Richardson recalled that de Guingand tried to persuade

Montgomery to do so at the morning briefing on 29 October, after Ultra showed that 90th Light Division had moved north. 'No, he won't have it,' said de Guingand on his return. He then discussed the matter with McCreery when the latter came up with Casey and Alexander, and de Guingand said, 'Look I will go and talk to Monty about it again – don't you, for goodness sake, because if you do there'll be – he won't do it. But if one can persuade him it's his own idea, so to speak, then I'm sure it's the right thing to do.' The second attempt was successful, and there was a sigh of relief among the staff.[4]

Having been relieved by the South Africans on the night of 27/28 October, the New Zealanders had enjoyed two days' rest. 'We had a real holiday,' recalled Murray Reid, 'and made up for many an hour of lost sleep. The YMCA truck called and made a distribution of fruit, chocolate and cigarettes to all ranks.'[5] At 2nd New Zealand Division conference the following day, Freyberg made clear why the break into the Axis positions was to be made by formations attached to his division from others: 2nd New Zealand Division had already lost 97 officers and 1,481 men since the battle had started and, as reinforcements were few, could no longer afford casualties without endangering its role in the pursuit for which it had trained.[6] Indeed, he first refused to accept Montgomery's plan to lead the assault. When Montgomery offered him a British brigade he still shook his head, although he was 'clearly weakening'. 'Very well, Bernard,' said Montgomery, 'I'll give you two infantry brigades . . . I could see,' said Montgomery later, 'that the old war-horse was itching to fight again. This sort of show was very much his cup of tea and I knew he was the right man for it.'[7] With 151st Brigade from 50th (Northumbrian) Division and 152nd from 51st (Highland) Division, and a re-equipped 9th Armoured Brigade, Freyberg would smash a passage westward to Tel el Aqqaqir on the Rahman Track – the original objective of 10th Armoured Division in Lightfoot.

Montgomery wanted the attack to begin on the night of 31 October, but when Freyberg visited the troops he was struck by the exhaustion of many of the infantrymen, the strain on the gunners who would be switching without a break from supporting the Australian operations, the difficulties inherent in the co-operation of the various troops from different divisions, and the short time allotted to them for route reconnaissance and preparation of start lines. On top of these factors was the still chaotic congestion of the area shared with Aussies, Jocks and armour through which most of his troops would have to pass on their way to those start lines, and he called on Leese to tell him that a 24-hour postponement was essential. Leese agreed.[8] This provided a brief respite for Rommel, during which time he began seriously to consider withdrawal and plans to hold a secondary position at Fuka using 90th Light Division. But such thoughts were complicated by the immobility of most of his Italian infantry. He also knew that mobile warfare was no longer a panacea in the face of Allied air superiority. Nevertheless, that afternoon he ordered the withdrawal of all administrative troops to Matruh, even further to the west.[9]

However, at 2330 hours he received news that *Luisiana*, carrying 1,459 tons of fuel on which he was counting following the sinking of the 2,388-ton tanker *Arca* off Crete by a British submarine on 26 October, had been sunk off Greece by aerial torpedo. This seemed to have an effect in Rome and Berlin, where OKW had until now believed the Alamein position could be held, Kesselring having stated that the British offensive had been launched more for political than for military reasons and that it was unlikely to bring about a fundamental change in the situation. Only on 30 October did serious misgivings arise, when Rommel reported that all his reserves were committed and that if his front gave way there was nothing to prevent the British driving as far west as they wanted to go. However, while Cavallero agreed that there was no option but to hang on, the ever optimistic Kesselring inspected the front on 1 November and reported that the danger had passed.[10] That day the *Tripolino* laden with fuel and ammunition was sent to the seabed northwest of Tobruk, and a Beaufort torpedoed the *Ostia* in the same convoy. When fuel was flown in from Crete, 205 Group RAF renewed its attacks on the main airfield at Maleme used by the Ju-52 transports.[11]

On 1 November, Montgomery wrote to Brooke:

> I am enjoying the battle, and have kept fit and well . . . Tonight's battle I have called Supercharge and I enclose a copy of the orders for it. If we succeed it will be the end of Rommel's army . . . Lumsden has been very disappointing: he may be better when we get out into the open. But my own view is he is not suited to high command, but is a good fighting Div[isional] commander. He is excitable, highly strung and easily depressed. He is considerably at sea in charge of a corps and I have to watch over him very carefully. The best of the lot is Oliver Leese, who is quite first class.[12]

Stuart Hamilton had been in the left-out-of-battle party of 8th Royal Tank Regiment but was moved 'up the blue' on the same day. He had stopped to ask for directions from four Kiwi anti-aircraft gunners when there was a sudden scream and six or more shells fell all around them, enveloping everything in dust. When it cleared it revealed the Kiwis piled on top of each other in a slit trench and Hamilton standing with his hands in his pockets and his pipe in his mouth. 'They got up and started to dust themselves down and wanted to know what the fucking hell I thought I was doing and that I wasn't going to be standing around for fucking long if I was going to do that stupid sort of fucking thing!' What they did not know was that Hamilton had clenched his fists 'so tightly in my pockets that I broke the linings of my shorts so that my fists were stuck tight and I just couldn't get my ruddy pipe out of my mouth!'[13]

With the end of genuine attempts to breach the southern part of the Axis line, XIII Corps had spent its time attempting to distract the enemy with a demonstration by 1st Greek Brigade and use of dummy tanks now under command of 4th Light Armoured Brigade, while 4th Indian Division collected its transport and drove it back and forth and 7th Indian Brigade made visible preparations for an assault. This included putting a borrowed piper in a carrier belonging to 4th/16th Punjab Regiment, in the hope that the enemy would hear him and perhaps think that 51st (Highland) Division was at this front. The enemy reacted to these demonstrations with artillery fire and machine-guns on fixed lines, which Headquarters 4th Indian Division regarded as 'a good reaction'.[14] 'Our job,' wrote Tuker, 'is to hold a huge front and make noises to keep the Boche interested. A poor sort of business, but someone has to do it. I don't think he has moved a man from our front.'[15] This, in all honesty, was probably due more to shortage of petrol than to effective deception measures. The demonstrations were then taken up by 50th (Northumbrian) Division on the night of the actual assault in the north.[16]

In this operation 2nd New Zealand Division would attack on a front of about 4,000 yards behind a creeping barrage put down by 192 guns. A barrage was fired on this occasion because not enough detailed infor-mation was available about all enemy positions. A further 168 guns fired concentrations on known enemy localities in and on the flanks of the advance, involving a total of 13 field and three medium regiments.[17] The New Zealanders were not impressed by the conference held by 151st Brigade. Kippenburger thought it a disgrace, and Captain Roy Blair found it 'the most amusing I ever attended and certainly the most unrehearsed . . . I can distinctly remember the Brigadier apologising for his staff who had incorrectly drawn an enlargement of the battle area and he asked the conference to visualise the whole map "up another square".'[18] The armoured plan was for a reconstituted minefield task force comprising 2nd Rifle Brigade with three troops of Crusaders, engineers and other necessary troops to follow up the infantry as far west as possible in three parties clearing routes based on the Diamond,

Boomerang and Square tracks. These would be followed first by 2nd Armoured Brigade, with 90 Shermans and 68 Crusaders, then by 7th Motor Brigade, also in three columns and with four of the new Churchill tanks,* and finally by 8th Armoured Brigade, with 62 Shermans and 47 Crusaders, which would pass through the Motor Brigade and form up on the left of 2nd Armoured Brigade.[19]

Before H-Hour on the night of 1/2 November 7th Indian Brigade once more created a demonstration to pin down forces south of the main attack, and succeeding in drawing fire.[20] The real action was all to the north, however. The DAF operated constantly: on the night of the assault, 68 Wellingtons (25 making second sorties) and 19 Albacores flew a seven hour attack on targets in the Tel el Aqqaqir area, dropping 184 tons of bombs and completely wrecking DAK's signals system, while night-flying Hurricanes kept up patrols over the battle area for a total of 1,094 sorties and 199 tons of bombs during 1 November.[21] The first formations to move were the Durham battalions of 151st Brigade, which left Tel el Eisa in lorries at 1900 hours along Diamond track, led by 28th (Maori) Battalion. They were supported by 34th New Zealand Anti-Tank Battery (plus E Troop 32nd New Zealand Anti-Tank Battery) and 244th Anti-Tank Battery Royal Artillery, and a company and platoon of 27th (Machine Gun) Battalion. Engineers from 7th New Zealand Field Company moved with the forward troops; the 44 Valentines of 8th Royal Tank Regiment brought up the rear. Forward observation officers from 5th New Zealand Field Regiment were distributed among the four battalions.

The start line began at Trig 29 and ran south through defences held by 26th and 24th Battalions. The Maoris would be on the right, linking with the Australians in their salient with 8th and 9th Durham Light Infantry in the centre and left respectively. Following close behind the lead battalions, 6th Durham Light Infantry would wheel right on the objective and fill the gap between the Maoris and their 8th Battalion. Seventh New Zealand Field Company would extend Diamond behind them into two branches, A and B. To the south was 152nd Brigade, comprising 5th Seaforth Highlanders on the right and 5th Cameron Highlanders on the left, with 2nd Seaforth Highlanders refusing the left to cover the southern flank, supported by 8th New Zealand Field Company and 38 Valentines from 50th Royal Tank Regiment. Once

---

*These belonged to a special experimental troop. One broke down on the way, one was knocked out later in the day and the others retired with guns out of action.

again the brigade had its men tie strips of rifle flannelette on to their backs to form a St Andrew's cross. In contrast to the men of the Tyneside Brigade, who still wore summer dress of shirts and shorts with pullovers, they would go into battle in full battledress. Responsibility for protecting the southern face of the area of penetration was given to 51st (Highland) Division, which in turn gave the task to 133rd Brigade, allocated from 10th Armoured Division for the purpose. Since it already held a portion of the line, this brigade planned to send 2nd Royal Sussex Regiment to occupy the old Woodcock position (the 4th Battalion, reduced to two weak platoons and an anti-tank platoon, was under its command) and link with 2nd Seaforth Highlanders, while 5th Royal Sussex Regiment would fill the flank back to 153rd Brigade's defences. Wary about losses in vehicles, the Sussex battalions were to advance on foot behind a special barrage fired from 20 minutes after the main operation (at 0125 hours), carrying only digging tools. They would bring forward only essential vehicles in due course.

When, in preparation, Lieutenant Norman Craig's unit was relieved by another unit of 51st (Highland) Division coming through, the newcomers brought up a meal with them which they insisted on sharing. Halfway through, a Jock came up to complain about the food. 'The officer laughed and told him to "bugger off". He slouched away cursing. The complaint – in the forward salient on the eve of an attack – was a ridiculous one. Yet it had a certain ring of defiance about it. When the Day of Judgement comes, the British soldier will vanish into the ultimate chaos with a complaint about the food on his lips.'[22] He should perhaps have considered himself lucky to be fed at all. The transport of 2nd Seaforth Highlanders had been unable to get forward, so 50th Royal Tank Regiment donated 80 battle rations it had been saving for itself.[23]

At 2330 hours, the 151st and 152nd Brigades de-bussed close to their start lines and prepared to follow the barrage. A 'deception' barrage had already been fired on the northern part of the front. There, 90th Light Division's communications were in order, whereas DAK's were in chaos after the bombing, so Panzerarmee only received news of the deception. Having previously witnessed engineer activity in the area, it was expecting an attack in this direction. Instead, the most concentrated barrage thus far began in front of the assault brigades at 0055 hours. From the first lift, it moved 100 yards every two and a half minutes until 0220 hours, when it halted for half an hour before moving again at the same rate to the final objective until 0345 hours. From then on it continued a curtain of fire at slow rate (two rounds per gun per minute), after which the barrage for 9th Armoured Brigade would begin.[24] 'The whole night to the east was broken by hundreds of gunflashes stabbing into the darkness,' recorded the history of 8th Durham Light Infantry, by now an experienced desert battalion but for which this was the first major operation of the battle. 'The shells whistled overhead to burst with a deafening crash in the target area, and from then on, until the barrage closed about three hours later, the frightful shattering noise went on continually.'[25] As Lieutenant Colonel D. I. Watson, commanding 6th Durham Light Infantry, noted, 'It was as if the giants of some other world were cracking their huge whips and hurling lumps of metal through the air. In every twelve yards there was shell hole.' Watson himself was a Territorial of 20 years service, whose father and great-uncle had commanded the battalion before him.[26]

As soon as the barrage began, the infantry stepped off and closed up as near as possible to the line of bursting shells ahead. When smoke rounds indicated the lift, they moved forward as a line. On the far right, the Maoris met opposition almost immediately from both German and Italian positions. Although they cleared these, C Company on the right suffered heavily. B and D Companies met another line of enemy posts, which they charged with bayonets and grenades, breaking through and collecting many prisoners in the process. They then formed a defensive box, where they were joined by the survivors of C Company, who found they were too few to hold their objective. A Company, which had been following up C Company, met a great deal of unsubdued opposition and only a few wounded where C Company was expected to be, so it dug itself in on its rather exposed position, under fire from three sides. When dawn greeted the battalion – now two groups out of touch with each other and their neighbours – so did snipers and machine-guns. The attached anti-tank gunners were badly shot up but managed to site two of their weapons, and B Squadron 8th Royal Tank Regiment managed to find cover of sorts to the rear. Casualties in the battalion amounted to around 100, including the commanding officer and the second in command, but many of the posts had resisted to the last and dozens of the enemy had perished especially among the Germans; another 162, together with 189 Italians, had been captured. The Maoris held their tenuous positions throughout daylight under constant fire, earning a Distinguished Service Order, a Distinguished Conduct Medal and two Military Medals in the process.

To the left of the Maoris, 8th Durham Light Infantry advanced with A and B Companies leading, while C Company was tasked to pull up on the right of A Company as soon as the Maoris had dealt with a known strongpoint just to the west of the start line. They immediately came under heavy fire as they ran into a line of posts. 'Things were looking pretty grim here and it was only the audacity of an NCO that got us out of it, which cost him an arm,' J. E. Drew wrote later to his mother.

> Joe and I had got our [Bren] gun going again and we began to advance with the section. The next thing I knew there was a tremendous crash behind us and as I fell forward I caught a glimpse of Joe going down. Picking myself up, I discovered that except for a few scratches, I was OK. I then walked over to Joe and found there was nothing I could do for him.

He did not get to see his brother buried.[27] As the battalion pressed on, it overcame these positions and broke through to overrun a head-quarters area which included a dressing station and a panzer recovery park. The defenders were too demoralized by the barrage to offer effective resistance, and many prisoners were taken. C Company was ordered to pass through, and reached the final objective at about 0400 hours, having taken another 50 Italian prisoners. As the men were digging in, feeling somewhat isolated, they were joined by the rest of the battalion with support weapons and a few tanks. Contact was estab-lished with its neighbours, but, having lost 5 officers and over 100 men in the lead companies, the battalion was not well sited for defence. On the left, 9th Durham Light Infantry had advanced with Major Teddy Worral, seconded from the Somerset Light Infantry, keeping his company under control with his hunting horn.[28] The first objective was quickly secured, but they then encountered dug-in tanks and gun posi-tions. Fortunately these were not defended very resolutely, and by 0400 hours this battalion too was on its final objective and being reinforced by its support arms, forming a continuous front through which 9th Armoured Brigade would pass through.

Sixth Durham Light Infantry allowed its sister battalions to get some 500 yards ahead before crossing the start line, and met desultory shell-ing and mortaring but no direct resistance for the first 800 yards. But once beyond the area cleared by the Maoris it came under heavy machine-gun fire from the north. One platoon from D Company was sent to deal with this, but became pinned down and eventually the whole company had to be detached. While this went on, A Company came up from reserve and, with C Company on its left, overran scat-tered infantry and Italian artillery positions to reach the final objective in the rear of 8th Battalion, where it set out a defensive front. The medical officer, Captain J. Gibson – an American volunteer much liked by the battalion – was himself already wounded as he attended to Regimental Sergeant-Major A. Page, who had accounted for one pos-ition with his rifle and bayonet. Watson recalled that 'we must have walked over some Italians who lay doggo as we advanced and undoubtedly one of them killed my RSM, the doctor tending the wounded and a sergeant who played cricket down in Dorset'.

Once D Company rejoined the main position it left the infantry very thin on the ground, with a wide gap between the Durhams and Maoris, but the brigade had achieved its task and had taken 350 prisoners from the German 115th Panzergrenadier Regiment and Italian Littorio and Trento Divisions, at a cost of 50 dead, 211 wounded and 87 missing.[29] At 0200 hours 15th Panzer Division had lost communications with 8th Panzer Regiment and 115th Panzergrenadier Regiment, whose headquarters were overrun, as were those of the Italian 65th Infantry Regiment.[30] When daylight came, there was little the Durhams could do to improve their defences or communications, because they found a fierce tank battle raging just beyond their positions.

Behind them, the sappers of 7th New Zealand Field Company, supported by two Scorpions, worked to extend the end of the Diamond track. On the B extension, most of the sappers' transport and kit was destroyed by a salvo of shellfire, and when the commander of 151st Brigade, Brigadier J. E. S. Percy, complained that the sappers were not working a relief party had to be called up. Some of 8th Royal Tank Regiment's Valentines then missed the route indicators and ended up among mines, having to be rescued by a Scorpion, all of which caused Freyberg to suggest to Leese that X Corps's armour should be directed to follow 152nd Brigade, whose mine clearing appeared to be progressing smoothly. However, the problems were overcome before any changes could be made, and 8th Royal Tank Regiment was able to offer close support to the infantry across the front by dawn.

On the left, 152nd Brigade had a much easier task: 5th Seaforth Highlanders met little opposition before the first objective, and bypassed some dug-in tanks en route to the final objective, which was reached just after 0400 hours with extremely light casualties. Captain George Green, commanding Headquarters Company, remembered a rum bottle:

> I'd been dishing out the ration on the start line, and then the barrage opened up, and there I was with this bottle in my hand. It was still half full. I couldn't possibly drink it all. I took one good swig out of it, and then laid it down very carefully all by itself in the middle of the desert. I've often wondered what happened to it.[31]

'Suddenly we were on our feet and moving forward,' remembered Roy Cooke.

> As far as could be seen, to both left and right of us, men were advancing with their rifles in the porte position, their bayonets glinting in the pale moonlight.

Full moon had been days ago so it was quite dark . . . As we advanced, the
feeling of pride and exhilaration was unmistakable. We didn't realize or think
of the danger we were in; we were doing a job and the thought of being killed
or wounded was far from our minds . . . I remember seeing forms sink to the
ground but our orders were to keep going and not to stop for wounded or
dying. Later we passed slit trenches with forms slouched over them facing in
our direction . . . Above all the din, the sound of the pipes could clearly be
heard, and even an Englishman can feel proud to belong to a Scottish regiment when he hears the shrill warlike sound of a pipe tune above the racket
all around him. It sounded so incongruous, yet it was just what was needed to
keep up one's spirits for what lay ahead.[32]

On the left, 5th Cameron Highlanders met dug-in tanks in greater
depth, but it clung to the barrage and reached its final objective just
before 0400 hours, with only around a dozen casualties. To the rear, 2nd
Seaforth Highlanders advanced with all four companies in line across
the brigade frontage and found that everywhere opposition had 'melted
away'; even the dug-in tanks had retreated or their crews were so
demoralized by the barrage that they surrendered. In all, some 30 prisoners were taken from the Italian Ariete and Littorio Divisions. Once it
reached the rear of 5th Camerons, 2nd Seaforths swung south to form
a front which later joined 2nd Royal Sussex Regiment to the south-east.
Major Christopher Nix, now commanding this battalion, noted that
'the attack was completely successful, although I had some very anxious
moments. The Battalion was magnificent and fairly tore into the enemy
and after an hour's fighting on the enemy position, all opposition died
away.'[33]

The sappers of 8th Field Company operating behind 152nd Brigade
had a relatively straightforward task extending the Square track,
although they suffered ten casualties in the process. Murray Reid noted
that the German machine-guns were using less tracer than before. 'The
bullets made a continuous zipping noise as they tore past, and I disliked
the idea of not knowing from where they were coming. Do what I
might I could not walk upright, but went ahead with my head down as
if facing a strong wind.'[34] Fiftieth Royal Tank Regiment, which followed
the brigade, began with 38 Valentines operational, but by the time the
infantry crossed their start lines this number was down to 24 through
breakdowns, scattered mines and enemy fire.[35] On the objective,
George Green of 5th Seaforth Highlanders arrived at 0430 hours to
find the regiment already digging in. 'The ground was like iron, and it
was impossible to dig down more than two feet without striking solid
limestone. We couldn't get down at all. For the next five hours my group
just lay as the shells came over heavily and accurately. They were dead

on the range. All this time we were trying to dig. It was the worst ever.' He and the medical officer finished the battle as the only unwounded captains in the unit. By the end of the battle it had lost 12 officers and 165 men.[36]

So far the attack had gone well, reaching its objective nearly 4,000 yards from the start line on time and without serious losses. The sappers had cleared lanes through the minefields, and at once the two armoured-car regiments, the Royal Dragoons and 4th/6th South African Armoured Car Regiment, tried to slip out into the enemy's rear areas. Although they met with no success near Tel el Aqqaqir, the Royals managed to get two squadrons through further south and set off to cause havoc, like the first spray of water from the fissures in a dam about to burst. An officer described how over the next four days while they caused mayhem they were in turn pestered by enemy aircraft, one of which had a novel form of bombing. 'He had probably grown tired of aiming at the small target offered by an armoured car and, attaching a bomb to a piece of rope suspended from his Me-109, flew over us hoping to bump the bomb into our turrets. After twenty-four unsuccessful attempts the bomb hit the ground and exploded, causing irreparable damage to his piece of rope.'[37]

By 0200 hours A and C Squadrons of 4th/6th South Africans were in a position to follow immediately behind the infantry. 'The attack goes favourably,' the regiment recorded, 'a steady advance is maintained and the noise is deafening . . . Hell let loose. The infantry are held up, then forced slightly back – but only slight. It is getting late and dawn is not far off and we must break through.' Unfortunately, when daylight came they were exposed to fire from 90th Light Division, and Lieutenant-Colonel R. Reeves-Moore had to call off the attempt, ordering B and C Squadrons to stand by to make another.[38] If Supercharge had been launched a little further to the south, so as to miss 90th Light Division opposite the Australians, very few Germans would have been encountered. At dawn, 9th Durham Light Infantry was hammered by artillery and suffered heavily. Forced to withdraw, it did so through 27th (Machine Gun) Battalion's 11 Platoon, which nevertheless held its own positions throughout the day.[39] To its front charged 9th Armoured Brigade.

Brigadier John Currie was told that he must be prepared for 100 per cent tank casualties, and decided he could not exempt himself from the risk. He therefore posted himself in the van. He was a 'dynamic, courageous and excellent Brigadier who worked harder than anyone', wrote

Clive Stoddart, who saw Currie just before they went up to the start line. Currie said, ' "Well Clive, how is everything" and he then asked my gunner where his first shot would land and I wish you could have seen his face when the boy answered, quick as a flash, "On the target, sir." He shook hands and said "We can't fail", and went off in a cloud of dust.'[40] Freyberg's plan called for a creeping barrage to begin at 0545 hours, behind which 9th Armoured Brigade would advance some 2,000 yards and 1st Armoured Division would pass through. However, the plan had been laid in difficult circumstances, since 4th New Zealand Field Regiment, which was to support the brigade thereafter, was already in action, and the arrangements for tying up the regiments with battery commanders and forward observation officers broke down, and not all of these were available. This might not have proved so critical had the advance gone according to plan, but it was thrown off schedule almost immediately.[41]

Lieutenant-Colonel Sir Peter Farquhar Bt, commanding 3rd Hussars, later described 9th Armoured Brigade's approach march:

> We were horribly shelled by guns and mortars whilst passing through the gaps in our own minefields and most of the soft-skinned vehicles and carriers were knocked out including all the anti-tank guns. In addition, all the officers, except one, of A Company 14th [Sherwood] Foresters and the New Zealand anti-tank troop were either killed or wounded with the result that this very important part of the regimental group was for all practical purposes eliminated very early on in the proceedings.

The loss of mine markers meant some tanks went astray, and in all some 29 failed to reach the start line in time. At 0520 hours Farquhar received a message that ' "the Meet of the the Grafton Hounds" had been postponed for half an hour. It was not stated whether the postponement was due to frost or fog, but the latter – war variety – was strongly suspected.'[42] In fact it was because the Warwickshire Yeomanry had been held up and Currie had requested a delay of 25 minutes. 'A creepy feeling crawls up our spines and our hands are somehow clammy,' noted the Royal Wiltshire Yeomanry's historian. 'That half-hour may make all the difference!'[43] Indeed, it meant the brigade would now be advancing in daylight. As it jockeyed into position despite desultory fire from guns and mortars, nobody was deceived that the growl of tank motors and the creaking of tracks went unheard by the waiting enemy; unlike their cavalry forebears, they could not muffle the jingle of their harness.[44]

At 0615 hours the barrage renewed and the tanks began to move forward into the receding darkness, there being enough light now to see about 100 yards faintly.[45] All three regiments quickly found themselves in fierce engagements. The tank tracks added to the dust and haze created by the barrage in front. Nevil Warner was a Grant driver with the Warwickshire Yeomanry. 'Tanks were brewing up all around us but we didn't get hit that morning. There were flashes from guns on all sides and it wasn't until the sun came up that we knew which direction we were facing.'[46] The three regiments advanced with 3rd Hussars on the right, the Royal Wiltshire Yeomanry in the centre and the Warwickshire Yeomanry on the left.

Third Hussars found themselves right in the middle of the Axis anti-tank-gun line. Two troops found themselves among 50 mm gun positions and accounted for eight of them, but 88 mm guns were further back and soon began to take a toll. Most of A Squadron was quickly knocked out, and the battlefield was thick with black smoke from burning tanks.[47] There was little control in C Squadron, as both the squadron leader's tank (and a replacement) and his second in command's went up on mines, leaving the rest to fight individually, while the supporting battery commander had been severely wounded and the accompanying observation post could not establish communications.

The Royal Wiltshire Yeomanry was at first held up by a line of Hawkins mines planted by British infantry, and these had to be cleared by 6th Field Company New Zealand Engineers. Led by the Crusader squadron in their newly issued tanks, the Yeomanry also found itself in the middle of the Axis anti-tank gun line and were engaged by guns on all sides while surrounded by masses of infantry. The commanding officer, second in command and squadron leaders' tanks were all among the early casualties, depriving the unit of any measure of control.[48] Yet here there was almost a breakthrough. B Squadron's attack was a complete success, getting right in among the enemy positions on the Rahman Track. Major 'Tim' Gibbs thought the battle won as his tanks went up and down crushing the trails of enemy guns. But as the sky paled 'the whole world seemed to blow up at once', and in two minutes the squadron was reduced to just two tanks.[49]

On the left the Warwickshire Yeomanry soon accounted for four Italian guns. For some 1,200 yards all seemed to go well as it approached the Rahman Track. But, as the unit advanced, the fire directed upon it intensified to a terrible fury. Clive Stoddart's tank was the first to be hit, turning white on impact and bursting into flames. Four of the crew managed to get out and sheltered in a trench from which they evicted a German and watched as several more tanks were hit. 'I just looked and shivered,' recalled Stoddart.[50]

Lieutenant H. S. Robertson of 5th Seaforth Highlanders literally had a worm's-eye view:

> At dawn our tanks came up and began fighting their battle right in amongst us, manoeuvring for position and firing while what seemed like every tank and anti-tank gun in the Afrika Korps fired back. Solid shot was ricocheting all over the place and there was H[igh] E[xplosive] too. The whole show was fantastic. Some of our lads had to skin out of their trenches several times to avoid being run over. One Sherman backed towards me. The Tankie saw me, worked round my trench, and stopped a yard or so away. I looked up, and there was a ruddy great gun-barrel hanging over my head. There was one hell of a bang, and showers of sand came down on top of us. The Boche fired back, but missed: we heard the shell go by a few feet away.[51]

'During the morning,' noted 90th Light Division's war diary, 'the fighting reached a climax. Smoke and dust covered the battlefield, and visibility became so bad that the general picture was of one immense cloud of dust and smoke. Tanks engaged in single combat; in these few hours the battle of Alamein was decided.'[52] Each surviving tank was fighting its own individual battle, engaging guns, tanks and machine-guns at close range.

Making his way back, Stoddart found a damaged tank and used the radio to ask what the situation was. 'My call-sign on air was "Charlie" . . . I was answered in English by a German who said "Charlie you have been *very* quiet lately, I hope you haven't been in trouble, but isn't it nice to see all your beautiful new toys going up in smoke – over!" ' Stoddart was ordered to take over C Squadron, and found Major John Lakin on the way. After a hasty swig of the latter's whisky, they boarded another tank. When Stoddart reached Lieutenant-Colonel Guy Jackson's tank,

> [Jackson] was looking bigger and more ferocious to the Germans than ever – quite by himself – and his horse so lame that he couldn't do anything *except* look big and ferocious. Nothing would have induced him to go back, and so the Germans went back. Several more of us joined Guy, we shot, and the Germans went back further, they shot at us and Guy still wonderfully cheerful on the wireless kept on saying 'The fox will break cover any moment now and the hunt will start – don't go back a yard.'[53]

The dwindling number of survivors kept firing, defying the enemy guns.

The 3rd Hussars started the morning with 35 tanks, but by 1000 hours 'had only seven tanks left in action including my own and my rear link's', reported Farquhar. 'In addition my only means of communication with these tanks was for either myself or Captain Eveleigh, who I had picked up, to walk round and give each one orders individually. I told them we would not withdraw and that they were to form line on either side of my tank, and conform to my movements.'[54]

Throughout the battle, Currie was in the thick of the action. Seeing one tank take evasive action after several near misses, he drove his own tank alongside and shouted above the din, as armour-piercing shot whistled between them, 'Where the hell are you going, you windy little . . .? Get on!'[55] But there is only so much that flesh and blood can stand, and the tanks' armour offered little protection. With only 19 tanks left in the brigade, Currie finally ordered their withdrawal east of the Rahman Track shortly after 0900 hours, whence they continued to engage the Axis guns while waiting for 2nd Armoured Brigade to move forward and exploit the gaps they had created.

People at home could hear the battle for themselves, as Godfrey Talbot of the BBC reported the advance. With the sound of 9th Lancers' tracks rattling in the background throughout, he described the scene. 'It's the night of Sunday/Monday November 1st/2nd and it's the early hours of the morning, and now on this desert, with the sand clouds whirling up behind each vehicle, British tanks are moving into battle.'[56] Second Armoured Brigade began to come forward slowly, with the 9th Lancers and 10th Hussars leading the Queen's Bays echeloned to the right.[57] But they were soon halted by anti-tank fire. 'When the mist lifted and it became fully light,' noted the Queen's Bays' historian, 'the enemy guns were clearly visible, and it was possible to see their gun-crews reloading after each shot.' Briggs wanted 2nd Armoured Brigade to push on, although his orders were to not to support 9th Armoured Brigade's advance but to engage the enemy's armour on ground of his own choosing. Brigadier A. F. Fisher, however, could see that his regiments were as well deployed as possible and that there was no further progress to be made. He came up in his Grant and told them to 'stick it out where they were'.[58]

'From then on the day was about the worst we ever had,' recalled the 9th Lancers' history. 'For hours on end the whack of armour-piercing shot on armour plate was unceasing. Then the enemy tank attacks started. Out of the haze in serried lines they came, the low, black tanks . . . It went on like this throughout the day, tanks regularly running out of ammunition and the lorries rushing forward to replenish them.'[59] Behind the Lancers, 8th Armoured Brigade was facing north and 7th Motor Brigade deployed into the heavily shelled salient. At 1037 hours Montgomery intervened, directing that 8th Armoured Brigade be relieved from its position ('I will take care of that') and move west around the southern flank of 2nd Armoured Brigade. The Staffordshire Yeomanry was engaging enemy tanks to the north, but 3rd Royal Tank Regiment and the Sherwood Rangers were able to conform. It was obvious by now that a large tank battle was brewing as 21st Panzer Division assembled, its moves traced by Y intercepts.[60] Jack Merewood of the Queen's Bays recalled that, as the fighting grew fiercer, 'the barrel of our machine-gun began to glow and then became white hot as the bullets passed through it. Ron worked like a demon, and I was firing the guns as fast as we could load them. We moved like robots – no time to think.'[61]

The remains of 9th Armoured Brigade were now under command of 1st Armoured Division, and fought all day in what Freyberg described as 'a grim and gallant battle right in the enemy gun line'.[62] Generalmajor Gustav von Värst, the commander of 15th Panzer Division, had ordered counter-thrusts as early as 0400 hours, but these had made slow progress. At 1100 and again at 1400 hours von Thoma himself led attacks in a desperate and violent attempt to restore the line. 'The British did not make any more ground during the day but all our counter-attacks broke against the solid wall of English tanks . . . which used their superior weapons and never allowed our tanks to get within effective range.'[63] In this battle 8th Panzer Regiment's tank strength was finally wiped out, and Oberst Willy Teege died with his men. Thirty-third Panzer Artillery Regiment almost suffered the same fate, although a few men managed to escape the cauldron with seven guns.[64] The Axis lost 77 panzers and 40 Italian tanks to the combined fire of tanks, anti-tank guns and artillery: it was a crippling loss.

By 1530 hours on the afternoon of 2 November, Rommel was considering beginning to pull back his front line that night. He only awaited von Thoma's report from DAK, which when it came was bleak: 'The line is intact but thin. And tomorrow we'll only have thirty or at most thirty-five panzers fit for action. There are no more reserves.' Rommel decided he had no choice but to fall back, although this was not something he would admit explicitly to Rome and Berlin.[65]

The Royal Wiltshire Yeomanry had been practically destroyed for the second time and its four remaining tanks joined the Warwickshire Yeomanry, while its attached company of 14th Sherwood Foresters, under Captain R. M. Dick, established a defensive area incorporating some anti-tank guns from other units. This held its ground until after dark, when Dick was ordered to withdraw.[66] The brigade lost 31 officers and 198 men killed wounded or missing, but claimed to have destroyed 40 anti-tank guns and 18 tanks and to have taken 400 prisoners.[67]

19

The Beginning of the End

The full story will never be told since so many of those that
could fill in the details are no longer here to recount them.
This action, condemned by many as an incorrect and costly
method of using armour, was fought to a finish with great
gallantry and devotion to duty.

Brigadier John Currie[1]

In an account in 1967, Montgomery wrote that 'if the British armour
owed any debt to the infantry of Eighth Army, the debt was paid on
November 2nd by 9th Armoured Brigade in heroism and blood'.[2] His
handling of armour throughout the battle has been criticized, and never
more so than in this instance. But Supercharge had driven a rectangular
wedge into the Axis positions. Montgomery later complained that
'every gun was reported as an 88 mm', but tankies knew the difference –
50 mm rounds flashed red as they went past; 88 mm rounds were white
and known as 'tennis balls'.[3] Most British tank casualties came from
smaller weapons, including the extremely effective 7.62 cm weapon that
the Germans mounted on old Panzer Mark II chassis. This was
extremely dangerous, being less conspicuous than the 88 mm but very
powerful.[4] DAK had started the battle with eighty-six 88s and sixty-
eight 76.2s, but also 290 of the excellent 50 mm Pak 38 guns.[5] Now their
numbers had been severely written down, and with panzer strength also
critically low it was difficult to see what the gap in the Axis line could be
plugged with. Von Thoma was to attribute Rommel's defeat to the
British gunners' destruction of half his anti-tank guns.[6]

During the day, 39 Squadron RAF, half of which had moved from
Malta to Egypt a month earlier, carried out an Ultra-directed attack on
the small merchantman *Zara* (1,976 tons), which had been spotted by
Wellingtons of 221 Squadron and torpedoed by others of 38 and 458
Squadrons, then taken into tow as part of a convoy that had been
temporarily 'lost'.[7] Tedder gave the squadron a pep talk stressing the

importance of attacking Rommel's supply position at this crucial stage, and the six worn-out Beauforts with time-expired crews, escorted by six Beaufighters from 272 Squadron, took off at 0625 hours on the hunch that the convoy had turned west to avoid the search and would probably be hugging the coast. 'We had guessed right,' recalled Charles Grant:

> we found the ships where we had hoped and in the right position, our 'turn in' position had been bang on and we were able to get between the ships and the shore and dive to the attack from an unexpected quarter and drop the torpedoes before the defences were fully alert. Then we were on our way and out to sea – but nevertheless we lost two Beauforts in the ensuing mêlée.

A third of the torpedo bombers had been lost in one morning. (The chances of a strike crew surviving a tour were a paltry 17.5 per cent, and of surviving a second tour only 3 per cent – the lowest chances of any aircrew.) The *Zara* certainly went down, and a similar ship, the 1,987-ton *Bironi*, loaded with fuel, was reported to have blown up in Tobruk harbour during an air raid by five US Liberators.[8]

Horrocks, on a visit to Eighth Army Headquarters, found Montgomery sitting in a deckchair with a cap over his eyes when a formation of bombers flew overhead. 'They are winning this battle for me,' said Montgomery.[9] The DAF flew 233 light-bomber and 651 fighter sorties on 2 November, and by dusk had dropped a total of 352 tons of bombs (100 tons more than during the first 24 hours of Lightfoot). 'So accurate and effective was the bombing – and so rapid the communications between our forward positions and Air Support Control,' noted 3 Wing SAAF's operational record – 'that on one occasion even before 3 Wing's bombers had landed, a flash signal came through that as a result of that raid 200 enemy troops had immediately surrendered.' This was later confirmed by a message from X Corps to Eighth Army that 'at 1534 hours the 1st Armoured Division reported that the last bombing raid was extremely effective and 200 of the enemy surrendered.' This particular raid comprised 18 Bostons of 12 Squadron SAAF dropping seventy-two 250 lb bombs.[10] The Luftwaffe throughout continued to try to interfere – once with 12 Stukas and once with 40, both groups escorted by fighters. But the first attack was met by Hurricanes of 33 and 239 Squadrons RAF and the second by 213 Squadron RAF and 1 Squadron SAAF. Outnumbered and outfought, the Axis air forces could manage only one sortie for every five flown by the DAF.[11] The effectiveness of Allied air control was attested by the captured diary of a German artillery officer: 'Where are our fighters, our Stukas and AA? Can't see a thing of them. Tommy comes every quarter of an hour with eighteen heavy bombers.'[12]

Montgomery wanted 1st Armoured Division to continue applying pressure north of Tel el Aqqaqir while features to the south of the funnel formed by Supercharge would be seized in order to pass 7th Armoured Division through.[13] The immediate objective entailed 2nd Seaforth Highlanders taking Skinflint, a ring contour 1,500 yards south of the funnel. This was attacked by 50th Royal Tank Regiment at 1815 hours, supported by eight regiments of artillery. Soon after, 2nd Royal Sussex Regiment finally secured Snipe; both operations 'went like a drill' and, significantly, all the prisoners taken were Italians.[14]

Although this had not been apparent at first light on 2 November, the launch of Supercharge had also relieved the pressure on The Saucer, and, apart from sporadic shelling, it proved a quiet day in the Australian sector. Patrols that night could not seriously interfere with organized withdrawal by the Axis forces, and much vehicle noise was noted. Daylight patrolling on the 3rd soon revealed that positions opposite were being abandoned, and the battalion diarist noted that it was the first day that 2/17th Battalion of 20th Australian Brigade had not been shelled since 23 October.[15]

The main effort during the night of 2 November – an attempt by 7th Motor Brigade to seize the Rahman Track along a 2-mile front stretching north-east from Tel el Aqqaqir – ended in failure. The decision to attack was not taken until 2030 hours, and there was no opportunity for reconnaissance. The London Rifle Brigade had remained in its unpleasant location for four days when 2nd Rifle Brigade – having had only a short time to recover from its ordeal at Snipe and now commanded by Tom Pearson – moved up to take its place on 29 October, in order to serve as the minefield task force for Supercharge. After reorganization, the London Rifle Brigade had then returned to 7th Motor Brigade. It was clear that the Axis forces were giving way and that at any moment the next minefield might be the last. The armour was held up once more by anti-tank guns, and the infantry in the funnel – including the two Rifle Brigade battalions – took their share of punishment from enemy shelling. Seventh Motor Brigade would now attack at 0200 hours. The objective of 2nd/60th Rifles would be Tel el Aqqaqir, the London Rifle Brigade was to secure the Rahman Track, and 2nd Rifle Brigade was to advance some 1,000 yards beyond it – all presupposing that the defenders opposite had evacuated their positions.

The 2nd/60th's attack was successful, covering some 2,000 yards against negligible opposition before digging in. But the battalion was soon counter-attacked by a dozen or so tanks, and held on only after a severe fight in which half the Axis tanks were knocked out for the loss of five out of eight anti-tank guns from the accompanying battery.[16] The London Rifle Brigade, with D Company leading, followed a compass bearing. When they reached what the company commander thought was the objective, the commanding officer thought they should go slightly further forward to make sure. When they did so, they ran straight into a wall of fire that the defenders had been holding until the last possible moment. Sergeant Main recalled that 'Above the sound of the explosions I heard the company commander, Major Trappes-Lomax, shout: "Up the Rifle Brigade! Charge!" ' With no cover to protect them, the lead platoons plunged into the darkness and contact with them was soon lost. 'Trappes-Lomax disappeared through a hail of tracer bullets. I felt he couldn't go in by himself so I gave the order to charge,' said Main. 'I went through the enfilade fire and I couldn't understand how I had not been hit. It was like daylight with the flares and mortar explosions. Sergeant Brine had run straight into a German machinegun. He was hit all over and before he died he asked to be placed facing the enemy.'[17]

Any attempt at movement brought down heavy fire, and no progress could be made. Sergeant Main found himself in the rear of the German position with two other riflemen.

> We heard a German NCO shout 'English swine right, fire!' Fortunately the machine-gun fired just over our heads as it could not be lowered to fire into the slight depression in which we were lying. From where I lay we could see an 88 mm gun at least fifty yards away. I decided to go for this and as I ran with rifle and bayonet, tracer from a German machine-gun was going all around me. However, I considered that if I continued running I would not be hit and eventually reached the gun followed by several riflemen.[18]

In the confusion, the anti-tank guns began to drive slowly up to the position, thinking that the success signal had been fired. They were soon disillusioned into beating a hasty retreat and, with Brigade Headquarters realizing that the position was untenable, the battalion was ordered to withdraw. D Company had a difficult time, sustaining some 50 casualties in total, but when the roll was called it was found that, overall, losses had been miraculously light.

Meanwhile, 2nd Rifle Brigade had advanced with two companies leading and the third to mop up. Once again the fighting proved tough, as the defence came to life after the lead companies had passed and mopping up proved more than a single company could cope with. The anti-tank guns were unable to come forward in the face of withering mortar and machine-gun fire, and the forward infantry were then counter-attacked by ten tanks, assisted by flares dropped by the RAF west of Tel el Aqqaqir. At about 0400 hours, with no anti-tank guns to counter the threat of enemy tanks, Pearson obtained permission from brigade to withdraw. At Snipe, an epic action had cost 10 officers and 38 men. Now, the regimental historian recorded bitterly, 'in this trifling, inconsequent, nameless battle, of which no one has ever heard and which ended in undignified retreat, the casualties were nearly as many and individually quite as important. Such is the fortune of war.'[19]

But failure did not end there: 4th/6th South African Armoured Car Regiment, under the impression that the infantry had taken Tel el Aqqaqir, ran into many obstacles such as scattered mines and disused gun pits. C Squadron first failed to get forward, and when B Squadron tried to take over the lead it also failed, making the unit doubly determined to succeed.[20]

Despite this disappointment for the Allies, 3 November was to be a grim day for the Axis forces. Even where seeking only local decisions, their counter-attacks had failed and, unlike the British, they could not replace their losses. Rommel had already been thinning out his rear elements for 48 hours, but now he recognized that the moment he had known to be inevitable for several days had arrived. On the evening of 2 November he had signalled Comando Supremo that it was unlikely that much of the Italian infantry could be saved, owing to its immobility; nevertheless, that night they had started to march to the west.[21] Sottotenente Michele Ciudolo was the medical officer of 19th Infantry Regiment. He recalled a bitter sense of this being 'the beginning of the end'. His unit was ordered to withdraw across the desert, starting at midnight, and his own responsibilities were to pick up any casualties from the long column, although he was desperately short of both medical supplies and water.[22]

Now on the morning of 3 November, Rommel sent his aide Berndt personally to inform Hitler that 'the African theatre of operation is probably lost to us. Ask for complete freedom of action for Panzerarmee.'[23] Rommel had authorized the Italians in the south to withdraw when at 1300 hours on 3 November he received an order from Hitler. The Führer told him that there could be 'no other thought but to stand fast, yield not a metre of ground, and throw every gun and every man into battle', and that to his troops 'you can show no other road than that to victory or death'.[24] Unwilling or unable to circumvent Hitler's more lunatic pronouncements at this stage of the war, Rommel ordered the army halted and the issuing of weapons and hand grenades to his staff. 'You are to fight to the utmost,' he signalled von Thoma. 'You have got to instil this order into your troops – they are to fight to the very limit.' That night Major Elmar Warning sat up with Rommel as he argued with his conscience. 'If I *do* obey the Führer's order then there's the danger that my troops won't obey me.' Then suddenly he snapped. 'The Führer is crazy . . .' He had reached a turning point in his life.[25]

The difficulty for the Axis was illustrated in a message issued by DAK to its subordinate formations at about 1100 hours: 'The only measure left to us is to initiate a mobile defensive policy and withdraw a little to regain to regain freedom of manoeuvre . . . We can do this without abandoning our main policy of defending the Alamein front.' But Rommel was not at this stage prepared to deceive Hitler, and he issued his own order authorizing DAK to fall back to its first bound, which was to be defended 'to the last man', followed soon after by more exhortations 'to retain possession of the battlefield'. Later Rommel would claim that had he only circumvented Hitler's order he could have saved Panzerarmee.[26] But this ignores the parlous state of Axis communications, particularly where Italian headquarters were involved; the task of halting the withdrawal – which had in any case begun some 15 hours before the halt order was received – was an impossible one. Unfortunately, many of the records of lower-level units and formations were lost or destroyed at this stage in the battle, and the detailed effects of Rommel's orders on the ground is obscure. Certainly German units continued to resist fiercely whenever they were encountered, but many Italian units were already on the move and continued to withdraw.

Hitler's order completely upset the effective use of transport to ferry the men back. In the rear areas, transport was being loaded with whatever stores could be carried, and dumps that could not be cleared were being prepared for demolition. Rommel's indecision over how to handle Hitler's directive led to disorder, as some convoys were allowed to proceed while others had to halt or were turned back and railway wagons were left without locomotives – all of which increased the congestion on the supply routes and offered tempting targets for the DAF. Armin Köhler of the Luftwaffe wrote in his diary:

> Nine British armoured cars drove up six kilometres south of the landing ground. We flew to Quotifiya. The latter half of the day was made a hell for us at Quotifiya. Continuous bombing attacks with eighteen to twenty-four four-engined aircraft with fighter-bombers and low-flying aircraft rattled our nerves. We never got out of our slit trenches. The Tommies were playing cat and mouse with us. Aircraft above aircraft in the sky – but never a German.[27]

During the afternoon and evening of 3 November, Panzerarmee was completely off balance – protected only by a thin line of rearguards – while DAK was by now reduced to 24 battle-worthy panzers.

Montgomery knew nothing of Hitler's disastrous intervention, but Australians patrolling near the coast found abandoned and booby-trapped positions. Only when they moved towards Sidi Abd el Rahman did they meet opposition. Further south, observation suggested a major withdrawal, but, having negotiated the complicated and still heavily mined and booby-trapped line of outpost positions, patrols were invariably stopped by strongpoints covering the minefields. Most of XIII Corps advanced into the outpost zone, but nowhere was the enemy forced back against his will other than where 2nd Fighting French Brigade overran a strongpoint around Point 104. Horrocks considered several plans to overwhelm these rearguards, but without armour, and with only enough transport to sustain his corps, no major action could be made that would fit into Montgomery's plans.[28]

At the beginning of the battle, 8th Armoured Division had been temporarily broken up. It had never possessed a lorried infantry brigade, and 24th Armoured Brigade had been posted to 10th Armoured Division. Similarly, its divisional troops had been designated 'Hammerforce' (after the Royal Artillery commander Brigadier A. G. 'Hammer' Mathew), and this had held and administered various units not immediately required in the battle line. On the evening of 3 November, Hammerforce was dissolved, most of its component parts reverting to command of 8th Armoured Division to prepare for Operation Grapeshot – a plan that had been made for rapid exploitation should the Axis suddenly abandon its positions. This intended that a mobile force would rush to seize Tobruk within six days, and was expected to include a strong RAF element, but was never carried out.[29] The force began to assemble on 3 November, but was steadily drained of troops for other more immediate tasks and the whole plan was eventually cancelled.[30]

Although it was now true that the battle could not be lost by the Allies, it could not be won until the enemy was broken, and there was still no sure sign of this. Montgomery had decided that another assault was necessary to crack open the Axis line, although he was now desperately short of infantry with which to make it. Also, the strong moon that had lit the way early on was both waning and rising later. It was now D+11, and nervous and physical strain approaching the level of exhaustion affected everyone in Eighth Army as much as on the Axis side. Still the supply services brought forward the essential ammunition, fuel, food and water without which the battle would grind to a halt, churning in low gear through axle-deep dust, eyes strained through lack of sleep. Equally the staffs – so often maligned by those who have never experienced the pressure of their work – continued to prepare plans and monitor their fronts. For Brigadier George Walsh, Leese's BGS, the battle had been ten days of constant crisis, and there had been no time to wonder whether it was being won or lost. 'It was all very well for Monty to express his confidence, but for most of us it was really touch-and-go to the end.'[31]

Montgomery entrusted the final assaults to 51st (Highland) Division, with 5th Indian Brigade under command. The first of its tasks on 3 November fell to 5th/7th Gordon Highlanders, which would attack with 8th Royal Tank Regiment south-westward across the Rahman Track through the position that 2nd Seaforth Highlanders had taken the night before. During the day there had been great controversy over the location of the feature to be attacked, which the Seaforths maintained they were already sitting on. Their supporting gunners, who, being sur-veyed in, professed they could not be wrong, fired some rounds to prove their contention, but these fell among the Seaforths' leading companies and the armour had their own ideas.[32]

H-Hour was set for 1800 hours, but only one squadron of tanks arrived on time. A message was then received from 152nd Brigade (to which the battalion was now attached) that the enemy was withdrawing and no air or artillery barrage was needed, but that smoke would be laid. The commanding officer decided that the quickest course would be to send forward some of his Jocks mounted on the tanks while the rest of the battalion followed at best speed, and the remainder of 8th Royal Tank Regiment arrived as B and C Companies were eagerly mounting the lead tanks. They drove forward, but were almost immediately struck from both flanks by anti-tank guns and machine-guns and were in des-perate need of artillery support, which for once was not forthcoming. Six tanks were destroyed and another 11 damaged, while the poor bloody infantry suffered, as ever, even more grievously; 4 officers and 14 men were killed, and another 4 officers and 46 men wounded.[33] Wimberley 'saw these tanks coming out of action and they were covered with the bodies of my Highlanders'. He was deeply moved, and said over the telephone to Leese, 'surely it's not necessary to continue like this'. Leese replied, 'It surprises me that you of all people should say this.'[34]

During the night of 2/3 November 2nd Fighting French Brigade had relieved 69th Brigade, and the latter took over positions on Ruweisat Ridge from 7th Indian Brigade, which in turn relieved 5th Indian Brigade, which went into XXX Corps reserve the following morning. This formation would now attack south-west towards the Rahman Track in conjunction with and under command of 152nd

Brigade. Once more, a narrow frontage would be cleared by a heavy artillery barrage.

Fifth Indian Brigade was faced with an approach march of 12 miles over unknown tracks, followed by another 5 miles at night to bring it to its battle position. Trudging through the deep and powder-fine dust in the confusion of tracks, it was spotted by enemy aircraft and dive-bombed. By 0100 hours it became apparent that the brigade would not be ready in time, and the commander – Brigadier D. 'Pasha' Russell – requested a delay of one hour. The delay was arranged, but 3rd/10th Baluch Regiment was bogged in soft sand, and only two incomplete battalions – 1/4th Essex Regiment and 4th/6th Rajputana Rifles – supported by 50th Royal Tank Regiment, managed to cross the start line, covered by the most intense barrage yet.

It was described thus by an Indian Army public relations officer:

> It looked like a cloud had suddenly risen out of a fissure in the earth, a steady and constant thickness of smoke and dust, where 400 guns cast their shells, one gun to every two yards of ground. It was a cataract of steel which poured down out of the air, churning the earth into powder. Down each side fireworks ran – Bofors guns firing tracer as flank guides. Minute by minute the crescendo heightened and deepened until at 0400 hours, slowly, inexorably, like a machine when power surges into its dead metal, the Wedge began to move. The drive had begun . . . The men who led the advance told me that in that thirty minutes while they waited for the curtain of steel to be woven, there came to them a wonderful feeling of confidence. The Wedge was so exact that they felt the barrage to be part of themselves; a weapon in their hands; as an airman feels when the earth has slipped away from him, when his engines beat sweet and true and he knows he has great power within his grasp. The Indians moved forward not as men ahead of guns but as men behind a shield.[35]

There was little fighting to be done: it was largely a case of collecting the demoralized occupants of dugouts and trenches, although a few panzergrenadiers sought to sell their lives dearly. According to one young officer of the Essex Regiment, it was 'engrossing' to follow a storm of fire for over three hours, 'but after a while, it seemed a bit lonely. I was rather pleased when, a little before dawn, I saw some shapes in the gloom, and realized that we had somebody with us.'[36] That 'somebody' was the armoured cars of 4th/6th South African Armoured Car Regiment.

In the early hours of 4 November 5th Indian Brigade made the decisive breakthrough 5 miles south of Tel el Aqqaqir at the southern end of the gun screen, although only 1/4th Essex Regiment and two companies of 4th/6th Rajputana Rifles actually gained the objective.[37] In the process, however, they took 351 prisoners (1/4th Essex Regiment took 237), at a cost of 80 casualties.

At 0540 hours on 4 November, Lieutenant-Colonel Reeves-Moore finally led his South African armoured cars into the Axis rear area, 'the eager children of any mechanized pursuit . . . scampered at dawn into the open desert beyond the mines and trenches and guns, to make their exuberant mischief amid the disintegrating enemy'.[38] They passed through a mass of enemy vehicles, whose occupants obviously thought the Springboks were friendly, until by 0630 hours they were in the open desert. They soon started causing the havoc they had been sent for: A Squadron captured two 88 mms, two 105 mm guns, two 110 mm guns, a Breda portee, six trucks and 130 prisoners, while B Squadron picked up five trucks and a staff car, one 105 mm, one 150 mm gun and 100 prisoners.[39]

Meanwhile the artillery was switching to support an attack by 7th Argyll and Sutherland Highlanders on Point 44. The battalion left its position in the El Wishka area, north of its old position on Nairn, at 0130 hours and marched for some 5 miles before finding itself in 5th Cameron Highlanders' area somewhat too far to the right when the barrage opened. It therefore began to advance immediately on a bearing of 280 degrees instead of the 203 degrees originally intended. At 0615 hours after covering about 1,000 yards, it found itself disappearing into the smoke laid by the guns to cover it over half way to the objective, which was reached some half an hour later – the position being almost entirely unoccupied. Unfortunately, however, the Highlanders had lost 8 killed and 23 wounded mostly to some British guns that were firing short. Tragic though this was, it was hardly surprising given that they approached from an unexpected angle and after the colossal number of rounds that had been put through the barrels during the preceding 11 days of battle, which had created tremendous wear on them – hence the tendency to fire short. On the objective they found an abandoned divisional headquarters with valuable documents, Chianti and champagne: a newspaper at home reported, 'The Boche got the wind up and the Argylls got the wine.' The Jocks also invested their commanding officer with the Iron Cross from a stock they found on the position, and others were later seen wandering around similarly decorated.[40]

Steadily over the preceding nights 1st South African Division had relieved 51st (Highland) Division for its new tasks. On the night of 1 November, 1st Natal Mounted Rifles took over from 5th Black Watch on Stirling, where some of the positions were only 500 yards from the enemy. Major A. Blamey, who had long experience in East and North Africa, could not help thinking that the Jocks could have saved themselves many casualties had they learned to dig deeper and site their automatic weapons better.[41] Elsewhere, 1st/2nd Field Force Battalion relieved 5th/7th Gordon Highlanders, whose affiliated regiment, 1st Cape Town Highlanders, took over from 7th Black Watch north-west of The Beehive on the night of 31 October, the latter having lost 78 dead (including 6 officers) and 183 wounded (13 officers).[42] Further moves followed as the enemy front began to break up and the threat of counter-attack receded, until on the morning of 4 November, after a night that was shattered by an intense barrage fired over their heads in support of 5th Indian Brigade's attack, 1st Cape Town Highlanders awoke to an eerie quiet. The enemy had gone, and shortly the desert was filled with every type of vehicle, armoured or otherwise, moving forward.[43]

Dawn on 4 November brought Eighth Army news of victory and, in the heavy morning mist, a traffic jam that surpassed all experience. With one exception, the armoured brigades had reverted to their original parent formations (4th Light Armoured Brigade was attached to 2nd New Zealand Division to replace 9th Armoured Brigade), and all three armoured divisions were trying to get through the same narrow funnel south of the Supercharge salient. It was almost 0800 hours before the mist cleared and armoured cars of 12th Lancers crossed Tel el Aqqaqir Ridge to see what barred the way to El Daba – it was the remains of DAK.

In the air it had also been a complete victory for Tedder, who had throughout involved the entire Middle East Air Forces. Between 23 October and 4 November the DAF flew 10,405 sorties, with the Americans adding 1,181. British losses had been 77 aircraft, and the Americans had lost 20. Axis sorties totalled 1,550 German and an estimated 1,570 Italian, with losses of 64 and 20 aircraft respectively.[44] However, the Desert War was a 'war for aerodromes', and the DAF continued to concentrate on battlefield support rather than harassing the column of retreating Axis transport: before striking further west, its commanders preferred to wait until ground troops had cleared the landing grounds at Sidi Haneish and El Daba, thus reducing the risk of being intercepted by enemy aircraft.[45]

Defeat was never going to weaken the resolve of the Axis rearguards, and one of the first casualties was the tank carrying Briggs, commanding 1st Armoured Division. So Briggs was forced to withdraw the armour and to bring up artillery to deal with this line of resistance, which slowly but inevitably was driven off.[46]

While the morning battle was in progress, Kesselring arrived once more at Rommel's headquarters, where he received an extremely cold reception. Rommel suspected that he had been sent to ensure that Hitler's 'crazy' order was being carried out, and was overcome with bitterness, having always felt that Hitler trusted him. Instead he was surprised to discover that Kesselring agreed with his sentiments, if not his choice of words. 'I would be inclined to regard Hitler's order as an appeal, rather than a binding order,' he said, and went on to point out that Panzerarmee was no longer holding the line referred to in the order but was now in the open desert. When Rommel replied that he regarded the directive as binding, Kesselring was emphatic: 'The Führer cannot have intended for your army to perish here.' Both marshals then sent messages to Berlin requesting that the order be withdrawn.[47]

At Führer Headquarters the gravity of the situation at Alamein had not been apparent for some time. A dispatch sent at around 1000 hours on 2 November in which Rommel reported the British breakthrough as a result of Supercharge and requested permission to withdraw 60 miles to Fuka did not reach Generaloberst Alfred Jodl, head of the operations branch, until the morning of 3 November. A reserve major who was duty officer had received the message at 0300 hours and had scanned the contents only superficially, failing to notice that it differed significantly from its predecessor by announcing that the retreat had begun. He filed it for use in compiling the morning situation report, and it was noticed only at 0800 hours, whereupon it was reported to Jodl, who in turn told the OKW chief, Generalfeldmarschall Wilhelm Keitel, and they then told Hitler.[48]

Jodl knew that Hitler's order of 2 November had been drafted several days earlier with the aim of stimulating morale and that it was based on the assumption that, although it was serious, the situation was not catastrophic. Hitler was becoming increasingly irrational, however; he had dismissed Halder as Chief of the General Staff in September, and was beginning to use words like 'annihilate' in his orders.[49] In his private quarters, the latest news prompted an explosion. 'Why have I only just received Rommel's report on the situation? Why was it not shown to me last night? Why wasn't I woken? Why?!?' he screamed. When Jodl began, 'the major thought . . .' Hitler cut him off. 'Couldn't he see that the order I had just sent put me in the wrong on the African position?' By the day's end the major was on his way to a punishment battalion as a private.[50] Hitler also dismissed his head of section, Generalmajor Walter Warlimont, but some time later was persuaded to restore both officers to their former positions.[51]

Von Thoma had personally organized the DAK Kampfstaffel (Headquarters Escort Group) and the remains of 90th Light Division into a rearguard line. When DAK's Chief of Staff, Oberst Fritz

Bayerlein, found his chief, von Thoma was wearing his medals – something nobody did in Africa. 'The Fuhrer's order is unparalleled madness,' von Thoma told Bayerlein. 'I can't go along with this any longer.' He then ordered Baylerein to establish DAK Headquarters at El Daba, declaring that 'I shall personally take charge of the defence [line].' At 1100 hours von Thoma's aide-de-camp, Leutnant Hartdegen, arrived at the newly established DAK Headquarters to report to Bayerlein that von Thoma's force was all but destroyed. Bayerlein jumped into a small reconnaissance car and raced back to the front, and from the crest of a dune he saw that this was true. Von Thoma was standing beside a burning panzer amid rattling machine-gun fire, and it seemed a miracle to Bayerlein that he was unscathed. Von Thoma was then approached by a scout car backed by two Shermans. At the same time, 150 fighting vehicles poured forward like a flood. 'I ran off westwards as fast as my legs could carry me,' recalled Bayerlein.[52]

Captain Grant Washington Singer – 'an officer of exceptional charm and outstanding gallantry', commanding 10th Hussars' Internal Communication Troop – had been alerted to the panzer's presence and arrived at the tail end of the battle in his scout car.[53] The panzer put a shot through the back of his driver's seat, and Singer directed the fire of a supporting British Grant tank, which disabled the panzer, whose crew baled out. When the firing died away, the scout car approached and was met by a dusty figure. 'I thought I might as well collar him,' said Singer.[54] Reginald Vine of the Royal Wiltshire Yeomanry's Light Aid Detachment was watching. 'A distinguished looking chap, rather forlorn, came out of the dust cloud, wearing field uniform and equipment, not like a British brass hat. He looked quite a gentleman, I did not know who he was at the time.' Trooper Lindsay was Singer's driver, and later recalled him as 'the finest officer I ever served under'. Singer and Lindsay went forward to collect the prisoner, who 'walked forward, then stopped, saluted Captain Singer and handed over his pistol. Both officers then shook hands.' Von Thoma introduced himself in English, and took his field glasses from around his neck and hung them on Lindsay's. Singer and Lindsay then drove him to Eighth Army Tactical Headquarters, before returning to the battle.[55] Bayerlein ran to the west. When he told the story to Rommel and Westphal, the latter exclaimed, 'For God's sake, Bayerlein, keep it to yourself – otherwise Thoma's entire family will have to suffer for it.'[56]

The day after taking the surrender of the commander of the Deutsches Afrikakorps, Captain Grant Singer was killed.* In the

---

*On hearing the news, von Thoma wrote a touching letter of sympathy to Singer's father.

meantime there was still much bitter fighting on 4 November. To the south, 7th Armoured Division drove south of the Rahman Track through the area taken by 5th Indian Brigade; 22nd Armoured Brigade ran headlong into Ariete Division, which still had 100-odd tanks and was in touch with 15th Panzer Division on its northern flank. If the Italian armour was qualitatively less formidable than that of the Germans, this formation was still most effective and clearly too much for Roberts to deal with. Harding was forced to bring forward the remainder of his division, and an artillery battle raged for most of the morning and into the afternoon with hardly any manoeuvring from either side. At last light the Axis forces withdrew, leaving the field to the British with the shells of 29 Italian tanks and some 450 prisoners. Effectively, the entire Italian motorized XX Corps – including the Ariete and Littorio Armoured Divisions – had been destroyed, and the repair shops had to blow up 40 tanks before making good their own escape.

Elsewhere Freyberg had been convinced that the enemy was cracking as early as the afternoon of the 3rd, and as soon as he heard news of the Argylls' occupation of Tel el Aqqaqir he set off on a personal recce to try to find a way through to the south. At this point 4th Light Armoured Brigade was reported as being at Alamein station, whereas he wanted it to drive straight to Fuka, some 55 miles to the west. Somehow, the armoured cars and tanks of 2nd Derbyshire Yeomanry and the Royal Scots Greys managed to thread their way through the salient, and Freyberg pressed on to the south and west, avoiding the battle being fought by Harding's 7th Armoured Division. He was desperately keen to get clear of the morass around the salient and from other formations and their battles, and he ordered that water and rations for eight days should be carried, along with 360 rounds for each field gun and petrol for 200 miles. Once he judged he was south of El Daba, he halted to allow the remainder of his column to catch up. Kippenburger's 6th New Zealand Brigade arrived at midnight, when a group of some 70 German parachutists attacked the rear of the column – probably with the aim of capturing transport to make good their escape. Eight Kiwis were killed and another 28 wounded, and Freyberg decided it was important to remain concentrated in this open, featureless and unmapped waste, populated by wandering groups of desperate men.[57]

20

The End of the Beginning

Live and let live.
No matter how it ended,
These lose and, under the sky
Lie befriended.

For foes forgive,
No matter how they hated,
By life so sold and by
Death mated.

John Pudney, 'Graves: El Alamein'

The Battle of Alamein was over. Eleanor Roosevelt recalled a dinner at Buckingham Palace at which Churchill was notably distant. Finally he excused himself and went to telephone Downing Street. He returned singing 'Roll Out the Barrel' with gusto. Later Brooke found Churchill busily dictating signals – including one to Alexander in which he referred to Montgomery not as 'your Monty', but as 'your brilliant lieutenant Montgomery'. The public, however, were painfully used to disappointment. First a defeat would be followed by optimism in the press indicating that matters were in hand and all would soon be well; then another defeat would follow. They expected the worst even now. But when on the night of 4 November the BBC announcer on the radio interrupted the programme to warn listeners not to switch off as the best news in years would be given at midnight, his voice shook with genuine excitement.[1]

'Great News from Egypt' ran the headline in the *Daily Express* on 5 November, and the BBC announcer that morning was unable to conceal his glee: 'I'm going to read you the News and there's some cracking good news coming in . . .' Moyra Charlton, a Wren, woke on 5 November to hear the radio 'jubilantly declaring "The Eighth Army are advancing and the enemy is in full retreat all along the line" . . . Dad was so excited at breakfast that he consumed the whole of his butter ration (that was to last till Saturday) on two pieces of toast.'[2] In America, the journalist C. V. R. Thompson reported that 'there is little talk about America's elections today, it is all about the defeat of Rommel. Montgomery has driven the election off America's front page.'[3] Lillian Bell, a young evacuee in the west of England, had listened to the news of the barrage, the battle and the victory, and later remembered a line in the school play: 'The finest sight in all the world; the Union Jack flying over Benghazi.'[4] There was, however, some way yet to go to reach Benghazi.

Success was less apparent to others. Les Symonds wrote to his wife, 'Ambulance train. Another nursing sister. Another needle. More sleep. An ambulance, a hospital, a ward. A sister is cutting what is left of my clothes. I am washed. Yet another prick in my arm followed by sleep. That is it, Peg darling. My first battle was short and sharp, and I don't think I did much good . . .'[5] Henry Ritchie also found himself in a hospital in Alexandria. 'Christ it was different from the fearful raw life of the gun pit. I couldn't get used to sleeping in a soft bed and I couldn't dispel, or I imagined that I couldn't dispel from my mouth, the acrid taste of cordite.'[6] Battlefield medical arrangements had proved satisfactory, and 7,500 battle casualties and 3,000 sick passed through the casualty system during the period 24–30 October.[7] But it was not surprising that there should be an 'amazing' amount of terror-inspired stuttering among patients in an Australian hospital after the ordeal through which 9th Australian Division had passed.[8] Although comprising only 6 per cent of Eighth Army, the Australians had suffered 22 per cent of its casualties. Jack Craig rejoined his unit immediately after the battle: 'God! They all looked tired and worn out. They were nearly white with dust and sand and all old and ashen faced. There were no boys left now. They had aged years.' Later he was able to buy a case of beer and have 'a good session with Cobber. Yarning of our experiences and those that "bought" it an[d] never came through the battle and finally singing our heads off to blot out the sorrow of losing our mates.'[9]

Rommel had by now realized that further sacrifice was pointless, and, following a conversation with Bayerlein, who had again taken command of DAK, had set off for Fuka. Organized resistance in front of the British ceased, and DAK armour retired to laager until dawn. Allied plans were drawn up for 5 November on the basis that Panzerarmee would offer battle the next day, but reports soon came in from LRDG patrols that Axis traffic was streaming westward, and it was quickly realized that everything must be directed to cutting off as large a portion of Panzerarmee as possible.[10]

On 5 November there were still large bodies of men wandering around the battlefield. According to Lieutenant-Colonel Roper-Caldbeck of 1st Black Watch, it

> was very strange. There was no shelling and no gunfire. The seething mass of
> vehicles had disappeared. The desert all round which for fourteen days had
> been a milling mass of tanks, trucks and lorries was empty. We suddenly real-
> ized that the whole battle had swept forward and we were completely out of
> it . . . it was a very strange feeling . . . we washed ourselves and went to sleep
> again in the sun.[11]

Some among the British did not forget that it was Guy Fawke's Day, and
celebrated by setting off Axis signal flares. The groups of Italian and
German prisoners arriving in a steady flow convinced many on the
British side that this really was it – the war in the desert was finally over:
it was goodbye to the Pam Pam and Sister Street. Certainly very few
would ever return to Cairo or Alexandria.

For many units left behind on the battlefield, these were days of shortage and hard living. Supplies for the front were given priority over units'
ration and water trucks, so that men whose nerves had been steadied by
cigarettes suddenly found there were none available, and very little
water. But others prospered in the immediate aftermath – ironically,
often by relying on the prisoners they were taking, who had no such
problems. It was clear that the Axis quartermasters had thrown open
the stores: the prisoners had cigarettes and wine, bread and Danish
butter.[12] 'We all wallowed in scrumptious food from captured enemy
ration trucks,' wrote Major Lindsay of the Sherwood Rangers – 'fruit,
Macedonian cigarettes, cigars, chocolate washed down with brandy,
Liebfraumilch, Chianti and Champagne.'

Nevertheless, the work of clearing up was essential. Driver Thomas
Rose of 552nd Company RASC 'saw dead Germans laying around,
some blown up and black'. The British dead had already been taken
away. 'We started towing [captured] wooden-wheeled guns towards
Alexandria and Italian rifles, but most never got to their destination.
The wheels collapsed. The road was full of pot holes through shelling,
so many of our Bedford [lorries] had broken front and rear springs.'[13]

It was not until 5 November that pursuit operations were properly
organized. One problem was that, although it had been formed to be
used as a *corps de chasse*, X Corps had taken a large part in the battle and,
even with 7th Armoured Division now under command, was exhausted.
The dogfight had been so long and so bitter that the petrol reserves set
aside for the immediate follow-up had been partially used up. The motor

battalions, whose mobility would have been invaluable in cutting off the retreating enemy, had suffered heavily, and the formations to which they belonged were not in a fit state for an immediate and prolonged advance.[14]

On the Axis side, vehicles were arriving at Fuka up to four abreast along the narrow ribbon of road, with every truck, tank, and gun tractor full or covered with troops, few of whom were still in cohesive formations. Rommel knew there was no time to prepare defences while the aircraft overhead were universally hostile. Twice during the day his headquarters was bombed, and news arrived that an enemy outflanking force was in the desert. He had no choice but to withdraw again, but had little idea of where he might stop:

> It was a wild helterskelter drive through another pitch-black night. Occasional Arab villages loomed up out of the darkness, and several vehicles lost contact with the head of the column. Finally we halted in a small valley to wait for daylight. At that time it was still a matter of doubt as to whether we would be able to get even the remnants of the army away to the west.[15]

But his luck was about to change.

The outflanking force was Roberts's 22nd Armoured Brigade, which Harding had sent on his own responsibility in a 'long hook' past Fuka. It was delayed for a short time by the passage of the tail of Freyberg's force, before being held up by a minefield which also stopped the New Zealanders to the north. For well over an hour 11th Hussars tried to find a way through or around it, until some attached engineers discovered it was in fact a dummy – and, moreover, one laid by the British in June. By this time Roberts had been given clear orders to assist Freyberg in clearing the airstrips at Sidi Haneish; but he still needed to pass through the minefield, and it was not until 1800 hours before his brigade was across. As 131st Brigade was some 15 miles behind and he was short of fuel, he ordered his brigade into laager to enable the infantry and supply vehicles to catch up. To the north, Freyberg remained unaware that the minefield was a dummy and was still trying to get 4th Light Armoured Brigade through a gap under fire, which he managed to do before he too decided to wait until morning before advancing further.[16]

Lumsden had by now realized the ineffectiveness of short hooks to outflank the enemy, and ordered 1st Armoured Division to make a long one of 70 miles to Matruh. However, although the order was issued at 1430 hours, Brigadier Fisher of 2nd Armoured Brigade was unable to get moving until six hours later. Led by 12th Lancers, the brigade struggled through the night for 55 miles and was halted at 0900 hours on 6

November, strung out in a long column and short of fuel. Supplies did not get forward for another two hours (those for the Queen's Bays had gone astray and been bogged in soft sand), and it was 1330 hours before Fisher could set off again. Freyberg had by now traversed the minefield and intercepted a column which yielded 500 prisoners. Also, 8th Armoured Brigade had reached Galal on the 5th and had established a roadblock which destroyed almost 50 tanks and captured several guns, some 100 lorries and over 1,000 prisoners (which probably formed the remnants of de Stefanis's Italian XX Corps). But this was an isolated success.[17] And then on 6 November the heavens opened.

The rain rendered the landing grounds at El Daba unusable. Wheeled vehicles began to sink up to their hubcaps, and tracked vehicles to use far more petrol than normal, with Shermans at one point needing 3 gallons per mile.[18] The New Zealanders' experience was typical: first the trucks with only rear-wheel drive, then those with four-wheel drive began to flounder, those at the rear being first to succumb as they drove over ground whose crust had been churned up by those ahead. To begin with, carriers and tanks could tow some of the wheeled vehicles out, but soon these too were becoming bogged down, and by late afternoon the advance had ground to a standstill.[19] Furthermore, the weather badly disrupted radio communications, which then experienced a complete blackout. Even worse conditions arrived from the north. Not knowing the locations of most units and unable to do more than exhort them to press on, command at all levels was effectively paralysed – and with this the last possibility of cutting off Panzerarmee slipped from Eighth Army's grasp.

Further back, Montgomery visited 10th Armoured Division, telling it to hurry up clearing the rear area of enemy stragglers and send every spare drop of petrol to Briggs's 1st Armoured Division. 'A detour round the left flank would doubtless have resulted in the occupation of Matruh and the capture of many prisoners and some equipment,' noted an 8th Armoured Brigade report of 7 November bitterly, 'but the brigade was not allowed to carry out this operation as other troops were thought to be coming in from the west and south.'[20]

Rommel, like Auchinleck before him, was showing the mettle in the face of adversity that is the mark of a great commander. With the ground behind him treacherous in the extreme thanks to uncharted minefields, and with the sand now pulverized by traffic and turned into a quagmire by the rain, he knew the dangers of being cut off and set about ensuring that this did not happen. When an emissary from Cavallero had appeared on 6 November to enquire about plans for the future, Rommel was able to reply acidly that, with fewer than 20 tanks, fewer than 20 anti-tank guns and fewer than 5,000 men, there was no point in making any plans except to retreat as far and as fast as possible. Fortunately for him, the next day he met up with Generalleutnant Karl Bülowius, Panzerarmee's chief engineer – a man with a genius for demolitions and booby traps that would turn the pursuit into a nightmare. Mines, which had been such a feature of the battlefield, had no less significant an effect, especially psychologically, on the ensuing mobile operations. Many miles behind the front a truckload of reinforcements would blow up on a Tellermine; men out for a walk from a transit camp might be killed by an 'S' mine. Eighth Army learned to tread carefully, and some men subconsciously avoided verges even when walking in an English country lane many years later.[21]

Also appearing out of the blue was Generalmajor Ramcke with 600 of his men who had made an epic crossing of the desert from their battle positions. They had ambushed and captured a British supply column and appropriated its lorries, and Ramcke greeted Rommel with a metallic and sardonic smile – metallic because his false teeth were made of stainless steel, and sardonic because, as *Fallschirmjäger*, his parachutists were Luftwaffe troops, and there remained mutual distrust between them and the Army.[22] Most German stragglers, however, had been rounded up by Allied tanks and armoured cars soon after the pursuit began. Karl Eisenfeller, also from the Ramcke Parachute Brigade, was in a group of stragglers who surrendered to a troop of British tanks. Having no facilities to deal with them, the tankies simply disarmed them, gave them water, and told them to march east until they could be dealt with by other troops. Once the tanks disappeared, however, they started to march west, hoping to be able to elude the British. They were recaptured by another tank troop, given water, and again told to march east. Again they set off to the west. But their efforts proved futile for they were not so lucky the third time, being intercepted by a lorried unit which did have the means to transport them to a prisoner cage.[23]

On 8 November, Rommel began to feel a measure of confidence that he could extricate himself and that a swift dash might be made out of Matruh to Sidi Barrani, 70 miles to the west. Then at midday came news of the Allied invasion of North Africa at Algiers, Oran and Casablanca – raising the prospect of being crushed between two massively superior forces. Of more immediate importance, however, was getting his forces across the escarpment, which would take two days even without interference from the DAF and the pursuing Eighth Army. He therefore directed what little remained of Italian XX Corps together with 3rd Reconnaissance Battalion to Habata to watch the British and keep them from the tops of the passes.

As British tanks entered Matruh on 8 November, church bells were rung in Britain for the first time in three years. A great victory had been won. Hitler, in his annual speech to commemorate the Beer Hall Putsch, dismissed the Torch landings, preferring to concentrate on the capture of Stalingrad. But Rommel declared to Generalmajor C. H. Lungershausen, commanding what was left of 164th Division, 'We must get the remnants of our army back to the mainland. In Africa, we have lost.'[24] The following day there remained a thousand Axis vehicles under constant air attack on the plain below the Halfaya and Sollum passes, while British and New Zealanders were reported to be assembling at Buq Buq in preparation to launch a concerted drive along the coast. But Bülowius's fiendish ingenuity prevented the pursuers approaching too quickly, and Rommel, having had an opportunity to assess the situation in its entirety, decided that, despite Mussolini's exhortations not to surrender a metre of his precious empire, he had no choice but to retire to Tunisia and the Gabes–Wadi Akarit position. He evacuated Tobruk on 12 November, and sought to regroup at Mersa el Brega.

Initially there was nothing to contain the threat posed by the Allied invasion of North Africa. Having been practically unopposed, the vanguard of this was within 150 miles of Tunis by 12 November. However, on 11 November the German 5th Parachute Regiment had landed in Tunisia, and, as the Allied advance stalled (despite the defeat of 5th Parachute Regiment at Medjez el Bab in north-west Tunisia), German and Italian reinforcements began arriving in quantity. By 22 November they had succeeded in establishing a thin perimeter which managed to hold, and at the end of the month this was bolstered by 10th Panzer Division under Generalmajor Wolfgang Fischer, who inflicted a serious defeat on the Allies on 1 December, forcing them into a humiliating retreat. Rommel's back door was shut, and he was saved – at least for the time being. However, it also meant the Nazis pouring hundreds of thousands more men into North Africa, which was not a prospect Rommel welcomed.[25]

Montgomery's pursuit has been portrayed as a series of missed opportunities, although this ignores the fact that only a tiny amount of the Axis forces actually escaped. Rommel criticized Montgomery's cautious pursuit, but he also recognized that Montgomery was too canny to risk serious rebuff, and referred to him, with some bitterness, as 'the Fox'.[26] Panzerarmee had lost over 55,000 men (including some 30,000 prisoners), 450 tanks, 1,000 guns and 84 aircraft. Eighth Army had lost 110 guns to shellfire and some 500 tanks, but all but 150 of the latter were repairable, and the distance that Eighth Army advanced (778 miles from Alamein to Agedabia between 4 and 23 November – an average of 39 miles per day) was by any standards remarkable.[27] Nevertheless, this rate of advance could have been better had not vital convoys of supplies become stranded in traffic jams.[28] For the supply columns struggling to bring forward petrol – the essential fluid of the pursuit – the narrow Supercharge salient became increasingly nightmarish. The tracks were feet deep in powder-fine dust which was getting deeper by the hour. Traffic control broke down, as the small numbers of military police were now spread along a vastly increased distance. The inadequacy of the traffic-control arrangements once the battle was over became rapidly apparent on the solitary metalled road. Despite the attention of large numbers of officers – senior and junior – all the bad habits of the Dunkirk withdrawal were noticed: double or treble banking instead of proceeding in single file; cutting in from side tracks; bunching nose to tail until movement was practically impossible.[29] The restraining effect of the logistic snarl-up was swiftly and increasingly felt – compounded by Eighth Army having trained exclusively for the break-in battle, and by the need to reorganize and recuperate after so debilitating a fight.

However, once it was apparent that Rommel and the remnants of his army were trying to get away, Montgomery decided that they would not stop before the El Agheila position on the edge of Tripolitania. While appreciating the need to keep pressure on the enemy, he now turned his mind to how he might defeat them there. Montgomery gave precise instructions to Lumsden about the pursuit to El Agheila, and kept a firm hand on the operations to prevent it being '"mucked about" by subordinate commanders having ideas inconsistent with it'.[30] These plans were finished by 29 November, by which time it was found that Benghazi harbour was not as badly damaged as had been feared and that ammunition dumps abandoned during the retreat through the Djebel Akhtar 11 months before had been left largely undisturbed. Montgomery was gearing up once more for a set-piece battle, and despite assurance through Ultra of Rommel's continued weakness, opportunities for a repeat of Beda Fomm were never seriously considered. Montgomery later claimed that he bluffed Rommel out of the El Agheila position, whereas Rommel bluffing Montgomery seems nearer the truth. He had over-insured by trying to get too many formations through the narrow bottleneck of the Alamein battlefield, and paid the price of trying to maintain too many formations in the pursuit operations. Indeed, over-insurance would be the keynote of the pursuit all the way to Tripoli, which was eventually occupied only three months later.[31]

The attack at El Agheila was delayed until 14 December and at

Buerat until 15 January. Given that Montgomery had full intelligence of Rommel's weakness from Ultra, Army Y and air reconnaissance, Correlli Barnett's assertion that the pursuit was a 'mere ghost' of O'Connor's daring march of 1941 seems rather accurate.[32] Tedder knew what Montgomery knew, and with his eyes fixed firmly on the airfields around Benghazi he was galled by the sluggishness of the advance. He had taken steps to ensure a rapid advance could be achieved once the breakthrough had been made by ensuring that Force A (the spearhead fighter force) lacked nothing and was organized to achieve maximum mobility, unburdened by any aircraft or vehicle that it could not repair within 48 hours. It was kept up to strength from Force B (the remaining air forces), and the chief engineer of Eighth Army, Brigadier F. H. Kisch, had undertaken to clear captured landing grounds of mines and obstacles as a matter of priority, in which he would be assisted by flights from the new RAF Regiment* also incorporated into Force A.[33] Together with Coningham, he deeply and rightly came to resent the boastfulness with which Montgomery claimed the victory as his alone – a boastfulness that would have sorry consequences for Montgomery's relations with other senior officers – and his reputation – two years later.[34] At least in the meantime the occupation off the Maturba airfields enabled the vital Stoneage convoy to reach Malta. The island was relieved for the last time, never again to be imperilled.

Rommel visited Europe, but this was not a success. Questions were now asked about his resolve, and his reception by Hitler at Rastenburg on 28 November was chilly in the extreme. His suggestion that, although a delaying action might be fought in Tunisia for a while, the end in Africa had surely come brought on a typical Hitler tantrum: retreat and evacuation were all that his generals ever suggested he screamed; he had had exactly the same trouble the previous year with his commanders on the Russian Front, and now they were talking the same way about Stalingrad. But they would stay where they were, and so would Rommel in Africa. The man chiefly responsible for Rommel's needs was Mussolini, and he should move on to Rome at once, accompanied by Göring. With that he was dismissed, to spend the following two days in Göring's personal train listening to the fat fool's boasting and his bland dismissal of all his problems – the product, in Göring's opinion, of Rommel's exhaustion and weakness.[35]

Fortunately for Rommel, Montgomery concentrated on his own

---

*This had been formed in the United Kingdom in February, but it was not until September that the 7,800 'ground gunners' in the Middle East had been formed into flights of the new regiment.

logistic problems rather than those facing the Axis. They were indeed considerable, largely as a result of the distances involved. Although the harbours of Tobruk and Benghazi were soon working, the former was 800 miles in the rear and it would necessarily take time to build up the stocks needed for six divisions. This also gave Panzerarmee time to recover, however limited that recovery might be, and so the slow slog across Libya continued. While lorries roared continually along the narrow roads and engineers worked feverishly to maintain them and risked their lives to clear Bülowius's masterpieces (losing 170 of their number in the process), 1943 and the next stage of the campaign approached.

Although the summer battles had halted Panzerarmee they had not thrown it back, and too many of them had been tactical failures. While Auchinleck's reputation was eventually rehabilitated, his right-hand man Dorman-Smith was ultimately ostracised by the army he had devoted himself to. He returned to Ireland full of bitterness and, taking the old family name of O'Gowan, dabbled with the IRA while fighting for recognition of the part played by Auchinleck in saving Egypt. If Auchinleck was a director of operations, Alexander took the role of chairman, with Montgomery as managing director choosing subordinates he trusted and could rely upon, and whose judgement in this respect proved more effective than Auchinleck's. However, it would probably been have impossible for Montgomery to have worked under Auchinleck's direction without the complete freedom of action within his remit that Alexander gave him. Montgomery certainly considered himself the military superior of both these men, but successful generalship is not merely the direction of soldiers on the battlefield.

Montgomery was promoted to general on 11 November and appointed a KCB as a result of his achievement. Alamein made 'Monty' a household name the world over, and when he was subsequently ennobled he styled himself by it. But from now onward he would have to be a team player, and he quickly proved incapable of sharing gracefully either responsibility or the laurels that attended victory. He sacked Lumsden and Gatehouse, because he had no time for officers whom he believed 'had shown signs of wilting under the strain'.[36] Shortly after arriving back in London, Lumsden reputedly entered his club in a bowler hat and said, 'I've just been sacked because there isn't enough room in the desert for two cads like Montgomery and me.'[37] Montgomery revelled in the description, because he understood that only an autocrat could make the British military system work efficiently. This system was a result of the peculiarly British view of themselves as men of 'character', which they were expected to show in adversity and was supposed, in the absence of battle drills and uniform doctrine, to make them well suited to battlefield challenges.[38]

Many years later, at a dinner in his honour at the Royal Hospital, Chelsea, Montgomery said that he owed his success to three things: 'the courage and initiative of the British soldier, the unfailing support and wise advice of my old friend Sir Alan Brooke, and the untiring work of my Chief of Staff, Freddy de Guingand'. Afterwards he excused himself: 'Gentlemen, as you know, I am a teetotaller and I like to go to bed early; so you will forgive me if I leave you.' Alexander and Marshal of the Air Force Sir William 'Dickie' Dickson, chairman of the Chiefs of Staff Committee, were talking near the door as he went to leave. Alexander said quietly, 'Monty, when you made your speech acknowledging the help you had received in achieving your victories, didn't you forget something?' 'No,' replied Montgomery, 'I don't think so.' 'Yes you did, you forgot me,' said Alexander.[39] He was by no means alone in this respect. It was a mild rebuke and perhaps indicative of the personalities of both men.

The effects of success on Montgomery's already difficult personality were not pleasant, and subsequently generated considerable distaste among many who were not his fans, to the point where some have sought to denigrate or belittle his achievement, and even to suggest that it was not truly his – that he had done little more than implement Auchinleck's plans. This is plainly not true: the battle was Montgomery's, and its success and its failures were his alone. But he could not have achieved what he did in isolation, as he sometimes seems to have imagined. Manfred Rommel said many years later that his father little respected Montgomery.[40] Nevertheless, some eight months after the battle Rommel wrote, 'The war in the desert ceased to be a game when Montgomery took over.'[41] Conditions for a total victory had been created at Alamein and expanded by Torch. 'Monty' had become the most famous British soldier since Haig and Allenby and had turned Eighth Army into a force with pride in its achievements. But he had failed to knock 'Rommel for six out of Africa' as he had promised he would.[42]

For Eighth Army, victory at Alamein marked the beginning of a long road which would not end until Vienna two and a half years later. A film, *Desert Victory*, was made at the behest of Churchill and the War Office to commemorate the battle. It was edited by Roy Boulting from 1.5 million feet of film shot by 20 cameramen of the Army and RAF

Film Units (of whom three were killed and two badly wounded). 'They are the men who deserve credit for the film,' said Boulting:

> No one knew *Desert Victory* was being made . . . We were given a completion date and we finished it in three days and nights without sleep with several bottles of whisky to keep us going. I carried the film myself down to the Odeon, Leicester Square, for the press view. I sat in the foyer absolutely exhausted and I heard a roar from inside and they were cheering.[43]

The desert victory been won at a cost of 13,560 men, killed wounded and missing. Sergeant D. F. W. Smith recalled the emotion of hearing a lone piper playing a lament after the battle.[44] As always, the highest price was paid by the infantry, and especially by the Australians, who bore a greater burden than any other formation both in attack and in defence. They had withstood no fewer than 25 German attacks on Trig 29. Tuker wrote, 'Every divisional commander who fought at Alamein will salute the memory of Morshead and his 9th Australian Division for their great achievements during nine days of solid fighting when they beat to a standstill those worthy enemies, 90th Light and 164th Divisions.'[45] Horrocks, watching events in the south, certainly thought that the success of Supercharge was largely due to the Australian effort in the preceding days. Afterwards he went to congratulate Morshead on the magnificent performance of his division. 'Thank you, general,' replied the tough little Aussie with typical understatement, 'the boys were interested.'[46]

Montgomery had not simply reverted to Haig's methods of 1918. He kept a tight grip on attacks carried out on narrower frontages; his use of deception to achieve surprise benefited enormously from a superb intelligence service. The long overdue development of battle drills, beginning with minefield breaching, combined with the skilful mounting of offensive operations at night, greatly enhanced British capabilities.[47] But Eighth Army's infantry strength was not so superior that it could have afforded a ding-dong struggle against prepared and fortified defences had it not been for one additional factor – the artillery.[48] British artillery and air-support techniques were far superior to those of the Axis, and Alamein was significant as the first great artilleryman's battle in the Second World War. Using for the first time all the technical aids which had been developed, and on a grand scale, it was possible by careful planning and with centralized control to put into practice the principles governing the employment of artillery which would play such a decisive part in the later stages of the war. During previous operations in the desert the control of artillery had been dissipated, but at Alamein it was centralized, with the fire of the maximum possible number of guns being concentrated to support the infantry at the decisive place. Surveying and aerial photography were essential to success in the early stages of the battle. Counter-battery fire was organized to an extent previously unknown, and divisional and corps concentrations were put down at a few minutes notice as a routine of battle for the first time in history. The action of the artillery was a decisive factor, and Alamein restored the Royal Artillery to its rightful place on the battlefield.[49]

The legacy of Alamein could be detected in the destructive power of the British artillery during the Normandy campaign.[50] The 25-pounder was as feared by the Axis as was the '88' by the British. Many prisoners asked to see the 'artillery machine-gun' that could fire so fast and so accurately, and refused to believe it was not automatically loaded, that it was merely the skill of the gunners that enabled it to fire at a dozen or more rounds per minute.[51] A Royal Artillery report later stated that 'a really heavy concentration will so neutralize the enemy that infantry, unsupported by armour, will be able to gain their objective without undue casualties . . . nearly all prisoners speak of the great effect of our artillery fire'. Even against armour it was effective: 'Probably in many cases no tanks were destroyed or even hit, but as far as is known on every occasion on which a heavy concentration of artillery fire was put down on enemy tanks, they either withdrew or changed direction.'[52]

Having made an immeasurable contribution to the success of the attacks which put the infantry on their objectives, it was undoubtedly also the artillery that made the biggest contribution to defending the ground taken. Throughout the battle, some artillery action was always taking place at both day and night. In 12 days, more than a million rounds of 25-pounder ammunition were fired at a daily average of 102 rounds per gun. On XXX Corps's front this average was 159 rounds per gun, and 9th Australian Division's regiments fired 50 per cent more than that.[53]

Tuker later criticized the failure to concentrate the artillery yet further, and pointed out that, compared with the wasteful and imprecise creeping barrages that others used, 9th Australian Division had more success by firing concentrations against known Axis strongpoints, which, given the coverage by air reconnaissance and survey, was equally feasible elsewhere. Only where time and lack of reconnaissance later on in the battle prevented the accurate location of strongpoints was a barrage justifiable.[54]

The value of XIII Corps's operations early on is also questionable, especially as there was no infantry reserve for XXX Corps. This meant that 2nd New Zealand Division had to be withdrawn and rested while brigades from 4th Indian, 44th, 50th and 51st Divisions were fed into the northern part of the battle to try to create the elusive breakthrough for X Corps. This showed a miscalculation of the artillery necessary to drive an infantry assault into a prepared defensive position across a four-division frontage, and it was therefore a creditable achievement by Eighth Army's artillery commanders to concentrate 360 guns for Supercharge. The 6-pounder also proved its worth, being more than a match for any armour the Axis then possessed – blunting Panzerarmee's early and fruitless counter-attacks.

Eventually, it was Eighth Army's persistence that won, and in this respect the battle was certainly a 'dogfight'. However, the battle was not a victory for Eighth Army alone, but the culmination of all that had gone before – particularly the sustained operations of the Middle East Air Forces and the Royal Navy against the Axis supply routes, which left Panzerarmee short of every vital commodity.[55] Yet even had the Axis secured these routes it would not have guaranteed Rommel success in his drive on Egypt. Of vital importance though she was, Malta was not the decisive factor in Rommel's supply problems: that was Libya's inadequate port facilities. Even with Malta out of the way, the capacity of Tobruk was so small (and more vulnerable from Egypt than Malta) that it could not easily sustain him. As Halder pointed out as early as 1940, the only realistic alternative to trickling supplies across the Mediterranean was to build up sufficient forces and supplies to take Alexandria in one go, solving the port-capacity problem at a stroke and for ever and leaving Malta as a strategic backwater. But Libya's ports could not supply the necessary forces. And it is not true, as many have suggested, that Hitler did not support Rommel: Rommel received all the forces that could be maintained in Africa, and more – including incomparably generous motor transport given the limited capacity of the German motor industry.[56]

For all his undoubted tactical brilliance, Rommel failed to understand what Wavell knew: that modern warfare is a matter of administration, and that unlike tactics – certainly in the desert – administration is the art of the possible.[57] Thus Alamein, like Stalingrad and the Marne, would become, in the words of the American Brigadier-General S. L. A. Marshall, a 'monument of the supreme folly of over-extension'.[58] Rommel's administrative weakness, coupled with a failure to husband his armour for a concerted blow, meant that he was never able to threaten Montgomery's precious 'balance', although the only Eighth Army manoeuvre that really made him dance was the series of blows struck by the Australians against 164th Division towards the coast.[59] But such criticisms are the matter of the military professional, and not strictly relevant to the wider importance of the victory. Certainly they were not relevant to the people of Britain, for whom Alamein was the first *permanent* victory. Churchill, with his unrivalled ability to coin a phrase, in a speech at the Mansion House on 10 November said, 'Now this is not the end, it is not even the beginning of the end. But it is perhaps the end of the beginning.'[60]

APPENDIX

Orders of Battle, 23 October 1942

Panzerarmee Afrika – Generalfeldmarschall Erwin Rommel
Battle Echelon [*Kampfstaffel*]; 10th Signals Regiment; V, VI, XII, 'Tripolis' Army Radio Stations; Special Operations Radio Troop 'Afrika'; 937th Signals Platoon; 15th Brigade Staff zbV [*zur besonderen verwendung* – for special purposes]; Air Staff Libya; Special Messenger Staff (Luftwaffe); 2nd Reconnaissance Headquarters (Army)/14th Panzer Division; 288th Special Group [Sonderverband – an ad-hoc formation]; SS Regiment 'Speer'; 13th Company, 800th 'Brandenburg' Regiment; 575th Army Map Store; 721st, 722nd, 723rd, 724th, 725th, 726th, 727th, 728th, 729th, 730th Survey and Mapping Troops; 73rd Army Construction Unit; 85th Construction Battalion; 585th Supply Regiment, Staff; 619th Supply Battalion, Staff; 792nd, 798th Supply Battalions zbV; 681st Unloading Staff zbV; 148th (Italian), 149th (Italian), 529th, 532nd, 533rd, 902nd, 909th Supply Battalions; 548th Vehicle Repair Battalion; 542nd, 543rd, 544th, 545th, 546th, 547th Ammunition Administration Platoons; 12th Petrol Analysis Troop; 5th Army Petrol Oil and Lubricants Administration Platoon; 781st, 979th, 980th Petrol Oil and Lubricants Platoons; Technical Stores Administration Service; 560th, 566th Army Mechanical Transport Parks; 1st, 2nd, 3rd Ordnance Stores Platoons; 554th Bakery Company; 445th Butchery Company; 317th, 445th, 'Afrika' Supply Depots, Staff; 556th Commandant Rations Office; 592nd Medical Company; 705th Hospital Transport Company; 542nd, 667th, 'Tripolis' Base Hospitals; Light Base Evacuation Hospital; 531st Medical Equipment Park; Patrol Headquarters, Secret Field Police, Military Police Troop; Local Defence Guard Battalion 'Afrika'; 615th 'Misurata', 619th 'Barce', 958th 'Tripolis', 959th 'Benghazi', 'Derna' Garrison Commanders; Tripoli Depot Commander; 782nd Prisoner of War Transit Camp; 659th, 762nd Field Post Offices; Field Post Office (Luftwaffe); Army Postal Services zbV

19th Flak Division
11th Observation Battalion
606th, 612nd, 617th Anti-Aircraft Battalions

135th Anti-Aircraft Regiment (Luftwaffe)

102nd Anti-Aircraft Regiment (Luftwaffe) [II Battalion, 25th Anti-Aircraft Regiment; I Battalion, 33rd Anti-Aircraft Regiment]

104th Artillery Command

1st and 2nd Africa Artillery Regiments [organized around Staff, 221st Artillery Regiment (motorized); Staff, 408th Heavy Artillery Regiment (motorized); 364th, 408th, 528th, 533rd, 902nd Artillery Battalions]

Deutches Afrikakorps – Generalleutnant Wilhelm Ritter von Thoma
Corps Combat Escort Group
605th Anti-Tank Battalion
300th Oasis Battalion

21st Panzer Division – Generalmajor Heinz von Randow
Divisional HQ and Signals Battalion; 531st Bakery Company; 309th Field Police Troop [military police]; 735th Field Post Office
3rd Reconnaissance Battalion
5th Panzer Regiment [2 battalions]
104th Panzergrenadier Regiment
155th Artillery Regiment [2 battalions]
39th Anti-Tank Battalion
200th Engineer Battalion

15th Panzer Division – Generalleutnant Gustav von Värst
Divisional HQ and Signals Battalion; 33rd Field Replacement Battalion; 33rd (Motorized) Supply Battalion; 33rd Ambulance Company; 33rd Field Hospital; 33rd Butchery Company; 33rd Bakery Company; 33rd Field Police Troop; 33rd Field Post Office
33rd Reconnaissance Battalion
8th Panzer Regiment [2 battalions]
115th Panzergrenadier Regiment [3 battalions]
33rd Artillery Regiment [3 battalions]
33rd Anti-Tank Battalion
33rd Engineer Battalion

90th Light Division – Generalleutnant Theodor Graf von Sponeck
Divisional HQ and Signals Battalion (190th); 190th Field Replacement Battalion; 190th (Motorized) Supply Battalion; 638th Ambulance Company; 535th Bakery Company; 517th Butchery Company; 190th Field Police Troop; 190th Field Post Office
580th Reconnaissance Battalion
155th and 200th Panzergrenadier Regiments [3 battalions each]
361st (Motorized) Light Africa Regiment [2 battalions]
190th Artillery Regiment [2 battalions and 1 company, 613rd Anti-Aircraft Battalion]
190th Anti-Tank Battalion
900th Engineer Battalion

164th Light Africa Division – Generalmajor Carl-Hans Lungershausen

Divisional HQ and Signals Battalion; 220th Workshop Company; 220th Supply Depot; 220th Butchery Company; 220th Bakery Company; 220th Field Police Troop; 220th Field Post Office

220th Reconnaissance Battalion

707th and 708th Infantry Gun Companies

125th Panzergrenadier, 382nd and 433rd Regiments [3 battalions each]

220th Artillery Regiment [2 battalions]

220th Anti-Tank Battalion

220th Engineer Battalion

609th Anti-Aircraft Battalion

Parachute Brigade Ramcke – Generalmajor Bernard Hermann Ramcke

3 infantry battalions, 1 artillery battalion

X Corps – Generale di Corpo d'Armata Edoardo Nebbia

9th Bersaglieri Regiment [28th and 57th Battalions]

49th, 147th Artillery Battalions

10th, 31st Engineer Battalions

17th Pavia Division – Generale di Brigata Nazzarono Scattaglia

Divisional HQ and Supply Detachments; 207th Motor Transport Section; 21st Medical Section [66th and 84th/94th Field Hospitals]; 679th Corpo Carabinieri Regio Reali [Royal Carabinieri] Section; 54th Post Office

V Light Tank Battalion and 6th Battalion, Lancieri Aosta [armoured cars] [attached]

27th, 28th (Pavia Brigade) Infantry Regiments

26th Artillery Regiment

77th, 423rd Anti-Aircraft Batteries [20 mm AA guns]

17th Mixed Engineer Battalion

27th Brescia Division – Generale di Divisione Brunetto Brunetti

Divisional HQ and Supply Detachments; 328th Motor Transport Section; 34th Medical Section [35th Surgical Unit, 95th Field Hospital]; 127th Corpo Carabinieri Regio Reali Section; 96th Post Office

19th, 20th (Brescia Brigade) Infantry Regiments

55th Artillery Regiment

401st, 404th Anti-Aircraft Batteries [20 mm AA guns]

27th Mixed Engineer Battalion

XX Corps – Generale di Corpo d'Armata Guiseppe di Stefanis

600th Post Office

357th Light Artillery Regiment

2nd Bersaglieri Company [motorcycle]

164th and 620th Corpo Carabinieri Regio Reali Sections

24th Engineer Battalion

132nd Ariete Armoured Division – Generale di Brigata Francesco Arena

Divisional HQ and Supply Detachments; 672nd Corpo Carabinieri Regio Reali Section; 132nd Post Office

3rd Armoured Group – 1st Nizza Cavalry Regiment, 32nd Armoured Regiment; 8th Bersaglieri Regiment [3rd, 5th, 12th Mobile and 3rd Anti-Tank Battalions]

132nd Artillery Regiment

31st Heavy Anti-Aircraft Battalion [88L56 and 90L53 guns]

161st Self-Propelled Artillery Battalion [75L18 self-propelled guns]

32nd Mixed Engineer Battalion [132nd Pioneer Company; 232nd Signals Company]

133rd Littorio Armoured Division – Generale di Divisione Ceriana Mayneri

Divisional HQ and Supply Detachments; 133rd Medical Section [142nd and 147th Field Hospitals]; 85th Corpo Carabinieri Regio Reali Section

3rd Armoured Group 'Lancieri di Novarra' – 133rd Armoured Regiment [VI, XII, LI Armoured Battalions]; 12th Bersaglieri Regiment [23rd and 36th Battalions]; 21st Bersaglieri Anti-Tank Battalion

Semovente Battalion [self-propelled guns]

3rd Mobile Artillery Regiment (Duca d'Aosta), Anti-Aircraft Battalion [5th and 46th Batteries]

101st Trieste Motorized Infantry Division – Generale di Brigata Francesco La Perla

Divisional HQ and Supply Detachments; 85th Heavy Motor Transport Section; 175th Supply Section; Medical Section [65th, 214th, 242nd Field Hospitals; 16th Surgical Unit]; 22nd Corpo Carabinieri Regio Reali Section; 56th Post Office

9th Bersaglieri Regiment [8th and 11th Battalions]

65th, 66th (Valtellina Brigade) Infantry Regiments

21st Artillery Regiment, Anti-Aircraft Battalion [146th, 411th Batteries]

32nd Enginer Battalion [28th Pioneer, 101st Signals Companies]

101st Anti-Tank Battalion

185th Folgore Parachute Division – Generale di Divisione Enrico Frattini

Divisional HQ and Supply Detachments; 185th Corpo Carabinieri Regio Reali Section; 260th Post Office

185th, 186th, 187th Parachute Regiments

185th Artillery Regiment

8th Engineer Battalion

XXI Corps – Generale di Corpo d'Armata Enea Navarini

7th Bersaglieri Regiment [10th and 11th Mobile Battalions]

8th Artillery Regiment [331st, 52nd, 131st Battalions]

27th and 65th Engineer Battalions

25th Bologna Division – Generale di Divisione Alessandro Gloria

Divisional HQ and Supply Detachments; 135th Motor Transport Section;

Medical Section (96th, 528th Field Hospitals; 66th Surgical Unit; 308th Field Ambulance); 73rd Corpo Carabinieri Regio Reali Section; 58th Post Office
39th, 40th (Bologna Brigade) Infantry Regiments
205th Artillery Regiment
4th, 437th Anti-Aircraft Batteries [20 mm AA guns]

102nd Trento Motorized Division – Generale di Divisione Luigi Nuvoloni
Divisional HQ and Supply Detachments; 51st Medical Section [57th and 897th Field Hospitals]; 160th/180th Corpo Carabinieri Regio Reali Section; 109th Post Office
61st, 62nd (Sicilia Brigade) Infantry Regiments
46th Artillery Regiment
412th, 414th Anti-Aircraft Batteries [20 mm AA guns]
7th Bersagleri Regiment [10th and 70th Battalions]
51st Mixed Engineer Battalion [161st Pioneer Company; 96th Signals Company]

GHQ Middle East Forces – General the Hon. Sir Harold Alexander

Notes: The prefixes 1/ and 2/ before the numbers of British batttalions are used to distinguish between units formed from the same parent – for example, 1/6th and 2/6th Battalions Queen's Royal Regiment (West Surrey) were both formed from the 6th (Bermondsey) Battalion when the Territorial Army was doubled in 1939. Other British battalions are amalgamations – for example, 5th/7th Battalion Gordon Highlanders is an amalgamation of the 5th and 7th Battalions. Also, as part of the Second Australian Imperial Force, all Australian units below have the prefix 2/ to distinguish them from militia units with the same number and from units of the First AIF formed during the First World War.

It has not been possible to ensure that all the vitally important but small service sub-units have been listed below. For example, every division would have a signals detachment (Royal Corps of Signals), an ordnance field park (Royal Army Ordnance Corps), a provost unit (Corps of Military Police) and a postal unit (provided by the Corps of Royal Engineers in British formations), and each brigade had a workshop company (from the newly formed Corps of Royal Electrical and Mechanical Engineers in British formations, but elsewhere provided by the Australian Army Ordnance Corps, South African Technical Services Corps etc.).

Eighth Army – Lieutenant-General Bernard Law Montgomery
Eighth Army Signals, Royal Corps of Signals

Corps of Royal Engineers: detachment, 1st Camouflage Company; detachment, 114th Mechanical Equipment Workshop and Park Company; 566th and 588th Army Field Companies; 655th General Construction Company; 3rd, 62nd, 72nd, 82nd (Airfields) Works and Staff (Royal Engineers); 5th Boring Section; 517th Field Survey Company; 13th Field Survey Depot; 4th and 5th Mobile Landing Ground Construction Parties; 17th Railway Operating

Company, 18th Army Troops Company, 27th Mechanical Equipment Operating Company, New Zealand Engineers; 22nd Workshop and Park Company, 25th Road Construction Company, 27th Road Construction Company, 32nd Road Maintenance Company, 36th Water Supply Company, detachment, 46th Survey Company, 85th Camouflage Company, 95th Bomb Disposal Company, South African Engineer Corps

Royal Army Medical Corps: 10th Casualty Clearing Station; 2nd (Indian) Casualty Clearing Station; 1st (New Zealand) Casualty Clearing Station Hygiene Section; 2/3rd (Australian) Casualty Clearing Station Hygiene Section; 6th Field Surgical Unit; 3rd Field Transfusion Unit; 5th Mobile Bacteriological Laboratory; 1st Mobile Opthalmological Unit; 14th Field Ambulance; 200th Field Ambulance; 1st Motor Ambulance Company; 18th MAS; 7th Advanced Depot Medical Stores

Royal Army Service Corps: 14th, 17th, 19th, 36th, 50th, 97th, 142nd, 163rd (Mauritian), 168th, 179th [2 platoons], 180th, 240th, 241st, 287th [3 platoons], 288th, 309th, 345th, 384th, 385th, 401st, 402nd, 462nd (Palestinian), 549th General Transport Companies [3-tonners]; 4th and 6th New Zealand Reserve Mechanical Transport Companies [3-tonners]; 101st Australian General Transport Company [3-tonners]; 203rd, 209th South African Reserve Mechanical Transport Companies [3-tonners]; 127th, 244th, 258th, 286th General Transport Companies [10-tonners]; 11th Ambulance Car Company (485th Company); 78th Bulk Petroleum Transport Company; 130th Water Tank Company; 148th (Palestinian), 220th, 261st, 262nd, 475th, 558th Water Tank Companies; 15th, 143rd, 144th, 335th, 372nd, 373rd Tank Transporter Companies; 13th, 15th, 38th, 41st and 'P' Detail Issue Depots; 12th Field Bakery; 2nd Field Butchery and Cold Storage Depot; 1st South African Field Bakery, South African Service Corps

Corps of Military Police: 105th, 112th, 113th, 202nd, 204th Provost Companies; 50th Traffic Control Unit

Royal Army Ordnance Corps: 128th, 129th Salvage Units; 510th Lines of Communication Vehicle and Stores Convoy Unit; 6th Salvage Unit, Indian Army Ordnance Corps

Pioneer Corps: 44th, 54th, 62nd Group HQs; 1204th, 1205th, 1208th, 1209th, 1213th, 1214th, 1216th, 1217th, 1250th, 1251st Companies, Indian Auxiliary Pioneer Corps; 1501st (Mauritius), 1502nd (Mauritius), 1503rd (Mauritius), 1504th (Seychelles), 1505th (Mauritius), 1506th (Mauritius), 1507th (Rodriquez), 1509th (Seychelles) Companies, Pioneer Corps; 1907th, 1917th, 1930th Companies, African Auxiliary Pioneer Corps (Basuto); 3rd Battalion, Libyan Arab Force

Tank Reorganization Group
1st Armoured Brigade Signals, Royal Corps of Signals; 1st Armoured Brigade Workshops, Royal Electrical and Mechanical Engineers; 67th and 307th

Companies, Royal Army Service Corps; Royal Armoured Corps Tank Delivery Regiment

1st Army Tank Brigade [elements]
42nd (7th (23rd London) Battalion, East Surrey Regiment) Battalion, Royal Tank Regiment
44th Battalion, Royal Tank Regiment

21st Indian Infantry Brigade [airfield security]
21st Indian Brigade Signals, Indian Signal Corps
2nd Battalion, 1st Punjab Regiment
4th Battalion (Wilde's), 13th Frontier Force Rifles
2nd Battalion, 8th Gurkha Rifles

2nd Anti-Aircraft Brigade
2nd Anti-Aircraft Brigade Signals, Royal Corps of Signals
69th (The Royal Warwickshire Regiment) Heavy Anti-Aircraft Regiment, Royal Artillery
2nd Light Anti-Aircraft Regiment, Royal Artillery

12th Anti-Aircraft Brigade
12th Anti-Aircraft Brigade Signals, Royal Corps of Signals
198th Company, Royal Army Service Corps
88th and 94th Heavy Anti-Aircraft Regiments, Royal Artillery
14th (West Lothian, Royal Scots), 16th, 27th Light Anti-Aircraft Regiments, Royal Artillery

X Corps – Lieutenant-General Herbert Lumsden
X Corps Signals, Royal Corps of Signals, 570th Corps Field Park Company, Royal Engineers; 5th Line of Communications Transport Column; 50th General Transport Company, 40th Detail Issue Depot, Royal Army Service Corps; X Corps Stores Convoy Unit, Royal Army Ordnance Corps; 12th and 151st (Sunderland) Light Field Ambulances, Royal Army Medical Corps; 8th (South African) and 15th Casualty Clearing Stations; 1st New Zealand Casualty Clearing Station Light Section; 6th and 8th Light Field Hygiene Sections; 11th and 15th American Field Service Ambulance Car Companies; 1st, 2nd, 5th Field Surgical Units; 7th Field Transfusion Unit, Royal Army Medical Corps; 115th Provost Company, Corps of Military Police

1st Armoured Division – Major-General Raymond Briggs
1st Armoured Divisional Signals, Royal Corps of Signals; 1st Armoured Division Provost Company, Corps of Military Police
12th Royal Lancers (Prince of Wales's) [armoured cars]
4th Royal Horse Artillery
11th Royal Horse Artillery (Honourable Artillery Company)
78th Field Regiment, Royal Artillery (Lowland)
76th Anti-Tank Regiment, Royal Artillery (Royal Welch Fusiliers)
42nd Light Anti-Aircraft Regiment, Royal Artillery

7th Field Squadron, 1st Field Park Squadron, Royal Engineers
9th Field Squadron, 572nd Army Field Park Company, Royal Engineers

2nd Armoured Brigade – Brigadier A. F. Fisher
2nd Armoured Brigade HQ and Signals Company, Royal Corps of Signals; 2nd
  Armoured Brigade Workshop, Royal Electrical and Mechanical Engineers;
  1st Field Squadron, Royal Engineers; 910th and 925th Companies, Royal
  Army Service Corps
The Queen's Bays (2nd Dragoon Guards)
9th Royal Lancers
10th Royal Hussars (Prince of Wales' Own)
The Yorkshire Dragoons (The Queen's Own) [motor battalion]

7th Motor Brigade – Brigadier T. J. B. Bosvile
7th Motor Brigade HQ and Signals Company, Royal Corps of Signals; 7th
  Motor Brigade Workshops, Royal Electrical and Mechanical Engineers;
  550th Company, Royal Army Service Corps
2nd Battalion, King's Royal Rifle Corps
2nd Battalion, Rifle Brigade (Prince Consort's Own)
London Rifle Brigade (7th Battalion, Rifle Brigade)
Special Tank Unit [6 Churchill tanks]

'Hammerforce' (from 8th Armoured Division)
4th/6th South African Armoured Car Regiment
146th Field Regiment, Royal Artillery (Pembroke and Cardiganshire)
73rd Anti-Tank Regiment, Royal Artillery
56th Light Anti-Aircraft Regiment, Royal Artillery (East Lancashire)

8th Armoured Division – Major-General C. H. Gairdner
HQ staff only
145th Field Park Company, Royal Engineers; A and B Companies, 8th Armoured
  Division Troops, Royal Army Service Corps; 8th Armoured Division Provost
  Company, Corps of Military Police

10th Armoured Division – Major-General Alec Gatehouse
10th Armoured Divisional Signals (Middlesex Yeomanry), Royal Corps of
  Signals; 10th Armoured Division Provost Company, Corps of Military Police;
  3rd, 6th, 8th, 168th Light Field Ambulances, Royal Army Medical Corps;
  332nd, 334th, 543rd Companies, Royal Army Service Corps
1st The Royal Dragoons [armoured cars]
1st, 5th, 104th Royal Horse Artillery (Essex Yeomanry)
98th Field Regiment Royal Artillery (Surrey and Sussex Yeomanry, Queen
  Mary's)
84th Anti-Tank Regiment, Royal Artillery
53rd Light Anti-Aircraft Regiment, Royal Artillery (King's Own Yorkshire Light
  Infantry)
3rd (Cheshire) Field Squadrons, 141st Field Park Squadron, Royal Engineers
571st and 573rd Army Field Companies, Royal Engineers [attached]

8th Armoured Brigade – Brigadier E. C. N. Custance
8th Armoured Brigade HQ and Signals Squadron, Royal Corps of Signals; 8th
    Armoured Brigade Workshops, Royal Electrical and Mechanical Engineers;
    552nd and 911th Companies, Royal Army Service Corps; 2nd (Cheshire)
    Field Squadron, Royal Engineers
3rd Battalion, Royal Tank Regiment
The Nottinghamshire Yeomanry (Sherwood Rangers)
The Staffordshire Yeomanry (Queen's Own Royal Regiment)
1st Battalion, The Buffs (Royal East Kent Regiment) [motor battalion]

24th Armoured Brigade – Brigadier A. G. Kenchington
24th Armoured Brigade HQ and Signals Squadron, Royal Corps of Signals;
    24th Armoured Brigade Workshops, Royal Electrical and Mechanical
    Engineers; 332nd Company, Royal Army Service Corps; 6th Field
    Squadron, Royal Engineers
41st (Oldham), 45th (Leeds Rifles), 47th Battalions, Royal Tank Regiment
11th King's Royal Rifle Corps (1st Queen's Westminsters) [motor battalion]

[attached] **133rd (Royal Sussex) Lorried Infantry Brigade** – Brigadier A. W.
    Lee
133rd Brigade HQ and Signals Company, Royal Corps of Signals; 133rd
    Brigade Workshops, Royal Electrical and Mechanical Engineers; 133rd
    Brigade Company, Royal Army Service Corps
2nd, 4th, 5th (Cinque Ports) Battalions, Royal Sussex Regiment
W Company, 1st Battalion, Royal Northumberland Fusiliers [machine-gun]

XIII Corps – Lieutenant-General B. G. Horrocks
XIII Corps Signals, Royal Corps of Signals; 14th Casualty Clearing Station, 186th
    Field Ambulance, 4th Field Surgical Unit, 6th Field Transfusion Unit, 2nd Motor
    Ambulance Company, 9th MAS, Royal Army Medical Corps
118th and 124th Battalions, Royal Tank Regiments [dummy tanks]
4th (Durham) Survey Regiment, Royal Artillery [HQ and composite battery]
576th Corps Field Park Company and 578th Army Field Company, Royal Engineers

7th Armoured Division – Major-General A. F. Harding
7th Armoured Divisional Signals, Royal Corps of Signals; 7th Armoured Division
    Provost Company, Corps of Military Police; 2nd and 14th Light Field
    Ambulances, 7th Field Surgical Unit, 25th Field Transfusion Unit, Royal Army
    Medical Corps; French ACL; 10th and 67th Companies, Royal Army Service
    Corps; 4th and 21st Field Squadrons, 143rd Field Park Squadron, Royal
    Engineers
The Household Cavalry Regiment [armoured cars]
11th Hussars (Prince Albert's Own) [armoured cars]
2nd Derbyshire Yeomanry [armoured cars]
3rd Royal Horse Artillery
65th Anti-Tank Regiment, Royal Artillery (Suffolk and Norfolk Yeomanry)
15th Light Anti-Aircraft Regiment, Royal Artillery (Isle of Man)

4th Light Armoured Brigade – Brigadier M. G. Roddick
4th Armoured Brigade HQ and Signals Company, Royal Corps of Signals; 4th
  Armoured Brigade Workshops, Royal Electrical and Mechanical Engineers;
  5th and 58th Companies, Royal Army Service Corps
The Royal Scots Greys (2nd Dragoons)
4th Queen's Own Hussars/8th King's Royal Irish Hussars [composite regi-
  ment]
1st King's Royal Rifle Corps [motor battalion]

22nd Armoured Brigade – Brigadier G. P. B. Roberts
22nd Armoured Brigade HQ and Signals, Royal Corps of Signals; 22nd
  Armoured Brigade Workshops, Royal Electrical and Mechanical Engineers;
  432nd Company, Royal Army Service Corps
1st and 5th Battalions, Royal Tank Regiment
4th County of London Yeomanry (The Sharpshooters)
1st Battalion, Rifle Brigade (Prince Consort's Own) [motor battalion]
4th and 97th (Kent Yeomanry) Field Regiments, Royal Artillery
44th Regiment, Reconnaissance Corps [attached]

1st Fighting French Brigade Group
1st Fighting French Brigade HQ and Signals
2nd Battalion, French Foreign Legion
3rd Battalion, Infanterie Marine Pacifique
2nd Anti-Aircraft Company
1st Fusiliers Marine
2nd Fighting French Anti-Tank Company
22nd North African Anti-Tank Company
1st Fighting French Field Engineer Company
3rd Field Regiment, Royal Artillery [attached]
1st Fighting French Flying Column: Armoured Car Squadron and Anti-Tank
  Troop
1st Morroccan Spahis
1st Fighting French Tank Company
Anti-Aircraft Troop, 1st Battalion French Foreign Legion

[attached] **131st (Queen's) Lorried Infantry Brigade** – Brigadier W. D.
  Stamer [incorporated into 7th Armoured Division on 1 November]
131st Brigade HQ and Signals Company, Royal Corps of Signals; 131st Brigade
  Workshops, Royal Electrical and Mechanical Engineers; 507th Company,
  Royal Army Service Corps, 11th Field Company, Royal Engineers
1/5th, 1/6th, 1/7th Battalions, Queen's Royal Regiment (West Surrey)
57th Field Regiment Royal Artillery (Home Counties)
2 batteries, 57th Anti-Tank Regiment Royal Artillery (East Surrey)

44th (Home Counties) Division – Major General I. T. P. Hughes
44th (Home Counties) Divisional Signals, Royal Corps of Signals; 44th Division
  Provost Company, Corps of Military Police; 131st and 132nd Field
  Ambulances, Royal Army Medical Corps; 503rd Company, 168th General

Transport Company, Royal Army Service Corps; 209th and 210th Field Companies, 211th Field Park Company, 577th Army Field Park Company, Royal Engineers

58th (Sussex) and 65th (8th London) Field Regiments, Royal Artillery

57th Anti-Tank Regiment, Royal Artillery (East Surrey)

30th Light Anti-Aircraft Regiment, Royal Artillery

6th Battalion, 22nd (Cheshire) Regiment [machine-gun]

132nd (Kent) Brigade – Brigadier L. G. Whistler

132nd Brigade HQ and Signals Company, Royal Corps of Signals; 132nd Brigade Workshops, Royal Electrical and Mechanical Engineers

2nd Battalion, The Buffs (Royal East Kent Regiment)

4th and 5th Battalions, Queen's Own Royal West Kent Regiment

50th (Northumbrian) Division – Major-General J. S. Nichols

50th Divisional Signals, Royal Corps of Signals; 50th Division Provost Company, Corps of Military Police; 149th Field Ambulance, Royal Army Medical Corps; 233rd and 505th Field Companies, 235th Field Park Company, Royal Engineers

74th (Northumbrian), 111th (Bolton), 124th (Northumbrian) 154th (Leicestershire Yeomanry) Field Regiments Royal Artillery

102nd Anti-Tank Regiment, Royal Artillery (The Northumberland Hussars)

25th Light Anti-Aircraft Regiment, Royal Artillery

2nd Battalion, 22nd (Cheshire) Regiment [machine-gun]

69th Brigade – Brigadier E. C. Cooke-Collis

69th Brigade HQ and Signals Company, Royal Corps of Signals; 69th Brigade Workshops, Royal Electrical and Mechanical Engineers; 522th Company, Royal Army Service Corps

5th Battalion, East Yorkshire Regiment (The Duke of York's Own)

6th and 7th Battalions, Green Howards (Princess Alexandra's Own Regiment of Yorkshire)

151st (Tyneside) Brigade – Brigadier J. E. S. Percy

151st Brigade HQ and Signals Company, Royal Corps of Signals; 151st Brigade Workshops, Royal Electrical and Mechanical Engineers; 524th Company, Royal Army Service Corps

6th, 8th, 9th Battalions, Durham Light Infantry

1st Greek Brigade – Colonel Katsotas

1st, 2nd, 3rd Greek Infantry Battalions

1st Greek Field Artillery Regiment

1st Greek Field Engineer Company

1st Greek Machine-Gun Company

1st Greek Field Ambulance

2nd Fighting French Brigade Group – Lieutenant-Colonel Allesandrie

5th and 11th Battalions de Marche

21st and 23rd North African Anti-Tank Companies
2nd Fighting French Engineer Company

XXX Corps – Lieutenant-General Sir Oliver Leese Bt
XXX Corps Signals, Royal Corps of Signals; Y Lines of Communication Transport
  Column; 52th and 61st Detail Issue Depots, Royal Army Service Corps; XXX
  Corps Stores Convoy Unit, Royal Army Ordnance Corps; 2/3rd Casualty
  Clearing Station Light Section, Australian Army Medical Corps; 16th Motor
  Ambulance Company, Royal Army Medical Corps; Corps Defence Squadron,
  Royal Armoured Corps; 3 troops, 4th/6th South African Armoured Car
  Regiment; 7th, 64th (London), 69th (Carnarvon and Denbigh Yeomanry)
  Medium Regiments, Royal Artillery; HQ and 2 section, 66th Mortar Company,
  Royal Engineers; 11th and 13th Field Companies, 22nd Field Park Company,
  South African Engineer Corps

23rd Armoured Brigade – Brigadier G. W. Richards
23rd Armoured Brigade HQ and Signals Squadron, Royal Corps of Signals; 23rd
  Armoured Brigade Workshops, Royal Electrical and Mechanical Engineers;
  Provost Unit, Corps of Military Police; 7th Light Field Ambulance, Royal
  Army Medical Corps; 331st and 333rd Companies, Royal Army Service Corps;
  295th Army Field Company, Royal Engineers
46th and 50th Battalions, Royal Tank Regiment
121st Field Regiment, Royal Artillery (West Riding)
168th Light Anti-Aircraft Battery, Royal Artillery

51st (Highland) Division – Major-General D. N. Wimberley
51st (Highland) Divisional Signals, Royal Corps of Signals; 51st Division Provost
  Company, Corps of Military Police; 174th, 175th, 176th Field Ambulances,
  Royal Army Medical Corps; 458th, 525th, 526th, 527th Companies, Royal
  Army Service Corps; 274th, 275th, 276th Field Companies, 239th Field Park
  Company, Royal Engineers
126th (Highland), 127th (Highland), 128th (Highland) Field Regiments
61st Anti-Tank Regiment (West Highland) and 40th Light Anti-Aircraft
  Regiment, Royal Artillery
51st Reconnaissance Regiment, Reconnaissance Corps
1/7th Battalion, Middlesex Regiment (Duke of Cambridge's Own) [machine-
  gun]

152nd (Highland) Brigade – Brigadier G. Murray
152nd Brigade HQ and Signals Company, Royal Corps of Signals; 152nd
  Brigade Workshops, Royal Electrical and Mechanical Engineers
2nd and 5th (Sutherland and Caithness) Battalions, Seaforth Highlanders
  (Ross-shire Buffs, Duke of Albany's)
5th Battalion, Queen's Own Cameron Highlanders

153rd (Highland) Infantry Brigade – Brigadier D. A. H. Graham
153rd Brigade HQ and Signals Company, Royal Corps of Signals; 153rd
  Brigade Workshops, Royal Electrical and Mechanical Engineers

5th (Angus and Dundee) Battalion, Black Watch (Royal Highland Regiment)
1st and 5th/7th (Buchan, Mar and Mearns) Battalions, Gordon Highlanders

154th (Highland) Infantry Brigade – Brigadier H. W. Houldsworth
154th Brigade HQ and Signals Company, Royal Corps of Signals; 154th
   Brigade Workshops, Royal Electrical and Mechanical Engineers
1st and 7th (Fife) Battalions, Black Watch (Royal Highland Regiment)
7th Battalion, Argyll and Sutherland Highlanders (Princess Louise's)

2nd New Zealand Division – Lieutenant-General B. C. Freyberg VC
2nd New Zealand Divisional Signals, New Zealand Corps of Signals; 5th and 6th
   New Zealand Field Ambulances; 166th Light Field Ambulance, Royal Army
   Medical Corps; 1st Ammunition Company, 2nd Petrol Company, 3rd Supply
   Company, New Zealand Army Service Corps
2nd New Zealand Division Cavalry Regiment
4th, 5th, 6th New Zealand Field Regiments, New Zealand Artillery
7th New Zealand Anti-Tank Regiment, New Zealand Artillery
14th New Zealand Light Anti-Aircraft Regiment, New Zealand Artillery
6th, 7th, 8th Field Companies, 5th New Zealand Field Park Company, New
   Zealand Engineers
27th (Machine-Gun) Battalion

5th New Zealand Infantry Brigade – Brigadier H. Kippenburger
5th New Zealand HQ and Signals Company, New Zealand Signals; 5th New
   Zealand Brigade Workshops, New Zealand Electrical and Mechanical
   Engineers
21st, 22nd, 23rd Battalions
28th (Maori) Battalion

6th New Zealand Infantry Brigade – Brigadier W. Gentry
6th New Zealand HQ and Signals Company, New Zealand Signals; 6th New
   Zealand Brigade Workshops, New Zealand Electrical and Mechanical
   Engineers
24th, 25th, 26th Battalions

9th Armoured Brigade (UK) – Brigadier J. Currie
9th Armoured Brigade HQ and Signals Squadron (Middlesex Yeomanry),
   Royal Corps of Signals; 9th Armoured Brigade Workshops, Royal Electrical
   and Mechanical Engineers
3rd The King's Own Hussars
The Royal Wiltshire Yeomanry (Prince of Wales's)
The Warwickshire Yeomanry
14th Battalion, Sherwood Foresters (Nottinghamshire and Derbyshire
   Regiment) [motor battalion]

9th Australian Division – Lieutenant-General L. J. Morshead
9th Divisional Signals, Australian Corps of Signals; 9th Division Provost
   Company, Australian Corps of Military Police; 10th, 11th, 12th Companies,

Australian Army Service Corps; 9th Division Salvage Unit, Australian Army Ordnance Corps; 2/3rd, 2/8th, 2/11th Field Ambulances, 2/4th Field Hygiene Section, Australian Army Medical Corps; 2/3rd, 2/7th, 2/13th Field Companies, 2/4th Field Park Company, Royal Australian Engineers
9th Division Cavalry Regiment
2/7th, 2/8th, 2/12th Field Regiments, Royal Australian Artillery
2/3rd Anti-Tank Regiment, Royal Australian Artillery
2/4th Light Anti-Aircraft Regiment, Royal Australian Artillery
2/3rd Pioneer Battalion
2/2nd Machine-Gun Battalion
40th (The King's) Battalion, Royal Tank Regiment [attached]
1st and 3rd Sections, 66th Mortar Company, Royal Engineers [attached]

20th Australian Infantry Brigade – Brigadier W. J. V. Windeyer
20th Brigade HQ and Signals Company, Australian Corps of Signals; 20th Australian Brigade Workshops, Australian Army Ordnance Corps
2/13th, 2/15th, 2/17th Battalions

24th Australian Infantry Brigade – Brigadier A. H. L Gadfrey
24th Brigade HQ and Signals Company, Australian Corps of Signals, 24th Australian Brigade Workshops, Australian Army Ordnance Corps
2/28th, 2/32nd, 2/43rd Battalions

26th Australian Infantry Brigade – Brigadier D. A. Whitehead
26th Brigade HQ and Signals Company, Australian Corps of Signals, 26th Brigade Workshops, Australian Army Ordnance Corps
2/23rd, 2/24th, 2/48th Battalions

1st South African Division – Major-General D. H. Pienaar
1st South African Divisional Signals, South African Corps of Signals; 12th, 15th, 18th South African Field Ambulances, South African Medical Corps; 1st, 2nd, 3rd, 5th Field Companies, 19th Field Park Company, South African Engineer Corps
1st (Cape Field Artillery), 4th and 7th Field Regiments, South African Artillery
1st South African Anti-Tank Regiment, South African Artillery
1st South African Light Anti-Aircraft Regiment, South African Artillery
Regiment President Steyn [machine-gun]
1 company from Die Middellandse Regiment [machine-gun]

1st South African Brigade – Brigadier C. L. de W. du Toit
1st South African Brigade HQ and Signals Company, South African Signals; 1st South African Brigade Workshops, South African Technical Services Corps
1st Battalion, Royal Natal Carbineers
1st/3rd Battalion, Transvaal Scottish Volunteers
1st Battalion, Duke of Edinburgh's Own Rifles

2nd South African Brigade – Brigadier W. H. E. Poole
2nd South African Brigade HQ and Signals Company, South African Signals; 2nd South African Brigade Workshops, South African Technical Services Corps
1st Battalion, Natal Mounted Rifles
1st Battalion, Duke of Connaught and Strathearn's Own Cape Town Highlanders
1st/2nd Field Force Battalion

3rd South African Brigade – Brigadier R. J. Palmer
3rd South African Brigade HQ and Signals Company, South African Signals; 3rd South African Brigade Workshops, South African Technical Services Corps
1st Battalion, Imperial Light Horse
1st Battalion, Royal Durban Light Infantry
1st Battalion, Rand Light Infantry

1st South African Division Reserve Force
2nd Battalion, Regiment Botha
3rd South African Armoured Car Regiment [less 2 squadrons]
1st South African Anti-Tank Battery, South African Artillery
8th Battalion, Royal Tank Regiment [attached]

4th Indian Division – Major-General F. I. S. Tuker
4th Indian Divisional Signals, Indian Signals Corps; 17th Mobile Workshop Company, Indian Army Ordnance Corps; 4th Indian Division Troops Transport Company, 220th Detail Issue Depot, Royal Indian Army Service Corps; 17th and 26th Indian Field Ambulances, 15th Indian Field Hygiene Section, Indian Army Medical Corps; 75th Light Field Ambulance, Royal Army Medical Corps
4th Field Company, King George's Own Bengal Sappers and Miners
12th Field Company, Queen Victoria's Own Madras Sappers and Miners
21st Field Company, Royal Bombay Sappers and Miners
11th Field Park Company, Queen Victoria's Own Madras Sappers and Miners
1st, 11th, 32nd Field Regiments Royal Artillery
149th Anti-Tank Regiment (Lancashire Yeomanry) and 57th Light Anti-Aircraft Regiments (King's Own Yorkshire Light Infantry), Royal Artillery
6th Battalion (Machine-Gun), 6th Rajputana Rifles

5th Indian Brigade – Brigadier D. Russell
5th Indian Brigade HQ and Signals Company, Indian Signals Corps; 5th Indian Brigade Workshops, Indian Army Ordnance Corps; 5th Indian Brigade Transport Company, Royal Indian Army Service Corps
1/4th Battalion, Essex Regiment
4th Battalion (Outram's), 6th Rajputana Rifles
3rd Battalion (Queen Mary's Own), 10th Baluch Regiment

7th Indian Brigade – Brigadier A. W. W. Holworthy
7th Indian Brigade HQ and Signals Company, Indian Signals Corps; 7th Indian Brigade Workshops, Indian Army Ordnance Corps; 7th Indian Brigade Transport Company, Indian Army Service Corps
1st Battalion, Royal Sussex Regiment
4th Battalion (Bhopal), 16th Punjab Regiment
1st Battalion, 2nd King Edward VII's Own Goorkha Rifles (The Sirmoor Rifles)

161st Indian Motor Brigade – Brigadier F. E. C. Hughes
161st Indian Brigade HQ and Signals Company, Indian Signals Corps; 161st Indian Motorized Brigade Transport Company, Royal Indian Army Service Corps; 161st Indian Brigade Workshops, Indian Army Service Corps
1st Battalion, Argyll & Sutherland Highlanders (Princess Louise's)
1st Battalion, 1st Punjab Regiment
4th Battalion, 7th Rajput Regiment

Headquarters Middle East, Royal Air Force – Air Marshal Sir Arthur Tedder
No. 1411 Meteorological Flight, Royal Air Force [Gladiator]; No. 2 Photographic Reconnaissance Unit [Spitfire, Hurricane, Beaufighter]; No. 60 Squadron, South African Air Force [detachment] [Maryland]; 162 Squadron, Royal Air Force [Lodestar, Wellington]

201 Group
No. 1 General Reconnaissance Unit [Wellington]; Sea Rescue Flight [Wellington, Fairchild Ambulance]; 15 Squadron, South African Air Force [Blenheim]; 47 Squadron, Royal Air Force [Beaufort]; 203 Squadron, Royal Air Force [Blenheim, Baltimore, Maryland]; 230 Squadron, Royal Air Force [Sunderland, Dornier 22]; 459 Squadron, Royal Australian Air Force [Hudson]; 701 Squadron, Fleet Air Arm [Walrus]; 821, 826 Squadrons, Fleet Air Arm [Albacore]; 815 Squadron, Fleet Air Arm [Swordfish]

235 Wing
13 (Hellenic) and 47 Squadrons, Royal Air Force [Blenheim]
459 Squadron, Royal Australian Air Force [detachment] [Hudson]

247 Wing
203 Squadron, Royal Air Force [detachment] [Maryland, Baltimore, Blenheim]
221 Squadron, Royal Air Force [detachment] [Wellington]

248 Wing
38 and 221 Squadrons, Royal Air Force [Wellington]
458 Squadron, Royal Australian Air Force [Wellington]
39 Squadron, Royal Air Force [Beaufort]

203 Group
1412 Meteorological Flight, Royal Air Force [Gladiator]
15 Squadron, South African Air Force [detachment] [Blenheim]

205 Group
Special Liberator Flight, Royal Air Force [Liberator]

231 Wing
37 and 70 Squadrons, Royal Air Force [Wellington]

236 Wing
108 and 148 Squadrons, Royal Air Force [Wellington]

238 Wing
40 and 104 Squadrons, Royal Air Force [Wellington]

242 Wing
147 and 160 Squadrons, Royal Air Force [Liberator]

245 Wing
14 Squadron, Royal Air Force [Marauder, Boston]
227 Squadron, Royal Air Force [detachment] [Beaufighter]
462 Squadron, Royal Australian Air Force [Halifax]

207 Group
34 Flight, South African Air Force [Anson]
35 Flight, South African Air Force [Blenheim]
1414 Flight, Royal Air Force [Gladiator]
1433 Flight, Royal Air Force [Lysander]
16 Squadron, South African Air Force [Beaufort, Maryland]
209 and 321 Squadrons, Royal Air Force [Catalina]

246 Wing
41 Squadron, South African Air Force [Hartebeeste, Hurricane]

216 Group
117 Squadron, Royal Air Force [Hudson]
173 Squadron, Royal Air Force [various]
216 Squadron, Royal Air Force [Lodestar, Hudson, Bombay]
267 Squadron, Royal Air Force [various]

283 Wing
163 Squadron, Royal Air Force [Hudson]

1st Bombardment Group (Provisional), United States Army Air Force
9 Squadron, United States Army Air Force [Flying Fortress]
Halverson Squadron, United States Army Air Force [Liberator]

98th Bombardment Group, United States Army Air Force
343, 344, 345, 415 Squadrons, United States Army Air Force [Liberator]

Air Headquarters, Malta – Air Vice-Marshal Keith Park
1435 Flight, Royal Air Force [Spitfire]
89 [detachment] and 227 Squadrons, Royal Air Force [Beaufighter]
69 Squadron, Royal Air Force [Wellington, Baltimore, Spitfire]
126, 185, 249 Squadrons, Royal Air Force [Spitfire]
229 Squadron, Royal Air Force [Spitfire, Hurricane]
828 Squadron, Fleet Air Arm [Albacore]
830 Squadron, Fleet Air Arm [Swordfish]

Air Headquarters Egypt

234 Wing
889 Squadron, Fleet Air Arm [Fulmar]

259 Wing
89 Squadron, Royal Air Force [Beaufighter]
94 Squadron, Royal Air Force [Hurricane, Spitfire]

252 Wing
46 Squadron Royal Air Force [Beaufighter]
417 Squadron, Royal Canadian Air Force [Hurricane, Spitfire]

Air Headquarters, Western Desert – Air Vice-Marshal Sir Arthur Coningham
No. 1 Air Ambulance Unit [De Havilland 86]

240 (Reconnaissance) Wing
No. 2 Photographic Reconnaissance Unit [detachment] [various]
208 (Army Co-operation) Squadron, Royal Air Force [Hurricane]
40 Squadron, South African Air Force [Hurricane]
60 Squadron, South African Air Force [Baltimore]
1437 Strategic Reconnaissance Flight, Royal Air Force [Baltimore]

3 Wing South African Air Force
12 Squadron, South African Air Force [Boston]
21 Squadron, South African Air Force [Baltimore]
24 Squadron, South African Air Force [Boston]

232 Wing
55 Squadron, Royal Air Force [Baltimore]
223 Squadron, Royal Air Force [Baltimore]

12th Bombardment Group, United States Army Air Force
81, 82, 83, 434 Squadrons, United States Army Air Force [Baltimore]

211 Group
6 and 7 Squadrons, South African Air Force [Hurricane]

233 Wing
2, 4, 260 Squadrons, South African Air Force [Kittyhawk]
5 Squadron, South African Air Force [Tomahawk]

239 Wing
112 and 250 Squadrons, Royal Air Force
3 and 450 Squadrons, Royal Australian Air Force [Kittyhawk]

244 Wing
92, 145, 601 Squadrons, Royal Air Force [Spitfire]
73 Squadron, Royal Air Force [Hurricane]

57th Fighter Group, United States Army Air Force
64, 65, 66, Squadrons, United States Army Air Force [Warhawk]

212 Group [protected by 94th Heavy and 16th Light Anti-Aircraft Regiments, Royal Artillery]

7 Wing, South African Air Force
80, 127, 274, 335 (Hellenic) Squadrons, Royal Air Force [Hurricane]

243 Wing
1 Squadron, South African Air Force
33, 213, 238 Squadrons, Royal Air Force [Hurricane]

Notes

Abbreviations for archives

AWM   Australian War Memorial, Canberra
BWA   The Black Watch Museum Archive, Perth
IWM   Imperial War Museum, London
LHCMA   Liddell Hart Centre for Military Archives, King's College London
PRO   Public Record Office, Kew
RLCM   Royal Logistics Corps Museum, Deep Cut, Surrey
SWWEC The Second World War Experience Centre, Leeds
WL   The Wellcome Library, Archives and Manuscripts, London
WSRO   West Sussex County Record Office, Chichester
WYM   Warwickshire Yeomanry Museum, Warwick

Full details of books cited in short-title form may be found in the Bibliography.

Introduction

1. SWWEC, Army/ R. I. Blair; Aileen Clayton, *The Enemy is Listening*, p. 223.
2. Terraine, *The Right of the Line*, p. 385.
3. Bates, *Dance of War*, p. 10.
4. For a detailed discussion on Montgomery's personality see Dixon, *On the Psychology of Military Incompetence*, esp. pp. 355–69.
5. Lucas-Phillips, *Alamein*, p. 185.
6. Greacen, *Chink*, p. 308.
7. N. Hamilton, *Monty: The Making of a General*, p. 553.
8. R. Walker, *Alam Halfa and Alamein*, pp. 6–7.
9. Ibid., p. 7.
10. Greacen, *Chink*, pp. 341–2.
11. D. French, *Raising Churchill's Army*, p. 186.
12. PRO WO 216/1: 'Memorandum: The Need for Administrative Services as an Integral Part of the Field Army, 21 Jan 1941'.
13. D. French, *Raising Churchill's Army, passim.*

14. Van Creveld, *Supplying War*, pp. 141–201; D. French, *Raising Churchill's Army*, pp. 121, 278.
15. Wilmington, *The Middle East Supply Centre*, p. 1.
16. Carver, *El Alamein*, p. 9.
17. J. Lucas, *Panzer Army Africa*, p. 3.
18. Churchill, *The Second World War*, vol. III, p. 5.

Chapter 1: Britain and Egypt
1. Forty, *The First Victory*, pp. 11, 68–9.
2. See Packenham, *The Scramble For Africa*, pp. 72–85, 123–140.
3. B. Pitt, *The Crucible of War: Western Desert 1941*, p. xvii.
4. For details of Britain's dealings with Egypt between the wars see Anthony Clayton, *The British Empire as a Superpower*, pp. 112–17, 130–4, 466–70.
5. Kiernan, *Colonial Empires and Armies*, p. 83.
6. Richard Lamb's *Mussolini and the British* presents a complete and revisionist study of Anglo-Italian relations between the wars.
7. G. Orwell, 'The Lion and the Unicorn', in *Collected Essays, Journalism and Letters*, vol. II, pp. 88, 93.
8. See M. Knox, 'The Italian Armed Forces, 1940–43', in Millett and Murray, *Military Effectiveness*, vol. III, pp. 136–72.
9. Ibid., p. 164.
10. Madeja, *Italian Army Order of Battle*, p. 37.
11. McGuirk, *Rommel's Army in Africa*, p. 50.
12. Bates, *Dance of War*, pp. 19–20.
13. For a complete description of the Italian Army in the Second World War, see Trye, *Mussolini's Soldiers*.
14. Caccia-Dominioni, *Alamein 1933–1962*, p. 43.
15. Wilmington, *The Middle East Supply Centre*, p. 2.
16. PRO AIR 41/50: 'The Middle East Campaign, vol. IV: Operations in Libya, the Western Desert and Tunisia, July 1942–May 1943'.
17. Bond, *British Military Policy between the Two World Wars, passim*.
18. D. French, *Raising Churchill's Army*, p. 281.
19. Bates, *Dance of War*, p. 29.
20. Bond, *British Military Policy between the Two World Wars*, pp. 35–71. The lamentable consequences are underlined in Fraser, *And We Shall Shock Them*, pp. 2–23. See also Dixon, *On the Psychology of Military Incompetence*, pp. 110–29, 288–301.
21. B. Pitt, *The Crucible of War: Western Desert 1941*, pp. 10–12.
22. Bidwell, 'After the Wall Came Tumbling Down', p. 60.
23. For a discussion of the differences in approach to officer training between the British and the Germans, see Whiting, *The Poor Bloody Infantry*, pp. 130–3.
24. D. French, *Raising Churchill's Army, passim*. This book provides the most complete analysis of the British Army's strengths, weaknesses and development before and during the Second World War.
25. Fletcher, *The Great Tank Scandal*, pt I, *passim*.
26. D. French, *Raising Churchill's Army*, p. 222.
27. Majdalany, *The Battle of El Alamein*, pp. 22–3.
28. Neillands, *The Desert Rats*, pp. 35–7.
29. Warner, *Alamein*, p. 117.

30. A. Gilbert, *The Imperial War Museum Book of The Desert War*, p. 39.
31. Messenger, *The Unknown Alamein*, pp. 34–5, 37.
32. A. Gilbert, *The Imperial War Museum Book of The Desert War*, p. 41.
33. Lucas-Phillips, *Alamein*, p. 21.
34. A. Gilbert, *The Imperial War Museum Book of The Desert War*, pp. 30–1.
35. Warner, *Alamein*, p. 54.
36. Clifford, *Three Against Rommel*, p. 36.
37. Warner, *Alamein*, p. 54.
38. A. Gilbert, *The Imperial War Museum Book of the Desert War*, p. 31.
39. Moorehead, *African Trilogy*, pp. 68–71.
40. Correlli Barnett asserted in *The Desert Generals* that had O'Connor been allowed to proceed he would surely have taken Tripoli. Considering that the British forces that reached Beda Fomm were out on their feet, this is wild speculation, and his excited claim in the 1983 edition of *The Desert Generals* that Ultra subsequently justified this is refuted by Ralph Bennett (*Ultra and Mediterranean Strategy*, p. 29).
41. PRO WO 201/2586: 'Middle East Training Pamphlet No. 10'.
42. Playfair, *The Mediterranean and Middle East*, vol. II, p. 3.
43. Liddell Hart, *The Other Side of the Hill*, pp. 233–4.
44. Trevor-Roper, *Hitler's War Directives*, pp. 85, 99.
45. Playfair, *The Mediterranean and Middle East*, vol. I, p. 317.

Chapter 2: Rommel

1. Caccia-Dominioni, *Alamein 1933–1962*, p. 51.
2. Fraser, *Knight's Cross*, p. 28. Fraser gives a detailed account of Rommel's First World War career based largely on Rommel's own recollections and notes for *Infanterie Greift An*.
3. Irving, *The Trail of the Fox*, p. 22.
4. McGuirk, *Rommel's Army in Africa*, p. 15.
5. Liddell Hart, *The Other Side of the Hill*, pp. 76–8.
6. Van Creveld, 'Rommel's Supply Problem', p. 67.
7. Barker, *Afrika Korps*, p. 15.
8. Irving, *The Trail of the Fox*, pp. 60, 67.
9. McGuirk, *Rommel's Army in Africa*, pp. 16–17.
10. Irving, *The Trail of the Fox*, pp. 70–1.
11. Hinsley, *British Intelligence*, vol. I, pp. 389–92.
12. Behrendt, *Rommel's Intelligence in the Desert Campaign*, pp. 42–3.
13. Dupuy, *A Genius for War*, pp. 4, 302.
14. Bates, *Dance of War*, pp. 21–2.
15. Barker, *Afrika Korps*, p. 12.
16. Hunt, *A Don at War*, p. 41.
17. D. French, *Raising Churchill's Army*, pp. 19–20.
18. PRO WO 287/226: 'Tactical and Technical Notes on the German Army No. 11, May 1939'.
19. D. French, *Raising Churchill's Army*, pp. 58–9.
20. B. Pitt, *The Crucible of War: Western Desert 1941*, p. 304.
21. PRO CAB 146/10: 'Enemy Documents Section, Axis Operations in North Africa, Part I: The New Battle Tactics Developed by the Panzer Formations, Nov. 1941'.

22. Roberts, *From the Desert to the Baltic*, p. 51; Carver, *Dilemmas of the Desert War*, pp. 23–3.
23. D. French, *Raising Churchill's Army*, pp. 218, 239.
24. Behrendt, *Rommel's Intelligence in the Desert Campaign*, p. 76.
25. Bean, *Official History of Australia in the War of 1914–1918*, vol. V, p. 301.
26. Address by Morshead to 26th Brigade Group, 12 August 1945, quoted in Maughan, *Tobruk and El Alamein*, pp. 11–12.
27. Macksey, *Kesselring*, p. 106.
28. Van Creveld, 'Rommel's Supply Problem', p. 67.
29. See W. B. Kennedy-Shaw, *Long Range Desert Group*. This book tells the story of probably the best, most professional and effective of the 'private armies'.
30. Bennett, *Ultra and Mediterranean Strategy*, pp. 38, 43.
31. PRO WO 201/358: 'Eighth Army Draft Report on Operations, 1941 Sept–Nov'.
32. PRO WO 169/996: 'Eighth Army Advanced HQ War Diary, 1941 Sept–Dec'.
33. Playfair, *The Mediterranean and Middle East*, vol. III, p. 15.
34. W. G. Stevens, *Freyberg VC*, p. 81.
35. A. Gilbert, *The Imperial War Museum Book of The Desert War*, p. 137.
36. See McLeod, *Myth and Reality*; J. Ross, *The Myth of the Digger*; M. Johnston, *At the Front Line* and *Fighting the Enemy*; Barter, *Far Above Battle*.
37. Bates, *Dance of War*, p. 25.
38. For an analysis of Australian attitudes to their enemies and vice versa, see M. Johnston, *Fighting the Enemy*.
39. AWM 3 DRL/6643/1/2/Bii: 'GHQ MEF, Daily Intelligence Summary No. 612, 22 January 1942: Report of 25 August 1941, by II Bn., 104th Lorried Infantry Regiment in Reply to Divisional Questionnaire'.
40. A. Gilbert, *The Imperial War Museum Book of The Desert War*, pp. 131–2.
41. Doherty, *A Noble Crusade*, p. 14.
42. PRO WO 201/358.
43. Doherty, *A Noble Crusade*, p. 16.
44. Fraser, *And We Shall Shock Them*, p. 167.
45. Doherty, *A Noble Crusade*, p. 25.
46. Ibid., pp. 26–8.
47. Parkinson, *The Auk*, p. 128.
48. Lewin, *Rommel as Military Commander*, p. 129.
49. Doherty, *A Noble Crusade*, pp. 29–32.
50. Trevor-Roper, *Hitler's War Directives*, p. 164.
51. Irving, *The Trail of the Fox*, pp. 79–80, 88–9, 104, 160; Kesselring, *Memoirs*, p. 132.
52. Doherty, *A Noble Crusade*, p. 33.
53. Tuker, *Approach to Battle*, p. 65.
54. Van Creveld, 'Rommel's Supply Problem', p. 68.
55. Barker, *Afrika Korps*, p. 86.
56. Playfair, *The Mediterranean and Middle East*, vol. III, pp. 150–3.
57. Hunt, *A Don at War*, pp. 68–9.
58. Tuker, *Approach to Battle*, p. 81; Carver, *Dilemmas of the Desert War*, pp. 56–8.
59. N. Hamilton, *Monty: The Making of a General*, pp. 403–7.

Chapter 3: Eighth Army

1. D. Johnston, *Nine Rivers From Jordan*, p. 24.
2. The full story of the song appeared in 'A Song for All Armies' by Derek Jewell in the *Sunday Times* in 1967 and was reprinted in Forty, *Afrika Korps at War*, vol. II, pp. 34–51.
3. Milligan, *Rommel? Gunner Who?*, p. 94.
4. J. Lucas, *War in the Desert*, p. 58.
5. Nalder, *British Army Signals in the Second World War*, p. 258.
6. Bishop, *One Young Soldier*, p. 95.
7. Carver, *Dilemmas of the Desert War*, p. 144.
8. PRO WO 277/25: 'Signals Communications 1939–1945'.
9. PRO WO 106/2223: 'Pamphlets: Notes from Theatres of War, Cyrenaica'.
10. Douglas, *Alamein to Zem Zem*, pp. 115–18.
11. Behrendt, *Rommel's Intelligence in the Desert Campaign*, p. 50.
12. See Kahn, *The Codebreakers*, for a complete version of this story. Khan reproduces many examples of Fellers's reports.
13. Richards and Saunders, *Royal Air Force 1939–1945*, vol. II, pp. 190–1.
14. Macksey, *Kesselring*, pp. 114–5.
15. Van Creveld, 'Rommel's Supply Problem', p. 69.
16. *Die Oase*, No. 8, August, 1968, p. 3.
17. Richards and Saunders, *Royal Air Force 1939–1945*, vol. II, pp. 195–6.
18. Doherty, *A Noble Crusade*, p. 39.
19. Ibid., pp. 40–1.
20. Heckstall-Smith, *Tobruk*, p. 201.
21. Douglas, *Alamein to Zem Zem*, p. 129.
22. Barnett, *The Desert Generals*, p. 148.
23. Doherty, *A Noble Crusade*, p. 49.
24. Agar-Hamilton and Turner, *Crisis in the Desert*, p. 38.
25. Farran, *Winged Dagger*, p. 144.
26. Fraser, *And We Shall Shock Them*, p. 220.
27. PRO CAB 44/97, Section I, Chapter J: 'German Assault on the Gazala Position: The Fall of Tobruk, 1942 May 26–June 21, by Brigadier J. C. Moloney [1952]'.
28. Heckstall-Smith, *Tobruk*, p. 211.
29. Connell, *Auchinleck*, p. 499.
30. Agar-Hamilton and Turner, *Crisis in the Desert*, pp. 74–9.
31. Connell, *Auchinleck*, pp. 568–9.
32. De Guingand, *Generals at War,* p. 182.
33. Auchinleck, 'Despatch', p. 378, col. 1.
34. Tedder, *With Prejudice*, p. 240.
35. De Guingand, *Generals at War,* p. 182.
36. Kennedy, *The Business of War*, p. 243.
37. Mellenthin, *Panzer Battles*, p. 139.
38. Orpen, *South African Forces, World War II*, vol. III, p. 288.
39. Heckmann, *Rommel's War in Africa*, p. 280.
40. Bernstein, *The Tide Turned at Alamein*, p. 104.
41. A. Cunningham, *A Sailor's Odyssey*, pp. 464–5.
42. P. Lewis, *A People's War*, p. 86.

43. Bryant, *The Turn of the Tide*, p. 408; Churchill, *The Second World War*, vol. IV, pp. 317–18.
44. L. Lucas, *Malta*, p. 130.
45. Richards and Saunders, *Royal Air Force 1939–1945*, vol. II, p. 202.
46. Mellenthin, *Panzer Battles* p. 150.
47. Barker, *Afrika Korps*, p. 112.
48. Heckmann, *Rommel's War in Africa*, p. 281.
49. Ibid., pp. 282–3.
50. Carver, *El Alamein*, pp. 40–1.
51. Ciano, *Diaries*, p. 483.
52. Shulman, *Defeat in the West*, p. 59.
53. Detweiler, et. al., *World War II German Military Studies*, vol. XIV, pt IV, MS# T–3 P1, pp. 46, 60.
54. Orpen, *South African Forces, World War II*, vol. III, pp. 330–1.
55. Barnett, *The Desert Generals*, p. 169.
56. In fairness to Ritchie, he subsequently proved a successful commander, first of a division and then of a corps. It was not his fault that he had been asked to command an army before he was ready to. Norman Dixon discusses his character in *On the Psychology of Military Incompetence* (pp. 126–9), while Michael Carver mounts a defence of him in an appendix to *Dilemmas of the Desert War*.
57. N. Hamilton, *Monty: The Making of a General*, p. 539.
58. Alanbrooke, *War Diaries*, p. 224.
59. B. Pitt, *The Crucible of War: Year of Alamein 1942*, pp. 119–20.
60. Maughan, *Tobruk and El Alamein*, p. 536.
61. Doherty, *A Noble Crusade*, p. 57.
62. PRO AIR 41/50: 'The Middle East Campaign, vol. IV: Operations in Libya, the Western Desert and Tunisia, July 1942–May 1943'.
63. Richards and Saunders, *Royal Air Force 1939–1945*, vol. II, pp. 211–15.
64. Mitcham, *Rommel's Desert War*, pp. 86–9. Mitcham, as an American using mainly German sources, tends to swallow some of the wilder claims of their operational success without question. For example, that the British used 1,200 guns in one concentration during the Alamein offensive, which as we shall see is wildly exaggerated.
65. Carrell, *The Foxes of the Desert*, pp. 233–4.
66. PRO CAB 44/98, Section I, Chapter K: 'Retreat to El Alamein, 1942 June 22–August 30, by Brigadier J. C. Moloney [1952]'.
67. Scoullar, *Battle for Egypt*, pp. 143–4.
68. R. Clarke, *With Alex at War*, p. 51.
69. Greacen, *Chink*, pp. 204–10.
70. Parry, 'Eighth Army – Defeat and Disgrace', p. 145.
71. Playfair, *The Mediterranean and Middle East*, vol. III, p. 374.
72. Ciano, *Diaries*, p. 495; Bates, *Dance of War*, p. 14.
73. Behrendt, *Rommel's Intelligence in the Desert Campaign*, pp. 167, 233–5.
74. B. Pitt, *The Crucible of War: Year of Alamein 1942*, p. 132.
75. A. Cooper, *Cairo in the War*, pp. 192–4.
76. Amery, *Approach March*, pp. 306–7.
77. J. Lucas, *War in the Desert*, pp. 30–1.
78. B. Pitt, *The Crucible of War: Year of Alamein 1942*, pp. 146–9.

Chapter 4: The Alamein Line

1. D. Johnston, *Nine Rivers From Jordan*, p. 20.
2. Pakenham-Walsh, *The Corps of Royal Engineers*, vol. VIII, pp. 374–6.
3. Birkby, *The Saga of the Transvaal Scottish Regiment*, p. 276.
4. Orpen, *South African Forces, World War II*, vol. III, p. 40.
5. Majdalany, *The Battle of El Alamein*, p. 19.
6. Carver, *El Alamein*, pp. 13–15.
7. Clausewitz, *On War*, p. 352.
8. R. Walker, *Alam Halfa and Alamein*, p. 5
9. Behrendt, *Rommel's Intelligence in the Desert Campaign*, p. 161.
10. Lucas-Phillips, *Alamein*, p. 46.
11. Warner, *Alamein*, p. 24.
12. C. Richardson, *Flashback*, p. 105.
13. Bates, *Dance of War*, p. 10.
14. Maughan, *Tobruk and El Alamein*, pp. 537–43.
15. Oakes, *Muzzle Blast*, pp. 93–4.
16. Goodhart, *The 2/7th Australian Field Regiment*, p. 151.
17. B. Pitt, *The Crucible of War: Year of Alamein 1942*, p. 160.
18. Quoted in Agar-Hamilton and Turner, *Crisis in the Desert*, p. 275.
19. Maughan, *Tobruk and El Alamein*, p. 547.
20. Agar-Hamilton and Turner, *Crisis in the Desert*, p. 277.
21. Bernstein, *The Tide Turned at Alamein*, pp. 107–8.
22. D. Johnston, *Nine Rivers From Jordan*, p. 19.
23. Pollock, *Pienaar of Alamein*, p. 142.
24. Connell, *Auchinleck*, p. 628.
25. Tedde, *Fiamme nel deserto*, pp. 206–7.
26. Bernstein, *The Tide Turned at Alamein*, p. 110.
27. The loss in this action of 2/5th Essex Regiment – coming on top of the loss of Norfolks, Suffolks, Cambridgeshires and 5th Bedfords, together with the Bedfordshire and Hertfordshire Yeomanry at Singapore in February – meant that a large proportion of the soldiery of East Anglia was incarcerated. The North Essex Boys of 2/5th (by no means the modern conception of an 'Essex Boy') remain unaware of the value of their stand and the losses they inflicted (I. Hook, curator, Essex Regiment Museum, letter to author 15 January 2001).
28. Bates, *Dance of War*, p. 88.
29. Playfair, *The Mediterranean and Middle East*, vol. III, p. 342.
30. McKee, *El Alamein*, p. 67.
31. Churchill, *The Second World War*, vol. IV, pp. 323–34.
32. Heckmann, *Rommel's War in Africa*, p. 305.
33. PRO WO 277/32: 'Rearmament, vol. II'.
34. IWM AL 879/1: '90 Light Div (Afrika) Ia, War Diary, 05.09.42–31.12.42 plus translation (extracts only)'.
35. PRO AIR 41/50: 'The Middle East Campaign, vol. IV: Operations in Libya, the Western Desert and Tunisia, July 1942–May 1943'.
36. Guedalla, *Middle East 1940–1942*, p. 191.
37. PRO AIR 41/50.
38. Bates, *Dance of War*, pp. 99, 109.
39. Playfair, *The Mediterranean and Middle East*, vol. III, p. 360.

40. Bennett, *Ultra and Mediterranean Strategy*, p. 130. Was Rommel stopped or did he 'run out of steam'? Correlli Barnett proposes the first in *The Desert Generals*, but Lord John Harding, who was then Deputy Chief of Staff to Auchinleck, suggests the latter. The evidence from Ultra shows stiffer British resistance as well as waning Axis strength, but significantly favours Harding's belief (Bennett, op. cit., pp. 132–3).
41. Mellenthin, *Panzer Battles*, p. 129.
42. Bidwell, *Gunners at War*, pp. 184–5.
43. Maughan, *Tobruk and El Alamein*, p. 554.
44. Parkinson, *The Auk*, p. 208.
45. Maughan, *Tobruk and El Alamein*, p. 552.
46. Greacen, *Chink*, p. 217.
47. Bates, *Dance of War*, pp. 123–4.
48. Orpen, *South African Forces, World War II*, vol. III, p. 364; Maughan, *Tobruk and El Alamein*, pp. 555–6.
49. Bates, *Dance of War*, pp. 131–2.
50. Doherty, *A Noble Crusade*, p. 64.
51. Orpen, *South African Forces, World War II*, vol. III, p. 366.
52. Maughan, *Tobruk and El Alamein*, pp. 559–65.
53. Behrendt, *Rommel's Intelligence in the Desert Campaign*, pp. 168–78. Behrendt discusses at length the demise of this important little unit, and then describes the British analysis of its value (pp. 178–87).
54. Hinsley, *British Intelligence*, vol. II, pp. 402–3.
55. PRO AIR 41/50. Portal had been forced to intervene with Churchill in the autumn of 1941, when Churchill wanted to recall Tedder from the Middle East. Portal's faith in Tedder was to be well rewarded.
56. Bates, *Dance of War*, pp. 143–7.
57. This is a confusing battle to decipher. See Bates, *Dance of War*, ch. 13, Kippenburger, *Infantry Brigadier*, pp. 165–70.
58. ATL OHInt-0204/1: 'Interview with Denver Fontaine'.
59. Kippenburger, *Infantry Brigadier*, pp. 173–4.
60. Douglas, *Alamein to Zem Zem*, p. 20.
61. Liddell Hart, *The Tanks*, pp. 211–12.
62. Quoted in Doherty, *A Noble Crusade*, p. 49.
63. Baker, *Yeoman-Yeoman*, p. 52.
64. Majdalany, *The Battle of El Alamein*, pp. 25–7.
65. WL RAMC 1762: 'J. D. P. Graham MD DSc FRCP FRSE, "A Time in the Sand: A True Account of Some Personal Experiences with the RAMC in the Western Desert 1941–1943"', pp. 20–1.
66. Liddell Hart, *The Rommel Papers*, p. 257.
67. Orpen, *South African Forces, World War II*, vol. III, p. 363.
68. Barker, *Afrika Korps*, p. 130.
69. Caccia-Dominioni, *Alamein 1933–1962*, p. 67.
70. Maughan, *Tobruk and El Alamein*, pp. 576–7.
71. McKee, *El Alamein*, p. 75.
72. Bates, *Dance of War*, p. 197.
73. B. Pitt, 'Monty's Foxhounds', p. 34.
74. McKee, *El Alamein*, pp. 76–9.

75. S. D. Hamilton, *50th Royal Tank Regiment*, p. 38.
76. Maughan, *Tobruk and El Alamein*, p. 579.
77. Barnett, *The Desert Generals*, p. 212. Barnett dates this incident to 22 July, but Morshead's diary gives it as the 21st, and the attack of 24 July to which Barnett refers was in essence a repeat of the abortive attack launched on the afternoon of the 22nd. (See Maughan, *Tobruk and El Alamein*, p. 579.)
78. Maughan, *Tobruk and El Alamein*, pp. 580–8.
79. S. D. Hamilton, *50th Royal Tank Regiment*, p. 32.
80. Scoullar, *Battle for Egypt*, pp. 375–6.
81. PRO CAB 44/98, Section I, Chapter K: 'Retreat to El Alamein, 1942 June 22–August 30, by Brigadier J. C. Moloney [1952]'.
82. De Guingand, *Operation Victory*, pp. 132–3.
83. D. Young, *Rommel*, p. 165.
84. B. Pitt, *The Crucible of War: Year of Alamein 1942*, pp. 204–5.

Chapter 5: Malta

1. Ciano, *Diaries*, p. 496.
2. There are many books on the history of Malta: see B. Blouet, *The Story of Malta* (London: Faber, 1967). Of particular interest is *Malta* by Sir Harry Luke, who was governor from 1930 to 1938, and describes the particular economic and political problems of the period (London: Harrap, 1960).
3. Of this siege Voltaire wrote, 'Nothing is better known than the siege of Malta' (Bradford, *Siege*, p. xv). This may have been true of those who spoke languages other than English, but remarkably little was written about it in the UK before the twentieth century. See E. Bradford, *The Great Siege: Malta 1565* (London: Hodder & Stoughton, 1960); T. Pickles, *Malta 1565: Last Battle of the Crusades* (London: Osprey, 1998).
4. Bradford, *Siege*, pp. 7–10. This is a rounded account of the 1940–43 siege. Bradford lived in Malta for many years.
5. Bates, *Dance of War*, p. 33.
6. Spooner, *Supreme Gallantry*, pp. 14–15. This book describes Malta's offensive role.
7. Mars, *Unbroken*, p. 33.
8. See Wingate, *The Fighting Tenth*, for a full account of the flotilla's actions. See also Simpson's recollections, *Periscope View*.
9. Spooner, *Supreme Gallantry*, pp. 82, 95, 105.
10. Ibid, p. 55n.
11. L. Lucas, *Malta*, pp. 13–14, 33. Lucas's account is a largely personal one of the part played by the RAF in the island's defence.
12. Richards and Saunders, *Royal Air Force 1939–1945*, vol. II, pp. 193–4.
13. Spooner, *Supreme Gallantry*, p. 119.
14. L. Lucas, *Malta*, pp. 43–4, 65.
15. Spooner, *Supreme Gallantry*, p. 122.
16. Richards and Saunders, *Royal Air Force 1939–1945* vol. II, p. 197.
17. McKee, *El Alamein*, p. 106.
18. Bradford, *Siege*, p. 189.
19. Woodman, *Malta Convoys*, p. 357.
20. Spooner, *Supreme Gallantry*, pp. 159–68.

21. McKee, *El Alamein*, p. 108.
22. Spooner, *Supreme Gallantry*, pp. 176–7.
23. Santoni, *Il vero traditore*, p. 76.
24. McKee, *El Alamein*, pp. 112–13. For a description of this flamboyant character, see Spooner, *Warburton's War*.
25. Bradford, *Siege*, p. 202; Playfair, *The Mediterranean and Middle East*, vol. III, p. 316.
26. Roskill, *The War at Sea 1939–1945*, vol. II, p. 302.
27. For the most complete account of Pedestal, see Smith, *Pedestal*.
28. Woodman, *Malta Convoys*, p. 397.
29. Smith, *Pedestal*, p. 112.
30. Ibid., p. 120.
31. Woodman, *Malta Convoys*, p. 406.
32. Smith, *Pedestal*, p. 149.
33. Bradford, *Siege*, pp. 211–13.
34. Roskill, *The War at Sea 1939–1945*, vol. II, p. 307.
35. Spooner, *Warburton's War*, pp. 180–2.
36. Smith, *Pedestal* p. 175.
37. Kesselring, *Memoirs*, p. 135.
38. Mars, *Unbroken*, pp. 119–26.
39. Smith, *Pedestal*, p. 191.
40. Woodman, *Malta Convoys*, p. 445.
41. Ibid., p. 454. The story of the *Ohio* – and in particular the last 24 hours of this incredible voyage – is told in more detail in Shankland and Hunter, *Malta Convoy*.
42. Mars, *Unbroken*, pp. 127–8.
43. McKee, *El Alamein*, p. 52.
44. Roskill, *The War at Sea 1939–1945*, vol. II, p. 308.
45. Playfair, *The Mediterranean and Middle East*, vol. III, p. 325.
46. Bennett, *Ultra and Mediterranean Strategy*, p. 149.

Chapter 6: Monty

1. See ch. 1 of Keegan, *Six Armies in Normandy*, for a discussion of the development of American ideas and British objections.
2. Churchill, *The Second World War*, vol. IV, p. 357.
3. Ibid., p. 41; Bates, *Dance of War*, p. 170.
4. Amery, *Approach March*, pp. 308–10. Brooke described Amery as 'a most objectionable young pup' whose opinion was based on nothing more than 'conversations with a few officers in the bar of Shepeard's Hotel in Cairo'. Afterwards he told Churchill that Amery was a 'bar-lounger', but Amery had flattered Churchill and impressed him (Alanbrooke, *War Diaries*, pp. 276–7).
5. Bryant, *The Turn of the Tide*, pp. 431–3, 439.
6. Lewin, *Rommel as Military Commander*, p. 143.
7. N. Hamilton, *Monty: The Making of a General*, pp. 537–8.
8. Carver, *El Alamein*, pp. 25–6.
9. Greacen, *Chink*, pp. 236–7.
10. Bryant, *The Turn of the Tide*, p. 443.
11. Bates, *Dance of War*, pp. 233–5.
12. N. Hamilton, *Monty: The Making of a General*, pp. 548–9.

13. Maughan, *Tobruk and El Alamein*, pp. 606–7.
14. Keegan, *Six Armies in Normandy*, p. 56.
15. Bryant, *The Turn of the Tide*, pp. 107–8.
16. N. Hamilton, *Monty: The Making of a General*, pp. 376–7.
17. Rees, *A Bundle of Sensations*, p. 150.
18. R. Clarke, *With Alex at War*, p. 47.
19. N. Hamilton, *Monty: The Making of a General*, pp. 551–2.
20. Ibid, pp. 720–1.
21. McKee, *El Alamein*, p. 142.
22. Connell, *Auchinleck*, pp. 708–9.
23. N. Hamilton, *Monty: The Making of a General*, p. 554.
24. Nicolson, *Alex*, p. 157; N. Hamilton, *Monty: The Making of a General*, pp. 556–7.
25. B. Pitt, *The Crucible of War: Year of Alamein 1942*, p. 205.
26. N. Hamilton, *Monty: The Making of a General*, pp. 557, 562.
27. Montgomery, *Memoirs*, p. 97.
28. De Guingand, *Operation Victory*, p. 139.
29. Montgomery, *Memoirs*, p. 100.
30. PRO WO 169/3910: 'Eighth Army Tac HQ Logs, 1942 May–Aug'.
31. Kippenburger, *Infantry Brigadier*, p. 257.
32. Freyberg was saved from having to break up 6th New Zealand Brigade for a general reinforcement pool only by the news that 5,500 drafts would be sent from home – R. Walker, *Alam Halfa and Alamein*, pp. 12–13, 38–40.
33. Platt, *The Royal Wiltshire Yeomanry*, p. 121.
34. N. Hamilton, *Monty: The Making of a General*, pp. 117–18.
35. Ibid., p. 522.
36. Mellenthin, *Panzer Battles*, pp. 173–4.
37. N. Hamilton, *Monty: The Making of a General*, pp. 583–4.
38. R. Walker, *Alam Halfa and Alamein*, p. 27.
39. N. Hamilton, *Monty: The Making of a General*, p. 362.
40. Carver, *El Alamein*, p. 23.
41. Maughan, *Tobruk and El Alamein*, pp. 598–9.
42. Doherty, *A Noble Crusade*, pp. 77–8.
43. De Guingand, *Operation Victory*, pp. 136–7.
44. PRO CAB 106/654: 'Western Desert: Account of the Battle of Alam el Halfa Sept 1942 written by Lieutenant-General Sir Brian Horrocks, commanding 13th Corps'.
45. Barnett, *The Desert Generals*, p. 262.
46. PRO CAB 44/99, Section II, Chapter L: 'German Assault on the El Alamein Position, 1942 Aug 31–Sept 7, by Lieutenant-Colonel M. E. S. Laws, 1945'.
47. Maughan, *Tobruk and El Alamein*, p. 610.
48. Mollo, *The Armed Forces of World War II*, p. 120.
49. Peniakoff, *Popski's Private Army*, p. 211.
50. Majdalany, *The Battle of El Alamein*, p. 58.
51. B. Pitt, *The Crucible of War: Year of Alamein 1942*, p. 217.
52. Peniakoff, *Popski's Private Army*, p. 211.
53. Correlli Barnett wrote that Alam Halfa 'was fought on a plan conceived by Dorman-Smith, approved and initiated by Auchinleck and from fixed defences largely dug before Montgomery left England' (*The Desert Generals*, p. 259). As

Michael Carver puts it, this is, to say the least, 'very misleading' (*Dilemmas of the Desert War*, p. 145).

54. Auchinleck, 'Despatch', p. 54.
55. Barnett, *The Desert Generals*, p. 262; N. Hamilton, *Monty: The Making of a General*, p. 595.
56. PRO WO 169/4034: 'XXX Corps G Branch 1942 July–Aug'.
57. Kippenburger, *Infantry Brigadier*, p. 257.
58. PRO WO 169/4006: 'XIII Corps 1942 Aug'.
59. 'How would I shape as a corps commander, I wondered? It was a big step up from command of the 2nd Battalion, The Middlesex Regiment during the withdrawal to Dunkirk' (Horrocks, *A Full Life*, p. 103). Since then Horrocks had seen no active service: he had been promoted to brigade and divisional commands while training in the UK.
60. N. Hamilton, *Monty: The Making of a General*, p. 606.

Chapter 7: Alam Halfa

1. P. J. Jones, *The Reluctant Volunteer*, p. 108.
2. McGuirk, *Rommel's Army in Africa*, p. 38.
3. Douglas, *Alamein to Zem Zem*, p. 67.
4. Jackson, *Alexander of Tunis as Military Commander*, p. 155.
5. Bryant, *The Turn of the Tide*, p. 512.
6. WYM: Capt. C. B. Stoddart, letters, October 1942.
7. Bowyer and Shores, *Desert Air Force at War*, pp. 117–18.
8. PRO AIR 37/760: 'AOC-in-C Air Chief Marshal Leigh-Mallory: Direct Air Support of Army in the Field: Miscellaneous Reports 1944'.
9. Macksey, *Kesselring*, p. 112.
10. Caccia-Dominioni, *Alamein 1933–1962*, p. 84.
11. R. Walker, *Alam Halfa and Alamein*, p. 86.
12. Richardson and Freidin, *The Fatal Decisions*, p. 78.
13. R. Walker, *Alam Halfa and Alamein*, p. 13.
14. Churchill, *The Second World War*, vol. IV, p. 454; Roskill, *The War at Sea 1939–1945*, vol. II, chs. 2, 13.
15. R. Walker, *Alam Halfa and Alamein*, p. 45.
16. Caccia-Dominioni, *Alamein 1933–1962*, pp. 69–70.
17. Mellenthin, *Panzer Battles*, p. 172.
18. Liddell Hart, *The Rommel Papers*, pp. 269, 274.
19. Ibid., p. 267.
20. Majdalany, *The Battle of El Alamein*, p. 42.
21. Liddell Hart, *The Rommel Papers*, p. 272.
22. Bennett, *Ultra and Mediterranean Strategy*, p. 149.
23. Hinsley, *British Intelligence*, vol. II, pp. 419–20.
24. Nehring, *Der Feldzug in Afrika*, p. 65.
25. Bennett, *Ultra and Mediterranean Strategy*, pp. 149–50.
26. Rommel, *Krieg ohne Hass*, pp. 201–2.
27. Bennett, *Ultra and Mediterranean Strategy*, pp. 142–6.
28. Lewin, *Ultra Goes to War*, p. 265.
29. N. Hamilton, *Monty: The Making of a General*, p. 650.
30. Caccia-Dominioni, *Alamein 1933–1962*, p. 35.
31. Warner, *Alamein*, p. 203.

32. Horrocks, *A Full Life*, pp. 116–19.
33. PRO WO 169/4251: '22nd Armoured Brigade HQ 1942 Jan–Dec'.
34. Maughan, *Tobruk and El Alamein*, p. 626.
35. De Guingand, *Operation Victory*, p. 146.
36. Behrendt, *Rommel's Intelligence in the Desert Campaign*, p. 192.
37. PRO WO 201/423: 'Planning Offensive Operations 1942 Aug–Nov'.
38. Liddell Hart, *The Rommel Papers*, p. 277.
39. Richards and Saunders, *Royal Air Force 1939–1945*, vol. II, p. 230.
40. Liddell Hart, *The Rommel Papers*, pp. 279–81, 284–6.
41. PRO AIR 41/50: 'The Middle East Campaign, vol. IV: Operations in Libya, the Western Desert and Tunisia, July 1942–May 1943'.
42. Doherty, *A Noble Crusade*, pp. 78–84.
43. Carver, *El Alamein*, p. 58.
44. Liddell Hart, *The Tanks*, pp. 221–3.
45. Majdalany, *The Battle of El Alamein*, p. 55.
46. R. Walker, *Alam Halfa and Alamein*, p. 111.
47. Mellenthin, *Panzer Battles*, p. 176.
48. Irving, *The Trail of the Fox*, p. 193.
49. Kesselring, *Memoirs*, p. 131.
50. Maughan, *Tobruk and El Alamein*, pp. 630–4; Austin, *Let Enemies Beware!*, pp. 126–52, includes Horton's own account of his feat. A famous painting of the exploit was made by Ivor Hele and is displayed at the Australian War Memorial – AWM (27559) 408.
51. Goodhart, *The 2/7th Australian Field Regiment*, p. 192.
52. Liddell Hart, *The Rommel Papers*, p. 280.
53. N. Hamilton, *Monty: The Making of a General*, p. 651.
54. Ibid., pp. 653–5.
55. The account in Chaplin, *The Queen's Own Royal West Kent Regiment*, glosses over the shambles that occurred – a result of lack of planning due to lack of time (Colonel H. B. H. Waring OBE, curator, QORWKR Museum, letter to author, 16 March 2001).
56. Doherty, *A Noble Crusade*, p. 86; R. Walker, *Alam Halfa and Alamein*, p. 128.
57. N. Hamilton, *Monty: The Making of a General*, p. 660.
58. R. Walker, *Alam Halfa and Alamein*, p. 179.
59. Underhill, *Queen's Own Royal Regiment The Staffordshire Yeomanry*, p. 5.
60. Maughan, *Tobruk and El Alamein*, p. 634.
61. Mellenthin, *Panzer Battles*, p. 172.
62. R. Walker, *Alam Halfa and Alamein*, pp. 176–7.
63. Majdalany, *The Battle of El Alamein*, p. 57.
64. R. Walker, *Alam Halfa and Alamein*, pp. 180–1.
65. Kesselring, *Memoirs*, p. 133.
66. Detweiler et. al., *World War II German Military Studies*, vol. XIV, pt IV, MS# T–3 P1, pp. 63–4.
67. Horrocks, *A Full Life*, p. 125.

Chapter 8: Lightfoot

1. Greacen, *Chink*, p. 227.
2. PRO AIR 41/50: 'The Middle East Campaign, vol. IV: Operations in Libya, the Western Desert and Tunisia, July 1942–May 1943'.

3. R. Walker, *Alam Halfa and Alamein*, pp. 209–13, 215.
4. Montgomery, *Memoirs*, pp. 112–13.
5. Barnett, *The Desert Generals*, p. 321.
6. PRO WO 169/3988: 'X Corps and Delta Force HQ 1942 Jan–Jun, Sept'.
7. Fearnside, *Bayonets Abroad*, pp. 257–8.
8. N. Hamilton, *Monty: The Making of a General*, p. 702. Correlli Barnett argues that the Battle of Alamein was not even necessary, that Torch would have been enough to force Rommel's retreat and end the war in Africa (*The Desert Generals*, p. 272). This speculation ignores, among other things, the plight of Malta. If neither Montgomery nor Eisenhower moved quickly enough, wondered Churchill, 'God knows how we are to keep Malta alive' (Bennett, *Ultra and Mediterranean Strategy*, p. 155).
9. De Guingand, *Operation Victory*, p. 158.
10. Kennedy, *The Business of War*, p. 257.
11. Churchill, *The Second World War*, vol. IV, p. 450.
12. Lucas-Phillips, *Alamein*, p. 61.
13. Maughan, *Tobruk and El Alamein*, p. 613.
14. Ibid., p. 614.
15. Lumsden was killed by a kamikaze attack on the bridge of the USS *New Mexico* in January 1945 while acting as liaison officer to General MacArthur, so his version of events has never been fully recorded.
16. N. Hamilton, *Monty: The Making of a General*, pp. 346.
17. McNish, 'El Alamein in Perspective', p. 5; McCreery, 'Reflections of a Chief of Staff', p. 40.
18. Lucas-Phillips, *Alamein*, pp. 62, 91–2.
19. McCreery, 'Reflections of a Chief of Staff', p. 40.
20. Montgomery, *Memoirs*, p. 113.
21. B. Pitt, *The Crucible of War: Year of Alamein 1942*, p. 273.
22. IWM Briggs MSS 66/76/1: 'Eighth Army Training Memorandum No. 1, The Approach to Training, 30.08.42'.
23. N. Hamilton, *Monty: The Making of a General*, pp. 184, 302, 383, 456, 676.
24. Stewart, *Eighth Army's Greatest Victories*, p. 82.
25. Majdalany, *The Battle of El Alamein*, pp. 63–4.
26. N. Hamilton, *Monty: The Making of a General*, pp. 687–8.
27. B. Pitt, *The Crucible of War: Year of Alamein 1942*, p. 18.
28. PRO WO 201/432: 'Operation "Lightfoot" Planning 1942 Aug'.
29. A full account of this action is G. Landsborough's *Tobruk Commando*, although Peter C. Smith's *Massacre at Tobruk* is more thorough on the naval and Royal Marine aspects.
30. See Peniakoff, *Popski's Private Army*, and Maclean, *Eastern Approaches*, for personal accounts of this raid.
31. PRO CAB 44/163, Section VI, Chapter J: 'Western Desert Maintenance and Supply 1942 July–1943 May, by Brigadier W. P. Pessell [1950]'.
32. Majdalany, *The Battle of El Alamein*, p. 71.
33. Lucas-Phillips, *Alamein*, pp. 48, 98; PRO WO 201/433.
34. PRO WO 201/646: 'Eighth Army Operations "Lightfoot" Planning 1942 Oct'.
35. PRO CAB 44/100, Section II, Chapter M: 'Battle of El Alamein, pt I: Preparation for the Battle, 1942 Sept 8–Oct 23, by Lieutenant-Colonel M. E. S. Laws, 1949'.

36. R. B. Johnson, *The Queen's in The Middle East and North Africa*, p. 46.
37. B. Pitt, *The Crucible of War: Year of Alamein 1942*, pp. 271–2.
38. De Guingand, *Operation Victory*, p. 186.
39. R. Clarke, *With Alex at War*, p. 61.
40. PRO WO 163/85/ECAC 51: 'QMG and VCIGS, Re-organization of RASC Transport Units, 7 July 1941'; *The Story of the Royal Army Service Corps*, pp. 128–9.
41. C. F. French, 'The Fashioning of Esprit de Corps in the 51st Highland Division', p. 287.
42. Whiting, *The Poor Bloody Infantry*, p. 137.
43. C. F. French, 'The Fashioning of Esprit de Corps in the 51st Highland Division', p. 278.
44. Salmond, *The 51st Highland Division*, p. 31.
45. Samwell, *An Infantry Officer with the Eighth Army*, p. 23. This excellent book appears to have been largely forgotten.
46. Bates, *Dance of War*, p. 123.
47. N. Hamilton, *Monty: The Making of a General*, pp. 117–18, 387.
48. PRO WO 201/452: 'Notes on Main Lessons of Recent Operations in the Western Desert, July 1942'.
49. Bidwell, *Gunners at War*, p. 189.
50. PRO WO 201/424: 'The October Battle of Alamein and the Advance to Tripolitania 1942 Oct–Nov'.
51. W. E. Duncan et al., *The Royal Artillery Commemoration Book*, p. 228.
52. Maughan, *Tobruk and El Alamein*, p. 653.
53. PRO WO 201/426: 'GHQ Situation Reports 1942 Oct–Nov'.
54. PRO WO 106/2223: 'Pamphlets: Notes from Theatres of War, Cyrenaica'.
55. Mure, *Master of Deception*, pp. 138–9.
56. Montgomery, *Memoirs*, p. 119; N. Hamilton, *Monty: The Making of a General*, pp. 712–13.
57. Maughan, *Tobruk and El Alamein*, pp. 645, 658, 661–2.
58. BWA 0727/3/1: Brigadier J. A. Hopwood, 'History of 1st Battalion 1939–1945, Quassasin to El Alamein'.
59. Murphy, *2nd New Zealand Divisional Artillery*, p. 373.
60. Playfair, *The Mediterranean and Middle East*, vol. IV, p. 5.

Chapter 9: In the Line

1. J. Lucas, *War in the Desert*, p. 54.
2. B. Pitt, *The Crucible of War: Year of Alamein 1942*, p. 218.
3. IWM AL 1349/3: 'Memo of a Conference with Marshall Cavallero, 23.09.42'.
4. IWM AL 1349/2: 'Reception of General Rommel by Mussolini, 24.09.42'.
5. Richardson and Freidin, *The Fatal Decisions*, pp. 90–1.
6. Irving, *The Trail of the Fox*, p. 198.
7. Boatner, *The Biographical Dictionary of World War II*, pp. 547–8.
8. Kesselring, *Memoirs*, p. 134.
9. IWM AL 898/3: 'Panzer Armee Afrika, Fuhrungsabt., War Diary Appendices Band II, 20.09–23.10.42'.
10. Liddell Hart, *The Rommel Papers*, pp. 299–300.
11. Maughan, *Tobruk and El Alamein*, p. 642.
12. R. Walker, *Alam Halfa and Alamein*, p. 197.
13. Kesselring, *Memoirs*, p. 135.

14. R. Walker, *Alam Halfa and Alamein*, p. 198.
15. Mellenthin, *Panzer Battles*, p. 178.
16. Caccia-Dominioni, *Alamein 1933–1962*, p. 169.
17. IWM AL 898/3.
18. Maughan, *Tobruk and El Alamein*, p. 643.
19. R. Walker, *Alam Halfa and Alamein*, p. 200.
20. Hillgruber, *Kriegstagebuch des Oberkommandos der Wehrmacht*, vol. II, p. 108.
21. Maughan, *Tobruk and El Alamein*, p. 623; Bennett, *Ultra and Mediterranean Strategy*, p. 135.
22. Richards and Saunders, *Royal Air Force 1939–1945*, vol. II, p. 228.
23. McKee, *El Alamein*, pp. 101–4. Foulis won a DFC and bar in a three-month tour before embarking on a second which he did not survive.
24. Playfair, *The Mediterranean and Middle East*, vol. III, p. 327; PRO AIR 37/760: 'AOC-in-C Air Chief Marshal Leigh-Mallory: Direct Air Support of Army in the Field: Miscellaneous Reports 1944'.
25. PRO ADM 223/89: 'Report of Mediterranean Operational Intelligence Centre 1939–1945'.
26. Piekalkiewicz, *Rommel and the Secret War in North Africa*, p. 180.
27. Irving, *The Trail of the Fox*, p. 198.
28. Bates, *Dance of War*, p. 46.
29. Spooner, *Supreme Gallantry*, p. 152.
30. R. Walker, *Alam Halfa and Alamein*, pp. 205–6.
31. Playfair, *The Mediterranean and Middle East*, vol. IV, p. 26.
32. Heckmann, *Rommel's War in Africa*, p. 324. Heckmann goes on to relate the story of a glider pilot and his mate. They crashed one glider at Athens and had to wait ten days for a replacement. They then landed in a sandstorm in Africa, where their glider was bombed almost immediately by the DAF (pp. 325–9).
33. McKee, *El Alamein*, p. 122.
34. Barker, *Afrika Korps*, p. 143.
35. Bates, *Dance of War*, p. 22.
36. McGuirk, *Rommel's Army in Africa*, p. 57.
37. D. Young, *Rommel*, p. 133.
38. Behrendt, *Rommel's Intelligence in the Desert Campaign*, p. 42.
39. Armstrong, 'Water Supply Problems in Egypt during the War 1939–45', p. 180.
40. Rainier, *Pipeline to Battle*, pp. 115–16.
41. McGuirk, *Rommel's Army in Africa*, p. 88.
42. R. Walker, *Alam Halfa and Alamein*, pp. 3–4.
43. Warner, *Alamein*, pp. 63–4.
44. 'Record of Service of the Regiment during the War', *XII Royal Lancers Journal*, 1946, p. 36.
45. Llewellyn, *Journey towards Christmas*, p. 247.
46. Barker, *Afrika Korps*, p. 144.
47. J. Lucas, *Panzer Army Africa*, p. 119.
48. Cody, *28 (Maori) Battalion*, p. 225.
49. R. Walker, *Alam Halfa and Alamein*, pp. 4–5.
50. A. Gilbert, *The Imperial War Museum Book of The Desert War*, p. 65.
51. J. Lucas, *Panzer Army Africa*, p. 61.
52. B. Pitt, *The Crucible of War: Year of Alamein 1942*, p. 281.

53. J. Lucas, *Panzer Army Africa*, pp. 56, 62.

54. Crisp, *The Gods Were Neutral*, p. 15.

55. Guntrip, 'Trooper In, Trooper Out', p. 123.

56. Bates, *Dance of War*, p. 24.

57. B. Pitt, *The Crucible of War: Year of Alamein 1942*, pp. 158–9. Pitt witnessed the scene and made the mistake of laughing – receiving a split lip and two cracked ribs for his trouble.

58. Aileen Clayton, *The Enemy is Listening*, p. 217.

59. R. Walker, *Alam Halfa and Alamein*, pp. 2–3.

Chapter 10: Final Preparations

1. PRO WO 201/552: '1st Greek Brigade: Report on Operations 1942 Nov'.

2. Clay, *The Path of the 50th*, pp. 92–3.

3. Warner, *Alamein*, p. 156. For a brilliant description of this 'routine' military activity see Fred Majdalany's novel *The Patrol*. Although set during the Tunisian campaign of 1943, it could just as easily apply to any other.

4. Douglas, *Alamein to Zem Zem*, p. 110.

5. Warner, *Alamein*, p. 39; Ellis, *The Sharp End of War*, p. 293.

6. RLCM: 'Expansion of the RASC Services and Operation in the War 1939–1945, Book 7: GHQ Base Installations and Area (also WD incl. Eighth Army)', p. 2.

7. Ibid., Book 45: 'WE DDST (Sups) CPO (Food, Spec. Ration Packs, Barracks)', p. 20.

8. Wilmington, *The Middle East Supply Centre.*, p. 118. Wilmington's book provides a complete account of this unique and unusual organization.

9. RLCM: 'Notes on the Maintenance of the Eighth Army and the Supporting Royal Air Force by Land, Sea and Air from El Alamein to Tunisia'.

10. Terraine, *The Right of the Line*, pp. 305–6; Warner, *Alamein*, p. 219; Guedalla, *Middle East 1940–1942*, p. 192.

11. Jacobs et. al., *South African Corps of Signals*, p. 75.

12. PRO WO 277/25: 'Signals Communications 1939–1945', pp. 382–3.

13. For a full account of this unique organization see Hills, *Phantom was There*.

14. Playfair, *The Mediterranean and Middle East*, vol. IV, p. 15n.

15. RLCM: 'Expansion of the RASC Services and Operation in the War 1939–1945, Book 7', p. 30.

16. Tatman and Kennet, *Craftsmen of the Army*, pp. 91–2.

17. RLCM: 'Expansion of the RASC Services and Operation in the War 1939–1945, Book 47: DDSI (Sups) Middle East and Libya', p. 28.

18. RLCM: 'Expansion of the RASC Services and Operation in the War 1939–1945, Book 7', pp. 33–8.

19. Crew, *The Army Medical Services, Campaigns*, vol. II, pp. 204–6, 213.

20. *RAF Middle East Review*, vol. II, pp. 85, 89.

21. PRO WO 201/2596: 'Middle East Training Memorandum No. 8, Lessons from Operations 1942 Oct–Nov'.

22. R. Walker, *Alam Halfa and Alamein*, pp. 111–12; Behrendt, *Rommel's Intelligence in the Desert Campaign*, p. 191.

23. Bates, *Dance of War*, p. 130.

24. G. R. Stevens, *Fourth Indian Division*, p. 189.

25. Howard, *British Intelligence in the Second World War*, vol. V, p. 42.
26. Mure, *Master of Deception*, pp. 120, 130.
27. Cave-Brown, *Bodyguard of Lies*, p. 118.
28. Maughan, *Tobruk and El Alamein*, p. 673.
29. PRO WO 201/2023: 'Scheme Bertram: Notes on Deception Practised by 8th Army prior to Its Offensive 1942 Nov'.
30. PRO CAB 154/2: '"A" Force Permanent Record File Narrative War Diary: 1 Jan–31 Dec 1942' (undated).
31. PRO WO 201/434: 'Operation "Lightfoot": Deception Plans 1942 Oct'.
32. Maughan, *Tobruk and El Alamein*, p. 648.
33. Barkas, *The Camouflage Story*, p. 198.
34. *The Story of the Royal Army Service Corps*, p. 147.
35. J. Lucas, *War in the Desert*, pp. 135–6.
36. PRO CAB 44/99, Section II, Chapter L: 'German Assault on the El Alamein Position, 1942 Aug 31–Sept 7, by Lieutenant-Colonel M. E. S. Laws, 1945'.
37. Warner, *Alamein*, p. 213.
38. PRO CAB 44/163, Section VI, Chapter J: 'Western Desert Maintenance and Supply 1942 July–1943 May, by Brigadier W. P. Pessell [1950]'.
39. Barkas, *The Camouflage Story*, pp. 198–200, 204–5.
40. M. Young and R. Stamp, *Trojan Horses*, pp. 70–1.
41. Barkas, *The Camouflage Story*, pp. 200–3.
42. W. E. Duncan et al., *The Royal Artillery Commemoration Book*, pp. 228–9.
43. Maughan, *Tobruk and El Alamein*, p. 649.
44. Pakenham-Walsh, *The Corps of Royal Engineers*, pp. 384–5; Mure, *Master of Deception*, p. 135.
45. PRO WO 201/2024: 'Camouflage Operations in the Western Desert 1942 Aug–Dec'.
46. Barkas, *The Camouflage Story*, pp. 210–11.
47. PRO CAB 154/2.
48. SWWEC, Army/N. P. MacDonald.
49. R. Walker, *Alam Halfa and Alamein*, pp. 218–19.
50. Liddell Hart, *The Rommel Papers*, p. 299.
51. R. Walker, *Alam Halfa and Alamein*, p. 201.
52. IWM AL 834/1: 'DAK Ia, War Diary, 03.08–22.11.42'.
53. Behrendt, *Rommel's Intelligence in the Desert Campaign*, pp. 197–8.
54. IWM AL 834/1.
55. R. Walker, *Alam Halfa and Alamein*, pp. 204, 207.
56. B. Pitt, *The Crucible of War: Year of Alamein 1942*, pp. 292–5.
57. Richards and Saunders, *Royal Air Force 1939–1945*, vol. II, p. 232.
58. Bennett, *Ultra and Mediterranean Strategy*, pp. 160–1.
59. Herington, *Air War Against Germany and Italy*, p. 368.
60. Caccia-Dominioni, *Alamein 1933–1962*, p. 210.

Chapter 11: Barrage

1. McKee, *El Alamein*, p. 146.
2. A. Gilbert, *The Imperial War Museum Book of The Desert War*, p. 161.
3. Whetton and Ogden, *Z Location or Survey in War*, pp. 72, 101–3, 106.
4. Warner, *Alamein*, pp. 107–8.

5. Lambert, 'Tin Triangles', pp. 330–4.

6. Pakenham-Walsh, *The Corps of Royal Engineers*, vol. VIII, p. 370. For a detailed description of the drill, see Lucas-Phillips, *Alamein*, pp. 73–9.

7. Lambert, 'Engineers at the Battle of Alamein', p. 23.

8. McKee, *El Alamein*, p. 154.

9. A. G. Brown et al., *A History of 44th Royal Tank Regiment*, p. 77.

10. Playfair, *The Mediterranean and Middle East*, vol. IV, p. 14n.

11. Pakenham-Walsh, *The Corps of Royal Engineers*, vol. VIII, p. 385.

12. C. E. Lucas-Philips, Alamein, pp. 112–12.

13. BWA 0799/1: 'Account of 1 BW at Battle of El Alamein, 23.10.42, Lt-Col William Noel Roper-Caldbeck (CO)'.

14. McCallum, *Journey With a Pistol*, p. 44.

15. S. Hamilton, *Armoured Odyssey*, p. 63.

16. AWM 3DRL2632: 'Papers of Lieutenant-General Sir Leslie Morshead'.

17. Thomas, *Ambulance in Africa*, p. 133.

18. Bolté, 'Our American Officers', pp. 19–20.

19. Birkby, *The Saga of the Transvaal Scottish Regiment*, p. 608.

20. P. J. Jones, *The Reluctant Volunteer*, p. 115.

21. J. Lucas, *War in the Desert*, p. 59.

22. B. Pitt, *The Crucible of War: Year of Alamein 1942*, p. 281.

23. *A Short History of the 57th Light Anti-Aircraft Regt, Royal Artillery*, p. 62.

24. W. E. Duncan et al., *The Royal Artillery Commemoration Book*, p. 234.

25. Warner, *Alamein*, pp. 157–8.

26. PRO AIR 41/50: 'The Middle East Campaign, vol. IV: Operations in Libya, the Western Desert and Tunisia, July 1942–May 1943'.

27. Herington, *Air War Against Germany and Italy*, p. 369.

28. Irving, *The Trail of the Fox*, p. 202.

29. Playfair, *The Mediterranean and Middle East*, vol. IV, p. 33.

30. PRO AIR 41/50.

31. R. Walker, *Alam Halfa and Alamein*, pp. 222–3.

32. Sheffield, *The Redcaps*, pp. 111–13.

33. Majdalany, *The Battle of El Alamein*, pp. 89.

34. Platt, *The Royal Wiltshire Yeomanry*, p. 130.

35. J. Lucas, *War in the Desert*, pp. 143–4.

36. 'The 5th Camerons at El Alamein', *The Queen's Own Highlander*, vol. 32, no. 83, winter 1992, p. 159.

37. PRO CAB 44/101, Section II, Chapter M: 'Battle of El Alamein, pt II, vol. I: Operation "Lightfoot", 1942 Oct 23–24, by Lieutenant-Colonel M. E. S. Laws [1950]'.

38. R. Walker, *Alam Halfa and Alamein*, p. 227.

39. PRO CAB 44/101.

40. W. E. Duncan et al., *The Royal Artillery Commemoration Book*, pp. 233–4.

41. Bennett, *Ultra and Mediterranean Strategy*, p. 163.

42. A. C. Martin, *The Durban Light Infantry*, vol. II, p. 283.

43. Hastings, *The Rifle Brigade in the Second World War*, pp. 150–1.

44. McKee, *El Alamein*, pp. 144–5.

45. PRO CAB 44/101.

46. IWM AL 834/1: 'DAK Ia, War Diary, 03.08–22.11.42'.

47. SWWEC, Army/T. S. Bigland.
48. Orpen, *South African Forces, World War II*, vol. III, p. 415.
49. McKee, *El Alamein*, pp. 145–6.
50. Barrett, *We Were There*, p. 225.
51. Rainier, *Pipeline to Battle*, p. 133.
52. From the poem 'Beach Burial' in K. Slessor, *Poems* (Sydney: Angus & Robertson, 2nd edn, 1957), p. 109.
53. Maughan, *Tobruk and El Alamein*, pp. 665–6.
54. Majdalany, *The Battle of El Alamein*, pp. 77.
55. Forty, *Afrika Korps at War*, vol. II, pp. 71–3.
56. McKee, *El Alamein*, pp. 144–5.
57. Bedeschi, *Fronte d'Africa*, pp. 189–90.
58. R. Walker, *Alam Halfa and Alamein*, p. 254.
59. J. Lucas, *War in the Desert*, p. 152.
60. McKee, *El Alamein*, p. 145.
61. IWM AL 834/1.

Chapter 12: Assault

1. Trigellis-Smith, *Britain to Borneo*, p. 110.
2. Maughan, *Tobruk and El Alamein*, pp. 667–8, 672.
3. *The Eighth Army: September 1941 to January 1943*, p. 77.
4. Ward-Harvey, *The Sapper's War*, p. 80.
5. Glenn, *Tobruk to Tarakan*, p. 145.
6. Maughan, *Tobruk and El Alamein*, pp. 668–70.
7. Fearnside, *Bayonets Abroad*, p. 260.
8. Liddell Hart, *The Rommel Papers*, p. 303.
9. Maughan, *Tobruk and El Alamein*, pp. 670–1.
10. Wimberley, *Scottish Soldier*, vol. II, p. 41.
11. B. Pitt, *The Crucible of War: Year of Alamein 1942*, p. 302.
12. J. Lucas, *War in the Desert*, p. 160.
13. Lucas-Phillips, *Alamein*, p. 129.
14. Fergusson, *The Black Watch and the King's Enemies*, p. 128.
15. Salmond, *The 51st Highland Division*, p. 39.
16. Lucas-Phillips, *Alamein*, p. 129.
17. Miles, *The Gordon Highlanders*, pp. 18–19.
18. Ibid., pp. 136–7.
19. Warner, *Alamein*, p. 101.
20. BWA 0799/1: 'Account of 1 BW at Battle of El Alamein, 23.10.42, Lt-Col William Noel Roper-Caldbeck (CO)'.
21. Fergusson, *The Black Watch and the King's Enemies*, pp. 129–30.
22. Chartres, '7th Field Squadron RE in World War II', p. 76.
23. Cameron, *The Argyll and Sutherland Highlanders 7th Battalion*, pp. 43–4.
24. Samwell, *An Infantry Officer with the Eighth Army*, p. 32.
25. Grant, *The 51st Highland Division at War*, p. 57.
26. Cameron, *The Argyll and Sutherland Highlanders 7th Battalion*, p. 44.
27. Doherty, *Only the Enemy in Front*, pp. 28–9.
28. Salmond, *The 51st Highland Division*, pp. 41–2.

29. Russell, *War History of 7th Bn., The Black Watch*, pp. 17–18.
30. IWM AL 1657/1: '15. Panzer Div. Ia War Diary and Appendices, 23.10–25.11.42'.
31. King, *New Zealanders at War*, p. 200.
32. P. W. Pitt, *Royal Wilts*, p. 136.
33. A. Ross, *23 Battalion*, pp. 199–209.
34. Burdon, *24 Battalion*, pp. 125–9.
35. Cody, *28 (Maori) Battalion*, p. 238.
36. BWA 0727/3/1: Brigadier J. A. Hopwood, 'History of 1st Battalion 1939–1945, Quassasin to El Alamein'.
37. Fergusson, *The Black Watch and the King's Enemies*, p. 127.
38. Cody, *21 Battalion*, pp. 197–204.
39. Henderson, *22 Battalion*, pp. 203–10.
40. J. Lucas, *War in the Desert*, p. 169.
41. IWM AL 1657/1.
42. Norton, *26 Battalion*, pp. 188–96.
43. Puttick, *25 Battalion*, pp. 225–30.
44. Orpen, *South African Forces, World War II*, vol. III, p. 426.
45. Reid, *The Turning Point*, p. 188.
46. Orpen, *The Cape Town Highlanders,* pp. 179–82.
47. Blamey, *A Company Commander Remembers*, pp. 187–9.
48. Ibid.
49. Orpen, *The Cape Town Highlanders,* pp. 422–4.
50. A. C. Martin, *The Durban Light Infantry*, vol. II, pp. 286–91.
51. PRO CAB 44/101, Section II, Chapter M: 'Battle of El Alamein, pt II, vol. I: Operation "Lightfoot", 1942 Oct 23–24, by Lieutenant-Colonel M. E. S. Laws [1950]'.
52. Tuker, *Approach to Battle*, p. 233.
53. Hingston and Stevens, *The Tiger Kills*, p. 156.
54. G. R. Stevens, *Fourth Indian Division*, pp. 192–3.
55. Most of the Greeks were recruited in Egypt and had little previous military experience. They were trained at the New Zealand Divisional School at Maadi (ATL OHInt-0204/1).
56. PRO CAB 44/101.
57. J. Lucas, *War in the Desert*, p. 136.
58. PRO CAB 44/101.
59. Lambert, 'Engineers at The Battle of Alamein', p. 26.
60. R. B. Johnson, *The Queen's in The Middle East and North Africa*, p. 50.
61. J. Lucas, *War in the Desert*, p. 150.
62. R. B. Johnson, *The Queen's in The Middle East and North Africa*, p. 50.
63. Hastings, *The Rifle Brigade in the Second World War*, p. 149.
64. Carver, *El Alamein*, pp. 126–8.
65. A. G. Brown et al., *A History of 44th Royal Tank Regiment*, p. 78.
66. Hastings, *The Rifle Brigade in the Second World War*, p. 152.
67. B. Pitt, *The Crucible of War: Year of Alamein 1942*, p. 322.
68. Warner, *Alamein*, pp. 131–3.

Chapter 13: The Armour Stalls

1. WL RAMC 1762: J. D. P. Graham MD DSc FRCP FRSE, 'A Time in the Sand: A True Account of Some Personal Experiences with the RAMC in the Western Desert 1941–1943', p. 20.
2. Warner, *Alamein*, p. 133.
3. WL RAMC 1762, p. 136.
4. Warner, *Alamein*, p. 133.
5. Thomas, *Ambulance in Africa*, p. 144.
6. McKee, *El Alamein*, p. 151.
7. Warner, *Alamein*, p. 133.
8. BWA 08001: 'Letters of Maj H. A. C. Blair-Imrie, 5 BW, to his wife after being wounded at El Alamein'. Blair-Imrie was killed commanding 5th Cameron Highlanders in Normandy in August 1944.
9. Agnelli, *We Always Wore Sailor Suits*, p. 85.
10. Forty, *Afrika Korps at War*, vol. II, p. 73.
11. Crimp, *Diary of a Desert Rat*, p. 146.
12. PRO CAB 44/101, Section II, Chapter M: 'Battle of El Alamein, pt II, vol. I: Operation "Lightfoot", 1942 Oct 23–24, by Lieutenant-Colonel M. E. S. Laws [1950]'.
13. PRO AIR 41/50: 'The Middle East Campaign, vol. IV: Operations in Libya, the Western Desert and Tunisia, July 1942–May 1943'.
14. IWM AL 743/1/1: 'Deutsche-Italienische Panzerarmee Ia, Sclachbericht I, 23.10.42–15.01.43'.
15. Playfair, *The Mediterranean and Middle East*, vol. IV, p. 36; Liddell Hart, *The Rommel Papers*, p. 302.
16. Caccia-Dominioni, *Alamein 1933–1962*, pp. 212–15.
17. IWM AL 834/1: 'DAK Ia, War Diary, 03.08–22.11.42'.
18. Tedder, *With Prejudice*, p. 357.
19. Hastings, *The Rifle Brigade in the Second World War*, p. 155.
20. Maughan, *Tobruk and El Alamein*, p. 679.
21. Dawnay, *The 10th Royal Hussars in The Second World War*, p. 80.
22. BWA 0799/1: 'Account of 1 BW at Battle of El Alamein, 23.10.42, Lt-Col William Noel Roper-Caldbeck (CO)'.
23. Crimp, *Diary of a Desert Rat*, p. 148.
24. J. Lucas, *War in the Desert*, p. 189.
25. Chartres, '7th Field Squadron RE in World War II', p. 76.
26. Beddington, *The Queen's Bays (The 2nd Dragoon Guards)*, p. 102.
27. Sheffield, *The Redcaps*, p. 109.
28. J. Lucas, *War in the Desert*, p. 60.
29. Bolté, 'Our American Officers', p. 20. Bolté's leg had to be amputated.
30. Doherty, *Only the Enemy in Front*, p. 29.
31. BWA 0799/1.
32. Russell, *War History of 7th Bn., The Black Watch*, p. 18.
33. Craig, *The Broken Plume*, pp. 62–3.
34. R. Walker, *Alam Halfa and Alamein*, pp. 268–72.
35. Baker, *Yeoman-Yeoman*, pp. 48–9.
36. P. W. Pitt, *Royal Wilts*, p. 139.
37. Ibid., p. 140.
38. W. E. Duncan et al., *The Royal Artillery Commemoration Book*, p. 231.

39. Begg and Liddle, *For Five Shillings a Day*, p. 186.
40. Lucas-Phillips, *Alamein*, pp. 145–8.
41. Sheffield, *The Redcaps*, pp. 111–13.
42. R. Walker, *Alam Halfa and Alamein*, pp. 274–5.
43. Ibid., p. 298.
44. Carrell, *The Foxes of the Desert*, pp. 285–7.
45. McMeekan, 'The Assault at Alamein', p. 327. This is an excellent personal account of sapper operations during the battle.
46. Douglas, *Alamein to Zem Zem*, pp. 46–7. Keith Douglas was killed in Normandy in 1944.
47. Delaforce, *Monty's Marauders*, pp. 112–13.
48. Henderson, *22 Battalion*, p. 212.
49. Cody, *21 Battalion*, p. 205.
50. Blamey, *A Company Commander Remembers*, p. 192.
51. Orpen, *South African Forces, World War II*, vol. III, pp. 429–30.
52. Wake and Deedes, *Swift and Bold*, p. 105.
53. Hastings, *The Rifle Brigade in the Second World War*, p. 157.
54. PRO CAB 44/101.
55. J. Lucas, *War in the Desert*, p. 191.
56. Warner, *Alamein*, p. 207.
57. R. Walker, *Alam Halfa and Alamein*, pp. 298–1.
58. PRO WO 169/3990: 'X Corps and Delta Force HQ 1942 Oct–Dec'.
59. N. Hamilton, *Monty: The Making of a General*, p. 741.

Chapter 14: Crisis Conference

1. PRO WO 201/537: 'X Corps Training Instruction No. 1, 11.09.42'.
2. Tuker, *Approach to Battle*, p. 250.
3. De Guingand, *Operation Victory*, p. 200; Montgomery, *Memoirs*, p. 129.
4. Montgomery, *Memoirs*, p. 129.
5. PRO WO 169/3990: 'X Corps and Delta Force HQ 1942 Oct–Dec'; R. Walker, *Alam Halfa and Alamein*, pp. 302–4.
6. PRO WO 201/425: 'Battle for Egypt Report 1942 Oct–Nov'.
7. Tatman and Kennet, *Craftsmen of the Army*, p. 95.
8. PRO WO 201/471: '23rd Armoured Brigade: Operations "Lightfoot" and "Supercharge" 1942 Oct–1943 July'.
9. Platt, *The Royal Wiltshire Yeomanry*, p. 146.
10. IWM AL 834/1: 'DAK Ia, War Diary, 03.08–22.11.42'.
11. R. Walker, *Alam Halfa and Alamein*, p. 305.
12. IWM AL 834/1.
13. Fraser, *Knight's Cross*, p. 367.
14. Irving, *The Trail of the Fox*, p. 199.
15. PRO AIR 41/50: 'The Middle East Campaign, vol. IV: Operations in Libya, the Western Desert and Tunisia, July 1942–May 1943'.
16. Maughan, *Tobruk and El Alamein*, pp. 680–1.
17. *What We Have We Hold!*, p. 164.
18. Hastings, *The Rifle Brigade in the Second World War*, p. 156.
19. Lucas-Phillips, *Alamein*, p. 170.
20. Miles, *The Gordon Highlanders*, pp. 140–2.

21. Cameron, *The Argyll and Sutherland Highlanders 7th Battalion*, pp. 45–7.
22. Norton, *26 Battalion*, pp. 198–200.
23. WYM: Capt. C. B. Stoddart, letters, October 1942.
24. Forty, *Afrika Korps at War*, vol. II, p. 78.
25. Loughnan, *Divisional Cavalry*, p. 232.
26. R. Walker, *Alam Halfa and Alamein*, pp. 306–7.
27. De Guingand, *Operation Victory*, p. 199.
28. McCreery, 'Reflections of a Chief of Staff', p. 40.
29. N. Hamilton, *Monty: The Making of a General*, pp. 743–4.
30. De Guingand, *Operation Victory*, p. 200.
31. Ryder, *Oliver Leese*, p. 111.
32. Kemp, *The Staffordshire Yeomanry*, p. 102; Lucas-Phillips, *Alamein*, p. 184.
33. Tuker, *Approach to Battle*, p. 251.
34. Delaforce, *Monty's Marauders*, pp. 113–14.
35. Moore, *Panzer Bait*, p. 110.
36. Ibid.
37. Warner, *Alamein*, p. 68.
38. Tuker, *Approach to Battle*, p. 251.
39. N. Hamilton, *Monty: The Making of a General*, p. 748.
40. Delaforce, *Monty's Marauders*, pp. 114–15.
41. Norton, *26 Battalion*, pp. 202–3.
42. Maughan, *Tobruk and El Alamein*, p. 683.
43. J. Lucas, *War in the Desert*, pp. 191,193.
44. Lucas-Phillips, *Alamein*, pp. 187–8.
45. R. Walker, *Alam Halfa and Alamein*, p. 316.
46. PRO WO 169/4117: '10 Armd Div G and A/Q Branch, 1942 Jan–Mar, Mar–Jul, Sept, Dec'.
47. N. Hamilton, *Monty: The Making of a General*, p. 754.
48. Ibid., pp. 755–7; Carver, *Dilemmas of the Desert War*, p. 139.
49. Forty, *Afrika Korps at War*, vol. II, p. 86.
50. A. Gilbert, *The Imperial War Museum Book of The Desert War*, p. 170.
51. Hastings, *The Rifle Brigade in the Second World War*, p. 157.
52. IWM AL 834/1.
53. Fearnside, *Bayonets Abroad*, p. 274.
54. *What We Have We Hold!*, p. 164; 'Silver John', 'Target Tank', p. 226.
55. Fergusson, *The Black Watch and the King's Enemies*, p. 132.
56. Orpen, *South African Forces, World War II*, vol. III, p. 432.
57. Clay, *The Path of the 50th*, pp. 96–7.
58. Crookenden, *The Cheshire Regiment in the Second World War*, p. 68.
59. Synge, *The Green Howards*, pp. 151–4.
60. Nightingale, *The East Yorkshire Regiment*, p. 118.
61. Synge, *The Green Howards*, p. 155.
62. Crookenden, *The Cheshire Regiment in the Second World War*, p. 68.
63. Clay, *The Path of the 50th*, pp. 98–9.
64. Carver, *Second to None*, pp. 63–4.
65. R. B. Johnson, *The Queen's in The Middle East and North Africa*, p. 51.
66. Warner, *Alamein*, p. 103.
67. R. B. Johnson, *The Queen's in The Middle East and North Africa*, pp. 51–3.

Chapter 15: Crumbling

1. Private R. J. Anson, 2/17th Battalion, diary, 24–6 October 1942, quoted in M. Johnston, *At the Front Line*, p. 43.
2. Fearnside, *Bayonets Abroad*, p. 274.
3. Lucas-Phillips, *Alamein*, pp. 174–5.
4. *What We Have We Hold!*, pp. 166, 168.
5. Pakenham-Walsh, *The Corps of Royal Engineers*, vol. VIII, p. 387
6. Warner, *Alamein*, p. 148.
7. Maughan, *Tobruk and El Alamein*, p. 687.
8. Lucas-Phillips, *Alamein*, p. 205.
9. N. Hamilton, *Monty: The Making of a General*, pp. 758–9, 762–3.
10. Dawnay, *The 10th Royal Hussars in The Second World War*, p. 81.
11. Fraser, *Knight's Cross*, p. 372.
12. Richardson and Freidin, *The Fatal Decisions*, pp. 96–7.
13. D. Young, *Rommel*, p. 136; W. Warlimont, 'The Decision in the Mediterranean', in Jacobsen and Rohwer, *Decisive Battles of World War II*, p. 203.
14. Liddell Hart, *The Rommel Papers*, p. 299.
15. IWM AL 834/1: 'DAK Ia, War Diary, 03.08–22.11.42'.
16. Behrendt, *Rommel's Intelligence in the Desert Campaign*, pp. 61, 198.
17. Mitcham, *Rommel's Desert War*, p. 143.
18. Liddell Hart, *The Rommel Papers*, p. 306.
19. Glenn, *Tobruk to Tarakan*, pp. 149–56.
20. Maughan, *Tobruk and El Alamein*, pp. 688–92.
21. Fearnside, *Bayonets Abroad*, p. 279.
22. PRO AIR 41/50: 'The Middle East Campaign, vol. IV: Operations in Libya, the Western Desert and Tunisia, July 1942–May 1943'.
23. Caccia-Dominioni, *Alamein 1933–1962*, pp. 212–15.
24. PRO AIR 41/50.
25. McKee, *El Alamein*, p. 144.
26. Liddell Hart, *The Rommel Papers*, p. 308.
27. Hinsley, *British Intelligence*, vol. II, p. 442.
28. Playfair, *The Mediterranean and Middle East*, vol. IV, p. 202.
29. McKee, *El Alamein*, p. 123.
30. PRO AIR 41/50.
31. McCallum, *Journey With a Pistol*, p. 49.
32. McGregor, *The Spirit of Angus*, p. 41.
33. W. E. Duncan et al., *The Royal Artillery Commemoration Book*, p. 234.
34. Samwell, *An Infantry Officer with the Eighth Army*, pp. 47–50; Cameron, *The Argyll and Sutherland Highlanders 7th Battalion*, pp. 47–8.
35. R. Walker, *Alam Halfa and Alamein*, pp. 333–4.
36. Orpen, *The Cape Town Highlanders*, p. 183.
37. Norton, *26 Battalion*, p. 205.
38. Puttick, *25 Battalion*, p. 238.
39. R. Walker, *Alam Halfa and Alamein*, pp. 337–9.
40. Orpen, *The Cape Town Highlanders*, pp. 183–5.
41. Lucas-Phillips, *Alamein*, pp. 206–9.
42. G. R. Stevens, *Fourth Indian Division*, p. 193.
43. Carver, *Second to None*, p. 65.

44. J. Lucas, *War in the Desert*, pp. 158, 162.
45. WYM: Capt. C. B. Stoddart, letters, October 1942.

Chapter 16: The Defence of Outpost Snipe
1. Playfair, *The Mediterranean and Middle East*, vol. IV, p. 53.
2. Hastings, *The Rifle Brigade in the Second World War*, p. 166.
3. PRO CAB 44/103, Section II, Chapter M: 'Battle of El Alamein, pt III, vol. I: Operation "Supercharge", 1942 Oct 26–29, by Lieutenant-Colonel M. E. S. Laws, May 1953'. Contrary to the Rifle Brigade's war diary (WO 169/5055, on which Hastings's account is largely based), which stated that 239th Battery brought 11 guns but could get only six into action, they brought only six in two troops already depleted through casualties.
4. Lucas-Phillips, *Alamein*, p. 216.
5. Wake and Deedes, *Swift and Bold*, pp. 111–12.
6. 'The . . . Battalion at the Battle of Alamein', *The King's Royal Rifle Corps Chronicle*, 1943, p. 68.
7. PRO CAB 44/103.
8. Miles, *The Gordon Highlanders*, p. 142.
9. Hastings, *The Rifle Brigade in the Second World War*, p. 167.
10. Lucas-Phillips, *Alamein*, p. 218.
11. Hastings, *The Rifle Brigade in the Second World War*, p. 168.
12. Lucas-Phillips, *Alamein*, p. 221.
13. Hastings, *The Rifle Brigade in the Second World War*, p. 179.
14. 'The Snipe Position', p. 150.
15. Lucas-Phillips, *Alamein*, p. 223.
16. Hastings, *The Rifle Brigade in the Second World War*, p. 170.
17. Crimp, *Diary of a Desert Rat*, pp. 152–3.
18. Lucas-Phillips, *Alamein*, p. 225.
19. Hastings, *The Rifle Brigade in the Second World War*, p. 171.
20. Ibid.
21. Hastings, *The Rifle Brigade in the Second World War*, pp. 171–2; Lucas-Phillips, *Alamein*, pp. 226–7.
22. A. Gilbert, *The Imperial War Museum Book of The Desert War*, p. 171.
23. IWM AL 834/1: 'DAK Ia, War Diary, 03.08–22.11.42'.
24. Lucas-Phillips, *Alamein*, p. 228.
25. 'The Snipe Position', p. 151.
26. Lucas-Phillips, *Alamein*, p. 229.
27. Ritchie, *Fusing the Ploughshare*, pp. 235–6.
28. PRO AIR 41/50: 'The Middle East Campaign, vol. IV: Operations in Libya, the Western Desert and Tunisia, July 1942–May 1943'.
29. Hastings, *The Rifle Brigade in the Second World War*, p. 174.
30. Lucas-Phillips, *Alamein*, pp. 230–31.
31. Liddell Hart, *The Rommel Papers*, p. 310.
32. Hastings, *The Rifle Brigade in the Second World War*, p. 174.
33. Lucas-Phillips, *Alamein*, p. 232.
34. Ibid., p. 233.
35. J. Lucas, *War in the Desert*, p. 222.

36. Crimp, *Diary of a Desert Rat*, pp. 156–7.
37. Lucas-Phillips, *Alamein*, pp. 233–4.
38. Ibid., p. 235. Lucas-Phillips's account comes mainly from the report of the committee of investigation which was set up a month later and made an exhausting analysis of the battle, official reports of the action made by Bird and Marten (incorporating a report by Flower), accounts by Turner in the *British Army Journal* and the *Rifle Brigade Journal,* as well as personal narratives to him by Turner, Bird, Marten, Atkin and Swann.
39. 'The Snipe Position', pp. 152–53.
40. Hinsley, *British Intelligence*, vol. II, pp. 443–4.
41. Glenn, *Tobruk to Tarakan*, pp. 156–7.
42. Ibid.
43. IWM AL 879/1: '90 Light Div (Afrika) Ia, War Diary, 05.09.42–31.12.42 plus translation (extracts only)'.
44. Glenn, *Tobruk to Tarakan*, pp. 156–7.
45. IWM AL 879/1.
46. PRO CAB 44/103.
47. Orpen, *South African Forces, World War II*, vol. III, p. 194.

Chapter 17: Thompson's Post

1. Field Marshal Earl Wavell, 'In Praise of Infantry', *The Times*, 19 April 1945
2. IWM AL 834/1: 'DAK Ia, War Diary, 03.08–22.11.42'.
3. J. Lucas, *War in the Desert*, p. 212.
4. Fraser, *Knight's Cross*, p. 375.
5. Maughan, *Tobruk and El Alamein*, p. 697.
6. WSRO RSR MS (147): '27–28 October 1942. Diary of Attack by 133rd Infantry Brigade on Positions known as "Woodcock" and "Snipe" during the Battle of El Alamein. Compiled by Brigadier Lee'.
7. SWWEC, Army/C. N. Barker.
8. McNish, 'El Alamein in Perspective', p. 6.
9. WSRO RSR MS (147).
10. McNish, 'El Alamein in Perspective', p. 6.
11. WSRO RSR MS (147).
12. Miles, *The Gordon Highlanders*, p. 142.
13. McNish, 'El Alamein in Perspective', p. 7.
14. IWM AL 1657/1: '15. Panzer Div. Ia War Diary and Appendices, 23.10–25.11.42'.
15. Lucas-Phillips, *Alamein*, p. 239.
16. McKee, *El Alamein*, p. 163.
17. WSRO RSR MS (147).
18. *A Short History of the 45th/51st (Leeds Rifles) Royal Tank Regiment (TA)*, pp. 17–19.
19. Carver, *El Alamein*, p. 155.
20. IWM AL 834/1.
21. Miles, *The Gordon Highlanders*, p. 143.
22. *A Short History of the 45th/51st (Leeds Rifles) Royal Tank Regiment (TA)*, p. 19.
23. Maughan, *Tobruk and El Alamein*, pp. 698–9.
24. Caccia-Dominioni, *Alamein 1933–1962*, p. 229.

25. IWM AL 879/1: '90 Light Div (Afrika) Ia, War Diary, 05.09.42–31.12.42 plus translation (extracts only)'.
26. Lucas-Phillips, *Alamein*, p. 244.
27. Fearnside, *Bayonets Abroad*, pp. 282–4.
28. Austin, *Let Enemies Beware!*, p. 167.
29. Shore, *Mud and Blood*, pp. 216–22.
30. AWM PR00906: 'Cpl J. Craig, 2/13th Bn, Diary 29.10.42'.
31. Oakes, *Muzzle Blast*, p. 114.
32. Maughan, *Tobruk and El Alamein*, pp. 701–5.
33. IWM AL 834/1.
34. Bryant, *The Turn of the Tide*, p. 512–13; Alanbrooke, *War Diaries*, pp. 335–6.
35. N. Hamilton, *Monty: The Making of a General*, p. 777.
36. Tedder, *With Prejudice*, p. 359.
37. PRO CAB 44/104, Section II, Chapter M: 'Battle of El Alamein, pt III, vol. II: Operation "Supercharge", 1942 Oct 29–Nov 1, by Lieutenant-Colonel M. E. S. Laws, 1953 May'.
38. PRO CAB 44/103, Section II, Chapter M: 'Battle of El Alamein, pt III, vol. I: Operation "Supercharge", 1942 Oct 26–29, by Lieutenant-Colonel M. E. S. Laws, May 1953'.
39. Maughan, *Tobruk and El Alamein*, pp. 708–9.
40. Ibid.
41. PRO CAB 44/104.
42. Glenn, *Tobruk to Tarakan*, pp. 159–61.
43. IWM AL 1657/1.
44. PRO AIR 41/50: 'The Middle East Campaign, vol. IV: Operations in Libya, the Western Desert and Tunisia, July 1942–May 1943'.
45. Fearnside, *Bayonets Abroad*, p. 286.
46. Anderson and Jackett, *Mud and Sand*, p. 302.
47. Trigellis-Smith, *Britain to Borneo*, pp. 113–9.
48. Serle, *The Second Twenty-Fourth*, pp. 219–20.
49. Glenn, *Tobruk to Tarakan*, p. 169.
50. 289th Battery was from 102nd Anti-Tank Regiment Royal Artillery (The Northumberland Hussars), commanded by C. E. Lucas-Philips during the battle. He describes 289th Battery's contribution in detail in *Alamein*, pp. 253–7.
51. Maughan, *Tobruk and El Alamein*, pp. 710–8, 720.
52. Anderson and Jackett, *Mud and Sand*, p. 309.
53. Liddell Hart, *The Rommel Papers*, p. 315.
54. PRO AIR 41/50.
55. Anderson and Jackett, *Mud and Sand*, pp. 310–12.
56. Ibid.
57. Glenn, *Tobruk to Tarakan*, p. 171.
58. Serle, *The Second Twenty-Fourth*, p. 222. 'You'll be sorry' was something of a catch-phrase among the AIF.
59. Maughan, *Tobruk and El Alamein*, pp. 720–3.
60. Sergeant F. Legg, 2/48th Battalion, diary, 1 November 1942, quoted in M. Johnston, *At the Front Line*, p. 45.
61. PRO AIR 41/50.
62. Bowyer, *Men of the Desert Air Force*, pp. 160–2.

63. Masel, *The Second 28th*, p. 112.
64. Ibid., pp. 135–6.
65. Maughan, *Tobruk and El Alamein*, p. 724.
66. Combe et al., *The Second 43rd Australian Infantry Battalion*, p. 129.
67. Corporal J. H. Lovegrove, 2/43rd Battalion, diary, 14 November 1942, quoted in M. Johnston, *At the Front Line*, p. 194.
68. Fearnside, *Bayonets Abroad*, p. 280.
69. Maughan, *Tobruk and El Alamein*, pp. 724–7.

Chapter 18: Supercharge
1. R. Walker, *Alam Halfa and Alamein*, p. 383.
2. Badman, *Australians at War*, p. 158.
3. 'Silver John', *'Target Tank'*, p. 249.
4. N. Hamilton, *Monty: The Making of a General*, pp. 779–81.
5. Reid, *The Turning Point*, p. 201.
6. R. Walker, *Alam Halfa and Alamein*, p. 367.
7. Lucas-Phillips, *Alamein*, p. 265.
8. R. Walker, *Alam Halfa and Alamein*, p. 368.
9. Fraser, *Knight's Cross*, p. 377; Irving, *The Trail of the Fox*, p. 206.
10. W. Warlimont, 'The Decision in the Mediterranean', in Jacobsen and Rohwer, *Decisive Battles of World War II*, p. 201.
11. Playfair, *The Mediterranean and Middle East*, vol. IV, p. 62.
12. N. Hamilton, *Monty: The Making of a General*, p. 787.
13. S. Hamilton, *Armoured Odyssey*, p. 76.
14. PRO CAB 44/105, Section II, Chapter M: 'Battle of El Alamein, pt III, vol. III: Operation "Supercharge", 1942 Nov 1–2, by Lieutenant-Colonel M. E. S. Laws, 1953 May'.
15. G. R. Stevens, *Fourth Indian Division*, p. 193.
16. PRO CAB 44/104, Section II, Chapter M: 'Battle of El Alamein, pt III, vol. II: Operation "Supercharge", 1942 Oct 29–Nov 1, by Lieutenant-Colonel M. E. S. Laws, 1953 May'.
17. PRO CAB 44/105.
18. Kay, *27 (Machine-Gun) Battalion*, p. 290.
19. R. Walker, *Alam Halfa and Alamein*, p. 381.
20. G. R. Stevens, *Fourth Indian Division*, p. 193.
21. Playfair, *The Mediterranean and Middle East*, vol. IV, pp. 65–6.
22. Craig, *The Broken Plume*, p. 76.
23. S. D. Hamilton, *50th Royal Tank Regiment*, p. 48.
24. R. Walker, *Alam Halfa and Alamein*, pp. 384–6.
25. P. J. Lewis and I. R. English, *8th Battalion The Durham Light Infantry*, p. 148.
26. Rissik, *The DLI at War*, pp. 101–2; Ward, *Faithful*, p. 493.
27. McKee, *El Alamein*, pp. 152–3.
28. P. J. Lewis and I. R. English, *8th Battalion The Durham Light Infantry*, pp. 149–52.
29. Moses, *The Faithful Sixth*, pp. 206–112; Rissik, *The DLI at War*, p. 103; A. Gilbert, *The Imperial War Museum Book of The Desert War*, p. 173.
30. IWM AL 1657/1: '15. Panzer Div. Ia War Diary and Appendices, 23.10–25.11.42'.
31. Borthwick, *Sans Peur*, pp. 33–4.

32. J. Lucas, *War in the Desert*, p. 237.

33. McNish, 'El Alamein in Perspective', p. 9.

34. Reid, *The Turning Point*, p. 206.

35. R. Walker, *Alam Halfa and Alamein*, pp. 387–91.

36. Borthwick, *Sans Peur*, p. 36.

37. *The Eighth Army: September 1941 to January 1943*, p. 90.

38. Klein, *Springboks in Armour*, pp. 302–3.

39. Kay, *27 (Machine-Gun) Battalion*, p. 292.

40. WYM: Capt. C. B. Stoddart, letters, October 1942.

41. PRO WO 201/554: '9th Armoured Brigade Report on Operations 1942 Nov'.

42. PRO WO 201/424: 'The October Battle of Alamein and the Advance to Tripolitania 1942 Oct–Nov'.

43. P. W. Pitt, *Royal Wilts*, p. 152.

44. Lucas-Phillips, *Alamein*, p. 280.

45. 'Account of the Action of The 3rd The King's Own Hussars at El Alamein', p. 34.

46. Baker, *Yeoman-Yeoman*, p. 57.

47. 'Account of the Action of The 3rd The King's Own Hussars at El Alamein', p. 35.

48. PRO WO 210/554.

49. Lucas-Phillips, *Alamein*, pp. 283–4.

50. WYM: Capt. C. B. Stoddart, letters, October 1942.

51. Borthwick, *Sans Peur*, pp. 36–7.

52. IWM AL 879/1: '90 Light Div (Afrika) Ia, War Diary, 05.09.42–31.12.42 plus translation (extracts only)'.

53. WYM: Capt. C. B. Stoddart, letters, October 1942.

54. PRO WO 201/575: '3rd King's Own Hussars 1940–1942'.

55. In *Alamein*, chs. 16 and 17, C. E. Lucas-Phillips gives a detailed account of 9th Armoured Brigade's epic action written from personal accounts by many participants and describes 2nd Armoured Brigade's follow-up.

56. SWWEC, Army/ Godfrey Talbot.

57. Dawnay, *The 10th Royal Hussars in The Second World War*, p. 84.

58. Beddington, *The Queen's Bays (The 2nd Dragoon Guards)*, p. 108.

59. Bright, *The Ninth Queen's Royal Lancers*, p. 113.

60. Lucas-Phillips, *Alamein*, pp. 295–8.

61. Merewood, *To War with The Bays*, pp. 67–8.

62. Baker, *Yeoman-Yeoman*, pp. 57–8.

63. IWM AL 1657/1.

64. Carrell, *The Foxes of the Desert*, p. 292.

65. Irving, *The Trail of the Fox*, p. 209.

66. Barclay, *The Sherwood Foresters*, p. 75.

67. PRO WO 201/554.

Chapter 19: The Beginning of the End

1. PRO WO 201/554: '9th Armoured Brigade Report on Operations 1942 Nov'.

2. Platt, *The Royal Wiltshire Yeomanry*, p. 148.

3. Montgomery, *Memoirs*, p. 131.

4. PRO WO 201/545: '24th Armoured Brigade: Notes on Armoured Fighting Vehicles on Operations 1942 Oct'.

5. Lewin, *The Life and Death of the Afrika Korps*, p. 168.
6. PRO WO 201/431: 'RA Notes on the Offensive by Eighth Army, 23.10–4.11.42, El Alamein Position, 14.12.42'.
7. PRO AIR 41/50: 'The Middle East Campaign, vol. IV: Operations in Libya, the Western Desert and Tunisia, July 1942–May 1943'.
8. McKee, *El Alamein*, pp. 115–17.
9. Horrocks, *A Full Life*, p. 139.
10. PRO AIR 41/50.
11. Herington, *Air War Against Germany and Italy*, p. 374.
12. Rust, *The 9th Air Force in World War II*, p. 20.
13. Barnett's assertion that this move, six days after Rommel had moved 21st Panzer Division up from the south, was 'Montgomery dancing to Rommel's tune' is absurd (*The Desert Generals*, p. 289).
14. Lucas-Phillips, *Alamein*, pp. 301–2.
15. *What We Have We Hold!*, p. 172.
16. Wake and Deedes, *Swift and Bold*, p. 114.
17. A. Gilbert, *The Imperial War Museum Book of The Desert War*, p. 174.
18. Ibid.
19. Hastings, *The Rifle Brigade in the Second World War*, pp. 158–60.
20. Klein, *Springboks in Armour*, pp. 303–4.
21. Fraser, *Knight's Cross*, p. 380.
22. Bedeschi, *Fronte d'Africa*, pp. 69–70.
23. Richardson and Freidin, *The Fatal Decisions*, pp. 104–5.
24. Ibid.
25. Irving, *The Trail of the Fox*, pp. 213–14.
26. Liddell Hart, *The Rommel Papers*, p. 327.
27. Ring and Shores, *Luftkampf zwischen Sand und Sonne*, p. 378.
28. R. Walker, *Alam Halfa and Alamein*, pp. 415–16.
29. PRO CAB 44/106, Section II, Chapter M: 'Battle of El Alamein, pt III, vol. IV: Operation "Supercharge", 1942 Oct 29–Nov 2–4, by Lieutenant-Colonel M. E. S. Laws, 1953 May'.
30. C. Richardson, *Flashback*, p. 123.
31. Lucas-Phillips, *Alamein*, pp. 306–7.
32. J. M. Sym, 'Brigade Major at El Alamein', p. 153.
33. Miles, *The Gordon Highlanders*, pp. 143–4.
34. Ryder, *Oliver Leese*, p. 115.
35. *The Eighth Army: September 1941 to January 1943*, p. 92.
36. G. R. Stevens, *Fourth Indian Division*, pp. 194–6.
37. T. A. Martin, *The Essex Regiment*, p. 237.
38. Majdalany, *The Battle of El Alamein*, p. 128.
39. Klein, *Springboks in Armour*, p. 305.
40. Cameron, *The Argyll and Sutherland Highlanders 7th Battalion*, pp. 50–2.
41. Blamey, *A Company Commander Remembers*, pp. 195–7.
42. Russell, *War History of 7th Bn., The Black Watch*, p. 18.
43. Blamey, *A Company Commander Remembers*, p. 198; Orpen, *The Cape Town Highlanders*, p. 186.
44. Terraine, *The Right of the Line*, pp. 385–6.
45. Doherty, *A Noble Crusade*, pp. 110–11.

46. B. Pitt, *The Crucible of War: Year of Alamein 1942*, pp. 421–2.

47. Detweiler et. al., *World War II German Military Studies*, vol. XIV, pt IV, MS# T–3 P1, p. 76.

48. Ibid., MS# D–172, pp. 8–9.

49. Bennett, *Ultra and Mediterranean Strategy*, pp. 164–5.

50. Carrell, *The Foxes of the Desert*, p. 299.

51. Hillgruber, *Kriegstagebuch des Oberkommandos der Wehrmacht*, vol. II, pp. 894–8.

52. Richardson and Freidin, *The Fatal Decisions*, pp. 106–7. See also Carrell, *The Foxes of the Desert*, pp. 296–7. Wolf Heckmann notes that, over the years, recollections of many of these little incidents have become clouded and sometimes romanticized. He suggests that von Thoma waited in a slit trench for the British, and Westphal reports that Bayerlein afterwards told him not to relate the tale to anyone (*Rommel's War in Africa*, pp. 340–1).

53. Lucas-Phillips, *Alamein*, p. 318. As with many stories of the battle, there are numerous versions of Singer's capture of von Thoma, all subtly different.

54. *The Eighth Army: September 1941 to January 1943*, p. 90.

55. J. Lucas, *War in the Desert*, p. 256; McKee, *El Alamein*, p. 172.

56. Irving, *The Trail of the Fox*, p. 215.

57. B. Pitt, *The Crucible of War: Year of Alamein 1942* pp. 423–6.

Chapter 20: The End of the Beginning

1. Calder, *The People's War*, p. 351.

2. Binns et al., *Britain at War in Colour*, p. 93.

3. N. Hamilton, *Monty: Master of the Battlefield*, pp. 3–4.

4. J. Lucas, *War in the Desert*, pp. 258–9.

5. Warner, *Alamein*, p. 134.

6. Ritchie, *Fusing the Ploughshare*, p. 240.

7. Crew, *The Army Medical Services, Campaigns*, vol. II, p. 213.

8. M. Johnston, *At the Front Line*, p. 46.

9. AWM PR00906: 'Cpl J. Craig, 2/13 Bn, Diary 9–11.11.42'.

10. B. Pitt, *The Crucible of War: Year of Alamein 1942*, p. 427.

11. BWA 0799/1: 'Account of 1 BW at Battle of El Alamein, 23.10.42, Lt-Col William Noel Roper-Caldbeck (CO)'.

12. J. Lucas, *War in the Desert*, pp. 257–8.

13. Delaforce, *Monty's Marauders*, pp. 117–18.

14. Hastings, *The Rifle Brigade in the Second World War*, pp. 161.

15. Liddell Hart, *The Rommel Papers*, p. 339.

16. B. Pitt, *The Crucible of War: Year of Alamein 1942*, pp. 430–1.

17. Carver, *El Alamein*, p. 191.

18. B. Pitt, *The Crucible of War: Year of Alamein 1942*, pp. 432–3.

19. R. Walker, *Alam Halfa and Alamein*, pp. 445–6.

20. PRO WO 201/437: 'Operation "Lightfoot" and "Supercharge" Reports 1942 Oct–Nov'.

21. Lambert, 'Tin Triangles', p. 335.

22. B. Pitt, *The Crucible of War: Year of Alamein 1942*, p. 436.

23. Doherty, *A Noble Crusade*, p. 109.

24. Heckmann, *Rommel's War in Africa*, p. 346.

25. Mitcham, *Rommel's Desert War*, pp. 167–72.

26. Fraser, *Knight's Cross*, pp. 384–6.
27. Macksey, *Kesselring*, p. 132; PRO WO 277/11: 'Maintenance in the Field, vol. II', p. 89.
28. PRO WO 201/2596: 'Middle East Training Memorandum No. 8, Lessons from Operations 1942 Oct–Nov'.
29. WSRO RSR MS (148): '5 November 1942. Lessons Learnt from the Phase of Operations 23 October–5 November 1942'.
30. Montgomery, *Memoirs*, pp. 141–2.
31. Carver, *Dilemmas of the Desert War*, p. 139.
32. Hinsley, *British Intelligence*, vol. II, pp. 453–4.
33. Playfair, *The Mediterranean and Middle East*, vol. IV, pp. 16–17.
34. Barnett, *The Desert Generals*, p. 264; Terraine, *The Right of the Line*, p. 387.
35. Irving, *The Trail of the Fox*, pp. 224–6.
36. LHCMA, Alanbroooke MSS 14/63: Alexander to Brooke, 10 December 1942; Montgomery to Brooke, 13 December 1942.
37. LHCMA, Sir R. O'Connor MSS 11/14: 'Obituary of General Sir R. McCreery'.
38. D. French, *Raising Churchill's Army*, pp. 279–80.
39. Wheatley, *The Deception Planners*, p. 108.
40. D. McGuirk, letter to author, 16 April 2001.
41. Chalfont, *Montgomery of Alamein*, p. 156.
42. Bennett, *Ultra and Mediterranean Strategy*, pp. 167–81.
43. P. Lewis, *A People's War*, p. 193.
44. J. Lucas, *War in the Desert*, p. 160.
45. Tuker, *Approach to Battle*, p. 249.
46. Horrocks, *A Full Life*, p. 140.
47. D. French, *Raising Churchill's Army*, p. 282.
48. Tuker, *Approach to Battle*, p. 237.
49. W. E. Duncan et al., *The Royal Artillery Commemoration Book*, p. 227.
50. See George Blackburn's account of a Canadian field regiment in Normandy and beyond, *The Guns of War*.
51. J. Lucas, *War in the Desert*, p. 101.
52. PRO WO 201/424: 'The October Battle of Alamein and the Advance to Tripolitania 1942 Oct–Nov'.
53. Maughan, *Tobruk and El Alamein*, p. 743.
54. Tuker, *Approach to Battle*, p. 258.
55. Richards and Saunders, *Royal Air Force 1939–1945*, vol. II, p. 239.
56. Van Creveld, 'Rommel's Supply Problem'. To say, for example, that 'the material resources of his force were outside his control' and talk of 'neglect of military leaders in Germany' (M. Cooper, *The German Army 1933–1945*, p. 353) is at best an oversimplification. Rommel's disregard of orders meant he put himself beyond *matériel* support.
57. Wavell, *The Good Soldier*, pp. 10–11.
58. Lucas-Phillips, *Alamein*, p. 35.
59. Tuker, *Approach to Battle*, pp. 242–4, 256–7.
60. Churchill, *The Second World War*, vol. IV, p. 487.

Bibliography

'Account of the Action of The 3rd The King's Own Hussars at El Alamein', *The 3rd The King's Own Hussars Journal*, 1946

Addison, P., and Calder, A. (eds.), *Time to Kill: The Soldier's Experience of War in the West 1939–1945* (London: Pimlico, 1997)

Agar-Hamilton, J. A. I., and Turner, L. C. F., *Crisis in the Desert: May–July 1942* (Oxford: Oxford University Press, 1952)

Agnelli, S., *We Always Wore Sailor Suits* (London: Weidenfeld & Nicolson, 1975)

Alanbrooke, Field Marshal Lord, *War Diaries 1939–1945*, ed. A. Danchev and D. Todman (London: Weidenfeld & Nicolson, 2001)

Alexander, Field Marshal Viscount, *The Alexander Memoirs*, ed. J. North (London: Cassell, 1962)

——'Despatch: The African Campaign from el Alamein to Tunis, 10 August 1942 to 13 May 1943', supplement to the *London Gazette*, 3 February 1948

Amery, J., *Approach March: A Venture in Autobiography* (London: Hutchinson, 1973)

Anderson, J. A., and Jackett, J. G. T. (eds), *Mud and Sand: The Official War History of 2/3 Pioneer Battalion A.I.F.* (Sydney: 2/3 Pioneer Battalion Association, 1955)

Armstrong, Colonel. S. J., 'Water Supply Problems in Egypt during the War 1939–45', *Royal Engineers Journal*, 1948

Auchinleck, Field Marshal Sir Claude, 'Despatch: Operations in the Middle East from 1 November 1941 to 15 August 1942', supplement to the *London Gazette*, 13 January, 1948

Austin, R. J., *Let Enemies Beware! 'Caveant Hostes': The History of the 2/15th Battalion, 1940–1945* (McCrae: The 2/15th Battalion AIF Remembrance Club/Slouch Hat Publications, 1995)

Badman, P., *Australians at War: North Africa 1940–1942 The Desert War* (Sydney: Time-Life Books (Australia) 1988)

Baker, P., *Yeoman-Yeoman: The Warwickshire Yeomanry 1920–1956* (Warwick: The Queen's Own Warwickshire and Worcestershire Yeomanry Regimental Association, 1971)

Barclay, C. N., *The History of The Sherwood Foresters (Nottinghamshire and Derbyshire Regiment) 1919–1957* (London: William Clowes, 1958)

——*On Their Shoulders* (London: Faber, 1964)

Barkas, G., *The Camouflage Story* (London: Cassell, 1952)

Barker, A. J., *Afrika Korps* (London: Bison Books, 1978)

Barnett, C., *The Desert Generals*, 2nd edn (London: Allen & Unwin, 1983)

Barrett, J., *We Were There: Australian Soldiers of World War Two* (Ringwood, Vic.: Viking, 1987)

Barter, M., *Far Above Battle: The Experience and Memory of Australian Soldiers in War 1939–1945* (Sydney: Allen & Unwin, 1994)

Bates, P., *Dance of War: The Story of the Battle of Egypt* (London: Leo Cooper, 1992)

——*Supply Company* (Wellington: War History Branch, Department of Internal Affairs, 1955)

The Battle of Egypt: The Official Record in Pictures and Maps (London: HMSO, 1943)

Bean, C. E. W., *Official History of Australia in the War of 1914–1918*, vol. V (Canberra: Australian War Memorial, 1937)

Beckett, D., *1/4th Essex Regiment: A Battalion of Eighth Army* (London: Wilson & Whitworth, 1945)

Beddington, W. R., *A History of The Queen's Bays (The 2nd Dragoon Guards) 1929–1945* (Winchester: Warren & Son, 1954)

Bedeschi, G., *Fronte d'Africa: c'ero anch'io* (Milan: Mursia, 1979)

Begg, R. Campbell, and Liddle, P. H. (eds.), *For Five Shillings a Day: Personal Histories of World War II* (London: HarperCollins, 2000)

Behrendt, H.-O., *Rommel's Intelligence in the Desert Campaign* (London: William Kimber, 1985)

Bennett, R., *Ultra and Mediterranean Strategy 1941–1945* (London: Hamish Hamilton, 1989)

Bergo, E., *The Afrika Korps* (London: Alan Wingate, 1972)

Bernstein, B. L., *The Tide Turned at Alamein: Impressions of the Desert War with the South African Division and the Eighth Army, June 1941–January 1943* (Cape Town: Central News, 1944)

Bidwell, S., 'After the Wall Came Tumbling Down: A Historical Perspective', *Journal of the Royal United Services Institute*, 135 (1990)

——*Gunners at War* (London: Arrow Books, 1972)

Bingham, J. K. W., and Haupt, W., *North African Campaign 1940–1943* (London: Macdonald, 1968)

Binns, S., Carter, L., Wood, A., et. al., *Britain at War in Colour* (London: Carlton Books, 2000)

Birkby. C. (ed.), *The Saga of the Transvaal Scottish Regiment 1932–1950* (Cape Town: Timmins, 1950)

Bishop, T., *One Young Soldier: Memoirs of a Cavalryman*, ed. B. Shand (Norwich: Russell, 1993)

Blackburn, G., *The Guns of War* (London: Constable & Robinson, 2000)

Blair, S. G., *In Arduis Fidelis: Centenary History of the Royal Army Medical Corps* (Edinburgh: Scottish Academic Press, 1998)

Blamey, A. E., *A Company Commander Remembers* (Pietermaritzburg, 1962)

Boatner, M., *The Biographical Dictionary of World War II* (Novato, Cal.: Presidio, 1996)

Bolitho, H., *The Galloping Third: The Story of The 3rd The King's Own Hussars* (London: John Murray, 1963)

Bolté, Lieutenant C. G., 'Our American Officers', *The King's Royal Rifle Corps Chronicle*, 1943

Bond, B., *British Military Policy between Two World Wars* (Oxford: Oxford University Press, 1980)

Borman, C. A., *Divisional Signals* (Wellington: War History Branch, Department of Internal Affairs, 1954)

Borthwick, A., *Sans Peur: The History of The 5th (Caithness and Sutherland) Battalion, The Seaforth Highlanders 1942–5* (Stirling: Eneas Mackay, 1946)

Bowyer, C., *Men of the Desert Air Force 1940–43* (London: William Kimber, 1984)

Bowyer, C., and Shores, C., *Desert Air Force at War* (London: Ian Allen, 1981)

Bradford, E., *Siege: Malta 1940–1943* (London: Hamish Hamilton, 1985)

Brander, M., *The 10th Royal Hussars (Prince of Wales's Own)* (London: Leo Cooper, 1969)

Brett-Smith, R., *The 11th Hussars (Prince Albert's Own)* (London: Leo Cooper, 1969)

Bright, J. (ed.), *The Ninth Queen's Royal Lancers 1936–1945: The Story of an Armoured Regiment in Battle* (Aldershot: Gale & Polden, 1951)

Brookes, S. (ed.), *Montgomery and the Eighth Army: A Selection from the Diaries and Correspondence and Other Papers of Field Marshal the Viscount Montgomery of Alamein, August 1942 to December 1943* (London: Bodley Head, 1991)

Brown, A. G., Dodwell, K. C. E., Honniball, F. E., and Hopkinson, G. C., *A History of the 44th Royal Tank Regiment in the War of 1939–1945* (Brighton: 44th Royal Tank Regiment Association, 1965)

Brown, R., *Desert Warriors: Australian P-40 Pilots at War in the Middle East and North Africa* (Maryborough, Qld: Banner Books, 2000)

Brownlow, D. G., *Checkmate at Ruweisat: Auchinleck's Finest Hour* (North Quincy, Mass.: Christopher Publishing House, 1977)

Bryant, A., *The Turn of the Tide* (London: Collins, 1957)

Burdon, R. M., *24 Battalion* (Wellington: War History Branch, Department of Internal Affairs, 1953)

Caccia-Dominioni, P., *Alamein 1933–1962: An Italian Story* (London: Allen & Unwin, 1966)

Calder, A., *The People's War: Britain 1939–45* (London: Panther, 1971)

Cameron, I., *History of The Argyll and Sutherland Highlanders 7th Battalion* (London: Thomas Graham & Son, n.d.)

Carrell, P., *The Foxes of the Desert* (London: Macdonald, 1964)

Carver, M., *El Alamein* (London: Batsford, 1962)

——*Dilemmas of the Desert War: A New Look at the Libyan Campaign 1940–1942* (London: Batsford, 1986)

——*Second to None: The Royal Scots Greys, 1919–1945* (Doncaster: Military Publishers, 1998)

Cave-Brown, A., *Bodyguard of Lies* (London: W. H. Allen, 1986)

Chalfont, A., *Montgomery of Alamein* (London: Weidenfeld & Nicolson, 1976)

Chaplin, H. D., *The Queen's Royal West Kent Regiment 1920–1950* (London: Michael Joseph, 1954)

Chartres, J., '7th Field Squadron RE in World War II', *Royal Engineers Journal*, 1981

Churchill, W. S., *The Second World War*, vol. III: *The Grand Alliance* (London: Reprint Society, 1954)

——vol. IV: *The Hinge of Fate* (London: Reprint Society, 1954)

Ciano, Count G., *Ciano's Diaries* (London: Heinemann, 1947)

——*Ciano's Diplomatic Papers* (London: Odhams, 1948)

Clarke, D., *The Eleventh at War* (London: Michael Joseph, 1952)

Clarke, R., *With Alex to War: From the Irrawaddy to the Po 1941–1945* (Barnsley: Leo Cooper, 2000)

Clausewitz, C., *On War* (Harmondsworth: Penguin, 1968)

Clay, E. W., *The Path of the 50th* (Aldershot: Gale & Polden, 1950)

Clayton, Aileen, *The Enemy is Listening* (London: Hutchinson, 1980)

Clayton, Anthony, *The British Empire as a Superpower 1919–39* (London: Macmillan, 1986)

Clifford, A., *Three Against Rommel: The Campaigns of Wavell, Auchinleck and Alexander* (London: Harrap, 1943)

Clifton, G., *The Happy Hunted* (London: Cassell, 1952)

Cody, J. F., *New Zealand Engineers, Middle East* (Wellington: War History Branch, Department of Internal Affairs, 1961)

——*21 Battalion* (Wellington: War History Branch, Department of Internal Affairs, 1953)

——*28 (Maori) Battalion* (Wellington: War History Branch, Department of Internal Affairs, 1956)

Combe, G., Ligertwood, F., and Gilchrist, T., *The Second 43rd Australian Infantry Battalion 1940–1946* (Adelaide: Second 43rd Battalion AIF Club, 1972)

Connell, J., *Auchinleck: A Biography of Field Marshal Sir Claude Auchinleck* (London: Cassell, 1959)

Cooper, A., *Cairo in the War 1939–1945* (London: Hamish Hamilton, 1989)

Cooper, M., *The German Army 1933–1945: Its Political and Military Failure* (London: Macdonald & Jane's, 1978)

Craig, N., *The Broken Plume: A Platoon Commander's Story 1940–45* (London: Imperial War Museum, 1982)

Craven, W. F., and Cate, J. L. (eds.), *The Army Air Forces in World War II*, vol. II: *Europe: Torch to Pointblank August 1942 to December 1943* (Chicago: University of Chicago Press, 1949)

Crawford, R. J., *I Was an Eighth Army Soldier* (London: Gollancz, 1944)

Crew, F. A. E., *The Army Medical Services, Campaigns*, vol. II: *Hong Kong–Malaya, Iceland and the Faroes, Libya 1942–43, North-West Africa* (London: HMSO, 1957)

Crimp, R. L., *Diary of a Desert Rat* (London: Pan, 1974)

Crisp, R., *Brazen Chariots: An Account of Tank Warfare in the Western Desert, November–December, 1941* (London: Frederick Muller, 1959)

——*The Gods Were Neutral* (London: Frederick Muller, 1960)

Crookenden, A., *The History of The Cheshire Regiment in the Second World War* (Chester: Cheshire Regiment, n.d.)

Cropper, A., *Dad's War* (Thurlstone: Anmas, 1994)

Cruickshank, C., *Deception in World War II* (Oxford: Oxford University Press, 1979)

Cunningham, A., *A Sailor's Odyssey* (London: Hutchinson, 1951)

Dawnay, Brigadier D. (ed.), *The 10th Royal Hussars in the Second World War 1939–1945* (Aldershot: Gale & Polden, 1948)

De Guingand, F., *Generals at War* (London: Hodder & Stoughton, 1964)

——*Operation Victory* (London: Hodder & Stoughton, 1947)

Dear, I. C. B. (ed.), *The Oxford Companion to the Second World War* (Oxford: Oxford University Press, 1995)

Delaforce, P., *Monty's Highlanders: 51st Highland Division in World War Two* (Brighton: Tom Donovan, 1997)

——*Monty's Marauders: Black Rat and Red Fox: 4th and 8th Independent Armoured Brigades in WW2* (Brighton: Tom Donovan, 1997)

——*A View from the Turret: 3 RTR in World War II* (Brighton: Tom Donovan, 2000)

Detweiler, D. S., Burdick, C. B., and Rohwer, J. (eds.), *World War II German Military Studies*, vol. XIV, pt IV: *The Mediterranean Theater, continued* (New York: Garland 1979)

Dixon, N., *On the Psychology of Military Incompetence* (London: Futura, 1979)

Documents Relating to New Zealand Participation in the Second World War, 1939–1945 (Wellington: War History Branch, Department of Internal Affairs, 3 vols., 1949)

Doherty, R., *A Noble Crusade: A History of Eighth Army 1941–45* (Staplehurst: Spellmount, 1999)

——*Only the Enemy in Front: The Recce Corps at War 1939–1946* (London: Tom Donovan, 1994)

Douglas, K., *Alamein to Zem Zem* (Harmondsworth: Penguin, 1967)

Duncan, T., and Stout, M., *New Zealand Medical Services in Middle East and Italy* (Wellington: War History Branch, Department of Internal Affairs, 1956)

Duncan, W. E., Ellis, H. F., Banks, R. L., and Scarfe, N. (eds.), *The Royal Artillery Commemoration Book 1939–1945* (London: G. M. Bell & Sons, 1950)

Dupuy, T. N., *A Genius for War* (London: Macdonald & Jane's, 1977)

Edwards, J. (ed.), *Al-Alamein Revisited: The Battle of Al-Alamein and Its Historical Implications* (Cairo: American University in Cairo Press, 2000)

The Eighth Army: September 1941 to January 1943 (London: HMSO, 1944)

Ellis, J., *The Sharp End of War: The Fighting Man in World War II* (London: Corgi, 1982)

Farran, R., *Winged Dagger* (London: Fontana, 1956)

Fearnside, G. H. (ed.), *Bayonets Abroad: A History of the 2/13th Battalion A.I.F. in the Second World War* (Swanbourne, WA: John Burridge Military Antiques, 1993)

Fergusson, B., *The Black Watch and the King's Enemies* (London: Collins, 1950)

Fernyhough, A. H., *A History of the RAOC, 1920–1945* (London: William Clowes, 1958)

Fletcher, D., *The Great Tank Scandal: British Armour in the Second World War*, pt I (London: HMSO, 1989)

Flower, D., and Reeves, J. (eds.), *The War 1939–1945* (London: Cassell, 1960)

Forty, G., *Afrika Korps at War*, vol. I: *The Road to Alexandria* (Shepperton: Ian Allen, 1978)

——vol. II: *The Long Road Back* (Shepperton: Ian Allen, 1978)

——*The Armies of Rommel* (London: Arms & Armour, 1997)

——*Desert Rats at War* (Shepperton: Ian Allen, 1975)

——*The First Victory: O'Connor's Desert Triumph* (Tunbridge Wells: Nutshell Publishing, 1990)

Foster, R. C. G., *History of the Queen's Royal Regiment*, vol. III: *1924–1948* (Aldershot: Gale & Polden, 1953)

Fraser, D., *Alanbrooke* (London: Collins, 1982)

——*And We Shall Shock Them: The British Army in the Second World War* (London: Book Club Associates, 1983)

——*Knight's Cross: A Life of Field Marshal Erwin Rommel* (New York: HarperPerennial, 1995)

French, C. F., 'The Fashioning of Esprit de Corps in the 51st Highland Division from St Valéry to El Alamein', *Journal of the Society for Army Historical Research*, vol. LXXVII, no. 312, winter 1999

French, D., *Raising Churchill's Army* (Oxford: Oxford University Press, 2000)

Gibson, P. S., *Durban's Lady in White: An Autobiography* (Northaw: Aedificamus Press, 1991)

Gilbert, A., *The Imperial War Museum Book of the Desert War 1940–1942* (London: Sidgwick & Jackson, 1992)

Gilbert, M., *The Churchill War Papers*, vol. II: *Never Surrender, May–December 1940* (London: Heinemann, 1994)

——*Winston S. Churchill: Finest Hour* (London: Heinemann, 1983)

——*Winston S. Churchill: Road to Victory* (London: Heinemann, 1986)

Glenn, J. G., *Tobruk to Tarakan: The Story of a Fighting Unit* (Adelaide: Rigby, 1960)

Goodhart, D. (ed.), *The History of 2/7th Australian Field Regiment* (Adelaide: Rigby, 1952)

——*We of the Turning Tide* (Sydney: F. W. Preece, 1947)

Graham, A., *The Sharpshooters at War: The 3rd, 4th and 3rd/4th County of London Yeomanry, 1939–1945* (London: Sharpshooters Regimental Association, 1964)

Graham, F. C. C., *History of the Argyll and Sutherland Highlanders 1st Battalion (Princess Louise's)* (London: Thomas Graham & Son, 1948)

Grant, R., *The 51st Highland Division at War* (Shepperton: Ian Allen, 1977)

Greacen, L., *Chink: A Biography* (London: Macmillan, 1989)

Gudmundsson, B. I., *Stormtroop Tactics: Innovation in the German Army, 1914–1918* (New York: Praeger, 1989)

Guedalla, P., *Middle East 1940–1942: A Study in Air Power* (London: Hodder & Stoughton, 1944)

Guntrip, D. J., 'Trooper In, Trooper Out: A Day to Day Account of the Warwickshire Yeomanry During World War II' (Warwick: The Warwickshire Yeomanry Museum, unpublished)

Halstead, E., *Freyberg's Men* (Auckland: Heinemann Reed, 1985)

Halton, M., *Ten Years to Alamein* (London: Lindsay Drummond, 1944)

Handel, M. I. (ed.), *Intelligence and Military Operations* (London: Frank Cass, 1990)

——(ed.), *Strategic and Operational Deception in the Second World War* (London: Frank Cass, 1987)

Hamilton, N., *Monty: The Making of a General 1887–1942* (London: Coronet, 1984)

——*Monty: Master of the Battlefield 1942–1944* (London: Hamish Hamilton, 1983)

Hamilton, Stephen D., *50th Royal Tank Regiment: The Complete History* (Cambridge: Lutterworth Press, 1996)

Hamilton, Stuart, *Armoured Odyssey: 8th Royal Tank Regiment in The Western Desert 1941–1942, Palestine, Syria, Egypt 1943–1944, Italy 1944–1945* (London: Tom Donovan, 1995)

Harris, J. P., and Toase, F. H., *Armoured Warfare* (London: Batsford, 1990)

Harrison, F., *Tobruk: The Great Siege Reassessed* (London: Arms & Armour, 1996)

Hastings, R. H. W. S., *The Rifle Brigade in the Second World War 1939–1945* (Aldershot: Gale & Polden, 1950)

Haupt, W., and Bingham, J. K. W., *Der Afrika Feldzug* (London: Macdonald, 1968)

Heckmann, W., *Rommel's War in Africa* (St Albans: Granada, 1981)

Heckstall-Smith, A., *Tobruk: The Story of a Siege* (London: Anthony Blond, 1959)

Henderson, J., *RMT: Official History of the 4th and 6th Reserve Mechanical Transport Companies* (Wellington: War History Branch, Department of Internal Affairs, 1954)

——*22 Battalion* (Wellington: War History Branch, Department of Internal Affairs, 1958)

Herington, J., *Australia in the War of 1939–1945: Air: Air War against Germany and Italy 1939–43* (Canberra: Australian War Memorial, 1954)

Hillgruber, A. (ed.), *Kriegestagebuch des Oberkommandos der Wehrmacht*, vol. II (Frankfurt am Main: Bernard & Graefer, 1963)

Hills, R. J. T., *Phantom was There* (London: Edward Arnold, 1951)

Hingston, W. G., and Stevens, G. R., *The Tiger Kills: The Story of the Indian Divisions in the North African Campaign* (London: HMSO, 1944)

Hinsley, F. H., *British Intelligence in the Second World War, Its Influence on Strategy and Operations*, vols. I and II (London: HMSO, 1979, 1981)

Hodson, N., *Home Front* (London: Gollancz, 1944)

Horrocks, Sir B., *A Full Life* (London: Collins, 1960)

Howard, M., *British Intelligence in the Second World War*, vol. V: *Strategic Deception* (London: HMSO, 1990)

Howarth, T. E. B. (ed.), *Monty at Close Quarters* (London: Leo Cooper, 1985)

Hunt, D., *A Don at War* (London: William Kimber, 1966)

Irving, D., *The Trail of the Fox* (Ware: Wordsworth, 1999)

Jackson, W. G. F., *Alexander of Tunis as Military Commander* (London: Batsford, 1971)

——*The North African Campaign 1940–43* (London: Batsford, 1975)

Jacobs, F. J., Boucch, R. J., Du Preez, S., and Cornwell, R., *South African Corps of Signals* (Pretoria: S.A.W, 1975)

Jacobsen, H. A., and Rohwer, J. (eds.), *Decisive Battles of World War II: The German View* (London: André Deutsch, 1965)

Jellison, C. A., *Besieged: The World War II Ordeal of Malta, 1940–1942* (Hanover, N.H.: University Press of New England, 1984)

Jewell, D. (ed.), *Alamein and the Desert War* (London: Sphere Books/*Sunday Times*, 1967)

Johnson, R. B., *The Queen's in The Middle East and North Africa* (Guildford: Queen's Royal Surrey Regiment Museum, 1997)

Johnson, R. F., *Regimental Fire: The Honourable Artillery Company in World War Two 1939–1945* (London: HAC, 1958)

Johnston, D., *Nine Rivers From Jordan: The Chronicle of a Journey and a Search* (London: Derek Verschoyle, 1953)

Johnston, M., *At the Front Line* (Cambridge: Cambridge University Press, 1996)

——*Fighting the Enemy: Australian Soldiers and Their Adversaries in World War II* (Cambridge: Cambridge University Press, 2000)

Jones, A. F., *The Second Derbyshire Yeomanry: An Account of the Regiment during the War 1939–45* (Bristol: White Swan Press, 1949)

Jones, P. J., *The Reluctant Volunteer in Service with the Ninth Division, 1940–1945* (Loftus: Australian Military History Publications, 1997)

Kahn, D., *The Codebreakers: The Story of Secret Writing* (London: Weidenfeld & Nicolson, 1968)

Kay, R., *27 (Machine-Gun) Battalion* (Wellington: War History Branch, Department of Internal Affairs, 1958)

Keegan, J., *Six Armies in Normandy* (London: Penguin, 1983)

Kemp, P. K., *The Middlesex Regiment (Duke of Cambridge's Own) 1919–1952* (Aldershot: Gale & Polden, 1956)

——*The Staffordshire Yeomanry (Q. O. R. R.) in the First and Second World Wars 1914–1918 and 1939–1945* (Aldershot: Gale & Polden, 1950)

Kennedy, J., *The Business of War* (London: Hutchinson, 1957)

Kennedy-Shaw, W. B., *Long Range Desert Group* (London: Greenhill, 2000)

Kesselring, A., *The Memoirs of Field Marshal Kesselring* (London: Greenhill, 1997)

Kidson, A. L., *Petrol Company* (Wellington: War History Branch, Department of Internal Affairs, 1961)

Kiernan, V. G., *Colonial Empires and Armies 1815–1960* (Stroud: Sutton Publishing, 1998)

King, M., *New Zealanders at War* (Auckland: Heinemann, 1981)

Kippenburger, H., *Infantry Brigadier* (Oxford: Oxford University Press, 1949)

Klein, H., *Springboks in Armour* (Cape Town: Purnell, 1968)

Laffin, J., *Middle East Journey* (Sydney: Angus & Robertson, 1958)

Lamb, R., *Mussolini and the British* (London: John Murray, 1997)

Lambert, Colonel J. M., 'Engineers at the Battle of Alamein: The Southern Sector', *Royal Engineers Journal*, 1954

——'Tin Triangles', *Royal Engineers Journal*, 1952

Landsborough, G., *Tobruk Commando* (London: Cassell, 1956)

Leach, B., *Massacre at Alamein?* (Upton upon Severn: Square One, 1996)

Lewin, R., *Hitler's Mistakes* (London: Leo Cooper, 1984)

——*The Life and Death of the Afrika Korps* (London: Batsford, 1977)

——*Montgomery as Military Commander* (London: Batsford, 1971)

——*Rommel as Miltary Commander* (London: Batsford, 1974)

——*Ultra Goes to War: The Secret Story* (London: Hutchinson, 1978)

Lewis, M., *The History of the British Navy* (Harmondsworth: Penguin, 1957)

Lewis, P., *A People's War* (London: Methuen, 1986)

Lewis, P. J., and English, I. R., *8th Battalion The Durham Light Infantry 1939–1945* (Newcastle upon Tyne: J. & P. Bealls, 1949)

Liddell Hart, B. H. (ed.), *The Other Side of the Hill* (London: Cassell, 1948)

——*The Rommel Papers* (London: Collins, 1953)

——*The Tanks: The History of the Royal Tank Regiment and Its Predecessors*, vol. II (London: Cassell, 1959)

Lindsay, T. M., *Sherwood Rangers: The Story of the Nottinghamshire Sherwood Rangers Yeomanry in the Second World War* (London: Burrup & Mathieson, 1952)

Llewellyn, S. P., *Journey towards Christmas (1st Ammunition Company)* (Wellington: War History Branch, Department of Internal Affairs, 1949)

Lloyd, H. Pughe, *Briefed to Attack* (London: Hodder & Stoughton, 1959)

Loughnan, R. J. M., *Divisional Cavalry* (Wellington: War History Branch, Department of Internal Affairs, 1963)

Lucas, J., *Panzer Army Africa* (London: Macdonald & Jane's, 1977)

——*War in the Desert: The Eighth Army at El Alamein* (London: Arms & Armour, 1982)

Lucas, L., *Malta – the Thorn in Rommel's Side: Six Months that Turned the War* (London: Stanley Paul, 1992)

Lucas-Phillips, C. E., *Alamein* (London: Pan, 1965)

Lushington, F. *Yeoman Service – The Kent Yeomanry 1939–1945* (Aldershot: Gale & Polden, 1947)

McCallum, N., *Journey with a Pistol* (London: Gollancz, 1959)

McCreery, R. L., 'Reflections of a Chief of Staff', *XII Royal Lancers Journal*, 1959

McGregor, J., *The Spirit of Angus: The War History of the County's Battalion of the Black Watch* (Chichester: Phillimore, 1988)

McGuirk, D., *Rommel's Army in Africa* (Shrewsbury: Airlife Publishing, 1987)

McKee, A., *El Alamein: Ultra and the Three Battles* (London: Hutchinson, 1991)

McKinney, J. B., *Medical Units of 2 NZEF in Middle East and Italy* (Wellington: War History Branch, Department of Internal Affairs, 1952)

Macksey, K., *A History of the Royal Armoured Corps 1914–1975* (London: Newton Publications, 1983)

——*Kesselring: German Master Strategist of the Second World War* (London: Greenhill, 1996)

——*Rommel: Battles and Campaigns* (London: Arms & Armour, 1979)

Maclean, F., *Eastern Approaches* (London: Four Square, 1965)

McLeod, J., *Myth and Reality: The New Zealand Soldier in World War II* (Auckland: Heinemann Reed, 1986)

McMeekan, Brigadier G. R., 'The Assault at Alamein', *Royal Engineers Journal*, 1949

McNish, R. R., 'El Alamein in Perspective', *Rousillon Gazette*, winter 1993

Madeja, W. V., *Italian Army Order of Battle 1940–44* (Allentown, Pa.: Valor, 1990)

Majdalany, F., *The Battle of El Alamein* (London: Weidenfeld & Nicolson, 1965)

Mars, A., *Unbroken* (London: Frederick Muller, 1953)

Martin, A. C., *The Durban Light Infantry 1854–1960*, vol. II (Durban: HQ Board DLI, 1960)

Martin, T. A., *The Essex Regiment, 1929–1950* (Brentwood: Essex Regiment Association, 1950)

Martineau, G. D., *A History of the Royal Sussex Regiment: A History of The Old Belfast Regiment and The Regiment of Sussex 1701–1953* (Chichester: Moore & Tillyer, n.d.)

Masel, P., *The Second 28th: The Story of a Famous Battalion of the 9th Australian Division* (Perth: 2/28th Battalion and 24th Anti-Tank Company Association, 2000)

Maughan, B., *Australia in the War 1939–1945: Army: Tobruk and El Alamein* (Canberra: Australian War Memorial, 1966)

The Mediterranean Fleet: Greece to Tripoli: The Admiralty Account of Naval Operations April 1941 to January 1943 (London: HMSO, 1944)

Mellenthin, F. W. von, *Panzer Battles: A Study of the Employment of Armor in the Second World War*, trans. H. Betzler (London: Futura, 1977)

Merewood, J., *To War with the Bays* (Cardiff: 1st The Queen's Dragoon Guards, 1992)

Messenger, C., *The Unknown Alamein* (Shepperton: Ian Allen, 1982)

Miles, W., *The Life of a Regiment*, vol. V: *The Gordon Highlanders 1919–1945* (Aberdeen: Aberdeen University Press, 1961)

Millett, A., and Murray, W. (eds.), *Military Effectiveness*, vol. III: *The Second World War* (Winchester, Mass.: Allen & Unwin, 1988)

Milligan, S., *Rommel? Gunner Who?* (Harmondsworth: Penguin, 1976)

Mitcham, S. W., Jr, *Rommel's Desert War* (New York: Stein & Day, 1982)

Mollo, A., *The Armed Forces of World War II* (London: Orbis, 1981)

Montanari, M., *Le Operazioni in Africa Settentrionale*, vol. I: *Sidi el Barrani (Giugno 1940–Febbraio 1941)* (Rome: Stato Maggiore dell Esercito Ufficio Storico, 1990)

——vol. II: *Tobruk (Marzo 1941–Gennaio 1942)* (Rome: Stato Maggiore dell Esercito Ufficio Storico, 1993)

——vol. III: *El Alamein (Gennaio–Novembro 1942)* (Rome: Stato Maggiore dell Esercito Ufficio Storico, 1989)

Montgomery, B. L., *El Alamein to the Sangro* (London: Hutchinson, 1948)

——*The Memoirs of Field-Marshal The Viscount Montgomery of Alamein, K.G.* (London: Collins, 1958)

Moore, W., *Panzer Bait: With the 3rd Royal Tank Regiment 1940–1944* (London: Leo Cooper, 1991)

Moorehead, A., *African Trilogy* (London: Cassell, 1998)

——*The End in Africa: A Personal Account of the African Campaign from El Alamein to the Fall of Tunis* (London: Hamish Hamilton, 1943)

Morris, G. A., *The Battle of El Alamein and Beyond* (Lewes: Book Guild, 1993)

Moses, H., *The Faithful Sixth: A History of the Sixth Battalion, The Durham Light Infantry* (Durham: County Durham Books, 1995)

Mure, D., *Master of Deception* (London: William Kimber, 1980)

——*Practise to Deceive* (London: William Kimber, 1977)

Murphy, W. E., *2nd New Zealand Divisional Artillery* (Wellington: War History Branch, Department of Internal Affairs, 1966)

Nalder, R. F. H., *The History of British Army Signals in the Second World War* (London: Royal Signals Institution, 1953)

Nehring, W., *Der Feldzug in Afrika* (Pretoria: Union of South Africa War Histories Translation, 1948)

Neillands, R., *The Desert Rats: 7th Armoured Division 1940–1945* (London: Weidenfeld & Nicolson, 1991)

Nesbit, R. C., *Torpedo Airmen* (London: William Kimber, 1983)

Nicolson, N., *Alex: The Life of Field Marshal Earl Alexander of Tunis* (London: Weidenfeld & Nicolson, 1973)

Nightingale, P. R., *A History of The East Yorkshire Regiment (Duke of York's Own) in the War 1939–1945* (York and London: William Sessions, 1952)

Norton, F. D., *26 Battalion* (Wellington: War History Branch, Department of Internal Affairs, 1952)

Oakes, B., *Muzzle Blast: Six Years of War with the 2/2 Australian Machine Gun Battalion A.I.F.* (Sydney: 2/2 Machine Gun Battalion War History Committee, 1980)

Orpen, N., *The Cape Town Highlanders 1885–1970* (Cape Town: Constantia, 1970)

——*South African Forces, World War II*, vol. III: *War in the Desert* (Cape Town: Purnell, 1971)

Orpen, N., and Martin H. J., *Salute the Sappers* (Johannesburg: Sapper Association, 1981)

Orwell, G., *The Collected Essays, Journalism and Letters of George Orwell*, vol. II: *My Country Right or Left, 1940–1943* (Harmondsworth: Penguin, 1970)

Packenham, T., *The Scramble For Africa* (London: Weidenfeld & Nicolson, 1991)

Pakenham-Walsh, R. P., *History of the Corps of Royal Engineers*, vol. VIII: *1938–1948* (Chatham: Institution of Royal Engineers, 1958)

Parkinson, R., *The Auk: Auchinleck, Victor at Alamein* (London: Granada, 1977)

Parry, D. F., 'Eighth Army – Defeat and Disgrace' (London: Imperial War Museum, unpublished)

Parsons, M., *We Were the 2/12th: 1940–1946* (Carnegie, Vic.: 2/12th Australian Field Regiment Association/McKellar Renown Press, 1985)

Peniakoff, V., *Popski's Private Army* (London: Reprint Society, 1953)

Perrett, B., *The Valentine in North Africa 1942–3* (London: Ian Allen, 1972)

Piekalkiewicz, J., *Rommel and the Secret War in North Africa 1941–1943: Secret Intelligence in the North African Campaign*, trans. E. Force (West Chester, Pa.: Schiffer, 1992)

Pitt, B., *The Crucible of War: Western Desert 1941* (London: Jonathan Cape, 1980)

——*The Crucible of War: Year of Alamein 1942* (London: Jonathan Cape, 1982)

——'Monty's Foxhounds', *War Monthly*, vol. IX, no. 3, 1981

Pitt, P. W., *Royal Wilts: The History of the Royal Wiltshire Yeomanry, 1920–1945* (London: Burrup & Mathieson, 1946)

Platt, J. R. I., *The Royal Wiltshire Yeomanry 1907–1967* (London: Garnstone Press, 1972)

Playfair, I. S. O. et. al., *The Mediterranean and Middle East*, vol. I: *The Early Successes against Italy* (London: HMSO, 1954)

——vol. II: *The Germans Come to the Help of Their Ally* (London: HMSO, 1956)

——vol. III: *British Fortunes Reach Their Lowest Ebb* (London: HMSO, 1960)

——vol. IV: *The Destruction of Axis Forces in North Africa* (London: HMSO, 1966)

Pollock, A. M., *Pienaar of Alamein* (Cape Town: Cape Times, 1943)

Puttick, Sir E., *25 Battalion* (Wellington: War History Branch, Department of Internal Affairs, 1960)

Qureshi, M. I., *The First Punjabis: The History of the First Punjab Regiment 1759–1956* (Aldershot: Gale & Polden, 1958)

RAF Middle East Review, vol. II (London: HMSO, 1944)

Rainier, P. W., *Pipeline to Battle* (London: Hamish Hamilton, 1944)

Rees, G., *A Bundle of Sensations* (London: Chatto and Windus, 1960)

Reid, H. M., *The Turning Point: With the New Zealand Engineers at El Alamein* (Auckland: Collins, 1944)

Reit, S., *Masquerade: The Amazing Camouflage Deceptions of World War II* (London: Robert Hale, 1979)

Rhodes-Wood, E. H., *A War History of The Royal Pioneer Corps 1939–1945* (Aldershot: Gale & Polden, 1960)

Richards, D., and Saunders, H. St G., *Royal Air Force 1939–1945*, vol. II: *The Fight Avails* (London: HMSO, 1954)

Richardson, C., *Flashback: A Soldier's Story* (London: William Kimber, 1985)

Richardson, W., and Friedin, S., *The Fatal Decisions* (London: Michael Joseph, 1956)

Ring, H., and Shores, C., *Luftkampf zwischen Sand und Sonne* (Stuttgart: Motorbuch Verlag, 1969)

Rissik, D., *The DLI at War* (Brancepeth Castle: The Durham Light Infantry Depot, 1952)

Ritchie, H. R., *Fusing the Ploughshare* (Dunmow: Henry Ritchie, 1987)

Roberts, G. P. B., *From the Desert to the Baltic* (London: William Kimber, 1987)

Rommel, E., *Krieg ohne Hass* (Heidenheim: Heidenheimer Verlaganstalt, 1950)

Roskill, S. K., *The War at Sea 1939–1945*, vol. II: *The Period of Balance* (London: HMSO, 1956)

Ross, A., *23 Battalion* (Wellington: War History Branch, Department of Internal Affairs, 1959)

Ross, J., *The Myth of the Digger: The Australian Soldier in Two World Wars* (Sydney: Hale & Iremonger, 1985)

Routledge, N. W., *History of the Royal Regiment of Artillery: Anti-Aircraft Artillery 1914–55* (London: Brassey's, 1994)

Russell, D. F. O., *War History of the 7th Bn, The Black Watch (RHR) (Fife Territorial Battalion) August 1939 to May 1945* (Markinch: Markinch Printing, 1948)

Rust, K. C., *The 9th Air Force in World War II* (Fallbrook, Cal.: Aero Publishers Inc., 1970)

Ryder, R., *Oliver Leese* (London: Hamish Hamilton, 1987)

Sadkovich, J. J., *The Italian Navy in World War II* (Westport, Conn.: Greenwood Press, 1994)

Salmond, J. B., *The History of the 51st Highland Division 1939–1945* (Edinburgh and London: William Blackwood & Sons, 1953)

Samwell, H. P., *An Infantry Officer with the Eighth Army* (Edinburgh and London: William Blackwood & Sons, 1945)

Santoni, A., *Il vero traditore* (Milan: Mursia, 1981)

Schmidt, H.-W., *With Rommel in the Desert* (London: Constable, 1997)

Scoullar, J. L., *Battle for Egypt*, Official History of New Zealand in the Second World War (Wellington: War History Branch, Department of Internal Affairs, 1955)

Serle, R. P. (ed.), *The Second Twenty-Fourth Australian Infantry Battalion of the 9th Australian Division: A History* (Brisbane: Jacaranda Press, 1963)

Shankland, P., and Hunter, A., *Malta Convoy* (London: Collins, 1961)

Sheffield, G. D., *The Redcaps* (London: Brassey's, 1994)

Shore, P., *Mud and Blood: 'Albury's Own' Second Twentythird Australian Infantry Battalion Ninth Australian Division* (Perth: John Burridge Military Antiques, 1991)

Shores, C., with Bull, C., and Malizia, N., *Malta: The Hurricane Years 1940–41* (London: Grub Street, 1987)

——*Malta: The Spitfire Year 1942* (London: Grub Street, 1991)

Shores, C., and Ring, H., *Fighters over the Desert* (London: Neville Spearman, 1969)

A Short History of the 45th/51st (Leeds Rifles) Royal Tank Regiment (TA) and 466th (Leeds Rifles) LAA Regt, RA (TA) (London: Reid Hamilton, 1955)

A Short History of the 57th Light Anti-Aircraft Regt, Royal Artillery (Aldershot: Gale & Polden, 1947)

Shulman, M., *Defeat in the West* (London: Secker & Warburg, 1947)

'Silver John' [J. N. L. Argent], *'Target Tank': The History of 2/3rd Australian Anti-Tank Regiment, 9th Australian Division, AIF* (Parramatta: Cumberland, 1957)

Simpkins, A., *The Rand Light Infantry* (Cape Town: Howard Thomas, 1965)

Simpkins, B. G., *Rand Light Infantry* (Cape Town: Timmins, 1947)

Simpson, G. W. G., *Periscope View* (London: Macmillan, 1972)

Smith, P. C., *Massacre at Tobruk* (London: William Kimber, 1987)

——*Pedestal: The Convoy that Saved Malta* (Manchester: Crécy, 1999)

'The Snipe Position', *The Rifle Brigade Chronicle*, 1943

Spooner, A. J., *In Full Flight* (London: Macdonald, 1965)

——*Supreme Gallantry: Malta's Role in the Allied Victory 1939–1945* (London: John Murray 1996)

——*Warburton's War* (London: William Kimber, 1987)

Stevens, G. R., *Fourth Indian Division* (Toronto: McClaren & Son, 1948)

Stevens, W. G., *Freyberg VC: The Man 1939–1945* (Wellington: A. H. & A. W. Reed, 1965)

Stewart, A., *Eighth Army's Greatest Victories: Alam Halfa to Tunis 1942–1943* (Barnsley: Leo Cooper, 1999)

The Story of the Royal Army Service Corps 1939–1945 (London: G. M. Bell & Sons, 1955)

Strawson, J., *El Alamein: Desert Victory* (London: Dent, 1981)

Sweet, J. J. T., *Iron Arm: The Mechanization of Mussolini's Army 1920–1940* (Westport, Conn.: Greenwood Press, 1980)

Sym, I. M., *Seaforth Highlanders* (Aldershot: Gale & Polden, 1962)

Sym, Colonel J. M., 'Brigade Major at El Alamein', *The Queen's Own Highlander*, vol. 32, no. 83, winter 1992

Synge, W. A. T., *The Story of the Green Howards, 1939–1945* (Richmond: The Green Howards, 1952)

Tatman, J. A., and Kennet, B. B., *Craftsmen of the Army*, vol. I (London: Leo Cooper, 1970)

Tedde, A., *Fiamme nel deserto* (Milan: Cisalpino, 1962)

Tedder, A. W., *With Prejudice* (London: Cassell, 1966)

Terraine, J., *The Right of the Line: The Royal Air Force in the European War 1939–1945* (London: Hodder & Stoughton, 1985)

Thomas, E. W., *Ambulance in Africa* (New York: Appleton, 1943)

Tobler, D. H., *Intelligence in the Desert: The Recollections and Reflections of a Brigade Intelligence Officer* (Victoria, BC: Morriss Printing Co., 1978)

Todd, A., *The Elephant at War: 2nd Battalion Seaforth Highlanders 1939–1945* (Bishop Auckland: Pentland Press, 1998)

Trevor-Roper, H. R., *Hitler's War Directives 1939–1945* (London: Pan, 1966)

Trigellis-Smith, S., *Britain to Borneo: A History of 2/32 Australian Infantry Battalion* (Sydney: 2/32 Australian Infantry Battalion Association, 1993)

Trye, R., *Mussolini's Afrika Korps: The Italian Army in North Africa 1940–1943* (Bayside, N.Y.: Axis Europa Books, 1999)

——*Mussolini's Soldiers* (Shrewsbury: Airlife, 1995)

Tuker, F., *Approach to Battle* (London: Cassell, 1963)

Tungay, A. W., *The Fighting Third* (Cape Town: Unie-Volkspers, 1947)

Tute, W., *The North African War* (London: Sidgwick & Jackson, 1976)

Underhill, Major D. F., *Queen's Own Royal Regiment The Staffordshire Yeomanry: An Account of the Operations of the Regiment during World War II, 1939–1945* (Stafford: Staffordshire Libraries, Arts and Archives)

Van Creveld, M., 'Rommel's Supply Problem, 1941–42', *Journal of the Royal United Services Institute*, 119 (September 1974)

——*Supplying War: Logistics from Wallenstein to Patton* (Cambridge: Cambridge University Press, 1977)

Verney, G. L., *The Desert Rats: A History of 7th Armoured Division* (London: Hutchinson, 1954)

Wake, Sir H., and Deedes, W. F. (eds.) *Swift and Bold: The Story of the King's Royal Rifle Corps in the Second World War* (Aldershot: Gale & Polden, 1949)

Walker, A. S., *Australia in the War 1939–1945: Medical: Middle East and Far East* (Canberra: Australian War Memorial, 1953)

Walker, R., *Alam Halfa and Alamein*, Official History of New Zealand in the Second World War (Wellington: War History Branch, Department of Internal Affairs, 1967)

Ward, S. P. G., *Faithful: The Story of The Durham Light Infantry* (London: Thomas Nelson & Son, 1962)

Ward-Harvey, K., *The Sapper's War: With Ninth Australian Division Engineers 1939–1945* (Neutral Bay, NSW: Sakoga/9 Division RAE Association, 1992)

Wardrop, J., *Tanks Across the Desert: The War Diary of Jake Wardrop*, ed. G. Forty (London: William Kimber, 1981)

Warner, P., *Alamein* (London: William Kimber, 1979)

——*Auchinleck: The Lonely Soldier* (London: Buchan & Enright, 1981)

Wavell, A. P., *The Good Soldier* (London: Macmillan, 1948)

We Were Monty's Men: With the Green Howards of the 50th Division from Gazala to Tunis (Richmond: Green Howards Museum, 1997)

West, F., *From Alamein to Scarlet Beach: The History of 2/4th Light Anti-Aircraft Regiment Second AIF* (Geelong: Deakin University Press, 1987)

Westphal, S., *The German Army in the West* (London: Cassell, 1951)

What We Have We Hold!: A History of 2/17 Australian Infantry Battalion, 1940–1945 (Loftus, NSW: 2/17th Battalion History Committee/Australian Military History Publications, 1998)

Wheatley, D., *The Deception Planners* (London: Hutchinson, 1980)

Whetton, J. T., and Ogden, R. H., *Z Location or Survey in War: The Story of the 4th (Durham) Survey Regiment, R.A., T.A.* (privately published by R. H. Ogden, 1977)

Whiting, C., *The Poor Bloody Infantry* (London: Guild, 1987)

Wilkinson-Latham, J., *Montgomery's Desert Army* (London: Osprey, 1977)

Wilmington, M. W., *The Middle East Supply Centre* (London: University of London Press, 1971)

Wimberley, D. N., 'Scottish Soldier' (Glasgow: Mitchell Library, unpublished)

Wingate, J., *The Fighting Tenth* (London: Leo Cooper, 1971)

Woodman, R., *Malta Convoys* (London: John Murray, 2000)

Young, D., *Rommel* (London: Book Club Associates, 1973)

Young, M., and Stamp, R., *Trojan Horses: Deception Operations in the Second World War* (London: Bodley Head, 1989)

Fiction

Denholm-Young, C. P. S., *Men of Alamein* (Stevenage: Spa Books/Tom Donovan, 1987)

Forrester, C. S., *The Ship* (Harmondsworth: Penguin, 1949)

Greenfield, G., *Desert Episode* (London: Hamish Hamilton, 1955)

——*Rich Dust* (London: House of Stratus, 2001)

Hull, C. Macdonald, *A Man from Alamein* (London: Corgi, 1973)

Joly, C., *Take These Men* (Harmondsworth: Penguin, 1956)

Majdalany, F., *The Patrol* (London: Longmans, Green & Co., 1953)

Index

Ranks and titles are generally the highest mentioned in the text